There's a FISH in the COURTHOUSE

By
GARETH (Gary) L. WEAN

CASITAS BOOKS

THERE'S A FISH IN THE COURTHOUSE

Copyright © 1987 by Gary L. Wean

All rights reserved. No part of this book may be reproduced or utilized in any form or by any means without permission in writing from the author, except by a newspaper or magazine reviewer who wishes may quote brief passages in connection with a review.

Library of Congress Catalog Card Number 87-071436

ISBN: 0-9624194-0-0 1st edition 1987
ISBN: 0-9624194-1-9 2nd edition 1996 with prologue and synopsis

Published and Printed in the United States of America by Casitas Books,
Address:
Order from:
Gary L. Wean
P.O. Box 1857
Cave Junction, Oregon 97523

Telephone for retail orders:
541-592-4406

FOREWORD

At first what only appeared to be a plot by a veiled group of local politicians and financiers to defraud the people was about to be exposed. Their indictment through a secret investigation by the Ventura County Grand Jury was imminent.

Then treachery, betrayal by a member of the Grand Jury brought swift orders from the corrupt presiding judge of the Superior Court to kill the investigation.

But, the judge's evil command to subvert the due process of law triggered a succession of murderous, treasonous events: a trail that led to the highest offices of the land....

DEDICATED TO

Evil men and
their total destruction.

PROLOGUE

This book was first printed and sold in 1987. The actual writing of it commenced nearly twenty years before that.

The author was honorably discharged as a Gunners Mate 2/c at the U.S. Naval Base, San Pedro, California on December 7, 1945, four years after Pearl Harbor, December 7, 1941.

In January 1946 the author joined the Los Angeles Police Department and after graduation was assigned to uniform patrol, the morning watch, midnight to 8:00 a.m. at University Division.

The story begins at this time, 1946, and relates events (not quite all of them) that occurred up to 1987 the time of printing and sale of the book.

In the fall of 1987 the author and a man he had just become acquainted with, Michael A. Thomas, traveled to Washington, D.C.

There in the nation's capitol, amid the sanctimony of the hallowed halls of Congress, where our dedicated representatives do their thing....we hand delivered to each of the one hundred U.S. Senators a copy of this book along with a 'Petition' from the people asking them to investigate judicial corruption of both federal and state courts in the Federal Ninth Circuit Court of Appeals. This judicial corruption involved murder of citizens and theft of their real estate and personal property, denial of due process of law and destruction of the American judicial system as set forth in the Constitution and Bill of Rights.

We had conferences and consultations with the top staff members of Senator Joseph Biden, the Chairman of the Senate Judiciary Committee, and direct written guarantees from Biden that he had ordered Senator Howlin Heflin to activate a sub-committee and to fully investigate the peoples 'Petition' charging judicial corruption. At this time Biden and Heflin were given documents and evidence verifying and exposing crimes that the people were suffering at the hands of judges.

But instead of investigating and conducting hearings on the citizens pleas for justice Joseph Biden and the members of the Judiciary Committee joined and combined with the rest of the United States Senate to bury and cover-up all the evidence and the peoples 'Petition' and particularly the author's book, 'There's a Fish In The Courthouse.'

Some of the most evil members of the Senate Judiciary Committee were Joseph Biden, Arlen Specter, Strom Thurmond and unexplainably Teddy Kennedy.

All of these Anti-American Senators are still in office, more powerful than ever and Specter has done untold damage to the citizens with his phony sub-committee white-wash cover-ups of Ruby

Ridge, Waco, Oklahoma City and lies about the Civil Militias.

In 1988, knowing that the U.S. Senate was covering-up the judicial corruption the author filed a (RICO) Racketeer Influenced and Corrupt Organization Act lawsuit, charging each and every one of the U.S. Senators with violations of the Civil Rights Acts of 1981 and 1964, Title 42 U.S.C. 1983 - 1986, 20002 (3).

This case, Number 88-0-346 was read by District Court Judge Beam, 8th Circuit, Omaha, Nebraska, before it was filed. This was witnessed by Chief Court Clerk Lyle E. Strom, Michael A. Thomas and others, Judge Beam proclaimed the lawsuit to be an excellant case and gave verbal orders to the U.S. Clerk to file it.

The case scheduled for trial in June 1990 had proceeded for nearly two years and was going very well, in fact too well to suit the defendants - a million dollars was secretly sent from lawyers in Oxnard, California to influential lawyers in Omaha and reached the hands of Magistrate Richard G. Kopf who had done most of the sabotage to the case. Shortly afterward Judge William G. Cambridge dismissed the case.

Then my appeal was dismissed by none other than Judge Beam who in the meantime had been promoted to the 8th Circuit Court of Appeals.

No valid reason could be found to dismiss the case so Judge Beam simply called it scandalous. This was in the face of the fact that Judge Beam had declared the case to be excellent and should be brought to trial. It was also after the million dollars had been split.

Ventura County Counsel James McBride and lawyer Stanley Cohen were behind the million dollar bribe. During the proceedure of the case McBride had exhibited his incompetence by failing to answer the complaint for defendant Susan Lacey, a Ventura County Supervisor and the author had filed a multi-million dollar default judgement against her.

Present California Governor Pete Wilson was a U.S. Senator in 1987 and was a major conspirator involved in the Senators cover-up. Wilson had filed an involved 'Motion for Extension of Time to Respond to the Complaint,' and Federal Judge Harry Pregerson was filing frantic 'Motions to Dismiss' along with William P. Clark, the former National Security Director and Secretary of the Interior.

The following is a list of the United States Senators in office in 1987 who were handed a copy of the authors book,'There's a Fish in the Courthouse' and a 'Petition and desperate Plea' from the people to protect them, their health, safety and welfare from a murderous gang of thugs who had usurped the judicial system and were murdering the citizens and stealing their property.

The Senators named in this list were deeply involved in the cover-up of heinous crimes and felonious abuse of their office.

Almost all of these traitorous persons are still in office as senators, some have become governors, ambassadors and others hold powerful political positions.

The loyal citizens of America must take notice of these traitors and do everything in their power to remove them from any and all positions of power in our country.

The damage to America and its citizens done by these thieving traitors is exposed in every chapter. The horrific, dreadful results of the Senators cowardly, treasonous cover-up since 1987 shocks not only America but the entire world. A synopsis of revelations follows at the end of the book.

Adams, Brock, (Wash)
Armstrong, William (Colo)
Baucus, Max (Mont)
Bentson, Lloyd (Tex)
Biden, Joseph (Del)
Bingaman, Jeff (N. Mex)
Bond, Christopher (Mo)
Boschwitz, Rudy (Minn)
Boren, David L. (Okla)
Bradley, Bill (N.J.)
Breaux, John B, (La))
Bumpers, Dale (Ark)
Burdick, Quentin N. (N. Dak)
Byrd, Robert C. (W. Vir.)
Chafee, John (R. I.)
Chiles, Lawton (Fla)
Cochran, Thad (Miss)
Cohen, William S. (Me)
Conrad, Kent (N. Dak)
Cranston, Alan (CA)
D'Amoto, Alfonse (N.Y.)
D'Concini, Dennis (Ariz)
Danforth, John C. (Mo)
Daschle, Thomas (S. Dak)
Dixon, Alan J. (Ill)
Dodd, Christopher, (Conn)
Dole, Robert (Kan)
Domenici, Pete (N. Mex)
Durenberger, Dave (Minn)
Evans, Daniel J. (Wash)
Exon, James (Neb)
Ford, Wendell H. (Ky)
Fowler, Wych (Ga)
Garn, Jake (Utah)
Glenn, John (Ohio)
Gore, Albert (Tenn)
Graham, Bob (Fla)
Gramm, Phil (Tex)
Grassley, Charles E. (Iowa)
Harkin, Tom (Iowa)
Hatch, Orrin (Utah)
Hatfield, Mark O. (Ore)
Hecht, Chic (Nev)
Heinz, John (Pa)
Heflin, Howell (Ala)
Helms, Jesse (N.C.)
Hollings, Ernest F. (S. Car)
Humphrey, Gorden (N.H.)
Inouye, Dan (Hawaii)
Johnston, Bennett J. (La)
Karnes, David K. (Neb)
Kassebaum, Nancy Landon (Kan)
Kasten Jr., Robert W.(Wisc)
Kennedy, Edward (Mass)
Kerry, John F. (Mass)
Lautenberg, Frank (N.J.)
Leahy, Patrick J. (Ver)
Levin, Carl (Mich)
Luger, Richard G. (Ind)
Matsunaga, Spark (Hawaii)
Mc Cain, John S. (Ariz)
Mc Connell, Mitch (Kty)
Mc Clure, James H. (Ida)
Melcher, John (Mont)

Metzenbaum, Howard (Ohio)
Mikulski, Barbara (Md)
Mitchell, George J. (Me)
Moynihan, Daniel P. (N.Y)
Murkowski, Frank R. (Alaska)
Nickles, Don (Okla)
Nunn, Sam (Ga)
Packwood, Bob (Or)
Pell, Claiborne (R.I.)
Pressler, Larry (S. Dak)
Proxmire, William (Wisc)
Pryor, David (Ark)
Quale, Dan (Ind)
Reid, Harry (Nev)
Riegle, Donald W. (Mich)
Rockefeller, John (W. Vir)
Roth, William (Del)
Rudman, Warren (N.H.)
Sanford, Terry (N.C.)
Sarbanes, Paul (Md)
Selby, Richard C. (Ala)
Sasser, Jim (Tenn)
Simon, Paul (Ill)
Simpson, Alan (Wyo)
Specter, Arlen (Pa)
Stafford, Robert T. (Ver)
Stennis, John C. (Miss)
Stevens, Ted (Alaska)
Symms, Steven D. (Ida)
Thurmond, Strom (S. Car)
Trimble, Paul S. (Vir)
Wallop, Malcom (Wyo)
Warner, John W. (Vir)
Weicker, Lowell P. (Conn)
Wilson, Pete (Cal)
Wirth, Timothy (Colo)

CHAPTER 1

MURDER!!...... The paper's headlines blared large and black, "BARTENDER MURDERED, Merle Harter, night bartender at the Captain's Table killed, knifed many times and left lying in a pool of blood behind the bar."

There weren't too many murders occurring in the beautiful city of San Buenaventura by the Sea, but even so I didn't read the entire story because it didn't seem to be much different from what was happening every day of the week a little farther south down the coast in the metropolis of Los Angeles.

One thing passed through my mind, the police would most likely come up with a suspect and I would get the task of investigating to prove that the suspect was innocent. Since September of 1966 I had been the Chief Investigator for the Office of Public Defender for Ventura County, a new department which had just been formed by the supervisors of the county. After a lot of thought the local politicians had come to the conclusion that it would be far more economical to create the county department of Public Defender than to have the judges appointing private attorneys to represent indigent people. There was a belief that maybe the court was playing favorites in the selection of certain lawyers and law firms and possibly these attorneys had been conducting far too many unnecessary courtroom appearances in behalf of their clients. Each separate appearance called for higher fees and expenses.

2 THERE'S A FISH IN THE COURTHOUSE

This wouldn't be the first murder case that I'd been involved in through the years, but it sure as hell was destined to be one of the most involved and far-reaching cases to me personally--changing my whole existence and future.

Our offices were on the third floor of a newer building which had been constructed behind the original courthouse. The older more elaborate building was situated on a site overlooking the old section of Ventura. Walking out of the massive front doors you looked down California Street, on across Main to the white sands of the beach and the blue ocean and sky. Usually a fat oil tanker lay anchored out beyond the fishing pier. Indeed, this beautiful view met your eyes as you left the front doors of the stately old courthouse--at least it did before the purveyors of cement and steel proceeded to build their master size freeway including the exits and on ramps at the foot of California Street. All this within several hundred feet of the white sand and blue ocean. Now all you could see was Greyhound busses and huge smoky trucks hauling their enormous loads of merchandise from San Francisco and Los Angeles interspersed with Volkswagens and Winnebagos. Progress, what would we do without it?

I parked the county car up on the hillside and walked down to the newer building that housed our offices. I decided to walk up the several flights of stairs thinking a little exercise won't hurt. Starting up the second flight I heard somebody coming down. Looking up I saw it was Woodruff J. Deem, the District Attorney. I gave a friendly "Hi," he nodded as he kept going at a fast pace down the steps. I figured Woody was doing the same thing, trying to get a little workout. But knowing how he pushed himself with his duties, he probably just didn't have the patience to wait for the one and only elevator to arrive. Woody, as he was known to almost everyone, was of average height and athletic build. Turning to watch him for a moment I noticed he still had a butch haircut and thought Lord, why doesn't he get a new suit.

I had known Woody for a long time, having taken many criminal investigative files to him to read and issue complaints on while I was a Det. Sergeant with the Ventura Police Department and he'd been a Deputy D.A. He was a shrewd lawyer, very fair while considering both sides of a case and whether there was sufficient good evidence to warrant taking a defendant to court and trying to convict him. You could expect a knowing, extremely long, sharp look, if he felt that you as the investigating officer had come up with a poor report. I started on up the stairs nursing a feeling that Woody didn't seem quite so friendly since I was with the Public Defender's office. On the other hand I'd heard rumbles that there was a strong antagonistic feeling being nurtured amongst the staff of the Public Defender against the District Attorney, this in a loud, boisterous and quite profane manner by Richard E. Erwin, the lawyer who was appointed to the position of Public Defender by the Board of Supervisors. In fact, Erwin had been appointed in a hurry and under pressure by the Board because the attorney they really wanted for the position had decided at the last minute not to take the job. Unless the position was filled in a hurry the courts would start using court appointed lawyers and this would create considerable problems with funds and clients cases.

It was early afternoon yet and I could see several of the deputy Public Defenders standing in the large front office discussing their problem cases and hoping for advice and encouragement from their fellow lawyers. Beyond them was a desk where sat Claire Brotherton, the woman that Erwin had selected for his executive secretary. She was an average-height female with mousey blonde hair, apparently at the age where a woman starts getting unwanted bulges in fairly obvious places. She had placed her desk in a very strategic corner of the room where her eyes from behind a pair of powerful glasses could see every object, moving or otherwise with one swift upward glance from her typewriter. I received one of these upward glances as I entered the main door, only she stared at me for what seemed like a longer period than she gave most individuals, and I was sure I detected a hostile gleam behind the glasses, along with the start of a sneer on her thin, tight lips. Just to the right of her desk was a door, gold letters announced, 'Richard E. Erwin, Public Defender.'

I was about to proceed to my left and go on back to my own office, but I could see Erwin standing inside his doorway, he was beckoning for me to come in with a *right now* gesture of his arm. I changed directions to head for his office, and Claire sensing where I was going leaped from her swivel secretary chair to intercept me before I could enter the sacred chambers. The heavy chair banged loudly against some metal files behind her, the attorneys who were engrossed in their conversation became suddenly still and turned to observe what was going on. I speeded up as fast as I could and still not appear that I was running. I passed through the door of the sanctum a breath ahead of Claire. Erwin just stood in the middle of his office staring at our maneuvers. I glanced back to see Claire standing in the doorway holding a bunch of papers, the blood had drained from her face leaving her very pale. This time I could see her hatred glaring at me with no thought of concealment. I had to wonder why she felt like this toward me because I had never tried to be anything but polite and helpful to her as we had struggled to organize the new office of Public Defender.

I was brought back to the present by a loud rasping voice saying, "Sit down, I want to talk to you!" I sat down on a couch and looked at the owner of the voice. Richard E. Erwin was a tall, thin man with graying hair and he combed it in a conventional mans manner except for a strange curley-cue in the front. He was standing there staring out the window with a paper clip in his hand. He had opened one end of the clip, with the loop end he was probing into his right ear fiercely at an extraordinary depth. Shortly he removed the clip from his head and stepping closer to the window where the light was brighter he examined the results of his probe on the loop end of the clip. I thought, what in hell can he be looking at because from that distance I couldn't see anything on the end of the clip. I was feeling squeamish when he suddenly threw the clip in the wastepaper basket and sat down. He said, "I want you to do something for me. I am just getting settled in my new house out in the east end of Ventura and my flowers and grass are coming up beautiful."

I figured I was going to get roped into some kind of gardening project. A couple of months before I had been invited out to his house for lunch, he wanted me to see what a beautiful location he had picked. It was very nice and was in a cul-de-sac along with six or seven other homes. As I stood on the sidewalk looking at the scenery I heard a powerful truck turning the corner, it was a large furniture van and it pulled up in front of Erwin's house. We had a lunch served by Mrs. Erwin, and I finished the afternoon helping to carry five rooms of furniture to upstairs bedrooms.

"Yeah! My flowers and grass were coming up beautiful until the people started moving into these other houses. Everyone of those bastards must have at least a dozen shit-assed little kids and their mothers send every one of them outside to play in my yard. They are killing all my grass and flowers, you have to do something about it. You were on the Ventura Police Department and you have friends over there. Get hold of some of your buddies and have them go up there in black and white cars and harass those people, pick up those little bastards, take them over to juvenile hall and make their parents come to the hall to get them."

I noticed that he was really serious and getting madder by the minute as his face was dark red and his small black eyes flashed behind his gold-rimmed glasses. I could see Claire's shadow on the floor in front of the door, I realized she must be out there listening to every word. I reached over and pushed the door shut. The whole conversation was making me nervous and I was feeling a slight touch of anger when I said, "Christ! Mr. Erwin, I can't go ask men on the Police Department to do things like this, *first of all they'd think I was nuts,* and second, they wouldn't do it anyway. Besides, now I am working for the Public Defender, and as well as I know them and they like me, they still don't trust our motives. It's like being friends with a soldier from another country, but your countries are about to declare war on each other." He stood up straight and stared at me.

"Alright, goddamn it! Then you take one of our cars with the county emblem on it and go up there in the cul-de-sac and sit there and watch them, maybe they will think you are from the sheriff's office." Anxious to leave his office, I assured him I'd do something about his neighbors and their kids.

Retreating from his office I saw Claire behind her desk trying to give an impression she was just a normal secretary doing her job. I continued down the hall toward my own office. On my right were several cubicles which served as the offices for the Deputy Public Defenders, I could see that most of them had returned from their combat duties in the courtrooms and were relaxing in their shirt sleeves. John Russell was in his shirt sleeves, but he wasn't relaxing. He was talking to a young Mexican, trying to interview him and get facts relating to the bust the cops had put on him. John looked up as I passed and yelled, "Hey, Gary, come in here for a minute. Meet Jesus Lopez." I looked at Jesus and said, "Hi." Jesus just stared at me. John said, "Jesus has a problem and I would like for you to get a police report from the Oxnard Police Department if you will. Jesus tells me the police busted him for nothing. All he was doing was sitting on a dark street about midnight last night smooching with his chick when two cholos came running around the corner and threw a bunch of loot in the back seat of his Chevy and kept on running. About this same time two cops came running around the corner, opened the front door of his Chevy, jerked him out on the street and handcuffed him."

"Yeah, sure sounds like a bum beef. Listen Jesus," I said, "will your chick swear that you were just sitting there smooching and you didn't know anything about the two other guys?"

"Well...man, she wasn't *actually there* when it happened..."

"What do you mean she wasn't there? Didn't you just say you were smooching when it happened."

"Naw man, she got mad and left just before the cholos came around the corner."

"You told me that you were smooching with your chick when it happened and *now you say she wasn't there.*"

Jesus tensed. *"Hey man, what's the matter? You on my side or you one of those cops?"*

"Alright, what kind of loot did they find in your car?"

"Man, those dirty cops found a TV set, two stereo speakers and a bag of golf clubs."

I looked at John, "Okay, I'll get a police report for you first thing in the morning, it sure sounds like you got a bigger problem than Jesus."

John was one of the first lawyers hired by the Public Defender's office. I had investigated quite a few cases for him and I had found him to be a fine and extremely able trial attorney. Along with a very analytical mind he had an amazing memory for statements which prosecution witnesses made on the stand while being questioned by the prosecuting attorney. Under John's patient cross-examination, if they were telling anything but the truth it was certain to come out in a manner quite devastating to the prosecution's case. The most important thing about him I found to be, was his dedication to a client if he had determined that the client was indeed innocent. I knew that he spent many hours after getting home at night studying the evidence, reading technical interpretations of law and preparing his defense for the next day in court.

Beyond Russell's cubicle I passed into a large room which served as the Bureau of Investigation headquarters. At this time there were only two desks in the room besides my own and a large file cabinet behind my desk in which I kept investigative files. The only other piece of furniture was a table about six feet long and several hard backed chairs which we used for clients while interviewing them.

James Hronesh, one of the two investigators besides myself, was already at his desk talking on the phone. He had his back to me and you could tell at first glance he was quite husky, but when he stood up it seemed like he must have stretched himself to make the height requirements for the police department. James had been a Ventura Policeman when I first met him, he worked as court officer in the morning, taking all the misdemeanor prisoners who were arrested overnight to court for arraignment. He'd help me with investigations in the afternoon when his court duties were over. We both said "Hi" as he hung up the phone, picked up some papers and left the room heading for the attorneys offices to give them some information they had requested. As Chief Investigator I was the first investigator hired by Erwin, Glen Kuhn was hired a couple months later. He was a Los Angeles Police Department officer but had to wait until he had all his time in to retire from L.A. before he could report to Ventura.

After a few phone calls to tie up some loose ends on a couple of minor cases I noticed that it was getting darker outside. Looking down from the window I could see that the clock watchers were pouring out of the courthouse rear door into the parking lot and were wasting no time getting their cars down the driveway to Poli Street. My wristwatch indicated it was thirty seconds after five pm. Heading down the hall to the main entrance of our office I saw Paul Clinton standing by the door of his cubicle.

"Hi Paul, how did things go in court today?"

He nodded, "Well you know how it is, you do your best then you hope for the best." Paul and John had come to the Public Defender's office about the same time. Paul was an impressive individual, fairly tall and husky with gray hair and a gray mustache that gave him an aura of distinguishment. Paul like John was an accomplished trial lawyer. He believed that a client should get the benefit of all the knowledge and effort that he could put forth.

"Paul, I see you've got a new sport coat, that Scottish plaid looks real sharp on you."

He smiled, then entered his cubicle to wind up his days work. Clinton was the sharpest and most stylish dresser in the office, he looked the part of a competent attorney which he was indeed. When reaching the main entrance of the office to leave I took a quick backward glance. A number of attorneys and office girls were also preparing to leave.

I saw that Glen Kuhn, the other investigator, had come in. He was sitting back against the wall next to Claire's desk and they were engaged in a private conversation. Kuhn was doing most of the talking. Claire's face was alternating with smiles then frowns in accordance with Kuhn's efforts to inform her of the occurrences throughout the day that would surely be their own little secrets. I'd noticed lately that this cozy little scene between the two had been occurring with greater frequency and going down the stairs I was beginning to wonder if this little *tete-a-tete* had anything to do with Claire's feelings toward me. I thought no, it couldn't be anything that

Glen was telling her. Glen had called me numerous times and asked me for assurances that I wouldn't hire any other investigator before him and he was doing everything he could to expedite his retirement with the L.A.P.D. so that he could report for duty in Ventura. I had assured Kuhn that Mr. Erwin and I would wait for his retirement and that he would be the next investigator hired. No, it couldn't be Kuhn would try to undermine me with Claire after I had kept my promise to hire him.

The next morning I left my desk to go into the front office and pick up some crime reports I needed. Coming down the hall directly toward me was Erwin. "Hey Gary, you're just the guy I was looking for." He lowered his voice to a more confidential tone and took a quick look around, no one else was in sight. "Here, take this piece of paper, it has a bunch of license plate numbers on it. I want you to get the owners names and check them *all* out for criminal records." The paper had eight license numbers scribbled hap-hazardly on both sides.

"Sure, I can check them out for you. Is it one of the cases I have been working on?"

"Christ no," he rasped, and his voice got back to its normal loud level, I could see that he was working himself up over something. *"That rotten son-of-a-bitch next door to me is making my life plain miserable, and goddamn it, I've told you I want you to do something!"* His name is Bruce Dodd, he's a bookmaker or narcotic peddler or something like that. He never works, just loafs around his place day and night. Last night there were cars all over the cul-de-sac, it looked like a bunch of hippies come up from Los Angeles to buy narcotics. So I got my dog on a leash and we walked around the houses. When no one was watching I wrote down those license plates."

"Mr. Erwin, if you are convinced this guy Dodd is really bad I'll talk to a detective friend on the Police Department and let them check it out."

"No, goddamn it! I want *you* to do it. And something else, that friggin' Woody Deem is just as crooked as they come. You know Gilliam, the colored guy we just made a deal for and got him second degree murder?"

I remembered Gilliam, a colored man that had been working in the lettuce fields in Oxnard. He had shot and killed another worker during a late hour argument in the barracks where they lived. Gilliam was a completely illiterate black man with low mentality. His past criminal record disclosed that he'd spent a long stretch in the state penitentiary in Tennessee for murder. As he put it, "I done bashed that black man's 'haid' in with a ball bat." It had happened so long ago he couldn't even remember why he did it. Erwin always referred to Gilliam as the baseball player, which to him was exceedingly funny to liken our client to Jr. Gilliam, a major league player who was also quite dexterous with a ball bat, but on the baseball diamond.

"I've told you guys a million times, Deem is in cahoots with a head shrinker up in Santa Barbara. Every time there is a killing Deem calls Dr. Battson down here to Ventura, the Dr. talks to the suspect before anybody else does and gets him all screwed up. He then turns in a report to Woody with statements that the suspect made. There is hardly anyway we can get around these statements and Deem beats us in court every time. We could have gotten the baseball player off on self defense if it hadn't been for that rotten head-shrinker."

"Well, how do you figure that makes Woody a crook? I've known him for a long time and there has never been even a whisper of such a thing about him. I know that he's very religious and he stands quite high in the Mormon Church."

The mention of Deem's standing with the Mormons served to set Erwin off into a frenzy of profanity. He was getting louder as we continued this conversation in the hallway, but he suddenly seemed to control himself. Lowering his voice he said, "Woody never calls any doctors in Ventura. He's always calling Dr. Battson from Santa Barbara. I know they have been splitting the money the Doctor gets from the County for interviewing the suspects and Woody gets the statements just the way he likes them. I want you to get to Santa Barbara and check this Doctor's past history, see if he is connected with Deem. I also want you to find out how high up he is in the Mormon Church. I want to know which of them is the big pooh-bah in the hierarchy, then I will know who is boss. You get on this right away."

"This puts me on the spot Mr. Erwin. I have quite a few cases I am working right now and our attorneys need the information as soon as possible."

"Don't worry about them. They will get by one way or another. You just get moving on this deal with Woody and Dr. Battson right away."

For several days I'd been doing my best to get some critical work out for the attorneys to assist them in their courtroom appearances. At the same time I avoided Erwin, who I was hoping had forgotten about his orders regarding the District Attorney, the Doctor and also Mr. Dodd, his neighbor. I thought, Erwin must have some kind of super-sensitivity that tells him when I am in this hallway...here he comes heading right at me. I could see the look in his small black eyes behind the gold-rimmed glasses, a look such as a small child might have on his face when he catches sight of Santa Claus and is waiting for the magnificent gift to be handed to him. "What did you find out? Let me have it," he said.

Christ, how I wished I was some place else. "Mr. Erwin, I spent two whole days here and in Santa Barbara trying to tie Deem and Dr. Battson into something together. There just isn't anything that goes along with your information. In fact, Dr. Battson isn't even a Mormon." Though Erwin was getting red in the face I figured I might as well give him the rest of the bad news. "Your neighbor Mr. Dodd moved to Ventura from up north around San Luis Obispo or Santa Maria where he was at one time a city councilman and a successful businessman with a good reputation. The car license numbers you gave me all checked out to reliable citizens down in Los Angeles."

I could see by Erwin's face that my information was going over like a lead balloon. I knew he'd been waiting for his gift all wrapped up in beautiful Christmas paper. He was sure it would contain all sorts of goodies that would incriminate Deem, the Doctor and Dodd. The information would put them away in cold, dark cells forever, where they could *never* bother him or his flowers again. His face got redder and his black eyes got smaller. His lips started to move, he screamed, "Damn it, you're a helluva' investigator, you couldn't find anything if it was right in front of you."

I was real glad that he turned around and walked off before I could completely formulate the answer I wanted to give him. Things kind of quieted down with Erwin for the next couple of days. The few times I saw him from a distance he just sort of looked at me and then cast his eyes down at his hands where I could see that he had a paper clip and that it had been opened on one end.

I had been at my desk for a while when I heard Hronesh coming into the investigator's room. My watch said 8:30 am. Some of the attorneys had been complaining to me that James had been dogging it and wasn't making decent reports on the information they had requested. Now...here he was walking into the office a full half hour late. "Jim, what's with you being late all the time? Also, the lawyers are complaining about your piss-poor reports or complete lack of them."

Banging a briefcase down on his desk he said, "Shit, I've been up all night over at Erwin's house, me and Kuhn too."

"What in hell happened over there?"

"Right after dinner Erwin called me at home and told me to get over to his place quick, that he needed me. I jumped in my car and dashed over there, Kuhn had already arrived. It seemed Mrs. Erwin had assaulted Mrs. Dodd over the fence, the police had been called and Mrs. Dodd wanted to file a criminal complaint."

"Lord, how bad was it?"

"Oh hell! Mrs. Erwin turned her hose on Mrs. Dodd. For some reason the cops became peed-off at the whole damn affair and I couldn't talk them out of taking a report."

"What in the world was Erwin doing?"

"Everyone was arguing and the cops were coming in and out of the house and that silly son-of-a-bitch sat there playing the piano all through the whole scene. After the cops left, Erwin made Kuhn and me go out into his garage which is attached to the house, and sit in the dark watching the Dodd's place through the window."

"What in hell did he want you guys to watch for?"

"Damn if I know, but his silly-ass daughter kept coming out to the garage with black coffee to make sure we didn't go to sleep."

"Where's Kuhn now?"

"He called Claire and told her he was going to take a sick day off. Erwin told us we could take overtime for all the time we were there, but my wife is pretty sore about it."

"Hell! I've got work stacked up on my desk a foot high, the lawyers are screaming for help and Erwin is using you guys for bullshit like this...and all you can do is cry about how mad your wife is." I put a pile of cases on his desk, "Here, damn it, get started."

CHAPTER 2

/ John Russell had a tough case he was defending in court, a loser. The D.A. was really pushing it hard to put Lee Smith, John's client away. They'd charged him with armed robbery. Randy Siple, a Dep. D.A., and a very ambitious prosecuting attorney, wasn't sparing the horses. It was at a time when the position of Chief Assistant D.A. was up for grabs. Siple knew that by *winning* this case he'd greatly enhance his chances for the appointment. Russell had asked me to contact Smith in the county jail and see what he had in mind. The jailer let me through the main door to the jail and yelled at one of the trusty's to get Smith who was being kept in a felony holding tank. I entered one of the interview rooms and sat down to wait for him.

You really couldn't call it a room, it was barely four feet wide, containing two chairs and a tiny table. There was mighty little space to move after you closed the door. Including the door there was glass on three sides. A wall on the fourth side had one small window with iron bars. The trusty returned with a man dressed in blue denim jail clothes, he indicated to Smith where I was sitting in the interview room. I watched him approach, he was tall, about six feet, well built, his black hair was neatly combed and he was clean shaven. Sitting down he stared out the lonely window. I told him, "John Russell sent me down to talk to you."

"Well, I'm glad you're here, I sure as hell need some help. You wouldn't have a spare smoke would you?" I offered him a cigarette from a pack I kept for just this sort of occasion since I had quit the smoking myself.

"Lee, I'm gonna' ask you right flat out...did you pull that job they busted you on?"

"No! Honest to Christ no, I did not do it."

"Alright Lee, I'll tell you what I'm going to do. I want to know minute by minute where you were for twenty-four hours before the robbery. I'm gonna' tell you another thing, if I find out you're lying or trying to *use me* to set up an alibi for you, by Christ you won't have to worry about Randy Siple, I'll personally see that you go to the joint. You know what I mean?"

"Yeah, I get you pretty clear."

"Okay. The hold-up occurred about 9:00 am, so let's start about 9:00 am the day before."

"I had shacked up with my girlfriend. After getting up I went outside and started to work on my car. The generator had gone out, so I worked on it most of the day. I went to a parts house and got a new one. That evening I got cleaned up and my girlfriend and I went out for a few beers, then we went back to her apartment. Next morning, the day of the robbery, I got up early and went down by myself to a restaurant and had breakfast."

"Wait a minute... As near as you can remember, what time was it when you left the restaurant?"

"Well, as near as I can recall, it was just about 8:00 am."

"What did you do then?"

"I drove back to my girlfriend's apartment."

"Where was the restaurant?"

"In San Fernando Valley, there's a little cafe by a gas station at Saticoy and Whiteoak."

"Just thinking real quick - from the restaurant to Santa Susanna Pass would take about fifteen to twenty minutes, then over the pass and out to Simi where the hold-up had occurred, another thirty to thirty-five minutes. It's cutting it pretty close Lee. You could have made it. As it stands now, Siple will have a timetable and he'll show that jury just how you made it with no trouble."

"Yeah, I'll tell you I am plenty worried. I've been listening to Siple and his witnesses in court the last couple days and so help me Christ he almost has me believing I did it myself."

"I'll go down to the Valley and see what I can shake loose." Next morning at 7:30 I was at the restaurant Lee told me about. I ordered coffee from a young girl waiting on the counter. She wasn't like the ordinary waitress. About twenty years old, her hair was done up very neatly in some sort of a fashion with an orange colored ribbon, and she was wearing a freshly starched uniform.

I asked, "Waitress, could I talk to you for a moment?" Quickly I explained who I was.

"Sure, I will be able to come around on the other side of the counter in just a few minutes, I get off at 8:00." Setting her cup of coffee at the place next to me she came around and sat down. Looking at me she said, "I know just about what you want to ask me."

"How do you know?"

"Because, several days ago an investigator from the Ventura D.A. came and talked to me."

"What did you tell him?"

"I told him I knew Lee Smith, not personally, only because he came in here quite often for coffee or a coke."

"What else did you tell him?"

"I remembered Lee got up to leave, he paid me and I know it was 8:00 am because the day waitress came in to relieve me so I went home. Also that D.A. investigator came back yesterday and served a subpoena on me to appear in court as a witness."

This would just about cook Smith's goose. This waitress could testify that Smith paid her and was leaving the restaurant at 8:00 am, which would give him not plenty of time, but sufficient time to get to Simi and pull the hold-up. With just his girlfriend's testimony that he came back to her apartment from the restaurant, Smith's alibi would never hold up in court. Someone sat down on the stool on my left, it was the chef who had been busy cooking while I was talking with the waitress.

"You know," he said, "I've been listening to you talk to Judy, I recall that morning when Lee Smith was getting ready to leave the cafe. I got here right as Judy was leaving and Smith walked out at the same time, but he ran into somebody he knew outside, after a few minutes they both came back in and sat down. They had a coke, Smith paid for the check and they left. That must have been a good fifteen or twenty minutes after 8:00." It turned out the chef was the owner of the restaurant and was willing to testify to what he knew.

"Listen Joe," the cafe owner had told me his name was Joe, "I'll be back with a subpoena for you first thing tomorrow morning." This was good news. It cut the driving-time element down to about fifty minutes, which meant that Smith would have had to drive like a bat-out-of-hell to get to Simi in time for the stick-up. Smith wasn't out of the woods yet. Siple would still be able to show the jury that it could be done.

Judy, the waitress, was poking my arm. "How about it?"

"How about what?"

"Can you cancel my subpoena? There's no use in me going up to Ventura if Joe saw Lee here after I left to go home."

"No, I can't cancel a subpoena that the D.A. served you with, but you and Joe can come up at the same time so you won't have to drive your car." I thanked them and left the cafe.

I was feeling pretty good...not only because of what Joe could testify to, but because it looked like Smith was leveling with me. I had always tried to stick to the rule of looking at both sides of a story before drawing any conclusions, even so, this is pretty hard to do when you've found through experience that most people who get arrested are guilty. That is, they are guilty of some violation of the law, leaving only the specific violation or degree to be determined by a jury. But every once in a while you come upon that rare instance when someone arrested is wholly innocent, but circumstances are sucking him into a vortex from which he cannot escape. Lee told me, "Look, I sure ain't no angel. I've been involved in lots of crazy things in the past, but I simply just did not have anything to do with this stick-up."

The only thing that concerned the Public Defender's office was to prove that he was innocent of the specific charges that had been placed against him. It was getting plenty hot for this early in the morning, climbing into the county car I sat thinking for a moment. Taking a yellow legal tablet out of my briefcase I wrote down the mileage that appeared on the speedometer including the tenths and jotted down the exact time. I drove away from the restaurant at as great a speed as possible without inviting a traffic ticket. Taking the shortest route possible I again jotted down the mileage and time when I reached the foot of the Santa Susana Pass. Further up the pass the traffic slowed to almost a snail pace and I saw that heavy construction work was being done in the area. It took nearly twenty minutes to reach the summit. Pulling over to the side of the road I got out of the car. I approached a construction worker standing by the side of his pickup truck.

"How ya doing? You got a minute to talk?"

Looking at my car and the county emblem on it's side he said grudgingly, "Yeah, I suppose so."

"Just what are you people doing here?"

"Our company has the blasting contract up here to prepare the way for the new freeway over the Santa Susana Pass."
"How long have you been up here?"
"Over six months now."
"Is the traffic slowed down like this all the time?"
"Yeah, we start about 8:00 am, and sometimes traffic is stopped completely for nearly fifteen minutes at a time."
"What is your name?"
"Martin....Deke Martin. Why? What's all the questions for?"
"Deke, I am going to have to subpoena you to court to explain the blasting and the construction work that has been going on up here, also how it has slowed down the traffic over the pass. We will arrange it so you can take the stand soon as you get there. We won't tie you up any longer than is necessary. I'll even send your company a letter and explain the situation and thank them for your help."
"Thanks a lot but I have work to do." Jumping in his pickup he headed down the pass.

In the afternoon I sat in John Russell's office explaining what I had learned. We examined all the possibilities of the driving time. Plainly it was a physical impossibility for Lee Smith to have left the restaurant at 8:00 am and still make it to the scene of the hold-up at 9:05.

"Alright Gary, subpoena all the witnesses we'll need for the day after tomorrow at eight am. The trial won't resume til ten am, that will give me a chance to talk to them first."

Closing arguments were made by both prosecution and defense. The judge instructed the jurors as to their responsibility. They retired to deliberate and there was nothing more Russell or I could do but sit in the corridor outside of the courtroom and wait. Lee Smith was returned to his cell by a deputy sheriff, where all that he could do was sit, sweat and await his fate.

I was feeling a weight of bitter frustration...while investigating Smith's where-abouts at the time of the hold-up I had come up with the suspects who had actually committed the robbery. Three men, prisoners in the Ventura County Jail had escaped. They had 'holed up' in an apartment across the street from the store that was robbed. At the same time as the crime they had abandoned the apartment.

During Smith's trial the three escapees, heavily armed, were arrested by the Los Angeles Police Dept. in Encino. They had held up another branch of the same chain stores as was robbed in Simi. Also they had in their possession a car, the same make, model, year and color as the get-away vehicle Siple accused Smith of using. I wanted to get 'mugs' of the three bandits and display them to the robbery victims in Simi but there wasn't enough time left.

During a recess in Smith's trial I had approached Siple with these facts...blustering and turning red in the face he rejected the information. He said, "Bull-shit," then muttered, "*anyway* it's too late, I've already got Smith convicted." Siple had left me standing in the middle of the hallway.

As of now Smith faced ten years in the pen for something he had not done. The jury returned to the courtroom late that night... Russell and I were there, Randy Siple was there, in dead silence we waited for the deputy sheriff to bring Smith from his cell, the verdict: "Not Guilty." Whether it had anything to do with it or not...Randy Siple was *not* appointed Assistant D.A....he blamed me for it.

It was almost quitting time the next day when I walked into the investigations office. Hronesh was talking on his phone with his back to me. I sat down and leaned back in my chair to relax for a minute. Something in Jim's tone of voice caught my attention, I listened. He was extremely agitated, his knuckles were white from holding the receiver so tight. "Listen Jon, you and Lola have got to do something quick and I mean it! Kuhn told me this afternoon Erwin was going to fire me if I didn't get it done. Alright, I know you guys have to take it easy, but hurry up and do it." He listened for a minute, said "Okay," and hung up. Looking at me he left the room, I watched him head for Erwin's office.

I realized Jim had been talking to Lt. Jonas Hopman and Lola, a policewoman, they were both on the Ventura P.D., I wondered what the devil he was up to. The next morning Glen Kuhn and I had been out in east Ventura talking to some witnesses on several cases. While driving back to the office I said, "Glen, I've been wanting to talk to you about several things. For one, what are you and James doing out all hours of the night using a county car? You can't be working on cases because I assign your cases and I haven't seen any written reports."

"Yeah, I know. Erwin is real unhappy with you because you wouldn't do anything about his neighbor Mr. Dodd. He was fit to be tied when you didn't come up with something on Woody Deem and Dr. Battson from Santa Barbara. Erwin has ordered me to get a dossier on every top official in the Ventura Courthouse."

"What in hell did he order you to get?"

"He wanted a *dossier*...a file with all the dirt he can get on all the big shots in Ventura. He has been raising hell with Hronesh because Jim has been around here all his life and he knows the scoop on everybody. Erwin found out that Charlie Reiman, the Ventura City Manager and Geary, the Chief of Police were going to fire Jim from the Police Department, so Erwin has been putting the squeeze on Hronesh."

"I know. Jim came to me when I first got this job and pressured me to hire him. He told me that a couple of years ago he and Lane Martin, a Lt. on the P.D. had bucked Reiman and Geary trying to get a pay raise for the whole department by going to the citizens and voters of the city. I guess they raised a lot of hell and got Reiman and the Chief down on them real bad. The voters turned down the pay raise and backed Reiman. Jim says Reiman has been trying to nail his ass ever since."

Kuhn laughed, "Hell, I knew that, but that wasn't why Reiman and Chief Geary were going to fire Hronesh."

"What are you getting at?"

"Hronesh was working plain clothes on night shift when a patrol sergeant caught him messing with a policewoman in the radio car. He got a warning to cut it out or else. It wasn't long after that the sgt. caught him in the police car again with the same policewoman and the stupid ass had parked in the same location they caught him the first time."

"Why that lying son-of-a-gun, Jim never told me any of this." Pulling around behind the courthouse I located a parking spot and turning off the ignition I said to Kuhn, "This goddamn dossier shit that Erwin wants is big trouble, I'm telling you right now to cut it out." Kuhn said nothing, we got out of the car and headed for the office.

I was working about twenty cases at once, but this one I was checking into right now was really a dilly. I was sitting in the front room of a small modest home in Montalvo. A young housewife sat in a chair across the room.

"Mrs. Hugginson, this copy of the police report I have here says you were arrested for shoplifting at a large department store. Why don't you go ahead in your own words and tell me what happened."

Flushing slightly when I said shoplifting she commenced talking. "I went to the beauty parlor at the store to have my hair done. My husband and I had planned to go out that night. All the girls were busy so I stepped outside the beauty parlor and was looking at some books in the book section. It appeared I would have to wait for quite a while so I took one and went back into the beauty parlor." When she hesitated for a minute I looked at the report. According to it a female security officer had been watching Mrs. Hugginson at the book rack and had observed her carry the book into the beauty parlor. Composing herself Mrs. Hugginson continued, "I finally got a seat, while the girl was working on me I vaguely remember the book being on my lap, then a phone rang."

Becoming tired of watching Mrs. Hugginson and the book, the security woman had returned to her office and called the hair dresser telling her she thought her customer was a shoplifter. The officer requested that she be notified when the lady was ready to leave. The beautician became alarmed, thinking she might not get paid she asked Mrs. Hugginson if she was going to pay in cash. She said no and gave her a credit card. The girl called the credit office to verify the card and was told not to accept it as it was overdrawn. The operator then demanded cash payment on the spot.

Mrs. Hugginson had only a small amount of change with her so the hair dresser ordered her out of the chair. She pleaded, "But you are only half done with my hair, it's all wet and hanging all over my face." Adamant, the beautician refused to do anything until she had been paid. Mrs. Hugginson asked to use the phone to call her sister to have her come down to the store with some money, but she was refused. Finally locating a pay phone she frantically called her sister who said she'd be there as soon as possible. It was about half an hour before she arrived, but all she had was a check which the beautician refused to take. Assuring the beautician she would contact relatives and return immediately with the money the sister left. By now it was getting late. Mrs. Hugginson was becoming a nervous wreck. She told the hair dresser, "I'm sorry, but I am going home and I will pay you later."

Immediately upon her stepping outside the entrance of the store the female security agent took hold of her arm demanding to look in her purse. Mrs. Hugginson opened her purse and the book was there. It was a small paper-back book which in her emotional state brought on by the events she had forgotten all about putting in her purse. The security agent advised Mrs. Hugginson she was under arrest and ordered her to come to the office. There the department store agent further searched and interrogated her. A Ventura police officer arrived. After conversing with the store agent the officer placed handcuffs on Mrs. Hugginson and led her out through the store. At the police station she was booked for petty theft.

In the meantime Mr. Hugginson arrived home from work and could not find his wife. He called the department store trying to locate her. Contending with a lot of hedging and frustrating answers he finally learned that his wife had been taken to the police station. After the necessary formalities he affected his wife's release about 11:00 pm. I verified our client's story by talking with many of the people involved. Even the department store security people and the police department seemed to have little to say that varied from the statement of Mrs. Hugginson. I made a complete report and turned it in to the office files so the attorneys would have it available for the client's court appearance.

The initial appearances were made by Public Defender Harrison Dunham in Municipal Court. Dunham, an ex-Hollywood lawyer, was hired by Erwin who had been extolling Dunham's legal experience as being extremely valuable to the other lawyers. According to Erwin, Dunham had been a *big-time* attorney in Beverly Hills and had handled many celebrities and their problems with great finesse. Dunham's story was that he wanted to come to work for the Public Defender's office to get away from the pressure of the Hollywood scene, even though it meant he would take a fantastic cut in his income.

Mrs. Hugginson's experience had been quite unusual in an odd way. I was used to odd-ball cases, but I made a mental note to keep tabs on it to see how it came out. Dunham was a big heavy-set man with graying hair and a large, round, florid face. A fat green cigar was clamped in his teeth constantly. In court he removed the cigar only when the bailiff announced in a loud voice that court was in session and the judge was sitting down in his seat. The smelly cigar would be lodged in the nearest convenient spot Dunham could find. Anywhere, from the hardwood rail separating the jury chairs from the court, to the chalk rack under the blackboard. This smelly, soggy piece of tobacco which was Dunham's constant companion, was laid by Dunham in a last minute emergency upon the arm of one of the chairs lining the courtroom wall. The cigar was rolling back and forth, I watched it from where I sat at the attorneys table in front of the judge's bench. It slid off the chair's arm and fell on the seat.

A group of lawyers stood near the row of chairs conducting one of their customary ultra-important little conversations in a very discreet and confidential manner. The judge entered the courtroom and sat down. The attorneys became quiet and backed up to sit down in the chairs along the wall. I noted with just a touch of perverted interest, one of the attorneys, a real dapper-dan and also quite an overbearing personality had both his hands on the arms of the chair, he was lowering himself in a very dignified manner directly down onto Dunham's cigar. I thought hell, if that damn thing is still burning there is going to be some fireworks for sure. I was watching his face close waiting to see if there was going to be any real action when he raised himself slightly and reached under his light beige, well pressed pants. He brought forth the remains of the flattened, foul-smelling cigar which lucky for him had not been burning. He held it at arms length looking at it, then stared icily at Dunham. Only his fear of the judge kept him from busting Dunham in the face with the cigar.

The court recessed and I went out into the crowded corridor. Dunham was standing next to the marble-lined wall unconcernedly lighting a fresh cigar. "Hi Harrison, I thought that case with Mrs. Hugginson and the department store was coming on today, but I didn't hear anything."

Dunham blew a cloud of cigar smoke and said, "No, it's been postponed."

"How come? It seems to me the D.A. would be trying to get rid of that one. It was pretty bad."

Mumbling Dunham said, "I'll see you later."

Back in the office I mentioned to the clerk, "Pearl, I can't find that file on Mrs. Hugginson, the gal who was pinched down at the department store." Pearl was the secretary in charge of all the reports in the office. She kept the active files with up-coming court appearances in a large metal cabinet, they were indexed so that they were very easy to find ordinarily. A tiny woman, Pearl was very friendly and easy to get along with.

"No, it isn't in the file. Claire took it out yesterday and put it on Erwin's desk." I glanced at Pearl, she stared back at me for a second with what I thought was a *knowing look* of some kind. I left the office with a briefcase full of cases to check on and didn't get back until around 4:00 pm. Dunham was on his office phone. He waved to me to come in and told the person on the other end of the line to hold on for a minute. Putting his hand over the mouthpiece he said, "Gary, I'm busier than hell on this phone. Do me a favor and take this letter down to the Municipal Court. Caton Machamer is down there. Give it to him, you'll have to hurry before he leaves."

Dunham handed me a large white envelope, it was thick and sealed tight. Taking the envelope I walked downstairs and through a passageway that connected our new office building to the original courthouse. The Municipal Court had just recessed for the day but there were still a few small groups of defendants and their attorneys standing around discussing their upcoming legal entanglements. I didn't see Machamer anywhere in the corridor, a quick glance into the courtroom revealed it was empty. Machamer, a private attorney, was a slim man with long hair and gold-rimmed glasses. Of late I had seen him frequently talking with Erwin and hanging around the Public Defender's office. Back at Harrison's office I tossed the envelope on his desk. Dunham was just hanging up the phone, I told him I couldn't find Machamer. Clamping his teeth on the cigar his face grew redder. It was quite obvious he was extremely upset over something.

"Alright! I'll take care of it myself," he picked up the envelope and placed it in a pocket inside his coat.

The next morning I was standing in the courthouse corridor watching for a guy from the Simi Valley area who was supposed to show up in court. I wanted to drop a subpoena on him, it would save me a long drive and a whole day over in Simi looking for him. I noticed Machamer leaning back against the wall, Caton was all by himself. He kept looking at his watch and down the hall like he was waiting for someone. Sure enough! He was waiting for someone. I saw Dunham bulling his way down the hallway heading over to Machamer. I remembered the envelope episode of yesterday afternoon and was getting mighty curious. A large group of people were walking behind Dunham, joining them I walked up to within a few feet from where Dunham and the lawyer were talking.

Slipping the long white envelope from his coat pocket Dunham handed it to Machamer who tore it open and removed some papers. I could see that it was a Public Defender investigative file. Examining the *pink colored papers* for a few seconds Machamer put them back in the envelope. Nodding at Dunham he reached inside his coat and removed a white envelope smaller than the one he had received from Dunham and handed it to him. The hallway was jammed with people, waiting for the court to open session. Dunham and Machamer were so engrossed in their conversation that they hadn't seem me. I'd moved toward them until only one man stood between us. Harrison opened the envelope, I saw a large sum of money in it before he quickly put it in his pocket. I faded away quickly, luckily so because Dunham turned and headed for our office.

Passing Claire's desk without a word he entered Erwin's office.

I caught a quick glimpse of Erwin before the door closed behind Dunham. Feeling a strong urge to get clear out of the building I went out the large front doors of the old courthouse, down California Street to a restaurant and ordered a cup of coffee. It couldn't be much clearer. *Dunham and Erwin were stealing confidential Public Defender investigation files and selling them to private attorneys.* Finishing my coffee I realized that my keys to the county car were still on my desk. Heading back to my office I went through the main doors of the courthouse, up the winding stairs and into the corridor. Glancing down the hall I suddenly had the whole picture. Christ! Down past the Municipal Court entrance I saw Dunham introducing Mrs. Hugginson to Caton Machamer. The sneaky shyster had sold the investigation report I had made detailing the events between Mrs. Hugginson and the department store. I'll bet Dunham and Machamer already had it figured out how much they could take the department store for. *Sometime later I learned that Machamer made an agreement out of court, for a large cash settlement.*

CHAPTER 3

/ My office had been moved temporarily to a glass-enclosed room adjacent to the main office. From where I sat in my chair I could see Claire's desk and into Erwin's office, also into the office to the right. Tilting back in my chair and reading some arrest reports I could see the clock hanging on the wall, it said seven minutes til noon. Claire was standing behind her desk talking to a tall young girl wearing an extremely short skirt, and the skimpy, tight fitting blouse she wore didn't conceal a hell of a lot either. She was quite attractive. Several of the attorneys leaving their office's to get a head start to their favorite lunch spots swiveled their heads about 180 degrees trying to get a last look as they went out the main door. I recognized the girl, a secretary from the County Executive's department whose offices were across the hall from ours. Claire and the girl were conversing very amiably, Claire must have found a friend. The girl cast a quick look at the clock and said, "Oh! I must go, I have an *appointment.*"

Watching the young secretary until she disappeared through the outer door, Claire dashed into the office to the right of Erwin's. I hadn't noticed Kuhn in there, he was sitting just to the right of the window. Looking out from his position a person could survey the entire county parking lot. Kuhn was telling Claire to look in a certain direction, she did, then squealed excitedly, "There he goes, there's Hugh Dreever getting into his car now. Quick Glen, get down there fast. She'll be coming out any minute. Dreever is pulling away."

Kuhn moving quickly from his chair told Claire, "This time I'll find out for sure where they go. Where in hell is Hronesh? I need him. That asshole is never around when I need him." Kuhn left in a hurry, Claire remained watching out the window, she didn't see me. I walked down to Dunham's office, it was empty, from there you could see the parking area. The secretary walked across the lot popping into a Volkswagen. Kuhn was coming out of the court house now, quickly he went to his car and followed the girl's VW down the drive at a discreet distance. I returned to my office. Claire was back at her desk, I knew she would sit there in a highly keyed-up state waiting for Kuhn to return to give her all the lurid details.

Hugh Dreever was an assistant to Loren Enoch, the County Executive. Enoch was an extremely powerful figure in the county government. It didn't take too much *deep thinking* for me to realize that Dreever and the tall sexy secretary had something going for themselves on their lunch hour. They couldn't have gone too far to meet. It was only about ten minutes when I saw Kuhn coming back with a big smile on his face. Claire and I were the only ones in the office. Kuhn sat down in the chair next to her desk and leaned back comfortably. Claire was coming out of her skin waiting for him to start talking. He was taking his time, I knew he was doing it just to annoy her.

"I followed her car, she went east of the courthouse a couple of blocks, turned north one block, made a left turn on the next street and parked in front of an apartment house. They must feel pretty secure, because she parked right behind Hugh's car and waltzed into the apartment house."

The next day Glen and Jim walked into the investigators room. Hronesh was telling Kuhn something, when he saw that I was on the phone he continued, "Don't worry Glen, I was parked in a real good position waiting for them to get there this noon. I got pictures of Dreever and the girl both going into the apartment house."

"Good, I checked the apartment building and found out a friend of Hugh's has an apartment there, he lets them use it at noon. We're lucky we got the pictures and other stuff now, because another week or so would be too late."

"How come?"

"Well, the secretary's husband moved down south of Los Angeles where he got a new job, and his wife is leaving to go down with him."

"Glen I was working half the night last night checking on Enoch's wife, I got all the dope on her and the policeman she's been having an affair with. But I'm getting tired of being out every night like we have for the last couple weeks."

Kuhn snapped, "What are you crying for? You know Erwin told us to turn in all the overtime."

"Yeah, but my wife's getting pissed off about it."

"Listen! Are you sure you got the *straight dope* on Enoch's wife? You know Erwin is real interested in that."

"Yeah, I got it."

"Alright, we'll take it easy for a few days."

Listening to them talk I was getting madder by the minute, but I didn't want to show it. I said, "You assholes keep screwin' around with *your dossiers* and one of these days you'll get messed up good." Hronesh grabbed his phone and Glen left the room.

I sat there angrily staring at the wall when I overheard Jim say, "Jonas how are you coming with that Thurman deal? Yeah, I know it takes time, but get Lola working on the warrant and bust that woman. Kuhn was telling me again today that Erwin is going to fire me if I don't get her arrested. Okay, okay...I'll call you later." He slammed the phone down. I was just about to get on Hronesh heavy over the stuff he was pulling when I heard a strange noise coming from the hallway.

"Oooh, yoo hoo, yoo hoo, Glen baby. Yoo hoo, Glen baby, where are you?" The voice was coming closer. "Yoo hoo, Glen baby." A face peered around the corner of the door. You couldn't see the body, just the face. The eyes were sparkling behind the glasses with the anticipation of seeing Glen Baby.

Claire's eyes roamed around the room and she said, "Oh! Has anybody seen Glen Baby?" Jim and I both just stared at her. The face disappeared and we could hear her going down the hall hoping to find Glen Baby.

"What the hell gives with her Jim?"

"She's been getting her jollies over following people and learning about their sex lives, Kuhn's been stirring her up with stories. She's enough to make you sick."

"Well, if you feel that way about it, how come you're pulling all this bullshit you're involved in? And how come you're after Lt. Jon Hopman and Lola all the time?"

Looking square at me he said, "Goddamn it, Erwin threatened me if I don't do it he is going to fire me and I'll never get another job...not in this county at least."

I was working in my glass-enclosed office about ten the following morning. Several secretaries to my right were pecking busily at their typewriters. I knew something was up again. Hronesh was in and out of the office whispering confidentially to Claire, and Kuhn had taken up his position again at the window in the office next to Erwin's. I left my office with some papers in my hand as if I had not been paying any attention to their actions. Down the hall out of Claire's sight, I stepped into Dunham's office which was empty and looked out the window onto the parking lot. I thought if those three assholes spent as much time working for the county as they did looking out the windows, we could get a lot of work done.

The only person in view they could be interested in was Ben Martinez who was standing by his car. He was talking to the county parking lot attendant. Returning to the main office I saw that Claire and Jim had joined Kuhn in their observation room. They were completely engrossed in watching Martinez. Kuhn was saying to Jim, "Get yourself down to the lot and follow Ben, I want to know where he goes."

Hronesh left the office in a hurry. Ben Martinez was County Supervisor Robby Robinson's Administrative Assistant. I had heard Jim and Kuhn a couple days before talking about following Robinson two nights in a row. Jim had told Glen, "I talked with a friend of mine. He's working on some other angles on Robinson for us."

Glen had replied, "Good, keep it up."

Jim returned shortly, he reported, "I followed Martinez. He went to see Herb Ashby, the County Counsel, in his office."

"Very good Jim. Now get a car, pull around in front of the building and wait for me." The County Counsel's office was on the same floor as ours but about fifty feet down the hall. Claire went into the secretaries area, from there she could see the door to Ashby's office.

Suddenly Claire came out fast and said to Glen, "Martinez and two other people came out of Ashby's office. They went down the stairs instead of using the elevator."

"They must be heading for the front entrance, I'll go down and meet Hronesh." As soon as Kuhn left the office Claire sat down at her desk.

I eased out of the office door, hurried over to the connecting corridor to the main courthouse. The courts had been dismissed for lunch time. I entered one of the empty Superior Court rooms overlooking the main entrance of the building. I could see Martinez walking with another man and a woman. I recognized the woman as a secretary of Herb Ashby's. I had known her for a long time, she used to be a secretary at the Ventura City Hall before she came to work for the county.

Martinez and his two campanions had crossed Poli Street and were passing the statue of Father Junipero Serra, which stood in a small grassy plot in front of the courthouse. Kuhn had come out and got into the car with Hronesh. Concentrating on Martinez and his companions Jim followed them slowly down California Street. I left the courtroom, walked down the spiral staircase to the first floor, crossed the alleyway between the two buildings to the parking lot. The attendant Martinez had been talking to was there checking cars for overtime parking violations. "Hi Joe. How are you doing?" I'd kidded him many times in the past about being a traffic cop.

He broke into a smile, "Oh I'm just working myself into trouble putting parking tickets on 'big-shots' cars."

"Uh huh, I saw you talking to Ben Martinez a few minutes ago, what are you trying to do, make a few points?"

Joe's smile faded and he said, "I don't know what's wrong with Ben. He was real serious and awful nervous. He said something very strange."

"Why, what did he say?"

"Well, something about, 'how those people are *trying to steal the courthouse,* and he was going to see some friends to try and stop them.'" Suddenly Joe said, "Look, I gotta get to work. See you later," and he hurried off among the parked cars.

I stood there for several minutes, wondering, what in hell could Hronesh and Kuhn be up to now!

CHAPTER 4

It was Saturday afternoon and hot. Looking for some small household items my wife had been wanting I wandered into one of those surplus import type stores. I hoped it would be cooler than outside. It was nice to have a weekend off and get away from the crazy intrigue Erwin was fomenting among his own staff along with the help of Kuhn and Hronesh. Pushing it from my mind I wandered up and down aisles loaded with a myriad of items, most of them from China and Taiwan. Suddenly I was aware that a man's voice had yelled, "Hey buddy. How you doin'?" Turning I saw Lt. Hopman coming down the aisle. I had known him about fifteen years, a nice guy, we had always gotten along great.

"Hi Jon. Oh, just window shopping, how about you?"

He looked around, saw no one was near, "I'm working security here on weekends. The Akron stores have been losing a lot of stock to shoplifters, we are trying to catch some of them. I'm glad I ran into you. I've been wanting to talk to you for quite a while. You're head of the investigators over at the Public Defender's office, do me a favor, tell Hronesh to stop calling Lola and me over at the police station. If the chief catches on, Lola and I are going to get our ass in a sling. Tell him we know Erwin wants Betty Thurman busted so bad that he can't stand it. We are working on it as fast as we can. Ask him from now on to call me at home." I thought, Jon must figure I'm in on this deal or he wouldn't be talking so loose. This was the second time I had heard the name Betty Thurman mentioned.

"Yeah Jon, I haven't paid too much attention. What's going on?"

"Well, Erwin's daughter lives next door to Mrs. Thurman and they don't get along. Erwin's daughter raises hell with him all the time telling him all sorts of stories about Mrs. Thurman and that he has to do something about her. Erwin jumps on Hronesh and tells him to get Mrs. Thurman busted for something or he is going to fire him. He has Jim scared shitless and Lola and I promised we would help him."

"It sounds like the same thing that Erwin and his wife stirred up with *his* neighbors where they live in the cul-de-sac."

Chuckling, Jon said, "I heard all about that deal. This guy Erwin and his whole family sounds like a bunch of real squirrels."

"Well, I've got to be going. I'll tell Jimmy what you said Jon. See you later." I could smell real trouble. Why can't people just stick to the job they've been hired for and be glad they've got a good one with a decent salary. I could sense my authority with the investigators evaporating.

Kuhn had just bought a new house in the east end of town, and a Deputy D.A. had spotted him Saturday and Sunday at a building supply company loading his county car up with bags of cement and lumber. The Deputy made a complaint to Loren Enoch, the County Executive. Enoch then sent the complaint on down to my office. I went to Erwin and discussed the matter, recommending that some disciplinary action be taken. After all, Kuhn knew better than to pull such a stunt. The car was painted a county color and had emblems on both sides. Erwin refused to back my recommendation, condoning Kuhn's actions by saying, "Well, Kuhn's been helping me a lot. I'll have a talk with Enoch and square the beef."

More big black headlines, "MURDER SUSPECT ARRESTED."

I read further. William Clinger had been picked up in a southern California county for the murder of Merle Harter, the bartender at the Captain's Table Restaurant in Ventura. Clinger had been living a few blocks from the murder scene with his girlfriend Didi Castro when the murder occurred. They moved from Ventura to Orange County shortly after the killing. The Ventura P.D. had been unable to come up with any clues for months after the killing. Down in Orange, Clinger and Didi had been out drinking one evening, both got pretty drunk and Clinger beat the devil out of her. While still drunk and madder than hell she confided in a girlfriend named Vera.

"I'll fix that son-of-a-bitch. He better not forget that I know he killed a bartender up in Ventura."

Vera was shocked, "For Christ's sake Didi, do you know what you are talking about?"

"You're damn right I know what I'm talking about. Bill came home late one night and he had blood all over him. He said, 'I was in a fight. A bartender got killed.' I even washed his shirt to get the blood out and we left town in a hurry."

The following day Vera tried to get Didi to go to the police to tell them what happened, but Didi said, "Forget what I told you, I mean forget it," and wouldn't talk about it any more. Vera became pretty upset with the information she had about a murder. Fearing she would become involved, she contacted the police. The Orange County Police picked up Didi and Bill who both denied any knowledge of the murder. Ventura P.D. detectives were sent to Orange to pick them up and bring them back.

Claire called on the extension, "Erwin wants you and the other investigators to come to his office."

Kuhn and Hronesh were both at their desks. "Come on you guys. We've got a call from the boss. He wants us right now."

Hronesh screamed, "For Christ's sake, its 4:30. What does he want now? My wife is just plain going to raise hell with me if I'm late tonight."

"Come on Hronesh. Get off your ass." Sitting in the office with Erwin was Hark Paik. He was a Deputy Public Defender, a short, pudgy man of Asiatic descent. He had never tried to hide the fact that he was *extremely ambitious* and went to great lengths in court to impress judges and lawyers with his legal ability. In court, when desired he could talk at a machine-gun pace. With a confusing accent and a gross misuse of words and sentences, he would throw the courtroom into a minor melee, with the judge, deputy D.A. and Paik all screaming at the same time.

During a preliminary hearing I sat in the courtroom while things got so hot and heavy between Paik and a Deputy D.A. George Eskin, that he yelled at Paik, "You're nothing but a damn Korean butcher."

Paik objected, "That's a lie. I'm a Jap." With a great sense of timing Paik let out with a high pitched combination laugh and giggle. It was instantly contagious and the entire courtroom burst into laughter. The deputy was so completely frustrated and plain mad at Paik that his face turned dark red and tears were coming to his eyes. Paik got about ninety-five percent of the charges dismissed at the preliminary hearing and made a hell of an agreement to plead his client guilty to a minor misdemeanor charge.

The harsh, rasping voice brought me back to the present. "Sit down. I want to talk to you guys." Erwin continued talking. "This is just the opportunity I have been waiting for. I just got word the Ventura P.D. picked up Didi Castro in Orange County and they are bringing her back to book her. I want Paik and Kuhn to get right down there...make sure the police department is advised we are her attorneys. And *no one* is to talk to her until Paik can advise her not to say anything to Deem's investigators, especially that Goddamn Dr. Battson. This is *one* murder case Deem is not going to win. I'm going to see to that! Gary, you take Hronesh and head back down the highway to the county line and see if you can spot the police car that's bringing Didi back. I want to make sure they don't transport her to some other jail and give Battson a chance to force a statement from her."

All four of us left Erwin's office in a hurry. I drove south on 101 highway keeping my eyes peeled for the police car that was bringing Didi to Ventura. "I sure can't understand Erwin's hatred for Woody Deem," said Jim.

"Me neither, I've never seen anybody use such foul language about a religion like Erwin does against the Mormons. As far as I can tell, Erwin never even heard of Woody before he came to Ventura. I remember shortly after we opened the office, I was standing by the main door and saw Woody coming down the hall. We shook hands, 'I came down to see Mr. Erwin. I wanted to see if we could discuss a case and make a suitable settlement.' Just then Erwin came around the corner of the secretaries office and I said, Mr. Erwin, the D.A. wants to talk to you for a minute about a case. Woody put out his hand to shake, Erwin looked straight at him for a second, then turned and walked away without a word. A couple of secretaries were sitting there watching the whole scene. I didn't know what to say. Woody turned and left. It was embarrassing I'll tell you."

Jim and I spotted the car carrying Didi before we got too far, we turned and followed them to the parking lot of the P.D.. Kuhn and Paik were sitting there waiting when we pulled in. Parking by the rear entrance of the detective bureau an officer stepped out the drivers side and a policewoman got out of the rear seat with Didi. We walked over to them, the policewoman was Lola, we told her we wanted to talk to Didi as the Public Defender was representing her. The officer had unlocked the back door and was urging Lola to bring the prisoner in and to get Didi away from us. Lola said, "All I can tell you now is to come around to the front desk and we will see what we can do."

Paik and Kuhn headed to the front entrance, Jim and I followed. A deputy D.A. was already in the booking office. Paik and the D.A. proceeded to get into a shouting match over who was going to talk to Didi first. Since she was entitled to talk to an attorney, Paik and Kuhn were allowed a couple of minutes with her. Then the four of us returned to our office. Erwin called us into the law library where Paik informed him that he had convinced Didi to say *absolutely nothing* to anyone, especially any psychiatrist who might attempt to talk to her. We sat around the conference table, Erwin, Paik, Kenny Cleaver, Kuhn and myself. Cleaver was the man Erwin had chosen for his assistant Public Defender. A short stocky man with heavy gray hair, he wore fancy shoes with metal buckles and high heels. To give himself even more altitude he wore lifts inside the shoes. When he appeared in court wearing a lavender shirt, green tie, a yellow jacket and pants, and squinted over his half-lens bifocals, he definitely was highly visible.

"It's real simple," Erwin was saying, "I have the defense all figured out. Deem's got no physical evidence whatsoever. They've never even found the knife that did the killing. All the police have is the story that that Vera woman told them and they can never get her on the stand except to rebut anything Didi says. And we are not going to let Castro ever testify. Alright Kuhn, I want you to get next to this Didi gal. Get friendly or anything you have to do, but convince her that if she says *nothing at all* on the stand, the D.A. just doesn't have a case."

Kuhn did a real good job on Didi, she took the stand refusing to answer any questions. She was given immunity by the court against anything which might be self-incriminating. She was again put on the stand and asked if she knew any of the facts regarding Clinger's involvement in the murder of the bartender. Didi still refused to talk and the judge remanded her to the custody of the county jail for contempt of court. The trial was postponed for a period of time and the jurors were sent home. The plan that Erwin had devised meant that *all the chips* were on the table. Didi could spend years in jail on contempt of court charges while her boyfriend enjoyed complete freedom on the street. If she did talk, Clinger could go to the gas chamber as the charges against him were first degree murder.

The phone rang as I walked into my office. "Hello," a voice said, "Is this Gary? I thought I recognized your voice. This is Lee Smith."

"Hi Lee. Haven't heard from you since your trial."

"I've been reading about that Clinger trial in the newspaper. I have some information you might be interested in."

"Let's have it."

"When my trial was going on there was a guy in my cell who told me he knew who *really* killed the bartender."

"What's his name?"

"His name is Dillon, but he's up north in the state penitentiary now."

"Give me your phone number, I'll tell Erwin what you said and call you back."

The next day I called him, a girl answered, then shortly Lee came on. "Yeah Lee, Erwin and Cleaver are interested in what you know. I am going to see Dillon at the joint in Mariposa. I thought if you would go along it might help break the ice with the guy."

"I'll help if I can. When do you want to go?"

"I'll pick you up at five tomorrow morning."

"Are you kidding?"

"No, I'll be at your place at five sharp."

It was still dark when Lee came out of his apartment house and climbed into the county car. We drove north on Highway 99. "Tell me...what do you know about this guy Dillon."

"Well, he's a young guy and he's been in and out of jails on all kinds of beefs. We got to talking in our cell one night about the murder of the bartender, and Dillon told me he knew who did the knife job on the victim."

"What do you think, was the guy bull-shitting?"

"No, I don't think so."

We left Highway 99 and traveled east to Mariposa, a small town nestled at the foothills approaching Yosemite. We turned left at Mariposa and headed up a paved road into the hills. Dillon was doing time at a state CYA camp at Mt. Bulyon. We drove into the camp grounds. There were no guards or high fences. I parked in front of a one story building that had an 'office' sign by the door. A state employee in khakis was sitting at a desk. I introduced myself and explained the purpose of my visit. The state man sent a runner to get Dillon. Lee greeted him as he entered, then introduced me. The three of us went through a side door of the office into a small courtyard and sat down on a bench. We were at a fairly high altitude and the mountains surrounding Yosemite National Park stood high and clear to the east. The sky was an azure blue that you never see anymore in the Los Angeles basin. The pine trees on the sides of the mountains stood out a true green against the bright multi-colored rocks and shadowed canyons. Dillon asked what I wanted.

"Any information you have on who killed the bartender at the Captain's Table."

Dillon then stated, "I was in the bar the night of the murder." I knew that if this was true it could be invaluable to Clinger's defense. The D.A. had witnesses who had accounted for all the patrons at the bar just prior to closing except for one man. Nobody knew this man by name, but the physical description fit that of Clinger. The D.A. was maintaining that this stranger was Clinger and that he had remained in the bar after closing time and had stabbed the bartender and robbed the bar.

"Dillon, when did you leave the bar?"

"Oh...five to ten minutes before closing. They close at 2:00 am. Listen, if you can get me out of this place and back to Ventura, I'll testify to what I know."

"Dillon, you told Lee you knew who did the stabbing."

"Well, not exactly. Go see Bob Ackerd in the county jail. He can give you the names of two narco pushers, they're from New York. They sold Ackerd a stolen Corvette and he got busted for it. They know who did the killing. I know Clinger was there, but a guy with him did the actual stabbing."

Back on Highway 99 we headed south toward LA, Lee had been mighty quiet since leaving the state camp at Mt. Bulyon. "What's your opinion of Dillon's story Lee?"

"I would go see this Ackerd guy at the county jail and see if he knows the names of the two dudes from New York."

"What I meant was about Dillon being in the Captain's Table the night of the killing. If that's the truth, it messes up the D.A.'s theory completely."

"I believe Dillon wants to get out of that camp so bad he would do anything."

"Alright, what I'll do is see Ackerd tomorrow. If he can give me the names of the two New York pushers, and the stolen car story is true, I'm going to find out who Clinger was with that night."

Lee spoke up, "I don't believe that Erwin is going to be able to keep Didi from talking on the stand."

"I don't either, I realize that Erwin is gambling Clinger's life that Didi will hold out. If another guy did the stabbing and Clinger was there, it would still be a lot better for him to tell the D.A. the truth and make a deal for second degree murder, or whatever he could get. The real problem is that *Erwin wants to sand bag Woody Deem so bad* that he doesn't care what happens to the case."

The next morning I reported to Erwin and Cleaver what Dillon had told me, they were both very interested. Erwin remarked, "This will blow Mr. Deem's theory all to hell," and told Cleaver to make arrangements to bring Dillon to the Ventura jail.

Leaving the office I hurried on over to the county jail. Ackerd verified Dillon's story about the stolen car and said the two guys from New York were named Dennie and Lennie. He didn't know the Corvette he bought from them was stolen nor did he know that they were dealing in narcotics. Ackerd said, "I have found out a lot about it since I have been in the jail. I'll tell you the name of a guy right here in jail who knows the name of the dude who did the killing. His name is Allen Jaeman, he used to work for the killer."

I went back to the jailer's office and requested them to send out Jaeman. He was a small, thin guy with a foreign accent. I came to the point. "Jaeman, do you know William Clinger, the guy they have in jail here for murdering the bartender?"

"Yes, I know him when I see him."

"I'm told that you know who he was with when the bartender was killed."

Jaeman became extremely nervous and was breaking out with sweat. He kept looking around making sure no one was near. I gave him a cigarette and he commenced talking. "I got out of a narcotic addiction hospital down south a few days before the murder. I hitch-hiked to Ventura and was wandering around on Seaward Avenue down by the beach. There was a hippie art shop across from the Captain's Table and I went in and looked around. I got acquainted with the guy who ran the shop, his name was Sam. He asked me if I would do some odd jobs and said he would pay me. I did some cleaning up and painting around the place. Sam was always in a bad mood. Young guys and girls were always coming in to see Sam. He would take them over to a corner and I could see them give him money, but they never carried anything out with them."

"Do you think he was selling grass or pills to them?"

"I'm postive he was. He was always complaining about how he *needed* a lot of money. After working there seversl days I got up enough nerve to ask him for a couple of dollars. Sam started cursing me something terrible. He just kind of flipped his lid and screamed he was going to kill me. Sam picked up a long sharp piece of metal from a table and started after me. I ran out the front door and down Seaward toward the beach. It was broad daylight. He was chasing me and trying to stab me with the metal and screaming he was going to kill me. I finally got away from him and went to the beach and sat down. Later on I went to a house a couple doors from Sam's place. There were some young guys living there that I had become friendly with. They weren't home so I sat down on the doorstep to wait for them. I was sure they would let me sleep on the floor or anyplace I could find. While sitting there I saw Clinger and Sam over in front of the Captain's Table. They were talking, after a few minutes they went inside."

"What time was that?"

"Oh, it was still daylight. It must have been 3:00 or 4:00 in the afternoon. I don't know anything more. The next day I hitch-hiked to San Francisco. I stayed there awhile. I came back to Ventura and they picked me up for violation of parole."

"Thanks a lot Allen. I will probably be back to see you later."

Erwin and Cleaver were talking in his office, I entered and sat down. "Mr. Erwin, I have done a lot of checking around and I know that there was somebody else with Clinger when the killing took place. Why don't we take all the information to the Police or to the District Attorney and let them investigate it. Clinger could come out a lot better that way than he will if he continues to lie and say he doesn't know anything about the murder."

"No. We are going to do it just like I said, Kuhn has convinced Clinger that Didi will *never* talk. This is the way Clinger wants it. We have Dillon down in the county jail and we'll get him to testify that he was in the bar almost until closing time. That will take care of Woody's witnesses that say Clinger was there. Clinger and Dillon are both about the same size and age."

"Mr. Erwin, *all I know* is that Dillon says he was there that night. There is no way that I could verify this. He is demanding that the Public Defender get him out on the street in return for his testimony in this case. The only thing he has told me that checks out was about Ackerd and the stolen car. He doesn't know Clinger or the other guy involved in the killing. I believe you should send him back to the camp."

"No, I want him right where he is and you go down there every once in a while and take him cigarettes. Keep him happy any way you can."

I left Erwin and Cleaver and went back to my office and closed the door. I felt sure that Erwin's hatred for Woody Deem was going to create real trouble before this is all over.

Didi Castro had been put on the stand several times. Each time she refused to talk, and Judge Lewis continued to remand her to the county jail for contempt of court. The whole procedure was causing continuances and delays of all kinds. Erwin would sit in his office and *laugh* at Deem's predicament, bragging about how he was going to ruin Deem's record for convictions *one way or another.*

CHAPTER 5

I walked into the office a little bit before 8:00 am, Erwin was standing by his door talking to Paik. He yelled, "Hey Gary, come with us we are going to Oxnard. Let's get going, I'm in a hurry."

Getting into Erwin's car we hit the freeway south, he said, "I just got a phone call from John McCormick over at the Oxnard Courier. John's got good information that Judge Lewis and Deem had Didi brought secretly to the judge's chambers and they were trying to compel her to talk. McCormick has been pissed-off at Lewis because the judge has been holding back on the testimony to the press and won't let McCormick in his chambers. In fact, John went to LA and filed a suit in court to prohibit the judge from restraining the press. The only trouble is the murder trial will be over before his suit can come up. Believe me, McCormick is plenty mad. He wants to get with me and make up a story to put in his paper that will burn Deem and Judge Lewis. Gary, you know John McCormick pretty good don't you?"

"Yeah, I know him."

"When we get to the newspaper office I want you to go in and bring him out. I don't want *anyone to see me* in there."

Yeah sure, I knew John McCormick alright. I'd picked him up *plenty of times* and brought him to the police station when I was working the detective bureau. John had been passing bad checks all over the county for years. Sgt. Doug Paxton, with the Sheriff's Dept.

and I had been working on some check cases involving John for quite a while when Paxton finally got a warrant and busted him. John was convicted of a felony and served time. Before Doug arrested John I remembered that he used to come down to the Green Mill, a large dance hall in West Ventura where the Mexican people held dances on Saturday nights. He was always drunk and causing trouble and the officer working security had to throw him out repeatedly. John had held a grudge against me ever since Doug and I had investigated him for bad checks.

Erwin pulled up in front of the Press Courier and said, "Gary, go in and bring McCormick out here." I located John and we went out to the car.

Erwin asked, "John how did you find out about Deem and Lewis bringing Didi to the judge's chambers?"

"I got a call from a secretary that I know in the courthouse."

"John, we've got to make up a story and put it in the paper about these bastards conspiring to deny Didi her rights. That Judge Lewis is as crooked as hell."

John looked at Erwin and said, "Just wait until you see the story I'll write."

"Good. Just so you don't back out."

"I ain't going to back out. It will be in the next edition."

"Very good, I'll see you later John."

On the way back to the courthouse Erwin started laughing, loud and rasping. "By God Paik, we are going to *kill two birds with one stone*. We are *going to nail* us a Goddamn Jew Judge and a friggin' Mormon preacher at the same time." I looked over at Paik, he had turned an absolutely pale white shade.

In a low voice Paik said, "Jesus Erwin, *this whole thing is crazy.*" Erwin parked behind the county building, Paik got out in a hurry and disappeared without saying a word. Sure enough, McCormick wrote the story just like he and Erwin planned.

At that time Judge Lewis was in Palm Springs for a few days. I figured when he got back and saw the newspaper there'd be some fireworks. Judge Marvin Lewis ordered a conference to be held in his chambers. The D.A. Woody Deem, Erwin and a private attorney named DeWitt Blais, also known as 'Red' Blais, were there. Blais had brought Ed Patton with him. Patton was now a private investigator working with Blais. Ed had once been a detective sergeant with the Oxnard P.D. He and I, along with Doug Paxton from the sheriff's office had teamed up many times to work narcotics cases that had spread from one city to another and on out into the county area.

Judge Lewis chastised Deem and Erwin, "I am fed up with all these shenanigans between the Public Defender and the District Attorney. An investigator from the Public Defender's office has been pounding on Didi Castro for months now trying to convince her *not* to take the witness stand and tell the truth, and investigators from the D.A.'s office have been hounding her to talk. Now, I am making a court order. I am releasing Didi from the county jail. She is being placed in the custody of DeWitt Blais, who is to act as her attorney and who is ordered by this court to place her in lodgings known *only* to himself and Mr. Ed Patton. The court will pay expenses for food and lodging. Mr. Blais is instructed that he is to be concerned only with Mrs. Castro's interest and welfare and *under no circumstances* is he to allow members from either the D.A.'s office or the Public Defender's office to come in contact with her."

The trial resumed and Didi was put on the stand again. She answered just enough questions to keep her from being in contempt of court, which would have caused her to be returned to the county jail. However, she answered enough questions to allow her girlfriend Vera to come on the stand in a rebuttal and tell the entire story that Didi had told her when she had been drunk and angry at Clinger. After Vera had given her testimony there was a court recess. Erwin, Paik and Cleaver were talking quietly in the corridor just outside the courtroom doors. I was standing nearby listening and Erwin was doing most of the talking.

"Listen Paik, since that girlfriend of Castro's got on the stand and told her story Clinger doesn't stand a chance. Have you looked at the faces of the jurors? Good Christ, they have already made up their minds."

Paik shrugged, "Well there's nothing more we can do now except make a hell of a good final argument."

Erwin then forced the issue, "There's just one more chance. Put Dillon on the stand to testify that he was in the bar until closing time. Deem has had all those witnesses testifying that a man fitting Clinger's description was in the bar until it closed. So if Dillon was there, then Clinger could not have been in the bar."

Paik, who hadn't been his own exuberant self since he had been a witness to Erwin's and McCormick's scheme to burn Deem and Judge Lewis, suddenly became quite excited and yelled, *"No Erwin. We can't do it. I have defended Dillon in the past, he is a liar and you can't believe a word he says."*

"What's the difference Paik. It can't hurt anything. As it stands right now Clinger is dead anyway."

Erwin turned to Cleaver and said, "How about it Kenny. What do you say?"

"Well, I have to go along with you Erwin. I don't see where it can hurt the position Clinger is in now."

Paik was definitely upset by this time, but apparently he figured he couldn't argue against Erwin and Cleaver both. Erwin looked at me and said, "How about Dillon. Will he testify?"

"I don't know. I haven't seen him for a couple of weeks."

"I thought I told you to keep him happy."

I felt myself getting hot under the collar. "Damn it Mr. Erwin, I told you and Cleaver a long time ago there was *absolutely no way* to verify Dillon's story about being in the bar at closing time. I wanted to take the information to the police about another man having been involved, but you wouldn't let me. Hell, I knew you could *never* keep Didi from eventually talking on the stand."

"Alright, alright." Erwin was getting mad now.

"You go down to the jail and see if Dillon will testify."

As I turned to go I had a quick glance at Paik's face. He was puffed up like a fighting cock and fuming to himself, but he said nothing.

The prisoner came into the tiny interview room, "Listen to me good Dillon. Erwin sent me down here to see if you would testify today."

He was very sullen and simply said, "Yeah, I'll do it. I returned to where Erwin, Cleaver and Paik were still standing. I repeated what Dillon had said.

Erwin decided, "Alright, go back to the jail and have a deputy bring Dillon down here. I want to talk with him before putting him on the stand."

I returned to the jail again and advised the sergeant that Erwin wanted Dillon brought to the courtroom. The deputy arrived with Dillon shortly after I got back. Cleaver and Paik were present when Erwin explained to the witness that they were going to put him on the stand and have him testify to being in the bar shortly before closing. Then Erwin said to Dillon, "You do remember, *don't you?*"

Dillon gave a small grin and said, "Yeah, I remember."

"We'll have you brought back down here this afternoon to take the stand."

Holding Dillon by the arm the deputy had started him down the corridor toward the jail. Paik, a highly emotional person, apparently could not continue containing his temper any longer. Trotting alongside Dillon he was screaming, "I can't put you on the stand. I know you from before. *You are nothing but a liar.*" Paik was so excited he became like a jumping jack. The deputy's mouth dropped open with sudden astonishment. The hall was jammed with people and John McCormick, the reporter, was standing right next to me.

Dillon looked at Paik and smiled, then said, "Screw you Paik." The deputy hustled Dillon quickly down the hall, back to his cell.

I went down a narrow hall, it led to the outer office of Judge Lewis's chambers. Three people were loitering in the outer office, buzzing amongst themselves about Dillon being put on the stand. A court recorder was talking and a secretary and a D.A. investigator were shaking their heads, agreeing. The gist of their conversation was, *how can Erwin put that guy on the stand...*Christ, even Paik knows what a liar he is.

I headed for the parking lot, got into the car and drove down to the county fairgrounds. A large semi-truck and trailer filled with cattle was being unloaded by some cowboys into a corral. At least they looked like cowhands, with their big cowboy hats and boots. I thought, those guys don't know how good a simple life can be. They were joking and kidding and smacking the steers on the rumps to hurry them down the ramp from the truck.

I sat there deep in thought. There really has to be something wrong with a guy like Erwin. He hates all his neighbors, he hates his daughter's neighbors and wants them all put in jail. He hates Woody Deem and he curses all Mormons. The only ones he seems to get along with are those like Glen Kuhn and Claire. People who constantly report to him about all the other employees activities and whispering in his ear what a great man he is. I recalled Kuhn asking me once to come down to the coffee shop with him, he explained, "Erwin is down there and I'll show you how to get along with him."

"Hell Kuhn, I ain't interested in getting along with him by kissing his ass. I got work to do, you go on down and do your thing." Kuhn didn't like the inference, he gave a short laugh and continued on down to see Erwin.

Reluctantly I left the peaceful fairgrounds and returned to the courtroom. *I couldn't forget Paik screaming at Dillon in the corridor and Dillon's retort.* Just as I sat down a deputy brought Dillon into the room, he took the stand and was sworn in. I looked for Erwin but he'd disappeared. Hark Paik's aggressive stance was gone, his *forcefulness* which he loved to affect was an integral part of Paik's courtroom demeanor. I wondered what was wrong with him. Cleaver was sitting at the attorney's table absolutely motionless.

Paik asked some normal preliminary questions then he brought Dillon's attention to the night the bartender was killed. "Now Mr. Dillon, do you remember where you were the night of the murder?"

"Yes I do."

"Will you please tell the court where you were about 1:30 a.m. on that date?"

"Yes, I was in jail in Holbrook, Arizona."

The courtroom became silent as a tomb. It seemed that everyone had stopped breathing. All I could think was...that stupid Erwin. *First* he was going to get Clinger completely free by having Didi refuse to talk...*now* his plan to have Dillon testify that it was *him* in the bar and *not Clinger* had just blown up in his face like a ton of nitro.

Considering the strange way that Cleaver was acting and Paik's actions, I wondered, was it possible they had known Dillon had been lying all the time? But if so, how could they have discovered it?

Leaving the courtroom I returned to our offices. Cleaver and Paik would be up shortly, there was going to be a lot of unhappy people. Erwin called everyone into the law library, we all sat around the table saying nothing. Erwin spoke up, "Tomorrow morning Paik I want you to put Gary on the stand. Let him explain how we first contacted Dillon and the story Dillon told about being in the bar on the night of the murder. That's all we can do now."

I was on the witness stand, Judge Lewis was sitting on my right. He was sitting higher than I was. In front of me and just to my left sat the twelve most important people in the courtroom. I glanced at them and twelve pair of eyes stared at me intently. Paik had gone down the line with questions and had me explain how we had first contacted Dillon and the story he told. Now it was Mr. Deem's turn to ask me questions. He was standing up and holding a tablet that he repeatedly referred to. Woody didn't seem to be real interested in Dillon's story. He was asking what day I went to the State Camp at Mt. Bulyon. I told him what time I had left Ventura and the time I arrived at the camp. I told him what day of the week it was and the date. Woody then asked what day I had interviewed Jaeman, the addict in jail. I answered that I had talked to him in the county jail the next day *after* Dillon had told me about him. Deem went on to pin me down for sure on the dates and who I'd talked to first. He then asked if I'd kept a daily log which would verify the date that I went to Mt. Bulyon. I said yes I had.

"Where is it?"

"It is in my desk in my office."

"Well, if I request a short recess would you get it and return it here to the court?"

"Yes, I would be glad to." The court recessed for fifteen minutes and I went upstairs to get my log sheet. I was wondering what Deem was up to. Had I made a mistake in the day or the date I testified to? Christ, with all the crazy things that had happened on this case I was beginning to have doubts about my own memory. I took the daily log from my desk drawer and scrutinized it quickly and half warily. No, I had *not* made any mistake. There it was in black and white, the *correct* day and date. I hurried to the courtroom with my log and took the stand again. Deem asked if I'd found the log and I replied I had.

"Would you read the day and date that you went to Mt. Bulyon please?" I read the day and date.

"Now, *you are sure* you have made no mistake?"

"Yes I'm positive." Christ, what is he up to anyway? I could feel Judge Lewis peering at me from my right. I glanced at the jury, each and everyone of them were staring at me. I had been on the stand many times in important cases, but I'd never had the feeling I was beginning to get now.

Woody said, "Are you sure that you went to Mt. Bulyon on the day and date you say you did, saw Dillon, and then went to the jail the next day and saw Allen Jaeman?"

"Yes."

Woody turned himself partly toward the jury and said in a loud, confident voice, "Are you sure you did not go to the jail first and contact the narcotic addict, and he told you to go to Mt. Bulyon and see Dillon and *he would testify to anything you asked him?* And the next day you did drive up to Mt. Bulyon. In other words, what really happened was just the reverse to what you have testified to."

"No, absolutely not. I went to Mt. Bulyon the first day and talked to Dillon. The next day I went to the county jail."

Triumphantly the D.A. said, "Alright, can I see your daily log sheet?" I handed it to him. He examined it and said, "Your Honor, I would like to submit this daily log sheet and to have it marked as evidence." Judge Lewis ordered *the evidence* excepted by the court. Deem dismissed me and called a sheriff's sergeant to take the stand. The sergeant testified he worked in the jail office and that a log was kept of all lawyers and defense investigators who visited the jail. He had with him a copy of the jail visitor log for the day and date I'd testified I was at Mt. Bulyon. Woody asked him if my signature was on the log the day and date that I had sworn I was at the camp.

The sergeant testified, "Yes, Gary signed the log on that day to visit Allen Jaeman the addict."

Deem requested, "Your Honor, I want to introduce this jail log as *evidence*." Judge Lewis so ordered. I couldn't believe my ears. What in hell was Deem trying to do. I'd known him too long. There wasn't any way he would pull something phony. I gave a quick glance at Woody. He had a very confident look on his face. I would say almost a smug look if he was capable of smugness, which I didn't believe he was. I only knew that he was an honest, hard working prosecuting attorney, because that was his job and he recognized the fact that the public was paying him to do a job. I knew this had been a very tough case for Deem to try. There was no physical evidence to present and Erwin had been blocking him at every turn to *prevent* Didi Castro from testifying. Now I could tell from Deem's expression he believed he'd moved the chessmen into a position where he was not only going to convict Clinger, he was also going to annihilate the public defender's office at the same time. It was close to 5:00 p.m., so Judge Lewis proceeded to recess court until 9:00 the following morning.

I waited in Paik's office for him to arrive. Cleaver came in and sat down but he said nothing. Paik entered the room and threw his briefcase on the desk. I could tell Paik was getting ready to jump on me, so I beat him to the punch. "Paik, Goddamn it, *I told you and Erwin and Cleaver* a long time ago to send Dillon back to the joint. There was no way for me to check his story about being in the bar that night."

Paik admitted, *"I know that,* I know Dillon is a liar."

"Well *why in hell* did you put him on the stand? For Christ's sake, everyone in the courthouse heard you screaming at him in the corridor."

"Yeah, I know. Erwin *ordered* me to put him on. What else could I do? But what is this shit about you being in the jail when you said you were at Mt. Bulyon talking to Dillon?"

"Listen Paik, I'll tell you something. I've *never* lied on the stand in my life and I ain't lying now. I don't know what Deem is up to, but I'm going up to the jail right now and look at those records." I wanted one of them to go with me, but I could see Paik was about to explode. I said, "Cleaver, will you go with me?"

"Yeah, let's go."

I rang the buzzer at the jail door, a deputy came over and let us in. It was real quiet in the jail, dinner time was just ending. One deputy was working behind the booking desk. He knew me, I asked for the jail log, he laid it up on the desk. I turned back to the date where my name appeared. Sure enough, there was my name, it was on the date when I'd testified that I was at Camp Bulyon. Cleaver sort of whistled, "Man, it looks like we have had it."

"Bullshit Cleaver, you just hold on. There's something Goddamn wrong here."

"You don't believe Deem is trying to frame you do you?"

"No, I don't believe anything like that. Look at this log. There's an entry in front of me, an attorney named Maxwell, from Oxnard. Then directly below my name is B. Jackson, a State Parole officer."

Cleaver suggested, "We can get hold of them and see what day they actually signed into the jail."

"No, I've got a better idea. Notice Maxwell's entry, he signed in here to see a female prisoner. That means he went up the elevator to the womens section on the next floor. There he has to sign again into the womens visitor log."

We jumped into the elevator and went up to the womens jail. A female deputy was on duty, I asked, "Mary, could I see your visitor log?"

"Sure." She brought it from under the counter and said, "Help yourself." I turned back to the same date Maxwell's name appeared on the log at the mens jail. It wasn't there. I continued to the next day. Maxwell had signed into the womens jail on the *day folowing* the date that the mens jail log reflected.

"Mary, would you take this one log sheet and hold on to it until tomorrow morning? I'll be here with a supoena bright and early to get it. Come on Cleaver, let's go back down to the mens jail. I think I know what happened."

The deputy in the mens jail handed me the log again and asked, "What are you guys up to?"

"There seems to be something wrong with these records."

"All I know is last week Woody's investigator was here going through them. He took that log you're looking at and made a copy, then brought it back. He was very excited, *he kept repeating, 'Wait until I show this to Woody.'*"

"Tell me, who puts the dates on the log sheet?"

"The deputy who comes on at midnight writes in the new date when he gets here."

"Well, take a look here. One date is missing."

"Yeah, the deputy must have forgotten to put in the date when he came on duty. That can happen if you are real busy, like booking a bunch of prisoners or something."

"Cleaver do you get the picture now?"

"I hope to tell you. Not only were *you telling the truth* all the time but Deem has made a horrible mistake. In fact, he has put his foot in his mouth clear up to his knee cap."

"Yeah, if the D.A. investigator had looked just a little further to the next date, he would have seen that one date was missing." Back at Paik's office Cleaver and I advised him what we had discovered. The Korean's face lit up and he began to exhibit a little of his old exuberance. They were laughing, thumping the desk and joking how they would screw the great Deem the next morning. I left the office and headed for home. I wasn't happy at all. I felt relief that I would be able to prove I'd told the truth about when I first visited Dillon, but this whole case was being turned into a *three ring circus*. I had gathered plenty of evidence and information that another man was involved in the killing. I realized that I was working for the Public Defender's office now, but all my old training and experience as a police officer just could not quite go along with letting a killer off completely to roam the streets with renewed confidence and allow him to *repeat murder* upon another innocent person. Actually our only concern and obligation was to defend Clinger. We had no legal responsibility to anyone else involved in the murder.

The next morning the courtroom was filled to standing room only, and the corridor was packed with people trying to get in. I had been up to the womens jail early with a supoena. Holding a copy of the jail records I walked over to Paik sitting at the attorney's table and handed it to him. Examining the record closely Paik appeared satisfied. Judge Lewis entered and the court came to order.

Paik commenced, "Your Honor I want to bring the sergeant who testified yesterday back to the stand and ask him some questions."

Deem had learned the true facts of the jail records before court started. His D.A's investigator had received a call from the deputy sheriff in the jail after Cleaver and I'd been down there inspecting the records. The D.A.'s man had dashed down to the jail and found out the mistake he'd made. He realized he was responsible for his boss, the D.A., going off on a disastrous tangent, it was a terrible embarrassment, it gave him the 'shakes' just thinking about it but he must notify Deem immediately. Woody was going to be absolutely *fit to be tied.*

Upon Paik's request to bring the jail sergeant back to the stand Deem came to his feet quickly and said, "Your Honor, the sergeant was *my* witness. I move that the court strike his testimony from the record and remove the jail record from evidence. I've learned that there was an error in the records which has made the testimony of the sergeant unnecssary."

Jumping to his feet Paik yelled, "Your Honor, I protest...! Mr. Deem placed this witness on the stand and had him testify to the veracity of certain jail records and on the basis of these records he has cast certain doubts regarding our investigator's whereabouts on a specific date. These allegations have been made before the jury. I move the court allow me to question the sergeant."

Judge Lewis looked at Deem, he said, "You put the sergeant on the stand and you requested the jail records be placed in evidence. I deny your motion to remove the witness or the evidence. The court orders the sergeant to take the stand. Proceed with your questions Mr. Paik."

"Alright sergeant. Yesterday you testified that your jail records showed that our investigator was not in the county jail on the day he said he was."

"Yes sir, that's right."

"Has anyone from the District Attorney's office talked with you this morning and explained that there was a *serious error* in the jail records?"

"Yes sir, they have, but I knew it before this morning." Paik was stunned for a moment. Getting his composure back he attacked...

"Sergeant, you mean you knew there was an error on those jail records *before* you testified?"

"Yes sir."

I looked at the jurors. They had an altogether different look on their faces now. They were sort of hunched forward in their seats and they were staring at the sergeant like they had stared at me the day before when I was sitting in the 'hot seat.'

Paik realized suddenly that he was in the drivers seat. Slowing down his rapid-fire speech he began talking loud and clear. "Well now sergeant, just *when* did you actually first realize that there was an error in the jail records?"

"Yesterday, when Mr. Deem asked me to look at the jail record to verify it was actually a Ventura County jail document."

"Now sergeant...if you knew there was an error on those records why did you testify yesterday that our investigator was not in the county jail on the day he said he was?"

"Well sir, uh, because I thought that was what I was supposed to say."

Paik could hardly believe his ears and his good fortune. This amazing testimony by the sergeant had indeed bolstered his spirits. He was puffed up again with confidence. Strolling toward the jury box, and when he was certain the testimony had soaked in good he said, "Your Honor, I need nothing further from this witness."

Judge Lewis said quietly, "You may step down sergeant."

I looked at Woody. He sat forward on the edge of his chair. I'd seen him turn his head to look back into the courtroom. I scanned the room quickly trying to spot his investigator. If he'd been there during the sergeant's testimony, *he was gone now.* Several days later the trial ended, the jurors simply couldn't agree on a verdict, it was a hung jury. Erwin ordered Kuhn to get all the newspaper clippings of the murder trial and anything else he could dig up. He wanted to present evidence to the court that due to the newspaper coverage Clinger would be unable to get a fair trial in Ventura County and to make a motion for the next trial to be moved to L.A. County.

Things had quieted down somewhat, I was sitting in my office catching up on the never-ending supply of arrest reports that had been piling up on my desk.

"Hey! What are you doing in there?" I knew who it was without looking up, it was Ed Patton, the officer from Oxnard I had worked with ten or twelve years ago.

"Hi Ed. Come on in and sit down." He plunked down on one of the chairs against the wall. He had one of his usual infectious grins. I could see he had something on his mind.

"What's up Ed?"

"Well something's bothering me real bad."

"So, let's have it."

"Would you mind telling me why Erwin put Dillon on the stand when *he knew* he was lying?" I looked closer at Ed. There was no grin on his face now.

"What do you mean, *he knew* Dillon was lying?"

"Didn't Erwin tell you about the polygraph?"

"What in hell poly are you talking about?"

"Wait a minute, didn't Erwin ever tell you about the poly Red

Blais gave Didi Castro?"

"Hell no! He doesn't tell me anything."

"And Kuhn didn't tell you anything about it either?"

"Are you kidding? Kuhn's got his nose so far up Erwin's rear end there is a good chance he will suffocate one of these days." Red hot pins were jabbing into me, all over my entire body, I was swiftly losing my temper, I fought to control myself. "Listen Ed, there's *no loyalty* in this office whatsoever. Kuhn is trying to get my job for himself. He's scared the hell out of Hronesh so bad by telling him Erwin is going to fire him that he'll do anything he's told. He has Erwin's silly secretary eating out of his hand. She runs around here like a nut squealing for 'Glen Baby.' The whole office is sitting back trying to mind their own business and just keep themselves out of trouble. They are all afraid of Claire and Kuhn, because nobody can get to Erwin except them."

Getting up, Ed looked carefully down the hall, then closing my office door and sitting down he asked, "You do remember when Judge Lewis appointed Blais to represent Didi and her interests only?"

"Of course I remember."

"Well, Blais and I had a talk, his thoughts were if Didi really knows nothing about the murder we can safely put her on the stand and let her talk. There is no way Deem can break her down if she *does not* know anything, but yet on the other hand, if she is *lying* it wouldn't take Woody long to tear her apart on the stand. Blais said, 'There is one way of finding the truth for sure. We could give her a polygraph, if she's clean Woody can question her from now on.'" Ed paused for a minute.

I urged, "Go on Ed, what happened?"

"Well, we got a polygraph operator from Los Angeles to come up. He is one of the best in the business, and we had been allowed expenses to be paid by the court for Didi's welfare, so there was no problem with costs. The poly operator drove up to Oxnard one day and we watched him question Didi."

"Who was there beside you Ed?"

"Red Blais, another attorney and the operator."

"What happened?"

"Christ, the test indicated that Didi *not only had knowledge* that Clinger was in on the murder, but she knew another guy was there also. The other guy did all the stabbing."

I could hardly believe what he was telling me. "Ed, you mean

Erwin and Kuhn *knew this all the time* and didn't tell me?"

"I knew Blais had told Erwin and Kuhn, but I figured they must have told you about it. Don't you remember when Erwin and Kuhn drove down to L.A. and contacted the State Supreme Court trying to get a writ prohibiting Deem from putting Didi on the stand?"

"Sure I remember that but I thought it was just another one of Erwin's crazy ideas."

"You know his whole defense plan was based on Kuhn keeping Didi from testifying on the stand. Well, when the Supreme Court turned down his request for a writ, that meant Didi had to take the stand or risk going back to jail. Even Blais knew that for his client's welfare he couldn't advise her *not* to talk on the stand."

"Ed, you realize Blais and Erwin violated every court order that Judge Lewis laid down. Involving Didi with the polygraph was bad enough but when he told Erwin about it so that he could try to get a writ to prohibit her from talking, they contrived a conspiracy to violate the court order and to obstruct justice." I could see Patton was getting perburbed over the whole conversation. I knew him well enough to know he didn't like this situation any better than I did. "One more thing, who was the poly operator?"

Sharply Ed said, "What do you care?"

Something about the way he said it aroused my curiosity to the point that I insisted he tell me. "Alright, but for Crist's sake don't repeat me. It was Kenny Scantlan."

I knew Scantlan, he was a retired L.A. police sergeant who had worked in the crime laboratory for years. When he retired he went to work for the L.A. District Attorney's Bureau of Investigation. He had set up a new scientific laboratory for the D.A.'s office. Kenny and I had worked several cases in conjunction for the L.A. District Attorney's Criminal Intelligence in the past.

"Ed, did Kenny know what this was all about when he came up here and gave Didi the poly?"

"Of course he did, and he specifically *did not* want you to know about it."

"This is really hard to digest. How did Blais and Erwin become so friendly?"

"Blais doesn't particularly like Erwin but he definitely does not like the D.A. He's had run-ins with Deem and law enforcement in general throughout the county."

"Ed one of the most important elements is, if *Erwin knew* that Clinger was in on the murder, then *he knew* it was Clinger who was in the Captain's Table late the night of the murder. And if it was Clinger who was in the bar, then Erwin was *aware* that Dillon could not have been there. Yet, Erwin *ordered* Paik to put Dillon on the stand to testify he'd been in the Captain's Table on the night of the murder."

"Yeah Gary, that brings us right back to why I dropped in to see you. If Erwin knew that Dillon was lying, why did he order Paik to put him on the stand?"

"You realize that this poly information fits right in with what I have been maintaining all along, that my investigation showed that another man was involved in the murder. Erwin's trying to get the new trial moved from Ventura County. He doesn't want any part of it up here next time."

"I can see why, I'm getting out of here, see you later."

"Hey Patton." He turned to look at me. "Thanks a lot for coming by."

Erwin succeeded in having the trial transferred down to L.A. County. He sent Kuhn with the defense files, ordering him to assist the L.A. Public Defender assigned to the case. Woody decided it would take him away from his office too many hours to personally prosecute Cinger so he assigned Dick Hanawalt to try it. A young deputy D.A., Hanawalt had developed a reputation as a formidable foe in the courtroom. At least the Public Defender's office had him so catalogued. Anyone from the D.A.'s office who had distinguished himself, at least to this degree of efficiency, had earned himself the undying hatred of Richard E. Erwin.

Some months previous Hanawalt had been prosecuting a felony case in a Superior Court jury trial. He'd gotten under Erwin's skin by deftly maneuvering the trial to a point of a one hundred percent sure conviction. Hronesh, anxious to ingratiate himself with Erwin and to further prove his valuable services had informed Erwin that Hanawalt was always in the habit of carrying a concealed weapon upon himself, even while court was in session. Supplied with this information Erwin had proclaimed a master plan. It would so startle the judge and the jury that it might discredit Hanawalt to the point that the jury at least would be unable to reach a verdict.

Erwin called me into his office and explained the plan. Hronesh, Kuhn and the attorney handling the case were already there. "Gary, Jim Hronesh has told me that Hanawalt is carrying a gun during the court proceedings. Tomorrow I want you to sit at the counsel table with our attorney. Hanawalt will be addressing the court, when he returns to the counsel table I want you to stand up and accidently bump into him. You're bigger than he is, when you knock him off balance grab him like you are trying to keep him from falling down. It will give you an opportunity to frisk him. When you feel the gun he is carrying, look over at me, I'll be sitting in the front row. Give me the high sign, I'll jump up and accuse Hanawalt of carrying a dangerous weapon in court." Erwin cackled, "Before I get through I'll create such an uproar that even the judge won't know what to do."

I remained silent a few seconds, then looked across the room at Hronesh. "Mr. Erwin, it sounds like a hell of a good plan, but since Hronesh has come up with such a valuable 'scoop' he should have the honor of frisking Hanawalt and giving you the high sign." There was silence, and more silence. Getting up and leaving the group I thought, Christ, every time I open my mouth I make big points with Erwin. Apparently Jim weaseled out of the honor of frisking Dick Hanawalt the next day because nothing more was ever said about it. Personally I was a little bit curious about Hanawalt maybe carrying a gun in court. I made a few discreet inquiries about the slightly obvious bulging Hanawalt had at his waistline. I learned that Dick had hurt his back in a ski accident and was wearing a metal brace. Thank God I had turned down Erwin's plan. I could just see myself waltzing around the Superior Court room frisking Hanawalt, trying to give Erwin the high sign...no gun Erwin, it's a back brace he is wearing. Shit, I was getting sick. Erwin had to be nuts.

Clinger's second trial had begun in L.A., Kuhn had been there for about two weeks. What in hell he could be doing down there all this time I couldn't figure out. I'd asked Erwin several times when Kuhn was returning to help with the enormous case load that was building up. I never got much of a reply.

It was late Friday afternoon, Kuhn had returned from L.A.. He and Hronesh came into the office, they were deep in conversation. Kuhn was cursing Hanawalt, "That s.o.b., I had everything all setup, my operator was waiting in the cocktail lounge where Dick does his drinking after court. She was going to get acquainted with him, have a few drinks, when she had a chance she'd slip Hanawalt a mickey and he would end up in jail for drunk driving or plain drunk. We could care less, just as long as he got booked."

Hronesh said, "Well, what happened?"

"My gal waited for two hours and Hanawalt never showed. We found out later that it was payday and he had left Los Angeles and drove to Ventura to get his paycheck."

Hronesh was very sympathetic, "Don't worry Glen. I'll fix it for you up here in Ventura. My friend on the police department hates Hanawalt. Dick caught him lying in a trial and refused to go along with his story. I'll talk to this guy, we'll fix him yet, don't worry." Jim must have felt a strong obligation to keep his word to Kuhn. Dick Hanawalt was busted for drunk driving. He was found asleep in his auto along the freeway and the officer staked out on him until he started to drive. It delayed the trial but did not do near the damage it would have done if Hanawalt had been arrested in Los Angeles where the large circulation of newspapers and the TV would have played it up big in a murder trial.

Didi Castro could not be found to testify during a second trial, it ended with another hung jury. It looked like maybe Clinger would get away clean, along with the other guy he was involved with in the murder. Hanawalt did not give up easy. There was a third trial, this time the D.A investigators located Didi working in Las Vegas. She was brought back to Los Angeles and in the third trial she took the stand and testified and Clinger was convicted.

No D.A. Investigators ever talked to Allen Jaeman the addict, about Sam the shop owner across the street from the Captain's Table...either about his attempt to kill Jaeman with a long, sharp piece of metal or about his selling narcotics to school age kids...

I couldn't explain it, maybe the D.A. Investigators just couldn't stand the thought of me, a Public Defender Investigator, breaking the case and getting the credit...

Anyway, the three ring circus had cost the taxpayers for three long, drug out, unneccesary trials, a terrible expense and clogging of the courts...

A killer was still stalking the streets and could kill again...

It was all terribly unprofessional...

CHAPTER 6

Soon as I entered the investigator's room Hronesh hurried over, "I've got to talk to you right now! It's real important!" Very excited he kept poking me on the chest with his finger. "I talked to Lane Martin this morning, he said he'd gotten *a big pile of money* from some guys in Ventura. They want us to *frame* Charlie Reiman, the Ventura City Manager, and County Supervisor Robbie Robinson." Gleefully he added, "And we're going to throw the Chief of Police Geary in on the deal free of charge."

Hronesh had declared his hatred of Reiman and Geary so many times in the past I was tired of hearing about it. He was saying, "Martin and I want you to help us. He got enough money for all of us."

"Okay, okay Jim. Get hold of Martin and tell him to come see me." Lane Martin and I had ridden motorcycle patrol many years before. I knew him well enough that I couldn't believe Hronesh was telling the truth. Several years ago when Martin and Hronesh had been trying to force Reiman to give the police department a pay raise, Reiman had won the battle and along with the Chief they had made things very uncomfortable for both of them.

Because of the whole situation Martin developed some kind of nervous condition. Whenever he went to the police station near the Chief he would break out with a rash. He was able to get a medical disability and a pretty good check from the retirement board. He'd obtained a state license to operate as a 'private investigator' and opened an office somewhere in town. A few hours after listening to Hronesh's story, Martin walked in the doorway. He was tall, with black hair, I saw he was getting gray on the sides. Dressed neat, he wore a natty dark blue sport jacket and a striped tie.

"Come on in Lane and sit down. Close the door while you are at it." He pushed the door shut and I noticed he was carrying a black briefcase.

"How you doing Gary, haven't seen much of you since you came back from Los Angeles."

"I've been pretty busy, what is this deal Hronesh was telling me about this morning?"

"Listen, this is a very important situation, it is extremely critical. I'm tied in with a group of very influential, wealthy and politically powerful people in Ventura. They've got a big deal working, these guys Reiman and Robinson are in their way, it's been determined that *they have to go*. I want you to help us, it'll be well worth your while. They gave me *$30,000 to fix* Robinson and Reiman."

"Jesus Martin, are you nuts? I don't want any part of a deal like this."

Martin tapped the side of his black bag, "That's a lot of money and these guys aren't pikers. They are wealthy and plenty powerful. Gary, Jim told me this morning that you have *something on* Charlie Reiman."

"Listen Lane, I don't know anything of the kind. When Jim told me this I thought it was just another one of his half-ass crazy ideas, but I've known you too long. I know you're not kidding. Now let's forget the whole conversation. I don't want any part of such a deal."

"Okay Gary, but I sure wish you were with us." He closed the door behind him as he left. I sat thinking for a few minutes, damn, this has gone too far. Kuhn and Hronesh following everybody in the county, Kuhn sending a woman down to L.A. to frame Hanawalt while he's trying a murder case and now this. I dialed the phone.

A secretary answered. "Let me speak with the Chief please."

"Who's calling?"

"Just tell him it's Gary."

A couple of seconds went by. "This is Jalaty speaking."

"Al, this is Gary. I wanted to see if you were in your office. I'm coming over to see you shortly. It's very important."

"Okay, I'll wait for you."

I drove to Port Hueneme, a small town about twenty miles south of Ventura, parking next to the old stucco building I went into the police station. A policewoman sitting behind a desk was detailing information to a patrol unit over the radio. When she was finished I said, "I have an appointment with the Chief."

She picked up the phone and in a second said, "Yes, the Chief is expecting you. Go right on in."

Going in I closed the door behind me. Jalaty leaning over the desk held out his hand, "Sit down Gary, make yourself comfortable." The Chief's office was small, not much over ten feet square, but it was comfortable, friendly yet business-like. Al's husky build made him appear shorter than he was. His hair was thinning on top. He was like his office, nothing pretentious. The Chief knew his officers and he knew what was going on in his small town. From experience criminals were aware they were facing a strong law enforcement policy in this town.

"Chief how do you manage to keep so tan over here in this fog country?" He smiled but before he could answer I said, "I've got a story I want you to hear. It's about some *insane* things that have been happening for quite a while and it's gotten to the point where I have to tell somebody. You are the only guy in the county I could come to."

"Okay let's have it." I told him the entire story. His face became increasingly grave as I continued. "It's not *only what they have done already,* believe me, *it's what they are planning yet to come.*"

So quiet I barely heard him, he said, "It is almost unbelievable. Let me ask you a few questions, first, do you know the name of the girl that Kuhn sent down to Los Angeles to *put the frame* on Dick Hanawalt?"

"No I don't. I just heard Hronesh and Kuhn talking, they said she's a waitress and lives in Thousand Oaks. They're *pretty cagey* around me now. They know I don't like what they are doing."

"Do your best to find out her name."

"Okay, I'll see what I can do."

"Gary, I'm having lunch tomorrow with Mal King. Do you mind if I tell him everything you have told me?"

"I wish you would, I couldn't go to Mal and tell him this story. Christ, with all the crazy things going on and the strained relations between the D.A. and the defender's office, Mal would think I was trying to mess him up in some way." King was Chief Investigator for the D.A.'s office, an honest, conscientious man.

"Chief, I've got to get back to the courthouse."

As I left he reminded me, "Be sure you let me know right away if you get the name of that gal Kuhn has operating for him."

Only a few attorneys were in the office, it was very quiet. Erwin walked in, "Gary I want to talk to you. I have made a decision. I am going to send you to our Camarillo office and I'm putting Kuhn in charge of the investigators."

Looking at Erwin my face must have reflected strong feelings. He was nervous, like he expected some sort of a hostile reaction on my part.

"What's the idea?"

"Well, Glen has been doing quite a few things for me that meets my approval, more than the way you do things."

"Yeah, I know some of the things Kuhn has been doing for you."

"This won't be so bad, you'll still have your classification and no change in your pay."

I thought maybe it will be better this way to get out of this rat's nest for a while. Next morning I was at the Camarillo office about 8:30, I greeted Bill Armstrong, the lawyer in charge, a nice guy. He went to law school at UCLA where he played football and later he played some pro ball.

Bill smiled, "I heard you were coming out, I'm glad. We can use some help."

Armstrong had only one lawyer to help him, together they were handling the entire east end of the county without an investigator. Though swamped with cases neither of them were full of psychotic hang-ups like Erwin and the small group of nuts he had surrounded himself with.

Armstrong and Dave Fitzsimmons were genuinely locked in with the people and their problems. There were those who had simply become seemingly irrevocably snared in minor legal entanglements, then there were those who with overwhelming evidence obviously were guilty of burglary, rape and other serious crimes. We fought unrelenting battles with the D.A.'s staff within the courtrooms but remained on civil and friendly terms on the outside. It was a relief being there even though it necessitated several hours of extra work a night on pre-trials and interviews. There seemed to be a simple understanding to get the work done and no bellyaching. I couldn't recall any of us in the Camarillo office ever turning in overtime for our efforts.

Things had been going smoothly. Bill, Dave and I usually went to the neighborhood hamburger stand around the corner for lunch and had a root beer or a malt and sandwich. We discussed the coming afternoon court problems and had short, friendly disagreements on the problems and tactics of police officers as versed to the problems of defense lawyers. They usually agreed with me on the subject of police departments, they were an absolute necessity for the safety and well being of a community. I even got them to admit one fact, the toughest kind of policeman to run up against, the one defense lawyers disparaged most was the hard working, conscientious officer who had his evidence and facts laid out in a manner that simply couldn't effectively be attacked by the defense.

Dave and I were standing in the hallway outside our office, it was noon, I looked into the cramped office that housed the three of us, our desks and a file cabinet that I kept our records in jammed the room. Bill sat at his desk reading a report. I asked, "Hey boss, are you coming to lunch with us?"

"No, I've got to familiarize myself with this report, you guys go ahead." Dave and I walked to a new taco stand that just opened up. I returned to the office early, Armstrong was still there. Gazing up quizzically he said, "You should have stayed here instead of going to lunch."

"Why, what happened?"

"Your old buddy Kuhn was here, he had a gal with him. He said she got busted for a 23102 Vehicle Code, drunk driving. He wanted me to make a court appearance for her. He claimed she was a good friend of his, she did a lot of work for him in the Clinger murder case."

Suddenly bells rang. Hell's bells, this must be the gal Kuhn had down in L.A. trying to frame Hanawalt. I tried to remain calm.

"Bill, do we have the file on her?"

"There isn't any file. Kuhn didn't want one."

"I believe that...what did she look like?"

"Well, not too bad. She was all dolled up and was hanging on to Kuhn like a clam. They left just before you returned. Kuhn didn't seem to be very anxious to be here when you got back."

"Thanks Bill, listen, I have to go over to the clerk's office. I'll be back before you need me." Hustling to the clerk's office I checked the records real quick. There it was! Right on the court calendar! Wilhelmina Chirp, drunk driving. Her plea: Not Guilty. 'Wilhelmina Chirp.' Christ, was Kuhn kidding? Yet this couldn't be a joke.... Nothing better to do I grabbed a phone book. A Chirp was listed in Thousand Oaks...right where Kuhn had told Hronesh the waitress lived. This was luck I hadn't hoped for. I went out the side door of the courthouse, down an alley about half a block to a gas station where there was a pay phone. I dialed the number for the police chief.

"Hello Al, this is Gary. Get this, the name of the gal Kuhn was using to *frame* Hanawalt was Wilhelmina Chirp...no damn it, I am not trying to be funny." I told him what had happened.

"Gary, I've got some news for you too, while talking to Mal King the other day I told him the whole story. He couldn't believe people like Kuhn and Erwin exist. You know Mal, he's so damn honest he's actually naive when it comes to vicious stuff like this."

"Yeah, that's what I was afraid of."

"Don't worry about Mal, what you've said fits right into certain things they know already. Mal talked with Deem and George Eskin, the Assistant D.A., they want a grand jury investigation, with no holds barred. Next week sometime I will make an appointment for you to meet with King at his house. He is *quite anxious* to record and document this whole story. In fact, I'm going to meet you there at his house."

"Jalaty I'll tell you, it's very encouraging and I appreciate what you are doing. You know there's damn few people who'd stick their necks out in a situation like this."

"Ah, it's nothing more than a matter of duty."

"Okay, I appreciate it anyway." It was 12:45, still fifteen minutes before Judge West was due to return to the courtroom. I went back to the office and sat down. Kuhn appeared in the open doorway. I didn't feel like talking to him, getting up I moved on out into the hallway. I could tell he had wanted to say something to me, make people believe that we were friends. I had come to the conclusion, this guy didn't have any friends, only acquaintances that could be used for his own purposes. When he realized that his acquaintances were getting wise to his modus operandi, the pat he gave them on the back was not an assurance of his friendship, he was feeling for the soft spot, the spot where the 'shiv' would go.

Out in the foyer Harrison Dunham was leaning against the door of the courtroom peering in. I came up behind him, "Hi Dunham, what are you doing way out here in Camarillo?"

Spinning around, a cigar clamped between his teeth, he stared at me. Startled by my sudden appearance he choked, "Oh...I just came out here to plead our client guilty to drunk driving."

"Hell, we've got two deputy public defenders out here who could take care of a simple problem like that."

"Well... This is kind of a *special client.*"

"You mean Kuhn's girlfriend, the one who *did so much* for him in the Clinger case?"

"That's her. Tell me, in the afternoon does a deputy D.A. usually come into court?"

"Not usually, why?"

"I've got to talk to Judge West as soon as he comes in. The D.A. is preparing to file a prior drunk driving conviction on this gal. That means she will get a mandatory sentence, suspension of her driver's license, and some jail time. I'll have to get in there and plead her guilty to this latest arrest and pay the fine before the D.A. finds out what we're doing."

"How can this woman be a client of our office? We don't even have a file on her, no request for attorney assistance, no financial statement, no nothing."

"*Kuhn set this up with Erwin,* he *ordered me* to come out here and 'snow' Judge West that we had made a deal with another judge in Ventura to plead her guilty, but the other judge was unavailable today so we needed West to do it in his court." Dunham was keeping a close eye into the courtroom. "There's the Judge now, I've got to get in there fast and talk to him before a D.A. comes in."

Harrison trundled over to the judge, after a second the jurist nodded his head, he then took the bench. From the counsel table Dunham quickly pled the woman guilty to drunk driving. The judge ordered a three hundred dollar fine and no suspension of license. Leaving the courtroom in a hurry Dunham met Kuhn in the foyer, they hustled over to the window where fines are paid. It took them only a minute, then swiftly they walked to the entrance and out to the parking lot where Wilhelmina was waiting in the county car. No wonder Kuhn wanted to get friendly in the office, he hadn't wanted me to go out to the courtroom and see what Dunham was up to.

I went to the clerk's window, studying the court calendar I saw Dunham had entered Wilhelmina's name to be called. The clerk let me see her record, they had paid the three hundred dollar fine with cash. That gal has really been doing something for Kuhn if he could get Erwin to order a stunt like this. Kuhn or Erwin hadn't come up with that money out of their own pockets, if I knew those crooked bastards it was county funds. Later when things had quieted down, I went to the pay phone. Listening to this latest chicanery Mal said, "I find these guys hard to believe, I'll check into this."

Early next morning on the drive to Camarillo I dropped off the freeway and hit a phone. King answered, "Gary right after we talked yesterday I discussed this with George Eskin. He contacted one of our deputies in Camarillo who managed an off-handed conversation with Judge West about Dunham's appearance in his court. According to West, Harrison worked it just like he told you he was going to. Another thing Eskin discovered, they lied about having made any arrangements with that other judge in Ventura. That judge said they had never contacted him. *Eskin is plenty upset* over this, it's just plain criminal obstruction of justice."

"Yeah, it's a pretty sick situation alright."

"This whole thing has to be presented to the grand jury, it's the only way to handle it. I want you to come to my house soon. I'll call Jalaty...have him let you know when."

Several days later Jalaty called me, he wanted to know if I could be at King's home that evening at six. "Sure Al, I'll be there." Mal lived in Santa Paula, when I pulled up at the house Jalaty's car was already parked in front. We sat in King's front room, I gave him the whole story, he was writing notes as fast as he could.

"I'm going to make a full written report to Woody, he wants to get it to the Grand Jury as soon as possible. He's already talked to Dr. Penfield, the Grand Jury foreman, *he was totally shocked.*" Mal appeared embarrassed, "Gary, I want to ask you something."

"Go ahead Mal, shoot."

"Well uh, would you be willing to take a polygraph?" I reasoned, hell, you can't blame them, in their place I'd ask the same question.

"No problem Mal, just set it up."

He seemed to feel better. "I was afraid you might get teed off." Al stayed after I left. I figured they'd discuss it among themselves. What was so utterly bewildering to me was the fact so many people were involved in all this crazy crap, yet *no where* along the line had any of these people stopped and said, hey, for Christ's sake, *this is insane,* we should stop doing these things.

CHAPTER 7

Out of a clear blue sky we received word the Camarillo office was to be closed. Everybody was being transferred to our branch office in Oxnard. The next morning before I reported to Oxnard I stopped in the main office in Ventura. There were some files that had to be taken to Superior Court in Oxnard. I was about to leave when Dunham came from his office saying, "Hold on a second, I'll ride over with you, I had to leave my car at the garage to be fixed." I took the back road to Oxnard, down by the beach and across the Santa Clara River.

Dunham was talkative, "You know I am going to be in charge of the Oxnard office. I'm replacing Paul Clinton, Erwin is pissed off at him. He says Clinton pleads too many of those illiterate Mexicans *not guilty*. Erwin wants to run them through court as fast as we can and stop having so many trials. There'll be *no more jury trials* from now on. You are going to be interviewing the prisoners first thing every morning. There will be an interpreter there for the ones who don't speak English, you're to tell them we will get them off with a small fine, probation, or as short a sentence as we can."

"I don't get it, from what I hear Clinton has been doing a hell of a good job in Oxnard. Even the deputy D.A.'s and police like and respect his ability."

"Yeah, the only trouble is Erwin hates him," Dunham chuckled, "Why do you think Erwin put Kuhn in charge over you?"

"I'll bite. Why?"

"Because...Kuhn would do what ever he wanted, even when he knew it was breaking the law."

"Uh huh, you mean like making life miserable for some poor widow and her family?"

Harrison looked surprised. "Oh, I see you know all about Mrs. Thurman."

"Yeah, I know."

"Did you also know that Kuhn finally got a warrant and had her arrested?"

"Is that right? I didn't know it."

"Sure, that's why Erwin put him in charge. Erwin was so tickled because Kuhn got Mrs. Thurman arrested that he couldn't sit still. He called me in and *gave me orders to make sure she didn't get a public defender* to represent her. Erwin ordered me to tell the court she didn't qualify financially."

"Did you do it?"

"Of course," revealing no remorse or embarrassment, Dunham admitted, "Sure...I told the judge she could afford her own attorney."

"Lordy, is that why Erwin is putting you in charge in Oxnard?"

"That's one of the reasons."

"I knew you had been doing other things for Kuhn and Erwin. I can't understand it, *why* do you do it?"

This seemed to stir some emotion in Dunham. "By God! I don't have any choice. When I was in my hey-day down in Hollywood I wouldn't have touched Erwin with a ten foot pole."

"I realize the top position in Oxnard pays a little more money Dunham, but not enough for a guy to sell his soul."

He made excuses, "Money is only part of it."

I was lucky, there was a parking space directly in front of the court building. Entering the office we saw Paul sitting at his desk. Obviously he was wanting to talk to Dunham, so I left. I went over to the Municipal Court. During arraignment the Oxnard police used the juror's box to 'corral' the prisoners while waiting for court to convene. In the back room I found some interview forms, grabbing a few sharp pencils I went out to the prisoners.

Rapping on the bannister I said loudly, "I am from the Public Defender's office. We will try to help you. Get your booking slips out, I want to see your name and what you have been booked for." Most of them were Mexican, several blacks and a few whites. I took the Mexicans first. If they couldn't speak English and they'd been arrested on some minor misdemeanor charge such as plain drunk, I sent them into the back room where an interpreter would fill out an interview form. After sending ten of them back I recalled Dunham's orders. Going there I saw the interpreter a young Mexican lady had them lined up clear around the table, she was still interviewing the first man I'd sent her.

Curtly I said, "Court is going to start in a few minutes. Harrison Dunham is the new attorney in charge. When he gets here he wants all these interviews on the counsel table in front of him. At the rate you're going you won't even be done with this first guy."

"But he says he is not guilty!"

More gently I said, "Alright, what was he arrested for?"

"Plain drunk."

"How long is it since he was last arrested?"

She rattled the questions off to him. "He says many years ago in Texas."

"Ask him if he has twenty dollars to pay the fine."

"He says yes, but he still insists he's not guilty. He only had one beer and fell asleep in a doorway. He'd just arrived in town and was going to the labor camp and get a job in the morning. The officer woke him up and took him to jail."

"Look, Dunham gave me my orders. He says it's a waste of time to fool around explaining to them how they can plead not guilty and put up bail and then have to come back to court for a trial. If they don't have money to put up bail they will stay in jail waiting for a trial and do more time than if they had pled guilty in the first place. Now, to start off, just get their names, what they are charged with and if they have enough money to pay the fine."

This worked pretty good with the transients and the non-English speaking prisoners. Dunham had a real mill going. He was dropping them 'down the tube' so fast that he had the jury box emptied out before anybody knew what happened. Prisoners with more serious charges we had to spend more time with. There wasn't any question about it, I knew from long experience of working both sides of the fence that some of them should be advised to plead *not* guilty and ask for a jury trial. It was the shits sitting there handing them a con job to plead guilty, and if they 'screamed' too loud, try to convince them that a court trial without a jury was their best bet. I began to notice that *all* the Mexicans were starting to act like they didn't understand English. They didn't want to talk with a public defender anymore. Some were demanding that the court should appoint them a private lawyer. I'd made up my mind, the next guy I interviewed who without question needed a jury trial, I was going to advise him to demand it before the judge.

When arraignments were over I walked upstairs to our office. Fitzsimmons and Dunham were there. Dave was an extremely easy going guy, I was surprised when I heard him tell Harrison angrily, "I'm assigned to this case. I determined that it was definitely to the best interest of my client to plead not guilty and ask for a jury trial."

Dunham's cigar was green and his face was red. He was almost screaming, "God damn it, I told you *nobody* was going to ask for a jury trial. *I'll decide* what's to the best interest of these *assholes.*"

Dave turned and left the room. I went to a desk and sat down. A client came in, a young fellow who talked to the secretary for a moment and she said to Dunham who was still standing there, "This gentleman is supposed to appear on a *traffic matter* tomorrow, but he won't be able to get here."

Dunham said, "We can take care of that," he told the secretary what to type up, then told the client, *"You just sign that paper* when she gets it done and you won't have to be here tomorrow. I'll make an appearance for you."

Next day in the courtroom I heard Harrison say, "Your Honor, I have here an affidavit signed by my client and I want to plead him guilty."

The judge had the case, I watched him reading it. He glanced at Dunham pointedly a couple times, then said, "Mr. Dunham, if I was to accept this guilty plea your client will *serve mandatory jail time.* Now I want you to withdraw it and move for a continuance, in the meantime advise your client to get his driver's license straightened out and I will place him on probation."

Withdrawing his plea Dunham left forgetting the affidavit on the counsel table, I read it. For expediency he had had the man sign an authorization pleading himself guilty. Dunham's *absolute unconcern* for anyone had just about put the poor bastard away for sure.

I called Mal on the phone and asked him how soon I could get to the grand jury. "You don't know how bad it really is." I told him about the reaction the Mexican people were having to the so-called legal representation they were supposed to be getting and the deal Dunham had just pulled in court. "That's only part of it. Two of our real good young attorney's are quitting. They can not go along with anymore of this crap."

"Who's quitting?"

"Well, Fitzsimmons for one, and another guy has turned in his resignation."

"That's too bad. It is a real shame for the county to lose good personnel like them."

"Mal, I am getting damn tired of this bullshit. All we are doing over here is crucifying these poor people."

"You've got to hang on. Dr. Penfield has it all set up for you to go before the grand jury. He wants the entire panel there, every last one of them."

"That will suit me fine. What about that polygraph you wanted me to take?"

"Don't worry about that, it's not necessary. We have been doing some investigating and *we know that everything you've said* is true. We know *a lot more* but I can't tell you about it now. Just hang in there until we get ready."

"Okay, I'll call you later."

Lunch was over and it was quiet in the office. Dunham came in, I told him if he didn't need me I was going over to the main office in Ventura and clean some of my stuff out of my old desk. He said, "Go ahead."

Entering the outer office Claire was the only one there. She sat at her desk looking down at some papers. If I wasn't aware of her ability to scan the room without anyone realizing it I might have thought she didn't even know I was there. In my office I discovered Claire had removed all my personal notes and files from my desk and had stacked them up on a small table by the door. There was a new swivel chair behind the desk. The old one I had been using was busted and I'd asked Claire for months to try and requisition a new one. Glen Baby was going to be living in style, Claire would see to that. It flashed through my mind, maybe I just didn't know how to operate. I should've taken lessons from Glen Baby and gone down to the coffee shop like he wanted me to and watched the 'M.O.' he used on Erwin. If that was the price of success around this joint I think I'll just continue on and take my chances.

Thumbing through the stack of papers Claire removed from my desk I noticed a small, blue colored piece of paper. The handwriting looked like Claire's. It said, 'Glen, Vol demote signed.' It was some kind of message from Claire to Glen. Even with the abbreviations she knew he would understand the message. It must be another one of their little secrets, *the strange message* had stirred my suspicious mind. I knew these two would never stop plotting. For years Claire had been in a dormant catalytic state, her vicious nature never really surfacing and becoming dominant until coming into contact with a chemical agent such as Kuhn's mental aberrations exuded. The blue piece of paper I folded and shoved in my pocket, the rest I pushed into a wastebasket.

Going down California Street after leaving the office I walked two blocks to the old building at the corner of Santa Clara Street. Formerly a furniture store it was now the County Personnel office. At the desk a clerk asked if she could help me. Giving her my name I requested to see my file. Going to a cabinet she returned with a folder. "Is there anything in particular you want to know?"

"Yes, has anything been added to it lately?"

She opened the folder, "Yes, there's a form called a Voluntary Demotion that has been placed in here with your signature on it."

"Let me see it."

"No, I can't let you have the file."

"Damn it, I never signed anything like that. I never even heard of such a form before."

"It's got your signature on it."

"Listen, I don't need the file. Make a copy on your machine and let me have it."

Running off the copy she remarked, "I thought there was something funny about this."

"What do you mean?"

"Last week Claire, the secretary in your office, brought one of these forms here to me, she wanted it put in your file, but it didn't have your signature on it. I told her we could not put a document like that in anybody's file without their signature."

"Do me a favor, on this copy you just gave me write your name and today's date."

"Sure, I don't see why not."

"Do me one more favor, please don't forget what you told me about Claire coming down here with an *unsigned form* and *trying to put it in my folder.*" Thanking her I left. I wasn't going to be able to hold it in much longer.

I was going down the corridor to the Public Defender's office, Kuhn Baby and I were going to get this straightened out one way or another. I almost ran directly into Paul Clinton without seeing him. He said, "I've been wanting to talk to you."

"Go ahead Paul."

"Several weeks ago, it was while you were still in charge of the investigators, I went to a dance in Oxnard, an annual event the legal secretaries put on for their bosses, it was held at the Colonial House Restaurant, everyone was having a good time drinking and dancing. Hanawalt was there, we were having a drink and talking, I glanced over to a corner of the room where there was a large potted plant standing against the wall. I thought I must be seeing things, I had to look twice to make sure. Kuhn was hiding between the plant and the wall. I saw his face through the foliage, he was watching Dick and me. It was the funniest thing I'd ever seen, just like one of those old 'B-rated' movies, where the house detective hides behind the potted plants in the hotel lobby." From the picture Clinton painted I could just see the fat detective hiding in the shrubbery. Mad as I was at Kuhn and Claire I had to laugh.

Paul continued relating the incident, "Sometime later I was out in front of the Colonial House getting ready to go home. Hanawalt and another deputy D.A. came out, Dick was feeling pretty good but the other D.A. was sober and I was glad when he got in the driver's seat and drove off with Dick. As they were driving away I saw Kuhn standing over in the parking lot watching them. Hronesh drove over and picked him up and they drove off following Hanawalt and the other D.A. The next morning when I came into the office I heard Kuhn reporting the whole evening's events to Erwin. Now...what I want to ask you is, did you know these clowns were up to this kind of bullshit?"

"Yeah, I had my suspicions but the way Erwin has been running things around here I lost all control of the investigators a long time ago. I've been unable to get any work out of them for months."

Showing Paul the blue piece of paper with Claire's handwriting on it, I told him the whole story about the voluntary demotion form. "Paul, so help me, *I never signed* any form like that, *I've never even heard of one* before. It's got to be forged."

"Maybe it's forged and maybe it isn't...I'll tell you the fast one they tried to pull on me. One day without any warning at all, Erwin called me into his office and accused me of the damndest bunch of crap you ever heard of. It was nothing but a bunch of lies. He told me that I was through, that I was fired from my job with the county. I didn't argue with him. I just told him to go ahead and file official charges against me, I wasn't worried about the pack of lies like he was spouting off about. A couple of days later Claire called me over to her desk, she said she had a form I must sign. Smiling at me she said, *'It isn't important Paul, it's just a notice* that I have to turn in regarding extra time off you took sometime back.' I told her I'd like to see it. She urged me, 'Come on Paul, it isn't important, just sign it, I'm in a hurry, I have a lot of work to do.' I knew she was up to something, I grabbed hold of the form, but she still wouldn't let go. I insisted...give me that form Claire, I want to read it first. I read it and if I'd signed that paper Erwin would have been able to fire me and he wouldn't even have had to file charges. It was *practically my own death warrant* so far *as my job was concerned.* Handing it back back to Claire I said forget it, I am not about to sign anything like this. The look on her face...believe me if looks could kill I would be dead right now. She snatched the form from my hand, jerking open the bottom drawer of her desk she threw the form into the drawer. I yelled, wait a minute Claire, damn it, what have you got in there? I'd caught a glimpse of a file. It had my name and picture on it, and a bunch of typewritten pages. She slammed the drawer shut. I said Claire you've got secret files in there on me, I demand to see them. She snarled, 'That belongs to me and you can't see it.' I was madder than hell, but what could I do?"

"Paul, did you see files on anybody besides yourself?"

"No but it was a large desk drawer and it was full of folders."

"Christ, that's what Hronesh and Kuhn have been doing all these nights when they are out until two or three in the morning. Erwin's been giving that pair *overtime* for following everybody in the county government. Paul, I'll see you later, I have to get back to Oxnard."

On the way back I was doing a whole bunch of deep thinking. It was a good thing I had run into Paul and heard his experiences. It wouldn't do any good to have it out with Kuhn now, that would just give them more ammunition to throw at me. If Claire had my signature on that *voluntary demotion form,* she'd pulled off a slick job. Everybody in the office had been in the habit of going to her desk and simply signing everything she shoved before them. It had been about a week ago, I was leaving the office in a hurry when she called me.

"Gary, come here and sign these automobile mileage forms and these other forms for office supplies."

How in hell could you ever combat the type of warfare Claire and Kuhn waged against you? If you were polite and cooperative with them they would catch you unawares. If you were constantly suspicious and belligerent they'd have everybody believing you were impossible to get along with. I was never easy to demoralize, but I was forced to admit to myself, they were kind of getting to me. If

Erwin was a real man and the type of administrator who wouldn't tolerate their type of crap there would've been no problems but he encouraged it. He surrounded himself with people of their mental propensities toward vagaries of the wildest kind. The best thing was for me to keep my mouth shut and get to the grand jury as soon as possible.

Never had I seen anything to compare with Erwin, Kuhn and Claire. Hronesh was actually a nothing, just a weak personality with no real loyalty to anyone. They had a squeeze on him right now, but if a grand jury got to him and gave him a break he would spill his guts all over the place.

I could hear Dunham talking on the phone in his office, which was next to mine. The temporary walls they had put up were as thin as paper. He was assuring somebody he'd take care of his financial obligations real soon. Harrison's secretary was sick one day and I answered the phone in her place. There was at least seven or eight calls that came in for Dunham from loan companies and collection agencies in L.A.. A couple of them wanted to know if he had filed bankruptcy yet. Erwin was squeezing Dunham the same way he was Jim Hronesh. Dunham's financial condition must be the twist Erwin has on him. I'd overheard Kuhn and Dunham arguing over money sometime ago and Kuhn had threatened him, "You son-of-a-bitch, I'm going to tell Erwin, he'll have your ass for sure."

I examined the pile of cases on my desk trying to forget all the damn back stabbing and intrigue. My phone rang, it was Kuhn, the sound of his voice was nearly enough to set me off. He was telling me that he was now the senior investigator. That since I had signed a voluntary demotion Erwin had promoted him to my job. Also that if I did not recognize the fact he was now the boss he was going to see to it that Erwin fired me. This did it! I had all I could take from him. "Listen Glen, it's too late in the afternoon for me to come over there now, but I am going to be in Erwin's office Monday morning and you better have yourself there too. I never signed any voluntary demotion or anything else. I have the note Claire wrote to you, and the clerk at personnel told me about her trying *to sneak a voluntary demotion in my file* without my knowing it, but you and that rotten secretary you are playing around with aren't going to get away with it." Banging the phone down I left the office. I walked downstairs, wandering around the hall and courtrooms I spotted the Coca Cola machine in the corner...maybe a coke would cool me off.

Returning upstairs I saw Dunham standing by his office door.

"Gary, come in here." I went in closing the door. Dunham seemed pleased about something, I soon learned why, "I just got a call from Erwin. He says you and Kuhn have got a personality clash and you are through in the Public Defender's office. He doesn't want to fire you. He's made arrangements for you to transfer to the Coroner's office."

"You can forget that Dunham, I'm not transferring anywhere. You call Erwin back and tell him that. If he wants to fire me I want him to file specific charges, because I haven't done anything wrong."

Harrison pleaded, "Listen to me Gary, why do you want to make trouble? Why don't you just do what Erwin wants?

"You call him Dunham and tell him what I've said. It's quitting time now and it's Friday night. I'm going home. I will be back here Monday morning."

Early Monday I was on the job in Oxnard. When I finished the arraignments I went up to the office. It wasn't long before Erwin came in. "Gary are you going to transfer to the Coroner's office like I told you?"

"No, I haven't done anything wrong. All I've done is refuse to do a lot of rotten bullshit for you like trying to get your neighbors arrested. Kuhn's been kissing your ass and doing all your dirty work and getting overtime for it for three years, while I've been working my butt off trying to help some of our clients. He spent ten months in Orange County screwing around with Didi Castro trying to *keep her from talking on the witness stand just so you could try to ruin Woody Deem, the D.A..*"

"Alright, I know you're mad about not having any help, but Glen does things the way I want and as long as he does what I tell him, I am going to keep him in charge."

"Erwin, I have always said that right is right and wrong is wrong. I haven't done anything wrong, so what are you going to do?"

"Alright, you are fired."

I removed my Public Defender's I.D. card from my wallet laying it on the desk. "I have the keys to the county car, I'm going to drive it back to Ventura and pick up my own." After driving a few blocks I pulled into a gas station and went to a pay phone. King answered, I told him what had taken place.

"That's too bad, I sure wish you could have held on a little while longer. Dr. Penfield set a date for you to appear before the Grand Jury about ten days from now."

"I know it. But this *phony voluntary demotion* thing and all the rest of the crap they are involved in is really making me sick to my stomach. I mean it really is."

"I can understand...what you better do is go over to the County Employees Association and see Al Palmer. He is the head man, a friend of mine and a real straight shooter. I'll call him now and let him know you are coming."

Palmer greeted me, "Good morning Gary, glad to see you. King gave me a little idea of what's going on." Al was a good listener. I gave him the story...the whole works, from the beginning right up until now. Al's ashtray was overloaded, continuously he had smoked until I finished. He remained silent nearly a minute, turning he said, "My Lord, that guy Erwin is running a Nazi Gestapo instead of a Public Defender's Office. We will have to file our demand for the 'specific charges' within a required amount of days and request a civil service hearing. But don't worry, I'll handle that part. Mal told me about the Grand Jury wanting all your information and *he wants you to appear* before them prior to the civil service hearing."

The following day Erwin filed dismissal charges against me with the county clerk. At Al's office we examined the documents. Palmer commented, "This is very interesting...there are only two pages here. Erwin just rambles on and on about you not liking Kuhn. He claims you knew you had been demoted a year ago and he was promoting Kuhn."

"That is a bunch of crap Al, I didn't know about any demotion for more than a year after talking with Erwin about transferring to Camarillo. Erwin is lying like hell, if what he says is true why did he wait a year to promote Kuhn?"

"That is right....now, here Erwin says *you* were responsible for putting Dillon on the witness stand."

"Do you remember me telling you Al, about Didi taking a poly and revealing Clinger was with another man who did the killing? Didi's lawyer Red Blais gave this evidence to Erwin months before Dillon ever took the stand, so, *Erwin had known immediately* Dillon was lying, still he gave the order for him to testify. It so enraged the little Korean that he went running down the corridor screaming liar at Dillon. Soon after that Paik took a job with a Public Defender's office in northern California. He wanted *to get away* from Erwin."

Al grunted, "Here on the second page Dunham states your work was completely unsatisfactory over in Oxnard."

"Dunham will swear to anything that Erwin tells him to, they've got a real crooked scam going, *selling investigative files* to private lawyers. Dunham was dead broke and heading for bankruptcy when Erwin brought him to Ventura. He still gets a half dozen calls a day from creditors demanding money or else..."

"At the end of the second page Erwin states that you are being dismissed for *incompetency...inefficiency...insubordination* and also *discourteous treatment* of other employees."

"Al, at this point all I can say is one thing. If you believe I am guilty of any of these charges just because I wouldn't take overtime money from the county to run around all hours of the night framing people and getting an innocent widow like Mrs. Thurman thrown in jail, then I'm willing to walk out of here and forget the whole thing."

"No no, don't get touchy. I believe what you've told me and Mal does too. I am going to a board of directors meeting of the Public Employees Association tonight, I am going to recommend that they give us as much money as possible to hire an attorney. Ordinarily I represent our clients at the Civil Service Board, but I hear Erwin is going to have his assistant Cleaver represent him at the hearing. It seems to me that Erwin is going all out to *get you* and I think we need legal help."

Leaving Palmer's office I drove north along the ocean on the Rincon Highway. It seemed like I was doing a lot of aimless driving and wandering lately, but I needed time to think, lots of time. The whole series of events from the last three years rushed through my mind. I wished I'd listened to Lane Martin a little longer. I could've discovered who those *wealthy, powerful men in Ventura were* who gave all that money to him and Hronesh. Maybe I could've learned how they intended to frame Robinson and Reiman, that would have really helped. Well, it was too late now. Hronesh had hardly spoken to me since I turned them down.

I remembered Palmer reading Erwin's accusations against me out loud. Incompetent and inefficient. That really rankled, in fact, it got to me 'really' bad. I recalled some of the commendations and letters I had received over the past years from top people in law enforcement, people like Thad Brown, Chief of Detectives of LAPD and Big Bill McKesson, Los Angeles District Attorney. I had been called lots of things over the many years, but *never* incompetent or inefficient.

A murder came to my mind. It wasn't big or important as cases go. Rather it was just *the speed* with which my partner Frank and I had wrapped it up. It was about 9:00 a.m., Frank and I were in the L.A. Police Headquarters Building. We'd stopped by Thad Brown's office and were shooting the breeze for a minute. "You know," Thad mentioned, "we have a murder case on our hands and Homicide has drawn nothing but blanks clear down the line for a month now. I thought perhaps you fellas from the D.A.'s office might have heard a rumble or something about it."

"Can you give us a few of the details Chief," Frank queried?

"The body of a man approximately forty years old was found up on Mulholland Drive. All we learned from the autopsy was that he was completely overloaded with heroin. An ex-con, he'd only been out of the pen for about a week. We don't know where he has been or who he was with since he was released."

We assured Chief Brown we would put out some feelers. Riding the elevator to the basement where the police cars and motorcycles were parked, Frank said, "Lets drive out to West Hollywood, I just got an idea. We haven't seen Iggy for quite some time."

I agreed it might be a good idea, anyway, even if Iggy doesn't know anything there's a couple of other guys we can hustle out that way. We drove out Sunset Boulevard to Fairfax Avenue and turned left. Half way down the short hill on Fairfax I parked in front of a fashionable apartment house. Out of habit from years of experience we didn't go in the front door of the apartment house. We walked down a long driveway to the rear of the building where a wide row of parking stalls had corresponding apartment numbers, no one was around.

We knew Iggy was home, his new Cadillac the Dragon Lady had just bought him was in it's stall. He was a pimp, a very successful one. Why not, his girlfriend Jeanie, who he affectionately called the Dragon Lady, was a beautiful girl, and she operated strictly for Iggy. At one time he'd been a top bass viola player in name bands before narcotics had gotten the best of him, he still knew who the big junk peddlers were in Hollywood.

We went through a rear entrance and walked quietly down the hall, the carpeting was thick and plush. Frank tapped on the door lightly. We heard movement inside and knew Iggy was looking at us through a small glass eye set in the middle of the door. He opened up greeting us effusively, "Why haven't you guys been out to see me more often? Come in."

Iggy was of medium height, well built and looked like he was in great physical shape. His thick brown hair was fashionably formed. The white cashmere sweater with a turtle neck and the light beige form-fitting trousers made him look like a fashion plate direct from

Fifth Avenue. He ushered us into the parlor. A flight of carpeted stairs spiraled elegantly up the far wall to the bedroom and bath. Frank and I made ourselves comfortable on a sofa.

"Look here you guys, what do you think of this? The Dragon Lady bought it for me for Christmas." Iggy, with his quick dancing movements had flitted over to a corner of the room where a small decorated tree was sitting. A litter of holiday gift wrap paper was pushed next to a large, red leather covered box. "It's a new type of vacuum sweeper fellas. Just look at this thing." He held up fittings with one hand and a glass jar with the other. "It's a paint spraying outfit." He was ecstatic. "Just think, I can even paint a car with this outfit if I wanted to."

We heard a voice faintly calling, "Iggy," from upstairs. Leaping to his feet obediently he dashed to the kitchen. Within a matter of seconds he came scurrying out carrying a silver tray covered with a white embroidered napkin.

"Excuse me fellas, the Dragon Lady wants her breakfast. I'll be right with you." He bounded soundlessly up the carpeted stairs and out of sight. I was about to suggest to Frank that we pin Iggy down and find out if he had any information about the murder when we heard a heavy crash upstairs. The Dragon Lady was screaming.

"You goddamn stupid pimp, you know I've been out frenching all night and you bring me a hot dog for breakfast. Get your ass out of here." Another crash and Iggy came flying down the stairs nearly wiping out at the bottom.

"Sorry fellas, the Dragon Lady's always in a bad mood when she first wakes up. I'll take her some orange juice and be right down." This time he made it back without any more commotion from the bedroom. Smiling he said, "Everything is wonderful, I told Jeanie we had company. She's such a lady."

Frank growled, "Okay Iggy, settle down, we want to talk to you." We told him of the ex-con's body being found on Mulholland Drive, loaded with heroin. Iggy's large eyes rolled in his head. He became serious and confidential.

"Maybe I can help you. I ran into Danny Eagle several days ago, he was madder than hell. He'd just gotten a new batch of 'H' from the East Coast some place. He was planning to make a lot of bread selling it. One day Danny left his pad for a little while and when he returned his stash had disappeared. He suspects his cousin Tommy Eagle put the snatch on his stash. Tommy's been on the junk pretty bad and he has been shacking up with some gal named Betty. She's an old time hype, a real living zombie."

"Alright, where is Tommy holed up?"

"I don't know but Danny's living down on Vine Street, you know the place."

"Okay, thanks a lot Iggy."

"You're welcome fellas. Come around once in a while and see me. Jeanie and I are just so happy together."

Iggy's voice faded as Frank quietly closed the door. I drove East on Sunset to Vine St. and turned south. A few blocks down was the Ranch Market, it stayed open twenty four hours a day. I pulled into the market's parking lot so we could observe the second rate hotel across the street. Danny's pad was on the third floor. It was noon and getting hot, Frank said, "I'll eyeball that joint and see if I spot any action going on if you'll walk over and get us something cold to drink."

Returning with the cokes I asked, "Anything going on?"

"Not a thing, let's go over and roust Danny." The hallway and staircase was dimly lit. A strong and distinctly unsanitary smell hung heavy in the place, I banged the door.

Danny on the other side said, "Who's there?"

"Open up Danny." The door opened a crack, when he saw who it was he pulled the door wider, "Come on in."

After a little preliminary yakking Frank said, "Danny, we hear that you lost a pretty good stash, worth quite a bit of bread on the street."

"What you guys mean? I ain't got no stash."

"Yeah, we know you haven't got one now but you did have and some one beat you out of it. Listen Danny, we heard that Tommy got himself a sackful of junk and he's living real high."

Danny cringed a little.

"Look Danny, we're not getting on you, we just want some info."

"So alright, I know that dirty bastard stole my stash, he left me absolutely broke."

"Do you know where he is now Danny?"

"Hell no, I've been looking every place for him. If I could find him I'd shove one of his rusty needles so far up his asshole they'd need a fish pole with radar to find it. All I know is that skinny bitch he's been shacking up with has this relative that just got out of the joint, and they have been living with him. Listen you guys, that stash Tommy swiped from me was some of the best 'H' I've ever had my hands on. I could a' thinned it out twenty times and it would still be better than anything you can buy around Hollywood right now."

"Danny we've got to get back to L.A., give us a call if you find out where Tommy is."

Back at the car I said, "It was a good idea when you suggested going out to see Iggy this morning Frank. It isn't too hard to figure out what happened to that guy they found on Mulholland. Tommy wanted to test out that 'H' but he was smart enough not to shoot it himself. He used that ex-con for a guinea pig. Christ, what a way to go."

We hit up on half a dozen of our old informants around town, inside an hour we learned Tommy and Betty had a hotel room near Melrose and Vine, about six blocks from Danny's hotel. They were both in the room when we arrived. Luckily they were in pretty good shape. It didn't take us long to squeeze the facts from Tommy. Just like we had figured. He'd given the ex-con a jolt of the stuff to test it out. They found out how strong it was the hard way. Tommy and his girlfriend saw the con was dead, loading him in their car they drove the body to Mulholland and dumped it. We convinced them the only thing to do was to go downtown to homicide with us and make a clean breast of the whole deal.

I stopped at a phone, called Thad, told him we were bringing a couple of suspects in on the murder case he had told us about that morning. At the Det. Chief's office two homicide detectives were waiting. While they were talking to Betty, Tommy complained, "I've got to go to the men's room real quick." I motioned, "Come on I'll take you." When we got back the detectives were ready to book the two of them. I said to Thad, "You better have the detectives take Eagle over to the hospital and let the doctor check him out. In the men's room he locked himself in one of the toilets, I think he has a keester stash."

"I sure do thank you guys," the Chief said, "this has saved us a lot of time beating the bush. We might never have gotten a lead in this case." Frank and I returned to the D.A.'s office and wrote out our reports. It had been nine when we were in Thad's office this morning and it was now four thirty in the afternoon. Frank looked at me and smiled.

"Not a bad day's work, eh?"

"I've seen a lot worse."

The phone rang, it was Thad. He said, "Gary, that was a good idea about having the doctor check Eagle. He had a keester stash with enough herion to screw up everyone in the city jail for a week.

Thanks again for all the help."

Suddenly I realized I'd driven up the Rincon Highway half way to Santa Barbara. The sun, a huge red ball was dropping right into the ocean. Turning around I headed back to Ventura. Perhaps the average person reading the investigation report would think nothing of it, all you had to do was go out and ask a few questions. I knew if anybody besides Frank or I had gone to Iggy and started asking questions they wouldn't have gotten the right time of day. It took years of cultivating people like Iggy and Eagle and the myriads of other people we knew to contact when we needed information. Just about back to Ventura now I turned off the Rincon, heading north toward home.

There is no statute of limitations for murder.
(Refer: page 74, para. 6)

A suspect in the killing of a policeman in a southern state almost fifty years ago, was recently arrested in New York City...the courts have taken action and the case solved.

A young girl was murdered, another young girl witnessed this crime but blanked out the terrible scene from her mind for years, recently her memory returned, the true facts were reported to the police...Her own father was arrested, tried and convicted....Case Solved.

The Captain's Table murder was a quarter of a century ago...the Ventura County District Attorney despite the herein related facts and others presented to him, including the suspect's name, refuses to take action.

Possibly this suspect had killed before and has killed since...over two dozen persons are still alive who if collectively appearing before a Grand Jury could indict the one who actually struck the blows...is the D.A. Michael Bradbury burying this deadly secret, knowing that the man has killed again and that his dereliction of duty amounts to murder itself.

Clinger left the Captain's Table through the rear door...forty feet across the restaurant on the front door of the Captain's Table a bloody palm imprint was left...just across the street was the shop where the killer was heading...the bloody palm was not Clinger's...

CHAPTER 8

The next afternoon I talked to Al Palmer on the phone, "Gary, I've got a little good news for you. At the board of directors meeting of the Employees Assoc. last night I explained how Erwin was trying to frame you. Unanimously, they voted to write a check for twenty five hundred dollars for your attorney expenses. One big thing that helped convince them was Erwin and Kuhn coming to the meeting to protest against the Association's helping you obtain a lawyer. My assistant, Ray Charles, and I have contacted a lawyer in Los Angeles. He'll be here tomorrow afternoon to talk with us. Can you be in my office by 2:00?"

"Right, I'll be there."

Ellen, the secretary for the Employees Assoc., was at the front desk. She smiled pleasantly, "Go right on back to Mr. Palmer's office, they are waiting for you." I thought, it's too bad Erwin couldn't have hired a pleasant, efficient secretary like this. Palmer introduced me to the attorney who'd driven up from L.A., his name was Dean Pic'l.

"It's pronounced Pitchell, just call me Dean."

Al Palmer got right to business, "I think we should discuss the financial angle first and see if Dean agrees."

Al explained, the Employees Assoc. was going to give me a check for twenty five hundred for expenses, provided the lawyer agreed to take the case. Any amount over that would have to be an agreement between Pic'l and me. Dean's agreed to the expense fund and stated that we had an extremely good case for a civil action against Erwin, the county and other people involved.

Pic'l added, "We will proceed with the civil service hearing first and *win or lose...we will file a civil suit against them.*"

Palmer spoke up, "There's another board of directors meeting tonight, Dean will you go with me and explain your position?"

"I'll be glad to. I am positive we can recover a substantial sum through a civil suit. If we do so we will reimburse the Employees Association the twenty five hundred they have given for expenses." That evening Pic'l repeated to the board his assurances of filing a civil suit and of repaying the expense fund in the event of winning the suit. The board was quite impressed with Pic'l and his plans to proceed with a civil action. They assured Palmer a check would be forthcoming soon.

Several days later I received a large brown manila folder in the mail. I could hardly believe it. Erwin had filed a whole new set of charges against me. I called Al. He was mad, "Yeah, I just received a copy also."

"Al, what he is doing is reversing things. He is accusing *me* of every God damn rotten thing he has had Kuhn and Hronesh doing."

"I know, I am sending a copy immediately to Dean."

"Good, advise Pic'l I'll be down to his office in a few days and discuss it with him." His office on Wishire Boulevard and Hobart was very plush...fast elevators, thick carpets, piped-in music, beautiful secretaries in short short skirts, the whole bit. I'd been working for a solid week gathering all the information for our defense. I asked Dean if he had received a copy of Erwin's new charges.

"Yes, it's right here in front of me."

"One question before we start, according to the Ventura County Civil Service Rules, as they are now, I'm *guilty* of everything Erwin has charged me with and it is *my responsibility to prove I am not guilty*. Do you as a lawyer know another place in the world, outside of Russia maybe, where a person charged with some offense has to prove he is not guilty?"

He thought a second, "No...I don't! Actually everywhere in law the agency placing the charges has total responsibility to prove their accusations."

"Pic'l, why don't we file a writ or something and turn this whole damned thing around so that the onus is on Erwin, make him *prove* his accusations. The way it is set up now all that Erwin has to do is accuse me of spitting on the sidewalk and I have to prove I didn't.

He doesn't have to say what time of day or night I did it or even if he has any witnesses, but I have to present witnesses who will swear I didn't spit on the sidewalk at anytime. How in hell can I prove I didn't spit on the sidewalk?"

"I see your point. I'll check into it. Let's go down the line with these new accusations."

"One more question Pic'l. How many chances does Erwin get to file new charges against me?"

"Actually I can prohibit him from presenting these latest charges at this hearing, but if you are found not guilty of the first ones he can re-file the second set of charges and start proceedings all over again."

"Alright, what's the first charge he's got there?"

"Erwin has a letter written by Eileen Chase, a secretary at your Oxnard office. She claims, in her opinion you are incompetent and lazy and that she once heard you refer to Kuhn, as a 'coon.' In a note at the bottom of her letter she states that Claire Brotherton, Erwin's secretary, came to the Oxnard office and *forced* her to write the letter which she hopes will be kept completely confidential."

"Dean, here is your answer to Eileen Chase. When Eileen was on the desk I had to stay around to check everything she did. She hadn't the vaguest idea of court or office procedure. She had been planning on going to Las Vegas for a vacation and for three weeks she did nothing but sew clothes to wear on the trip. She had a large box full of material, thread, needles and buttons in the corner of the office and she was sewing on a dress. It was about two in the afternoon, half a dozen clients were sitting on benches waiting for help when I came up from Municipal Court and saw what she was doing. I went into the back office to file a bunch of papers I had brought from court. While I'm in the back office Claire walked in catching her sewing on the dress, when I came out Eileen was crying. I asked what was wrong, she said Claire *had ordered* her to write a letter for Erwin or she'd be fired. She refused to tell me what Claire wanted her to write, but it's fairly obvious, you've got the letter in front of you." Dean went to the next accusation, "It's another letter, from a a hospital patient, he says you entered his room and threatened to break his leg. He had to call for a nurse to come and save him. He says Kuhn was there and was a witness to your threats."

"Dean, I had a conversation with that guy three years ago while he was in the hospital. There was nothing threatening about what I said. He is an ex-con and a known liar. Kuhn is just putting him up to more lies. If Kuhn was so upset over what I said to the guy why did he wait for three years to say anything about it?"

"That's a good question, we'll ask Kuhn. Now we have Dunham writing a letter, according to him you didn't handle the clients very well when he was in charge in Oxnard."

"That's partly true, so far as a couple of them were concerned. One client, a Mexican, Dunham pled him guilty without his knowing it, the judge threw him in jail. He had to go borrow every dollar he could scrape up to hire an attorney to straighten things out for him. The client came into the office after court was over, he was so mad he was ready to beat hell out of Harrison. I spent fifteen minutes calming him down. Hell yes, the guy was making a *big scene* in the office, but if I hadn't talked to him like a Dutch uncle he sure as hell would have kicked the shit out of Dunham. This guy Dunham is really something, he raised so much hell with the attorneys to plead all the clients guilty and get rid of them anyway they could that five lawyers quit while he was *in charge*. They were good, hard working personnel too."

"Dunham further says you were building a house and the Chief of Police in Ventura was furnishing trusties from his jail to work on it."

"That's so fantastic I can hardly believe that even Dunham could concoct such a lie. I didn't even know the Police Chief in Ventura. I have never talked to him in my life. In fact, I wouldn't even know him if I saw him. The only men who ever worked on my house were two older fellows from Ojai. Both staunch Mormons, they were the most completely honest men you could ever meet. Neither of them has ever been in jail in his life. Dunham's just plain sick to make up such lies. Let me tell you something about Dunham. I checked with the California State Bar Association and dug up his history. He is a *disbarred attorney*. He was disbarred for *lying* to his clients and to the judges. He stole stock certificates from a client and refused to return them even after being ordered to do so. A client, Mrs. Lynch paid him to obtain a divorce for her. He swore he had obtained her an interlocutory decree. Later he told her he had obtained a final divorce. Mrs. Lynch asked numerous times for her divorce papers. Dunham told her repeatedly they were in his office but there was a typographical error on them he had to change. After Dunham had assured Mrs. Lynch she was divorced she returned with Mr. Donald Tinkler, who was a clergyman. They informed Harrison they wanted to get married and *he told them to proceed, everything was just fine.*

He even took *more money* from Reverend Tinkler to straighten out some custody matters for Mrs. Lynch's three small children. About this time Mrs. Lynch's first husband filed suit for divorce and Mrs. Lynch discovered the lies the hard way, Harrison *hadn't filed* any divorce papers for her at all. Juvenile officers came to Mrs. Lynch's home and were going to take her children to juvenile hall. In front of her children she was accused of being not only a bigamist, but of several other unsavory activities by the juvenile officer.

From another lady client, Dunham received money to file legal papers in court which would have freed her husband from doing six months in jail on a minor charge, he never filed anything, it resulted in her husband serving six months in jail unnecessarily. Dunham has whined and cried to the bar investigators that he's been upset over his wife's terminal illness and that is one of the reasons for his lying and stealing. I inquired into Mrs. Dunham's health, she's in better shape than you are, he's been pulling that story about her having terminal illness for fifteen years. Christ, we all got terminal illness if we live long enough."

After an extensive and thorough investigation into this shyster's activity by the State Bar of Calif., Local Administrative Committee No. 17 for the County of Los Angeles, it was determined Dunham *had violated his oath* and duties as an attorney and counselor at law within the meaning of Sec. 6103 of Article Six of the Business and Professions Code of the State of Calif.. Also the same violation is prescribed by Sec. 6067 and 6068, Article Four of the Business and Professions Code of the State of Calif., in that *he committed acts involving moral turpitude and dishonesty* within the meaning of Sec. 6106, Article Six of the Business and Professions Code of the State of Calif.. There were a lot of other charges of acts involving moral turpitude and dishonesty filed against Dunham under other sections of the Business and Profession Code. *His guilt of these charges was determined by the following members of the committee:* Vincent C. Page, Esq., and Royal M. Miller, Esq.. Also present was Howard B. Weiner, Esq., Examiner for the Calif. State Bar.

In March of 1968, the disciplinary board imposed the following disciplinary action: That Dunham be suspended from practicing law for six months and be on probation an additional eighteen months. During the last eighteen months, he must write a complete report every month detailing his actions and account for each and every dollar he received from any client. If he should violate any of the conditions of his probation during the eighteen months he will then be disbarred for an additional year and a half. Voting to impose the disciplinary action were the following members of the Board: Baker, Andrews, Haley, Keegan, Madden, McDaniel, Reid, Rothert, Smith and Warburton.

"That is just a *quick rundown* on the type of a shyster Dunham really is Pic'l. Can you possibly believe any of the crazy lies he has written about me after reading these files from the bar association?"

"Lord no! Who could *believe* a guy like that?"

"Wait until I show you the rest of the deal. Dunham was hired in March of 1967, right in the middle of this investigation the bar association was making on him. Between March and June 23, 1968, Erwin discussed Dunham's corrupt activity with a member of the Disciplinary Committee and also several other attorneys who were acquainted with the action. It seemed Dunham's crazy antics were common lunchtime gossip among lawyers. On July 29, 1968 Richard Erwin wrote a letter, swearing under the 'penalty of perjury,' to the Honorable Roger Traynor, Chief Justice of the Supreme Court of the State of Calif., that he'd had no knowledge of the pendency of the proceedings against Dunham until July 24, 1968. In the letter to Traynor he maintained that Dunham was *valuable* in training young lawyers and should be placed under his supervision. I can subpoena three damn good lawyers who'll testify they resigned while working for Dunham in Oxnard because they couldn't stand his bare-faced lies to judges and the way he was forcing defendants to plead guilty just to get rid of them."

"*No wonder* Erwin wants to keep Dunham around."

"By writing his false letter to Traynor, Erwin caused the court to abrogate months and months of time consuming investigation by a State Bar Committee. After they turned all their findings over to the Disciplinary Board of the Bar, Erwin then caused the Supreme Court to abrogate the board's decision to suspend Dunham. Erwin knew Dunham was capable of continuing the same type of crooked operations if they placed him under his control, he would do exactly what Erwin told him. In another charge Erwin claims I was working for private attorneys and using county equipment to benefit myself. I will tell you what really happened.... Before the Public Defender's office first opened, William Todd, a private attorney, got himself appointed by the Superior Court to defend a man who was arrested for robbery. The defendant was claiming he'd been registered in a motel down in Covina, California, over eighty miles away when the robbery occurred in Ventura. Lawyer Todd *asked* Erwin if he could assign me to investigate his client's alibi and Erwin *ordered* me to assist with the case. I wrote letters to an investigator in the Covina area requesting a photo copy of the motel's register where Todd's client claimed to have been. The register's records revealed the man had not checked into the motel until the day after the holdup. I told the lawyer that his client was lying. Todd had a serious chat with his client and then pled him guilty. Claire, in her *clever little way,* had found the letters I wrote to the police investigators in Covina. She then looked in *our client file* and couldn't find any case under the name I had inquired about. The reason Claire couldn't find it was because it was Todd's case and he had the files. She ran to Erwin about her big discovery and boom, they had another charge to file against me."

Dean broke in, "It's pretty clear how they operate."

"Yeah, and Claire was given the prestigious task of typing the charges which Erwin filed against me."

Pic'l had to leave the room for a minute. I thought about how Claire must have relished her job typing up the charges. At long last she was in a position to *really* help Glen Baby in his pursuit of the department's top investigative position. Now she could prove to him her sincerity, her true devotion, her unwavering loyalty. How many times I wondered, did she have tantalyzing hot and cold flashes and goose pimples on her neck while she typed with a speed she never knew she was capable of. Her anticipation of Glen Baby's gratitude for the splendid job she was doing was overwhelming. It took her breath away.

Dean returned and I continued, "When I went to Todd's office and asked if he remembered the case, he said, 'It was so long ago I can't recall it now.' He asked his secretary to get the file. Thumbing through it a minute he said, '*Oh yes, now I recall that whole case.*' He looked up, I could see that the beautiful tan on his face which he got from spending every afternoon on a golf course, had changed to ash white. I wondered, what the hell is the matter with him. Then Todd said in a subdued voice, 'I've been reading in the paper about the trouble between you and Erwin. My God! You're not going to get me involved with *him* are you?' What the hell's the matter with you Todd, you don't work for him. He can't harm *you* in any way. 'Well, I have to live here in Ventura. I don't want to be involved.' Listen, you recall the case and it's recorded right there in front of you. You asked Erwin to order me to help you with the case, now Erwin's twisting it around trying to say I was working for you on my own and using county equipment. If that's what you want Todd, I'll subpoena *you and your file.* And Dean, that's all there is to Erwin's charges that I worked for private lawyers on county time. Damn it! Dean, I never received so much as a cup of coffee from Todd."

"Let's take this last charge Erwin has filed. He claims that two weeks after he fired you, John McCormick came and told him that during the Clinger trial he had heard you say that Dillon was going to take the stand and lie."

"John McCormick's an old newspaper reporter. Why in the hell would he wait for a whole year and a half to make a statement like that instead of writing it when it was hot? I'll tell you why, because McCormick was standing in the corridor when Paik was screaming at Dillon he was a liar and he could never put him on the stand. It was *Paik who said it,* not me. Paik, Erwin and McCormick were the ones who had conspired to ruin Woody Deem and Judge Lewis by printing a false article about them in John's newspaper, the Oxnard Press Courier. They knew I was there and heard them planning it. John's harbored a grudge against me for years, he blamed me along with Doug Paxton, for arresting and convicting him of a felony. This was the first real chance for him to get even. Erwin, Paik and John have cooked this thing up together. I'll tell you another thing Dean, it's mighty sick for a guy in a responsible, high office like Erwin, to go so far as to perjure himself in writing to the Supreme Court to keep a shyster like Dunham around him."

"I sure have to go along with you on that Gary. I'll be back up to Ventura one day next week and we'll put things together then."

"Alright Dean. In the meantime I am going to check out Erwin's background."

CHAPTER 9

Palmer's call came early, "Be in my office at nine this morning. Pic'l will be here, so will George Eskin and Mal King."

All four were there when I arrived. Eskin, who'd been promoted to Chief Asst. D.A., was recalling an incident which had occurred between him and Erwin. "I saw in the paper how Erwin's son-in-law was killed in an airplane crash. The next day I saw him in the hall of the courthouse. I offered my sympathy to him and his daughter for the death in the family. Erwin let out a roar of laughter in his loud course voice. 'Don't be sorry for that son-of-a-bitch. That plane crash was the best thing that ever happened. That bastard will never bother my daughter again.' The hallway was full of people staring, shocked, I just slipped away as fast as I could."

I added, "Eskin, that's merely *par* for the course. While you're on this particular aspect of Erwin's mentality I'll tell you another one that will make you wonder even more about him. During the period he was after me to make life miserable for his neighbors, I walked into the office about quitting time. Staff members were coming into the larger outer office eager to leave for the day. Erwin, bounding around the crowded room was yelling, 'Hey everybody, look at this.' Under his left arm was a bundle of newspapers, with his right hand he was waving more in the air. Shouting, he was shoving papers in everybody's hands. It was the holiday season and I wondered what could be making him so happy. It was a picture of an automobile on a railroad crossing with a giant locomotive looming over the twisted wreckage of a sedan. Its driver was returning home to his wife and children when the car was struck by the train and he was killed. The room was quiet except for Erwin's voice. *'How do you like that,* he's one of my neighbors that's been making my life so miserable. Well, that bastard won't be bothering me any more.'"

Eskin's face became a shade paler, he made no further comment. Palmer broke the silence, "George, will you explain to us what you and Mal have in mind?"

"Yes indeed...Mr.Deem, Dr. Penfield the Grand Jury Foreman, Mal and myself, have conferred several times. We *all agreed* there *definitely must be a Grand Jury investigation* of all these things that have been going on. We certainly cannot allow Dunham, a man with his background and record to continue in the county service. As an attorney his conduct has been more criminal than the people he is supposed to be representing. I myself checked into this matter of Dunham lying to Judge West and paying that woman's fine of three hundred dollars. Such corrupt actions simply will not be tolerated. Dr. Penfield is appalled at what he has heard so far. *He can hardly believe a man in Erwin's position can be using his staff for trailing and spying on other people in our government, then compounding his corruption even further by framing them."*

"Pic'l I told you last week I was going to investigate into Erwin's past. I've discovered very interesting things and *brought documents* to show all of you while we're gathered here. The Star Free Press, our local newspaper puts out a Sunday Special called 'Profile of the Week.' Erwin got a reporter, Rita Garfield, to write a big five page special about his honesty, ethics, morals and integrity and how he induced such a moral and experienced lawyer like Dunham to come here and help him improve the Ventura Public Defender's office. Look here, at the top of this newspaper, on page three where I've got it marked...Erwin says he received his law degree in 1942 from Southwestern Law School. I went to the law school at 1121 So. Hill St. in L.A. and talked to a Mrs. Harding, the Custodian of Records. Checking all their records she advised me, 'At one time we did have a Richard E. Erwin at this law school but he never came close to obtaining a law degree.'"

Inspecting the paper Mal commented, "I wonder how many lies he told when filing his application with the personnel department?"

"Hold on Mal, I am just getting started. Erwin told the reporter that he was married in 1939 and that a daughter was born in 1940.

I checked all the marriage records in 1939, there was nothing. But I found the birth certificate for his daughter on February 25, 1940. Continuing the search I finally found a marriage certificate for one Richard E. Fish, 'alias' Richard E. Erwin, it said he was married on October 2, 1941, which is two years later than he told Rita Garfield. *Nothing fits,* there are so many *outstanding discrepancies* between Erwin's article and the evidence I found it doesn't make sense. The marriage license shows that his wife's name was Lila Blodgett, she was born in Navajo County, Arizona. And on the birth certificate of his daughter it says his wife's name is Lylia Broggett, and she was born in Alaska."

Palmer glanced toward Pic'l who was still reading the news article about Richard Erwin, "What in hell do you think of all that crap in that Sunday section Dean?"

"All I can say is Erwin sure did con that poor gal reporter from the newspaper."

Eskin and King both examined the photo copies of the marriage and birth certificates. Al Palmer chimed in, "It sure looks to me like Richard E. Fish maybe *assumed another man's identity* and got his names, dates and places all mixed up."

Someone spoke up and said, "Well gentlemen, it sure looks like there's a 'Fish' in the courthouse."

Eskin reminded Mal, "We've got to get back to the office. Gary, we have the Grand Jury all set to talk to you tomorrow morning at nine thirty, will you make it?"

"I wouldn't miss it for the world George."

Mal quickly added, "I want to remind everyone here this morning that *Dr. Penfield is demanding strict secrecy.* Outside of us here in this room, Mr. Deem the D.A., is the only other person who knows there is to be a secret investigation by the County Grand Jury."

After King and Eskin's departure Dean remarked, "It looks like you've got it wrapped up in good shape Gary."

"Not quite, after I go to the Grand Jury tomorrow I'm driving to Arizona and see what I can find out about this Richard Fish thing. Erwin claims he lived in Arizona and his father died in 1918, during the flu epidemic."

"Your civil service hearing doesn't start for several weeks yet, so keep me advised on anything new turning up."

Leaving Palmer's office I walked west on Santa Clara Street. It wasn't quite lunchtime and City Hall was only two blocks away, maybe Reiman, the city manager would still be in his office. I'd known him about fourteen years, I was on the Ventura Police Department, and he was Asst. City Manager. Charlie had seemed straightforward and conscientious of his obligations to the citizens and taxpayers. I had been considering for some time of warning him regarding the pile of money that had been put up for the purpose of *framing* him and Robinson. Possibly he might be willing to shed some light as to why this mysterious group was trying to nail a city manager and a county supervisor.

At City Hall a clerk asked, "Can I help you?"

"Yes, I want to talk with the City Manager."

"I'm sorry, but Mr. Reiman is in Hawaii on vacation, he's not due to return until next week."

"Thank you." A brooding disappointment nagged at my brain, the more I thought it over the more insistent it became, I had to know why someone was so hot to destroy the two politicians. I considered going to Robinson, but I had never met him before. I dismissed the thought, no telling what kind of reaction he might have on learning what I knew.

It was the morning I was to appear before the Grand Jury... My briefcase was loaded with documents and verification of the information I was prepared to give them. It was early, so parking my car near Palmer's office I went in. Al nodded toward the coffee maker, "Grab yourself a cup and sit down, you've got a few minutes before you have to be there, so listen to this. Last night I ran across some lawyers I know at the Sportsman Cafe, we were having a few drinks, they were laughing and joking about Erwin's article in Sunday's Star Free Press. Do you remember how he claims he wrote a best seller book about drunk driving?"

"Yes, I remember."

"Well, one of the lawyers knew how the book actually came into being. He explained about an old time attorney down in L.A. who'd written the manuscript, when he died, Erwin who knew him, stole it and published the book as his own." Palmer chuckled, "Erwin sure did snow that newspaper lady. He must have written all of those lies on a piece of paper and handed it to her."

"It's pretty obvious he got it into the paper just before the Civil Service hearing, hoping to influence the public with his honesty and integrity. What I hope is we will be able to get the paper to tell the real truth as it comes out. It's about time for me to get going Al, I'll leave my car parked here and walk up the hill to the courthouse."

I rode the elevator up to the floor that housed the D.A.'s office.

I had to walk down a corridor passing through their entire office to reach the Grand Jury meeting room. A uniformed deputy sheriff at semi-attention stood before a large door. A sign hung on it, 'Grand Jury in session.' Mal King emerged from an office to my left. "Good morning," with tension he queried, "How are you?"

"Hell, I'm okay Mal."

"Come in here," motioning me into the office from which he had just come. "Have a seat, make yourself comfortable, I'll be back in a minute." He returned accompanied by another man. "Gary I'd like you to meet Dr. Penfield, the Foreman of the Grand Jury."

Dr. Penfield offered his hand. He appeared to be what could best be described as a gentleman from the old school. Shaking his hand I observed his ruddy face and iron gray hair. He wore a trim houndstooth jacket, white shirt, dark tie and an impressive jeweled tie pin. The handshake was firm and friendly, it helped confirm what Mal had told me about him. Here was a man worthy of the position of Foreman of the Grand Jury, one who could reassure confidence in 'due process of law' and procedure of the courts in a fair manner. Free of corruption and taints of any power structure from outside the frame of justice.

"I believe all the jury members are present," the Foreman said, "Come with me and I'll introduce you." Entering the jury room the door was closed by the deputy, he remained outside. The room was quite large, a table in the center had to be at least fifteen feet long. One man sat at the far end, the other jurors sat on each side. Dr. Penfield led me to the unoccupied end of the table and invited me to sit down.

"Now Gary, all the jurors have read the report made by Mal King when you first talked with him and Al Jalaty, but they would like to hear from you in person. I believe it would be best to start right at the beginning and run through the entire story."

I proceeded with the events up to the point where Hronesh and Kuhn followed Supervisor Robinson's Administrative Assistant Ben Martinez from the courthouse. The jurors had remained completely silent. Thinking maybe I'd lost them at some point along the way I asked, "Would any of you like to ask a question?" At the far end of the table the man spoke.

"Yes, I'd like to know when in hell those people do any work for the county?"

It was Marvin Sosna, Editor of the Thousand Oaks Chronicle, a newspaper in the eastern part of the county. He appeared to be an outspoken type of person with intelligence tempered by many years experience as a newsman. I continued with the story, finishing the part where I'd discovered that the lawyer for Castro had given her a polygraph and passed the results to Erwin. This had been in *direct violation* of a court order by Judge Lewis. I'd proceeded into other aspects when another juror to my left interrupted.

"How did you learn about the lie detector test given to Castro?" This juror was a fairly large man, he appeared to have spent much of his life out of doors. I knew him to be a wealthy farmer from the Oxnard area. He repeated, "How did you find out about Castro and the polygraph revealing she knew someone else did the stabbing?"

"I got the information from a friend."

"What is his name?" Hesitating I wondered about such a strong interest in my contacts at this stage of the game. He insisted, "Go ahead, tell us, this is a *completely confidential, secret meeting.* If we are to investigate this we'll have to know certain things."

I figured I might as well tell him, I couldn't see that it would hurt Patton, after all, everything was going to come out eventually. "The man who told me is an old friend of mine, Ed Patton."

Scraping forward in his chair the rancher asked, "You mean Ed Patton who used to be a Sgt. on the Oxnard Police Department?" I wondered about the deep glint of interest that flashed momentarily in his eyes. I said, "Yes, that's who I mean." This seemed to satisfy his curiosity, leaning back he asked no more questions. I continued on through the part of Hronesh and Martin getting a lot of money to frame Robinson, Reiman and the Chief of Police...and then into Dunham's activities and his record with the Bar Association. I saw that many of the jurors were busily scribbling notes. Glancing at my watch I saw it was noon, I'd been talking more then two and a half solid hours.

Dr. Penfield spoke, "Ladies and gentleman, I suggest we adjourn for lunch." He stepped to the door and knocked, the deputy opened it and looked in. King was standing just outside the door, he walked toward us, the jurors filed out and the three of us were alone.

Anxiously Mal asked, "How did things go?"

"Fine, Gary did an excellent job giving all the details. *I'm positive each of the jurors have now fully realized what has been going on."*

With a pleased look *Mal said,* "*That's great,* I'll be meeting with both Deem and Eskin this afternoon and I will advise them of the situation as it now stands."

Responding enthusiasticaly Penfield said, "You can further advise them *I intend to set up a special committee* and then proceed with a full investigation."

Leaving the building by the main entrance I walked down the hill away from the courthouse. The day was beautiful, a bright shining sky with a fresh invigorating breeze blowing in from the ocean. *Dr. Penfield's decision to utilize the power of the Grand Jury to bring some justice and fairness to the citizens of the county had removed a heavy load off my shoulders.* I was confident if the truth could be brought out at my Civil Service hearing it would not only clear me but would prevent a lot of innocent people from being ruined by the insidious activities of Kuhn and Hronesh.

Palmer was leaving when I arrived at his office. I informed him the Grand Jury was going to investigate. "That is great news, have lunch with me and we'll talk."

"No, I've got some things to do, I'm leaving tonight for Arizona. Remember the article that Rita Garfield wrote for Erwin? I want to see if I can get a lead on his father, he supposedly died during the flu epidemic. Nothing seems to tie in together...the names...Fish and Erwin."

"Okay, contact me when you return."

Five days later, I was back in Palmer's office, he was sitting at his desk having breakfast, coffee and cigarettes. He blew a huge cloud of smoke, "Did you find anything worthwhile on Mr. Fish or Erwin in Arizona?"

"According to the article, Erwin's father died in 1918 in northern Arizona. I went to the county seats of three counties in the north: Coconino, Navajo and Apache. I found no records of the death of anybody named Fish or Erwin. I checked from 1916 to 1919 but still found nothing. I also checked marriage records from 1900 to 1916 for anyone named Fish or Erwin but there just weren't any."

"Obviously your hunches were right on, there's something mighty, mighty strange about that guy."

"If I'd only had the time I could've checked him out all the way but the hearing starts next week."

"That reminds me...Pic'l was here while you were in Arizona. He said you'd done a great job of getting information and evidence to refute all of Mr. Fish's charges. Pic'l said he's positive he can win a Civil Suit, which *he will file* as soon as the hearing is over."

"Yeah, it starts next Monday morning Al. I'll see you then."

CHAPTER 10

It was eight fifty five in the morning. The hearing was scheduled to begin in five minutes. It'd been decided to hold it in a conference room at the new Juvenile Court building in East Ventura. Already a large number of people had arrived. I'd been advised it could be a closed hearing if I chose to. In other words, no reporters or public would be allowed. Hell no I told Pic'l, I want all the news reporters and anyone else who is interested to be allowed to hear the whole proceedings first hand. In a far corner I saw Fish, Kuhn and Kenny Cleaver in a tight huddle. Al Palmer had told me that Mr. Fish was planning to have Cleaver present the charges against me instead of doing it himself. That figured. Mr. Fish never did anything himself. Always it was someone else who handled the dirty work. Claire, his secretary, scurried through the door carrying a folder over to Glen Baby. Whispering a few minutes she left. I wondered, who in hell is helping the Public Defender's indigent clients with their problems today, it appeared that Mr. Fish's entire staff was either at his side or on call.

Phillip Cohen entering the room sat down at the big horseshoe shaped conference table. He was a lawyer from the County Counsel Office. Herb Ashby his boss, had appointed him to be Law Officer at the hearing. In the event any legal points had to be interpreted, Cohen would make the determination. There was a designated spot for me, Palmer who had just arrived took the chair to my right. He asked, "Have you seen Pic'l yet?"

"No, I haven't. He should be here any minute." Glancing around the room I noticed something rather encouraging. "Al, do you see those two women sitting in the back, next to the wall, that colored lady and the gray haired woman to her left?"

He spotted them. "What about it?"

"They are *Grand Jury members*. Penfield must have sent them here to get *evidence* for the investigation." Suddenly the room was quiet, people filled all the seats and stood along the wall. The three Civil Service Commissioners had entered the room and taken their places at a desk situated at the open end of the conference table. Sumner Padelford, a rancher from over in the eastern part of the county was the Chairman. Harry Maynard, manager of the Ventura Wells Fargo Bank and Thomas Boyd, V. Pres. of the Oxnard Bank of A. Levy, were the other two. Meanwhile, Dean Pic'l had slipped into the room and occupied the chair to my left.

The hearing was brought to order and Cleaver read the charges that Mr. Fish was alleging. As he read the trumped-up lies Mr. Fish had manufactured, I was beginning to realize more and more how precarious my position was, especially if they succeeded in getting anyone to believe all that crap.

Cleaver called Eileen Chase, his first witness to take the chair. She was the secretary in the Oxnard office that Claire had caught sewing when she was supposed to be working. Eileen repeated what she had written in the letter for Claire. It made me so mad I was strangling. Nudging Pic'l I whispered, "Damn it, all that crap she is saying about me calling Kuhn a 'coon' is a lie, she is twisting it all around. Glen used to strut his lard-ass around the office like he was a big comedian spouting off, 'I'm the only white coon in the office.' He loved pulling this stunt after some black clients had left. To him it was about the funniest routine outside of Abbott and Costello."

Pic'l let Eileen leave the witness chair without asking her single question. He whispered, *"Don't worry,* no one will ever believe she wrote all of that silly stuff without Claire forcing her. We will get to her later." I thought, maybe so, but what in the hell would it hurt to squeeze the truth out of her right now?

Cleaver called their ex-con witness, the one Glen Baby had dug up. Under Cleaver's direction he claimed that while he was in the County Hospital with a broken leg I had threatened him.

Pic'l asked three questions of the con, "Did Mr. Kuhn come to you three years after these so-called threats and ask you to testify?"

"Yes."
"Are you an ex-convict?"
"Yes."
"Are you noted for testifying to the truth in courtrooms?"
The ex-con couldn't hold back a big grin, "Well not really."
"Alright, thank you, as far as I am concerned you are excused." Cleaver seemed relieved when the ex-con left. I noticed him look at Kuhn and raise his eyebrows pleading, for Christ sake, don't bring any more of your jerks like him up here. He called Dunham to take the witness chair. Chairman Padelford interrupted, "It is very near the lunch hour. We'll recess and return at one thirty."

"Coming with us for lunch?" Palmer asked.

"No thanks. I have to meet a friend over in Oxnard." That was the quickest excuse I could come up with. I didn't feel like listening to all the usual lunch hour bull. I drove to the beach and parked, it was deserted, a cold winter wind blew from the ocean even though the sun was bright and the sky cloudless. A brown bag with a carton of milk and a sandwich sat on the car seat, a subconscious reminder that I didn't have a pocket full of money. It was extremely expensive eating in the plush cocktail restaurants where Al and Dean liked to go. There'd been no money coming in since Mr. Fish had fired me and I had spent a lot of time and cash in the last month and a half preparing my defense to his false charges. There was no question in my mind that Mr. Fish meant to not only take my job, he was going to *destroy everything* I had worked for in the past, present and the future.

Dunham would be on the witness stand this afternoon. From my briefcase I removed all of the files on him double checking to see if everything was there. Dean would have his chance to cross examine and expose Dunham for the liar and thief he really was immediately after his testimony for Mr. Fish. It was one twenty when I returned. People were gathering in isolated groups in the patio outside of the conference room. I saw Herb Ashby talking with Phillip Cohen. This was good. I felt Ashby would do everything in his power to see that legal fairness was maintained throughout the hearing.

The room was filling up. Al was seated, but I didn't see Pic'l. I went to a window, looking out on the patio I saw Dunham with his back to me, Dean was with him. Dunham was doing all the talking and gesturing with his hands. Pic'l's left side was toward me. He was saying nothing but his head was nodding up and down very slowly in concurrence with whatever Dunham was telling him. Turning from

Harrison he then walked toward the conference room. Hurrying, I got back to my chair next to Palmer before Pic'l entered. All three of the Commissioners were seated and the afternoon session came to order.

Cleaver called Dunham to the stand. His face was much redder than usual. I could see the sweat breaking out on his forehead. Had Pic'l told him about the Bar investigation files I'd dug up? Even so, Dunham had no choice, he'd been ordered by Mr. Fish to take the witness chair and repeat all the charges he'd written against me in his letter.

Now...it was Pic'l's turn to question Dunham. All my files on the shyster laid open on the table in front of me. Out of the corner of his eye Pic'l saw them, *deliberately excising the files from his mind as if they had never existed*, he asked Dunham a couple of insipid questions regarding the amount of work I had been doing while he was in charge of the Oxnard office. Elbowing him I whispered, "God damn it Dean, forget all this bullshit you're screwing around with, get to it. Prove to the Commissioners, show them what a shyster he is and the crap he is capable of pulling."

Dean whispered, "I want to hold back on this. We'll save it for the Civil Suit. Listen, I'm your lawyer, you've got to have confidence in me and *place yourself in my hands.*"

"But how in hell are we going to convince anybody I'm innocent of these damn lies if we screw around like this?"

"Shhhish, everybody's watching us, just take it easy, *I know what I'm doing.*" Pic'l then asked Dunham another inane question and let him leave the witness chair. Dunham wasted no time getting out of the room. Cleaver called Hronesh to take the chair.

I leaned over to Pic'l, "Are you going to allow this crumb to say everything he wants without getting on him? This is your chance to pin him down on all that sneaky, crooked crap he and Kuhn have been doing for Mr. Fish."

Pic'l was about to answer when Cleaver started talking. Hronesh had a large brown manila envelope in his hands. Cleaver was asking him to remove the contents from the folder, the room became quiet in expectation. I had to admit to a strong curiosity myself. Hronesh was being very slow and deliberate in opening the brown envelope. Straightening the small metal clips fastening the envelope's flap he placed his hand inside. Hronesh removed a white envelope and at Cleaver's directions he testified that it was addressed to me and it had been postmarked Detroit, Michigan. This evidence supposedly was to have substantiated the charges that I had been working for private attorneys on the side.

Pic'l asked Hronesh where he had obtained the envelope. "Well, I don't exactly remember. I think I found it laying around the office someplace."

"Was there a letter in it when you found it?"

"I don't think so. I can't really remember."

"What made you keep an empty envelope addressed to someone else for over a year?"

"I don't know. I just put it in my desk when I found it."

"Let me see the white envelope."

Hronesh got out of the witness chair and handed the envelope to Pic'l. I leaned over and looked at it along with him. A plain white envelope with my name typewritten on it, no return address, it was postmarked from Detroit, Michigan. Pic'l flashed me a questioning look. I whispered to him, "Hell...I don't know what it's about, your guess is as good as mine."

Pic'l handed the envelope back to Hronesh, "I have no further questions for you."

Padelford said, "It is getting late, if there are no objections from either side, we will adjourn until tomorrow morning at nine."

Dean *wouldn't answer* our *worried questions*, making excuses *he brushed us off*, "If you fellas don't mind, I'm dashing out of here. I gotta' appointment in L.A. early this evening."

Al just said, "Okay, we'll see you at nine in the morning."

When Dean left I asked, *"What do you think Al?"*

"You mean about *Pic'l letting both Dunham and Hronesh off* so easy?"

"Yeah, that for one."

"Well, *it sure isn't the way I'd have done it,* but he's a lawyer, and we've *paid him twenty five hundred dollars expenses to defend you,* so we better go along with him."

"Okay, I'll see you here tomorrow morning."

At eight forty five the next morning I drove into the parking lot across from the juvenile hall building. Rita Garfield, who'd written the news article about Erwin, was standing in front of the building talking to another female reporter from the Oxnard Courier. A car pulled in parking a few spaces from me. John McCormick got out and walked across the street. Nodding at the reporters he continued over to the patio where Cleaver, Kuhn and Erwin were standing. As I passed by them going into the conference room they all made like clams. Mr. Erwin must be giving McCormick last minute orders on what to say.

. Chairman Padelford brought the room to order, Cleaver called McCormick to the chair. John swore I had told him that Dillon was going to lie on the witness stand and that I had told him this when we were standing in the hall just outside the courtroom. McCormick went on to say that he had given this information to Paik the next day.

Cleaver was through and Pic'l began to question McCormick. "How long has it been since you claim you heard Gary make that statement?"

"About a year and a half ago."

"You mean you never told Mr. Erwin about it for a year and a half...but you told Mr. Paik?"

"Yes, that's right."

"Mr. McCormick, during that time were you a news reporter for the Oxnard Press Courier?"

"Yes."

"You were a reporter, covering a *sensational front page murder trial*, and *yet you never wrote a thing* about what you had heard?"

"No I didn't."

"Well, you never told the District Attorney about it either, did you?"

"No."

"What you're claiming is you never told anyone about it except Paik, *until* you heard of the trouble between Mr. Erwin and Gary?"

"That's right."

"Out of your sense of duty *you volunteered* this information to Mr. Erwin?"

"Yes."

"How long have you personally known Gary?"

"Oh, about five or six years."

I nudged Pic'l, whispering I told him, "He's lying like hell. I used to throw him out of the Mexican dance every Saturday night at the Green Mill for being drunk. Doug Paxton, from the sheriff's office, and I arrested John for check forgery fifteen years ago, and he was prosecuted and convicted of felonies and served time. Look at this Dean, right here, I have a copy of a report on John written by his probation officer, and this guy is a hell of a good officer. He talked to McCormick's father, and also his sister, she's Jane Tolmach, an Oxnard councilwoman." I read part of the probation report to him.

"John McCormick's *father and sister* both told the officer that *John was always writing bad checks and was an irresponsible liar, that he was a sodden alcoholic idiot and should be in an institution under psychiatric care.*"

"Okay, okay. *You've* got to let *me* handle this." Pic'l then said, *"No more questions,"* and McCormick left.

"What the hell are you doing Pic'l? How in the hell am I going to prove I'm not guilty with a half-assed defense like this?"

"Take it easy, like I told you...I want to save all that for the Civil Suit."

Paul Clinton and John Russell were both present, standing by to testify in rebuttal to Mr. Erwin's charges that I was incompetent in my investigations. Dean called Clinton to the stand, before taking the chair he advised the Commissioners that he was very willing to testify, but, his testimony would be in contradiction to Mr. Erwin's charges and also the testimony of all the witnesses that Erwin had brought forth. Paul felt that *for his own protection* a court reporter should be present to record any and all testimony that was given by him and John Russell. Chairman Padelford agreed. Recessing for lunch he instructed both Erwin and Phillip Cohen to arrange for a court reporter to be present at one thirty, at which time the hearing would resume.

I walked over to my car. The bag on the seat had a thermos of milk, a cheese sandwich and grapes, I hardly remembered eating. Something *really* bothered me, bad...*why* hadn't Pic'l, my attorney advised me of the need for this right at the very beginning? Why hadn't I realized I needed a transcript of the complete hearing. I wasn't exactly overjoyed at my position so far...something was very wrong...it was obvious, Pic'l just wasn't getting our evidence or the points we needed over the way he should.

A court reporter was *now* present, we resumed. Paul stated I'd investigated many cases for him, I was thorough and competent and never to his knowledge had I been insubordinate or threatened anybody. Paul also testified that *he himself* had been called by Erwin into his office and accused of serious offenses and told that he was fired. Clinton told Mr. Erwin his accusations were completely false and that Erwin would have to file charges because he wasn't about to resign. Clinton then repeated the story he'd told me about Claire trying to get him *to sign* some papers without his looking at them and also about the *secret files* he'd seen in her desk drawer.

John Russell testified that I had investigated many cases for him and that my services had proven to be invaluable. He also testified I *hadn't even investigated* one of the cases Mr. Erwin was accusing me of lousing up.

There were no more witnesses left from either side. Chairman Padelford advised the lawyers that he had discussed McCormick's testimony with the other two Commissioners, they wanted to hear Paik's testimony. They'd decided to summon Paik to the hearing. A subpoena would be sent today and the hearing would be adjourned for several days to give Paik time to appear. This was a real break, maybe Padelford was sincerely trying to get at the truth. I couldn't wait to get Paik in that witness chair. I would get the truth out of Paik one way or another, and Pic'l wasn't going to pull any more of his crap about waiting for a Civil Suit.

Driving home my mind was thinking clear for the first time in days. With Paik on the stand we could blow up their whole pack of lies. He wouldn't dare lie, there'd be no need for him to, he'd done nothing wrong. Erwin had *ordered* Paik to put Dillon on the stand. I'd subpoena the deputy sheriff who transported Dillon down to the courtroom, there was no way he'd ever forget the incident.

My mind flashed back to the Clinger trial, I could still see that deputy's face, his mouth dropping open in astonishment when Paik called Dillon a liar and followed them down the hall screaming that he didn't dare put him on the stand. But, later that afternoon Dillon was sitting in the witness chair. Paik began to ask questions leading up to his whereabouts the night of the murder. *Dillon dropped his bombshell:* "I wasn't even near the Captain's Table that night. I was in jail in Holbrook, Arizona." Paik stood frozen, his left hand flat on the table, bracing himself. Watching Paik's inscrutable countenance, I couldn't read the implacable oval face, but I easily fathomed the malice deep within his Oriental mind. The excruciating acupuncture technique that he would like to perform on Mr. Erwin would surely more than compensate Paik for the unforgivable position Erwin had placed him in.

Very distinctly Paik made his point, "Your Honor, at one time Mr. Deem made reference to a conversation I had with Mr. Dillon in the corridor. Because of that *confrontation* I request the court to allow my co-counsel Mr. Cleaver to continue the examination of the witness." Paik now appeared frightened...*no wonder* he wanted out! How could he possibly remain there *pretending* he believed Dillon was telling the truth, when everybody had heard Paik calling him a liar just before he took the stand.

Believe me, *I was all set.* I had the complete transcript of Paik's statements he had made in court on that day, page no. 5137, lines thirteen to twenty four.

Three days later Palmer called me on the phone. "Gary, I have some bad news."

"What's the matter Al?"

"This guy Paik is pretty sharp. He did a little researching and learned that a Civil Service subpoena is only good for two hundred miles. He is about three hundred miles from here and he has told the Commission that he does not intend to appear."

"Jesus, I've got a good notion to go up there and drag the lousy coward down here."

"No, the hearing starts again at nine tomorrow morning."

"Alright, I'll be there," I hung up. Waves of helplessness seemed to engulf me. What in hell can I do? The Civil Service Rules say it is my responsibility to prove I'm *not* guilty. Every time I can do it they slam the door in my face. Suddenly I recalled a guy, a lawyer who worked in the same office with Paik. Dialing long distance and with a little luck I got him on the phone.

"Doyle, what's cooking up there? We've been trying to get Paik to come down here and tell the truth about what happened." Doyle laughed.

"What's so funny?"

"Well, if you could have seen Paik's face and heard him when they served that subpoena on him you would have laughed too."

"I don't doubt it Doyle, but what happened?"

"Paik really flipped his lid. He called his old boss Erwin every rotten lousy name you can think of."

"What else did he say Doyle?"

"Paik was raving mad. He said, 'That God damn stupid Erwin was going to *open a can of worms* that would crawl all over them.'"

"Alright Doyle, thanks for the information."

That evening on the front page of the Star Free Press, where no one could miss it, was an article by Rita Garfield. According to her, Paik called her on the phone and backed-up John McCormick's lies. With the help of Rita and the Star Free Press, the cowardly little man from Korea hadn't only helped Mr. Erwin slam the door in my face, he'd crashed it shut while my head was still in the door. That entire night all I could think was, what right did Rita Garfield have to print a story like that! She'd reported a sneaky phone call from a sleazy little lawyer after he had cowardly refused to come to the hearing and testify to the truth.

The next morning everyone showed up at the hearing promptly. The Commissioners wasted little time. They agreed not to let the newspaper article Garfield wrote influence their consideration of John McCormick's testimony. Bullshit!...I'd been around courtrooms too long. How could you remove false information from a juror's mind once it was implanted? You sure as hell couldn't accomplish it by admonishing them to try to forget what they had heard.

Mr. Padelford, the Commission Chairman, advised attorneys for both sides that their final decision was to be handed down at their next regular meeting, two weeks hence. They adjourned the hearing and any and all proceedings accordingly.

Two weeks! Two weeks of what? I couldn't get a job for that length of time, and all my debts were mounting up. That was one thing I had, good credit. Always, I'd paid my bills. No one I owed had ever lost a dime, now it was different...I had no job, no income whatsoever. I didn't even have my reputation. How could I go to anybody and borrow money to carry me through? What if I lost the hearing? How could I possibly pay back anything I borrowed? When the Star Free Press printed the article stating that Paik, a lawyer, had verified John McCormick's story, they had crucified any of my chances.

CHAPTER 11

Mrs. Thurman, the widow, came to my mind. I'd been intending to contact her ever since all this bullshit had first started. After the hearing adjourned I went to my car and drove away in a maze of mental anguish and pure frustration. I remembered how friends had discreetly whispered in my ear that maybe I should have gone along with the things that Mr. Fish wanted done. To prove it they pointed out my present position as compared with that of Glen Baby. Even Hronesh was riding high, no one could touch them.

Betty Thurman resided in a modest tract home in a comfortable neighborhood. Walking up the driveway it was necessary to dodge a tricycle, an upended wagon and a clutter of small toys. My knock was answered by Mrs. Thurman, a slim lady with dark hair. When I introduced myself she smiled and opened the screen door.

"Come in! Please come in, I am awfully glad to see you. Have a chair over here at the dining room table. I've been reading all about your Civil Service hearing in the paper. I even thought of getting in touch with you, but I didn't know if I could help or not. My family has had a *lot of experiences* with Erwin and his daughter, she lived next door to me. Believe me, the two of them have put me and my family *through hell* and I haven't been able to get a lawyer."

"I can explain that real easy. You couldn't get a Public Defender because Fish had ordered Harrison Dunham to tell the judge you didn't qualify because of your financial status."

"How could that be? I have no money, I get Social Security since I've been a widow. I also went to a private lawyer here in Ventura. He said that he'd take my case for two hundred dollars but when he found out that it was Erwin and his daughter who were involved he refused to help me. I even went clear to Los Angeles to try and get an attorney. I went to court a couple times on my own. I still have to go to court and try to get it straightened out. The policewoman who came here to the house told me I hadn't done anything wrong, so I subpoenaed her to testify for me in court but she never showed up."

"That is understandable Betty, that was the same policewoman, Lola, who went to the judge and got the warrant for your arrest."

Betty was shocked at learning this. "I can't believe it! *Why* would she do such a thing to me?" Thinking a minute, she said, "Quite a few very strange things have happened since Mr. Erwin's daughter moved next door."

A teenager walked into the room. Betty introduced me to her son and said, "David, go ahead and tell this man what happened to you." David was reluctant to talk about his experience to a stranger but with a little urging and reassurance from his mother he began.

"One evening I left to go to Ventura to meet some friends. I had driven only a few blocks from the house when a detective car pulled me over to the curb. Two plainclothes policemen opened my door and told me to get out. I got out and they pushed me up against my car. One of them said, 'We've been told that you are bothering Mr. Erwin's daughter.' I told them I hadn't even so much as talked to her. One detective said that wasn't what they had heard and that if I even went close to either her or her house something was going to happen to me. Then they got in their car and drove away."

I thought for a moment, "David, what color was the car?"

"It was tan."

"Could it have been a county car instead of a city vehicle?"

"Yes, strange...I know most of the policemen in town but I had never seen those two before or the car. I was so scared when they grabbed me I wasn't thinking about them not being cops. I was just glad when they got back in their car and left me alone."

After leaving the Thurmans I drove down Main Street thinking about the widow and her family. David's description of the two men and car fit Hronesh and Kuhn perfect. Their crude operation was precisely how Fish had wanted *me* to harass his neighbors, Mr. and Mrs. Dodd, who lived in the cul-de-sac. This was what Hronesh had been up to when I overheard him pleading with Lt. Hopman on the phone to hurry up and 'fix' Betty Thurman or he was going to get fired. Erwin must have really leaned hard on Hronesh and Kuhn to get them to pull off a stunt like this. Anyway, according to Dunham, Kuhn *got credit* for getting Mrs. Thurman arrested and for his *good work* Fish put him in charge of the investigators. Jesus! No matter what my friends thought I was damn glad *I hadn't* done any of that crap for Mr. Fish.

There was no doubt in my mind, I just wasn't in a good position. No use trying to get a job for two weeks. Best thing for me to do is go home and paint the house and fix the yard up. We will have to sell everything we've got to get out of this predicament.

Two weeks later, in the forenoon, the phone rang. I expected it, the Commission met this morning and were to make their decision. It was Ray Charles, Assistant Manager of the Employees Assoc.. By the sound of his voice I knew the news was bad. Charles said, " The Commissioners threw out all the charges against you except the *one* where McCormick testified you had told him Dillon was going to lie on the stand."

"I have a long distance call in for Pic'l right now Ray. He better file a Civil Suit and damn soon."

Charles continued, "I was there when Padelford, the Chairman, read their decision and so was Phillip Cohen, the Law Officer. He couldn't believe it. He stood up and said he just couldn't understand how they could reach such a verdict."

"That's a big help, thanks for calling Ray. I don't feel much like talking and I have to tell my wife the news. She's been taking this whole thing pretty hard." Hanging up I sat there feeling like tons of dirt was burying me, deeper and deeper into the cold dank earth. I would never be able to stand upright again, I couldn't breath. The phone was ringing, as a matter of habit I picked it up.

The voice said, "Hi, this is Ernie Shaw."

"Hi Ernie, how you been?"

"Listen, I've got great news for you." Ernie was a good friend, a straight shooter. A Captain retired from the Ventura P.D., born and raised in Ventura, he knew everybody and everybody knew him.

"Alright Ernie, if you have good news let's have it."

"I've been trying real hard to contact you for a week, but nobody answered the phone."

"What's the good news Ernie, believe me I could use some right about now."

"Last week I was barbecuing a dinner at the Elks Lodge. Harry Maynard, one of the Civil Service Commissioners was helping me cook steaks and we got to discussing your hearing. Maynard told me that he was going to find you innocent. He said that after listening to all the witnesses stories, even if they were telling the truth, which he doubted, he just couldn't see where you'd done anything wrong. Not only that, he stated that the witnesses Erwin put on just weren't believable."

"Okay Ernie, that's real good news, there's only one thing wrong. Just ten minutes ago I got a phone call from Ray Charles. He told me that Harry Maynard had decided I was guilty of the charges that John McCormick made."

"My God, I can't believe it, that's impossible! Everybody knows McCormick has been trying to get even with you for years."

"Ernie I'm real glad you called, I really appreciate it. Do me one favor. Get hold of Harry Maynard and find out why he changed his mind."

"Yeah, believe me, I'm going to get hold of him right now!...there is something really wrong here. Harry was *absolutely positive* when I talked to him the other day."

Ernie called back the next afternoon, "Gary, you're going to find this hard to believe."

"Go ahead Ernie, the way it's been going I can believe just about anything."

"Harry told me Thomas Boyd, one of the other Commissioners, came to him and *put so much pressure on to find you guilty* that he just didn't have any choice."

"Christ Ernie, that is really sick. What kind of pressure did Boyd put on Maynard?"

"Well, Maynard didn't come right out and say it, but you know they're both vice presidents of their banks. Who knows what kind of deals they are cutting up. Big money talks you know."

"It sure as hell looks that way Ernie, thanks again."

"That's alright, I am glad to help. *Everybody knows* you're getting shafted on this deal."

"Ernie if you hear anything else just call me here at the house." This really tore things up. Why in hell would Thomas Boyd put all that kind of pressure on Harry Maynard to try to ruin me? I called Ray Charles and asked if he'd heard from Pic'l, our lawyer.

"Not a word. In fact I'm getting teed off about it. I hate to say this but I'm beginning to believe he's *trying to avoid us.*" I told Ray about the information Ernie Shaw had given me.

"My God, *can the Civil Service Commissioners be that corrupt?*"

"They sure as hell are Ray and listen, if you're unable to get Pic'l on the phone today then send a telegram to his office. I'll call you back tomorrow afternoon."

My suspicions flared, swift and harsh. Several times before the hearing even started Pic'l had let slip some indictions that he *didn't* relish the idea of bucking Fish and Dunham. *Surely he wouldn't run out*...not after telling Palmer and the Employees Association that he would file a Civil Suit and *assured* them he'd *repay* the twenty five hundred dollars expense money.

I thought about Thomas Boyd, it was strange, during the hearing he had sat through the entire procedure, non-committal. He never asked any questions and I hadn't seen him in any discussions with the other two Commissioners. What reason could he possibly have for doing such a thing?

Later that evening I turned off the TV and sat in the den with the lights out. Maybe I'd be able to think better in the dark. No use going to bed, I couldn't sleep. Since Ernie had called me this thing with Boyd and Maynard had been running wild in my brain. It just wouldn't stop. The name Boyd was beginning to ring a bell. Many years ago I'd shot and killed a man named David L. Boyd, he came from the midwest, the same area as Thomas Boyd, they would have been about the same age, close enough to be a brother or cousin.

CHAPTER 12

A rush of memories and recollections, my mind took me back to the L.A. Police Department, morning watch at University Station. Lt. A. J. Smith, watch commander, and Sgt. Haynes entered the roll call room carrying clipboards with the officers assignment sheet and a log of the crimes that had occurred on the preceding watch. The Lt. and Sgt. took their seats on a raised platform at the front of the room. The sergeant, known as 'Bookem' Haynes, was a policeman from the old school. If you brought a felony suspect to the station and asked the sergeant what to do with him, the only answer you ever got was a gravel-voiced, 'Bookem.'

I'd been working the morning watch nearly a year and a half, you seemed to get used to the bad hours after a while. Roll call started at eleven thirty and you were in the patrol car and on the street by midnight. The time passed fast, the honky tonks closed at two a.m., and then the after-hours joints came jumping to life.

Haynes was reading off the assignment sheet. He had assigned Ray Cooper and me to Car 37. Lt. Smith read off the list of crimes that had occurred, the usual thefts, cuttings and rapes. I wrote down a few notes on the last occurrence the Lt. gave us. A 211 PC, armed robbery had occurred in Long Beach, the victim had been shot and killed. The suspect was described as male caucasian, 26 to 30 years, black hair, 5'10", about 165 pounds, armed with an automatic pistol. He was last observed leaving the scene of the crime in a late model

Pontiac or a Buick, dark in color.

"Alright, that's it," the Lieutenant ordered, "Let's get out there and go to work." Grabbing their gear, clipboards loaded with report forms, hot sheets, and flashlights, etc., everybody jammed their way down a narrow flight of creaky wooden stairs and headed out to the parking area where the night-watch cars would soon be coming in.

'Chick' Macy and his partner Andy Drobatz, were going through their usual routine. Andy complained in mock anger, "I sure wish the Lt. would give me a cop for a partner instead of Macy."

Macy's round face opened in a big smile, he chuckled. Someone kept it going, "What's wrong with Macy? I heard he's a nice guy."

Drobatz moaned, "All I do the first hour is sit down at the chili stand at Main and Adams and watch that fat-ass eat half a dozen bowls of chili beans and a whole box of oyster crackers. All of you guys know what he does the rest of the night."

Someone suggested, "Why don't you eat some chili beans and get even with him Andy?"

Macy spoke up, "Hell, Andy doesn't need beans to get even. He's just like all of those foreigners, all he eats is sauerkraut and Polish sausage."

Car 37 from the night-watch rolled in, the driver said, "You guys are all set, we gassed up about an hour ago." It was the middle of June, a real nice warm night. Throwing my leather jacket into the back I got behind the wheel and drove south on Figueroa St.. Using his flashlight to see, Cooper recorded the car's mileage, our names and serial numbers on our log. My partner was a young officer, not too long out of the Police Academy. He was a big husky man with a friendly personality.

"Cooper, I've been thinking about that robbery and murder down in Long Beach. If the guy is from somewhere up here in L.A. there is a good chance he'll use Figueroa St.. Let's go down to the south end of our district and watch a little while."

"Sounds like a good idea." Our patrol car was a beat-up, faded maroon colored 1941 Chevy, I parked inconspicuously between two cars on the southeast corner of Figueroa and Vernon. While sitting there we had observed several outstanding traffic violations, we had just about agreed to grab the next one that came along. Suddenly a long black Buick coming from the direction of Long Beach pulled smoothly up to the boulevard stop. There were no passengers, just a driver. Easing our radio car from the curb I followed the sedan north on Figueroa. We crossed Santa Barbara Ave., Exposition Park was on our left, there were only a few lights but the huge outline of the Coliseum loomed up in the darkness over the tops of the tall fir trees.

"Cooper, this is a good place to pull him over. Be damn careful, if this is the guy that pulled the robbery in Long Beach, he's got an automatic and he's already killed one person."

Ray nodded he was ready. Our red light was a spotlight mounted on the driver's side. I flipped the switch on and honked the horn. The driver glanced in his rear-view mirror. When he spotted the red light he took off like a rocket. Our old Chevy trembled and bucked in rebellion when I floored the throttle. The Buick was pulling away from us. Cooper was on the ball, he had the mike, "Car 37 calling KGPL. We are requesting all frequencies to stand by. Car 37 is in pursuit, going north on Figueroa St. from Santa Barbara Ave."

Ray was broadcasting the pursuit over the radio like a veteran. I had plenty of troubles of my own. The old patrol car had gradually picked up speed, I had to be doing over eighty miles an hour. The siren was operated by a pedal next to the clutch, my left foot was pumping it like a six-day bike rider. The spotlight kept falling down and flashing a red glare off the hood. I was grabbing the handle to straighten it up. We must be doing eighty five now. There were no floor mats, and the metal floorboards were throbbing and banging. I hoped that they didn't fly up in our face. The Buick angled off of Figueroa onto Hoover St.. Ray was broadcasting to the other units, "KGPL, this is Car 37, Car 37, we are now on Hoover approaching Jefferson Blvd. at a high rate of speed."

University Police Station was on the northwest corner, across the street was an all-night coffee shop, heading there was our Lt., right out in the middle of Hoover, the careening Buick just barely missed him, and we were bearing down on him. We were going far too fast to swerve. Cooper whispered, "My God, I hope he runs in the right direction!" I caught a glimpse of the Lieutenant's startled face as we flew past him. The old Chevy was pushing ninety miles per hour for sure. Severance St. slid off to the right from Hoover, the Buick took it. The street was lined with two and three story houses. In bygone days they had been the homes of the very wealthy and social strata of L.A.. Since the end of World War 11 they had become fraternity and sorority houses for the students of the University of Southern California.

The Buick was still going full speed. Knowing that three blocks further on the street ended I let up on the throttle. You had to turn

Ofc. A.R. Cooper pointing at author's Sam Brown belt where bandit's bullet hit.

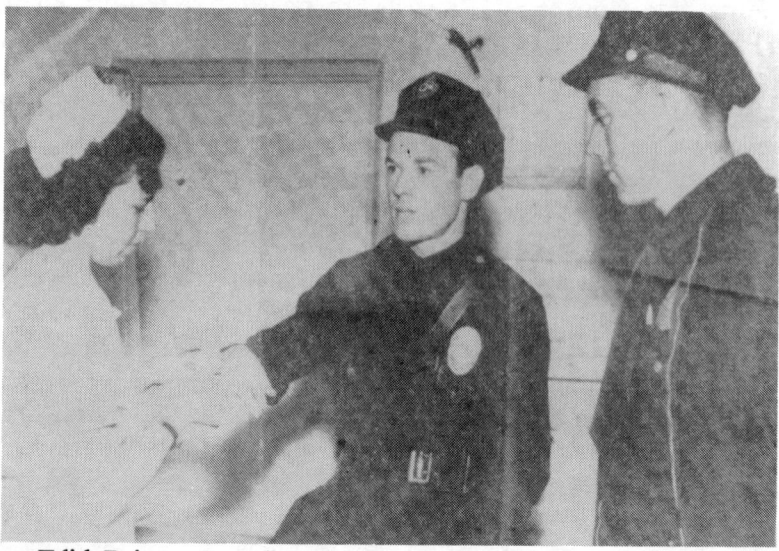

Nurse Edith Baier at Georgia Street Receiving Hospital treating bullet wound to author's hand.

right or left on Thirtieth Street, if that stupid bastard kept going at that speed he'd never make it. A large three story house was at the end of Severance, when he hit the curb he'd take off flying...right into that old building. Ray anticipated what was about to happen, "Car 37, Car 37, we'll be out at Thirtieth and Severence." Hanging the mike from a hook on the dashboard he grabbed for something solid to hold onto.

The Buick's brakelights blazed, I knew it was too late, he'd never make the corner. The curbs were lined with parked cars, bumper to bumper. The driver tried to turn right on Thirtieth doing sixty miles an hour. Broadsiding around the corner he caroomed into a solid line of parked cars on the far side, the speeding Buick disintegrated in a shower of metal and glass and sparks flying everywhere. A half dozen cars were smashed by the hurtling vehicle before it stopped. Barely making the corner we came to a screeching halt amongst the wreckage.

Miraculously the driver was thrown unhurt out the left side of the wreckage and ran up a driveway. Leaping from the patrol car I didn't have time to grab my flashlight. Cooper leaped out and ran around the far side of the house to intercept him as I raced up the driveway in pursuit. It was the darkest time of the night, the moon had disappeared and no light came from the houses. All I could see was the dark form fleeing swiftly up the driveway. A wooden gate stood partially open, as he sped through it I yelled for him to halt. I fired a warning shot in the air, he disappeared behind the gate. Dashing through the gate I jumped quickly to the left and halted. Standing silent and listening, I could hear no sound of running feet. My eyes slowly adjusted to the dark, the gnarled trunk of a large tree loomed a few feet to my right. Suddenly a slight movement by the tree caught my eye.

"Stand fast and raise your hands," I ordered. I moved toward the shadowy figure, damn but it was dark, I wished I had my flashlight, it threw them when you put that bright beam right in their eyes.

The shadowy figure said, *"Don't shoot, don't shoot."* My gun was ready as I approached him, he didn't raise his hands. I reached out with my left quick to grab his right hand. With a lightning move he jammed the gun he had concealed in his right hand hard against my belly and fired. A terrific shock knocked me backwards, a loud ring pierced my ears. Above the ringing I heard his gun firing again. A sharp pain struck my right hand and ran up my arm, my hand was numb. One thing for certain, if my gun wasn't blown clear out of my hand I sure as hell wasn't going to wait for him to shoot again. My 38 calibre S&W with a six-inch barrel boomed over the crack of his automatic weapon. Rapid-fire, five remaining rounds in my pistol were gone in a split second.

Most officers in those days alternated the rounds in their guns with a soft-nosed lead and a hard steel bullet with a flat nose. We called the flat-nosed rounds highway patrol bullets. When fired at a sloping trunk of a speeding car they didn't ricochet, they went right on through. The heavy slugs did terrible damage to flesh and bones. The bandit was blasted violently backward against the tree where he hung up, his gun still in his hand. Arriving from around the house, Ray whipped off two quick shots, the holdup man sliding away from the tree crumpled to the ground, a chrome-plated automatic pistol clutched in his right hand in a death grip.

Lights were snapping on in the houses. Behind me in an upper story window a young coed stood in her nightgown. Lights from the room behind her revealed the outline of her body. A frightened but curious voice behind her was asking, "What's going on out there?" Radio cars answering our pursuit call were arriving with their sirens growling. Officers were coming up the driveway swiftly.

Gene Stein in plain clothes, the only detective on the morning watch, was talking to Cooper, "Take your car and run Gary up to Georgia Street Receiving Hospital, I'll take your report when you return to the station." Light from windows of the house and flashing lights of the police cars illuminated the area. Cooper and I walked down the driveway to Car 37, blood ran down my hand and over my gun. Reloading I put it back in the clamshell holster and snapped it shut. I realized my hand was working all right despite the blood, it must be just a flesh wound. But my belly hurt like hell. I told Ray, "I'm scared to unbuckle my Sam Browne, maybe I'll come apart." I reached for my buckle to loosen the belt.

Cooper grabbed my arm, "No, no, just leave it alone. I'll get you to Georgia Street fast. Where in hell are the ignition keys?"

"I tossed them on the floorboards." Parking in the driveway at Georgia we took the elevator to the third floor. Emerging from it you could see into four of the receiving rooms, each one had what looked like an operating table covered with a white sheet. I walked into one of the empty rooms and climbed onto a table. I knew the Sam Browne had to come off sooner or later. I handed my belt and gun to Cooper standing nearby, then looked down cautiously at my middle, my regular belt holding my trousers was alright, I couldn't see a hole or any blood.

Ray was examining my Sam Browne, his face lit up, "Hell, would you look at this. The bullet hit your buckle, it made a groove down the belt. It didn't even go through."

Grabbing the belt I looked, Cooper was right. Jumping from the operating table I hooked the Sam Browne around my waist. "Come on Coop, we're getting out of here, I'll soak my hand in hot water when we get back to the station." In the past I had brought plenty stab and gunshot victims here and watched the doctors probe with long instruments into the small blue-colored holes probing deep for glass or lead. On the ride to Georgia Street I was thinking...now it's my turn. The doctor will have to probe and jab and cut my stomach looking for that piece of lead. I'll have to lie on that table with the white sheet.

Before Cooper and I could get out of the room a nurse appeared in the doorway, she blocked our exit, "Where do you think you are going?"

"Back to the police station."

"Oh no...you aren't going any place until the doctor takes a look at your hand and makes out an injury report." The nurse was young and pretty, she was also very firm. After washing the drying blood from my hand I could see that it was only a flesh wound. The bullet had torn up a lot of skin. The Doc taking a quick look ordered the nurse to apply some disinfectant and a bandage.

The sky was still black when we parked behind the station and walked up the back stairs to the locker room. Cooper had continued on through and into the detective bureau. Poking his head back in the locker room he said, "Stein wants to talk with us in the Dick's bureau."

Gene hung up the phone and looked at all the notes on his desk. "Well, you guys got a good one tonight. We've identified the guy as David L. Boyd, he originally came from Missouri. He's done time in state and federal penitentiaries for burglary, robbery, auto theft, even piracy on the high seas. This last time he got sprung on parole and his parole officer hasn't seen him since. The new Buick he had was stolen, it's now a total loss. We found an apartment house not too far from here where he has been holed up. Some officers just called me from there, they found the loot from about six different burglaries that they've identified. Our division records disclose that we have recovered more than seven stolen cars in just the last three weeks that have been dumped within the close vicinity of this guy

Boyd's apartment." Glancing up Stein said, "I wanted you to know how things are going. You guys better get your reports completed, Capt. Hayes will be in early and you know how he wants everything laid out on his desk."

The barking of a dog returned my mind to the present. The den was still dark, light from a tiny lamp behind the bar enabled me to see our German Shepherd standing by the door, he wanted to go out. Letting him out I returned to the couch. The vivid memories I had just resurrected had to be the reason for Thomas Boyd putting such *tremendous pressure* on Harry Maynard to change his decision. It had to be something of great importance for Bank Vice President Boyd to pressure Bank Vice President Maynard into such a criminal conspiracy. Their misuse and abuse of the power of the office of the Civil Service Commission was unconscionable.

The dog stood outside the door peering at me. I let him in, going to his favorite spot in the corner of the den he laid down. He was evidently satisfied that everything was secure outside.

CHAPTER 13

The next afternoon I got Ray Charles on the phone. "What have you heard from our attorney Dean Pic'l?"

"Not a thing, I've called his office several times, all I get is a big run around. Last night I sent a telegram to his home, but I haven't heard a word about that either. I'm so disappointed in him I don't know what to say. After all, I *personally recommended* him to you. When I was a Colonel in the Army Pic'l was a sergeant under my command, he was a law student at that time. Pic'l and his wife were guests of my wife and I in our home many times, we became great friends. Gary, I'll tell you, when I get through at five tonight I am going to drive down to West Covina where he lives and get hold of him personally."

"Okay, I'll call you in the morning." By now my mind was made up, we'd been *taken* by Pic'l but I might as well let Charles drive to Covina and find out for himself. There was still our one big chance, the Ventura County Grand Jury. This was a powerful organization of citizens set up by California State Law and mandated to protect the health, welfare and the civil rights of all the citizens of Ventura County. I called the courthouse and asked for the Foreman of the Grand Jury, within seconds he answered.

"Dr Penfield, this is Gary, I haven't heard a word from you, how are you proceeding with the investigation?"

There was *tense* silence, then Penfield said, "I hate to tell you this

Gary, but there isn't going to be any investigation."

"What in the world are you saying...*why* isn't there going to be an investigation...what about all the information and evidence you've been given?"

"I'm very sorry, but Judge Jerome Berenson, the Presiding Judge of the Superior Court, has given the strictest orders to the Grand Jury to kill all investigations of the evidence and information that was given to them."

"Just a minute, are you telling me that Judge Berenson *ordered you,* the Foreman of the Grand Jury, to *kill* your investigations? He has *no* authority to do that, that's *tampering* with the Grand Jury. Damn it, you know as well as I do that he is obstructing justice by covering up for Erwin and Dunham and the whole mess. So what about those people who put up the large amount of money to frame Supervisor Robinson and City Manager Reiman? Dr. Penfield, I'm telling you, Berenson has no legal right to cover up for these people just because they are lawyers."

Like a parrot he repeated, "I'm sorry Gary, but those are Judge Berenson's orders. There is nothing more I can do."

"Damn it Dr. Penfield, *you* are the Foreman of the Grand Jury, *you* have the authority to contact the State Attorney General and the Judicial Council in Sacramento."

"Like I said, I am sorry, but *I have received the Judge's orders.*"

"Well how about Mr. Deem, the D.A., have you discussed it with him?"

"Yes I have, he was very upset, but apparently he feels that Judge Berenson controls the situation and he can't go against him."

"Well Dr. Penfield, *a whole lot of people had faith* in you and the power of the Grand Jury to protect them and their property. They are going to be sick when they hear of this fiasco."

"As I said before Gary, all I can do is follow Berenson's orders."

I hung up. For the first time in my life I was feeling a complete, frustrated, utter helplessness. Why in the world was Judge Berenson so determined to take such vile means to cover up for such crooked people? What did he owe them? The *brotherhood of lawyers,* was it so powerful, so binding that Berenson's obligation to protect them over-rides the inherent rights of fairness and justice guaranteed to even the lowest person by the Constitution? I was mad and getting madder by the minute. I called the District Attorney's office and got King on the phone.

"Mal, I just talked to Dr. Penfield. He says there isn't going to be any Grand Jury investigation because Judge Berenson killed it."

"Yes, I know."

"What! You mean *you knew* this all along?"

"Well, Penfield told Deem and me a couple days ago. I've been meaning to call you."

"Meaning to call me...! For Christs sake! Mal, Berenson had *no right to interfere* with the Grand Jury when they're making secret investigations into corruption."

"*I know it* Gary. What Deem and I are trying to figure out is how Berenson was able to learn about the investigation."

"Even so King, there isn't any reason why Deem can't go ahead and investigate this mess himself."

"We discussed that, but Mr. Deem's afraid that as things stand he just wouldn't have enough power to do it. Berenson is the Presiding Judge of the Superior Court and he controls all the judges."

"That's horseshit, how about the rest of the Grand Jury members, are they all going to go along with a conspiracy like this?"

"Gary, I attended a meeting the other night and a group of the Grand Jurors came to me, they complained about Judge Berenson and Penfield *ordering* them to stop the investigation. One lady was in tears, she cried, 'I absolutely cannot understand how a man like Berenson could do such a terrible thing.'"

"What about the Judicial Council in Sacramento? *It is their duty to straighten out corrupt judges like Berenson.*"

His answer was in a very low voice, "Judge Berenson is a *leading and very powerful member* of the Judicial Council."

"I am beginning to get the picture strong and clear Mal. I've been around judges and courtrooms for a long time, but I've never seen anything to compare with this. I'll do some checking around, when I find out who went to Berenson I'll call you."

Their *depravity* was overwhelming. I went to bed but sleep didn't come. I continued to rack my brain, minutely examining all of my suspicions. It boiled down to a point where it had to be one of the Grand Jurors...one of them had betrayed his trust and his oath, I recalled one Grand Juror, the rancher from Oxnard. The minute I mentioned lawyer Blais and the polygraph he'd given Didi Castro, the Juror had shown a strong and unusual interest. He practically demanded to know how I had received the information. This had to be the answer. The pressure in my head eased up a little, a night of good sleep would help.

The next morning it proved quite easy to verify my suspicions. A few phone calls to friends in Oxnard gave me all the information I needed. The Juror frequented a local bar and restaurant in Oxnard. A couple people overheard him telling some of his drinking buddies how he'd given very important information to Red Blais who was to pass it to Berenson. It was still *hard to believe* that Judge Berenson would jeopardize himself to cover up for the likes of Mr. Fish and Dunham, even considering the fact they were 'brother's' of the Bar Association.

I wanted to discuss it with Ray Charles, we agreed to meet in a Ventura coffee shop for a talk before lunch. He was there when I arrived, within minutes I'd given him the story about the Juror. He just continued shaking his head and repeating over and over, "I just can't believe lawyers and judges are capable of this kind of criminal subterfuge."

"I'm going to write a letter to the State Bar Association in L.A.. I need a copy of the check for the twenty five hundred that I gave Dean, I wrote on the front that it was for expenses only. I want to send it along with my letter."

"Sure, come over to the office, I'll get you a copy now." We sat in his office while the secretary located the check and made a photo copy. Encouragingly Charles said, "I hope the Bar Association will do you some good."

"I don't believe they'll do a damn thing but I'm going to make an official record of how Pic'l *refused to bring out* the incriminating evidence at my hearing because it involved attorneys." The copy of the check was on the desk before me, something was wrong. "Wait a minute Ray, look at this copy, nothing's written on the upper left hand corner. On the original I put 'for expenses only.' I wrote it in Pic'l's office, he was watching me and commented, wanting to know why I did it. He seemed quite put out. I explained that it was my habit to write a note on my checks verifying what it was for. Ray, would you bring the original and let me see it?"

Taking the check, I held it up to the strong overhead lighting. It was easy to *detect the eradication* on the upper left corner. I told Ray, "Keep this check safe and do not let anyone destroy it. I am going down to the bank in Los Angeles and look at the microfilm to determine if it was erased before it was deposited or after."

He agreed to keep the check safe, then went on to say, "I've been unable to contact Pic'l, his secretary just gives me the *run around.* They got the telegram but he still refuses to answer."

"Let's face it, Pic'l *never* intended to live up to anything he said.

We have had it. Dean *erased* my notation on the check so he could say that we gave it to him for a retainer and not expenses."

"This is all extremely puzzling to me. What's the motive for the Grand Juror to go to attorney Blais and spill his guts?"

"He probably wanted to use it as a bargaining point. His daughter or niece, I'm not quite sure which, got busted for narcotics. She was peddling heroin for years, she wasn't a hype herself, just sold it to addicts. She didn't need money, her grandfather had left her a three hundred thousand dollar trust fund and she had a ninety thousand dollar house in Oxnard. Her uncle or father whichever, was trying real hard to keep her out of jail. He got a lot of prominent Oxnard people to write letters to the court trying to get her put on straight probation. Police found written records in her house revealing she'd peddled over fifty thousand dollars of heroin in a two month period. She even tried to blame the whole thing on her brother, who is at this time a fugitive from justice on narco charges, also for threating witnesses. The Juror is trying to get Blais to go to Berenson using this knowledge as a leverage to get his relatives off the hook."

"It's a hell of a mess, what do you intend to do now Gary?"

"I'm going to do some thinking." On the drive home I was doing some heavy pondering. There was one major snag...I knew that the Juror, the old rancher, had revealed the secret information to Red Blais wanting him to take it to Judge Berenson and barter to help his relatives. But...that's where the whole pattern broke down. Blais couldn't have gone to Berenson, he would have cut his own throat. His own serious acts in violating that court order during the murder trial would have come out. And even worse...it would have tied him in personally with the Fish. Judge Berenson *had to have gotten* his information from *another* source. I could sense it real strong, there was something else, *hidden,* far more evil behind all this than just the two bankers, Harry Maynard and Thomas Boyd having a hatred for me. It was to be many years later before I learned that it had been another Grand Juror who had so treacherously gone to Judge Berenson, also the sinister reason why.

But right now I knew there was one thing I had to do, I've got to find a job. I'm about to lose my home and everything else we own. I was in debt up to my ears and my wife's health was very poor. I had no insurance or hospitalization. Mr. Fish and his friends did a beautiful job so far as my future is concerned. There's no way I can get a Civil Service job again. I probably lost my security clearance with the Federal Government because of this hearing. So maybe my philosophy was all wrong, I could have operated just like Hronesh, Kuhn and Dunham and I'd still have my job and reputation. Never in my life have I ever felt lower and more depressed then I do right now, it's like the end of the world. But I knew one thing, people will probably think I am nuts, but I still don't want to be in their shoes pulling all that rotten stuff for the Fish.

The following morning I opened a phone book and looked under lawyers. No question about it, if I didn't get a lawyer to represent me, there wasn't much hope. I recalled the *reaction* of lawyer Todd. He almost passed out just thinking about getting involved. Another local attorney had turned Mrs. Thurman down as soon as he heard that Fish was behind her problems.

Somewhere along the way the name of a lawyer, William Herro had come up, I found him in the yellow pages. His secretary advised me Mr. Herro would see me in ten minutes if I could be there then. His office was on Santa Clara Ave. a few blocks east of California St.. After a short wait in the reception room I was ushered into Mr. Herro's office. In his late twenties or early thirties, he was very neat and fashionably dressed. Attentively he listened, at my conclusion Herro sat silent for a few minutes. He said, "As I look at it now we would file an appeal to the Civil Service Ruling."

"One *big* problem is the factor that Pic'l didn't record the entire proceedings."

He twiddled his thumbs, "I can't quite *conceive* an experienced attorney like Dean Pic'l failing to do that."

"Why can't you? Looking back at what transpired it's pretty damn obvious he *never at any time* intended to file a Civil Suit. He was *only concerned* with covering up for Fish and Dunham and all the other lawyers involved."

"Well Gary, an appeal would take several years and my fee would be ten thousand dollars or more and I would need cash to proceed."

"Hell, I don't want to spend years fighting to get an appeal based on some vague legal technicalities maybe we could prove and maybe we can't. All the crimes they've committed and the issues involved would have long been forgotten and lost. No justice would be served by that kind of procedure. I want a lawsuit, one that'll bring out all the facts to a jury and clear me of all the Fish's damned lies. I am willing to let a jury decide what's right and abide by their decision."

"But let's face some facts. You are bucking a lot of lawyers, plus Judge Berenson. That amounts to a lot of power and pressure that they can bring to bear."

"Mr. Herro, I realize they are powerful and are capable of pulling every rotten corrupt trick in the book. These crooks have already demonstrated that ability, but if I can take their depositions under oath then I can prove everything I've said. If they tell the truth it'll all come out, if they lie to cover up they'll end up in more trouble. Once the *truth* starts flowing they'll begin to bicker and fight among themselves, blaming each other for what has happened."

"There is one other way out for you."

"What is that?"

"Have you ever considered just plain walking away from the whole thing?"

Staring at the lawyer I saw a change coming over him. I recalled the suspicious feelings I'd encountered with Pic'l before the hearing. It was even more pronounced with Herro, he was younger than Pic'l but it wasn't taking him long to realize he could be jeopardizing his entire future and career as an attorney by *even* considering filing a suit involving Judge Berenson in criminal activity.

"Mr. Herro, *my* right to justice and due process of law means just as much to me as Judge Berenson's cover-up for a gang of shyster lawyers means to *him*." As I left Herro was mumbling something in a low voice...something like how sorry he was he could not help. I didn't feel much respect for Herro but I couldn't work up any anger against him either. My anger was against the Bar Association, the lousy system lawyers were caught up in. If they had aspirations to rise to the heights of legal success they knew sure as hell that they couldn't do it by filing a lawsuit against the most powerful Superior Court Judge in the county who was on the Judicial Council and had the power to *kill* a Grand Jury investigation by a mere wave of his hand.

The next few days I spent looking for a job. I'd take anything I could get, it was a matter of trying to keep food on the table and paying the gas and light bill. An ad in the paper said to see Jack at the V&S gas station in Ventura, they needed an attendant. At the cut-rate station I convinced Jack that I had experience pumping gas and could count change correctly. He explained that the shift they needed covered was from one in the afternoon to ten at night, six days a week and paid a dollar and ninety cents an hour. Jack took my phone number and said he'd think about it and call me later.

Early the next morning I called Dick Hanawalt's law office and made an appointment. Having resigned the D.A.'s office, Hanawalt had joined a private law firm in Oxnard. It was a *long shot*...but who knows, maybe he has enough guts to do something, he'd developed a lot of experience while handling many involved cases. Dick's office was in a modern building in the center of town. On the third floor you had a view of the city through large plate glass windows. Cute secretaries dashed around in a very efficient manner. One pointed to the location of Hanawalt's office, then from behind me someone grabbed my arm saying, "Come on I'll show you where it is." It was Hanawalt, we entered his office and closed the door.

I had a briefcase loaded with documents, he was examining them closely while I was filling him in on what had transpired. Dick had become quite absorbed in the Bar Association's files on Harrison Dunham.

"Gary, to start off let me explain something, I am associated with the other attorneys here, so first I will have to discuss it with them. Drop by in a few days and see me."

"Very good, I can't ask for much more then your word that you will consider the situation."

Bright and early two days later I sat in Dick's office. He started off, "Let me do the talking. Shortly after you left here the other day I phoned Harry Maynard. He *admitted to me* that he'd talked with Capt. Ernie Shaw and that *he'd made the statements to Ernie about your not being guilty and that Thomas Boyd had pressured him into changing his decision.*"

I felt elated, with Maynard himself *confirming* what Ernie Shaw had told me it was the first real good news in a long time. I thought of David Boyd, "Dick, when you talked to Maynard did he say that Thomas Boyd had given him any reason *why* he wanted Maynard to change his decision?"

"No he didn't, but I have to agree it'd be *real* interesting to know the reason why. There's a little bad news along with the good."

"What's that Dick?"

"Well, I had a conference with my associates in the office. They have been representing Maynard on some matters. Thus they feel it would be a conflict of interest if I was to represent you." Dick just sort of clammed up after that. Picking up his pipe he made quite a little operation out of lighting it. I knew that our conversation was finished.

"Thanks a lot for your time Dick." What else was there to say?

Being still early I decided to stop by the Employees Association. Al Palmer was standing on the sidewalk in front of the building. He listened to me dissertate on my efforts to obtain an attorney. I even told him about one lawyer I'd known for a long time. "I accidently ran into him in front of a reataurant on California Street. He was friendly enough, however, the entire time he was glancing furtively around making sure he wasn't seen talking to me. He gave me some real helpful legal advice, then quickly hustled off down the street. After all, a prominent member of the Bar like him couldn't be seen with a political leper like me, he could be disgraced.

Palmer had listened patiently, but he finally asked, "What in hell was the valuable advice that the lawyer gave you?"

"The eminent barrister's advice was that, 'I'd never be able to get an attorney in Ventura. I should go to Los Angeles and try to find a *lawyer who hates Mr. Fish.*'"

Al looked at me closely to see if I was joking then said, "Now, I'll tell you something strictly confidential. Last night I was contacted by a group of attorneys. Seven of them have grouped together and they want to represent you, they know through their own knowledge that you have been *framed* from one end to another. They feel if all of them stick together they'll be strong enough that no one will be able to ruin them."

"That sounds interesting Al. Lord, I'm pretty well convinced I'm not going to get an attorney by myself."

"We discussed it last night, they feel that if you stick to a lawsuit against Fish and Harrison Dunham you can win with no problem."

"Wait a minute Al, you mean they are wanting me to forget the part about Berenson and his ordering the Grand Jury to *kill* their investigation?"

"That's right. They want to stick strictly to Mr. Fish."

"Hell Al, that's the crux of the whole thing. Berenson is right in the middle. If we go to court against Fish and Dunham all the other stuff would still keep coming up, I'd have to lie every time I turned around. Things would get so screwed up I wouldn't even know what I was saying. Damn it Al, I know what the truth is and I also know who is involved right down the line. That's why I got screwed up in the first place because I wouldn't do any of the crooked crap that Fish wanted. I'm not about to get involved with a bunch of guys like that. The very first time something went wrong they'd throw me to the wolves and it would all be over. The truth is the only weapon I have. Can't you see it, if they could just once get me to lie on even one little thing, I wouldn't stand a chance. Besides Al, it makes me wonder...why are these lawyers so interested in helping me...who's behind them? If they want me to leave Berenson out of it they are obviously more interested in *his* welfare than they are in mine. I'll tell you Al, on my way over here from Hanawalt's office I did a lot of thinking. Lord knows I'm no lawyer but I'm going to go 'pro-per.' I'm going to file my own lawsuit. I'll do it somehow, somehow I will do it."

"Did you ever get an answer from the Bar Association regarding how Dean Pic'l doubled-crossed us?"

"Yeah, a lawyer from the State Bar wrote me a letter wanting to know if I had any more detrimental information on Dunham. Hell, they have enough evidence on that two bit shyster to put him away for ever. He also wanted to know if I had a written agreement from Pic'l regarding what he had agreed to do. Anyway, after reading the letter it wasn't hard to figure out they weren't going to do a damn thing. The Bar Association should be wiped out and a responsible agency formed to 'police' corrupt judges and lawyers. Harry Truman used to say, 'Only a stupid farmer would hire a fox to guard his hen house.' I also got an answer from Govenor Reagan's office. Here, take a look at this letter. Reagan instructed Richard K. Turner, his Assistant Legal Affairs Secy. to answer my letter. Read the second paragraph there. Turner states he spoke with Herb Ashby who used to be a Dep. D.A. and the Ventura County Counsel before he was appointed to a job with Governor Reagan's office in Sacramento. Ashby told Turner he was *very familiar* with all the facts in my case and confirms what I had written. Turner goes on to say, 'Governor Reagan is sorry to admit that there is very little he could do in my case as the Governor had no jurisdiction to intervene into matters pending in local administrative agencies.' I wrote a letter back to Gov. Reagan telling him that I wasn't asking his office to intervene in my behalf, but as Governor it was his obligation and his duty to order the Attorney General to investigate into Judicial corruption such as the Presiding Judge of the Superior Court, Judge Jerome Berenson, *killing a Grand Jury investigation* into county government corruption and the *rank violations* of citizens basic Civil Rights. Al I have to get going now. I got me a job in a gas station and I have to be there by one this afternoon. And I am going to be busier than hell trying to figure out how to be a lawyer and learn enough so I can file my own lawsuit."

CHAPTER 14

The next three weeks were gruelling, by seven every morning I hurried up the coast to the Santa Barbara County Law Library. As soon as the doors opened I would quickly enter and load a table with reference books, case law history, law decisions and what have you. And before I knew it, it was noon. Returning down the coast to my job I'd eat some of my lunch and save the rest for my dinner about six. That cut-rate station was plenty busy, you wolfed your food while running from one pump to another cleaning windshields and pumping gas. With the ridiculously low pay there was a quick turnover of employees. By closing time at ten, you were dragging more than your feet.

Arriving home about ten thirty, I wrote notes for several hours, than laid it all out so my wife could type on the complaint the next day. All too often the entire routine became almost unbearably depressing and discouraging as I realized my shortcomings as an ersatz lawyer. While reading and searching frantically through the myriads of cases and pondering their worth, I often broke out in a cold sweat. My ultimate goal was in filing the lawsuit and by that method provoke some of the justice and fairness which our country was *supposedly* so famous for. My salary didn't amount to even a small part of the income we needed to survive on. Realizing this did not help the waves of engulfing helplessness, the deep depression often descending upon me like a giant soaking wet blanket, blinding and suffocating, determined to destroy."

At long last my lawsuit was ready, typed properly, all twenty five pages were stapled neatly together, law required that each defendant receive a copy of the entire complaint. I ordered fifteen copies of it to be made up by a photo company. Normally the Recorder's office in the courthouse was a bustling place filled with lawyers, law clerks and process servers filing documents of one kind or another. Now there was only one clerk on duty, I was the lone customer. Coming to the counter she asked if she could help.

"Yes, I have a Civil Complaint to file." I put all the copies on the counter.

"Alright, I'll give you a file number, here's your receipt. And you will have to put up a *bond of five hundred dollars* for *every one of the defendants* before I can issue a summons."

"What are you talking about? There are twelve defendants listed on this complaint. Do you mean to say that I'll have to give you six thousand dollars before you'll issue the summons to serve them?"

"Yes, I'm sorry, but on all libel and slander suits the law requires a five hundred dollar bond for each defendant."

"Alright, just put the complaint number on each of these fifteen copies." Stamping the case numbers on them she kept the required amount of copies for the court records. Walking to my car in the parking lot I sat down. Good Lord...! All that time and effort for nothing. I couldn't help thinking about all the poor people in the country who had far more than enough legal cause to file lawsuits to protect their reputations but were prohibited because of a five hundred dollar bond. But worse yet, what if they came up with the thousands of dollars necessary then fell into the claws of shyster's like Dunham and Fish.

There was no time left to sit there bemoaning the situation, only a few minutes were left to get to work. The entire shift was nothing but a daze, a blur of heated motors and dirty windshields, my mind was working *double-time* in what seemed like a non-stop argument. Was there really any use in carrying on any further this maddening rage I felt to *clear my name* of those vicious false charges and to expose the corruption of the county officials involved? But no one seemed to really care one way or another, even so, that sure as hell didn't make everything all right.

Suppose I forgot *everything* that had transpired...went to some new place far from here...suppose I became financially successful in some business enterprise and made a million bucks...despite such a wonderful possibility it still could never relieve the terrible nagging problem of justifying to my own conscience and what's more to my family, why I'd run out when things got rough. I recalled a passage I'd read in a history book, it went something like..."A man who *runs* when accused of a wrong is either guilty, or a coward."

The next morning I was back at the law library, the clerk pushed opened the heavy oak doors and I entered. After one hell of a mess of research and reading through the enormous pile of law books I'd stacked on the table, I became convinced there was only one proper complaint to file. The one fitting the circumstances and events most particularly and accurately was 'Malicious Prosecution, Misuse and Abuse of Process, and Conspiracy to Commit the Same.' Another month was consumed traveling to the Santa Barbara law library and back to the gas station, then home to burn the midnight oil, and last but not least, get a few hours sleep.

Finally the new complaint was completed and all the necessary copies were prepared. The clerk put her stamp and signature on the original and all the copies. She entered the complaint in the court records, took my fee and issued a summons. This was just a starter. Now I'd have to *serve* each and every one of the defendants with a summons and copy of the complaint. Twenty minutes after leaving the County Clerk's office I was back at the cut-rate service station washing windshields. The telephone in the station office was ringing, I saw Jack the big boss pick it up, he glanced out the window at me, I could tell he was annoyed. Coming to the door he motioned me to come in and answer the phone. Who'd be calling me at this place? The voice said, "This is Bob Hamm, the County Clerk."

"Yeah Bob, what's on your mind?"

"Gary, you were in my office a little while ago and got a summons for a complaint that you filed."

"That's right."

"I want you to bring the summons back. It was not issued right. I'll fix it up and give you a new one."

"There wasn't a thing wrong with it when I read it Bob. I don't understand?"

"Listen Gary, you've *got* to bring it back."

"Nothing doing Bob. I like it just the way it is. Tell me something, how did you find out where to find me?"

"Well, I got the phone number from somebody."

"Yeah, I know who you got my number from..."

"What do you mean?"

"You got this number from Mr. Fish."

"Who's Mr. Fish?"

"You know damn good and well who Mr. Fish is, you've read the complaint I just filed in your office."

"Gary, *you've got to bring that summons back* or there is going to be trouble."

"Are you taking your orders from Mr. Fish now Hamm?"

"What are you talking about?"

"You know damn well what I'm talking about Bob, your sneaky secretary, Barbara Barham's been shacking up with Kenny Cleaver for years. When documents are filed in your office and she thinks it would help them to know about it she steals the file and takes it up to Cleaver and Fish for them to read. Less than five minutes after I filed that lawsuit today she *stole* it from your office and took it to them...Fish called you on the phone...he was madder then the devil and gave you orders to get that summons back from me."

"How do you know all of this?"

"I know Barbara has been a stoolie for Cleaver and Fish for a long time. She's been *stealing files* from your office that the D.A. and private attorneys have filed with the court and that is a very serious violation of the Penal Code, Hamm."

"Alright, I admit that Barbara is very close to Kenneth Cleaver, but I didn't know she was taking files from the office."

"Bull shit! How did Fish find out about the lawsuit so fast. You know what's going on Hamm. Fish gave you this number to call. He knows where I am because he's had Jim Hronesh following me."

"Gary please, bring that summons back."

"No. And don't call me here anymore, the guy who runs this place will get mad."

Next morning I took my summons to the Marshal's office and filled out the necessary forms to have them served on Fish and the rest of the defendants. Their office was quite efficient. They served Fish the same day and I received a copy of their service in my mail the next morning.

Shortly after the mail delivery the phone rang. "This is Sgt. Bob Jones from the Marshal's office. We served your summons on Mr. Fish and mailed the papers to you yesterday. Did you receive them yet?"

"Yes sergeant, they came in the morning's mail."

"There was a slight error when the papers were served, if you'll *return them* to our office *we'll rectify* the error and give them back to you."

"What exactly is wrong with the papers Sgt.?"

"Well, uh, I don't know, the secretary told me there was an error and she asked me to call you."

"I'm *real* curious about what specifically is wrong. Would you ask the secretary what the problem is?"

"Uh, well, uh, she isn't in the office right at the moment."

"Well, I'll tell you sarge, the papers look fine to me. You people did a real fine job. I'll just leave them the way they are and let the court decide if there is something wrong."

"But you don't understand. I was *ordered* to get the summons back from you."

"You have orders! *Orders from who*...you just said the secretary asked you to call?"

"That's right. The secretary asked me to call you."

"Sergeant, just tell me one thing, how did you get my home phone number? It's an unlisted number."

"Well, uh, I'll tell you, let me call you back, I'll get some more information." The sergeant hung up.

By gosh, someone's sure getting nervous over my lawsuit. They're doing everything they can think of to keep from having to answer my summons. Phoning a good friend in the courthouse I explained to her about the strange call I got from Sgt. Jones. She chuckled when I told her how Jones seemed more than a little upset when I questioned him about the orders he had received.

I asked, "Why are you laughing?"

"It's really kind of funny when you know the whole story. If you can meet me in Ventura before you go to work I'll tell you what is going on."

"Okay, I'll meet you at the White Bib Cafe in twenty minutes." On the way to Ventura it occurred to me that I was lucky to still have a few good friends around who were willing to help. She was waiting in a booth when I arrived.

"Hi Gary, I only have a few minutes, so I will make this brief. You knew Judge West didn't you?"

"Sure I knew him." There had been newspaper headlines about how Judge West and Hugh Gallagher, a lawyer from Santa Paula, were both drowned several weeks ago in a boating accident near the Santa Cruz Islands. Judge West, a popular Municipal Court Judge, had been running for election to the Superior Court. Robert Shaw, another Municipal Court Judge, had filed his papers to run against

West. It was after the filing period had closed that West was killed, making it too late for any other judges or attorneys to file for the judgeship. Governor Reagan then appointed Municipal Court Judge Pollack to the Superior Court position. All these facts had quickly run through my mind. My friends voice returned me quickly to the present. I asked, "What does all this about Judge West have to do with Sgt. Jones from the Marshal's office calling and wanting that summons back?"

She smiled, "That's where the funny part comes in. Soon as this guy Fish found out that Judge West was killed he supposedly did some legal research, he claims that West's Municipal Court position was up for grabs. At election time he had his assistant Ken Cleaver, and his secretary Claire Brotherton, Glen Kuhn, Jim Hronesh and probably even his wife write in his name for Municipal Judge on their ballots."

"You mean that shyster wants to be a judge? Can't you just see him up there on the judge's bench in a black robe looking down on people, sending them away for a maximum sentence just because he doesn't like their looks, or maybe their name happens to be Smith and he remembers fifty years back a guy by the name of Smith that he didn't like."

She laughed, "I told you it was funny, but that isn't all. On county time Claire has been typing all kinds of briefs and legal papers to present to the courts, and Cleaver's researched the law clear back to Cicero to convince the courts that Fish won the election. Fish is now demanding that the Clerk recount all the election ballots to see if anyone got more write-in votes than him. It's estimated the entire ridiculous farce of a recount will cost tax payers over $25,000.00."

"Lord, he wants to be a judge really bad."

"This is where the Marshal's office comes in. Municipal Court Judges have jurisdiction over the Marshal and they appoint him."

"Yes, I knew that."

"So Fish gave the Marshal the word, in no uncertain terms. Soon he'd be a Municipal Court Judge, and if the Marshal did not get the summons back from you damn fast he'd be looking for a new job." My friend left, I sat musing over a cold cup of coffee. Surely I've filed the correct lawsuit against Mr. Fish...could there be anything more fitting to file on him than...*MISUSE AND ABUSE OF LEGAL PROCESS AND CONSPIRACY TO COMMIT THE SAME?*

CHAPTER 15

An old friend in Hollywood, Audie Murphy, knew the troubles I'd run into trying to get a lawyer. He called early one morning to tell me that he'd made an appointment at ten the next day for me to meet with his attorney. This was a break, it made me feel good. Audie was a great person, one whose patriotism for his country had always stirred his emotions toward fairness and justice for everyone. He was well known in the movie industry and I was sure any lawyer connected with Audie would be the finest. I made arrangements to be off work the entire day.

The lawyer's office was in Beverly Hills. It was hot and smoggy, even at nine-thirty. Locating the address I parked at an angle into the curb and put change in the meter for two hours. Inside the door was a large glass-covered directory. The lawyer was Paul Caruso, he was listed there along with numerous associates. The receptionist's desk was on the second floor. Informing me Mr. Caruso was tied up in court the entire morning, she said, "However, he's arranged for you to talk to one of his associates, Mr. Tom Guerin."

A young guy, Guerin extended an aura of confidence. His open friendliness made it easier to tell my story and to present all the corroborating documents which I'd brought in a big cardboard box. Guerin was obviously intrigued with what I'd told him, but carefully withheld any hasty opinions. We agreed my documents should be left there allowing him time to familiarize himself with the situation.

Guerin said he would contact me within a few days.

In response to the summons served on Fish, I received notice that one James E. Dixon had filed an affidavit in Superior Court swearing he was a lawyer. Dixon also swore, he was representing Mr. Fish, who would *especially appear*....but yet, Mr. Fish will not make a *general appearance*... From Dixon's 'double-talk' I deduced that Mr. Fish was to appear, yet...on the other hand he would not appear.

At the specified time and date I was in the Superior Court of Judge Richard Heaton. The clerk called my case and I approached the attorney's table with a slight trepidation born from the fact of my inexperience in Civil Procedure. We were about ten feet from the judge's bench. Putting my briefcase on the table I watched as another man walked up with an extremely large briefcase. Zipping it open, he laid out an array of impressive looking law books. Each one had many small blue markers protruding from their pages. Mr. Dixon, I figured that's who he was, looked over his left shoulder. Staring at my meager supply of papers he sniffed, then looked back at the undeniably bigger and more impressive mound of books and papers on the table before him. Dixon was imbued with confidence and assurance that he could easily overcome the minor distress and the discomfort that my lawsuit was causing his client. He winked at the court clerk, smiled and waved at the bailiff. Turning, he shot a look of camaraderie toward a group of brother lawyers in the rear of the courtroom. Silently he was assuring them he would never let the legal brotherhood down in the forthcoming joust against such a brazen usurper who came to court to do battle in Propria Personae. Last but not least, his courtroom demeanor dictated that he give me a look that was a combination of smirk and condescending pity.

Lord, I wondered where Fish could have dug up this clown. It must have been a real bargain-basement deal.

Judge Heaton, occupied with details from the preceding case, was now tapping his gavel on the bench, indicating he was ready to proceed.

Mr. Dixon led off, he requested that the court dismiss each of the cases I had filed on the basis that both were libel suits and that I had merely put a different heading on the second complaint. He argued that no bond had been placed with the court and that the Summons in the Malicious Prosecution suit was *inadvertently* issued by the clerk's office, thus the court should order the return of the Summons and dismiss both of the cases. I addressed the court, "Your

Honor, I will stipulate that the first case I filed was a libel suit and I was unable to raise a bond of six thousand dollars to file with the court. I will not oppose the court's dismissing the first suit I filed. Now, Your Honor, regarding the second lawsuit. It is a legitimate complaint with cause and filed under the proper charges with more than sufficient merit and it requires no bond. Mr. Dixon is trying to lump the two cases together under the heading of a libel suit, which is not correct."

I continued, "But, even if the court were to agree with Mr. Dixon that both cases came under the heading of a libel suit there is still no cause at this time to dismiss either of them for lack of a bond. I have a Summons in my possession that was issued by the Superior Court Clerk of this county. Now, if the clerk feels that it had been *inadvertently* issued why isn't he here in court today to testify and request the court to order the return of the Summons? Dixon's only contention is that the Summons was *inadvertently* issued by the clerk and hence the court should order me to return it. Your Honor, in researching I've found a statute requiring that the Court Clerk file a bond amounting to ten thousand dollars when he is elected. Also, I've found case law that says the clerk is legally responsible for the actions of his deputy clerks. Any and all of the defendants in the complaint are more than protected and indemnified by the County Clerk's bond of ten thousand dollars which is four thousand more than they would be by my individual bond of five hundred each. By the absence of the County Clerk from this hearing I represent to the court that the clerk feels the Summons is in order and is entirely legal. If this court dismisses my second suit it would be setting a precedent by prohibiting the filing of complaints charging Malicious Prosecution and Abuse of Process, it would lump them all under the heading of Libel and Slander."

Judge Heaton said, "With everybody's approval I will dismiss the first complaint charging libel and we will have that out of the way. Now...I want to make it clear that I do not approve of the Plaintiff appearing here in Propria Personae. The proceedings are liable to be complex and the Plaintiff should have legal representation."

"Judge, I've made *every effort humanly possible* to obtain legal counsel, but to no avail. Mr. Pic'l absolutely *refuses* to acknowledge any type of communication with me. I've contacted numerous other attorneys to no avail. I've talked to a lawyer in L.A. who may agree to represent me but at the present I do not have his definite word."

Dixon got the Judge's attention. "Your Honor, I maintain that the clerk *inadvertently* issued a Summons and the court should order the Plaintiff to deliver that Summons to me at this time."

I spoke up quickly, "Your Honor, have you read my complaint charging Malicious Prosecution?"

"No, I'm sorry, the court hasn't yet had the opportunity to study the complaint."

"Well then, Your Honor, I submit that the court doesn't even have the necessary knowledge to determine if my complaint comes under the category of a libel suit. Thus, there is no way the court at this time can compel me to hand my Summons over to Mr. Dixon."

The judge was silent for several moments, then said, "I'm going to order the Plaintiff to return the Summons to the County Clerk."

Dixon interrupted, "Your Honor, the Plaintiff can give me the Summons right now and I will deliver it to the clerk myself."

It was beginning to dawn on me! It had taken a long time, but now it was coming through. Mr. Fish wanted that Summons in the worst way. This was the reason he had put all the pressure on Bob Hamm, the County Clerk, and the Marshal's office to retrieve the papers. That *Summons* was the only weapon I had had my hands on since all this crap started. Fish knew I could compel him to answer my complaint if I had a Summons, that was the one thing he'd never be able to survive. If only once I could get to the point of taking depositions from Fish and his cohorts under oath and to subpoena records I could expose their entire sinister machinations.

"Your Honor, I am here in this court in Pro-Per, I have no legal representation. Mr. Dixon definitely has me at great disadvantage due to his superior knowledge of Civil law. Accordingly I'm asking the court for a continuance until I can contact my lawyer in Los Angeles." Judge Heaton continued the case until two that afternoon, at which time I was to return with my attorney's decision.

On the phone I brought Guerin up to date on the situation. He said, "I talked with Mr. Caruso, *he agreed* our office would handle your case for a five thousand dollar retainer."

"That's great Tom, I can raise the money. I have some left in my pension fund and I can borrow the rest from friends and relatives."

"Tell Judge Heaton *we will take your case* and ask him for a two week continuance. We will get together in the meantime and chart our course."

"Thanks Tom, I'll call you tomorrow."

Upon returning to the courtroom the clerk said, "The Judge is still in his chambers."

"Please ask if I could see him for a moment?"

She gave a light rap on the door then entered. In a moment she returned, "The Judge says for you to go on in." Heaton motioned me to have a seat. I had known him for many years and had always felt at ease in his presence.

"Judge, I talked to my lawyer, he's taking my case. I'm going to Los Angeles soon and give him a retainer. He instructed me to call Mr. Dixon and see if he'd agree to a two week continuance. I called him, but he won't agree to anything."

"Alright, I will make a court order without his agreement. The case is continued for two weeks." He called his clerk and instructed her to make a record of the continuance.

"You know Judge, it bothers me...what in hell makes people do some of the things they do? Take Jim Hronesh for instance. He's likable, his friends have always gone out of their way to try and help him. I know I have. Then the first thing you know he stabs you in the back and is trying to ruin you."

"Gary, many years ago back east in college, an old professor used to tell the class, 'The *world* is full of bitchery.'"

"Judge, I can sure believe that."

"Gary, you are young and healthy, you could go out and make a living doing lots of things. Why do you *want to make trouble* for Berenson?" The Judge's question took me by surprise. At the same time it triggered a quick flash of anger.

"I will tell you Judge!...when Berenson *killed* that Grand Jury investigation he covered up serious criminal violations and gave a free rein to all his associates to continue their corrupt conspiracies. His orders were such a completely *deliberate obstruction of justice* directed against the rights and welfare of the people that it just *can't be* ignored."

Heaton didn't say anything. Rising from my chair I thanked him for continuing my case and left the chambers. Temporary quarters for the Superior Court had been erected a short distance to the east of the main courthouse. Stepping out of the courtroom I was in a small patio-like area surrounded by other temporary offices. A few yards to my right was a drinking fountain, I walked over and took a drink. Leaning against the building and relaxing a minute I suddenly realized I was awfully tired and beat. To my left the doors of the courtroom opened, Judge Heaton exited, he headed toward the east entrance of the courthouse. Walking in the same direction I entered the larger building at another location, and went swiftly up a narrow flight of stairs. From this location I had a view of the lengthy second floor corridor. Heaton was going down the hall, I watched him enter the office of Jerome Berenson, the Presiding Judge of the Superior Court. I recalled the story Heaton had told me..."*The world is full of bitchery!*" I wasn't so sure of the world, but this county courthouse sure as hell was full of it.

I went to the County Treasurer's office on the first floor where I withdrew the money that I had contributed toward my pension. It represented all my plans to retire, maybe do some fishing and a little traveling here and there. Nothing out of the ordinary, just being able to sense a small feeling of security and freedom. Well, tomorrow morning I would take the pension money and what I'd borrowed to L.A. and give it to the lawyer.

But before I left a call came from Tom Guerin. "Listen Gary, I thought I would call you early and save you a trip down here."

"Why, what's the matter?"

"Something has happened, at the very last minute yesterday in the afternoon Caruso called me into his office, he advised me that we *wouldn't* be able to handle your case."

I was getting so used to my heart thumping and dropping down into my stomach that it didn't bother me nearly so much this time when it hit the bottom. "Didn't Caruso give you any reason at all why he wouldn't handle the case Tom?"

"No, Caruso was pretty vague. I'm very sorry, there is nothing I can do, I'm a junior associate in the office."

"Alright Tom. I am going to drive down to your office and pick up my papers today."

Guerin wasn't in when I arrived, his secretary let me take the large box containing my records from his office. I was loading it in my car when Guerin walked up. He said, "I want you to know that I'm deeply sorry I can't handle your case. I studied it carefully and discussed the facts and evidence with several other lawyers in the office, they agreed with me that you *definitely* have a *great* case."

Guerin's sincerity and his legal evaluation of my problems took a little bit of the sting out of this latest blow. "Why at the very last moment did Paul Caruso change his mind?"

"I don't know."

"Could it be that he got a *long distance phone call* from Ventura yesterday afternoon?" This seemed to embarrass him. "That's alright Tom, the way I figure it, somewhere along the line in this country a man is entitled to legal representation."

"I feel very bad about this, I don't know the answer. I just don't know."

"Judge Heaton ordered I would have to get an attorney because he won't let me appear on my own behalf. You're a lawyer, tell me, how much time, effort and money is a person required to expend trying to get a lawyer?"

"I realize what you're getting at Gary, but I really don't know the answer."

I related the advice the lawyer in Ventura had given me, that I should go to L.A. and search for a lawyer that had known Mr. Fish in the past and who hated his guts. Tom laughed, he agreed, no one should be forced to search for an attorney with such a requirement necessary.

"The only suggestion I can possibly make may be odious to you, you could go to the ACLU."

"You mean the American Civil Liberties Union?"

"Yes, I just don't know what else to tell you."

Shaking hands with Tom Guerin I thanked him. I felt a genuine respect and liking for him. I was certain if he'd been in the driver's seat of that law firm things would've been much different. Driving east on Wilshire Blvd. toward downtown I pulled over to a phone booth in a gas station. A listing for the ACLU was in the book, the address was in central L.A.. I dialed, a man answered, he wanted to know what the problem was. I explained that it was a long story and quite complex. He agreed I should come to his office to discuss the matter.

It didn't take very long to eliminate the 'ACLU' as a possible source of representation for a citizen in dire need of legal assistance. The interviewer for the Civil Liberties Union informed me that they were only interested in cases that could be carried to the Supreme Court and would produce decisions to limit the investigative powers of police agencies. He described one case the ACLU was presently working very hard on. It involved a member of a minority group who had passed out in his car on an off-ramp of the freeway. Officers observed the car and while checking out the driver's condition they found narcotics in the vehicle. The occupant of the car was arrested for a narcotic violation. The ACLU maintained the defendant had parked far enough off the ramp that he wasn't a traffic hazard, thus the officers had no legal right to a search and seizure.

"Well, an investigation of my case would expose corruption in the Judicial System. That sure as hell is just as important as limiting police investigative power that you are so concerned about." He was appalled, he started waving his arms. I said, "Forget it pal, just forget that I was here and believe me...so will I." Christ, had I really fallen so low I had to come *begging* to scum like this. It was late, heading west toward home the traffic was jammed five lanes abreast. The smog hung in a heavy pall over the city, the sun was a huge fire ball dropping behind the Hollywood Hills, everything was swathed in a red glare. The car seemed to operate itself as everyone drove slowly bumper to bumper.

My mind drifted away from the traffic problems. I recalled the events that had occurred in Ventura the last several months. Things were going just as I'd told the Grand Jury they would. The Ventura City Manager was forced from office, County Administrator Enoch, his assistant and the head of the Planning and Zoning Department left overnight. Penfield's Grand Jury had been ripping into all of them at the same time they'd been making the secret investigation into Supervisor Robinson. A close-knit group of conspirators had gone to the Grand Jury and testified that Robinson took money for campaign funds but it was really a bribe to vote on zoning permits for a sand and gravel company. The Grand Jury served a Summons on Robinson's Assist., Ben Martinez, ordering him to appear before them. That night Martinez suffered a massive heart attack and died. Bob Hooks and Bill Jones were former employees of Robinson, they gave secret testimony to the Grand Jury that was extremely harmful to Robinson and Martinez.

It was a few months before this that James Hronesh and Lane Martin had told me about the *big sum of money* they'd gotten from the *secret group* of wealthy, powerful men in Ventura. This money was handed to them to *frame* Robinson and Reiman and the Chief of Police. Hronesh was a close friend of Bob Hooks, I had spotted Jim and Kuhn going into his office so often I'd become very curious why they were spending so much time with him, and Mal King *knew* more than eight months ago that Hronesh and Martin had all this money, he had made a report to Deem, and *they had told Penfield,* and on top of that...I'd appeared before the Grand Jury...they were *fully aware* of a giant conspiracy to frame the government officials.

A short time after Ben Martinez died the Grand Jury indicted Robinson for allegedly taking a bribe. Superior Court Judge Shaw was subpoenaed as a defense witness, *he swore* that a star witness for the prosecution had committed perjury. Kenneth Haymaker was representing Robinson, when Judge Robert Shaw made his *amazing statement* that a crucial witness was lying, Haymaker merely asked Shaw a few piddling questions and allowed him to leave the stand. I just couldn't believe Haymaker had passed up such an outstanding opportunity to bring out testimony regarding this lying prosecution witness. It could have been a turning point in the case. Anyway, if Judge Berenson hadn't *killed* the Grand Jury investigation the *entire conspiracy* would've been exposed and Ben Marintez would be alive today. It was murder...no matter how you looked at it...just plain murder. When Judge Berenson allowed the Grand Jury to serve the Summons on Martinez and to indict Robinson, all the time knowing a sinister group had placed a large sum of money on their heads to frame them, he'd *sentenced* Martinez to death, his heart and mind simply couldn't withstand the blow. And Robinson was found guilty and sentenced to prison.

My attention returned to driving the car, traffic had thinned out and was moving faster. I slipped to the right over several white lines and settled down into a slower taffic lane. My thoughts had become completely absorbed in reviewing these events. Now having to drive carefully, my thoughts returned to the present.

I had quit my job at the cut-rate gas station. Obviously it was impossible to exist on the income derived from all the hours I was working. Driving between home and work, I'd noticed an old dingy, grey building on a curve in the highway, it had two gas pumps in the front and a tiny auto repair shop in the rear. Occassionally I would stop to chat with the old gentleman who operated the gas station. Mervyn was his name, a nice old fellow. The property was very run down and Merv was doing little business. Getting to a point where his health was poor, he couldn't take the long hours.

By now the only asset my wife and I had left to our name was a trust deed of thirty five hundred on the house we had sold in L.A. when we decided to return to Ventura. We both agreed and vowed that we were not going to leave Ventura under the conditions that Mr. Fish had decreed for us. His decree having been that my family and I leave Ventura absolutely and completely destitute, head over heels in debt, and with no prospect of gainful employment for the present or future.

Accompanied with conflicting emotions, mainly a hell of a lot of plain old-fashioned consternation for our future, especially if I was to remain in Ventura County...I offered Merv the trust deed plus a monthly payment for a specified number of years for his gas station which also included the property. It was the middle of summer and

I suddenly found myself in the gas station and auto repair business. A beat-up old cash register had been included in the deal. I had to borrow thirty five dollars in change to put in the till for operating money.

The following months slipped by swiftly, I kept the station open from six a.m. until eleven at night, plus working in the garage after closing hours repairing tires and doing numerous other chores for customers who would be back early the next morning. I scraped and painted inside and outside the building, hauled away old junk and shrubs that needed to be trimmed down so the gas station could be spotted from the highway. The business was building up due partly to keeping long hours and the overall available service which I was offering. The highway passing in front of the station went to a lake and recreational area and we were picking up more customers from Los Angeles who came to camp and fish there. Cleaning up another section of the building I moved in some Pepsi and soda pop coolers. Then for seventy five dollars I applied for and received my license to sell beer and wine.

Leaving the warm, comfortable bed at five a.m. was rough, but pleasant compensation was attached to the shock of rising so early. Few people were stirring at the break of day, the air was clean and fresh. To the east the sky was miraculously turning from a pale blue to a warm rosy glow, it presaged the arrival of the sun over the hill behind the station.

As the sun arrived, so did the first customers of the new day. I pumped gas and washed windshields. Between gas customers I ran over to the store at the far end of the building and sold bread, milk, beer and toilet paper to grocery customers. Then promptly at seven thirty, George, the mechanic would arrive and we'd open the repair garage at the opposite end of the building.

My mind jogged back to the present as the freeway narrowed down and converged into the old two lane highway leading into Ojai Valley. A few more miles and I'd be home. The vagaries of the old highway would not permit the luxury of my thoughts returning to its dissection of the last few months events as I had been doing while cruising home on the freeway.

The next day I was back on the job. Increasing activity and the long hours at the station and small store had been paying off. We were starting to catch up on our debts which were overwhelming us. Summer was turning to winter and business slowed down some. It was a new year and a different Grand Jury would be in power.

I realized that Jerome Berenson had been the Presiding Judge of the Superior Court for the last *ten* years. And from this *powerful position* he *personally picked* most of the Grand Jurors, and he also approved the rest of them who were picked by the other judges who were under him. Naming a foreman was the *crowning touch* which gave Berenson *complete control* of the Grand Jury. From the lofty throne of Presiding Judge of the Superior Court, Berenson also had the power to *strategically assign* any critical case to the judges of his own choice. Theoretically all of the Superior Court Judges convened every year to choose their presiding judge. The *fact* that Berenson had been *chosen for ten successive years* didn't speak so much for his *judicial ability* as it did for the *raw political and financial powers* he wielded behind the scenes.

Berenson had already appointed his foreman for the new Grand Jury, I knew from *his choice* of David Donlon that I wasn't going to have any better luck than I'd had with Dr. Penfield. Donlon was a member of an old-line, wealthy ranching family in the Oxnard area and long time friend of the former Grand Juror, who had betrayed his trust to the people by revealing secret evidence to the Oxnard lawyer, Mr. Blais.

Even though realizing there was no way I could force the new Grand Jury to take any action, I wrote a letter to Donlon requesting and demanding that he contact the Judicial Council regarding Judge Berenson's misconduct. Also, I demanded that Donlon contact the State Attorney General's Office with a request that they assist the Grand Jury in making an investigation. I made copies of Dunham's record as a lawyer, and the results and determinations of the State Bar Association regarding the disciplinary action taken against him. I also sent documents regarding Fish and the alias of Erwin he was using and pointed out the discrepancies in the marriage and birth certificates used to establish his identity.

Berenson's *arrogance* and *his total disregard of judicial integrity* was fantasically reflected in *his appointing Harrison Dunham* to sit on the bench as a judge. I pondered if this was a *macabre* move on Berenson's part, relaying a hidden message to me that all my efforts to expose them were in vain.

My letter along with documents to Donlon were put in a large manila envelope. Sending them certified mail, I requested a return receipt. The four members of the Criminal Complaints Committee appointed by the Foreman Mr. Donlon, were each supplied with a copy of the letter informing them of the specific information and demands that I had mailed to Mr. Donlon.

Several months prior to sending the letter to Donlon, the same material had been sent to Ralph Bennett, County Supervisor of the district in which I lived. It was mailed certified, I received a signed receipt back from his office verifying the fact he got the letter. However, Supervisor Bennett refused to answer. Moreover, Bennett later denied that he had *ever received* the information or *had any knowledge* of it.

CHAPTER 16

A cold winter, even for coastal California had hit. The mountains towering above the Ojai Valley were snow covered and strong winds whistled down the mountain passes in icy blasts. By midmorning the mailman in his blue and white G.I. truck pulled alongside my store leaving his usual assortment of advertisements and bills in the mail box. More than a month and a half now of waiting expectantly and I still hadn't gotten an answer from the foreman of the Grand Jury. Apparently Donlon, in his *official arrogance,* backed by the extreme wealth of his family, felt he had no obligations to answer such an accusatory and rude letter. On the other hand, maybe he'd received orders from Judge Berenson not to give an answer. It didn't seem possible, by the standards of justice and equal protection of the law established by the founding fathers for the protection of the people that the foreman of a Grand Jury could scheme to 'cover-up' such serious crimes merely by *refusing* to acknowledge the evidence of their existence.

Thinking back to my early days as a policeman and my training at the L.A.P.D., it was deemed that an outright 'omission' of your sworn duty was just as serious as any other major criminal violation of the Penal Code. And beyond that, a definite ethical and moral infringement of your position of trust and fidelity. Our magnificent, so-called fair and equitable government was giving me the 'good old shaft.' Documentation of the entire proceedings as they progressed was the *only method* I had of ever being able to prove the events as they *truly happened.*

After waiting for the answer from Donlon which I realized would never come, I felt it reasonable to send another letter requesting acknowledgement of some sort. Another three weeks elapsed after sending my second letter to the Grand Jury. It was now more than two months from the time I sent my original letter to Mr. Donlon before I received the following terse communication:

"Dear Sir: I am writing to inform you that I have received your two letters to the Grand Jury dated January 17th and March 12th. Both of these letters *were referred* to the Complaints Committee for review. I am sure that you understand that *the deliberations* of the Grand Jury are *'secret'* and are kept in *'strict confidence'* by it's members.

Therefore, if the Committee *sees fit,* suggestions will be made to the proper county officials. No report of the Committee's findings will be made to you by the Grand Jury." Signed, David J. Donlon, Foreman Grand Jury, J. Cole, Secretary.

One of the four members of the Criminal Complaint Committee was Joan Cole who had supposedly studied the letters and evidence. She was also David J. Donlon's secretary in the Grand Jury. I did a little background check on Joan Cole. She had gotten a divorce not too long ago, her previous name was Joan Jones. After her divorce Joan married Carl Cole, a lawyer in the most prestigious law firm in Ventura County. The firm was owned by Ben Nordman, Berenson's law partner before Berenson was appointed a Superior Court Judge. I discovered that Ben Nordman was a powerful controller and legal advisor for the Bank of A. Levy. After all, his mother was Helen Levy before she married Ben Nordman, Sr..

Using the telephone and a little conversation, I contacted two members of the Criminal Complaints Committee. Both *vehemently denied* that Donlon *had ever* brought any evidence about Dunham or Fish or Berenson's corruption *to their attention.* Sure as hell, this whole thing was becoming more involved and smelling worse all the time. Berenson had not only appointed his friend David J. Donlon, Grand Jury foreman, he had also appointed Joan Cole. I wondered how many other phonies Berenson had slipped into this Grand Jury and other juries the past ten years since he had become Presiding Judge in perpetuity. No doubts remained in my mind...Donlon had joined in the conspiracy to cover up all the crimes of the past, now they were *faced* with concealing Berenson's evil corruption in *killing* the preceding Grand Jury's investigation.

I had plenty of evidence and knowledge of what was going on, but sometimes it was so hard to believe that I wondered if I wasn't really dreaming. Like a jigsaw puzzle, the pieces were all there, but they refused to fit into place like they should. One of the most persistent pieces refusing to fit was, *why* would Judge Berenson put himself out on such a flimsy, dangerous limb as he'd done merely to cover up for Fish and Dunham? Even a misguided loyalty to a brother lawyer surely couldn't compel Berenson to go as far as he had for those two shysters. All the worries and mental strain of the last few years had dulled my thoughts, exhausting any comprehensive concentration into the heart of the problem.

The letter Donlon had sent outlining what the Grand Jury *wasn't* going to do continued to irritate me no little bit. I had one of my strong feelings that everything about that letter was wrong, especially since two of the members of the Complaint Committee had denied receiving any information from Donlon. It took only a few days to discover that the letter sent to me by Donlon was not written on the typewriter available to the Grand Jury at the courthouse. Several more days of nosing around and I determined that the letter was typed by Joan Cole at the law office of Ben Nordman in Oxnard. Also at Nordman's office Donlon had engaged in conversation with Judge Berenson regarding the information I had sent to the Grand Jury. I knew that Berenson was mighty close to Nordman, they were law partners and had lived next door to each other for many years, but why the meetings with Donlon at Nordman's office? For now it had to remain just another piece of the jigsaw puzzle that wouldn't go into place.

Still working long hours and seven days a week, I'd learned that the Alcohol Beverage Control Department was planning to have a drawing for liquor store licenses the coming fall. The big obstacle stopping me was the six thousand dollars the State required as a deposit before I could enter the drawing. Weeks were spent going from one savings and loan to another with no luck. The last day to post the money with ABC was rapidly drawing close. Finally a bank I'd done business with for many years agreed to a short term loan with my house as collateral, however I'd have to furnish a letter of commitment from a S&L company that they'd increase the loan on my house in the event I drew a liquor license.

After spending one hell'uva lot of time running around making arrangements I finally had a certified check in my hand for over six thousand, made out to ABC. I sped to Santa Barbara and deposited the check with the District Office. Even if I was fortunate enough to win a license there'd still be a slue of hardships to overcome. There would be a terrific increase in my monthly house payments, plus the added interest on the short-term loan at the bank. I'd need a lot of money for the liquor it would take to stock the store. There was no guarantee that business would increase enough to pay all the added bills and expenses. And if I didn't win a license I'd be stuck with the interest on the loan anyway. With all these worries and conflicting nightmares rampaging in my head, I did indeed wonder if it wouldn't have been better to take the easy way out and gone along with the Fish's insane program.

Along with the population increase of Ventura County it had been determined that seven licences would be made available for the drawing. Shortly before the filing date was closed I learned that more than sixty-five people had put their money up and applied for the licenses. This meant I had about one chance out of ten to win. That was mighty poor odds for me. I couldn't ever remember in my life winning anything in a lottery or drawing. During the last days before the drawing my mind was plagued with anticipatory worries, both negative and affirmative. Summoning all my will power I wiped the thoughts of the lottery from my mind.

The next day after the drawing I called the Alcoholic Beverage Control and asked the secretary if she could give me the names of the winners.

"Yes, I have a list right here on my desk." She began reading the names, number one, number two, by the time she hit number six I was ready to hang up the phone. "And last, but not the least, here is number seven." The secretary proceeded to read off my name. In all reality I could hardly believe it. I knew it was going to cost me plenty of cash to stock the store and make payments on everything, but it was still forging a step ahead in my efforts to free me and my family from the Fish's hateful decree.

Number seven, lucky seven, the last chance, I'd won it. Perhaps it was an omen, encouragement from a higher source not to give up. Then again, maybe it was only a tidbit, tossed my way and designed to lure me into far deeper water before delivering the last and final heavy blow.

Several trips were necessary to ABC where I filled out affidavits swearing to the veracity of my personal and financial background, and as to the source of the money for filing my license application.

My fingerprints were taken, they would be checked in the FBI files in Washington, D.C. for any criminal background. A felony record as far as California was concerned was a cause to deny a person a liquor license. The secretary handed me a large sheet of paper with instructions that it was a Notice of Intention to sell liquor on my premises and by law it was necessary to post the sign in my window for a thirty day period.

Many weeks after the posting period was over and the sign had been removed, I noticed the sedan pull up and park in front. A man wearing a blue business suit entered and introduced himself as Cliff Lowen, an agent from ABC. His bearing was official but friendly and straight forward with what he had to say.

"Well Gary, it seems we have a serious problem. We received a letter from the Ventura County Planning Dept., notifying us your property is substandard and they request that we do not issue you a liquor license."

"What's the big idea? I've had my license several weeks now, the sheriff's office inspected my property and approved everything and the posting period is over, so what are they trying to pull?"

"You mean you've heard nothing about this from the county, you never received a copy of the letter they sent to us?"

"No, I've heard nothing from the county about this whatsoever."

"That's damned funny. They are required to send you a copy of everything they send us. I'll tell you what, tomorrow morning when I get back to Santa Barbara I'll call the Planning Department and check into it."

I thanked him and he left. *Here we go again!* I must have stirred them up with my letter to Donlon. Next morning my curiosity was bothering me, I called Santa Barbara and got Lowen on the phone. I asked what he had found out.

"There's something damn odd about this whole thing. I talked to a man in the Planning Department about their letter asking *us to deny* your license. When I told him we'd already issued the license to you and we didn't intend to take any action, the guy said, 'Well, I guess there's been a mistake. Do me a favor, just *tear* our letter up and *throw* it away.'"

I told Lowen, "There are certain people in the courthouse doing everything in their sneaky power to run me out of the county. This is another of their *under-handed tricks* trying to get you to close me up. Do me a favor and don't destroy the letter. Put it in your files and save it. I want you to know I really appreciate your honesty and the way you handled this problem."

The agent said, "Don't worry about it. I do my job just the way I'm supposed to, there's no one can influence me to do otherwise."

Two weeks later I went to Ventura on business, when I returned my wife said, "A man from the building department was here."

"What did he want?"

"He said he had orders from his boss to inspect our storeroom."

"Did he say why he wanted to inspect it?"

"No, he just said he had *orders* to look around for *something*, he was *real vague*. Finally he said he would go check with his boss." I knew they were up to something and I had better stay close to the store. The next day while working in the storeroom, my wife called back to me saying, "That county man is back again."

Out the window I saw a county car parked at the far end of the building. Two men peered in one of the windows. My wife pointed out, "The tall one wearing the sport shirt is the one who was here yesterday." The other man was shorter and wore a suit. I walked out where they stood by the window and asked if I could help them. The man in the suit came on real hard.

"Yeah, we have an order from the sheriff to inspect this place."

"An order from the sheriff! What are you talking about? Let me see this order you have."

He handed me a photo copy of a sheriff's department document. I looked at it, what the hell, it was a copy of the report the sheriff's department made six months ago when I first applied for my liquor license. I said, "Where did you get this paper?"

"I got it from Capt. De Sanno in the sheriff's office." Snatching the paper from my hand he gruffly ordered, "We're going inside and inspect this place."

"Hold on a minute, I want some identification from you." He had a business card with the county seal embossed in gold in the corner. It said he was Donald Wright, from the Planning Department. "This is your name, Donald Wright?"

"Yes, and I am running out of time, let's go inside, I am going to inspect this place."

"There isn't going to be any inspection. That piece of paper you have from Captain De Sanno doesn't mean a damned thing...you've been sent here for no other reason than to harass me!"

Coming on harder all the time, the man in the suit said, "Well, you can let me inspect...or I'm going to give it to you the *hard way.*"

I'd done my level best to keep my temper under control, but his *threat of the hard way* was too much. It completely blew the safety valve. "Come on you son-of-a-bitch, the *hard way suits me* just fine. Let's have at it," I moved toward him.

"No, no, I don't mean I'm going to fight you. *I mean I'm going to kill your liquor license with the ABC Department.*"

"You go ahead and try to do anything you want, but get your ass off my property, I mean now!" Barely controlling myself, I started toward the man in the suit, he jumped in his car. The other guy in the sport shirt had never spoken a word during the entire incident. They went south, heading toward town and the courthouse.

The phone rang early the next morning, it was Lowen, from ABC. "What's going on down there?"

"What do you mean?"

"Well, I just got through talking on the phone to a man in the Ventura Planning Dept., he called and swears you are a completely no good so-and-so and wants me to take action against your license."

"What are you going to do?"

"I have no intention of doing anything against your license just because that guy doesn't like you. But listen, why don't you cooperate with them, try to get along?"

"Hell, do you think I like this? They've got their orders from the big shots to harass me. They don't have *any intention* of trying to cooperate with me about anything. What was his reasons for wanting to inspect my building?"

"He claims he wanted to make sure there is a fire wall between your repair shop and your liquor store."

I reminded Cliff, "When I got my license you said in your opinion the gas pumps were too close to the liquor store, and it didn't seem compatible to combine gas and liquor sales in such close proximity. Even though I was fearful of losing the income from the gas station I agreed to cooperate with you, I removed the pumps, the car hoist and the repair equipment from the garage and now the entire area is nothing more than a storage room. There is no need for a firewall in the building."

"I know Gary, I was at your place just a few days ago and checked everything myself. But listen, just to keep everybody happy, will you let me phone the guy back and tell him you will let him inspect?"

"Alright, you have treated me fair and square, go ahead and call them." After talking to Lowen I got to thinking about the county guy in the suit, the more I thought about him the madder I got. Digging through my desk where I'd thrown his card yesterday I finally found it, Donald Wright, County Planning Department. Dialing the number I asked for the head man. Explaining to him who I was and what had happened yesterday, I told him that I sure as hell didn't intend to take any more crap from Donald Wright.

"Just a minute," he said, "We haven't had any reports or requests to inspect your store and your description doesn't sound like Don Wright. Let me do a little checking."

It wasn't ten minutes after I hung up when a county car pulled up in front. The driver came in, I'd never seen him before, he asked, "Are you the person who just called the planning department about Mr. Wright?"

"That's correct, I sure did."

"Well, I'm Donald Wright," he flashed his county identification card, it included his name and picture.

I showed him the business card with his name on it, "Is this your card?"

"Yes it is."

I told him about the tough guy from the county yesterday. He was extremely perturbed over the fact that someone was using his name and card to cover up their dirty business. Wright swore he would make a complete report to his boss and they would find out who the employee was who had impersonated him.

Within minutes after Wright was gone another county car pulled up and three men came in. A large heavy set, dark complexioned man introduced himself as Salvadore from the building department. He stated he was there to inspect my property. I didn't need a ton of bricks falling on me to clue me in that this whole operation was *a set-up* of some kind designed to put me *out* of business.

"Listen Salvadore, yesterday there was a county man came here saying he was from the planning department to inspect. He gave me a phony name...now you claim you are here from the building dept. to inspect. I want to know who in the hell gave you orders to come here and just what it is that you are looking for?"

Salvadore said, *"I've been sent here to inspect and it's none of your business who sent me."*

"It sure as hell is my business and I want to know who gave you these orders!" Salvadore headed for the storeroom, I leaped in front of him. "Nobody is going to be running around my property until I find out what's behind this thing."

Salvadore was madder than hell. "You mean you're not going to let me inspect this place?"

"You heard me the first time. Now get the hell out of here!"

Salvadore's face was red as a beet, he glared fiercely, "By God, *you'll be sorry*. I will get a court order and come back here and go through this place with a fine-tooth comb."

"Go ahead and get a court order. I can't wait to appear in court, I'll sure as hell find out who's behind you and why." Salvadore and his two men left.

Months rolled by, things were going smooth, business was on the increase, any loss of income from closing the gas station and garage was being overcome. I'd written letters to all five county supervisors and got back receipts from the post office verifying they had been received. But it was the same old bullshit. Never an answer of any description from those so-called *representatives* of the citizens and taxpayers.

I'd tried almost every avenue of procedure known and available to a citizen to expose the rampant corruption and political power that was being used to cover-up the criminal conspiracy in our local government. Buried deep in a recess of my mind I'd been thinking seriously of another approach to the problem. The *Grand Jury* was so completely corrupted and dominated by Judge Jerome Berenson it was a waste of time to consider contacting them again. Unless I could find a lawyer who was fearless, totally faithful to his client, and absolutely uncorruptible who would go ahead with my lawsuit there appeared to be no hope. I'd contacted the Governor's office by mail and phone practically begging him to order an investigation by the State Attorney General. What in hell else could a person do against the formidable roadblocks that were constantly being thrown in their path at every turn in the road.

A statewide primary election was coming up in June, it included election of local officials. There was still time to file for the position of County Supervisor. My house and business were both within the Third Supervisorial District. Maybe this was just what we needed, some real old-fashion American politics to return solid standards of justice and due process to the courthouse. After paying a filing fee and other costs the county required I had over five hundred dollars invested in my latest effort to bring the truth forth from darkness to light.

I knew full well it was going to be uphill all the way and would take a lot more money, time and effort plus neglecting my business and property before it was all over. A group of very knowledgeable, and patriotic citizens concerned over the sad condition our county government was in, made small cash donations, also contributions of their time and effort to my campaign. Two men besides myself were challenging 'Hoot' Bennett, the incumbent politician. He had never been elected by the voters. Governor Ronald Reagan had appointed him to the position at a time when it had been vacant.

Candidates had received requests from various civic groups and political organizations to appear before them and give a short, time controlled speech taking in their stance and philosophies on issues pertinent to the voters. A necessary part of a campaign was making these guest appearances before the groups and discussing every type problem imaginable hoping to land a vote.

One invitation I got appeared to offer just the right opportunity I had been waiting for. All four of us as candidates were invited to appear before an influential group of women. The political meeting was to be held at the home of a wealthy, socially prominent lady in Ojai, and conducted by the Ventura County Branch of the American Association of University Women. It was scheduled for eight in the evening, I noted it was a quarter to eight as I drove up the winding drive. It was truly a lovely setting. Approaching the summit of the sloping wooded drive I saw the tops of beautiful mountains that rose above the town of Ojai. The drive widened into large level grounds interspersed with groupings of shrubs and flowers. The parking area was full of expensive cars, people were strolling toward a building to the left of the main residence. It was late spring, the mild twilight glow ushered in a strong fragrance of flowers and fresh mown lawns extending a pleasant welcome.

I joined the movement towards the smaller building. Inside the furnishings were comfortable. It appeared it was once the original home, later converted into a combination summer cottage or guest quarters. In a corner of the large room I saw two of my politically aspiring opponents seated and drinking coffee, I took the chair next to them. A friendly lady appeared with a cup of coffee and a plate of cookies. The room filled with ladies, a few husbands had tagged along. Bennett, the incumbent arrived and we all four sat in straight-backed chairs together in the corner.

A small trim woman with short gray hair introduced herself as an officer of the association and coordinator of this evening's event. At the same time she acquainted us with the lady who was the hostess and owner of the home.

The first candidate, Jack De Long, a post office employee, spoke mostly in generalities, what he was going to do for the people when he became elected. Joe Bravo, the second speaker's background was solely in education, mainly at the grammar school and junior high level. He used his allotted time assuring the audience that, without any question, every child would be guaranteed a more than adequate education if he was successful in being elected as the supervisor.

Bennett utilized his five minutes touting the financial advantages for the county in taking over a large abandoned Air Force base to convert it into a modern commercial and passenger transportation center. He painted a beautiful picture of a giant air terminal in the county and the increased employment and monetary benefits that would accrue from a major airport. My mind traveled to the old air base and explored the dilapidated barracks, outmoded hangers and the lumpy landing strip from the World War 11 era. There were no sophisticated electronic systems available necessary to operate such a proposed airport. The entire project would run into hundreds of millions. And bucking this was a majority of citizens in the city of Camarillo dead set against the very idea of an airport so near their community. The landing pattern was directly overhead, the resulting noise, smog and increased vehicle traffic that would ensue would be to their notion, completely unacceptable.

There was no need to engage in a full blown disagreement with 'Hoot' Bennett over the airport issue at this time. After all, the air base wasn't even in his supervisorial district. Tonight I was prepared to utilize my three hundred seconds of speaking time discussing and explaining the incredible cover-up of corruption within our county government. I exposed the entire fantastic background of Harrison Dunham, and the huge sum of money paid to James Hronesh and Lane Martin to frame Supervisor Robinson, City Manager Reiman and the Chief of Police. And how Berenson had ordered the Grand Jury to kill it's investigation into this political corruption.

Bennett interrupted with loud indignation, "Why Judge Berenson doesn't have any authority over the Grand Jury. He couldn't halt a Grand Jury investigation if he wanted to."

"Well he sure did it Bennett, and you know it."

"What do you mean I know it?"

"I mailed all of this information to you and to each of the other supervisors and you people covered it up."

"I never knew *anything* about this until right now."

"The hell you didn't." I had the post office receipts in my hand along with copies of all the documents I had sent him. I thrust them toward him, "Here are the records right here, signed by your office staff. Look at them."

He refused to even glance at the papers I thrust toward him. His eyes ferreted around the room. Lying he said, "I *never* received any of the information you say you sent me."

"If that's so, how do you explain the fact that at several meetings you discussed these crimes with the other supervisors? Do you still deny right here and now you know nothing about these matters?"

The glib politician suddenly changed his tune. "By golly, if such corruption is true, I'll call a press conference first thing tomorrow. The public should certainly know all these facts."

"That's great...when and where are we going to have this press conference tomorrow?"

"Well, I'll give you a call in the morning and let you know."

The small trim lady, the coordinator of the meeting had leaped from her chair, she stood in the center of the room, shock on her face. Whether it was the subject I had brought up or the intensity of the discussion between me and Bennett that had upset her I could not tell.

"Gentlemen," she switched the subject, "I think we should stick with the airport issue. Maybe *our* Supervisor would give the ladies of this club some ideas on how they could participate in studying his airport proposal." Apparently as coordinator of the meeting she felt it should be conducted as more of a social get-together with tea and crumpets, but I had a strange feeling she was interposing, covering for Bennett. There was little doubt in my mind, I had brought up a sordidness and corruption that even though being true, had no place at any meeting of the American Association of University Women. Bennett proceeded to present the ladies with information describing the type of aircraft proposed for use at the airport and a relatively low level of noise they were capable of maintaining. The University Women resolved to form a committee to study Supervisor Bennett's plans.

As I left the meeting several husbands approached and shook my hand. They expressed deep interest in the subject I had brought up. "*Why* are our county authorities tolerating such a situation and *why* has nothing ever appeared in the Star Free Press?"

"Well you have seen and heard Bennett, with politicians of his stripe what else could you expect!"

The Public Employees Assoc. of Ventura County was presenting a 'Meet Your Political Candidate Forum' several evenings after the meeting in Ojai. They'd scheduled it to be held in the Ventura High

School auditorium. All candidates for U.S. Congress and the State Assembly were to be present along with all the candidates running for three of the Supervisorial districts in the county.

I parked as near the high school as possible and walked across Main Street to the auditorium. Glancing in the front door I saw the room was half filled already. The crowd milling around in front of the auditorium and the stream of others coming across the school lawn was sure to pack the house. Looking back in the door again I saw the huge stage of the auditorium, chairs were arranged across it with a microphone standing near the speakers podium. My briefcase held all the documents and receipts necessary in the event someone wanted verification, tonight I was ready, I intended to lay it right on the line.

Someone called my name, Ray Charles, Assist. Manager of the Employees Assoc. came toward me through the crowd. "Hi Ray, how have you been?"

"Oh pretty good. Listen, Palmer wants to talk to you before you go up on the stage."

"What does he want?"

"I don't know, but he gave me strict orders to find you and tell you to be sure and see him."

Wandering around I finally found Al standing in a corner near the entrance of the auditorium. "Ray says you wanted to see me Al, that it was important."

"Yes, I told him to find you." Al shook hands, at the same time he moved me further into a corner out of earshot of people standing nearby. "Gary, I don't know just how to say this..." he hesitated.

"How to say what Palmer? What cooks, you look upset." Chain smoking as always, he was definitely lacking his normal strong self reliance that was so reassuring to others.

"I've been *ordered* to tell you that if you get up on the stage and start telling all these people the story you told the other night up in Ojai, something is going to happen."

I could hardly believe what I was hearing from Palmer. "Lord Al! What are you talking about? Who gave you an order like that?" He seemed reluctant to talk, but finally he admitted receiving the order from Jim Farley. "You mean Farley, the lawyer working for Fish in the Public Defender's office?"

"Yeah, that's him."

"Who in hell is he to be giving you orders like that?"

"Maybe you haven't heard but Farley's gotten himself elected as

President of the Employees Association, he's in charge of this affair tonight. He came to me and said I had to stop you from giving that same speech you gave in Ojai the other night."

"How in hell did he expect you to stop me?"

Palmer paled, he said, "I guess they figured we are friends and you'll understand if I tell you."

"Of course we are friends. Al you were the only one who really went to bat for me when the Fish started this entire thing, I'm not about to forget that. So, what is it that's going to happen if I try to tell the truth about those crooks?"

"Farley says he'll pull the plug on you, he has somebody behind the stage all set to jerk the plug out on the mike and he, as master of ceremonies will start chattering and telling jokes, he'll break up your speech. You know...kind of make you look silly."

"I get the picture, what are they threatening to do, get rid of you also for helping me?" Palmer just looked at me. "Don't worry Al, I'd never do anything to hurt you. You and Ray were square with me. I can't forget that."

Since this entire crazy situation began I had fought hard to keep cool. I knew if my temper ever gave way despite all the provocations they'd be able to point at me and say, "Look at him, he's irrational, just like we've been saying, he's not stable, all it takes is one little thing to set him off." I went down the aisle toward the stage, at the end and to the left was a door, inside was a short flight of stairs. At the top I saw I was in the stage wings looking out upon the platform. Standing there I wrestled with what Palmer had told me. If I tried to go ahead with my speech on corruption in the county there was no doubt in my mind that Farley intended to do exactly what he'd told Palmer.

Out on the stage Jim Farley was busy shaking hands, promoting himself with the arriving candidates. He was a large pudgy man with a mod-hair style covering his ears, the hair-do and his small gold rimmed glasses made him a dead ringer for pictures of Ben Franklin I had seen in history books. Walking out on the stage I had just sat down on a chair when Jim Farley came bouncing over, he grabbed my hand. "Real good to see you again Gary, it's been quite a while since I last talked to you." He was gone before I could even think of something to say.

All the chairs were filled by the candidates except one. Checking them off fast I realized it was Bennett, my opponent for the Third District who was missing. He had never contacted me regarding the so-called press conference he said he would set up and I hadn't been able to get any answer from his staff the last couple days. Easily I understood why he had failed to show up tonight. There could be an explosive reaction to Farley's order, he was afraid to be here. Damn, the only thing stopping my going ahead and battling it out tonight was the position it would put Al in. But if I had known then it was already cut and dried they were going to fire Palmer and replace him with Farley, it would've been different. Later when I learned this I felt bad, I knew Palmer had lost his job for trying to help me.

But for now I had another subject matter I could substitute for my speech. There was the issue of the courthouse. A powerful, secret group was trying to move the old courthouse from it's original site to a new location about five or six miles east of downtown Ventura. Two times the proposition had been placed on the ballot before the voters, both times they soundly rejected the proposition. The voters decision was arrogantly cast out by this powerful, corrupt political clique. Accelerating their evil plans the conspirators continued to scheme to move the courthouse despite the voters mandate.

Through various machinations the supervisors were contriving to have the courthouse declared unsafe in the event of an earthquake. A firm of engineering consultants were hired at a fantastic cost to the taxpayers to inspect the building. Their final report claimed that the existing courthouse could collapse with serious loss of life and limb of county employees in the event an earthquake of any major consequence occurred.

The new courthouse was scheduled to be built on an eighty acre orange grove. I'd spent considerable time examining the proposal. Construction of the parking lot areas for the new courthouse alone would cost in excess of fifteen million dollars. At a political meeting several weeks prior to this evening, Bennett had conned the citizens that the entire cost of the new structure wouldn't exceed eighteen million. While I gave the audience the true cost of the new parking lots exclusive of the buildings and other appurtenances which I had estimated to be sixty million, Bennett suddenly leaped up screaming with mighty umbrage and angry cries that I was highly exaggerating the cost of construction. Tonight, with Bennett afraid to show up for the meeting, I'd be able to present my facts and figures without his interruptions and lies. When the meeting was over I headed toward the stage wings and left through a side exit, I didn't feel like hanging around for all the hypocritical hand shaking.

CHAPTER 17

On election night all the candidates had come to the Supervisor's room on the fifth floor of the courthouse. Voting results would be announced as fast as they came in from the precincts. Packed in the room, people were milling around waiting for the first results. There was a flurry of excitement as Bob Hamm, the County Clerk, stood by the blackboard, his hands raised asking for silence. According to Hamm there was a foul-up regarding the polls in the San Francisco Bay area. A *court order was issued* directing them to remain open one hour longer. Also the election officers of all the other counties were *ordered to withhold all election results* and to not make them public until *after the polls were closed in San Francisco.*

Fifteen minutes *before* the polls in Frisco were due to close I was in a seat next to the aisle, Bennett stood nearby talking to a group of people, his assistant and Hamm approached with big smiles. Both grabbed at Bennett's hand while Hamm blustered, "Congratulations 'Hoot,' *you have won the election."*

Two ladies who'd been helping me during the campaign rushed in the room. Out of breath they were very excited about something. "This is very important, we must talk to you right now."

"What is it, what's wrong?" We walked out to the hallway where there was more privacy.

They explained, "We have been at the election building on Main Street, we ran all the way up the hill to find you."

"Okay, tell me what happened."

"We were standing out in front of the building, deputy sheriffs were pulling up in their squad cars delivering the ballot boxes from the precincts and carrying them into the building."

"Go slow, you're all out of breath."

"We saw the deputies take the boxes through the main room of the building then they left. Within seconds several men *came back out carrying the same boxes* and the locks were still on them."

"Were they deputy sheriffs?"

"No, I do not believe so, at least they weren't wearing uniforms. They wore business suits."

"What did they do with the ballot boxes?"

"They walked down the street, put them in a car and drove away. A deputy sheriff was standing next to his squad car a few feet away from the men when they carried the boxes out. We asked him where those men were taking the boxes after they had just been delivered to the election department. He said he didn't know, all he had been ordered to do was deliver them here, what happened to them after that was not his responsibility."

"Alright, I'll go to the election department and see what I can find out." Walking down the hill I tried to think of a *logical reason* why the boxes would be *removed* from the election department as soon as they arrived. Considerable confusion reigned in the main office, clerks were dashing helter skelter. I tried to tell several clerks what I was trying to find out, but they assured me they had no idea why any ballot boxes would be removed from the building. I went to the rear of the office, one of the girls had told me that was where the ballots were being counted. A door was marked for employees only and I was told that only authorized personnel were allowed inside.

Back outside I stood there thinking, it was suspicious, *something was wrong*. I'd heard Hamm telling Bennett he'd *won* the election *before* he could have possibly counted the votes. The ladies who had told me about the ballot boxes being removed were absolutely above reproach, they'd never dream of telling anything but the truth about such happenings. Returning to the supervisors room a hub-bub was prevailing as election results were beginning to appear on the large viewing screen. It was not too long before it became quite obvious that Bennett *was going to win*, just like Bob Hamm had told him he would half an hour ago.

There was little traffic on the freeway, it was dark and quiet as I drove slowly home. It seemed the circumstances certainly warranted investigation and a recount of the ballots. Even if I could arrange to get a recount it would be under Hamm's supervision. Nothing could be accomplished that way. Considering all the *sad* experiences I had already had with the Grand Jury it was pretty obvious I'd be wasting my time contacting them. The District Attorney was responsible for investigating complaints in cases of *voter frauds,* but there was small chance of drumming up any action there. Things were still coming out just like I had told the Grand Jury they would.

Woody Deem, the D.A., was fighting for his political life. Judge Shaw, who'd stated from the witness stand in Robinson's trial that *crucial witnesses had committed perjury,* was now making angry and vile charges from his bench that the D.A. was involved in covering up drug crimes amongst his own family. It was one of the stories I'd heard Hronesh and Kuhn telling Fish three years ago when Fish was ordering me to harass and frame people he did not like. This *worn out* story was now being pressed before the Grand Jury. Deem was never indicted but shortly after this pillory by the virulence of the unproven charges, he informed the press he was resigning from his position as the D.A., and intended to take a job teaching law at a university in another state.

Coincident with all the other events a lawyer filed a suit against the Chief of the Ventura Police Department. It was for a vast sum of money. He was charged with violating the civil rights of a citizen of Ventura, as with Deem this charge was taken to the Grand Jury. *Again,* as with the D.A. they *didn't* bring an indictment, instead they *leaked the secret transcript* of their so-called investigation to the new City Manager of Ventura who had just been appointed by the City Council to replace Reiman. The new manager released cutting hints to the newspapers that the evidence against the Chief looked very bad, however he wasn't sure he was going to take any action against him. Shortly after the manager got the confidential information from the Grand Jury the Chief announced he had gotten an offer to teach police procedure at a university in another state. Soon as the Chief *left town* the charges were dropped. It was never learned who paid all the lawyer fees and costs, nor *why* the injured parties gave up a lawsuit wherein their avowed reasons were to uncover supposedly serious violations of citizens rights by the Chief. This same Grand Jury *was holding evidence of an existing plot* to frame the Chief, yet they covered up these facts completely.

All the city and county officials that Hronesh and Kuhn had been spying on had now disappeared. It appeared they'd earned the large sum of money the secret group of powerful people had paid them. The only person who had enough guts to fight back was Supervisor Robinson and he was found guilty and sentenced to jail. This was in spite of the fact that during the trial Judge Robert Shaw took the witness stand and *under pressure had blurted out* that prosecution witnesses were committing perjury.

By now I was completely convinced that there *was* a powerful and sinister master plan behind the entire operation. But I couldn't figure out how they were able to consistently use the Grand Jury to run all the top people clear out of the county. *Why...what in hell could be the motive?* Judge Berenson's covering up for other lawyers might be part of it, but things had progressed *far beyond* that point now. Maybe by pleading not guilty and fighting the secret group Robinson had put himself in a position of being made a *horrible example to frighten* the others. Anyway, nobody had seen fit to fight any of the *trumped up* charges leveled against them since Robinson was sent to prison. Somehow, or some way, I'd gotten myself mixed up right in the middle of the entire rotten mess.

With all these thoughts running through my mind I arrived home without realizing it. In the carport I switched off the lights and sat there thinking. For some reason it seemed necessary to convince myself, I had to become satisfied within my own conscience. It was not going to help one damn bit to make a report to the D.A. or the Grand Jury regarding how the ladies observed the ballot boxes being taken from the election department. Knowing from past experience that absolutely nothing would be done about it and would probably just bring more crap down on my head seemed to lend me sufficient justification to forget the events of the entire evening. Hell, it was late and I was dead tired, I walked into the house...it seemed that forgetting was the only logical solution available...at least for now.

CHAPTER 18

Time rolled by, it kept getting busier at the store. Things hadn't been easy by any stretch of the imagination. It took a lot of doing, plenty hours of hard work, but I was convinced a man could become a success if he applied himself and knuckled down. I'd been working hard and long, that was for sure, hadn't seen so much scraping and painting since I was a lowly seaman in the Navy, and that was a long time ago.

From my customers and people I dealt with every day I began to evolve many new insights into local problems and the problems of our country as a whole. No doubt of it, our country was still set up under laws allowing an honest, ambitious man a chance to make his fortune and attain any goal in life he desired. The establishment is basically sound. It is only when *unscrupulous people* seize control of our governmental administration and institutions and twist and turn and force our basic constitutional concepts into tools *for their own greed and evil uses* that the establishment breaks down.

But then again, perhaps that was just one of the hazards that are encountered by an honest and ambitious citizen of our country, one of the evils to be faced. If you were not realistic enough to accept these basic facts and stout enough of character to *challenge and fight* them there was little chance of reaching your goal. My thoughts were slightly embarrassing, seeming so simple and idealistic it sounded like a naive, small town Sunday school teacher who'd never faced any of the grim, harsh realities of life.

Arriving early at the store I'd been working several hours...being such a bright sun shiny day I decided to drive to Ventura with the bank deposit. Just to simply get away from the store a while would be refreshing. Heading down the freeway the sky was a crystal blue. Not a trace of the normal fog lay across the ocean, Santa Cruz and Santa Rosa Islands, vivid in deep hued green and purple colors stood out clearly on the horizon.

Pulling off the freeway at the downtown exit, I made a left onto Main Street, continuing east several blocks to California. A parking space stood empty right in front of the bank just waiting for me. The teller completing my business swiftly, I decided to walk across the street and have a cup of coffee, relax a bit before heading back. The restaurant was busy but there was one empty seat at the far end of the counter. While sipping coffee slowly, I gazed around the room. Over in the dining room section a familiar figure was standing by a booth, I recognized Judge Walter Fourt, though I hadn't seen him for a long time.

He'd been a Superior Court Judge in Ventura County for many years until being elevated to the California State Appellate Court. Fourt used to come to the Ventura Police Station and hang around in the squad room drinking coffee and hobnobbing with the officers. He had always evinced strong interest in the welfare of the general public as well as the street problems confronting police officers. His demeanor, even the name Fourt, had always rang synonymous with some sort of bastion, an unassailable citadel full of legal weapons to be used as the strong arm of the law in dispensing justice and equity. I had read in the paper that Fourt, retiring from the Appellate Court was returning to enter the private practice of law. His law partner was younger and married to a woman who held the job of Ventura County Counsel.

Fourt was walking away from the booth where he'd been talking to several people. I watched him leave the restaurant, stride across California Street and enter a side door of the bank building. There were law offices on the floors above the bank. Paying for my coffee, I went across the street and through the same door as Fourt. On the index I saw that he and his partner were located on the third floor. A lone elevator and a flight of stairs stood side by side, I chose the stairs. At the top a narrow hallway led to a reception desk where a secretary busily pecked away on her typewriter. Giving my name I asked to see Judge Fourt. Pointing down the hall she said, "Knock on that door over there and you will find him."

Walter Fourt looked up from some papers on his desk, "Come on in." He remembered me and invited me to sit down.

"Judge I have a story to tell you and I need some help real bad."

"Let's have it."

As I proceeded he emitted several sharp gasps of amazement and disgust but did not interrupt. Upon hearing the part about Judge Berenson ordering the Grand Jury to kill their investigation, Fourt reacted spontaneously. "By God!...that is a *criminal obstruction of justice*. Berenson hasn't any right to *interfere* with the Grand Jury." Slapping his desk loudly with the palm of his hand emphasizing his indignation at such an act by Berenson, he asked, "Who was it that told you Berenson had ordered the investigation killed?"

"Dr. Penfield, the Foreman of the Grand Jury and Mal King, the Chief Investigator at the D.A.'s office told me. Several members of the Grand Jury also complained to Mal King and Dr. Penfield about Judge Berenson killing their investigation."

Pausing, Fourt exclaimed, "I want to check some of these things out myself. I'll get hold of Ernie Shaw and talk to him, I've known him for years and he's straight as an arrow. You give me a call next week and we will discuss this some more."

"Okay, and thanks very much for listening to me Judge. It's been mighty rough trying to battle this thing alone, especially without an attorney."

"This is a terrible situation, *I certainly do intend to delve into it.*"

Going back to the store I was in a much better mood. Too bad I hadn't been lucky enough to talk with Fourt at the very beginning. There was no question of the Judge's judicial qualifications. He had been a Superior Court and Appellate Court Judge over thirty five years. I was particularly pleased by his *spontaneous* angry reaction to Berenson's cover-up. After all, that had been the crucial point in the entire situation. If Judge Berenson had allowed the *due process of law* to proceed, the ensuing Grand Jury investigation would have revealed the entire sinister plot. The whole set of false charges and lying witnesses the Fish had set up against me would have collapsed. A lot of other *innocent people* would have been spared the agony they'd been put through and Ben Martinez would still be alive.

Fourt had said to call him in a week. But time passed too slow, after six days I called his office. Fourt sounded very enthused, "Yes Gary, I got hold of Ernie, he *verified* what Harry Maynard told him about Thomas Boyd putting pressure on him to find you guilty even though Maynard didn't believe you were guilty of anything. He also explained about John McCormick wanting to get even with you for arresting him years ago. Shaw also filled me in on quite a few *other things* going on around here. I want you to stop by my office in the next couple days so we can formulate our procedure."

"That's great Judge, and don't worry, I'll be there for sure."

Two days later I was in Walter Fourt's office. The secretary was still pecking away at her typewriter. She slowed just long enough to inform me that he was in his partner's office conferring with a client, she expected him out shortly. I made myself comfortable in a large chair, I didn't mind waiting, at last it looked like I'd get some action.

A door opposite Fourt's opened, Thomas L. Schechter his partner, their client and Fourt were still conversing as they came down the hall toward me. Fourt hadn't noticed my presence yet, I stood up, he was only a few feet away when I said, "Judge, is it possible to talk with you now?" Whirling around he stared at me, his eyes grew large and his face paled, in a high breaking voice *he screeched,* "What are you doing here? Go away," he croaked, *"I can't help you. Go away!* Oh-oohh," the Judge clapped a hand to his chest, "I'm having a heart attack," he cried in a weak voice. Fourt then walked swiftly down the hall, the elevator door was standing open ready for use. He didn't bother with it, fleeing down the three flights of stairs he looked like a track star.

Aware my mouth was agape, I closed it. The secretary was trying to correlate her thinking with her mouth also. The client was walking down the hall toward the elevator, but the Judge had passed him and disappeared down the staircase. Schechter, the law partner watched the weird proceedings, with the disappearance of Fourt he retreated to his office without a word. I walked slowly down the hall and even more slowly down the stairs. I was still clutching my briefcase full of documents and evidence that I'd brought with hopeful anticipation that Fourt would examine them. Climbing into my pickup truck I sat there, I had to be dreaming, every bit of it had to be a dream, one hell of a bad one...*a nightmare,* there was just no other answer.

Back on the freeway I became aware it was an overcast, terribly gloomy day. Odd, I hadn't even noticed the weather when I'd headed for town. Everything had seemed bright, full of hope. The more I thought of the entire affair the madder I got, *a sickening disgust overwhelmed me.* Everyone of the lawyers and judges I had gone to and talked with had done nothing but doublecross me.

In books, newspapers, legal journals, stories written by lawyers and judges constantly brag about their codes of ethics and their moral standards. They boast of an inspiring oath they'd taken and sworn to uphold on their honor. You would begin to believe that they were mighty, powerful knights of the legal round table...dwelling in a great castle whose lofty spires reach ever upwards touching the purity of the sky, declaring with blaring bugles to suffering people that herein resides their *saviors...knights in shining armor* prepared to charge forth from citadels, riding mighty steeds, armed with legal knowledge as their spears, warriors ready to wage fierce uncompromising battle in the courtroom arena *against tyranny* and other unspeakable evils which constantly combine to destroy the people and their pursuit of happiness.

Bullshit, nothing but lies and bullshit, piss ants, that's what they were, nothing but a lousy pack of piss ants, it was really getting to me, *what in hell could be behind this whole crazy thing? Who could have frightened Fourt so bad he would pull a stunt like that?* Never before had I ever encountered anything like it...sure, I'd run across lawyers and policemen who had personal qualms of getting involved in some investigation that they were afraid could harm their image or pocketbook, but never anything like this. I'll get to the bottom of it if it's the last thing I do. So-help-me-God, I swear.

Not too long after the weird fiasco in Fourt's office I read in the newspaper he was politically backing a former mayor of Ventura for the position of California State Senator. The man was a local real estate broker, he'd resigned as mayor, fearful of a new law coming into effect that would force him to reveal any business dealings that would be a conflict of interest with his position as mayor. He had become a powerful man in local politics having built a strong clique of followers in the downtown business area. Fourt had been away from Ventura most of the time he was with the Appellate Court, I wondered...how could he have developed such close association with this man?

Rummaging through my memory I began vaguely recalling some things. After Lane Martin retired from the police department he'd obtained a license to operate as a private detective and opened an agency in the east Ventura area. Not long afterward he moved his operations to downtown Ventura in the same office with the former mayor's real estate company. It was during this same period of time that Martin had come to my office with his money bag wanting me to help him frame Robinson and Reiman. I wondered, for the first time were tiny pieces of an enormous jigsaw puzzle beginning to fall into their real places. But even if pieces were actually descending into some semblance of order, it still *did not* make any sense, that maddening question still remained....*why...what evil was behind it?*

CHAPTER 19

The same old grinding routine of long hours, seven days a week at the store continued. But since the crazy scene at Fourt's office, it had become increasingly difficult to focus my thoughts, or to force the mysterious events from my mind. Little words or incidents would pop up, sending my thoughts dashing off in an attempt to analyze and catalog that specific event within my brain for future reference. It had reached the point of being exasperating as hell. Nothing new materialized, even with all the harsh mental efforts I was putting forth. The same old elusive, and haunting question, why? It injected itself insidiously into each and every analyzation of each and every tiny recollection that my mind managed to traipse off in pursuit of.

Weeks passed under the same conditions of mental torment and strain, with the same old hopeless realization that I was no closer to a solution or key to the problem than I'd been at the very beginning. It was time to close up, I was glad to be locking the doors, I was completely exhausted.

On the drive home my mind returned to a few experiences I had been through in the past. All those years spent digging into crimes from murder on down, unearthing evidence and facts to take into court for the purpose of convicting a defendant of a specific crime. Then suddenly making the switch to Chief Investigator for a Public Defender's office I had found it was necessary to make the same investigation for the defense as for the prosecution. In the process of probing for a defense I'd more often than not suddenly come upon evidence and witnesses proving that the defendant was guilty of the crimes the police had charged him with. Okay...so what in hell was my duty when I reached this turn in the road? When does duty to a defendant end, and responsibility for the safety and welfare of the people and victims begin? There had to be a *cut-off*, it couldn't be simply discretionary.

It had been misting as I left the store, now it began raining, slow but steady. Inside the house was warm but dark. Wandering into the den I flipped the television on. A silvery flickering light bathed the room with an eerie cast. Leaning back in the corner of the couch I put my feet on the coffee table. It felt good just to sit here in the darkness and relax. Tired as hell, I was not real sleepy or ready for bed, too many thoughts had been coursing through my mind.

Having been totally unsuccessful in getting a lawyer to represent me seemed to place me in a special category of rejection. A class, a *low class*, wherein you *no longer* have *any* legal rights in a country that is famous for its homespun idioms, such as, "Okay,...so you got problems, go get yourself a good lawyer." But nobody could answer the riddle that had become my biggest dilemma. Where in hell do you get a *good* lawyer, and what in hell is a *good* lawyer? A severe gloom had settled on me lately. My spirit was sure as hell dragging in the mud. From their all-powerful political thrones these scum are capable of *removing* a person's lawful and historical weapons of legal redress and then proceed to *erase* them from the roll call of decent society.

A small, select, very elite group of landowners and financiers in Ventura had taken command, with Judge Jerome Berenson wearing the crown of Grand Oligarch.

Music from the TV disrupted my thoughts, Hollywood's Academy Awards were being presented. Liza Minelli was dancing and singing a song from her hit show Cabaret, her talent was fascinating. The black costume she wore added a strange ethereal quality combined with the European touch. The tune and lyrics she sang were catchy, "Money, money, money, money, money, money." Minelli continued singing, "money, money, money."

There came an astounding flash striking through my brain, an explosion, brilliant lights. *Money, money, money, money*...what else? *Money,... Money...that was it!* Money was behind it all. What was wrong with me anyway? Why had it taken so damned long to figure out something so damnably simple and basic? All along I had been thinking that Berenson had been covering up to protect the Fish and Dunham because they were brother lawyers, some sort of esprit de corps or something. Money, money, money...why hadn't it come to me? Hell...common sense should have told me Berenson wouldn't give a shit for those two shysters Fish and Dunham. Money, money, money, *lots of it* was involved somewhere *behind* all of his corrupt actions.

Liza was finishing her number, her image slowly fading from the screen. Like some enchanting sorceress she disappeared completely. Bright rays of confidence flared in my head, this was it! I knew that tomorrow I'd be able to ferret out some of the hidden secrets.

I headed for the County Recorder and Tax Assessor's office early the next day, it was as good a place as any to start. At the Assessor's I hit pay dirt. Nordman owned a parcel of land known as Montalvo Hill. Locating the legal description and map book I found that the 'Hill' was an eighty acre parcel fronting on Victoria Avenue. It lay just south of the eighty acres Berenson had arranged to purchase for the purpose of building the new courthouse. Leaving the tax office I drove to East Ventura to the new location of the Recorder's office. Examining the Montalvo Hill deed I knew the captivating sorceress of last night hadn't deceived me. Money, money, money, indeed...it was money, that was the answer.

Montalvo Hill was co-owned by Ben Nordman and R. H. Roussey, a real estate broker, land developer and the Mayor of Oxnard. An egotist who loved seeing his name in the newspaper with his life's story of success and raising hints that he possibly was a millionaire. In the old days shortly after World War 11, Roussey was developing housing tracts in Oxnard and Nordman and Berenson, law partners, represented him in land development and construction transactions. Back in those days it was a simple operation, Roussey would tie up a large parcel of farmland and Berenson and Nordman wrapped up the legal ends. They'd all proceed to Oxnard City Hall, where their old buddy Mayor Carl E. Ward would okay the zoning requirements, all a very simple operation...when you had the *right* connections.

Berenson was now a Superior Court Judge, while his law partner Nordman was the owner of the largest, most influential law firm in Ventura County. As time passed the Mayor's son Carl E. Ward Jr., became an *associate member* of the Nordman law firm. Shortly after Nordman and Roussey purchased Montalvo Hill, Berenson started a slyly-worded mouth campaign denigrating the adequateness of the old courthouse facilities. He *advocated* the movement of the entire county government to the east end. Holding the top position of the county's Criminal Justice Planning Committee, he used his influence to convince many unknowledgeable people that the entire County Jail facilities had to be incorporated with the new Administration Center. This was a very clever move on Berenson's part. It put the county in line for Federal Criminal Justice funds under the *pretext* that a new county jail was *absolutely necessary* for the protection of the citizens.

Bud Milligan, President of Bank of A. Levy, and Ben Nordman were cousins. Directors and controllers of the bank they exerted a tremendous social and financial control over the entire county. The movement to the Victoria Avenue location and the construction of a new administration and courthouse complex *including* the jail and sheriff's headquarters, garages, parking facilities etc., etc., brought Montalvo Hill into the prospectus of a multi-multi-million dollar development. Every land development and construction scheme that Berenson, Nordman and Roussey engineered in the past had turned into far more than just the average financial success. Their egos and arrogance kept apace with burgeoning bank accounts and influential positions. Charles Mc Grath, the son of wealthy and influential land owners, was appointed to the Municipal Court Bench. He was also a partner in Nordman's law firm, and being a younger man he was heir-apparent to the Superior Court position long held by Berenson. With Berenson's retirement Mc Grath would perpetuate the role of Grand Oligarch. Berenson, as a Presiding Judge appointed foremen to the Grand Jury *year after year*. William Petit Clark, land owner, real estate dealer and Grand Jury Foreman made recommendations urging construction of a new county center. His son Wm. P. Clark, was a member of the Nordman law firm. In the near future Clark would be appointed as a *Superior Court Judge* and soon afterwards be elevated to the *State Appellate Court* and then to the *Supreme Court* by Governor Ronald Reagan.

Next foreman appointed was Robert L. Mobley, a Vice President of the Bank of A. Levy. At that time he was *secretly* engineering the purchase of a piece of land on Victoria across from the proposed new County Complex. It was for the purpose of constructing a new Bank of A. Levy. Foreman Mobley began making forceful demands that the new county center be built immediately. Commencing his construction of the new Bank of A. Levy he was *so positive* that the new county center would be built directly across the street that he filed an application with the State Banking Department to designate the new bank the *County Center Branch.* Mobley's rise in the Bank of A. Levy organization was very rapid and after leaving the Grand Jury as the Foreman, he was then appointed to the Ventura County Civil Service Commission.

Overnight Judge Berenson and Nordman were hit by one of their first setbacks, it was a serious blow to their plot. They had slipped a bond issue onto the ballot which would have financed the County Center. But even after all the cunning ground work they'd laid trying to convince the taxpayers the center was an absolute necessity, the voters *still defeated* the measure soundly. Strong underground forces had sprung up in objection to the proposed *relocation* of the county government. It was quite obvious to even a novice, the public was being deceived by their proposed cost of the construction. A local architect had been hired at a cost of over a million just to draw the plans. His concept of the courthouse was an eight story cantilevered structure that drew red-hot opposition based on outrageous costs of the building alone, not to mention its total lack of functional utility. The conspirators original lies of eighteen million had now jumped admittedly to over forty or fifty million.

The architect was fired, but it was necessary to pay him the full million for the worthless plans. Another architect was hired, his fee was agreed on at nearly three million. To date there was over five million of taxpayers money down the drain. Berenson fully realized that he *had* to take stringent action. It was necessary that any force whatsoever threatening the construction of the new Center must not only be crushed immediately, it must be destroyed totally.

Judge Berenson appointed another of his cabal to be Grand Jury Foreman. Franklyn R. Jewett had definite financial interests in the area of the proposed new County Center. Not only a landholder, he also controlled the oil and mineral rights to a large parcel of land near the new Bank of A. Levy on Victoria Avenue.

Berenson and Nordman had concluded that the taxpayers voted down the financing of the proposed Center because they *already had a courthouse,* there was *no reason* for a new one. The plotters next reasoning brought forth a new scheme, if the people *didn't have the old courthouse,* they would *have* to vote to build a new one! Soon a rumor was spreading around, the *old* courthouse was a menace, completely unsafe in the event of an earthquake. A local structural engineer was hired at taxpayers expense to inspect the building. He reported dramatically, "*An average* earthquake could level the *old* courthouse, causing severe damage and endanger the life and limb of county employees.

Many stormy civic discussions were held, also *secret backroom meetings*. Berenson's puppets shouted long and lusty that it was far too expensive a project for the budget to renovate and refurbish the old courthouse. Now that they'd proven it to be not only dangerous but worthless as well, Berenson and Nordman had only one problem remaining, how to *dispose* of a worthless old courthouse?

After secret negotiations a deal was cut with the City of Ventura. The courthouse and jail, worth millions, was sold to the city for a *ridiculous sum* of one hundred thousand dollars. Then the county government was moved out of the courthouse and all of the various departments were scattered throughout the city in *high-price leased* buildings. The good-hearted city politicians then leased back space in their vacant old City Hall at an exorbitant cost to the county. I remembered Kuhn and Hronesh following Martinez and the woman from the County Counsel's office, and Martinez's odd remark to the parking lot attendant, *"They are trying to steal the courthouse."* Such a strange thing to say, it had been nothing more than a momentary puzzlement in my mind...but it made sense now...sure as hell, the old courthouse had been stolen!

The woman Martinez was walking with was formerly a secretary at City Hall, perhaps she had knowledge of the scam and was telling him how they had worked it. From what he'd said to the attendant, it was evident that Ben opposed the courthouse theft. As Grand Jury Foreman, Jewett was conducting a secret frame-up of Robinson and Martinez. Jewett then passed-on the conspiracy to Berenson's next Foreman, Dr. Douglas Penfield. This was where I unwittingly had come into the picture.

I'd given Dr. Penfield's Grand Jury all my information including the plot to frame Robinson, Reiman and the Chief. I had jumped to a conclusion that Berenson was covering up for Fish and Dunham. Actually it had been *my* information about the *frame-up* that had precipitated his order to Penfield to *kill the Grand Jury* investigation immediately. Berenson did not dare let them continue. If the secret group of conspirators who'd paid to frame Robinson and Martinez was unmasked, Berenson and Nordman's *evil scheme to steal* the old courthouse would have been exposed.

I could see now where I had tromped on powerful toes. Berenson sure as hell didn't want me around any longer. This was why Thomas Boyd, the Civil Service Commissioner and Vice-President of Bank of A. Levy, had gotten his orders to pressure Harry Maynard into firing me. Maynard, Vice-President of Wells Fargo Bank and dealing deep in banking circles was easy to convince it was to his benefit to go along with Boyd's pressure. After all, I was expendable...my future couldn't possibly be equated with that of mighty judges and lawyers. Obeying Berenson's command to kill the investigation, Dr. Penfield proceeded with the indictment of Robinson, who went to prison and Ben Martinez was dead.

Franklyn R. Jewett, Foreman of the Grand Jury involved in the framing of Robinson, was appointed to *replace* him as Supervisor. Jewett would take over the district in which the new courthouse was to be built. As the new Supervisor, Jewett quickly leased office space in the new Bank of A. Levy building on Victoria directly across the street from their proposed new complex. His office was separated from Robert Mobley's office by a thin partition that could be easily removed to enlarge the bank, which Mobley claims will be necssary when the new county complex is completed.

Mobley advanced swiftly within the Bank of A. Levy organization, and Jewett became County Supervisor overnight. Berenson went to a birthday party for Penfield at his home, there was much hugging and back slapping between the two old friends. For a birthday gift Judge Berenson *appointed* the Doctor to a prestigious position on the *County Criminal Justice Planning Board.*

They had everything lined up, the time was *ripe* now to *slip* the bond issue back on the ballot to finance the new courthouse. They were absolutely positive that it would pass this time just as a matter of routine, *especially* since the people no longer had a courthouse. But they were forced to reveal that the new complex estimate now came to over seventy five million. Angry voters again turned down the bond issue for the center. For Berenson and Nordman this was appalling, without the county complex all of their plans and schemes were wiped out. They'd lose millions, only one alternative was left. They would have to force it, proceed with their scam to build a new center whether the public liked it or not.

They formed their own group called the *Ventura County Public Facilities Corporation* to sell revenue bonds to raise money and the Board of Supervisors chose the corporate directors. The president, Ralph Cormany, a lawyer in Berenson and Nordman's law firm was in charge of obtaining funds. Another corporate officer was Barbara Henricksen, a former Grand Jury appointee of Berenson's. Delving further into county records I discovered that Ben Nordman and Bud Milligan, the president of Bank of A. Levy, had formed a company that was doing business as The Real Estate Investment Trust Corp.. This company also owned acreage in the Montalvo Hill area near the proposed county center. It was created for the express purpose of buying up property for speculation and then taking any clandestine action necessary to increase its value.

Berenson was the big fish in the courthouse, no doubt of it, *the brain, the force* behind the scenes. This fish had attained enormous size in the past years from feeding on the smaller fish. It was now capable of swallowing and digesting anyone so foolish as to interfere with its smooth sailing. After digestion of the unfortunate victims which took place deep within the dark recesses of the big fish, the residue was passed on out the far end, dropping down and down into the black, silent depths of the ocean floor, never to be heard from again. I admitted to myself that I had indeed been swallowed by the big fish and was wallowing around in the cavernous darkness, trying to discover a way out. By God, I may have been swallowed by the big fish, but I was not going to be digested and cast out the far end like the others. I was coming back out the same way that I went in. My fierce pounding and yelling inside the dark, dank digestion chamber was giving the Big Fish indigestion.

One of the Superior Court Judges in Berenson's organization had become frightened, he *refused to nominate* any more of his friends as candidates for the Grand Jury. The Judge told a newsman that in all fairness and for better all around protection and representation of the general public, the Grand Jury members should be chosen by selection from the roster of the voters register. The Judge later told a confidential source that Berenson's shady dealings as Presiding Judge over the past ten years had given him grave concern for the preservation of the judicial and due processes of the Superior Court system of the county.

Perusing countless records and entering book and page numbers of documents in my notebook for future reference I finally left the county offices. Getting into the old pickup I drove to the deserted county fair grounds, the gate was open. Coasting toward the ocean I turned right, past the stables and corrals, reaching a secluded spot I'd found in the past to be very restful. It was a good place to sit and think, trying to relate my thoughts to evidence and information that I had been digging up. Thinking back to the time of my civil service hearing, Pic'l, my lawyer, under one pretext or another had *refused* to bring out *any* of the documented evidence I had prepared for my defense. After losing my job he *refused* to communicate with me or the Public Employees Association.

After Robinson was found guilty his lawyer Ken Haymaker, who had botched Robinson's defense, was appointed to a judgeship. I remembered how Thomas Guerin, the lawyer in Paul Caruso's firm called at the last minute advising me that Caruso had changed his mind and wouldn't take my case. Checking, I discovered Caruso had been *appointed to a high position* in the California Criminal Justice Organization shortly after he *refused* to handle my case. I'd figured there was far more than just coincidence involved. Contacting an old friend in the County Communications Dept. I'd obtained a copy of their phone bills, it confirmed my suspicions. Within minutes after I had told Judge Heaton that Paul Caruso was going to represent me I had watched him go to Judge Berenson's office. Not five minutes later Berenson *made a long distance call* to Caruso in Beverly Hills. George Eskin, the Assist. D.A. under Woody Deem, had wanted the Grand Jury investigation real bad, but now, Eskin in private practice *was appointed* by Berenson to a committee to plan the lay-out of the new county center. In a scheme to grab off Criminal Justice money under the guise of new innovations, Eskin had come up with a weird proposal. He advocated the removal of jail responsibility from the Sheriff and combining jailers with the County Probation Dept., to form a *new* department which would place criminals under a more *social type* of environment. This new innovation would require an entirely new jail facility at their proposed Administration Center. Thus it would be in line for federal grants from the Criminal Justice Organization because of its supposed innovating concepts connecting it to a vague supposition that it would *remove* the criminality from the criminals.

Mal King, Chief Investigator for the D.A.'s office under Deem, had also wanted a Grand Jury investigation. He'd *assured* me that something was definitely going to be done about the corruption in the courthouse. But soon after the investigation was killed Berenson *appointed King* the Executive Director of the California Criminal Justice Planning Board, he became the *principal procurer* of federal funds and the *inventor* of new and innovating ideas such as Eskin's that supposedly would help peace officers make the streets safe for the citizens. Most of the federal money allocated for a new jail was *misappropriated and used* in the construction of the Administration Building which *did not* qualify for Criminal Justice funds under the Federal Omnibus Safe Street Act. California had a *strict mandate* from the Federal Government to use Criminal Justice funds to assist peace officers in making the streets safe for citizens in areas with high rates of serious crimes.

I had been giving the criminal justice money much thought. Far too many greedy politicians were *dipping* their hands into the funds for their own personal gain. The *basic purpose* of the federal funds was to make the streets safe for citizens. A simple reverse concept, an approach from a different angle could produce amazing results. First of all, change the name from *Criminal* Justice Association to *Citizen* Justice Association. The realization of the indisputable fact that the health, safety and welfare of honest, law-abiding citizens far out-weighed the so callled *rights* of the professional criminal would immediately switch efforts to the right direction.

From many years experience I knew that police departments in the state were performing an admirable, professional job. They have incorporated in training and practical procedures just about every type of so-callled innovative and technological techniques possible without becoming something other than a Law Enforcement Agency altogether. The *breakdown* in citizens justice has been building up over a period of several decades. A bushel of stupid courtroom legal theories complicated by the rise in *judicial corruption* is the primary cause.

The State Bar Association has long since ceased being competent in governing corrupt, half-assed lawyers and judges who are clogging the courts. The Bar should be completely reorganized, a law should require that *no judge* should sit on a bench in perpetuity. To wipe out the cancer cells in our judicial system, it should be required by law that well qualified lawyers be placed on *every election* ballot to run against any judge who has no opposition. Judicial election is a voters right. The theory that any lawyer who manages to get on the bench becomes indispensable to justice is an extremely dangerous myth. From the fear I'd seen expressed by lawyers for their futures if they *dared* to buck a powerful, wealthy judge, I had gained a vast insight into problems of justice and the *lack* of justice.

I began to suspect I had worn out my welcome for the day at this quiet friendly spot. A cold, dreary fog bank engulfing the ocean was now in the process of creeping through the small grove of pine trees. Having fallen so deep into thought I had not realized the length of time I'd been sitting there. Wispy tentacles of fog pursued my truck as I left.

CHAPTER 20

Finishing my business in town by mid-morning I decided to drive out to the proposed location of the *new* county center. Going north on Victoria Avenue to Foothill Road, which was as far as you could go, I turned around and parked heading south. Not too many years ago Victoria had been nothing more than a narrow blacktopped lane running through the orange groves. Many entrepreneurs were tying up property on Victoria, desiring to be in on the ground floor with the new county center. They also feared being left in the old and dying business area when the courthouse moved. Mobley from his strategic spot as Vice President of Bank of A. Levy and during the past year while Grand Jury Foreman had been spreading what he called *inside* information that this new location was indeed going to be, the financial hub of Ventura County.

Gazing south from my vantage point I could see the large orange grove on the left that constituted the eighty acres of the proposed center. Across from the grove was the Bank of A. Levy. Just a little further on lay Nordman's Montalvo Hill property. Victoria continued south under the freeway that connected Camarillo to the east with Ventura to the west, another freeway bordered on the orange grove connecting Ventura with the town of Santa Paula to the northeast. New rumors were spreading of plans being drawn to widen Victoria to eight traffic lanes and continuing directly south across the Santa Clara River right into the heart of the Oxnard City civic area.

More and more I was beginning to feel a *genuine* admiration for the fantastic plans of this powerful organization. When they owned and controlled property they didn't just sit around waiting for things to happen, they made them happen! Moving the government center to this spot was a catalyst that would develop the area far beyond dreams. They'd have control of everything. I could see the absolute genius in the entire scheme. If they could build the center and widen Victoria across the river to Oxnard, they would have all business and professional people from every city within a radius of twenty miles, not only vying but fighting amongst themselves for the privilege of paying astronomical prices for property and leases.

Their scheme would of course bring a financial blight to the old downtown business area. The thousands of acres of existing farmland adjacent to the center would be thrown open to development. No one would be able to stem the inevitable tide of growth. There was no problem visualizing the millions upon millions of dollars involved in the scheme. The *true genius* of their plot was how the taxpayers had been tricked into footing the bill. Even the widening of Victoria and all the improvements would be paid for with tax money.

It became plainer and plainer every second how I'd put my foot right smack in the *middle* of the big juicy apple pie when I told the Grand Jury about the *frame-up* to destroy key politicians.

Attempting to be a little more realistic about the situation than perhaps I had been in the past, I knew I would only bring more grief down on myself by going to the County Grand Jury. There was only one other possible chance. I could go to the Federal Grand Jury in Los Angeles. From what I had read in the newspapers, the Federal Grand Jury had not hesitated in their investigation and indictment of Spiro Agnew, the Vice-President of the United States despite his tremendous influence. Starting the pickup I headed down Victoria toward the freeway.

The remainder of the day and night I spent in a heated argument deep within myself. All that stinking mess of corruption had to be exposed without any doubt, but *who in hell was I* to try and do it all by myself? What made me think I'd possibly have any better success going to a Federal Grand Jury than when I had gone to the County Grand Jury? These people were formidably organized, it could be another trap, another *set-up* of traitorous jurors. What would I then be facing?

Conceivably they had things all sewed up. The new City Manager had wrapped up the takeover of the old courthouse for the City of

Ventura in great style. The newly appointed County Executive was given absolute authority to proceed with the plans for construction of the new county complex. The real powers behind the scenes had left no question remaining in the new County Executive's mind as to his accountability. If he failed his appointed task of constructing the new courthouse he was a dead race horse. There would be no more cushy, top executive jobs in his future.

Repeatedly my mind returned to Ben Martinez and that strange thing he had said, "They are trying to *steal* the Courthouse." They had stolen it all right, by outrageous fraud and evil conspiracy. The courthouse had been county property, as such it had belonged to the citizens and taxpayers. They were victims, their property had been stolen. They had indicated *twice* through the polls and also by other vigorous protests that in their judgement the only solution was to keep the *old* courthouse. By voracious means of sly trickery, fraud and conspiracy the people had been *permanently deprived* of their valuable property.

Years ago as a policeman when I caught a car thief the criminal went to jail and the stolen auto was returned to its rightful owner. This was a simple analogy however it basically described the existing problem facing the people. It presented the fact that the courthouse could be recovered through court action, the thieves sent to prison and held financially responsible for the problems their conspiracies had *put upon* the taxpayers.

With ruthless misuse and abuse of power their vicious conspiracy to obstruct justice was designed to propagate their own riches and power. Successfully they had removed and nullified all recourse to justice and the rights citizens are entitled to through due process of law. Here was the *major breakdown* in *citizen* justice. Good police officers can make the streets safe from common thieves but who is to make our Government safe from corrupt public officials who are *totally unrestrained* by prescribed rules or bounds?

This big, heated argument had been raging back and forth in my head for days now, gradually it burned down to a white hot pinpoint demanding that I make a decision one way or another. Through all of the struggle and hardship of the last few years, I had just begun to reach the position of being successful in business. I was paying my bills, *why should I* continue fighting the corruption I knew prevailed in our local government? *Why should I* put myself right back on the same spot I'd been on several years ago when I'd refused to frame people for the Fish? He still had his civil service job, his paycheck and some sort of a reputation. No one had dared to challenge the thieving, lying Dunham. This sinister organization was stronger and more powerfully in control than ever. The days of the indefatigable and adventurous crime breaking reporters with their noses digging up civic corruption and putting it on the front page for the public to read was a thing of the past, a lost art.

The biggest mystery of the entire affair, the *key* to the mess, was the identity of the secretive, politically powerful group who had put up the money for the frame-up. This remained an *unholy and dark* enigma. I had tried to uncover them many times but had run out of time, leads and money. There was *no one* left to go to for help with troubles like these.

There wasn't any reason in the world for me to get involved again. Why should I? All those years, everything that I had worked for, *my job, my pension* and *my reputation*...I had lost everything!

CHAPTER 21

Every night for weeks, when I read the paper it was full of phony propaganda promoting Judge Berenson's and Nordman's insidious scam to fleece the people. Their front, the Ventura County Public Facilities Corp. was setting it up to float sixty-five million dollars of bonds on the market to finance the first-phase of the construction of a new courthouse.

I had tried earnestly to talk myself into being sensible...sit back, relax...ignore the God damn rot and stinking corruption, go on about my own business, just make money and pay my bills. There had to be something wrong with me, I couldn't do it, I must be nuts to brood over it, the D.A., Grand Jury, the Bureaucrats, *no one* was going to help me if I stuck my neck out. Failing to heed all those warnings, a couple of days later I found myself wandering around at the old courthouse. Perusing the pile of Superior Court filings at random I selected several cases that appeared to be in the right categories. Studying them for guide lines they lent enough legal procedure and information for me to start outlining a pro-per lawsuit.

The *basis* of my lawsuit would be that of *prohibiting* the Board of Supervisors and Public Facilities Corp. from proceeding further with financial and construction plans involving the courthouse complex. It was June 1, 1976, the lawsuit was filed, I watched the girl stamp the Official Seal of Robert Hamm, County Clerk on the document, Superior Court file No. 60980. The *die was cast,* my decision to fight their corruption was irrevocable. As it turned out it was a *sentence to the fiery depths of hell,* far worse than anything I had dreamed of or allowed myself to expect. Ten dreadful years of total frustration, despair, and anguish, an *abyss* of dark intrigue, treason and murder.

In the past Judge Berenson had numerous times put himself *on record* with statements to the Board of Supervisors, local business men's groups, women's clubs and news reporters that, "The Ventura County Superior Court system was *so overworked, so under-staffed, and so clogged with criminal cases that civil cases were backlogged nearly five years. The situation was so serious that some of the cases had become so old they might never even be heard."*

But my Pro-per filing No. 60980 was not destined to receive their normal nonchalant Ventura County Superior Court treatment, it was not an ordinary civil case. At the time I didn't know it, but the case was put in the hands of Judge Berenson before I'd even reached my car in the parking lot. And before I could put the key in the door a cryptic command was received by Berenson's underlings to assemble immediately in his office.

The *dire emergency* created by case No. 60980 brought Dorothy L. Schechter, the Ventura County Counsel and her Chief Assistant James L. McBride scurrying to Judge Berenson's chambers. County Clerk Robert L. Hamm also arrived swiftly. His temper flaring, the Judge ordered Schechter to minutely research every legal aspect and take immediate measures to dismiss the suit. Hamm was summarily ordered to return to his office and for Christ sakes make sure Gary doesn't file any more of these dangerous lawsuits.

Shuffling in haste back to her office Schechter mobilized all the lawyers, clerks and typists. They were informed that an exigency of dreadful proportions existed, all other matters were to be dropped as of right now, this day, Tuesday June 1, 1976. The result of this frantic lawyer type activity was what they called, A DECLARATION FOR AN ORDER TO SHORTEN TIME and for a NOTICE FOR HEARING ON MOTION TO STRIKE AND DISMISS PRO-PER COMPLAINT NO. 60980. Signed by James L. McBride, Chief Assistant County Counsel *it was officially filed* by Robert L. Hamm, County Clerk, on Thursday June 3, 1976, *only two days after* I had filed my lawsuit. Schechter's people under heavy pressure and toiling with feverish haste also whipped out an, ORDER TO SHORTEN THE TIME FOR NOTICE OF A HEARING ON THE MOTION TO STRIKE AND DISMISS PRO-PER COMPLAINT NO. 60980. This order was signed by Superior Court Judge Robert Willard, and like the Declaration it was filed on Thursday, June 3, 1976 by Robert Hamm. There was also an order that I be served with a subpoena on that same day, Thursday, June 3, 1976 commanding me to appear in court the next morning, Friday June 4, 1976.

It was about closing time for the store on Thursday June 3, the small bell on the front door tinkled. A man clad in dungarees and plaid work shirt entered. He seemed to be just an average working guy seeking a six-pac of beer to take home after a hard day in the oil fields. Instead he reached over the counter and handed me some legal papers, a quick glance told me what they were. Taking a closer look at the process server I said, "The County must be in damn bad shape if they can't get a uniformed deputy to come out and serve papers, who are you?"

Sheepishly he answered, "I do jobs for the County maintenance department and I happened to be over in the courthouse late this evening. A couple big-shots with suits on dashed out of their office and grabbed me. They ordered me to come out to this address and serve these papers on you. It was a strange deal, they acted *awful* nervous and excited." As he left I locked the door. Switching off the lights I went back to my small office in the storeroom.

Under the light of the low desk lamp I read the papers that were just dropped on me. Along with the subpoena ordering me to be in court the next morning an extremely interesting document had been filed by McBride in the Clerk's office. It was especially enlightening since I'd learned only a few days before that McBride and Hamm were *both officers* in the so-called non-profit Public Facilities Corp.. McBride revealed in the document that there was a frenetic urgency to shorten time for the Court to hear their MOTION TO DISMISS case No. 60980. The Public Facilities Corp. was planning on selling thirty-five million dollars of revenue bonds Tuesday June 8, 1976. If my lawsuit was *still pending* on Monday June 7, 1976 which was the *day before* the planned sale, the potential bond bidders by law *would have to be notified* that a complaint for injunctive relief had been filed. According to this document of McBride's, such a notification would *prohibit* the P.F.C from *going ahead* with the bond sale. It meant a *total* financial catastrophe, a disaster to the P.F.C., and to Berenson and Nordman's slickly laid plans to rip-off the taxpayers. Lord...*no wonder* those big-shots who had grabbed that maintenance worker were nervous and excited.

Friday morning a large group of concerned taxpayers protesting and opposing the bond sale had shown up in court to back me at the hearing, several people brought tape recorders with them. It wasn't a bad idea, it was nearly ten and there was no sign of the required court reporter in the room. Coming from the chambers two deputy sheriffs ordered the people to remove the recorders from the court, it was an order from the judge. When satisfied all recorders were removed one of the deputies called the court to order.

It was a slight surprise when Judge Robert Shaw garbed in black robes came from the chambers. I'd been expecting Robert Willard, the judge who had signed the orders for the hearing. But Berenson was too cagey to put Willard on the bench where he could louse up the whole deal. Willard had *earned* the nickname of, 'Old Wishy Washy' throughout the years of his diligently screwing up just about everything he touched.

Shaw was the judge who'd been *caught lying* on the witness stand during Robinson's trial. In his desperation at being caught lying, he had lashed out wildly with vengeful charges against Deem, the D.A., who he'd blamed for putting him in his sniveling and embarrassing predicament. Shaw took his seat, there was still no official reporter present *as required.* Swiveling his chair to face the blank sidewall of the courtroom he pretended to be reading the complaint. Mumbling desultorially he flipped pages, his words were indistinguishable from more than five feet. I listened trying to pick up Shaw's words, I knew damn good and well Berenson had instructed him precisely how he was to handle the hearing. Suddenly I was positive I'd heard Shaw mumble, "DISMISSED."

I slammed a heavy book down on the table with a crack. In the shocked silence my words were heard throughout the room, "Judge, did I just hear you say, 'Case Dismissed?'"

Shaw jerked, swiveling around to the audience he stammered in a startled, frightened voice, "Oh, ah, no, I didn't say dismissed." He was chalk white, his face looked like maybe his head was completely devoid of blood. Extended eyeballs stared vacantly like small, black ball bearings. I knew this deal had him under terrific pressure, I was not too happy myself. Obviously their so-called judicial hearing was a lousy kangaroo court if there ever was one.

Tinged with a sarcasm I couldn't hide, I jabbed, "Judge, have you read this case?"

"Well, oh, no I haven't."

It was *hard* for me to use the *term of respect,* "Your Honor, I am requesting a continuance to try to get a lawyer. First of all I haven't had time to prepare an answer to the SHORTEN TIME ORDER.

Also, the court has not even *read* the complaint and consequently is completely unfamiliar with it which is cause for a continuance."

A lightning shaft darted from those black ball bearings, I read the *vicious hatred* aimed at me as the judge swiveled back facing a side wall. Staring at the blank wall he mumbled interminably, suddenly turning around he squeaked, "Case Dismissed." Springing from his chair Judge Shaw leaped like a kangaroo, disappearing through the door leading to his chambers. Close behind him, his deputy sheriff slammed the heavy door with unmistakable finality. Chief Assistant County Counsel James J. McBride and William Hair, a lawyer from Ben Nordman and Judge Berenson's law firm were jumping around victory patting each other on their backs for a *job well done*, with wide grins they exited the courtroom.

It was only ten forty-five, I spent the balance of the day trying to figure out how Berenson could wind up my lawsuit in a matter of minutes, according to him all the other Superior Court cases were running *five years behind* the schedule. I finally concluded the only *necessary* ingredient for this kind of *speedy* judicial chicanery was that it involved *his own* and *Nordman's* personal financial interests.

By nine the following night, Saturday June 5, 1976, I'd closed the store and was heading north on Highway 33 toward home. It was a clear warm night. Passing the small shopping center to the right I noticed the lights being switched off as they closed. A short distance further on I slowed to make a right turn onto a narrow private lane. Valley Meadow Dr. had no street lights, it wound upward, rounding curves lined with giant, beautiful old Spanish Oaks. Their dark bulks were outlined by a large yellow moon just appearing over a hilltop. Approaching my house I observed a car parked on the same side, a short distance up the hill. It was in a very dark spot under a tree. Suddenly I became completely alert, it didn't belong to any of my neighbors and seldom did strangers park on this narrow road.

Two ghostly figures loomed in the front seat of the car. All the old instincts and senses I'd developed from working many years as a policeman on dark streets and back alleys warned me something was *definitely wrong,* danger was lurking close. Turning left into my driveway it slanted down about ten feet lower than the street into a carport. Switching the motor and headlights off I grabbed my old 38 S&W snubnose which I always kept handy and slid out the passenger side of the pickup. Quickly moving across the dark carport I stood silently beside the trunk of a large oak in the middle of the yard. It was pitch dark, the moon's rays hadn't yet reached the front yard. I focused my eyes on a point about twelve feet above me toward my neighbors driveway. Through some large porous hedges I watched the lower portion of a pair of legs moving stealthily down the drive. The legs stopped, I could no longer see them, but I knew they were there.

Not even breathing, I wondered, could I be seen? Suddenly there was a sharp crack, a slug blasted a branch from the tree next to my head. The shadowy legs ran swiftly back to the parked car. I dashed toward my driveway, their car roared past me less then fifteen feet away with the lights off. I could have easily shot them through the window, but if I missed there was a house across the street. Rapid fire I slammed two slugs into the side of their car. Running to the middle of the road I fired a parting shot at the fleeing car, its lights didn't flash on until they reached a sharp curve a quarter of a mile down the hill.

I figured it would be useless to chase them in the truck, besides, prowl cars would be arriving soon. I made a quick reconnaissance around the house. Three patrol cars arrived parking directly in front of my driveway. From across the street a man and a woman came running, reaching the deputies before I did. A deputy asked who had called, the woman said, "We did, we heard what sounded like a shot and went to our balcony on the second floor where we had a good view of the street. A car came roaring down the road with the lights out, a muzzle blast came from it aimed at the man across the street." They explained how they then heard my shots but said that the first two they had heard were much louder than mine. A sergeant who had just arrived asked me, "Do you *know anybody who would want to kill you?*"

I knew Berenson without a doubt would sleep a hell of a lot better knowing I was dead, but just yesterday morning they'd dismissed my suit against the *new* Government Center. I couldn't believe they'd risk everything at this point trying to kill me if they didn't have to. "Sergeant, at this time I really do not know anyone who would have a motive to kill me."

Deputies were contacting other neighbors, some said they thought they'd heard firecrackers. Ultimately the sheriff filed a *final report* that in his opinion it was *nothing more* than innocent firecrackers. Nothing about the shooting ever appeared in the papers. One thing I knew for damn sure, I'd been around a hell of a lot of shootings in my police experience and I was a navy Gunners Mate before that. There wasn't anybody who could convince me that a firecracker had popped that branch off the oak tree next to my head.

Monday June 7, I was busy with early morning customers when the phone rang, "Hi Gary, I have been trying continually to get hold of you over the weekend."

"I was right here at the store all day Saturday and Sunday, I don't know why you couldn't reach me." I asked, "Who am I talking to?"

The voice said pleasantly, just like we were *old buddies,* "This is James McBride, from the County Counsel office. I just wanted you to know that even though *we dismissed* your suit against the County Center you have still *accomplished your purpose* of halting our sale of series 'B' revenue bonds tomorrow."

I thought quickly, something is damn fishy about this phone call, I recalled the haughty smirk McBride had flipped me when he and Bill Hair walked out of Shaw's courtroom. He continued his friendly approach, "The fact that you *have a right* to appeal Shaw's decision *prohibits us by law* from selling the bonds. I would like you to come down to our office and *sign off your right* to appeal."

"McBride, yesterday I contacted an attorney in Los Angeles who is going to check into this situation for me, my legal position is now in his hands." I gave him the phone number of Terrell Powell, my lawyer in Los Angeles.

The Chief Asst. Counsel was menacing, "I do not want to talk to your lawyer, I haven't time. We've flown a group of wealthy bankers in from New York. They're waiting here right now to negotiate the bond sale. In fact if you will come down right now I will show you any records you want to see to prove there's nothing crooked about this deal."

With that I burst into laughter, "McBride, there is no way in this world you can ever convince me that Judge Berenson and Nordman are not gangsters." McBride's tone of voice changed, the abrupt fury that involuntarily exploded from his mouth betrayed what had been his true intent. Berenson and Schechter were pouring on the heat while they whispered to McBride, exhorting him to get me to *sign off my right* to appeal.

It was too much for his raw nerves, McBride screamed into the telephone, *"You can not halt the legal and orderly processes of the County Government. I am going to the District Attorney, I will file felony charges of Malicious Prosecution against you, believe me, I am going to have your God damn ass in jail."*

A feeble light of warning had flickered in my brain ever since this conversation had begun, now it was flashing and clanging in my head like an old navy war ship sounding battle stations knowing a major attack is coming. Good Christ! This son-of-a bitch had known since Friday when Shaw dismissed my lawsuit that I had a right to appeal their kangaroo court ruling. It meant they were *still in the same boat* they were in to begin with so far as not being able to *legally* sell the revenue bonds.

With this startling revelation slamming through my brain I still managed to hold my temper. Quietly I said, "McBride, I gave you my lawyer's number, you'll have to call Powell," I hung up. McBride immediately dialed Powell who also refused his demand to have me sign any release of my appeal rights. McBride, overwhelmed with desperation then threatened my lawyer with the same fate of being feloniously prosecuted and jailed that he had threatened me with.

Back in the storeroom it was cool and quiet. Sitting down on a Pepsi box I leaned against the wall. It wouldn't take a *crystal ball* to figure out the *reason* they wanted to murder me last Saturday night. If I had become suddenly dead over the weekend Berenson and his partner Nordman's grandiose conspiracy to steal all those millions would have had free sailing. They'd become plenty damn desperate because they went ahead and sold the bonds anyway...*without even bothering* to give the legally required notification.

A few days later I walked into Terrell Powell's office in L.A. The only reason I had been able to retain Powell was because he'd just passed the bar. He had no conception he was about to plant his feet deep in the *quicksands* of one of the ugliest, most cunning, vicious rat races ever devised. It is called, the *Legal Profession*. The realm of legalese is comprised of people totally devoid of any mercy. So terribly enmeshed in a *mad quest* of power and gold that all their jabbering of ideals, ethics, morals and principals is as genuine as the false and diseased smiles that play upon their lips.

Terrell was a black man, he'd earned his law degree from Loyola, one of California's most highly regarded institutes of legal learning. Powell looked like Anthony Davis, a great running back for U.S.C. that I had admired. The purpose of my visit to him that day was in going over the appeal he was preparing in answer to the dismissal of my civil case, No. 60980, by Judge Shaw. The brief was addressed to the Second Appellate District of the California State Court of Appeal. His attack on Shaw's dismissal was based on Code of Civil Procedure violations, SHORTENING OF TIME, DENIAL OF REQUEST FOR CONTINUANCE TO CONTACT COUNSEL, DISMISSAL OF THE COMPLAINT WITH PREJUDICE, etc.

We had a short discussion of the basic facts of the case and some explanations by Powell as to the legal strategy of the appeal he had prepared. I read the brief, it appeared to comprehensively cover all of the errors, abuses of discretion, and legal insufficiencies of Shaw's ORDER OF DISMISSAL. Powell then assured me the brief would be filed the next day.

Shortly after talking to Powell, I received a large manila envelope in the mail. It was a NOTICE dismissing our appeal by a panel of three judges in Division Five of the Second Appellate District of the California State Court of Appeal. By this time I was accustomed and hardened to such routine cover-ups by judges. But after looking over the dismissal I began to readily discern even *more* startling evidence of the 'Modus Operandi' of corrupt judges. How they *joined in* with other corrupt judges in suppressing and destroying any sort of legal uprisings by honest citizens which would reveal the judges criminal misdeeds of Malfeasance and Incompetence.

In bold capital letters, on the front page of the documents I saw the order made by the 'Honorable' Appeal Court Judges that their dismissal of my case No. 60980 was "NOT FOR PUBLICATION." Hell, I didn't blame them, reading it I immediately understood why they would not want anybody else to see this abortion. These *noble guardians* of justice proceeded to cover-up for Judge Berenson and Nordman, by ordering that, "They saw no need in *further identifying* the *involved* judges by even mentioning their names in the dismissal."

So far as my complaint about Shaw's *refusal* to allow the hearing to be recorded they simply stated, "We will *assume* generally for the Appeal that the plaintiff's statements are a part of the record." The Appeal Judges noted that McBride had captioned his Motion as one 'TO STRIKE AND DISMISS' my complaint as a 'SPEAKING MOTION' which is *not permitted* in California (Vesely v Sager 1971 5 Cal. 3d 153, 167-168, and see 157, Fn. 4) however, the three judges deviously maneuvered around this by saying, "What County Counsel James McBride really had intended to do was file an ORTHODOX DEMURRER which made it alright."

Then after reading a few more lines it was *clearly evident* why the noted judges had changed McBrides's 'SPEAKING MOTION' to an 'ORTHODOX DEMURRER' which made it alright.

According to due process I should have had *fifteen days* notice instead of just the *three days* I received. After changing McBride's MOTION TO A HEARING ON A DEMURRER they then stated that, "GOOD CAUSE was shown to DISMISS because the pendente of the suit would have effectively prevented the sale of the revenue bonds and halted the orderly processes of the County Government." They further conspired to aid and abet the cover-up by ruling that McBride's, MOTION COULD BE HEARD WITHOUT A REQUIRED STATUTORY PERIOD OF FIFTEEN DAYS NOTICE.

However these revenue bonds were not being sold by the county, they were being *huckstered* by the Ventura County Public Facilities Corporation. Despite such a clever, misleading name it is a private, non-profit corporation owned and operated by Judge Berenson and his law partner Ben Nordman.

The bullshit put out by these *noble jurists* continued on and on, page after page until finally their last paragraph advised me, "My Complaint was Frivolous; my Appeal was without Merit; and Shaw's Trial Court had properly Dismissed the Action. THE JUDGEMENT IS AFFIRMED." Then on the last page lest anybody should forget, the three Appeal Judges *again* printed in large, bold, capital letters and underlined them, notifying everyone that the decision was, "NOT FOR PUBLICATION." The Presiding Judge was Otto M. Kaus, his ruling was concurred in by Clark Stephen and J.H. Hastings.

We Petitioned the State Supreme Court, within days Powell sent me notice, "The State Supreme Court Denied us a hearing on our Petition. Unfortunately, this ends whatever battles that could have been waged in court. But this should not end your fight for right in Ventura County. You will just have to fight in a different arena, your newspaper for one." Yours very truly, Terrell D. Powell.

I had organized a small town paper in an effort to enlightened the people of the vicious corruption within our county government. I'd hoped that the Star Free Press, the biggest newspaper in Ventura City would also delve into the situation to reveal to the public the true facts. But the opposite occurred, every time I tried to expose what was going on, even with documented evidence, the Star Free Press counteracted with editorials *praising* all the crooked politicians in county government and covered-up for them. The lies printed by the major paper negated all our efforts to reach a larger portion of the people.

My suit to halt the courthouse construction was filed the first of June, by the middle of August it was completely wiped out. In only two and a half months Berenson and Nordman had demonstrated their treacherous behind-the-scenes political power and evil influence all the way to the State Supreme Court in Sacramento. With a single imperialistic nod the California State Supreme Court had swept Due Process and any resemblance of Justice under a huge, dusty old rug they keep up there in Sacramento just for this purpose.

After this judicial debacle I went back to work at the store with the definite intent of swallowing the bitter pill of total frustration. Unquestionably, the judges are *all-powerful* in their evil. I resigned myself to the fact that I'd reached the end of all the rope of legal recourse that our just, benevolent, judicial set-up was going to give me.

FATE - that small, indescribably mysterious word, fate, it kept dashing around in my head. Had that final judicial ruling debauched with Prejudice and Denials of any further legal hope been from the very beginning...my predestined fate?

Had there been a mystical or cabalistic decree commanding that dreary failure was to be my inevitable and ultimate fate? Each of us in this world are infinitesimal, the earth upon which we live is only a vague speck in the middle of everlasting infinity. The spinning of that tiny word in my brain all the more proved to me that fate since the beginnings of time has *forever* been a mysterious, *uncontrollable* element in our short allotments of time on earth. Everyone had their destiny...at least throughout life we endure a seemingly unavoidable succession of events which inexorably leads us to our conclusive fate of failure or success.

Several months rolled by, long days of tedious work hadn't served the purpose of wiping out a deep, constant aggravation. I'd endured nearly eleven years of successive tribulations in various degrees of importance since my civil service hearing. All ending in failure and signifying that I'd probably about reached my final destiny or fate. Only then another event occurred, verily causing me to believe that a fickle, capricious fate was never finished with you until the final thread was cut.

In Greek mythology three comely sisters, Clotho, Lachesis, and Atropos, being Goddesses, were believed to have control of all our destinies. Clotho spun a mysterious thread, Lachesis then rolled the thread which represented the course of life on a spindle. Atropos held a pair of scissors and nothing could stop her from mercilessly cutting the thread when the final hour of fate struck.

The small copper bell on the front door jingled. A man entering proceeded to casually move around the room, he displayed a typical tourists interest in a small town store and its wares. There was not the slightest inkling at the time that I would later on consider this unexpected meeting to be a momentous event of fate. But it was to signal an entirely new era and arena of legal conflict in my war with the *Berenson gang* and *their* spurious Public Facilities Corp..

Later on I was to consciously give much thought to the fact that Atropos had indeed *not yet* applied her deadly scissors to my thread. A happy, encouraging thought struck, *perhaps* she was eyeballing Berenson's life thread with far more relish than mine.

With a deep southern drawl the tourist made queries, generally regarding the local area. Apparently he was seeking a place to live with a more peaceful, rural atmosphere than he was experiencing in Los Angeles. The tourist was friendly, making new acquaintances with ease. I quickly discovered myself engaged in far more than the average banal talk regarding the weather and time of day. Robert DuPre was an attorney from South Carolina. Not a member of the California State Bar he was not entitled to practice law here. He had attempted to consult with L.A. lawyers in his field as a specialist of Federal Civil Rights Law. Bob explained how he had first arrived on Wilshire Blvd., *also known as* Lawyers Row, with its myriads upon myriads of law offices stretching for miles, from L.A. clear through Beverly Hills.

To these professional denizens of 'lawyers scam-land,' a Beverly Hills Post Office address is top gun, a most highly prized possession. Considered a necessity by them, it is *suggestive* if not positive proof of their prosperity and prestige as legal wizards. Its weight carries an official connotation, a guarantee of their intimate connections among the wealthy social stratum of Hollywood's glittering, most glamorous personalities.

Bob had a Southerner's knack in dialoging the comical antics of the scam people he observed during his sojourn on lawyers row. He described towering office buildings encased with inscrutable black glass, lushly carpeted rooms compacted with lawyers by the square foot. Engaged in dramatic scenarios of boiler room activity it was a master setting for the incongruous escapades of scam-land deluxe. Lawyers Row was unquestionably a farcical affair, however, it was much too wild, too far from Bob's conception of legitimate practice of law. Seeing at first hand the intricate entanglements of lawyers with a *phony heart specialist* and *lab technicians* setting up scams defrauding Medi-Cal patients was the last straw. "What I really want to do is come to *a nice quiet, peaceful little county* like this where things are done *honest and legal,* out in the open."

I couldn't help it, I shouted, "Horseshit." My sudden unexpected crude outburst startled DuPre, he was shaken. "Bob I know all about those Hollywood and Wilshire Blvd. dingbats, hell, they are nothing compared to the organized corruption of the judges and the heads of Ventura County Government." Expressing amazment he mirrored disbelief at what I was saying. "Listen Bob, we have a judge here, Jerome Berenson, he's been the Presiding Judge of Ventura County for eighteen years. He has *never been elected,* in fact, he has *never even appeared on a ballot.* He's the absolute boss of everything that moves in the county, he was appointed by Governor Pat Brown, one of the lousiest governors California has ever had, that is with the *exception* of his whacko son Jerry, who is now the Governor. He's *appointed* more sick hypes and sex deviates to the Courts than his old man ever thought of."

Bob's face still registered disbelief, he kept on questioning what I told him. "I could go on telling you about these crummy Ventura crooks forever, but I have a lot better idea." Reaching beneath the counter I produced a stack of papers, I handed them over to him. "Here, I've been documenting all this crap I'm telling you about for over nine years now. Take these with you, read them, if you don't believe it, or it scares the hell out of you and I never see you again don't worry about it, I will understand."

Robert left the store clutching the papers and shaking his head. I gazed fixedly out the window, vaguely acknowledging the familiar flipping shadows of the late afternoon north bound traffic. Silently I agreed to myself, that's the last I'll ever see of Robert DuPre. The following morning I was taken by surprise. It was snappy cold, yet here he came in his shirt sleeves still clutching the stack of papers. "Good morning Bob, well it looks like I was wrong. Last night I bet myself I would never see you again."

He chuckled, "Hell no, I was up the entire night reading all this stuff you gave me, I couldn't put it down. Your lawyer at the Civil Service hearing was about as sad as anything I ever heard of."

"You mean Dean Pic'l?"

"That's him, and this character Jerome Berenson has to be right out of the past. I can't believe he's been able to *get away with* such criminal acts."

"The problem is that Berenson controls everything in the County Government. He and his law partner Ben Nordman and Nordman's cousin, Bud Milligan, the President of the Bank of A. Levy, own the land, the money, the County Government, and the law. They've *run things* around here for so damn long *nobody* dares to oppose them, especially other lawyers, that is if they don't want to be destroyed."

"Well, I've run into a few of these type of things back home but never anything this large and powerful or well organized. Every once in a while some big politician or judge would get crazy ideas in his head that he could organize and take control. But it just won't work back there because the counties are so small, everything's too close knit, everybody knows what's going on. They've been trying to sneak in a new County Courthouse back in my old hometown of Walhalla, for years and they still can't get it going. If they'd tried to pull what Nordman and Berenson have pulled with this Courthouse deal out here they'd have been in the state pen before they could ever stick a shovel in the ground."

I added, "There's another problem possibly you've never ran into before, the newspapers. They refuse to dig down deep and tell the people the true story of who runs things and how. The Ventura Star Free Press's editor, Judas Gius, always covers-up very cleverly for them. I have never figured out the editor's connections, however, knowing these crooked bastards I'm sure that money and power is the only possible answer."

"Yesterday when you were recounting all this corruption, my first reaction was probably about the same as the average citizen with no experience in government intrigue or how politicians operate. But I'll tell you, some things you've documented in these papers tipped me off. It has convinced me there sure as hell is something awfully wrong in Ventura County." DuPre wagged his head in dismay, "That part about Judge Berenson *killing* the Grand Jury investigation and all the *evidence that exposed* their conspiracy to *frame* government officials reveals that a very powerful, evil force is at work here. The County Judiciary is in it clear up to their necks. I'm speaking from considerable experience involving criminal conspiracy and intrigue within governmental circles."

Pausing, Bob continued, "I sort of got my start when I graduated from the South Carolina Law School in 1953 and passed the State Bar. I was sworn in that same year. After a few months of private practice I became interested in law enforcement, I joined the FBI. After graduating from the FBI Academy I was assigned to a squad investigating communist activities. Much of my time was spent out here on the west coast, particularly around East L.A.. Later I was transferred to New York City."

I finished with a customer. Bob continued, "After four years with the Bureau I got a job on U. S. Senator Strom Thurmond's staff as

Legislative Assistant. Believe me, in that post I got a barrel full of experience. My job and duty was to read and analyze, I mean fully analyze, all Senate and House bills for the purpose of enlightening and advising Strom Thurmond as to their legalities and merits. This was for his use in determining his vote and position in speaking pro or con before the Senate. Constitutionality was *always* the first and *most* vital determination in analysis of proposed bills. I will never forget...one of the most important and provoking bills I encountered was the 1957 Civil Rights Bill introduced by President Eisenhower. Basically it was focused on expanding the original 1871 Civil Rights Bill. It mainly provided negroes with rights to vote and protection from oppressive state laws."

I listened with great interest as Bob spoke on. "This new bill of 1957, actually it was aimed more directly at discrimination against negroes. But, however, in *my* legal analysis I came to a definite and startling conclusion. This new bill could *eventually* through case law evolve down to the fact that, all citizens, *regardless* of race or color would have the *right* to sue government entities. Through the courts they could attack officials who while *acting under* the *Color of Law*, misused and abused their official capacities and powers to deprive citizen's of their Constitutional Rights without Due Process. Some Rights being the protection of Life, Liberty and Property. I strongly believed these new avenues of redress were extremely necessary, a *rightful recourse* being legislated for the citizens. However, Strom viewed the bill differently, more in the light of its having granted strong, and to be more explicit, *very dangerous powers to the people* in that *they would have the right* to sue corrupt government officials for their misconduct. Perversely, Strom Thurmond blocked the bill by conducting a record filibuster of fifty seven hours on the Senate Floor. As a result most of the bill went down to defeat. However, Pres. Lyndon Johnson, in 1964 signed a Civil Rights Act containing everything that had been struck out of the 1957 bill. It was in 1961, after a number of years on Thurmond's staff, I got an opportunity that was to prove even more exciting and stimulating. But the work load on this job and the accompanying mental stress and physical tensions were notoriously known to be of monster proportion. I was appointed to the U.S. Justice Department by President Kennedy's brother, Atty. General Robert Kennedy. In September 1961 I was assigned as Federal Prosecutor to the Western Judicial District of South Carolina, headquarters were in Greenville."

I was astounded by the strangers background. "Gary, I have to tell you...some of those cases were really rough. I had been successful in prosecuting a lot of government officials. County attorneys, sheriffs, state circuit judges and minor federal officials, also private lawyers under the criminal provisions of the Civil Rights Act, which covers deprivations of Life, Liberty and Property. From what I've perceived at this point it appears your problems are distinctly symptomatic of the West Coast. I've found since being out here that with very few exceptions lawyers shy away from the Federal Courts."

"That's certainly understandable, the judges out here are a closed circuit. At one time in a fit of frustration and desperation I decided to write to the U.S. Attorney General in Los Angeles. I explained to them in full detail what was going on and that I wanted to make a formal complaint. I asked for a return receipt, I got one back from the Attorney General's office with a signature and an official stamp on it. After a couple months of waiting with no answer I drove to L.A. wanting to see if anything was being done. Hell, it turned out to be just one big ridiculous waste of time and money."

Bob kept nodding understandingly as I continued. "On one of the highest, most inaccessible floors of the Federal Building, the Atty. General has a small, glass enclosed desk and switchboard with one woman on the other side. Through a tiny hole in the glass you have to try to converse with her. She claimed to know nothing about my correspondence. But when I showed her my proof that the Attorney General had gotten my letter she condescended to call through her switchboard to what she said was the Mail Receiving Department. Then she wheezed through the small hole in the glass, 'I am sorry, the Mail room knows nothing about your letter.' Well, look at this receipt, see the name on it, call this person and see what they know about it."

Showing great annoyance, she responded, "Sir, I don't know that person, you see we have lots of people who work the Mail room."

"Bob, understand...while all this stupid double talk was going on a steady stream of both male and female lawyers had been coming up to the window, and each time she would push a buzzer and the door opened allowing them to enter into the main workings of this weird place."

Bob grinned, he knew the scene I described. "Each of these male and female attorneys appeared to have everything in common. All quite young, they wore beautiful tailored form fitting, gaily colored slacks flourishing their well rounded bottoms. With special emphasis both sexes were extravagantly coiffured. As with the male peacock, the male lawyers displayed an upper hand in the latest of fashions. Each of them, both male and female jealously coveted an expensive alligator skin, gold monogrammed briefcase. Lawyers dropping the names of the higher level federal personages concealed behind the buzzer operated door received considerably more respect from the woman behind the glass. I noticed she attached more prestige to the lawyers whose elegant briefcases appeared more fully stuffed with important documents. After more than an hour of door buzzing and my futile attempts at an intermittent conversation with the woman it became obvious I was getting nowhere. Andrea Ordin, the female U. S. Attorney appointed by Pres. Jimmy Carter, had securely and effectively insulated herself against the *detestable* public by erecting a barrier of glass and noncommittal front desk employees. I had the same old familiar feeling, they'd been prepared and waiting for my personal visit. Their story of never receiving any information from me was bullshit. I headed toward the elevator to get the hell out of the place when I heard a voice call. I looked back, the woman had half risen from her stool, leaning over she had her mouth close to the glass. Maybe she felt sorry for me, or was mocking, I couldn't tell, but she was shouting, 'Sir, if you come back next Thursday at two o'clock *maybe* someone will be able to talk to you.' I shouted back, lady this is Monday, I drove over a hundred miles down here from Ventura to talk with someone. I can't close my business again and come back next Thursday at two o'clock. She repeated, 'If you'll return Thursday at two maybe somebody will talk to you.' The door of the elevator closed, I could still hear her."

Bob said, "I know exactly what you were up against."

"DuPre, my instincts were not tricking me when I suspected that they were prepared for me to show up. So, doing a little checking I discovered that Andrea Ordin, the Federal Attorney General, is the wife of Robert Ordin, a U.S.Magistrate. Conveniently he happens to be a Federal Bankruptcy Judge who is involved in countless corrupt scams with Ben Nordman and Judge Berenson. And to top this all off Nordman also conveniently happens to be a Federal Bankruptcy Judge for Ventura County."

"I follow you, when Andrea Ordin received the evidence you had sent her regarding the corruption in Ventura County I'm damn sure it only took *a few seconds* before Andrea and her husband got hold of Berenson and Nordman. That of course explains why there isn't any record of your documents in their Mail Department. Gary, if it is alright with you I'd like very much to read and study what ever else you have. At this point *I can see* gross, outrageous Civil Rights violations deeply involving a criminal conspiracy *committed* under the Color of Law."

I felt new hope, "Hell Bob, that sounds great, come on." I led him through the store to a dark room in the far corner of the warehouse where I flipped a switch on the light bulb hanging from a cord in the ceiling. "DuPre, see all those old whiskey and beer boxes, they are full of newspaper clippings from ten years back. Over there in that corner are my Pro-per law cases plus a bunch of other official and court documents that I have filed and collected. In the others I have some more interesting material relating to this entire affair."

From the doorway he gazed around the room at the disorganized piles. The older ones were covered with thick coats of dust, smokey gray cobwebs profusely decorated the walls. The weak illumination from the encrusted light bulb didn't do much for the scene either. Bob said nothing. Experiencing sharp misgivings I thought, this time for sure I have seen the last of lawyer DuPre.

To the contrary, he was undaunted. In minutes he had swiped the miscellaneous collection of junk from the top of the dusty desk and replaced it with a yellow legal pad. An old stained coffee cup full of decrepit ball point pens was added. Bob had already seated himself in a rickety swivel chair. He started pulling documents from dusty, spider infested boxes.

CHAPTER 22

Shortly after the shooting on Valley Meadow we sold our house and bought the building next to the store. A nice five room Spanish stucco house, it had been built sometime in the 1920's. Outside of needing paint and general repairs it was in fair condition. Zoned for commercial use, it doubled the size of the store property. Cleaning it up, I put in a grill and deep fryer for onion rings and french fried potatoes for a sandwich stand in conjunction with the liquor store.

The only work requiring a county permit was a hood and fan over the grill. I phoned a building Inspector named Williams asking him to come out and make an inspection. He always asked me about the work then would say, "Okay, you're doing alright, it's not necessary for me to come out to see it." Meantime a Health Inspector, Lloyd Hughes, came by looking the place over. He said everything passed, then commented, "You are lucky, if that kitchen sink wasn't divided and stainless steel you would have to replace it."

Installation of the hood was finally complete. Williams was called at least ten times in two weeks, everytime he promised to come out, but he never did. I decided to go ahead and open for business. The hamburger stand had been in operation about seven months and I'd gotten all the county tax bills including personal property taxes for equipment etc. made out to the business, all were paid on time. One day a county building inspector walked in the restaurant and asked if he could look at the grease hood that we'd installed. "Go ahead, help yourself, I've made a lot of phone calls trying to get someone to come out."

"Yes, I am aware of that...I also know *why* no one has been out here. Everything looks fine, it's a good installation job, I am signing off the Final Inspection." I thanked him and he drove off. The next morning before the restaurant opened two men came knocking on the door, they claimed they were from the building department and wanted to go through the building to inspect. "It won't be necessary, a man from your department was here yesterday and approved the final inspection."

One of them lied, "We don't have any record of an inspection, we want to come in and look around."

"All you've got to do is go back to your office and talk with the Inspector yourself, you'll find that a Final Notice of Inspection has been filed, I have my copy." I was getting mad, "Hell...who you guys kidding? You know damn well inspection was made yesterday, that's why you're here. The Inspector who came out probably didn't know he wasn't supposed to okay anything for me. Now *you've* been *sent* out here to cover-up and write a phony report that will put me out of business. I got an honest inspection yesterday and there's no way I'm going to let you in here." Closing the door I walked over to the window, the pair were standing a few feet away, a surly voice said, "I know how to fix this son-of-a-bitch, let's go to Oak View."

A few months after buying this place I'd bought a neighborhood cocktail lounge on an acre of land about five miles north of here. It was in the small town of Oak View, it had another building on the property which fronted on Highway 33. At the rear a county road gave it additional access. The place could pay for itself, I figured in a few years I'd add some more units for additional income. When I heard the rough voiced guy say, 'Let's go up to Oak View,' I had a pretty good idea what he was planning on doing.

The cocktail lounge was already opened for the days business, I knew there was no way to keep them out even if I went up there. I worked around the restaurant a few hours then drove up to the bar. Soon as I entered the door the bartender let me know, "Hey Gary, we had a couple visitors, they left this." He gave me a large piece of paper. "These two guys went through the whole building, their noses were in everything for a solid hour. Then they slapped me with this paper, it's an Official Notice from the Building Inspector, he says he found over twenty code violations." I read the list, it was absolutely ridiculous. One of the violations stated that the inspector didn't like the paneling that was on the wall of the ladies restroom, he'd signed it, Inspector Bowling.

Several months before this I'd applied to the Sheriff for renewal of the annual permit for the pool table at the bar. It never came. Al Jalaty was now the Sheriff, he'd been Police Chief of Port Hueneme eight years ago when I'd told him about the *frame-up*. I hadn't seen him for a while, I decided to drop in and inquire what was going on with the permit. Al returning from lunch spotted me waiting in his outer office. He greeted me friendly, "Hi stranger, come on in," he motioned me to sit down. Looking around I noticed the room was only slightly larger than his chief's office in Pt. Hueneme. The only added prestige appeared to be the two average size windows with a view of the ocean. The Sheriff said, "I haven't seen you in quite a while, everything going okay?"

"Just a few problems, I stopped by to see what was holding up my renewal permit for a pool table at the Hilltop."

His big smile faded, he appeared apologetic, "Oh yes...I know, the renewal came across my desk, but I'm afraid I have some *bad* news for you."

"Alright I'm used to *bad* news, what is it?"

"I got a letter from Building and Safety, they say you are violating the building code. They asked me *not to* issue the permit."

"For Christ sake, since when does the Sheriff's Department take its orders from Victor Husbands in the Building Department?"

"The Supervisors have changed Husband's title, they've appointed him head of their Environmental Resources Agency, which includes the Building and Safety, Weights and Measures, Health Department, Zoning and Planning, Air Pollution, just about everything. He's very powerful."

"Al, that bar has *automatically* got a renewal permit for the pool table every year for thirty five years until now, when I own it."

"I know that...*believe me,* I am really sorry, but in the face of the letter I can't issue the renewal permit for you." I left, an odd feeling was coming over me, Sheriff Al Jalaty was *not* really as sorry as he professed.

On the way back to the store I was remembering, this is a replica of what happened about three years ago. A few years after I got the store going I had an opportunity to buy a large building across the highway from the store. A man getting along in years ran a second hand store there for many years, he was thinking of retiring. I saw many opportunities in cleaning up the place and combining a rural type country store with antiques and second hand stuff. I would add other items like hay and grain along with a garden machinery repair shop.

Well I bought the building, did a lot of work on the place making it real presentable. Plenty of hard work was involved, also a hell of a mess of running back and forth across the highway keeping both the liquor store and new place operating. It was picking up pretty good and we were holding our own financially. The way I'd painted and fixed up all our property had considerably up-graded the small business area that had badly deteriorated for many years.

Things were rolling fairly smooth...too smoothly I guess, the letter I'd just picked up in the days mail was from Capt. De Sanno, of the Sheriff's Department. It was the same Captain whose name was on the paper the two County Inspectors had used in their ruse trying to inspect the liquor store several years before. In his short, succinct statement Capt. De Sanno informed me he was *not* going to renew the business license for the new store.

I found De Sanno at his Headquarters in the old courthouse. Bill Meade, a Sgt. I had known for some time was present. Holding the letter out to the Captain I asked, "What's your reason for denying me a business license? The person I bought the property from has renewed that business license every damned year for fifteen years without any problem. Now that *I own it* the Sheriff is going to deny me a license." De Sanno began hemming and hawing around with a bunch of nonsense talk. "Forget all the bullshit De Sanno, I want to know the *reason* why *I can't* get a business license like *anybody else* around here."

He wouldn't look at me, "Hell Gary, you have been around City Hall and politicians a long time, you know all about the *Birds and the Bees,*" he snickered.

"Birds and bees your ass De Sanno," I bellowed, "What in hell are you trying to pull?"

Suddenly the Captain wasn't so sure of his ground, he mumbled, "The Sheriff's Office got a letter from Victor Husbands, head of the Planning Department, *to phase you out.*"

"PHASE ME OUT! By God De Sanno, I want to see that letter from Husbands."

"Oh no! That *letter is confidential and secret,* no way will I let you see it."

"Damn it! I demand to see that letter."

"Nothing doing, I am not giving you anything."

Terrible anger, I felt it coming on...I *had* to get out of there *fast*, there was no way I could take anymore of their rotten shit. I walked down the marble lined hall of the courthouse toward the door when Sgt. Meade caught up to me. Hesitating he said, "Gary, I'm sorry as hell about this, I want you to know the Sheriff's Department is not the one who is trying to get you."

Meade had always been a good officer and a nice guy, maybe his conscience was bothering him a bit. "Thanks Bill, but if the Sheriff's Department isn't trying to get me Capt. De Sanno is sure doing one hell of a good job."

I had no financial resources and God knows *what* they'd pull on me *next* if I fought back, even if I did no lawyer would take my case, it wasn't difficult to see the writing on the wall. Without the license I ended up losing the property, also considerable money, sweat and labor, not counting all the bitter disappointment involved. That deal with Capt. De Sanno was several years ago, there'd been no chance of getting an attorney at that time.

Things had changed slightly since then, I had Powell for a lawyer now. Since this *latest* permit denial by Jalaty I knew I had to make some documentation of what was going on. It wouldn't pay for me to file another lawsuit in Ventura, Berenson would simply have his judges dismiss it. About the only thing I could do was send a letter to the Board of Supervisors with a Post Office receipt proving they received it.

J. K. Mac Donald, the Supervisor in my district acknowledged my letter. He'd arranged a meeting with Victor Husbands, the Director of the Environmental Resources Agency, and Michael Bradbury an Assistant D. A. at that time. We were to discuss the accusations I'd made in my letter.

During the period of these events DuPre had been spending long days, months avidly reading, researching and cataloging the material and records stored in my back room. When he learned that Powell would be coming to Ventura for the meeting at Mac Donald's office Bob expressed a keen desire to be present. "I certainly have to take advantage of this opportunity in seeing and hearing such nefarious politicians and officials first hand. I've only been here a short time but in light of what I've learned about the outright corruption and intrigue and how they so *amazingly* are able to keep it *suppressed*, all I can say is...It's incredible...unbelievable."

It was nearly ten a.m. when Powell, Bob and I entered Supervisor Mac Donald's office at the new county center. Giving the secretary my name she came on very professional, "Oh yes, I shall inform the Supervisor you are here."

She walked into the adjacent room, within moments Mac Donald appeared in the doorway, "Good morning gentlemen, please come in my office." Ken, a short rotund individual, displayed a wide Bugs Bunny smile. I felt certain, in his inimitable way he must be firmly convinced his grin represented a friendly appearance calculated to disarm wary citizens. It was also a design to sooth and impress timid constituents with his sincere, kindly feelings toward them and their pressing problems.

Years ago Mac Donald got his start as a used car salesman in the small town of Ojai, fifteen miles north of Ventura. It was quite a prestigious jump for Mac Donald to politician. In those days, used car salesmen were at the bottom of the pole so far as honesty in dealings was concerned. Indicatively a recent public opinion survey reveals politicians have *slid* down the pole reaching dead bottom. Used car salesmen presently enjoy a rating for truth and integrity *much higher* than our leaders.

Ken Mac Donald had been busily working at setting up a glorious retirement plan for himself based on a mental and physical disability pension giving him a much greater amount of money than he had coming. At the same time he was also sowing active hatred within the Ventura County Civil Service Employees Assoc., by proposing plans to lower their annual wage increase scale and degrading their retirement benefit system. The Supervisor was basing this claim to a mental disability pension on his premise that, "During past years while in an official capacity as a politician struggling desperately to aid down-trodden people he'd permanently, mentally and physically disabled himself."

There was a probability Mac Donald could have indeed ruptured himself at some explicit period over the years as he clung frantically to that slippery public opinion poll. In a desperate struggle to halt this downward slide he had suffered excruciating mental pain and anguish as he passed in full review of his old buddies, the used car salesmen.

Crossing the room, Ken stationed himself behind his mahogany desk. Darting a glance at us he relinquished his bunny grin only a slight degree as he spoke. "Well gentlemen, what can I do for you?" I thought, what's with this character, pretending like he doesn't even know why we are here? Michael Bradbury then entered followed by Victor R. Husbands, the Director of the Environmental Resource

Agency. Husband's assistants were right behind him carrying heavy volumes of records. These politicians are pretty clever, I knew they had discussed my letter among themselves. This meeting was set up for *one* purpose only, so they could *later* state that they'd given me a fair opportunity to air my grievances. It would be a very expensive and futile meeting for me. However, I couldn't afford to put myself in the position of having to admit in the future that I'd turned down their magnanimous and unselfish offer to clarify the problem.

Powell fired off pointed questions at the Director about licenses, permits and inspection procedures. He was extremely arrogant and equivocal, muttering he motioned to the big stack of papers on his assistant's lap. The aide obediently picked up on his cue and started thumbing through the files. He flapped through the papers, at the same time he carried on a self-educational discussion wreathed in governmental gabble about regulations, requirements, procedurals, applicables, assumptions, etc., etc..

There was a silence, the aide had discontinued thumbing through the files. Evidently he was unable to locate what he was supposed to find. Nervously he gawked around the room, shooting a chagrined glance at Husbands he dribbled, "I am unfamiliar with this case, I haven't been employed here very long."

DuPre had quietly observed the oppressive duplicity of the sham meeting. Now looking directly at Husbands he said authoritatively, "Husbands are you acting under secret orders from Judge Berenson in harassing and refusing Gary business licenses and permits?"

Startled, Victor Husbands reacted quickly to this spur by DuPre. "Absolutely not, I *do not* even know Judge Berenson!"

DuPre had him going, "Hell man, this is a small county, you have been around here for years, you mean to say you have never even passed Judge Berenson in the hallway of the courthouse, never even exchanged a casual greeting with him?"

Husbands blundered, "That's correct, I wouldn't even *know* Judge Berenson if he walked in here right now!" The totally unexpected, astonishing lies brought a frightened hush over the officials.

Bradbury, the D.A., was quick to react, realizing that DuPre was about to trick Husbands into blowing the *whole* deal he interrupted shouting, "Hey, hey...just hold on there Mr. DuPre...you are cross examining Mr. Husbands."

Bob grinned, "Of course I am, that is the *only way* in the world I am going to get the truth out of him, that's the only way *any* of you people are going to tell the truth."

Bradbury was unnerved, unsure of his ground he asked Bob, "Are you a lawyer?"

Bob answered, "Yes I am."

"Do you have a business card?"

Bob retorted, "No, I'm just here as a friend of Gary's."

Bradbury was well aware that as an assistant D.A. his legal duties were to investigate and prosecute crimes. Yet, here he was, not only *defending* but actually *representing* corrupt public officials who were misusing and abusing their authority and public office. His mouth quivering, Bradbury leaned forward in his chair and whispered to DuPre, "Are you gentlemen *recording* this meeting?"

Powell observed, "It is quite apparent we are getting nowhere and I don't believe *things are going to get any better.*"

With that I said, "That's for sure," and headed for the door.

CHAPTER 23

Three months had passed since DuPre had plopped down on the rickety swivel chair in the dusty office and undertook his arduous, exhaustive scrutiny of all my documents and records. One day Bob yelled, "Hey, if you have a spare minute come on in here." The desk Bob had cleared was now strewn with papers. The yellow pad was full of lawyer type scribblings and doodles, the stained old cup was almost empty of ball point pens. But the room was still decorated with what appeared to be the same old cobwebs. "I want to explain some facts and convey a legal point of view I have arrived at."

"Okay, fire away."

"Considering everything that's happened, let's start back when you *first* went to the Dist. Attorneys Deem and Eskin, and Grand Jury Foreman Penfield with your knowledge of corruption, that happened to be about eight months *before* you were fired," DuPre waved his hands expressing his point, "many substantial, flagrant violations of your Civil Rights have occurred. The first and most important thing to consider is the fact that a government employee *has a duty,* and the *right* to testify before a Grand Jury exposing official corruption, and *not* lose his job as a matter of retaliation. Now, on top of being fired, we have severe complications over the fact that Judge Jerome Berenson *tampered* with those Civil Service Commissioners during your hearing. Then Judge Berenson committed an even *far graver* crime by *killing* the Grand Jury investigation. There were so many *sneaky deals* they pulled at that hearing, for one, the Civil Service Rules *wrongfully required that you testify and the burden of proving you were innocent of doing anything wrong was also yours...always* the burden of proof is on the *person making the charges*. The fact that *soon* after the hearing, the Supervisors took official action and changed that ruling *proves* they were aware it was illegal. Dean Pic'l should *never* have allowed the hearing to commence without a court reporter being present. He *knew* that you could never file a lawsuit without a transcript of what transpired."

DuPre halted a moment while adding some quick thoughts on his yellow pad before he continued. "One of the *next* violations against your Civil Rights was *extremely* noteworthy. It begins to reveal more of the participants involved in their conspiracy to destroy you and thus bury forever your knowledge and evidence of *vast corruption* in Ventura Government. Let me ask you something, do you recall at the time that Phillip Cohen, an attorney from the County Counsel office, was appointed as the legal officer for the hearing?"

"Sure, I remember that."

"Okay, after losing your job you filed a couple pro-per lawsuits asking for your job back. The suits were dismissed by Judge Richard Heaton. You also sent several letters to the Supervisors *demanding a review* of the hearing based on numerous irregularities and all of the illegalities that occurred at the hearings."

"Yeah, I remember all of that."

"I recognize at that time you were *totally unable* to obtain legal counsel or advice, but what *you accomplished* by writing the letters and filing the suits was to *legally demand* a Superior Court review of your Civil Service hearing under Section 1094.5 of the California Code of Civil Procedure."

I blurted, "Oh yeah, bullshit! I didn't get any review."

"I know, just hold on a minute...it was their *next* move that really began to reveal to me the extent of their *desperation and terrible fear* of being exposed. In your documents I discovered a *directive* from the County Counsel office to the Supervisors saying that you had *no* further legal recourse as to the final decision of the Civil Service Commissioner. Written and signed by Phillip Cohen it constituted a *legal decision* laid down by the County Counsel's office, this was *totally illegal and vicious* but it was *needed* by the Supervisors so they could *reject your demand* for a hearing."

"I remember that letter Bob, and *I realized* what they were doing to me, *but what the hell could I do without an attorney?"*

"Yes, that was *truly* a shame, however, one of the most important things about this letter is *the revelation* that Phillip Cohen is deeply involved...he has to be...by law he's *required* to notify you that you had the *right* to a Superior Court review. They were conspiring to put a definite and final lid on any more of your attempts to make public what's going on. You also had a *Constitutional right* to run for a public office along with the *right* of free speech to notify the people what was happening. Then sometime after Cohen's letter to the Supervisors you filed another pro-per case to prohibit the Public Facilities Corp. from spending any money on the new Courthouse. In essence you had actually filed a taxpayers lawsuit which in *no way* could *legally* be dismissed in the manner that it was by Judge Shaw."

"That was case no. 60980."

"Correct, and on top of that, the Appeal Dismissal by Judge Otto Kaus was *chock full* of legal errors. *Very cleverly* he falsely claimed the lawsuit had been heard when *no facts had at anytime ever been presented.* In regard to that same case, another outrageous violation of your Civil Rights was the *evil threat of false imprisonment* made against you and your lawyer Powell, by James L. McBride, the Asst. County Counsel. I have to say, *this entire set of facts* is fantastic...in all my years of experience I've never run across anything that equals it. Proceeding a bit further, I already talked with Powell, he agrees since he's had no experience in the field of Civil Rights laws he will consult with me in filing a Civil Rights complaint in Federal Court. That is of course if you'll agree."

"Hell yes, course I agree, it's damn obvious we aren't going to get anywhere against Judge Berenson and Nordman in *any* California Court!"

June 2, 1978, Powell and DuPre filed our Civil Rights Complaint No. C.V. 78-2158-HP in L.A. Federal Court charging a, "Conspiracy to Deprive of Constitutional Rights," Amendments 1st, 4th, 5th, 6th, 14th, Title 42 United States Code of Laws, Sections 1983 et. seq..

July 17th, 1978, Dorothy Schechter, in behalf of Ventura County and all the defendants named, filed a, NOTICE OF A MOTION TO DISMISS our complaint, etc..

I sat in the back room with Bob while he read aloud Schechter's, MOTION TO DISMISS. "What's your opinion of it Bob?"

"I'll tell you...as a legal document purported to be a MOTION TO DISMISS a valid lawsuit, it is just about the *poorest* damn thing I have ever seen. She's written page after page doing nothing but call you all kinds of names. On one page she professes to be not only an attorney but also a psychiatrist, as such she's taken it upon herself to diagnose and analyze your specific mental sufferings. Your dread maladies are numerous, conspiracy fetishes, vendettas, unbalanced approaches and so forth. She's particularly incensed because of your *refusal* to slacken your attacks against Judge Berenson, whom she personally and very emphatically proclaims is the finest, most noted Superior Court Presiding Judge in California. Gary, I must warn you to be wary, Dorothy Schechter says she's not only an attorney and psychiatrist, she's a surgeon as well and this time she has blood in her eyes. She says, 'In order to stop any and all of your future uses of Civil Rights laws she's become *totally dedicated to chopping you off at the knees!*'"

"Chopping me off at the knees! Good Lord Bob...is that woman crazy?"

"No, possibly she is not totally crazy, but you have to remember and understand, the *only reason* she has that job isn't because she's a competent lawyer, it's because *she follows* their orders. First she catches hell from you, then Judge Berenson raises holy hell giving her orders to put the stoppers on you. What is really making her so damned frustrated is that on a straight, honest legal basis there's *no way* for her to stop you. She has to revert to every lie, subterfuge and insane twisting of facts she can think of. If Schechter wants to keep that good paying, highly prestigious job, she has to perform for Berenson like a *monkey on a string*. What is really disturbing her is how *deeply* she has become personally involved in all of Berenson's corruption. She is beginning to feel the hot breath of fear blowing down her neck. I'll point out just a few of her tortured twistings and turnings. She attempts to have our Complaint dismissed by claiming that you *rejected your rights* to a Judicial review years ago."

"Hold it right there DuPre. *That's one hell of a lie, I didn't reject anything.* It was completely the opposite, *I did everything possible I could to get a review despite the fact I could not get a lawyer!*"

"Right, that's exactly what I'm saying. She's trying to *cover up* the fact that Phillip Cohen, who was a County Counsel, *misled you* into believing that you didn't have the right to a Judicial review. It's all part of their continuing criminal conspiracy to destroy you. She has done her very best to bring up case law saying there's no conspiracy involved. But when you read the cases she refers to you find she's deleted vital parts changing their real meaning. One of the silliest and craziest things Schechter maintains is that you should be *denied the right* to go to Federal Court simply because you have refused to accept the decisions of the Superior Court, the Appeal Court and Supreme Court of the State of California. In essence she's saying, in *her* opinion you have *no legal recourse* beyond the State Supreme Court."

"Jesus! I wonder if that's her idea of States Rights."

"Whatever she is thinking it's damn amateurish because actually the Superior Court at *no time ever allowed the merits* of any of the cases to be heard. We know how Judge Otto Kaus, from the Appeal Court, *covered up* for Berenson and hell, the State Supreme Court refused to *even listen* to our appeal. She is attempting to put a tag of ethical Judicial Justice on *all this butchery.* On August 7, 1978 at ten a.m. we have a hearing in Federal Court before District Court Judge Harry Pregerson in L. A. We are in very good shape, I can't see that Judge Pregerson can do *anything more* than to order us to amend the complaint and he should *rule* on our MOTIONS FOR DEPOSITIONS from Judge Berenson."

Bob and I sat midway in the audience section of the Los Angeles Courtroom. Powell chose a seat near the railing anticipating being called. The room was crowded, it became silent, everyone rose when the Bailiff called the Court to order. Judge Pregerson nattily attired in his flowing black robe strode uprightly and with mighty dignity to the bench. Then several hours of lawyers mumblings and arguments dragged by. The room had emptied, we were No. 14, as always, the *last* case to be called.

James L. McBride appeared in behalf of Ventura County and the defendants. Powell acknowledged he was present and prepared to proceed. Pregerson put forth a few superficial questions, suddenly he took us by surprise, "Mr. Powell, did James L. McBride *threaten* your client and you with *criminal prosecution and jail* if you *did not* relinquish *your right to appeal* a Superior Court Decision?"

Emphatically Powell answered, "Yes Your Honor he did."

Pregerson then asked, "What did he say to your client?"

"Basically the same threats that were put on me, that McBride was going to have his ass hauled into court and he'd be prosecuted and jailed for hindrance of justice, malicious obstruction, and for preventing their Public Facilities Corp from selling bonds."

Intimidatingly, Judge Pregerson *repeatedly* questioned Powell, a total of six times, each time *more harshly* as to whether he and his client had actually been threatened with prosecution and jail. Each time Powell stuck to his guns, *"Yes Your Honor,"* and he repeated McBride's threats again to the court.

Pregerson looked down at McBride, "Is there anything you'd like to say Counselor?"

Alarmed, the County Counsel stammered, "Your Honor, I do not know how...how exactly appropriate it is, Powell has testified as to what I told him. If I might add one or two items...number one, *I've never* talked with his client! When I talked to Mr. Powell I merely explained to him that the case was so lacking in merit that it might even come under the title of malicious prosecution if he continued with it."

Leaning over to Bob, I whispered, "McBride's a friggin' liar, right here in Federal Court he's lying like hell, he called me on the phone threatening that if I *didn't* sign off my right to appeal he'd have my ass thrown in jail. That was the very next morning after the shooting took place at my house."

"I know, I know, Pregerson is letting him lie, since he was unable to *frighten* Powell into changing his story he has no choice."

With a thud of his gavel Pregerson said, "Very well, this matter stands submitted." With a rustle of flowing black robes...the *illusion of Justice* vanished spectrally behind the solid barrier of mahogany paneling into dark, mysterious, forbidden chambers.

We fought through the noontime crush of bodies, gushing from overloaded elevators they moved inexorably toward their favorite lunch and drinking spots. We emerged from the building and into a dazzling display of August sunlight. With typical cool Powell said, "There's nothing we can do now except wait and see what Pregerson does." Shaking hands with him, Bob and I went south on Broadway to an underground parking area. I hit the nearest freeway on-ramp proceeding north toward Ventura. Traffic rolled smooth, we relaxed slightly.

Bob remarked, "I was *real proud* of Powell the way he stood right up there telling Pregerson that that lying McBride had threatened him and you. It takes an honest, straightforward man and a lot of courage for a lawyer to make such a serious charge against another lawyer."

"It's exactly as I told you, I don't care what McBride says, he was lying through his teeth when he said he has *never* talked to me."

"I know, and we'll prove it real easy when the proper time comes. McBride *trapped himself* good with his lies. Think back...when you went to court on that Friday before Judge Shaw and he dismissed your case, *you didn't have a lawyer,* isn't that right?"

"Yes. I phoned Powell over the weekend and we talked, and he agreed to represent me."

"Then *how in the hell* could James McBride call Terrell Monday morning and talk with him as he *swears* he did when he didn't even know that you had a lawyer. He *had to call you first* to learn about Powell and to *get his phone number.*"

"My God! *You're right,* mighty good thinking Bob."

"Maybe it is, but I am far more concerned, even shocked about what took place at that hearing this morning." DuPre's solemn tone subdued a slight trend toward enthusiasm for our legal posture I'd begun to develop. Staring straight ahead through the windshield, he spoke slowly as though thoroughly analyzing some specific problem and each word's meaning was of the utmost importance.

Very worried DuPre said, "We had a Motion before Pregerson to *take a deposition* from Judge Berenson, and Pregerson completely *ignored* that Motion. We are lucky he asked those questions about McBride's threats, they are *now* a matter of official record. But, in *no manner* is he supposed to attempt to try the case *nor* attempt to determine if the allegations are true, that is *strictly the juries duty!* They determine the evidence at a trial, and direct a verdict. I'll try to explain it simply, under the Federal Court Rules Judge Pregerson was *required* to determine *one* question...and that is...*IF,* remember, that is the big word, *IF... IF* what we have alleged in this complaint is true...would there be a *violation* of a person's Constitutional Rights under Section 1983 of the Civil Rights Laws? There's only one way a judge in his position can possibly legally dismiss such a case. That would be if the allegations were so outlandish, and so coupled with physical and scientific impossibilities that *obviously* they could *not* be true then the judge could dismiss the complaint basing it on that reason. But...he'd be *required to write an opinion* to that effect."

I started to speak, Bob said, "Hold on a minute, I'll give you an example of the type allegation you'd have to make to get dismissed at this point under Federal Rules 12 b, 6. Suppose you alleged that your mother-in-law hated you and she'd joined in a conspiracy with Berenson. They planned to put you in a rocket and shoot you on a one way trip to outer-space where you'd never again be able to drink beer. Further, they were lying in wait for you to fall asleep, so they could lock you in a straight jacket and blast you off into space."

"Okay, okay, I got it, I understand."

Bob grew more tense as he went on, "Pregerson brought up many *extraneous matters* that had absolutely *no bearing* what so ever on a hearing of this kind. His harsh repeated questioning of Powell about

McBride's threats gave me a sick feeling, obviously he was doing it to frighten Powell, make him change his testimony."

"Yeah, I had precisely the same feeling."

"Let me say it again. I'm extremely concerned, what comes to my mind is this guy Pregerson is so dumb he shouldn't even be a lawyer much less a Federal Judge, but *far* worse and even *more* frightening is the manifest possibility that he is *setting the stage* in a venomous scheme to extirpate your Civil Rights forever."

Robert's trepidations sure as hell were doing nothing whatsoever for my morale. I said, "We're in Federal Court now, it hardly seems conceivable that we are going to face *more* crooked judges."

I shot a glance toward Bob, with a slight shrug of his shoulder he said low, "We can only wait and see." DuPre had seriously broached an instinctive premonition of *judicial treachery and chicanery* on the part of Judge Harry Pregerson. I fully accepted the prophetic talents and abilities Bob had acquired as a result of many years of practical experience, he'd engaged in hard fought battles in open courtrooms and even more bitter legal conflicts and ethically delicate skirmishes fought within the solemn privacies of Federal Judges chambers.

Okay, sure I had been involved in law enforcement many years. I had spent plenty of time in state courtrooms but I'd had very little experience in Federal Courts, policemen rarely do. Most policemen along the way develop a sentiment that Federal Courts are sort of a *higher echelon* of Justice, a place you can go for *real* Justice when things begin breaking down. Despite all of DuPre's disheartening premonitions I *hopefully clung* to my optimism that we would get a fair shake in the Federal Courts.

Throughout the years, I had seen some mighty crazy shenanigans pulled off by local judges. Everything from, wife beating, extortion, narcotics and sex, yeh, good old sex, the Kissing Judge, for sure, how could I forget him? It was some years back, but I remembered the Kissing Judge case, the Judge had become very successful, an expert in his field. In fact he was getting so much good old fashioned, home style loving that he had become subliminally giddy and light headed, and to say the least, *quite forgetful.*

The Judge had grown increasingly fond of drunk driver cases. In fact, extremely fond if perhaps the unfortunate defendant happened to have a beautiful wife or charming girlfriend. Upon such a *relevant* judicial discovery the only further information needed by the Judge was did the lady *want* her boyfriend or husband *in* jail or *out?* Then a swift trip out the south bound Coast Highway with the lady to the

THERE'S A FISH IN THE COURTHOUSE   219

Kissing Judge's favorite motel in Seal Beach. It invariably ended in an agreement as to a justifiable sentencing.

The Judge's chronic giddiness along with *increasing forgetfulness* was becoming a problem. Amazed jailers had discovered one of their prisoners had been locked up so long that he was well on his way to doing a *life stretch* in the County Jail for his very first drunk driving conviction. He was a *long forgotten* victim. The Los Angeles D.A. ordered an investigation. A wife had been forced to go along with the Judge, she *had* no choice, she *had* to get her husband out of jail, he was the *sole support* for her and the kids. We caught the Judge in the motel...with his pants down. He was arrested for his vicious plundering and defilements, not to mention the *criminal misuse and abuse* of his judgeship.

Melvin Belli, a highly touted defense attorney was retained by the Judge. A devoutly narcissistic lawyer, Belli commanded huge legal fees for his reputed expertise in defending notorious and wealthy personages. In trial, Melvin ranting bombastically and unabashedly, threw his entire bag of tricks at the jury of twelve good citizens. A number of female victims took the stand to testify. Amid sobs and emotional outpourings dreadfully weighted with guilt, embarrassment and shame they tearfully related their stories. Disgrace heaped onto the housewives brought frightening dismay, a chain reaction of anger created havoc among the families of the women. The damage caused to innocent lives by the Kissing Judge were incalculable and lasting.

Reporters clamored over the *amoral exploits* of the Judge. Front page notoriety kept pace with the daily court events, arousing and aggravating spousal jealousy and jaundice. All the men unfortunate enough to ever appear before the Kissing Judge regardless whether they were freed or sentenced to jail were suddenly taking quizzing, second looks at their wives and their girlfriends. Nauseating visions of gross infidelities resulted in fights and bitter divorces.

Belli had his Private Eye working on the case. Freddie Otash was an L.A. policeman on the vice squad before he quit and became a *notorious* Sunset Strip Private Eye. During a recess he approached me in the hall, gushing with heartiness Freddie clapped me on the shoulder, "Hey, we don't have to stay mad just because we are on opposite sides. Tell you what, Belli is giving a hell of a bash tonight out at Dino's club on the Strip. You are invited, beautiful girls and all you can drink, it's all on Old Mel."

"Sounds great Freddie."

He beamed, "Yeh, you'll love it."

"Tell you what Otash, I'll take a rain check on the party, just till after the trial is over."

Freddie's face hardened, "Screw you, that invite is only good for tonight." He walked away.

Hell! Old Belli is really crude, he wants to get me to that party tonight, it would be a *set-up*. Tomorrow he'd call me to the witness stand, then start one of his famous cross examination extravaganzas. He would make me look like an idiot in front of the jury.

Belli would bear down, "Now, last night, weren't you at Dino's night club?"

"Yes."

"And did you have numerous alcoholic drinks?"

"Well, I had a few."

Belli would pour on the pressure, "You mean you had quite a few don't you?"

"Well..."

"And while drinking you were very friendly with a girl?"

"Well I was sitting at the bar, a girl sat down next me."

"And did you have a conversation with the young lady?"

"Well, yes, we talked."

"Isn't it true that you discussed the case with her?"

"I wouldn't say so, she brought it up." By now I'd be hedging and squirming helplessly, Belli would have me just where he wanted me.

He blasted on, "And while you were talking to the girl didn't you admit you knew this whole thing was a frame-up against the Judge?"

"No...I never said anything of the kind."

"You just said you talked to the girl about the case."

"Yes, but I never said anything about a frame-up." And that was the way it would go. Belli would run me off the stand. Then he'd put the lady on to testify. Sweetly calling me a liar she'd *parrot* anything Belli wanted.

Walking back to the courtroom I laughed to myself. Lordy! If that was the best the Great Lawyer Belli could dream up for a defense... Twelve solid citizens were grim of face, adamantly stern while the verdict was read aloud. One word came forth...*Guilty!* The Kissing Judge was, *Guilty!* Inquisitive, busybody courtroom gawkers slowly exited the scene of all the exciting, but wretched confessions. Their prying eyes missed nothing, their pervert minds working overtime.

CHAPTER 24

DuPre was on the phone when I entered his small office. "Yes, I understand Terrell, that's for sure, yes, I got it all." Hanging up he said, "That was Powell calling from L.A., he received a notification this morning that Pregerson dismissed our case on August 14, 1978, just one week to the day after the hearing."

Angrily I kicked an old chair, "It didn't take them long. What did Pregerson's ORDER OF DISMISSAL say?"

"It was damn short, Pregerson said *he'd considered* the Pleadings, Memoranda of Law and Oral Argument, then concluded that he was going to DISMISS WITH PREJUDICE."

"Did he *also consider* McBride's threats and his lies to the court? After all, it was Pregerson himself who brought out these facts. Bob tell me, what is all this damn DISMISS WITH PREJUDICE crap they are always putting on me, it sounds real bad."

"Last week on our way home from L.A. I told you that based on the way Pregerson conducted that hearing he was either the *most stupid* judge sitting on a Federal bench, or the *most crooked.* After analyzing his ORDER OF DISMISSAL I can only say that, he has got to be both."

"Both what?"

"*Both stupid and crooked.* Now, about the DISMISSAL WITH PREJUDICE thing they've been putting on all your lawsuits, that's something that only stupid and crooked judges do when they want to wipe someone out without giving them legal Due Process of Law. It is directed as a subtle hint, a little psychological warfare scaring the lawyers involved. It warns them they are pushing their case far too aggressively and are stepping hard on influential and powerful toes. The judge is telling the lawyer with no ifs or buts, it's now time for him to tell his client, 'I'm sorry, but we have proceeded as far as we can go legally. I can do nothing more for you.' Pregerson has ruled that you have no cause of action and has dismissed your suit, WITH PREJUDICE. It means you can file nothing more in this case. Some people get so mad at being screwed in such a devious way that they seek other attorneys. That's a big mistake, the citizen is just milked a bit, and more fees are extracted before the new lawyer sings that same old tune, you have been DISMISSED WITH PREJUDICE. Believe me Gary, I know from experience, it has left a hell of a lot of very unhappy citizens in this country with a damned unhealthy hatred for judges."

I got sicker to my stomach as Bob went on, "Actually DISMISSED WITH PREJUDICE as *clearly defined* in the Encyclopedia Corpus Juris Secundum states that there are only two instances wherein you cannot refile a lawsuit. One instance is when both parties, Plaintiff and Defendant arrive at mutual agreement and settle the case in finality. The other is after a trial, in which evidence and testimony have been presented, and examined, and the merits reached and a verdict is brought. Both of these instances are called Res Judicata, in lawyer lingo that means the case has already been adjudicated. Under these instances any attempt at refiling the same case could properly and legally be DISMISSED WITH PREJUDICE. But at *no time* have you *ever* reached an agreement of any kind with anyone, nor have you *ever* been allowed a trial where the merits could have been reached. It is *criminal* for them to continue dismissing your Constitutional Rights With Prejudice!"

"That's all well and good DuPre, it explains the legal part to me very clear. I've known all the time that Berenson is corrupt, but for Christ sake, now we're in Federal Court and Judge Harry Pregerson is coming on with exactly the *same* old shyster tricks...the law and Federal Rules mean nothing to any of them. *What in hell is wrong with these people?* All I have ever asked for was a trial where the facts could be brought out!"

"That's just the point, they cannot afford to have those facts and evidence come out, it would destroy them!"

"I see that...but how are they able to continue keeping us out of trial? How in the devil are *all* of these other judges like Berenson in the Superior Court, Otto Kaus with the State Supreme Court and Pregerson in the Federal Court System tied in together?"

"You just asked a couple of damn good questions, it gives me an idea." DuPre started dialing the phone. Our angry dissection and pondering over Pregerson's Dismissal, had consumed most of the forenoon. It was time I did some work in the store.

Later on in the day I again visited DuPre. Angrily thrumming his fingertips on the desk he spoke. "This morning I told you I had an idea. Having become very curious as to how a District Court Judge is assigned to his cases, I called Edward M. Kritzman, Clerk of the District Court in Los Angeles. Now this is what he told me, 'They have a *local* District Court Rule *set up by the judges* whereby they receive their cases in what is called a *blind draw,* the cases are then put in plain unmarked envelopes and the judges never know what case they are going to get.' I quizzed Kritzman on the mechanics of this blind draw system. Were the cases placed in the envelopes each day as they were filed? Does he conduct this drawing by himself? How often do the judges make a draw, once a week, once a month? I asked about our case, how the assignment was handled. Kritzman was lying like hell, he couldn't explain even the simplest mechanics of what he was calling the blind draw rule. The further I questioned him the less he knew. Reluctantly Kritzman *finally admitted* they do *switch* their cases around, trading with each other when they *really* want to get their hands on a *certain* case. While I was drawing out Kritzman it became *starkly evident* to me, Judge Harry Pregerson wanted our case *bad...real bad.*"

I shook my head...then again, even harder in hopes of jarring my senses free from this *nightmare, this deranged madhouse of judicial insanity.* "Bob, how in hell can Pregerson, a Federal Judge from Los Angeles, conceivably be *tied in* with Berenson and *all* the corruption here in Ventura County?"

"Who knows what his *connection* is up here. But considering his wanting our case, his clumsy illegal intervention at the hearing, and then his DISMISSAL WITH PREJUDICE, I have to tell you one thing...there is *one hell of a connection,* yes indeed!

"So, it appears we have simply uncovered more concatenation of overall *evil* Judicial conspiracy." It was 1978, more then ten years of their malignant abuse and pressure weighed heavy on my shoulders. Without the right to defend myself it became harder and harder to take. I said, "What this means is I'll have to spend a hell of a lot of valuable time and money I do not have, down in Los Angeles trying to ferret out Judge Harry Pregerson's *connections* with these crooks up here in Ventura."

Recognizing the flash of bitter anger in my voice Bob solemnly, and with grave retrospect added, *"We are on our own,* there isn't a soul in this world going to help us, but us."

CHAPTER 25

Detective work...coming up with information and evidence, it is sometimes a frolic, like Hollywood TV, 77 Sunset Strip and Freddie Otash, the celebrated Private Eye of Tinseltown. His office, a cozy, huge reserved table with phones near the beautiful rock fireplace at Dino's. Artful bartenders in white shirts and red vests pour his Irish Whiskey and soda, movie moguls, directors and stars dropped by his table just to be seen greeting Fred. Sensually accentuated blondes, starlets, stars and madams leaned over whispering spicy tales in his ear upon their breath of teasing, sexy excitement. Freddie was the main source and chief conduit of *inside* information for Hollywood's scandalous Confidential Magazine.

There was another way of scrounging evidence and information. Pounding blistering hot sidewalks in thin soled shoes, gulping acid smog swollen by the sweltering mid-August heat of downtown L.A.. Darting madly back and forth, in and out, from one county building to another, battling crammed elevators and escalators, floor upon floor, each a conglomeration of rooms containing official records, cross references, more records etc.. It's just another routine in the procedure of detecting information and evidence you diligently seek and desperately need. Five hectic strung out days from Monday to Friday, entirely consumed in the fiery furnace of the typical L.A. summer, sustained by peanut and coke lunches.

One and a half of those days totally devoured by walking, driving and looking for places to park left me only three and one half days for actual investigation and reasearching old records plus numerous intervening phone calls to friends...old time cops. We reached way back into past years, freshening my memory on *who had been doing what to whom* back in the good old days.

Heading north out Ventura Freeway, L.A. stretched far behind. Perceptibly, the huge haze shrouded sun ball drooped, sinking over the steering wheel rim. The ratio of hours I'd spent in the Big City were inescapable, but well worth it. Slowly, methodically my mind was roaming back and forth over the information I'd gleaned over the past five days. East of the central downtown section of towering government and business buildings, just across the dry L.A. river, a small knoll arises. Its narrow, winding spider web of up and down streets and tiny homes built on extraordinarily narrow lots give an odd appearanace of tying together this hill known as City Terrace.

From City View Ave., his neighborhood street, Harry Pregerson looked down on the teeming central part of Los Angeles City. But his young and avid gaze incessantly roamed ambitiously westward, toward Hollywood and Beverly Hills. Greedily he eyed Sunset Strip and Wilshire Boulevard, those legendary gold paved streets. Like a sailor lured onto the jagged rocks by the hypnotizing music of the sea nymphs, Harry became spellbound. Fantasies raced through his mind, great talents abounded, visions of Royal adulation and acres and acres of filthy lucre and unretractable judicial powers raging rampant stomped through his brain.

Sloping sharply to the south the winding streets of City Terrace soon fused with Brooklyn Ave., the main drag that traversed the old Boyle Heights district. To the north the Terrace sloped more gently, down to the antiquated, red brick buildings of the County Hospital then on to the North Main Street business area. Pregerson and his old pal, Sidney Bocarsky, whose family ran a small grocery store on City Terrace at the corner of Wabash and Stone, were well aware of the *gang and drug infested areas* of Boyle Heights. In those days most of the dope being smuggled across Tijuana's border hit Boyle Heights first. There it was cut up and sold to distributors and small time pushers throughout Los Angeles.

Harry and Sidney knew all about the gambling and sinister Mafia activities with its headquarters at the Dragna family store on North Main. Mickey Cohen, a young City Terrace hoodlum and a vicious embryo gangster with a fetish for stylish suits and soft brim fedora hats drew *inordinate* hero worship from Harry and Sidney. Keenly they watched this brash young Jewish gang leader outwit Mexican drug smugglers in Boyle Heights and on occasion even outsmart the classier Siciliano's up on North Main Street.

Abe Phillips and Nathan Turkebtahn, friends of Harry and Sidney, were also confederates of Cohen's and helped his gangland prestige burgeon. After all, how many young thugs on the City Terrace had his own personal bail bondsman constantly at his side? With such underworld connections Abe and his brother Hymie ran a thriving bail bond traffic.

Harry made his first move toward leaving City Terrace by getting married. He moved into a classy duplex next door to his in-laws on fashionable Los Feliz Boulevard in Griffith Park. After passing the State Bar, Harry inaugurated his long awaited law office in Beverly Hills.

Mickey Cohen's gangster operations had been paying off like Las Vegas one-arm bandits with the 'fix-in.' Amid front page gangland murders, beatings, and many trips to police stations, Mickey set up his new gang headquarters in a haberdashery shop on Sunset Strip just north of Beverly Hills.

With good connections and *mysterious financing* Pregerson started his swift climb up the noble ladder of unretractable judicial powers. Blatantly he decreed that Royal adulation, high praise, and filthy lucre be a constant attendant of his Immaculate Ascension. Indeed, Pregerson had the world by the tail, obtaining a house atop a knoll in Woodland Hills, it commanded a view of the entire San Fernando Valley. He also acquired two beach front lots in Oxnard Shores in Ventura County worth about half a million. Harry's son, Dean and his wife, both lawyers, had a law office only a few steps from Judge Berenson's headquarters in the old Courthouse.

Somewhere along the way Sidney Borcarsky, Harry's old buddy, changed his name to Bocarsly. Sidney was now an engineer living in North Hollywood, a suburb in the San Fernando Valley. Not too far from Sid's home was the Morely Construction Company, the outfit that got millions and millions of dollars from the Public Facilities Corporation for building the new Ventura County Center Buildings.

Not long after the sale of the revenue bonds, Borcarsly bought a home in Woodland Hills near Judge Pregerson for nearly a quarter of a million bucks. At this same time he acquired a beach house in the Pierpont area of Ventura at close to three hundred thousand dollars. Checking into Borcarsly's beach property some very strange, puzzling facts and events popped up. Directly across the street two more houses had changed title *shortly* after the *sale of the revenue bonds*. One was acquired by Charles Embrecht, a lawyer and State Assemblyman from Ventura County, the other one by Ron Gill, a lawyer from Ben Nordman and Jerome Berenson's law office.

A hell of a mess of unexplored theories and ideas clanked around in my head as I carefully, but automatically negotiated the entrance to my carport. In the den I picked up the phone and dialed. The far away gentle ringing at the other end was euphoric, relaxing drowsily I relinquished the sharp tenseness that had battered my belly the past five days in Los Angeles. DuPre came on the line. During our discussion of things I'd learned downtown our combining reasoning subconsciously kept returning in a mutual curiosity to the Morley Construction Co.. We decided that in two days we would drive to North Hollywood, agreeing that at least it would not hurt to take a look at the Morley Construction Company.

Sunday morning the freeway was meek, I pointed the Chevy east toward the San Fernando Valley. Easing off the freeway at Laurel Canyon, we wended our way northeast. Traversing the residential and industrial streets of the area we found Morley Co. on Saticoy Avenue. Everything was locked behind a high chainlink fence. We surveyed the hodge-podge of rundown small-job type equipment and machinery scattered all around the industrial lot. DuPre exclaimed, "Christ all mighty, this outfit could never even begin to qualify to build the largest proposed County Complex west of the Mississippi." On a weed covered vacant lot across the street I spotted a beat up house trailer with Morley Construction Co. painted across its side. I'd seen it sitting for months on Nordman's Montalvo Hill property, near the new Center. DuPre shook his head, "This Morley Co. thing just doesn't add up."

"I agree, let's drive into downtown L.A., from what I've learned, Morley has a hook-up of some kind with the Turner Construction Company at 445 S. Figueroa."

"Okay, I'm intrigued with this construction company angle." Using the freeway we were there in fifteen minutes. Parking across from 445 S. Figueroa, I stared skyward, up and up at the towering black glass building. The huge blue and white sign at the top declared the edifice as being, the Union Bank.

DuPre got out of the car, "I'll go take a look around, maybe I can get in." I watched as he shaded his eyes and peered into the wide plate glass of the foyer. The security guard in a light blue uniform opened the door a crack, after a brief conversation he allowed Bob to enter. I looked around, downtown Los Angeles was dead, a block north on Figueroa the only thing moving was a Yellow cab, hoping for a customer.

I was thinking of walking over to the Union Bank when the guard opened the door and let Bob out. Ambling back across the street he climbed into the car, with a wide smile he said, "I conned the guard into letting me in and I think I ran into a little good luck. Some big shots from the Turner Co. were having a meeting with Bocarsly and another guy who had come with him."

"No kidding...you mean Bocarsly is at the Turner Company?"

"Yep, up on the sixteenth floor, I got the other guys name, it was Wittenberg."

"Wittenberg! Christ! He's the Chief Administrative Executive of Ventura County. This *ties in* Pregerson and Bocarsly with Berenson and Nordman and the County Center. How about that...*no wonder* Judge Pregerson dismissed our case *with prejudice.* Why in hell do you suppose they are meeting so secretly like this on a Sunday?"

"I would say they are probably in there right now cutting up the big apple pie."

"I believe you just hit the nail right on the head. Some real odd things about Richard Wittenberg come back to me that I've never told you about because when it happened it didn't make any sense. Before things had heated up between the Fish and me I dropped by the Pt. Hueneme Police Station to say hello to Chief Jalaty. Al said, 'I'm going across the street to the City Hall, come on with me and have a cup of coffee.' Al introduced me to Richard Wittenberg, he was the Planner for the City of Pt. Hueneme. Not long after this he became what they called the Legislative Analyst for the County. He spent most of his time in Sacramento, mainly as a lobbyist for the county politicians. Later, just prior to my Civil Service hearing Al Palmer went to a Directors meeting of the Ventura County Public Employees Association, this had been arranged to request financial assistance in helping me fight the Fish. Wittenberg showed up, and with a vicious tirade against me he did everything possible to keep the directors from giving me assistance. But everybody else was in favor of it. I couldn't figure out what in hell was wrong with this guy Wittenberg, we'd never had any differences, why in the world would he try to bury me? Well, later on I discovered he'd been *a partner* in Berenson and Nordman's law firm, and it was Berenson who had elevated him to the position of Legislative Analyst, and then later on to County Administrative Executive where he became Berenson's chief ram-rod, promoting the new County Center. A strange thing cropped up about Wittenberg's attempt to prevent me from getting financial help, it was just *prior* to my testimony before the Grand Jury. Only a very few people knew I was going to give the Grand Jury evidence about the frame-up against Supervisor Robinson and City Manager Charles Reiman. Wittenberg had wanted to prevent me from having a Civil Service hearing for fear that I'd expose the frame-up. And Judge Berenson killed the Grand Jury investigation shortly after I appeared before it. The point I'm trying to make Bob is this, *someone* that I was confiding in told Berenson. And...it also reveals that Wittenberg has been *one* of the cogs in Judge Berenson and Nordman's powerful machinery right from the start. It's crazy, the most unexpected thing you and Powell accomplished by filing that Civil Rights case was forcing Berenson and Nordman to expose Judge Pregerson's connections with them and their County Center. They *had* to bring in Pregerson, it was a dire emergency to get the case Dismissed With Prejudice."

"This whole affair is taking on fantastic turns. In my experiences I've discovered if you keep prodding and fighting, justice sometimes prevails. It just happens that we are bucking extremely powerful and evil judicial forces, totally devoid of scruples or conscience. But they have failed to consider one deadly and fatal fact. I'll put it this way, under the 'cloak of authority' they have conspiratorially used their governmental powers to deprive the citizens of their Constitutional Guarantee of Due Process and Equal Protection of the laws. Here is their fatal mistake, they've got the governmental power under the 'color of law,' to *deprive* people of their Rights, but what they *don't* have is the 'legal authority' to *deprive* people of their Rights."

"That sounds real good...but what in the hell can we do about it?"

"The new Civil Rights Act of 1964, sec. 1983 and 1985, gives the citizen the *right to sue* governmental authorities, right up to the top, for damages due to deprivations of any Constitutional Right. What we've got to do now is proceed with an Appeal Brief to the Circuit Court asking for legal justice."

Days of research and preparations on the Appeal by Powell and DuPre was exhausting. But the *incredible detailed requirements* set down by the Court, as to specifications was almost insurmountable. The Brief's cover had to be a certain shade of blue with specifically designated size, shape and spacing of the letters. The pages must be printed on both sides and spaced in the center of the page with no letters closer to the edge than one and three sixteenths of an inch.

The specified dimensions of the overall Brief were so unusual that you couldn't buy typing or printing paper that size in any stationery or supply store in the county. They would be glad to order suitable paper from L.A. and make a special cut but that could take days and at prohibitive cost. A mess of time and money was wasted on typists and secretaries in experimenting and trying to make the required copies. It was soon obvious that it could not be done to the judges specifications even if I ordered the special size paper.

The ninety day deadline was rapidly approaching, with exploding exasperation I finally admitted we could not do it ourselves. There was no choice, somehow I had to raise some cash. Over in East Los Angeles, more than a hundred miles away, I finally found a company that did legal printing. Several trips were necessary for preliminary discussions. Then three more trips to accomplish complicated final consultations with the company agents as to proper composition, form, and legal requirements of the Brief. Down to the wire, in a mad dash we finally filed the Appeal with the Ninth Circuit Court in San Francisco, just ahead of the deadline in January 1979, Brief No. 78-3098. I sold some extra machinery and equipment I was hoarding at the store for emergency breakdowns. The three thousand dollars I got for it paid the printing company, traveling expenses and extra help needed to run the store while I was gone, but, the three grand didn't take care of the accumulating mental and physical anguish created by a despairing hope for eventual Judicial Justice.

JUSTICE!...just how much of this God Damn legal type Justice can mankind really stand. Embossed on Federal, State and County buildings the nation over are statues and replicas of a virtuous lady, chaste and undefiled. Protectively she clutches the sacred scales of Justice, promulgating the guarantee that within this building equal and everlasting rectitude is judicially dispensed.

The Justice Lady had begun to remind me of the young paper boy riding his bike. Every afternoon he passed a pretty woman waiting in front of a building. With great admiration for her beauty he'd stop and admire her captivating loveliness. He watched expensively dressed men approaching the pretty lady, they'd say, 'Here are my two dollars.' The nice lady smiled as arm in arm they entered the building. The newsboy was enchanted. With a resolute diligence he saved his pennies but after months of saving he still had only one dollar, he decided to take a chance. Surely the lady would recognize his honesty, loyalty and deep devotion, even though he was a dollar short. The paper boy brought his polished, shiny bicycle to a halt before the lady, with confidence he said, 'Mam, here is my dollar.' Snatching the boys dollar and grabbing him by the neck she shook him until his teeth rattled, bashing him alongside the head she then turned and entered the building. Wobbling dazedly down the street on his bike the boy passed some onlookers, he was heard mumbling, 'Jeesus Keerist! Thank God she didn't take me inside, I don't think I could stand another dollars worth of that.'

My weekly newspaper, The Oak View Journal, was developing a pretty fair circulation. I had found there was a definite desire by the public to learn the truth. They believed it was the responsibility of the newspaper media to keep them closely advised of the scams the local politicians and their cohorts continually cooked up to defraud the people. I had been digging into one of these deals.

The financial and land holdings of the Hoffman Family in Ventura County are vast. A huge earthen dam, two hundred eighty five feet high and two thousand feet across the top was built by the Federal Government at the southern end of the Ojai Valley. It was also the southern boundary of the Hoffman Ranch. Damming the Ventura River it flooded the lower part of their ranch creating Lake Casitas. The rolling hills above the water were retained by the Hoffman's, comprising what is called Rancho Mi Solar Trust. A portion of lake water is contracted by Ventura, it flows south via gravity to the city. The balance of the lake's water is pumped by a power station at the bottom of the dam, north up the Arnaz Grade and back into Ojai Valley.

The headquarters of Casitas Municipal Water District are located in the community of Oak View, situated generally in the center of the Ojai Valley. The lake had been formed for many years when in December 1976 as editor of the Journal I developed the startling information that secret proposals were being made to the Directors of the CMWD to sign an agreement with land owners to steal a big percentage of water for private use and development.

If the dope I got was right, something dangerously wrong was in the wind. In the event of a *series* of dry years Lake Casitas would *not* be able to supply the existing demand for domestic water much less handle new demands for huge developments and subdivisions. After a few discreet questions around town I discovered that Judge Berenson and his partner Ben Nordman were behind an involved scheme. They'd approached CMWD's Board with a scam to build and connect a direct line to a pumping station behind the CMWD office in Oak View. The pipeline would run about a thousand yards west on Santa Ana Blvd., a county road. It was to then proceed an unknown length up a winding private lane into the hills to a specific storage location on Rancho Mi Solar property.

It was crazy, but if Judge Berenson and Nordman were involved it was a scam of 'gigantic proportions.' Somebody was going to get *screwed* pretty bad, which was *usually* the general public. CMWD's regular meeting was scheduled for Wednesday December 15, 1976 at three p.m., I was there, all five members of the board were present. James D. Loebl, the Mayor of Ojai City was there as the attorney representing CMWD. Seventeen items were listed on the agenda. Sixteen were routine matters, but the seventeenth, the last one said, "Discussion of Proposed Water Pipelines with Haley." Katherine H. Haley was a Hoffman, also the owner and operator of Rancho Mi Solar, and sister of Walter Hoffman. Both were tightly involved with Berenson and Nordman in financial corporations and land ventures. The information I had appeared to be right on target!

The Board members were discussing item seven when the hearing room door opened. William Hair, a lawyer, quietly entered and sat down next to Loebl. Hair was the attorney Nordman dispatched to help James McBride, when Judge Robert Shaw dismissed my lawsuit to halt construction of the new County Center. Hair and McBride had their strict orders to protect Berenson and Nordman's Public Facilities Corp.. I hadn't forgotten the jeering sneers that they had turned on me as they left Shaw's courtroom. I comprehended their sneers, they were laughing at me and saying, you poor stupid ass, don't you have brains enough to know that we're *backed by powers* that 'nobody' can touch! Hair didn't amount to much as lawyers go, but could follow orders competently when Nordman had it all laid out for him. His legal dullness was masked and adroitly covered by an egotistical, pushy, blustering manner that well qualified him for his 'front man' role within Berenson and Nordman's organization.

Loebl leaned over whispering into Hair's ear. Hair slowly turned staring to the back of the room where I was sitting. Whispering back and forth, they slowly swiveled their eyes in unison to the rear in a scathing stare, I returned their scowls. Grasping their omnipresent briefcases protectively they quietly slipped from the hearing room. I thought, those twins are about the most un-clever, obvious pair of conniving conspirators I ever saw.

The Board had begun to deliberately drag out the piddling items on the agenda. If they wanted me to weary of their game and leave, they were wasting their time. I was going to see this show through.

I figured they had to get to item seventeen sooner or later. Their timing was perfect, Loebl and Hair returned at four p.m., just as the board members finished with item sixteen. Mayor Loebl addressed the directors, "The only change that Mr. Hair asks for is a larger water pipeline than was *originally* agreed to."

Hell, no wonder my presence here was spooking lawyer Hair and Mayor Loebl so bad. An agreement to *secretly* pump water to the Haley Ranch had already been quietly signed sealed and delivered by the CMWD Board. But one of Haley's engineers had made an alarming discovery. The size of the clandestine pipeline wasn't large enough to conduct all the water to Rancho Mi Solar necessary for the future development they covertly planned. It had become a dire emergency to alter the agreement. The diameter of the pipe had to be increased before they could start construction.

Loebl continued standing before the Board who were assuring him his requested change in the agreement would proceed immediately. Hair's reaction was an arrogant grin as he swaggered out the door. Loudly I demanded, "I want a copy of the original proposal made to the Board by the Nordman law firm. Also, I demand a copy of your contract with Kay Haley guaranteeing you are going to pump Lake Casitas water to her Rancho Mi Solar property."

The Board Chairman, a mean looking little guy named Campbell, feigned total surprise. He looked me straight in the eye, "Why the Nordman law firm has *never* at anytime made a proposal to pump water to the Haley Ranch."

"What are you pulling off Campbell, everybody in this room just now heard Loebl telling you and the Board that the Haley Ranch wants a 'larger' pipeline than *originally* agreed to. In fact, that lady right over there has officially recorded the entire meeting." I pointed at the clerk sitting just to the left of the Board members. As I did, she jerked the electric plug from the recorder. Swiftly she picked up the machine and left the room.

Chairman Campbell was becoming hotter, he repeated his lie, "I told you, there was *no* original proposal or agreement. I'll give you a copy of our next agenda."

"I don't want your next agenda. I am demanding that you give me a copy of the original proposal and agreement that CMWD's Board of Directors made with Nordman and Kay Haley. You directors are perpetrating a fraud on the people, your operation is a *conspiracy* to steal lake water."

Campbell until now had been acting smart alecky, but suddenly the wizened little Chairman became enraged, crashing his gavel hard on the Board Members table, he screamed, "We're going into executive session." Leaping from his chair he charged from behind the table brandishing his gavel like a war club. Pointing it at me he shouted, "That means *you* are excluded!" As Campbell stalked from the room, the members trailed compliantly, following him into a side room. I could hear the bolt slide in the door as it was solidly secured on the other side.

Robert Perkins, the Office Manager, was standing in the hallway outside the hearing room. "Mr. Perkins, how about you, what do you know in regards to this pipeline agreement?"

"Not too much, however, I know Nordman's law firm *did* make a written proposal to the District."

"What did it say?"

"I'm not sure, I've never actually seen it."

"Who has it now?"

"Robert N. Mc Kinney, the General Manager and Chief Engineer of CMWD, received the proposal from Nordman and his associate, Ralph Cormany. Mayor Loebl and Hair had been collaborating on the agreement for the pipeline quite a while. Loebl gave Mc Kinney *strict orders*, 'no one' was to see the contract until after the Board Members had voted on it."

"Now we are getting somewhere. The Board must have agreed to the contract months ago because what these lawyers Loebl and Hair are doing today is to simply have the Board okay a larger pipe."

"That's correct."

"I want a copy of the original proposal and the contract the Board agreed to."

"I'm sorry, but I don't have that authority."

"Alright, tell Mc Kinney I would like to talk to him."

"I'll inform him." Perkins came back in a minute, "I'm sorry, but Mc Kinney is tied up in his office."

"Who in hell tied him up, Chairman Campbell?"

A smile, but very faint, was the best I could raise from Perkins. Walking down the hall to leave I saw Loebl sitting in the hearing room. With his briefcase open, he appeared nervously preoccupied with the papers he was sifting through. I figured, what the hell, one more shot at these crooks ain't going to hurt anything.

I moved into the room, "Loebl, you're supposed to be an attorney, if so, you know the original proposal by Nordman, and the contract you and Hair worked out and secretly got the Board to agree to is nothing but an out and out fraud, a criminal conspiracy. You people are defrauding the public out of their future water rights. I demand a copy of that original proposal and the Board's agreement!"

Mayor Loebl, tall and balding, really caught me off guard...I was expecting him to mouth a bunch of legal type mumbo jumbo about contracts, non-conflicts of interest, vague legal issues, etc.. Loebl looked up from the briefcase. Peering at me over a pair of half-lens intelligentsia type glasses hanging on the end of his nose, he quite innocently, in a soft mocking voice said, "Why I don't know *anything* about any pipeline proposal or any other agreement being made by the Directors of the CMWD." Loebl's stupid lie was irksome. But thinking about it I realized that after all, when caught red-handed stealing...what is there really left to say. Hell, I had snatched plenty of damn thieves off the streets over the years, I couldn't remember any of them *ever* coming up with an *intelligent* answer either.

Having experienced Campbell's wrath and Loebl's lies, I thought, who knows, maybe McBride and Hair were right, maybe they were actually aware of sinister, powerful forces of corruption, and they had accepted the fact that these people were so powerful and high placed that a man was a fool to attempt to interfere with them.

Still, it was hard to digest...how in hell can they pull off a deal like this? *How do they control and manipulate so many people?*

In this case it was five directors of the CMWD. Director Marion Walker obviously was a Nordman and Berenson plant, and also a director of their Public Facilities Corp., deeply connected with the new Courthouse scam. One board member was just appointed to the Planning Commission, another was a county fireman angling for a promotion, and who knows the total value of Campbell's incentive, he sure as hell had made his position plenty clear.

Like in the old days of the wild west, ranchers fought for control of a strategic water hole. They knew that without water they were dead. The secretly planned future development of Rancho Mi Solar would also be dead without water being guaranteed from the lake. Nordman and Berenson had engineered their cunning agreement with CMWD Board members and no one would have been the wiser if they hadn't made that mistake and had to increase the eight inch pipeline to eighteen inches. And no one would have ever known that Rancho Mi Solar Trust was handed first rights to over fifty percent of the lake water, that is, the people would not get wise until the thieves began pumping water out of the lake through their eighteen inch pipeline.

The battle would begin over the 'water hole,' the residents of Ojai Valley would unite in anger, just as the settlers had banded together in the old days to protect themselves from the big ranchers. They'd fight for their water to the end. Raising large sums of money they would retain prominent lawyers to take their case to the courts. Not understanding who was behind the conspiracy they would probably end up by hiring the 'honest,' well established old law firm of Judge Berenson and Ben Nordman.

Years and years later, still not in court, some of the old settlers had died off and some had moved on to greener pastures. As the finances became depleted their attorneys finally got the case on the 'jammed Civil Court Calendar.' The Honorable Jerome Berenson, Presiding Judge for the past thirty seven years swiftly Dismissed the case With Prejudice, he had *suddenly* taken 'Judicial Notice' of the fact that the statute of limitations had run *before* the case was even filed. Then further, according to the Honorable Judge Berenson the *entire matter* had become 'Moot' due to the fact that there wasn't *any water left* in Lake Casitas anyway.

The Oak View Journal was demanding long hours, with the store and cocktail lounge I was on the go eighteen and nineteen hours a day, seven days a week. My wife reminded me that during the last ten years we had taken one vacation, a three day trip to Las Vegas which was actually business involving our store. Circulation of the paper was increasing, we had numerous news racks scattered around the Ojai Valley and several in Ventura. The most popular rack was the one in front of the White Bib Restaurant on California Street, a block down the hill from the old Courthouse. The White Bib and Sportsman's Lounge across the street, got most of the Courthouse and downtown business people's luncheon trade.

The Ventura Star Free Press *never* printed any of the down deep political and judicial corruption in the county. I had tapped a large segment of citizens whose curiosities became aroused after reading the Journal. A small operation like mine wasn't going to cut real deep into the Star's circulation, but lots of readers were plaguing Editor Judas Gius why his newspaper *never* exposed any corruption. It had become embarrassing for him.

Gius had a tight formula for running the Star Free Press, truth or accuracy had no part. His modus-operandi was to keep a very close, personal back-slapping association with affluent, dominant politicos. He loved to butter the *self-ordained* blue bloods, the haughty, local high-society clique. Gius' *major* contribution was in writing insipid editorials glorifying all these people. He excelled in cloaking their corrupt, disgraceful schemes. In covering up treacherous, cowardly judicial chicaneries of Judge Berenson, Judas Gius would come on with gushy, catchy phrases about him like, "and the works of great men," and on and on.

I had been ripping deep into county corruption. Judas *had* to do something about it, his next move took me by surprise. It was very sly, an insidious operation it was designed to injure my business and reputation. The Star Free Press like Pearl Harbor struck on Sunday morning. In bold captions, by reporter Clark Mason, "Prospect Of Sex Films Splits Casitas Springs."

Star reporter Mason penned a story about the large old building across the highway, it was the building I'd been forced to lose when they had refused to give me a license, I hadn't owned it for several years. Lately someone had been working on it, it was rumored to become a roadhouse of some kind. I didn't have any idea who the owner was. Mason claimed, "He had been told that the owner was going to screen sexually explicit adult films to paying customers." Mason went around town knocking on doors stirring up a hell of a furor among the residents, then he wrote, "One local business man welcomed the new business that roadhouse sex films will bring."

I wondered...why was this reporter running around town fanning the flames of sex rumors. Then several days later their reasons for spreading their weird stories in the paper became quite clear. The reporter galloping around stirring up tall tales of sex was laying the ground work for Judas.

In their 'Letters to the Editor' column, Gius played up a letter, purportedly from a man, Bill Porter in Casitas Springs. On the top of the letter section in extra large print was a title, "How Can Adult Films Help A Community?" In his letter Porter growled, "Sex films are completely out of line for a residential area." Further he stated, "The Star Free Press is aware of a local business man who owns the liquor store, and he is one of the people who will secretly benefit from all the Sex film operations."

I'd never heard of any guy in Casitas named Bill Porter. I called some of the old timer's around town, nobody had ever heard of Bill Porter...*he didn't exist.* An hour later I walked in the front office of the Star Free Press. A young secretary asked, "Can I help you?"

"Yes, I want to speak to somebody in charge of this rag."

She spoke into the intercom, soon a man appeared from an inner office. "What can I do for you?"

THERE'S A FISH IN THE COURTHOUSE   239

I held up the article, "I am the business man you are accusing of setting up 'Sex Films' in Casitas Springs. I want to see your original letter you say you got from this guy Porter."

He was tough, "We don't have to show you anything." I recognized him, he was Chuck Thomas, a Gius stooge. A method writer, like a method movie actor, regardless what kind of part he was portraying it always came out the same. In sucking up to his boss he was wont to start off by saying, "And now folks, from my Favorite newspaper, The Star Free Press," and on and on.

"The reason you refuse to show me the letter is because you don't have one. There's nobody named Bill Porter in Casitas Springs, you wrote the letter yourself."

Puffing up he said caustically, "We don't have to show you a damn thing!" Jesus, I wanted to rap him in the teeth. Driving back to the store I pondered over the amount of effort Judas had put into his crazy sex story in Casitas. By noon the next day I had the answer. For many years Gius and Thomas had been busily writing cloying, mawkishly misleading editorials *designed to convince* the downtown merchants that moving the Courthouse wouldn't harm their business or property values in Old Ventura.

The official document I had in my hand revealed that sometime ago Gius had quietly bought acreage near Victoria Ave. for John P. Scripps newspapers. Gius had known all along the paper was going to move from the old downtown area and build another plant near the *new* government center, he realized the need for secrecy. Hell, none of the merchants or property owners would have gone for his tricky editorials if they had known he was planning to pull the Star Free Press and its employees from the heart of old downtown. They would've resisted strenuously the theft of the courthouse. By God, Judas Gius' editorials may have appeared inane and mawkish, but they sure as hell weren't innocent of his perfidious design. He had been *leading* the people of Ventura by their hand, right down the primrose path the entire time, "The Old Judas Kiss."

Gius had arranged to buy the property for a paltry few thousand dollars. Now with the Government Center at Victoria Ave. the land was worth millions. This entire set of circumstances I'd reported in the Journal. Gius, trying to cover-up his shameful duplicity arranged for John P. Scripps attorneys from headquarters in San Diego to write a nasty, intimidating letter demanding my story be retracted. Scripps lawyers maintained that Gius had never at anytime allowed the Star Free Press to be other than "Objective and unbiased in any of his references to the movement of the county courthouse to the new location." With a return receipt requested I mailed copies of Gius' editorials to the lawyers wherein he'd conned the citizens into believing that *all* they'd need was ten million dollars to construct the new county center. The corporation lawyers for the Star Free Press never answered the letter. My newspaper's exposure of corruption brought fresh barbs of deadly vengeance from Berenson's onslaught to destroy all opposition to his evil schemes. I had graduated from being an annoyance to a *full fledged obstacle* in their plans for total control of Ventura County.

A letter from the County Fire Dept. came soon after DuPre and Powell filed our appeal of Judge Pregerson's dismissal of my Civil Rights lawsuit. In the letter Dennis Gage, a Fire Prevention officer, claimed that I had illegal underground gasoline tanks on my store property and must make arrangements with the Fire Department to remove them. Gage's office was in the new County Administration Building adjacent to Victor Husbands, Berenson's top hatchet man. The tanks Gage referred to were phased out over eleven years ago when I shut down the gas station and started the liquor store. One was a two hundred gallon tank and the other a one hundred fifty gallon. Very small, they had been in the ground for over fifty years. Being close to the surface and badly rusted they collapsed and were compacted when run over by a heavy tractor repairing the driveway for the store.

Getting Gage on the phone, I explained about the tanks, "Gage, nobody has given those old tanks a thought for years. Why are you suddenly starting this crap now. I want to know who is ordering you to do this?"

Quite hostile, Gage replied, "When I decide to tell you who gave me the information I will let you know. You are required by law to fill out proper forms and remove those tanks immediately according to fire department instructions."

"Gage, who put you up to this shit...I have a right to know."

"I don't have to tell you anything."

Christ! I knew it, here we go again, that same old song...'I don't have to tell you anything!' "The hell you don't Gage, we'll see about that!" Calling Fire Headquarters I got Captain Festerling, I advised him what was going on. "Captain, I've got a right to know who it is that's instigating this malicious crap against me."

"Yes, I agree about that, you are correct, I'll make an inquiry and call you back."

"Thank you."

An hour later I got a call, it was a Fire Chief named Mc Claren, "I'm sorry but I can not help you. I have talked with Fireman Gage, he absolutely refuses to tell me where he got his information."

"You are kidding, what are you talking about? You mean to tell me that Gage is refusing to answer his superior officer's questions, what in hell kind of an outfit are you running anyway?"

"I'm unable to find out anything," Mc Claren hung up on me. Well hell, that would be the end of that, or so I thought. A few days later I received another letter from Gage. He threatened, if I did not fill out the forms he'd sent and have the tanks removed under the Fire Department's supervision he was going to prosecute me with certain County Ordinances. Gage stated he was only giving me thirty days before going to the Dist. Attorney to prosecute me. I figured Judge Berenson must really be desperate if this kind of bullshit was all he could come up with.

Several months had slipped past since we filed the Appeal. Due to the full realization of Berenson and Nordman's evil, unrelenting efforts to 'phase me out,' very perturbing premonitions had created foreboding anxiety that the Ninth Circuit Court of Appeals was just toying with us. Misusing their official powers they could simply bury our Appeal under the massive and unescapable weight of time...time, an old judicial trick, unrelenting, implacable, corrosive time, fading shapes and forms, withering the facts and evidence. An artless but totally effective dismissal of my rights to Due Process of Law by a petty artifice.

DuPre said, "Gary, quite precisely my intuition is warning me. We have to file a 'Motion To Expedite the Calendaring' of our Appeal Brief with the Ninth Circuit, because they sure as hell are not going to hear it of their own volition."

"I understand what you're saying, we've got to stay right on top of this thing every minute."

"What I want to do is bring the court record up to date on all the threats and occurrences that have happened since the filing of your Civil Rights Case on June 2, 1978. That includes McBride's threats, his lies in the courtroom about how he has never even talked to you much less threatened you, and the shooting that took place at your house. It's damn clear to me that you screwing up their thirty five million dollar bond sale was a hell of a motive to 'kill' you. James McBride's phone threats the next day fit right in. I will put it all in an affidavit and have you swear to it before a notary public, also I want to put in all the facts about this fire department thing."

"I'll take care of it just as soon as you get the affidavit completed." On May 14, 1979 our Motion and notarized affidavit were filed in Federal Court, Case No. 78-3098.

McBride's response seven days later consisted of three pages of vituperative abuse. He commenced with a groveling apology to the court, "For taking up its valuable time with such frivolous matters." In attempting to cover-up his guilt, McBride resorted to extremely bizarre name calling. He told the court that our Motion should be viewed as nothing more than, "Concoctions by innuendo, conspiracy fetishes, jaundiced eye and poppy cock falsifications," etc. etc.. In conclusion McBride again toadingly, "apologized for taking up the courts very valuable time in such a frivolous case."

Bob laughed, "McBride is getting maybe a little smarter along the way, I noticed he was able to get Dorothy L. Schechter, the County Counsel, to sign his response." DuPre's analytical comments about McBride's answer were very interesting. I'd developed much more of an insight into a strategy that Bob appeared to be staging. I had observed that preliminary inter-play between opposing lawyers takes on characteristics of a master chess game. Jabbing and feinting, they feel each other out by making innocent appearing initial moves with their pieces.

"Gary, I'm starting to loosen up a little, at first you must be very careful you do not underestimate your opponent. To make such a mistake can be totally fatal to the ultimate judgement in a case. We have now proceeded far enough that I've detected very weak areas in the legal defense they are putting up. But even more encouraging I see substantial flaws in the legal experience and abilities of these people, particularly in the field of Federal Law. I'll give you sort of an analogy. You've got two fighters in the ring, one figures he's far stronger than the other. Coming out in the first round he's throwing punches all over the place, hoping for a quick knockout. And he has an ace in the hole, the referee is on his side, a fellow conspirator who has lots of money riding on the fight. The big guy lands a lucky punch. The little guy is flat on the canvas struggling to get up, the referee is coming on with one hell of a fast count but before he can reach ten the bell rings. Now understand, that bell is all important. In this analogy it represents one of the Federal Court Rules that prevents them from ending the fight. Without these Rules the little guy would have been finished in the first round. These are fixed and obligatory rules. To fight within this arena it is necessary that you understand them from A to Z. It is unconditionally mandatory, you have to adhere to and abide by them."

Emphasizing his point Bob waved his arms. "The little fighter has been following the rules. Though he suffered a fierce beating in the opening round he's ready and eager to come out for the second. He grows stronger by virtue of having survived the rigorous first round. The big guy, a heavy slugger, doesn't know shit about the Rules and furthermore he could care less. The crooked referee, 'the judge in this case,' has not seen fit to follow any of the Rules. In fact, he's been *making up his own Rules* as he goes along, he calls them 'Local Rules.' As the fight progresses you'll discern the unremittingly vital importance of the eighty five Federal Court Rules. Down through the multitudes of decades they evolved unto a degree of imparting a delicate balance within our Federal Judicial System. This balance protects and preserves our United States Constitution. It gives the unique form of Freedom that honest men in this country presently are fighting so desperately to maintain."

I was amazed, "Until now Bob, I never even knew there was such a thing as eighty five Federal Court Rules. In a way you're an artist, you've just painted a Michael Angelo masterpiece, an enlightenment that every patriotic American should be fully aware of."

"I dare say, you can actually and definitively look upon the Federal Court Rules as being a masterpiece. A perfect work by genius's, full masters of the law. As we utilize them you'll see us grow stronger, and more robust legally, while the inept slugger and crooked referee become weak and ailing under the implacable penalties imposed on them. This occurs not because of their ignorance alone...but more surely and justly for their conspiracy against the U.S. Federal Law."

Within a matter of a few days we received our answer from the Court of Appeals for the Ninth Circuit on our Motion To Expedite Calendaring Of Our Appeal. Judge James Browning mailed a trite one-liner as his judgement regarding our untenable and evilly forced legal situation:

"UPON DUE CONSIDERATION, MOTION DENIED."

"In our Motion DuPre, you informed Judge James Browning that Pregerson had *ignored and violated* the Federal Court Rules when he dismissed our case. You've cited cases from the Supreme Court that over-rule Pregerson, still Browning can wipe us out by merely saying...Motion Denied. What in hell has happened to the Federal Court Rules? It's damned evident the Appeal Court's intentions are to 'bury' our case deeper and deeper."

"About the best I can say right now is this is just another round. I'll admit it isn't fair and it sure as hell isn't legal, but we have little choice. If we are to survive these 'low blows' we have to continue fighting and following the Rules."

"I intend to obey the Rules Bob. I've been a sailor in the United States Navy, a policeman and a loyal American citizen too damned many years to do it any other way, but how long can we keep it up? How can we possibly maintain any sort of a fight for justice against these powerful evil forces? It's not only wiped out my finances but it's taken one hell of a terrible mental and physical toll, these judges are well aware of this."

"Of course they are. It is part of their modus-operandi, the way they operate to *destroy the people.*"

"DuPre, I remember we discussed this a long time ago. But I just have not been able to bring myself to understand these people, what in the devil is wrong with them?" I was struck with a grim, festering frustration. "Who in hell are these people wearing 'black robes' who are so powerful that they can *toy* with the Federal Court Rules, and the *lives* of the people?"

CHAPTER 26

At one o'clock in the morning, in a deep sleep, there's no shock like the shrill ring of a phone. It's never good news, but you've got to pick it up. A hysterical woman screamed, "Fire! Fire! Gary your place is on fire!"

"Lord...what place...who is this?"

"This is Helen, Gary, your restaurant in Casitas is burning, I can see the flames."

"Jesus! Okay Helen." She lived next door to the restaurant. "Call the fire department, I'll be right there." The flames were out when I arrived.

A fireman explained, "Due to the suspicious circumstances I've asked for an arson investigator." My neighbor, Richie, was relating information to a deputy sheriff for his crime report. Luckily he'd heard some stealthy noises, going outside to look around he saw the front door of the restaurant engulfed in flames. Thinking quick he got his garden hose, he put the fire out before it got a good start. While playing water on the flames Richie noticed a cream colored panel truck parked a short distance away. It sped off heading south on the highway. From the sound of the exhaust it had a powerful engine.

The deputy completed his crime report. Robert Burleson, Arson Investigator, said the fire had been intentionally set by a flammable liquid poured on the heavy wooden front door.

It was getting late, the excitement was over, the onlookers, the deputy, and the firemen had gone. I thanked Richie for his stout assistance. The front door was nearly destroyed. Flames had burned through the top and started licking at the ceiling inside the dining room. It was obvious, had Richie not taken such expeditious action the restaurant would have been severely damaged or even destroyed before the firemen arrived. Locating a piece of plywood and nails I secured the front door for the remainder of the night. Driving the few miles home up the deserted highway I knew I'd probably never be able to prove who'd set the fire, but it sure would have hurt me financially in my fight against Berenson if I'd had to shut down the restaurant. I wasn't sure whether to chalk this up as another round, or perhaps just a part of a round...it was strange, the blaze followed closely on the 'threats' of Gage to prosecute me, and the 'denial' to let me into court by Judge Browning. Well hell, hopefully that damn phone won't ring again tonight.

My mind traveled back. Nearly twelve years had gone by since Lane Martin had come to my office offering me money to help him frame Supervisor Robinson and Charlie Reiman. A hell of a lot of water had gone over the dam since then. Untold times that incident and the importance of discovering *who'd* put up the money besieged my mind futilely.

It was *something* Martin had said, "The dough was given to me *specifically* to frame Robinson and Reiman, but...Hronesh and I are going to throw in Police Chief Geary, free of charge." This was an indication that whoever put up the money had had no axe to grind with Chief Geary, they were after Robinson and Reiman.

I had definitely pinned it down...Robinson and Reiman were the top politicos behind relocating the Courthouse. It would necessitate the combined efforts of county and city powers to pull it off. If this was the motive for the frame-up, then clearly the money was from someone who *did not* want the County seat moved. Hell, that could be any number of people in Old Downtown Ventura! Many would lose money on their property if the county buildings and employees plus related businesses that always located close to the government facilities were pulled out. Plainly the proposed Government Center movement was a *powerful motivation* for all the evil connivance and intrigue.

Lane had told me something else, "Gary, believe me, the people behind this are extremely influential politically, and money isn't any object," that narrowed it down considerably. Over the years the trail had become colder than an iced herring. Lately a premonition or an intuition nagged and pestered me on the critical importance of what he'd said. I *had to* get on it. Martin was the only *direct connection* to the origin of the money but I knew damn well he wasn't going to tell me anything.

For months I scratched deep for leads. I contacted every font of information I could resurrect without stirring up a hornets nest by having it get back to the wrong people, I finally got a call. It was an old time policeman, Bill Strickland, we had worked together years ago. Having retired as Chief of the Ventura P.D., he was presently working part time for the County Treasurer's Office. It seemed that a certain lady, a friend of a friend, might possibly have some helpful information. The lady lived just off Victoria Ave., not too far from the new Government complex. Knowing Bill's ability for coming up with good information I made specific arrangements to contact her at seven thirty in the evening at her residence.

I tapped on the door with the light weight brass knocker. While waiting I admired the neatly trimmed lawns and shrubs surrounding the newly constructed condominum development. I was hoping that tonight didn't turn out just another dry run. After all the years that had passed you could hardly expect someone to remember too much. But, if I'd had even the *slightest inkling* of the startling story this lady would tell I'd have pounded on her door with a twenty pound sledge hammer instead of tapping with that flimsy brass knocker.

Hospitable, the slim, attractively attired lady indicated a seat for me on a comfortable divan. Not being sure how much my friend Bill had explained to her about the details I figured it couldn't hurt to start off pretty close to the point. "I'm well aware the subject I am bringing up happened many years ago. However, I'm in hopes that you might recall something, anything that'll help me to understand why somebody would hire men to frame Robinson to the degree of sending him to prison."

Her words came spontaneously, "I *defintely know* that Robby was threatened, because he told me about it."

"You mean *someone* actually threatened Robinson, what was the threat involving?"

"I remember Robby was asked by Mr. Lagomarsino to meet with him for dinner to discuss an *extremely* important matter."

"Are you talking about Robert Lagomarsino, the United States Congressman?"

"No, I mean his father, 'Red' Lagomarsino. When this happened

Bob was a California State Senator, he became a Congressman later on."

"Then you are referring to Emilio Lagomarsino?"

"That's right, well anyway, Robby met Emilio along with some other important people for dinner at the White Bib Restaurant, you know, the place on California Street."

"Do you recall who else was at the meeting?"

"Yes, Supervisor Ralph 'Hoot' Bennett and downtown businessman, Milam Cleck, he owns the White Bib. There was someone else but I can't recall now who it was, if I do I'll let you know."

"Good, what was the purpose of the meeting?"

"Robinson had been working a long time on a plan to move the Center, the downtown businessmen were very angry. Red's owned considerable real estate in Ventura for many years."

"I'm aware of that, the Ventura Realty Co. belongs to him, it owns and controls much of the property downtown."

"Robby told me that Red Lagomarsino and the other men there put tremendous pressure on him to change his mind about moving the Courthouse. Also, they *demanded* that he use his influence on Reiman to discontinue his effort in the movement. Red promised Robby 'if he'd *stop* the Courthouse move he would see to it Robby would remain Supervisor forever. But if he continued with the move he would be destroyed.' Robby told Lagomarsino that 'he did not intend to be intimidated, and he had no intentions whatsoever of changing his mind.' The men became furious and Red threatened him...'Robby, I'm telling you...you have just hammered all the nails into your coffin.'"

"I'll be damned, excuse me, it's just that this amazes me. First Emilio attempts to bribe a Supervisor, and when that doesn't work, he vows to destroy him, and threatened Robby that he'd just nailed his own coffin."

The woman said, "That is the way it happened."

I thought about it. "I don't recall at any time Robby's attorney, Ken Haymaker bringing up *any incidents of threats* at the trial."

"No, I don't believe they ever realized there was a connection."

I thanked her for the invaluable information. As I left she said, "If I recall anything else I'll call you at the number you gave me."

It was hard to believe my good fortune. After all the intervening years I was convinced I'd never discover who had put up the money for the frame-up. Sure as hell, this *had* to be the answer.

The next morning the phone rang, it was the lady from last night,

"I hope I'm not calling too early."
"No, not at all."
"I just recalled something else I'm sure you'd want to know."
"Certainly, I appreciate your call."
"After you left last night it came to me who the other man was at the White Bib meeting."
"Good, I'm very anxious."
"I didn't know him personally but I did know of him."
"Yes yes, that's fine, but what was his name?"
"He is the Editor of the paper, you know, The Star Free Press."
"You mean Judas Gius?"
"Yes, that's him, he was there." I thanked her profusely. Lord! The whole thing is crazy, the more I learn the screwier it gets. Judas Gius, Editor of the Ventura Star Free Press, a John P. Scripps paper, was involved in bribes and threats against a supervisor. When Robby wouldn't go along with them he was framed, tried and convicted and Gius still said nothing. I realized something else, even more amazing, Marvin Sosna, Editor of the Thousand Oaks Chronicle, also a John P. Scripps newspaper, was a member of the Grand Jury I'd appeared before. The *very same* Grand Jury I'd given direct evidence to that I'd been offered a share of a huge sum of money to frame Robinson.

Sosna and Gius were as tight as two Macaque monkeys in a tiny cage...together the pair of them *had known* that Judge Berenson had corruptly and criminally ordered that *very same* Grand Jury to *kill* its investigation into the frame-up of a Supervisor. Gius and Sosna, both editors, were the 'only persons' completely aware of the entire conspiracy. The others had only half of the pieces, and no way of putting them together. Both editors being self anointed heros and champions of the First Amendment, *forever* screaming about rights of the news media, and the rights of people *to know what is going on,* concealed and covered-up the most explosive political conspiracy in California... Why?

For months John P. Scripps papers were filled with testimony and courtroom pictures of Robinson's trial. WHY...why in hell did they cover-up all the facts and withhold and conceal from the people such an outrageous conspiracy? What in the world could possibly be in it for them? Scripps newspapers could have exclusively exposed a 'multimillion dollar fraud' that Judge Berenson and Ben Nordman were perpetrating on the citizens and taxpayers. Gius and Sosna were in it with Berenson and Nordman up to their eyeballs and they were *hoodwinking* the downtown businessmen and 'Red' Lagomarsino into believing Judas Gius was on their side.

Another crazy set of facts was gigging my brain...Berenson and Nordman was the force behind the Courthouse move...Robinson and Reiman must have been inadvertently helping them...Lagomarsino and his group were violently against moving the Courthouse...so why in hell did Judge Berenson kill a Grand Jury investigation that would have *cleared* Robinson and 'exposed' Lagomarsino's frame-up...? I mulled that one over for days. The most likely explanation was the simplest. The whole scam of relocating the Government Center had begun to generate so much public ire that Berenson and Nordman were in fear of a direct confrontation with Lagomarsino. It could create such a smell and so much heat that even Marvin Sosna and Judas Gius could not cover it up with their newspapers.

Actually Robinson meant nothing to them anyway. They decided to sacrifice Robinson and replace him with Franklin Jewett, one of Berenson's hand picked Grand Jury Foremen. Jewett would work out even better for them, he owned large parcels of land in the Victoria Ave. area and was eager to increase the value of his property. Now I better understood Gius' pernicious attacks against me in the Star Free Press...he sure as hell didn't want any of his connections in the corruption to be exposed. But, what in the world could Sosna's and his real participation be?

Lagomarsino's Ventura Realty Company tried to halt relocation of the Courthouse with a Superior Court lawsuit, but to no avail, Berenson simply ordered Judge Heaton to 'dismiss' Lagomarsino's case and Red was finished.

I'd begun to sense something *far more* intricately evil than just a bunch of local, town hall connivers, scheming, and stealing piles of taxpayers money. Mighty tentacles writhed *deep* within our judicial system, extending into the news media. They could destroy anybody, it was something damnably vile and terrifying.

It started with the Grand Jury testimony, my pro-per lawsuits, and Federal Civil Rights suit, fighting back we had accomplished a lot, we had forced more and more of their organizations's secret judicial and political figures to reluctantly but necessarily sacrifice themselves to exposure by their *corrupt judicial and administrative decisions*. The tenacious Civil Rights suit had sucked Judge Harry Pregerson right out of the woodwork. This fortuitous revelation had given us extremely valuable knowledge, but at the same time it was a completely devastating blow. Instead of having been elevated to the Federal arena of supposed legal equity and Due Process of Law for

American Citizens, we suddenly discovered we were up against a far more terrifying power than we *ever* dreamed of. Its sinewy tentacles were entwined into the Federal Government and Judicial system to the point that it was impossible to tell a loyal government employee from a deadly member of their secret organization.

It had to be an organization...what in hell else? My theory of being up against an influential, powerful Oligarch made up of Judge Berenson and Nordman controlling the local government and banks had *exploded* into a million pieces. I thought I'd been fighting the head of the octopus where it could possibly be destroyed, but, I was only tangling with the tip of a tentacle. Where in the world was the head...the controlling brain, how many tentacles did it have...how *far* did they reach? The tentacle I had been battling extended not only to Los Angeles, it slithered all through the State of California. God damn it, how in the name of hell did I ever get involved in this thing anyway? How in the hell was I ever going to get out...or was I?

CHAPTER 27

DuPre was on the East coast, I didn't expect him back for several months. Supervisor Ken Mac Donald had decided not to run for re-election. I knew it wasn't going to help my precarious predicament to just sit around waiting for a miracle to come along and solve all my problems. So, I paid the Court Clerk Robert Hamm, over five hundred dollars filing fee. I was in for months of rough campaigning from early morning till late at night in addition to taking care of my businesses. Without Mac Donald running as an incumbent it was a wide open field. Two candidates declared intentions of running for the office. However, I knew before it was over there would be four, including Jack De Long and me.

Jack De Long, a postal worker in the Ojai Valley, a follower and dedicated sycophant of the entrenched powers was forever poised to run for office whenever the need arose to split the votes. Eight years ago I'd learned about De Long. It was when I had first run against Supervisor Ralph 'Hoot' Bennett. De Long filed immediately after I did. With a little effort I discovered incumbent Bennett had paid for De Long's filing fees to split the vote.

Jack's backers never wanted him involved in an election...unless, a dangerous opponent sprang up. This meant he was always the last one to file. Over the years De Long devised a tricky little stunt to counteract this problem. Through his contacts in the elections dept. he'd arrange to be notified the minute I filed my papers. Quickly he would dash to the clerks office and file his papers. Then he'd spread the word throughout the entire Valley that I had filed *after* he did just for spite trying to destroy his long known aspirations to become a public official.

Jack's tricky stunt worked to get him sympathy votes. This time I was ready. Late afternoon, Friday February 29, 1980, the last day to file, I entered the Registrar of Voters office and filed my papers. I hung around until after closing time, De Long never showed. The following Monday March 3, the Star Free Press ran a story *claiming* De Long had filed to run for Supervisor last Friday, *before* I did.

As usual Gius was lying! I had been there until after closing time, Jack could not possibly have filed on Friday. I recalled a story a few years back involving Jack in a burglary of the Oak View Post Office. It was an inside job, the Postal Inspectors suspended him, ordering him not to enter the building. Political friends got him a transfer to the Santa Barbara Post Office, after a short time he quietly retired. To repay Jack for his services Supervisor 'Hoot' Bennett got him a job with the county, he was working in a building five or six miles from the County Clerk's office.

Jack received a call and was told that I was in the Clerk's office filing my Declaration of Candidacy form. He couldn't make it there before closing so Jack and the clerk *phonied* up his filing papers and *certified* them as being filed on Friday Feb. 29, 1980, the same day I filed. Gius had the type all set up for the story to hit on Monday.

One week later, Monday afternoon March 10, 1980, I went to the elections office. Candidacy forms being a matter of public record, I asked to see Jack De Long's file. On the upper right hand corner of my form the clerk had dutifully recorded the amount of the filing fee, $503.04, the date and paid by cash. On Jack's form nothing was entered. The same clerk who'd prepared and signed my papers had also signed De Long's.

I asked why she hadn't verified having received payment on Jack's form. Becoming very nervous and visibly shaken, the clerk could not explain the fact that if indeed she had received the money why she had not verified it on the form as required. I asked for the copy of the receipt a candidate is given for his payment. Searching the file she became flustered and frightened, claiming she couldn't locate it. Another clerk who'd been tuning in on our conversation, suddenly spoke, "I have a personal check from Mr. De Long, we're depositing it today."

"Are you telling me that you leave checks amounting to over five hundred dollars laying around almost two weeks before depositing them? Could I see the check please?" Removing it from the file she gave it to me. Stapled to the check a piece of paper stated De Long was given official receipt No. 58811 for his payment. My own receipt No. 58810 was issued prior to De Long's, and the clerk attested that these receipts were issued strictly in numerical sequence.

There was no question...De Long's papers were fraudulently filled out and certified as having been subscribed and sworn to before the clerk on Friday Feb. 29, 1980, when actually he couldn't have signed the documents or paid the fee until sometime during the following week. A forenoon spent at the Courthouse Law Library confirmed my suspicions, what Jack and the clerk had cooked up was a criminal violation. In fact, if we had an honest D.A. they would end up doing time in the joint for their dirty tricks.

California State Elections Code, Section 6553, Nomination Papers, Filing Fees, states:

"The filing fee required to be paid *shall be paid* to the County Clerk at the time that the forms for nomination are obtained from the County Clerk. The Clerk *shall not* accept any papers unless the fees are paid at the time required by this section."

Section 29303, states:

"False Nomination Papers or Declaration of Candidacy: filing or submission Penalty: *Any* person who files or submits for filing a nomination paper or declaration of candidacy knowing that it or any part of it has been made falsely is punishable by a fine not exceeding one thousand dollars, or by imprisonment in the State Prison for sixteen months, or two, or three years, or by *both* such fine and imprisonment."

The foregoing violations involving two or more persons conspiring to violate State Election Codes come directly under, "Crimes Against Public Justice." Sec. 182, Calif. Penal Code: Conspiracy. Definition & Punishment: If two or more persons conspire.

Section 1: to commit any crime.

Section 5: to commit any act injurious to public health, to public morals, or to pervert or obstruct justice, or the due administration of the laws, they shall be punishable by imprisonment in the County Jail for not more than one year, or in the State Prison for not more than three years or by a fine not exceeding five thousand dollars, or both."

All the facts and evidence of these crimes should be presented to District Attorney Michael Bradbury, with a demand for investigation and prosecution. After prudent consideration of Bradbury's political connections and commitments I knew such a course of action would not only be futile but also dangerous.

I recalled how Bradbury, as Assistant D.A., had *represented* and *protected* Supervisor Mac Donald and Planning Director Husbands at Ken Mac Donald's office. Also how Bradbury with his personal secretary came to my store on two separate occasions asking for my records exposing corruption. And, how at the time I'd envisioned an honest, law-abiding man capable of busting all of their political and judicial corruption wide open.

Shortly after Bradbury visited me an impressive article appeared in the Star Free Press. All about how Bradbury was going to run for District Attorney of Ventura County, it named a prestigious election committee. Jesus Christ! I read their list of names, Bradbury's avid interest in my records was immediately obvious, he'd *solicited* every crooked politician and judge involved in Ventura county corruption. What in hell kind of a *deal* could Bradbury be cooking...what was he *promising them in exchange for their money*.....was it his assurances that as D.A. he would protect them and make sure that I'd never be allowed to file criminal charges and appear before the Grand Jury again to expose them?

Judge Berenson and Nordman were enraged that I was going to run for Supervisor again. The familiar *tell-tale* signs discrediting me immediately sprung up. Fred Volz, Editor of the Ojai Valley News proclaimed, "Whether or not he will be a viable contender for office remains to be seen since he has refused to pay a filing fee debt of $230.73 which he has owed the county for four years." Very cleverly Volz pitched in with Judas Gius, they combined their viciousness to write, "Since there's no provisions in the election laws to reject his papers because he has not paid a filing fee owed the Election Dept. for four years, *our newspapers* have an *obligation* to notify the voters that he is a bad guy who does not pay his just debts." Christ! If I'd owed the County money, why in hell would they wait for four years before they started screaming about it?

March, April, May, it was three months til election day, June 3, 1980. I worked night and day contacting individuals, attending early morning and late evening social functions and political meetings set up for the candidates, some of them received thousands of dollars from the special interest groups...I had solicited no funds, everything was out of my own pocket. *In my book* it was more than impossible to believe that you could take thousands of dollars from a financial backer and still *not be indebted* to him. People handing out that kind of money to politicians sure as hell are not philanthropists, they are ruthless realists, hard headed businessmen who damned well expect *something* in return for their cash. Spelling it out, it simply means that *somewhere* along the line the politician will sell out the citizens and taxpayers.

It was the days of Howard Jarvis' Proposition 13. The people of California were sick to death of these high flying, arrogant, abusive politicians blowing all their hard earned taxes on every conceivable scam that cocaine and sex skewered brains could hallucinate.

My personal political beliefs and theories had always gravitated to the conservative area. However, the word conservative connotated one thing, spending tax money where it should be spent, and letting *none* of it to be swindled by rapacious and sick politicians.

Everything political evolves around money. Even sex is secondary, if you can control the money, then sex, a luxurious fringe benefit just comes naturally. I drew up flyers documenting the theft of millions and millions of county taxpayer money. Berenson's Public Facilities Corporation hucksters had repeatedly and unequivocally conned the people that the new Center would not cost over forty eight million. Documents revealed that the PFC had indebted the people with fifty eight and a half million dollars worth of revenue bonds they'd sold to the banks, plus interest on the bonds which amounted to another eighty million. Assistant County Auditor Controller, Thomas Mahon, and Deputy County Executive for the Budget and Finance, Michael McGee, agreed that they had on hand nineteen million, six hundred thousand of Federal Revenue Sharing funds dedicated to the new Government Center construction. But the County Executive argued that the true amount of the Revenue funds on hand should actually be twenty two million, two hundred thousand. A slight disappearance of only two million, six hundred thousand.

As California's Criminal Justice Committee head in Sacramento, Berenson, in a matter of just a few years directed more than twenty million dollars of Federal Criminal Justice money to spurious, falsely accredited law enforcement related construction at the new Center. Five million more was taken from property owners in tax increases to be used in the construction, plus one hundred million in interest taxpayers will be forced to pay on the loan against the courthouse property. Totaled up the Center would cost two hundred and eighty three million bucks, Berenson and Nordman were only stealing an insignificant amount of two hundred thirty five million.

All candidates were allowed an equal amount of time to address

THERE'S A FISH IN THE COURTHOUSE 257

the audience at the various forums from a speakers dais. My factual, vivid illustration of fraud and theft of enormous sums of taxpayers money was presented to them. Of all the candidates I was the only one backing an initiative advocating reduction of state income taxes.

We were drawing good crowds, my plugging away on the taxes was soaking in, people had begun to comprehend, if all of that Criminal Justice money had gone to law enforcement to make streets safe for citizens as mandated and if all the Revenue Sharing money had gone to senior citizens, crippled, blind and the truly needy, there'd still be millions left. My message was sinking in, people were contacting me by letter, phone and in person. I felt maybe I was beginning to do alright. In Camarillo the Daily News had given me several favorable write-ups as to my political views. Camarillo was an area that had just recently been added to the third district by a reapportionment, it comprised over fifty percent of the entire district's voters.

Three days before the election I got a call from some guy named Solkovits. "I'm a reporter for Camarillo Daily News. I want to know about this $230.73 that you have owed to the Election Department for so many years." I knew what was coming, Solkovits was going to repeat those same lies Gius and Volz had been up to. But this guy was worse, he screamed..."Robert Hamm, the County Clerk, has a warrant for you, it is laying on his desk right now. He went to the County Board of Supervisors and they gave him permission to sue you. You know you owe the money, why didn't you pay it?"

This was crazy, he was coming on like I owed him personally ten thousand dollars. "Hey fella...hold on...what's all your bullshit about Hamm having a warrant for me and he has decided that now is just the right time to serve it on me? Who told you all these lies?"

"I don't have to tell you."

"The hell you don't, by God I'll be down to your paper in twenty minutes and I'll damn sure find out."

"There's no one but me here, and I'll be gone, I am going home now, it's Saturday, my day off, I've been working long hours special on this story."

Quickly thumbing through the phone book on my desk I stalled him for a few seconds. I asked, "What's your interest in a so called special story about me in these last three days before the election?" I found a Gregg Solkovitz listed in Woodland Hills, before he could answer I said, "I know you live in Woodland Hills, if you are going home I'm coming down there right now."

"Wait a minute, you're not going to come to my house, this is my residence."

"What the hell do I care, I'll find out one way or another where you got your shitty information."

"Okay, alright, I heard it from a woman...a clerk in the Elections Department."

"What was her name?"

"Jacobson, that's her name, Geraine Jacobson, she's the one who gave me the story."

"Who ordered you to write this big 'expose' you've been working special on?"

"I can't tell you that."

I jammed the phone back on the hook, no use talking further to him. I knew he was going to write a story just the way he was told, he had his orders. I'd learned enough from him to make the whole picture come out clear as crystal. Jacobson, that was the clerk who spoke up saying she had De Long's personal check for his filing fee. This was good, it identified one of the clerks that Robert Hamm was using. Jacobson had to be the one who engineered all of De Long's filing fee chicanery.

Sunday morning, June 1, 1980, two days until election, Solkovitz's fearless expose appeared in the Camarillo Daily News, depicted in large black headings, "County Taking Board Candidate To Court." Solkovitz had become unnerved after our talk, in his article he put the *finger* on Jacobson as the one who gave him the story to print. When I first spoke to him he hadn't intended to reveal his source, now to *cover for himself* he had changed his story considerably. He now claimed Jacobson told him, "The Board of Supervisors approved taking Gary to court to recover the money, and she's only awaiting the go-ahead from County Clerk Hamm to file the complaint."

Their timing was perfect, the story appeared in Sunday's edition of Camarillo's Daily News, every voter in town read it. They had all Monday to spread the story around the district before voting started the following morning. Regardless of my inevitable loss at the polls I'd gained something. Never in a million years would County Clerk Robert Hamm have so imperiled his own personal, dearly cherished hide by setting up such virulently slanderous lies to emanate from his clerk's office, unless, first he'd gotten precise, un-refuseable orders from Judge Berenson commanding him to do so.

Judge Berenson and Nordman's extreme necessity for such vicious, sinister obstruction of the election's outcome spawned a momentous disclosure, a revelation, it unmasked their latent, vulnerable Achilles heel. Yes, for sure, I'd hit upon their weakness, a fatal weakness, an integral segment of *unrecantable* beliefs, a voluntary acknowledgment of *doom* buried deep into their consciousness. Anathema Maranatha, a *dreadful curse* lay upon them. The unthinkable fate of disbarment, the terrible, sickening, *divestiture of their aggregate swindlings*, total extirpation. All brought forth upon them by detested, insignificant, but unescapable truth and facts.

CHAPTER 28

Before starting my current political struggle I applied for a license to sell beer at my restaurant in Casitas. Customer's asking for beer as well as Coke indicated it would increase sales considerably. The ABC Office was in Santa Barbara, thirty miles north.

Wednesday October 10, 1979, my wife and I filed an application for an on-sale license. We showed Ventura County records to Agent Stanley Huntington, proving our business was zoned for consumption of alcoholic beverages. We paid a fee of over three hundred dollars. He handed us a large sheet of paper explaining, "This is your notice of intention to sell beer on your premises. It must be posted at the business for thirty days in open view of the public. This gives them the opportunity to file a protest if they have an objection."

When we left it was late afternoon, we arrived at the restaurant in about forty minutes. The looming mountain across the road had gobbled up the sun. In the remaining light I tacked the notice to the front of the building and filled in the date of posting.

Judge Berenson's intelligence system began to function the instant we walked out the front door of the ABC office. Agent Huntington immediately put in a long distance call to Victor Husbands office in the new Ventura County Courthouse. Husbands Resource Agency investigators went to work on me instantly. All my files were pulled out and thoroughly examined before I'd even posted the notice on my building.

Steve Solomon, County Environmental Health Agent was assigned my case and ordered to keep close contact with Agent Huntington. Early next morning, Thursday October 11, 1979 Solomon appeared promptly at the U.S. Post Office. He sent an official notice, a copy to me and my lawyer by certified mail, receipt No. 695950, I signed for it. Reading it I admonished myself, this was going to be only the beginning if I tried to fight for the beer license. They weren't going to let me ever get another license or a permit for anything.

They'd red-lined me everywhere in California and maybe further, Solomon's message was a command, "If you don't apply for a Health Permit within seven days of receipt of this notification the Resource Management Agency's enforcer will take immediate legal action as prescribed by State Law, Section 510 and County Ordinance 4605." A week later Agent Huntington phoned from Santa Barbara telling me that Ron Vogelbaum, agent for Husbands' Planning Department had notified him that ABC could not issue me a beer license until I applied to the County for a conditional use permit, also a planned development permit.

I talked to DuPre about the situation. After researching the legal technicalities he determined that ABC had the responsibility only to ascertain if the zoning was proper and conduct a hearing if anyone filed a formal protest during the thirty day posting period. Bob said, "Very simply, ABC has no legal authority or requirement to make an investigation or any legal determination as to county environmental procedures much less to deny a license based on county accusations of *alleged* violations of their ordinances." In reality DuPre had long ago made a choice, he realized that his fervid, abiding anger toward the malevolent evils of official abuse of power forever precluded him from the ranks of politically influential, prestigious, giant law firms, he was a loner.

DuPre was adamant, "For the county officials to use such vicious under-handed means to deny your license is wild. It's proof of their overwhelming criminal conspiracy to deny you Due Process of Law. Legally their only recourse is to file charges, take you to court and try to prove you are in violation of their ordinances, not to furtively block your license by conspiring with the ABC. We've rotated right back to the same old thing, they have no evidence to prove *anything* against you in court, rather it's proof that they have to do everything within their power to destroy your ability to fight their corruption."

November 8, 1979, two days before the posting expired a letter came from another one of the under-lying departments of Husbands

Ventura County Resource Management Agency. I was well aware of their talent for duplicity, but I struggled hard to digest their latest concoction. W. H. Korth, the Manager of Weights and Measures had written the letter. He sent copies to the ABC office, also to each of the five supervisors, District Attorney Michael Bradbury and one to Husbands, the person who had ordered Korth to write it in the first place.

I was reading it the third time when DuPre arrived. More than a little provoked I yelled, "Hey Bob, Good Lord, listen to what they're doing now! I don't have the faintest idea how in the world I ever got involved with Weights and Measures. Husbands must be running out of people to write his letters. Listen, this guy Korth says, 'I have no permits for the demolition of a previous building at my restaurant.' Damn it, there was no demolition on the restaurant property. Then he says, 'there is no building permit for construction work done on the premises.' That's another lie, the only work I did was to install the ventilator hood over the grill. I took out a permit and tried for months to have it inspected. Finally I got an inspector to come out, he approved it and signed if off. The very next day two other guys from the building department showed up, they claimed it had never been inspected. I told you how mad they got. I knew that they had come to put a bunch of violations against the restaurant. Becoming frustrated they went to my other property in Oak View where they filed a mess of ridiculous violations against me."

DuPre answered, "Yeh, how could I ever forget!"

"Listen to the next accusation Korth makes, 'There's no permit on file to abandon the gasoline storage tanks which at one time existed on the property.' Bob, never at anytime were gasoline tanks on the restaurant property. They were at another location altogether."

"It's obvious what they are doing. Desperate to obey Berenson's rabid order to block your license, Husbands has scrounged up every scrap of paper in your dossier, then lumped it all on your restaurant property."

"Damn it Bob, it isn't right to send all those lies to ABC."

"Absolutely not," with a short pause, he said, "Next week after the posting date has expired we'll go to Santa Barbara and see this guy Huntington. Let's see if we can't talk some sense with him. Really, this entire operation is crazy, I find it exceptionally hard to believe that Berenson can control state agencies so easily."

Without trying to set up an appointment, which I was sure would have been unsuccessful anyway, we went to Santa Barbara. Luckily

Agent Huntington was there. Bob reminded him the posting period had expired many weeks ago. "Do you have any formal protests or objections to the license?"

"Well no, but I have talked to one resident of the area who might object."

"What do you mean 'might' object, has he filed a written protest?"

"No he hasn't."

"Then what is the problem if he hasn't filed anything in writing? You're well aware that the 'protest period' has expired, why are you continuing to hold up issuance of the license?"

"Well, we have received information in writing from the County of Ventura." Huntington had my file on his desk, he held up a letter.

Looking at it DuPre said, "Yes, I've read that letter by Korth, it's nothing but a pack of lies, for instance the accusation regarding the gasoline tanks. Never at any time were they ever on the property in question, how can you even consider such an accusation when you have never come out to investigate any of these vicious charges? It appears to me that you are railroading the entire operation under direction of *certain people* in the Ventura County Government!"

Huntington perceived the conversation wasn't going well for him. "I am only an investigator, I've forwarded my report to Sacramento for deliberation."

"So, you've sent all those accusatory letters from the County and the memos of those malicious phone calls you got from people like Solomon and Vogelbaum, but have you seen fit to send any diligent, honest investigatory reports explaining that those gas tanks were not even on the restaurant property?" Huntington's face was blank. Bob added, "It would've been damn easy for you to verify that there has been no demolition on the subject property." Huntington by now was saying nothing, he had closed the file on his desk. Bob asked, "How long will Sacramento take to make some kind of decision?"

"I do not know." Averting his eyes Huntington mumbled, "I really cannot tell you anything more."

Bob had become increasingly perturbed with the agent's dip-shit attitude, the apprehensive clamping of Huntington's lips lent him an appearance of being frightened. Of what, who knows? Maybe for his job or was it the sting of DuPre's pointed questions. I nudged Bob, we got out of there.

A month had passed since our visit to ABC when a letter came. Huntington was trying to get tricky, his latest letter said, "You are in violation of a County zoning ordinance in that you do not have a planned development permit, such improper zoning constitutes the grounds to 'deny' the beer license." At this point the agent's deceit became plain, "I don't want to do that. Such a denial prohibits you from re-applying at the denied location for one year from the date of final Denial Order. Under these circumstances you may be best advised to *withdraw* your application. In doing so you wouldn't have a denial on your record, and you could re-apply for the license any time after you get the County Permit." He thoughtfully enclosed a "NOTICE OF WITHDRAWAL OF APPLICATION" form with his letter.

Upon reading the letter Bob howled derisively, "This guy makes it sound just like he sincerely has your best interests at heart."

"Yeh, he sure does."

"This is evidence that they know they're wrong. They are pulling every trick in their power to lull you into a voluntary withdrawal of your application. They're hoping to get off the painful hook of having to deny your application."

"I get it, but what scares me is how in hell do Judge Berenson and Ben Nordman have such awesome power to put a state agency on the hook in the first place?"

"When we talked with Huntington he said he had sent the file to Sacramento for a determination. If that's true, why is he sending a letter like this? I have a feeling he never sent the file anywhere."

Another month elapsed, again a letter came. Bob and I took heart, this time Huntington mailed a "PETITION FOR A CONDITIONAL LICENSE." It was now the middle of January 1980, three months since filing my original application. It appeared Huntington knowing he had no legality to deny my license was giving in. The next dirty trick he could do was put severe restrictions on the license to make it as tough on me as he could. Those conditions were as follows: "I would not be allowed to sell beer after eight p.m. or before eleven a.m. or serve beer on the patio or erect a fixed bar on the premises."

"Hell Bob, that was all I ever wanted in the first place."

"Yes, but hold on a second before signing it, I just don't trust this Huntington. He has never come on like a straight guy from the very start."

"I sure agree with that, what do you suggest?"

"Let me type a note next to where you sign the agreement." He put the Petition into the typewriter and banged away a few seconds, "I think this little appendage will forestall any deceptions Huntington has in mind." DuPre had typed, "Note: This petition is signed and submitted subject to this agreement by ABC to issue a conditional license forthwith."

"That is an excellent thought Bob, I like it."

"I have had a strange feeling, it has now been three months since Huntington said he sent the file to Sacramento for a determination. It shouldn't take them that long. If the file is in Sacramento like he says, then why in hell is he sending you a Petition for a Conditional License?" Bob's note got immediate reaction from Huntington. This time I didn't have to wait a month, he answered in two days.

His letter stated, "The 'addendum' you placed on the Petition for Conditional License at the bottom of the document, invalidates the Petition. No such agreement was made by ABC. The license cannot be issued forthwith." Bob's suspicions had proven to be right. It had been an elaborate guile, another ploy devised by Huntington. Shortly afterward something else occurred that allowed no room for further doubt as to ABC's evil intents.

Leaving a grocery store in Oak View, I headed across the parking lot toward my car. A quite voice said, "Hey Gary, haven't seen you for awhile, how you been doing?" I glanced around, sitting in a car was Cliff, the ABC agent who'd helped me years ago. I had never forgotten his steadfast refusal to acquiesce to those vicious Ventura officials who had demanded that he 'deny' my liquor store license. Shaking hands we chatted, "I wish you good luck in the election, my wife and I will be voting for you."

"That's great, you know the old saying...every vote counts."

"What about Santa Barbara, how are you coming along with your license?"

I'd become overly testy to that situation. I said quickly and a bit more harshly than I intended, "Hell, that guy Huntington really put the screws on my beer license. He's in deep with all those crooked Ventura bastards and I mean right to his eyeballs."

Shock sprang on Cliff's face at my anger. He said, "Huntington is actually a really nice guy, but *he's got his orders.*"

"Orders! You say he's got his orders to deny me a license? That makes him a bigger asshole than ever." Our friendly chat dwindled. I was wrong, it sounded like I was berating all the agents. "Cliff, I really appreciate you and your wife's votes, if I should just accidently win, I'll guarantee you one thing, there'll be some changes made in that damned Courthouse."

After wasting four months Huntington knew he'd failed with his tricks and guile to obtain a voluntary withdrawal of my application.

He had only one alternative. On March 6, 1980, the Department of Alcohol Beverage Control delivered notice that they were denying my application. "The issuance of a license to 'you' would be *contrary to the public welfare and morals,* as provided in Article XX, Section 22 of the Constitution of the State of California, and Section 23958 of the Business and Professions Code, and Rule 61.4 of Title 4, Chapter 1 of Calif. Administrative Code. The denial was signed by a Beatrice Smalley, their ABC attorney in Sacramento, Calif.. Also Beatrice let me know, "If I was not happy with any of their actions I could within ten days file a petition for a hearing in Sacramento."

DuPre wrote an Appeal stressing two facts:

1. No formal protest as required by law have been filed with the ABC by any resident of the area.

2. The ABC dept. had erroneously concluded that the Business and Professions Code confers legal authority upon it to carry out the intent of environmental laws. Where property itself is correctly zoned by the County for the operation of this type business, the fact that allegations of failure to obtain any type of permit has no bearing on ABC's decision. Particularly when as a fact the County has refused to adjudicate their allegations of zoning violations. Notice of Appeal was filed on March 14, eight days after the denial.

March 18, 1980 Beatrice acknowledged receipt of my Appeal by advising me she would schedule a hearing as soon as possible, and I would be notified of the date, time and place.

The last of March, DuPre unexpectedly left for Atlanta, Georgia, on personal business. He wasn't sure when he'd return. Without his legal guidance and reassuring presence, my future was mighty bleak. But election activities and pressing business duties managed to keep me fully occupied.

May 6, Beatrice Smalley mailed a notice that a hearing date was set. It would be held June 18, ten a.m. in the Multi-Purpose room, third floor of the new Ventura Government Center. Beatrice was very helpful, "If you're not skilled in speaking or understanding the English language, an interpreter will be made available for you at the hearing. Accordingly you are entitled by law to issue subpoena's to force the attendance of witnesses, and for documents and any other things." The only 'other thing' I could subpoena to help me would be an honest judge. Where in hell do you find one of those things?

A week into June DuPre returned from the east, "I was in Atlanta a while then went to Washington, D.C., left just in time to miss the summer swelter."

"Damn Bob, you don't know how glad I am to see you. I lost the election, which probably comes as no real surprise."

"No, no surprise, they didn't dare under any circumstance let you win. Something else, I've been gone for two months but this ABC thing never once left my mind."

"Believe me, it's been on my mind to, they've scheduled a hearing for June 18."

"I think you can forget that farce, you'll just be up before the same people who denied your license in the first place, how are you going to beat that?" I studied DuPre, he'd battled government chicanery and connivery many times before, it sure as hell wasn't anything new to him. I knew his brain was chewing on an idea, maybe a whole lot of ideas. I waited, not wanting to disturb his thoughts.

After a minute he spoke, "The practice of law is the matter of a concept evolving itself into a theory, you can never allow yourself to be enticed by an adversary into playing his game. It's been two years since Harry Pregerson dismissed our suit in District Court. For all intents and purposes the Appeal Court has 'buried us' forever. They now have us running in circles, spinning our wheels with the stupid idea of winning a lousy little administrative hearing that they've got completely wired up."

"I'm listening."

"That case does not belong in the Appeal Court, it belongs in the District Court for trial, because never at 'anytime' have the merits been reached. My theory is to file a new case in District Court. Set the entire legal process in motion again right from the start. If the Appeal Court is going to bury our Appeal, let them go ahead."

"I agree, it's plain bullshit waiting for years while they stall us off, meanwhile everybody dies."

"I'm familiar with most of the ABC stuff, give me a rundown on the election happenings while I was back east. I ran through all the crazy crap with Robert Hamm and Gregg Solkovitz the reporter.

"One thing, you had them scared to beat hell or they'd never have stuck their necks out so far. The facts you related are all *overt acts* involving new defendants in an *extension and continuation* of their *original conspiracy*. It is a new case, none of the merits have at any time ever been reached. I must talk with Terrell Powell, I need his approval on this just as soon as possible, our time is running out, I only have a few days."

"Alright...I'll contact Terrell, and anything else you need just let me know."

"Good...for the next five days at least I will be tied up in the law library from morning till night."

"One thing Bob, I don't understand the critical time element?"

He smiled, "That is part of my theory. We are going to the ABC hearing alright, but not to *beg* for a beer license. We'll be there to serve a lawsuit. A Federal Civil Rights Suit, Section 1983, charging ABC with being participants in the conspiracy. Let them go ahead and do whatever they want at the hearing. Our only chance lies in the Federal Courts." During the next ten days I saw little of DuPre. The date of the ABC hearing drew close.

It was time we talked with Powell, we left early the next morning. Exiting the San Diego Freeway we went east on Century Boulevard. The Hollywood Park race track was to our left, a swift glance at my watch, eight fifty five. Powell's office was another five minutes, we were right on time. Terrell studied the Civil Rights Complaint Bob had drawn up. It commenced at the very beginning, basically when Berenson *killed* the Grand Jury investigation. The Complaint aligned the entire conspiracy, including the latest defendants, Robert Hamm and Baxter Rice. Rice was Director of the Department of ABC.

It was noon when Powell and Bob concluded their legal colloquy. Powell commented, "It's very good, most comprehensible." He then signed the Complaint.

Bob shoved the documents into his briefcase and looked at me, "We better get rolling, this is June 17th, tomorrow is the hearing." Encountering heavy traffic on the inbound lanes of Harbor Freeway and parking problems on the busy surface streets it was a little after one thirty when we entered the Post Office building, we had to send a copy of the Complaint to each of the defendants, including one to ABC in Sacramento.

In the morning we'd *hand deliver* another copy of the Complaint directly to Beatrice Smalley, the ABC lawyer. We still had to get to the Federal Building at 312 N. Spring Street. Immediately inside the entrance a uniformed guard requested DuPre to open his briefcase for inspection. I pondered, was this need for precautional security the proximate indication of a rapidly declining respect for Federal Judicial integrity and honesty?

The Clerk of U.S. District Court, Central District of California, stamped his Certification of Filing on the Complaint, June 17, 1980, Civil Action No. 80-02582. He collected his fee.

Standing in the doorway I surveyed all the people gathered in the Multi-Purpose Room, third floor, new County Government Center.

Agent Huntington was over in a far corner huddling with a group of Casitas Springs residents. ABC can't use them to protest my license now, what the hell is going on? Not one of them had filed a formal protest within the required posting period. During the eight months Huntington stalled me on the license not one of these people had ever complained. Obviously ABC wasn't concerned with the law. All they knew was, they *had their orders*..."kill that beer license."

Leaving the huddle, Huntington crossed the room and conversed with a woman standing behind a table, it had to be Beatrice Smalley. Arrayed before her were high stacks of official documents. A sinster looking black briefcase was open a slight crack. Bob had been right, I'd seen set-ups before but this one appeared deadly. Beatrice was imposingly formidable, a heavy weight...a brick gate post clad in a Ukrainian peasant woman's attire, surely Beatrice is hiding an axe in the slightly opened briefcase next to her right hand. A copy of the Complaint I'd been gripping was taken from my hands, I heard Bob say, "Here, let me lay that Complaint on Beatrice." I didn't protest.

Smalley snarled at him, "You *can't serve that on me*," roughly she slammed the Complaint across the table. The judge had just taken his seat. He said to DuPre, "Let me see that Complaint."

After a moment he thrust it toward Beatrice, he ordered, "Here, you *better* read it."

Snatching it she commenced reading. Manifestly upset Beatrice clutched at Huntington, "Where's the nearest phone?" The Amazon growled, "I have to contact Sacramento headquarters, immediately."

Charging from the room Smalley hustled down the escalator with Huntington practically running up her back. They must have found a telephone down there, they didn't come back. We'd served them, it appeared there was nothing more DuPre or I could do...we exited the Multi-Purpose Room. Beatrice was furious, she'd prepared for and dreamed of nothing but her great impending legal confrontation for days and months, she'd gone all out, Beatrice was going to lower the boom. This would make her reputation, privately she understood how bad her boss really wanted this one. Traveling all the way from Sacramento, she'd been mentally prepared to finish me off once and for all. Beatrice felt it was unfair, "Damn it, it just ain't right to be cheated like this." However, Beatrice tolled her revenge. A few days later she sent a notice advising me, "Your beer license application has been denied since you abandoned your right to Appeal."

"There's no use to fret," Bob said, "You can't abandon something that you were not going to get."

Suit 80-02582 filed June 17, precipiated a swift series of events that Judge Harry Pregerson couldn't stem. The Appeal Court in San Francisco *forthwith* gave birth to a so-called, Judicial Notice of the situation. They well knew the merits of our original case had never at any time been adjudicated. We could continue filing lawsuits in District Court as fast as Judge Pregerson could dismiss them, also we could Appeal each Dismissal, it would be of no further avail for them to bury our Appeal. Within days a terse notice came from the Appeal Court in San Francisco. Our case was soon to be submitted *without* oral argument to a three judge panel, Sneed, Anderson and Tang.

Two days later Ventura County Counsel Schechter wrote a letter to the judges in a distorted attempt to influence them. She insisted that they join the old and new Complaint and Dismiss them on the grounds of Res Judicata, which means that, "the merits have been adjudicated." But the same Court hearing our Appeal ruled in Guam Investment Company v. Central Building Inc. 288 F. 2d 19, 24 Ninth Circuit, 1961, that, "Where the court has entered a summary-type Dismissal, without allowing more definite statements or amendments to the Complaint *the merits of the former case were not reached* and Res Judicata *would not* bar a subsequent suit." The Appeal Court then remanded the case for a trial on the merits. DuPre displayed an intense conviction that the Court should definitely impose a severe sanction on Schechter for her callous, interference with the Appeal Court's deliberation.

August 5, 1980, ABC filed a MOTION TO DISMISS my latest case. The hearing was set for September 15, 10:00 a.m., U.S. District Court, room 14, to be heard by Judge Manuel Real. James McBride, Assist. County Counsel, represented the County. Attorney General George Deukmejian would defend the ABC. Damn...! That sure did constitute one hell of a lot of legal power coming forth just to make certain I did not get a beer license.

For years Deukmejian promoted and nourished his self declared image as, "The Great Defender of Law and Order." I wondered how the devil he equated my small desire for a beer license to help me make a living in comparison to Judge Berenson's cravings to defraud the taxpayers of more than one hundred million dollars. Some of it ironically was Criminal Justice money. Gov. Duekmejian had a great opportunity to establish himself a true image by busting the judicial corruption in Ventura County. But reality churned my brain, he was probably *taking orders* just like ABC Agent Huntington.

Ten a.m., Sept. 15, 1980, I sat in Judge Manuel Real's courtroom. Powell and Bob were having a last minute strategy session across the aisle from me. In the rear of the room James McBride was talking with Elizabeth Koen, a Special Deputy Atty. Gen. that Duekmejian had assigned to handle our case. It was 11:00 before Real finished with his other court business. As always, we were the only ones left in the room when the clerk got around to calling our case. Walking through the gate McBride and Koen approached the lawyers table in front of judge Real's bench. Exhibiting normal affectations McBride crowed, "James L. McBride, I am ready and appearing for Ventura County." Duekmejian's Special Attorney spoke, "Elizabeth Koen, appearing for the State of California." Powell letting the gate swing shut behind him moved toward the table, and like the rest of them he said, "Terrell Pow...," CRACK!! Startlingly Judge Manuel H. Real had crashed his gavel on the bench, he hissed, "CASE DISMISSED." Scurrying from his dais Real vanished swiftly within the safety of his chambers.

Mouth agape, Powell was transfixed, he clung to his briefcase as if it were his solitary remaining possession. McBride slid his arms around Koen, sharing knowing glances, the pair smirked exultantly as they whispered in each others ears. Slipping through the doors, they disappeared into the marble lined halls of this mighty edifice that housed, FEDERAL JUSTICE. DuPre and Powell headed for the street, I followed. Out on Spring St. a bright sun did nothing to dispel the pall of darkness that Federal Judge Manuel H. Real had spread. A silent Powell took off across Spring St..

We were halfway to Hollywood on the north bound freeway when Bob said, "What do you think about it?"

"Jesus Christ! What do I think? How much money does it take to buy scum like Judge Manuel H. Real?"

"In all my years of experience in Federal Courts in the east I've just never experienced anything near so glaringly bad as this. By the Federal Rules, Judge Real is *required* to issue an order for summary judgement allowing us the right to Discovery and Depositions. It's the same old merry-go-round, *the merits have not been reached*, we can re-file and also Appeal Judge Real's Dismissal. I can only guess that their over-all strategy is based on their belief that you won't be able to withstand years of financial strain. Then there is their more kindly disposed, profound hope you will drop dead."

Eight days later more definite proof of Manuel Real's greasy, low grade character was openly evident. September 23, Real entered his order granting the Motion To Dismiss. In Judge Real's own words: "HAVING CONSIDERED THE PLEADINGS, THE EXHIBITS OF WHICH THE COURT TAKES JUDICIAL NOTICE, THE MEMORANDA OF LAW, AND THE ORAL ARGUMENTS OF THE PARTIES ON SEPT. 15, I CONCLUDE THAT THE CASE SHOULD BE DISMISSED WITH PREJUDICE."

For a week I had been assailed violently with upset intestines, the dreary illness had set upon me very shortly after watching Judge Real scurry from his bench and slink cowardly into his chambers. Now his signed document wherein *he swore* that *he had heard,* "THE ORAL ARGUMENTS OF THE PARTIES ON SEPT. 15," convulsed my tortured guts into a full eruption. I had to puke! Hell, Powell hadn't even gotten his entire name out of his mouth when Real crashed his gavel on the bench. Real's actions were a deplorably depraved misuse of Judicial power, striking a Supreme Court Ruling full in the face.

From Encyclopedia of Law, Corpus Juris Secundum 791 et. seq. comes the decision from the U.S. Supreme Court, 1957, Conley v. Gibson, the Court ruled that:

"Motions to Dismiss are granted sparingly, and that there are *Constitutional limits* on the *power of the Courts* to Dismiss an action, and thereby deprive a party of the opportunity for a hearing on the merits of his case."

After two and a half years, on Sept. 18, 1980 the Appeal Court, Ninth Circuit, overturned Judge Pregerson's premature Dismissal of my original Case No. 78-2158. Snead, Anderson and Tang, Appeal Judges, knew it was a meritorious case and that it *should not* have been Dismissed. To extricate Judge Berenson from his trap and at the same time cover-up Pregerson's involvement, they *tortured the facts* of the case and their own individual mentalities with clumsy chicanery. They ultimately determined the only possible way in which they could accomplish this act of extrication would be to *redefine* the laws of a Civil Conspiracy leaving only a few minor, separate charges that could never survive. The corrupt morals among Federal Judges always oozes to the surface when the matter of another corrupt judge comes before them.

DuPre and I discussed and thought for days about the reversal the Appeal Court made against Judge Pregerson, we'd arrived at a hell of a critical crossroads. Sunk deep within my own thoughts I heard DuPre's voice, "The next obvious step is loaded with traps. Ordinarily an average attorney, exultant from gaining a reversal by the Appeal Court will immediately begin drafting an Amended Complaint based

THERE'S A FISH IN THE COURTHOUSE   273

on his opinion of what *he thinks* the Appellate Court has said. We could proceed on that route but I've a strong feeling it would be a terrible mistake. Making a circumspect analysis of the Appeal Court opinion it is nothing more than an abominably extraneous, muddled piece of thinking. If we should even attempt to interpret what in hell they are thinking we will be in big trouble. They have remanded it, so, we should wait for the District Court Judge to issue orders for further proceedings based on what 'he' believes the Appeal Court has said."

Bob's background was engulfed extensively in Civil Rights actions, both Civil and Criminal. His great source of knowledge also sprang from exposure to both sides of the fence, defense and prosecution wise. Not long after the Appeal Court remanded our case back to District Court we learned Pregerson had again seized our case.

"This is damned disturbing," DuPre stewed, "now I understand why I was so leery of filing an Amended Complaint. Hell, he would have Dismissed us again in a week. I can not figure this guy Pregerson's motives. President Carter appointed him to the Appeal Court in San Francisco just recently, supposedly to ease an over burdened case load up there. Instead, he stays here in Los Angeles and *takes over* our case *again.*"

"He has to Bob, Pregerson's so damned involved in the corruption in Ventura County he doesn't dare let our case get out of his hands. He'll Dismiss it in District Court, when we file our Appeal against him he will fly to Frisco and as Appeal Court Judge he will Dismiss it again. Next if that stupid Carter appoints Pregerson to the U.S. Supreme Court in D.C., the son of a bitch can fly back there and he can Dismiss our last and final Appeal."

"Pretty damn frightening!"

"It's not only frightening, it's sickening, but that's the way he'll do it. When you think about it, who can stop him? That *gangster* is a judge for life."

A couple days later DuPre said, "Sit down for a minute and listen. From the very beginning something's plagued me about our case. It's the reason for the position we are in right now. We can never hope for success unless we do something about it. The problem itself is very simple, it's doing something about it that troubles me. The fact is, we follow and obey the Federal Rules meticulously, but the judges don't follow anything except their 'Local Rules' which they *make up as they go along.* I spent the last two days at the law library reading them, I've explained it to you before, it is necessary to delve deeply into your mind in terms of theory and strategy, it's not till then that you begin digging for law. My theory is this, if we can force them to follow the Federal Rules we can beat them. We have truth and facts on our side, all they have got is their guilt to hide."

I had to laugh, "Other than being a poet I am sure you must have something up your sleeve Robert."

"Well, at first I was toying with maybe a direct Appeal to the U.S. Supreme Court. It had seemed like our only hope since it's obvious Pregerson controls our case, both in the District and Appeal Court. Such a move could take many years, and they could bury it the same as the Appeal Court did."

"I'm staying with you Bob."

"But, a better theory has evolved. I'm talking about a Petition for Writ of Certiorari to the U.S. Supreme Court. Under Rule 12 (b) (6), Federal Rules of Civil Procedure, and Title 28 United States Code, Section 1254, the Supreme Court can exercise their *power of Supervision* over lower Federal Courts. Now, in our case those lower Courts have ignored Federal Rules of Civil Procedure so as to deny a Petitioner a determination of the merits of his case."

"Sounds good."

"One good thing is that it can be heard in the October 1981 term of the Supreme Court, also the entire file will be transmitted to D.C., for a review."

"That's amazing Bob, maybe there is some hope in the system for the people after all!" But it was not as simple as I thought.

DuPre worked for days creating the Certiorari. Again we ran into all those Local Rule requirements regarding the size of the typing, size of pages and how far the words must stay from the top, bottom and sides of the page. It was enough to drive you nuts, forty copies had to be compiled to send to the Supreme Court for distribution. I had checked several printing companies, the cheapest was over a thousand dollars, however, they wouldn't guarantee to complete the job before time to file expired. Such malevolent rules were scrounged up for one purpose only, discouraging the poor and disenfranchised and enriching lawyers.

December 2, 1980 we met with Powell in L.A.. After much perusal and study he approved and signed the Certiorari. Back in Ventura, Bob and I labored for days assembling the booklets and preparing them for mailing. In answer to the Certiorari we received two letters.

December 10, James McBride wrote to say, "In view of the fact that the subject case clearly does not warrant review by the Supreme

Court we waive our right to file a Brief in opposition."

Robert laughed, "What McBride is really saying is that he doesn't know how to answer the Petition for Certiorari without becoming more screwed up than he already is." The second letter arrived on January 5, 1981, we did not shrug it off so jauntily. We both felt the ominous portent in the brief two paragraph letter from Richard H. Deane, Clerk, U.S. Court of Appeal Ninth Circuit, San Francisco, California. We realized Deane now worked for Pregerson, the newly appointed Appeal Court Judge. The clerk stated, "We have received your request to certify and transmit this Court's record of your case to the Supreme Court of the United States. Rule 13.1 and 19.1 of the Supreme Court provides that the record shall be transmitted *when* the Supreme Court determines that the record is needed."

Decoding the sinister significance of Deane's letter DuPre and I realized Pregerson didn't intend to allow the file to *ever,* 'at anytime' reach the Supreme Court. The last two sentences further clued us in as to the dirty tricks Deane was up to. "We have *arranged* with the Clerk of the Supreme Court to advise us immediately when such a determination is made. Please be assured at that time the complete record will be transmitted without delay."

"Bob, what sort of *arrangements* do you believe Deane has actually made with the Clerk of the Supreme Court?"

"I don't know, but it sure can't be good. All those clerks get their orders straight from the judges and they can create more havoc and grief than you could possibly imagine. As it stands right now Deane, the Clerk in San Francisco, does not intend to transmit our case to the Supreme Court unless he has to. So, all we can do regarding that is wait until the U.S. Supreme Court's October term of 1981." Bob's theory of not attempting to file an Amended Complaint based on the screwy decision by Judges Snead, Anderson and Tang, brought action from Pregerson. On December 30, 1980, Pregerson filed his 'personal decree,' he was going to hold a 'Hearing on Filing and Spreading the Judgement' of the Court of Appeal, on Monday January 26, 1981 at 10:00 a.m., Courtroom 1600, Los Angeles, Calif..

"Alright, I give up, what in the name of hell is this Spreading the Judgement Pregerson is going to do?"

Bob grinned, "It's nothing but a ruse by Judge Pregerson. Since we haven't tried to file an Amended Complaint he can't figure out what our legal theory and strategy can be. It's bothering him, he intends to browbeat and twist the hell out of Powell trying to squeeze foolish statements out of him on which to base some sort of inane reasoning to Dismiss our case again."

"Damn it Robert, what sort of Federal Procedure do you call this kind of shit? Look at this form letter mailed by R. W. Johnson, the Deputy Clerk for Pregerson. He has crossed out District Court Judge and typed in Circuit Court Judge. We should be in District Court, with a different judge, the case was just returned from the Appellate Court in Frisco, why in hell are we still in the Appellate Court in Los Angeles? What in the world gives with this guy Pregerson?"

"You ought to know, you answered that question yourself not too long ago when you said, 'Harry Pregerson is so deeply involved in corruption in Ventura that he couldn't let go, even if he wanted to.'"

For some time Bob had brought up the subject of a dire need for additional legal assistance. We had become aware of further crimes involving Judge Berenson and Nordman in land development frauds and judicial corruption. Digging into this new case it became quite obvious it closely paralleled my own lawsuit and would be more than Powell could handle without help. DuPre had met an attorney while doing research at the County Law Library. The young lady, an L.A. lawyer had impressed Robert by her indications of strong personal distaste for judicial chicanery, a bit of which she'd already perceived in the Ventura Courts. After several conversations Donna M. Danks, the attractive, legally acute lady lawyer agreed to become additional counsel on my case and the new one which had just been filed.

At 10:00 a.m. Monday January 26, 1981, Bob and I were seated in Pregerson's courtroom. We awaited his momentous Spreading of the Judgement, of the Court of Appeal. Our lawyers Donna and Powell were prepared, Bob had conveyed to them his strategy, it was best to say as little as possible. Judge Pregerson was frustrated. Even with McBride's help he was unable to force or to tempt our lawyers into making any careless statements regarding their theories or strategy. Muttering that he'd set a date for a new hearing, Pregerson walked out. Leaving the room I asked Bob, "Is this what Pregerson made us come all the way from Ventura for? This is what he calls...Spreading the Judgement?"

"Remember, this hearing is extremely crucial to Pregerson, he is desperately searching for anything at all he thinks he can twist and use to Dismiss our case."

"I understand, but damn it Bob, is this what the law is all about? Just some shitty crooked judge searching for a way to get *himself* and his *gangster pals* out of trouble? Does a situation like this somehow make us the *bad guys* attacking the government or something?"

Donna approached us by the elevator, she nodded over to where McBride had Powell cornered in deep conversation. She gritted her teeth, "I tried to pry Powell away from McBride but didn't have any luck. I sure wouldn't talk to a lawyer like that who'd *threatened* to have me prosecuted and my ass thrown in jail."

I asked, "What are they talking about?"

"I didn't hear, they shut up when I got close."

I wasn't liking the way Powell huddled so cozy with McBride any better than Donna did. Walking over I tapped him on the shoulder, Powell spun around. I was certain I caught a flash of fear on his face before he recovered his composure. "Are you coming, we'd like to talk with you before heading back, and it's getting late." Ignoring me he turned back to McBride. I walked away.

On the front steps of the building Donna, DuPre and I waited for a few minutes before Terrell came out. Aggravated, I asked, "What did that asshole want?"

"Well, he was very upset about this new case I filed on Berenson and Nordman. He demanded to know if you have got anything to do with it. He thinks it's a lot more than just a coincidence that it was me who filed the new case."

"What did you tell him?"

Terrell seemed nervous, "Oh, I didn't tell him much." Leaving it at that we parted.

Discussing our on-going strategy, Robert explained, "We *must* sit tight, let Pregerson make a court order as to how we should proceed. It is impossible for him to make a straight forward, honest judicial order and still protect himself. This way we'll have something we can attack from a legal standpoint. At the present Harry is *desperate* to know how we intend to proceed. It's vitally imperative we *keep* him that way until he sets the next hearing date."

A week later we called Powell I listened on an extension, Bob was asking if Pregerson had set a new date for a hearing. "No, he hasn't set a date, but this guy R. W. Johnson keeps calling me raising hell wanting to know what I'm going to do on the case."

"You mean Pregerson's clerk, Johnson? He's been bugging you?"

"Yeh, he's called me half a dozen times."

"You don't have to tell him what we are intending to do, or what our strategy is, that's none of his business. By the way, what *did* you tell him?"

"All I said was we intended to *wait* until Pregerson made a court order directing how we were to proceed and..."

Bob choked, exploding, "Damn it Terrell, you didn't have to tell Pregerson's clerk a thing, it's none of his damn business to be calling you up asking what your client intends to do. You know you've *given* our strategy away. You told Pregerson *exactly* what he's been trying so hard to find out. He ain't about to write any opinion now." Terrell mumbled, I couldn't understand what he said. "Okay, forget it, there is nothing we can do except wait and see what he does." After that it didn't take long for Pregerson to make his move. March 9, 1981, Pregerson *again* Dismissed our Civil Rights case against Berenson and Nordman.

R. W. Johnson, Pregerson's clerk mailed Terrell a notice of the Dismissal, but not one to Donna Danks our new associate attorney. Luckily, a few days later Robert called Powell's office, his secretary informed him of the Dismissal and also that Pregerson gave us only twenty days to answer, fuming, Bob told me about the Dismissal and Powell's failing to let us know. We dared not waste time waiting for the secretary to mail us a copy. We left for Inglewood immediately, our talk kept returning to a specific subject...WHAT IN THE HELL WAS WRONG WITH TERRELL?

Bob was thinking out loud, "Several weeks ago Powell, Donna and I met in L.A.. We all agreed on a strategy that we would *hold tight* and let Pregerson make his court order as to how we should proceed in regards to the Appeal Court's decision. In the past Powell's made a few unfortunate statements at some of the court hearings. I began to think maybe he was just dumb, but then he proceeds to *reveal* our entire strategy to Pregerson. Now Pregerson realizes we were forcing him to commit himself to a court order which we'd be able to attack, so he's not about to give us another hearing, he simply dismisses our case and allows us only twenty days in which to prepare an answer. *And Terrell doesn't even call to let us know."*

This dismaying summary of Pregerson's evil conspiracy to destroy me fired salvos of icy shafts shooting through my entire body. It was unnecessary for Bob to illustrate further. I knew Harry was forcing us into making an incomprehensible answer he could dismiss again. He'd make sure we had no chance left in the Appeal Court. Halfway home I pulled off the freeway and parked at a Mexican restaurant on Ventura Boulevard. Staring at the piece of paper in his hand Bob gave it to me, it was Pregerson's 'Judgement.' March 9, 1981; "WITH NO ATTORNEYS PRESENT FOR THE PLAINTIFF--NO ATTORNEYS PRESENT FOR THE DEFENDANT--NO COURT REPORTER PRESENT--CASE DISMISSED" Alone in his chambers Pregerson had perpetrated this friggin, criminal, judicial abortion. The relentless sinister club wielded by this vicious, rotted judicial system battered hard at my resolve, it sapped my strength, then wildly, a tremendous wave of uncontrollable hatred and revenge flooded over me. Raging so bitter I didn't know how in hell I curbed the savage impulse to crash my fist into the heavy, carved oak door of the restaurant.

Inside it was dark and cool, wrought iron lamps cast their glow on luxuriant hanging ferns and thick carpets, it was peaceful. Drained mentally, I flopped on a bar stool. Bob ordered two beers, I downed the can of Bud, crushing the soft aluminum container I stared at its useless mangled carcass lying dead on the bar. I wondered, could our fragile Constitution withstand the crushing violence of such corrupt, feral judges any better then had the form of that helpless beer can? I saw our leaders, the Congressmen standing petrified, clutching each other desperately, speechless, frightened. As one, they stared down at the corpse, terribly mutilated almost beyond recognition our U.S. Constitution lay dead at their feet.

Futile cowardly attempts to hide their singly guilty responsibility hurled shocked terror blazing across their minds. With averted eyes they shrieked wild and accusingly at each other, "What on earth are we going to do now?" I watched the bartender removing the carcass. DuPre's glass was empty, I heard him say, "We don't even have ten days left to answer Pregerson's Dismissal. Lord knows I could use ten weeks for research alone."

"I'm ready to go if you are, let's head home."

The following day I met with DuPre, he moaned, "I spent the last twenty four hours just about as deep in theory and strategy as my poor brain would allow. A recap of what's happened since you first tried to get a court review twelve years ago has vividly familiarized me with the shenanigans of lawyers and judges here in California. Their strategy is one of abuse and harassment, screeming meemy, nerve racking, threatening, unmitigated harassment. They must teach it in the law schools out here. Their M.O. is to file reams of useless documents, duplications by the hundreds of worthless court records, motions for depositions and interrogatories and millions of totally inane irrelevant questions, not to mention threatening phone calls of court discipline and monetary sanctions against your attorney. Their scheme is to literally scare your attorney to death and to irrevocably muddle the case. I mean muddle it so damn bad nobody could ever begin to unravel it once the judge has said, Dismissed. These judges in this Ninth Circuit aren't attorneys, they're a bunch of plumbers." I knew how Bob felt.

He continued, "I will drop my theory on you, here it is, see what you think. At this point we have to agree the plumbers are laughing up their sleeves at us. They're positive they've adequately muddled the case and now we are going to help them by muddling it more by filing tons of paper in an Amended Complaint, trying to refute all the crap they have put into the record during the past twelve years. Okay let's go way back. At the very beginning what was it you were seeking?"

"I wanted a fair hearing, a court review of those charges the Fish had made against me."

"Now, by law you were *entitled* to that, let us stick to the law and issues. We'll make this case simple again like it should be. We'll just let the plumbers wade around in their own piles of manure:

No.1. Your Civil Service hearing was held under unconstitutional rules and procedures shifting the burden of proof onto you. In other words, they demanded that *you* had to prove by a preponderance of evidence that you *weren't guilty* of Fish's charges. This requires that you prove a negative which is inherently impossible. Lord, they could hang everybody in the country with laws and procedure such as that.

No.2. As positive evidence of the existence of their knowledge of wrong doing the Board of Supervisors *quietly changed* the Rules and Procedure on March 16, 1971.

No.3. We have the false, fraudulent document written and signed by Phillip Cohen, the Assistant County Counsel, which was designed to mislead you by conveying the false impression that *he,* Cohen, had made an administrative review, and that you were not entitled to a court review. These false and fraudulent representations were made with the full intent to deceive you and they were made to carry out the *official policy* of the County to deny you a court review.

No.4. It was not until *after* you filed your Civil Rights Complaint on June 2, 1978 and Schechter continued her efforts in concealing their *official policy* of denying you a court review that the scheme was discovered. In their numerous Federal Court filings Schechter concocted untold conflicting stories. On page seven of her Motion to Dismiss she sought to cover-up and conceal the original fraudulent scheme with false, misleading statements for the purpose to deceive the Court of Appeal. On page fifteen and sixteen of his brief to the Appeal Court, McBride 'covers-up' and conceals the fact you were purposely mislead as to your right to a Judicial review. I have drawn up an outline for an Amended Complaint that is based on what I've just explained to you. Will you read it?"

"Absolutely, let's see it." His Amended Complaint contained but seven pages of direct, explicitly to the point facts. As documentary evidence a copy of the unconstitutional Civil Service Rules used at my hearing and the injurious, deceiving document drawn and signed by Phillip Cohen, the Assistant County Counsel, were included. The signature of Harry L. Maynard, Commissioner, was still visible on the Civil Service Decision to fire me. Maynard, presently President of Emilio Lagomarsino's American Commercial Bank, is very much alive, still running around town posing as 'Old Honest Harry,' your friendly, home town banker. His cohort, Commissioner Thomas C. Boyd, Bank of A. Levy President is dead, Maynard no longer has to worry about Boyd telling the truth. The entire Amended Complaint including the documented evidence consisted of only twelve pages.

"Well, what do you think?"

"Bob, nobody could've done it better, I mean nobody. One thing bothers me, what about Berenson and Nordman and the others, and their corruption?"

"Okay, something should be done about them, but what I've done now is to make this a simple, easy to understand documented case Pregerson can't muddle even if he tries. Don't worry about the other crooks, the merits have still never been heard. We'll separate them from the Amended Complaint and file on them all over again."

"Alright, but time is running short."

On March 26, 1981, Donna approved and signed the Amended Complaint. We filed it at the Federal Court in L.A.. April 9, 1981, Schechter answered with her normal diatribe minus any appropriate law. Dorothy abandoned her earlier contentions that the Statute of Limitations pertained. Now her 'Motion to Dismiss' our Amended Complaint was predicated on Res Judicata. She was trying to create a false impression that the merits in my case had been adjudicated. First year law students would snicker at such an uninspired defense. Other than her improper legal objection of Res Judicata she wrote seven pages 'denouncing me and my outrageous impositions' upon her time and the time and energies of the Court.

Laughing, Bob commented, "Just read the next crazy long winded sentence Schechter has written."

I read it, Dorothy had, "Respectfully submitted that our Amended Complaint is an affront to the Processes of the Court, and grounds for striking our allegedly Amended Complaint with impositions, and appropriate disciplinary measures against any lawyers participating in its preparation or who had helped me in filing such a document."

"Bob, Schechter is like a rabid dog foaming at the mouth. She is saying that I don't have a right to file an Amended Complaint and further that *anybody* who files one in *my behalf or helps me* should be *put in jail* by the judge."

Making an effort to control his mirth Bob said, "Well, it is pretty crazy alright but Dorothy is becoming frantic just trying to keep her job. She doesn't really know what to do other than the fact that she is supposed to do something."

"She is definitely not a plumber, she's more like a trench digger for a plumber."

"Yep, further along amidst her diatribe and threat of disciplinary actions she complains about you...'embroiling her in your continued manipulations of the Judicial Process and your total disregard of the Courts.' She carries on with more of her acidic vituperations, on the last page Dorothy digs her grave deeper and deeper. Categorically she accuses that you have, 'demonstrated a blatant disregard for the Processes of the Federal Judicial system, therefore she respectfully submits it should not be countenanced by the Court, *you should be punished*, Dismissal Without Leave To Amend would clearly be an appropriate penalty.' She signs it, Respectfully submitted, Dorothy Schechter, Ventura County Counsel."

DuPre was shaking with unrestrainable laughter, stopping he said, "Actually, it isn't so funny, she's too dangerous to be comical." In his answer to Dorothy's Motion, Bob employed Points and Authorities totally destroying her feeble claims of Res Judicata. He noted that Dorothy's defense was improperly pleaded under the Federal Rules of Civil Procedure. Approving, Donna signed the 'Opposition to the County Counsel's Motion,' it was filed April 24, 1981.

A hearing was set for May 11, at 10:00 a.m. before Judge Harry Pregerson on the sixteenth floor of the Federal Building. When we arrived Pregerson's Courtroom No. 1600 was *locked* and was *dark inside*. Two women in the Clerk's office directly across the hall were surly, obviously lying they disclaimed any knowledge of Pregerson's whereabouts. Splitting up we started a search of the building for the missing Pregerson. After an hour of up and down the elevators and checking out courtrooms I learned the Judge was starting a trial on the second floor, the trial between the National Football League and Oakland Raiders. Noisy spectators and news media were jamming the room. I spotted the Court Clerk, R. W. Johnson.

"What about my scheduled hearing in Room 1600 at 10:00 a.m.?"
Sneering he asked, "Who are you?"
"You asshole, you know damn good and well who I am!"
"Oh yes...that has been taken off calendar."
"Who did that?"
"I don't know."
"Well why in the hell didn't you notify us? *Why* did you make us waste a whole day and run us all the way down here from Ventura?"
"I called Mr. Powell, he said he wasn't your lawyer anymore, and I couldn't contact Donna Danks."
"Horseshit, her *address and phone number* are on the *front* of the Motion she filed three weeks ago, you want to cause us all the grief you can. I see you made sure McBride and Schechter didn't have to make a useless trip down here." In the hallway I found Bob, a few minutes later Donna arrived, I told her what Johnson had said. She was surprised.
"If Schechter's taken the case off Calendar we can file a Default. Where's the clerk?"
I pointed, "That's him, the finky little queer over there wiping his glasses."
Donna walked over and asked, "Why has our hearing been taken off Calendar?"
"Oh, I didn't say it was taken off Calendar, I said Judge Pregerson had continued it."
"You're a damn liar, you told me it had been taken off Calendar!"
Donna intervened asking, "What's the new date?"
He sneered, "I don't know, maybe I can let you know next week."
"Here's my phone number and address." The finky clerk took the business card she proffered.
Out in the hall I asked Bob and Donna, "What's Pregerson trying to pull?"
A disgusted DuPre said, "It's more harassment."
"How long can he hold the case like this and refuse us a hearing?"
Bob wagged his head, "I just don't know, I have never run across any judges like the ones here in California."
"It is really a terribly sad thing when Federal Judges are so sick and caught up in corruption that they are forced to resort to such scurvy, miserable tricks trying to save themselves. It just seems like they pull our entire system of government right down their rat hole along with them!"
"Pregerson can't bury the case forever, eventually he will have to

do something."

"DuPre, I look for that gangster to Dismiss it just like he's always done before...no legal reason given, no one present...*NO ONE*...just the Honorable Federal Judge, Harry Pregerson!"

CHAPTER 29

The new case, No. 81-0148 CBM, it was filed in January 1981, it charged Berenson and Nordman with fraud and land development corruption. This was the case McBride had quizzed Terrell about. McBride had been totally unnerved over the possibility that maybe I was involved with its being filed. A set of very strange, coinciding circumstances surrounded the discovery of the facts and the ultimate filing of this new case. During the period of time DuPre was on the east coast I received an unexpected phone call.

"Hey Gahrie, is this you?" The voice could not belong to anybody except Eddie Cannizzaro. I hadn't talked with him in twenty years!

"Hey, Edwardo, you still alive?" Cannizzaro was old time Siciliano Mafia, I mean the *real* Mafia. It went back a long time ago. When I was a policeman in L.A. Eddie was Mafia enforcer for Vegas and L.A. under Jack Dragna. Eddie's moniker was the *Money Collector.* Lots of knee caps were busted in those days with a lead pipe. If this preliminary inoculation failed to work with a recalcitrant debtor, the treatment got a lot worse. When the subject of his occupation was broached by cops he'd laugh, "Naw, I'm just a bookkeeper, hee, hee." But in those days it was just part of the game, everyone knew, if you couldn't pay you shouldn't play.

"Yeah Cannizzaro, this is me...how in hell did you get my unlisted number?"

"Ah, I still got some friends around. I heard that you were up in

Ventura. I have lived here in Agoura, the eastern part of the county about twelve years."

"What are you doing now Eddie?"

"I'm retired but I monkey around in real estate a little. I thought since you've been in Ventura quite a while you might be able to help me. I've run into a bunch of crooked lawyers from up there, they're trying to screw me around."

"Hell you've seen crooked lawyers before, what's new about that?"

"Yeh, but these shysters are different...they've got *everything* sewed up."

"I could meet you around ten tomorrow morning."

"Good, come to Agoura, get off the freeway at Kanan Road, I'll be waiting at Denny's Restaurant."

I saw him in a booth. "Still keeping your back to the wall I see." Eddie smiled and shook hands.

"Sure, do you know a better way to stay alive?"

"Alright, but have you checked out the kitchen in this joint?" We laughed, it was a joke we easily recalled. Years ago I was sitting with Eddie and Joey Bello in a restaurant in San Fernando Valley when suddenly Bello jumped up screaming, "Jesus, they've got a telescope rifle." I looked quick in the direction Bello was staring. Through the opening into the kitchen, sure enough, two guys back there had what looked like a telescopic camera aimed right us. Jumping from our booth we ran through the kitchen, but we were too late, outside the car with two men sped from the parking lot.

Several days later the head of our Intelligence Division called me to his office, he appeared stern, "I just returned from a meeting with the FBI and the LAPD Intelligence Units, they ran a moving picture of Cannizzaro and Joey Bello eating in a cafe out in the Valley. The FBI is going all out trying to identify the third man in the picture." Grinning the Captain asked, "Do you know who he was?"

"So it was the FBI taking those pictures, man it scared hell out of Eddie and Joey, they thought it was a hit, someone with a gun trying to rub them out."

"When I told the FBI that the person they were trying to identify was you, they couldn't believe Cannizzaro or Bello would talk with an Intelligence Officer. They want you to 'duke' them in real bad."

"No way Captain, I couldn't do that. Those people don't trust any authorities, they've learned from bitter experience. It takes years of knowing them before they'll sit down and have coffee with you."

"I hate to advise the FBI we can't help them."

"I'm sorry Captain, but I just can't introduce them to other agents. If something went wrong they'd hold me responsible forever. That's the way they are." The Captain was disappointed but he knew it was a rule and I wouldn't budge.

In an east coast accent Eddie said, "Gahrie, I had a deal on some acreage over by Moorpark, the old Howard Estate. It was handled by a lawyer, William Hair and a real estate guy named John Conlon. They screwed the deal up for me and now they are holding the land and going to make the money for themselves."

"That's par for the course, I know 'em, John Conlon was a County Supervisor and Hair is a law partner of Ben Nordman."

"Nordman! This Hair and Nordman are partners?"

"Didn't you know that?"

"No, and that's strange because it's Nordman I wanted to ask you about." He patted the stack of real estate maps and brochures piled next to him. "Let me explain, my mother and dad bought the house here twelve years ago. I live with them, in Oak Dale Park, a tract of two hundred homes built on a hundred fifty acres by Metropolitan Development Company. Metro actually owns almost three thousand acres. The county gave 'em a permit for these houses but that was all because of an environmental impact on the area. Chopping these hills up will create so many engineering problems with flood control, mud slides, inadequate sewers and water facilities, that Building and Safety refused to zone any more of the land for development."

"It looks to me like they're building a million homes around here."

"Sure they are, and the damned mud pours down the streets, they can't even get sewer hook-ups or anything else, the black top on my street is all torn up. The residents here have banded together and complained to the Building Department but they laugh at us."

"You just said that Building and Safety would not allow Metro to cut up the hills and build more houses."

"That's right, but all of a sudden here comes Judge Berenson and Nordman and ZIP, Metro is allowed to do whatever they want. Fact is they have things sewed up to the point that inspectors don't even come out to check on what they're doing. Back when the county told them they couldn't build anymore, Rudy Schaefer, Pres. of Metro, hired a slew of Wilshire Blvd. lawyers and commenced suing Ventura County. It went on for several years and Metro was getting nowhere, then Rudy contacted Supervisor Conlon to get him to do something, so he set up a *meet* between Schaefer and William Hair. Suddenly Nordman's law firm *jumped in* and before anybody knew what the hell was going on Judge Berenson *over-ruled* the Building Dept. and Metro was back in business. Their stock *jumped* from only fifty five cents a share to *over* fourteen dollars as soon as Berenson made his ruling to let Metro build more houses."

Eddie was slapping real estate maps and brochures on the table. He pointed out obvious construction code violations, wrong roofing materials used in fire hazard areas, driveway paving shorted on the specified thickness, etc. "Look at this paper, Schaefer paid Nordman one hundred thousand dollars to *set-up this deal* for the zone change and approval of the 'Environmental Impact Reports.'"

"I see it Eddie, it's just more of Nordman and Berenson's normal crooked operations. I'll bet you the hundred grand is only the down payment on what Rudy agreed to pay them. Since the shares value took such a fantastic jump Berenson and Nordman are not going to settle for a measly hundred big ones."

"Yeah, I believe that."

Leaving Denny's we paused at Cannizzaro's car. I said, "Give me that paper, the one about the hundred grand payment to Nordman."

"I can't, these documents belong to a guy back east, he'll be out here in a few days and I have to give it all back to him...and don't forget, you promised to look at the Metro case for me."

"No, I won't forget." It was still early afternoon, having given my word, I went by the courthouse to get it over with. A clerk brought the Metro file, case No. 55879, filed July 16, 1973. It was almost a foot thick. Like Eddie said, Metro had been in a losing battle with the county for years. I got a *real* surprise...the *same* people involved in my case kept coming up. Judge Heaton was handling the Metro case, he'd ordered Victor Husbands of Building and Safety to give a deposition explaining the county's unyielding stance against Metro's future building plans.

Suddenly I was spurred by a penetrating impact of something I'd just read, with no warning Judge Berenson had walked into Heaton's court and *relieved* him of the Metro case. Shortly after this episode Husbands' scheduled deposition was *canceled*, and his Building and Safety Department's tough stand against Metro was *swiftly reversed*. Conlon, Presiding Supervisor, sponsored and passed a *new* County Ordinance allowing Metro to develop the three thousand acres to all intents and purposes *free* from any restrictions. Berenson approved a stipulation that the County would *no longer interfere* with Metro's activities, simultaneously with this action by Berenson Metro's stock took an *astronomical* leap.

Something about this whole business grabbed me real bad but I couldn't put a finger on it. Judge Heaton had always been a part of the organization, at least, he obeyed orders from Berenson without question. It was Husbands part in the plot that in some way bothered me. Going back over it, squeezing my memory, things commenced to return. It was at the meeting in Supervisor Ken Mc Donald's office. I was recalling the obvious fear Husbands had exhibited when Bob had quizzed him about his connections with Berenson. Then came Husbands weird statement that he didn't *know* Judge Berenson, and furthermore that he *didn't even know* what Judge Berenson looked like. And then the hushed silence in the room, everybody there had picked up on his lie. That must be it! Husbands was a weak sister in the organization. Maybe his conscience bothered him, but more than likely it was his acute dread that *one day* they'd all get caught and have to answer for their corruption. This could be why they'd sent Bradbury, a Dep. D.A., to protect Husbands. But this enlightenment only created another mystery. How *deep* was Bradbury involved in all this crap, why was he acting as a legal protector for Husbands? Fearing our accusations of corruption, was his presence there to nip any of their problems in the bud?

It could explain Bradbury's frightened concerns as to whether we were bugging the meeting. If they'd been simply nervous at Powell's presence all they needed was a deputy county counsel to be there. I knew one thing for sure, Bradbury had never put one foot forward in an effort to investigate or prosecute the corruption. He'd brought back Mal King as Chief Investigator for the D.A.'s office. King was well aware of the person responsible for the corruption. He should be, he'd worked for Judge Berenson for years as 'Chief Dispenser' for all the stolen Criminal Justice money gorging the slavering maw of the Public Facilities Corporation. That night I called Cannizzaro telling him what I had discovered.

"Damn it Gahrie, crooks on the street are one thing but crooks in black robes are something else, what can we do about gangsters like Judge Berenson?"

"Damned if I know, but sure as hell something should be done. DuPre just got back from the east, I'll see what he thinks about it."

"Well, let me know soon."

A week later we sat in Eddie's favorite booth at Denny's. DuPre was telling him what he'd learned about the Metro case. "The file's so thick I spent two entire days studying it. Nordman and Berenson handled it very cleverly, but the facts still remain. First, the Metro attorneys were beating a dead horse. They had charged the county with inverse condemnation of their property and estoppel and they also asked for damages from the County. But, the county's position was backed up by a Supreme Court decision. It upheld their power to zone property for its best use... That case was, <u>Village of Belle Terri v. Borass,</u> in New York State. Metropolitan's lawsuit should have been Dismissed immediately instead of dragging it on through court until the file became a foot thick. The hired attorneys for the county filed a Motion to Dismiss, stating there was, NO CAUSE OF ACTION. September 21, 1973 Nordman joined the case in behalf of Metro and asked for a continuance, shortly after this Berenson made two rulings in direct defiance of the Supreme Court decision. Feb. 13, 1974 in his thirteen page opinion the judge ruled against Ventura County's 'Motion to Dismiss' Metro's suit. The county's lawyers filed a Demurrer claiming that Metro had *No Cause of Action* and asked Berenson to reconsider the Supreme Court Decision of the 'Village of Belle Terri v. Borass.' On May 14, 1974 in his five page opinion Berenson stated he had taken into consideration the Village of Belle Terri v. Borass case, yet in the face of this decision he proceeded to rule against the county's Demurrer. This *unconscionable* judicial act *stripped* Ventura of its defense, forcing them into making a totally illegal agreement with Metropolitan, Berenson approved his corrupt stipulation on Dec. 30, 1974.

Cannizzaro was furious, "I see how Berenson and Nordman pulled it off but shouldn't the county have appealed instead of making an agreement?"

"Certainly they should've appealed, but that was up to the Board of Supervisors."

"I get it, that's where Conlon, Chairman of the Board, and Hair come in. Conlon wipes out any *Right to Appeal* then he passes a *new* ordinance for Metro's benefit, then they are right back in business again. It's clear why Judge Berenson wasn't afraid to rule against the Supreme Court's decision, he *knew* the County Counsel would *never* Appeal. Berenson and Nordman are old conspirators, buddies, living next door to each other for over thirty years. The entire scam was probably plotted out at their daily breakfast table. I know how these people work their deals, I wasn't born yesterday."

DuPre said, "You've got it right so far Eddie. To further muddle the court record and camouflage their guilty involvement these two employed *another* subterfuge. They brought in the San Francisco law firm of Goldstein, Barceloux and Goldstein. Using a pretext I called

Goldstein. I said I was a lawyer from the east coast dealing in land developments and zoning. I told him about running across the Metro case in Ventura and sure would like to know how in hell they had *by-passed* the Supreme Court Decision in the Village of Belle Terri v. Borass case. Goldstein *laughed*, 'Oh yes, that Metropolitan case, indeed that was a *bit unusual*, more like about one percent law and ninety nine percent politics.' It appears that muddling the record is an integral part of these peoples M.O., *never* allow any court record to remain clear or concise."

Listening to Bob and Eddie I reached a two fold comprehension, the Metro case had cost the taxpayers a quarter of a million dollars just paying for private lawyers. But, compared to the millions Judge Berenson's criminal misuse of the courts was costing along with its devastating effects of resulting log jams of criminal and civil cases, that was only a drop in the bucket. Shortly after Berenson's Metro decision the City of Thousand Oaks abutting Agoura, was sued by a land developer who used the same charges Metro had filed against Ventura. Thousand Oaks City hired lawyer George Kinkle who was the *same* lawyer who'd represented Ventura against Metro. Kinkle *again* used the Village of Belle Terri v. Borass case, but this time Berenson *immediately* Dismissed the developers suit against the city. The unlucky developer simply had *not* hired 'the right' attorneys to represent him. If he'd known the ropes in the county he would have gone directly to Nordman in the first place.

Eddie agreed that we'd meet with Terrell as soon as I could make arrangements, which we did a few days later at Cable's Restaurant in Woodland Hills. Bob and Eddie showed Powell real estate records and copies of court documents of Metro's case, explaining in detail the serious situation at Oak Park. Powell agreed to represent Eddie and asked Bob to consult with him in a Civil Rights Action. In mid January, 1981, Powell filed the Complaint.

Judge Berenson, Nordman, Metro and the County were charged with Conspiracy to Violate Title 42, United States Code 1983. Case No. 81-0148 was assigned to Dist. Court Judge Consuelo B. Marshall. They had twenty days in which to file their answer.

I picked up the phone, it was Bob, I knew it was urgent. "Eddie just called me and I mean he was screaming, madder than hell."

"What in the world happened now?"

"Powell has loused up the whole works something terrible, against Eddie's *explicit* instructions, he gave Metro a thirty day extension, supposedly to complete and file an answer to the Complaint. Instead they used the *extra time* to serve a subpoena for deposition on him. They've listed a million questions, they're demanding that he bring all his files. Everything that they have asked him for is available to them at the courthouse records, this is nothing but harassment. The subpoena was served just three days before the scheduled deposition. There's no way he can get copies of all those documents and prepare for a deposition over the weekend. Eddie's raving mad, Powell never mentioned a single word to him about this."

"Bob what in the devil is the matter with Terrell. It sounds almost like he's trying to set Eddie up. Do you suppose they've bought him off?"

"All I know right now is that something is *damn bad*, we'd better get to Inglewood and find out what it is real quick." Powell wasn't in his office. Bob and Flo, the secretary, began their usual kidding and joking. Using innocuous but searching questions in his banter, Bob soon learned that Powell had been under a *siege* of phone calls from Nordman and Metro attorneys. It was a constant *barrage of threats* and reminders of dire consequences for his impudence in daring to attack such prominent society people in the judicial and legal system. Flo was a tiny, very industrious, efficient secretary. Handing Eddie's file to DuPre it appeared she barely reached his elbow despite high heels. Wiping my smog ruined eyes I dozed on the office couch while DuPre examined the file. I heard him say, "Florence, will you copy this letter please?" Returning the file to her, Bob said, "Thank you," then abruptly to me he said, "I'm ready to go."

As I drove, Bob concentrated on the two page letter. "Well, here we have the *answer* to Powell's strange conduct, they didn't pay him off as we suspected...they simply frightened him to death. The fears of sanctions and penalties were bad enough but threats of contempt and *disbarment* if he didn't back off turned him to jelly."

"Well at least he didn't sell Eddie out for money. When you think about it those threats to snatch their license is mighty frightening, what in hell would lawyers do, get a job in a gas station?"

"Yeh it's tough, but you also have to *consider* what happens to a client. This letter was mailed by Ben Nordman's partner, Robert L. Compton shortly after Eddie's Civil Rights suit was filed. Compton signed it, but more likely it was contrived by Nordman and Judge Berenson themselves." Bob snorted, "Here's what Compton says, 'I am writing in behalf of my law partner Mr. Nordman, *demanding* that you forthwith dismiss your action and address a letter to Ben E. Nordman retracting statements you have made concerning him and

others in the alleged conspiracy. Court records available to you or anyone else show conclusively:
1. Judge Berenson was assigned to the case by Presiding Judge Richard C. Heaton.
2. Berenson took no part in a settlement other than to approve a settlement proposal worked out by the attorneys for the parties.'"
Bob interjected, "But we know these are lies, we have *copies* of the *two rulings* made by Berenson *wiping out* the county's legal defense."
"Sure we have copies, when they sent the letter they didn't *know* we had *discovered* how Judge Berenson worked the fraud."
"On page two, Robert E. Compton threatens, 'California case law provides Nordman with a remedy.' He states, 'Both Powell and his client are liable for damages for malicious prosecution under certain conditions, and we intend to pursue this remedy upon conclusion of this case. By filing this spurious action you have caused irreparable harm to the reputation of Nordman and others. We suggest that you minimize your exposure to damages for 'malicious prosecution' by *immediately* dismissing the Complaint as to all persons against whom a conspiracy is alleged and providing Ben Nordman a written letter of retraction.' Signed by Compton."
"Bob do you think that letter frightened Powell so badly that he'd throw Cannizzaro to the wolves?"
"Sure it did, that and *those* phone calls. Who knows how vicious they were with their threats. Look at this letterhead on Compton's letter. Nordman has an office with twenty attorneys, the largest law firm in the county, plus his powerful partner Berenson, the Presiding Judge of Ventura's Superior Court. Powell's also become alarmingly aware of their powerful *ties* within the Federal System in L.A.. Hell yes, you *better believe* Terrell is scared. This is something they sure as shit didn't teach him about in law school. It means one thing for sure, from this moment on Cannizzaro doesn't dare allow Terrell to represent him."
The urgency struck me, whipping off the freeway I hit the first phone I saw, calling Agoura I told Cannizzaro to meet us at Denny's in twenty five minutes. Eddie was waiting, briefing him we listened to his tirade of curses. "For Christ Sake, these God damn shysters are worse than the muggers in dark alleys, they'd cave your skull in and suck your last drop of blood for less than fifty cents. Okay, so I gotta have a lawyer, what about this lady attorney that you've added to Gary's case? Let's phone her, see what she says."
Returning from his call Bob said, "Okay Eddie, Donna's agreed

to represent you. We've got an appointment to meet her tomorrow morning, you and Donna will sign a substitution of lawyer. Gary and I have some other business with Terrell, we'll have him sign it."

"Alright, alright, God damn it, but how long do you think this poor little broad all by herself is going to hold up against these gangsters? They are gonna' eat her tender little body alive."

It was noon when DuPre and I arrived at Powell's office, he was gone but Florence expected him soon. "Flo, would you please bring me Gary's file?" I continued to be slightly amazed at the ease with which Bob so mysteriously established instant rapport with normally aloof and uncommunicative legal secretaries. Trying to pinpoint this minor phenomenon of personal magnetism it seemed to relate to the female instinct, an intuitional acceptance of his mien and maybe his very evident legal competency.

Bob's voice barely audible drew my attention. My file was open on the counter. Bob was staring into it ashen faced with disbelief, aghast at what was there.

"What in the world is the matter Bob?"

"Come and look at this," he wheezed. There in the middle of my file was a letter. It was addressed to Powell, in regards to me. Large print at the top identified the official communication as being from the Office of the Clerk, United States Supreme Court. It read:

Dear Mr. Terrell Powell;

In accord with our phone conversation, I am returning the postal money order of two hundred dollars since you have advised that the *intention* of filing a Petition for Certiorari has been *abandoned.*

The letter was signed, Alexander L. Stevas, Clerk of the Supreme Court of the United States and also by Assistant Clerk, Edward C. Schade. The un-cashed money order I had made out to the Clerk of the Supreme Court was clipped to the letter.

I must have turned paler then Bob. "Good Lord almighty, Powell has been sabotaging us for months. Damn it Bob, he's had this letter since right after we filed the Certiorari. They must have terrorized Terrell, completely demoralizing him to cause him to do a thing like this, *now* I understand what you meant when you said he was scared. Pregerson undoubtably went *berserk* on learning that we asked the Supreme Court to *supervise* the 'lawlessness and corruption' in the Ninth Circuit under *his* Local Rules."

Engrossed with the letter Bob gave no indication he'd heard me. I analyzed the message from the Supreme Court, the devious trail of Judge Pregerson's evil intrigue to destroy our Certiorari was not too difficult to trace. Pregerson ordered his clerk Richard W. Johnson to immediately contact Richard C. Deane, the Appeal Court Clerk in Frisco, and order him to hold up our records. I recalled the letter Deane sent soon after we filed the Certiorari, saying he would *not* send our records to D.C. until the Supreme Court asked for them. Hell, Deane knew the Supreme Court was *never* going to ask for our records to review them, because he *knew* that Johnson was going to make sure the Court never received our Certiorari.

Under Pregerson's orders Johnson burned up the phone wires to Alexander L. Stevas in D.C.. Stevas and Schade then viley forced my lawyer into treacherously abandoning and destroying my Certiorari. It attested to the degree of fear these evil people had inflicted upon Terrell. Damn, those federal clerks are nothing more than two-bit pimps in charge of dirty tricks for the judges. Violent phone calls, sabotaging cases with erroneous, misleading information, they don't even stop at destroying documents and evidence. I remembered the day that Bob and I drove to L.A. to file some documents, the clerk refused to file the papers because Bob had written them according to the U.S. Federal Rules. She informed Robert that the documents had to be written according to 'Local California Rules,' because *they* superceded the Federal Rules. Hardly believing this, Bob demanded someone in authority. Judge Consuelo Marshall's law clerk, Laura Cavin, also Corey Mc Meeking, the Supervising Clerk of the Court Clerks advised Bob that:

"The Local California Rules *supercede* the Federal Rules of the Supreme Court and Congress."

Two lawyers, Lane Vaughn and James Ortega from Dallas, Texas were waiting to file their documents, they had witnessed the entire conversation. DuPre said, "Gentlemen, you both heard those clerks, Texas is in the U.S. Fifth Circuit, has it ever been your knowledge that Local Rules set up by District Court Judges suspercedes Federal Rules?"

Incredulous, they both responded, "We heard what the clerks said alright, but can hardly believe they mean it!" The Texas lawyers gave Bob their phone numbers for future contact. Judge Marshall's clerk, Laura Cavin, was adamant, she had *orders,* she refused to file our documents. It was necessary we return to Ventura that evening and revise the documents to conform to Local Rules and repeat the trip back to Los Angeles the next day, a round trip of some one hundred and seventy fine miles each day.

I also recalled the scheduled hearing Pregerson ordered, his clerk

Johnson had lied, saying he'd tried to phone and tell us the hearing had been continued. A few days after having been tricked into the expensive round trip to L.A., Pregerson's pimp Johnson, called my attorney Donna Danks threatening to put me in jail if I ever talked nasty to him again. Donna became very frightened on my behalf, but DuPre assured her Johnson was lying again, he possessed no powers of arrest. A small amount of satisfaction was gleaned from the dirty tricks pulled by the clerks, it told us that Pregerson did *not* have a *pipeline* to any of the Justice's on the Supreme Court that he could call on in an emergency like he was now confronted with.

However, I knew they were *working* feverishly on this necessary adjunct to their complete power. Insidiously over many years they had maneuvered William P. Clark, an old partner and conspirator of Berenson and Nordman into the enormously powerful, and strategic position of Assistant Secretary of State.

Within the stringent political society of Wash., D.C., the general convictions were that Clark had been brought there by Reagan with intentions it would be a short jump from Assistant Secretary to the Supreme Court. Nothing could be more scary than the idea of Clark being on the Supreme Court. All this warped political intrigue was driving me nuts. Non-stop repetitious discourse reverberated in my aching head, never ceasing to berate me for becoming so damnably involved. What in hell was I ever going to accomplish for myself or anyone else by continuing this friggin' one sided fight...? My head spun like pins in a bowling alley.

One evening in hope of some kind of trusted, munificent advice and possible alleviation from the mounting problems, I had driven to San Fernando Valley. Tranquil winding streets in Toluca Lake with stately huge trees guarding the community like invincible, stalwart sentries were solemnly assuring. The heavy wrought iron gates stood open. A warm glow of amber light floating from the lanterns on the massive gate posts welcomed me as they'd done many years before.

It was a long time ago, away back in forty-six when I'd driven the owner of this beautiful, opulent estate to his door, depositing him for safe keeping with his wife, the other choice was to take him to Old Lincoln Heights Jail on North Ave. 19 and book him for drunk. Tod had left a social gathering about twelve a.m. and was flopping around the downtown L.A. streets trying to find his parked car.

After that incident I ran into Tod several times and we became good friends. Since his wife had died Tod lived here alone. He led the way through dimly lit rooms, I knew we were going to the den, his favorite haunt. The tall, spare man wrapped in his worn smoking jacket waved me to a chair. I'd never liked this room, the heads of all sorts of big game stared forlornly at me from dark paneled walls. Tod leaned back in his heavy, leather upholstered chair. The rug on which he fondly planted his feet had once been a fine specimen of the Royal King of Beasts, and the stand for the ashtray to the right of his chair was the foot of an elephant. Many times in the past I'd chided him about the dauntless, mighty hunters who with powerful rifles and scopes killed a defenseless prey from afar. Tod's answer was always an indulgent chuckle at my inexperience to the eminent pleasures of the African Safari. Now in his eighties, Tod hadn't been born into wealth. Oddly enough he'd made his basic fortune during the Great Depression, after the beginning of WW 11 his subsequent fortunes came easy.

In '29, the year of the stock market crash most people were going broke but Tod prospered in the car sales industry. He'd discovered an extraordinary secret to all sucess in business. He had mastered the delicate art of behind the scenes political string pulling. You did not fool around selling one car at a time, you sold loads of them to the county and city governments. The big secret was installing your own men in key political offices. For more than forty years Tod and his very select, elegant group of confederates had secretly controlled politics for their *own* personal and financial interests within Southern California. But only within the last twenty years had they developed connections clear to Washington, D.C.. It had taken them millions of dollars but they understood and accepted the plain fact that, it takes money to make money. I sipped from the small glass of fine Cognac Tod poured.

Always he was miles ahead when the subject was of intrigue and strategies. "Tod, I am just a little guy, an average American. For a while I foolishly believed I might get a fair break in Federal Court, but every time I take a step these bastards are right in front of me. How am I to ever get an honest hearing from the Supreme Court? I mean one free from the influence of these gangsters like Nordman, and Judges Berenson and Pregerson. Methodically forming a steeple with his long fingers Tod peered thoughtfully at them. Tasting my Cognac, I waited.

In a low drone he began, "Gary, the *poor* people of this country, and you *average* people, if you had a million years you would *never* comprehend what you are up against with politics. I am over eighty years old, after many decades of constant intrigue, throat cuttings and nerve racking ordeals I finally pulled out. My old associates in a once proud, powerful secret society are all over the hill, but they continue stubbornly to hang in there firmly believing in the status of their old powers. Sure, they have tons of money and maintain their powerful connections in the White House. However, they've become nothing more than *unwitting patsies* along with Ron Reagan. This *new* power has sprung up, a sinister, malignant thing. At my age I'm not fool hardy, I have no desire to aggravate them. Dick Nixon, the most powerful man in the world was a *victim* of their terrifying destructive force. Using only *one* judge from the U.S. District Court, out of the several hundred, this sinister organization *completely* destroyed the President of the United States and his entire staff."

"I knew there was something powerfully evil behind Watergate."

"But, never at *any time* did we ever consider the annihilation of America for any consideration. Our plans and designs for the future diametrically opposed this new force. Their evil schemes for power knows no boundaries, it's inclusive of the universe. This small hard core group sprang into being right here in Southern California much the same way as my group evolved under extreme economic, social strife during the Depression. A group of young Post war era people came together, already united in a close religious order, and racial bonds they evolved into this tight group of dedicated, sinister people. Studying the law in college they seized judgeships forming their basis of power, they now own the judicial branch of our government. Since its inception in the days of Thomas Jefferson it has been potentially the most powerful branch of the three. Thrusting their people into key positions of the Judicial System they are close to their goal of total control within the government."

Absorbing the significance of Tod's expoundings I realized he'd hit upon the subject of *all* my problems, the Federal Judicial System. Starting to ask a question I thought better of it.

Tod continued, "Sometime back I recognized their overwhelming power. This evil menace, I call it, The Black Robe Syndicate." Tod's tale was dismaying, he had revealed and verified a secret force, its existence I had fearfully suspected but had prayed did not exist...a depraved, treasonous *judicial cabal* designed to strip Americans of their Constitutional Rights to Due Process of Law.

"I tried my best to convince my old associates that the Black Robe Syndicate could destroy them at will, they scoffed at me. No Gary, my old associates in our once proud, untouchable secret society will learn the hard way. I'll tell you something, William P. Clark was *not* taken to D.C. to be put on the Supreme Court, he was sent because the Black Robe Syndicate has designated him as the *next* President of the United States. They'll then control the Judicial and Executive Branch. Congress they consider as an ineffectual, bungling rabble of petty politicians, alcoholics and queers who are incapable in any way of coping with the Black Robes and their mastery of the Judicial and Executive Branches. In any event they have already *placed* their key personal in the Senate and the House of Representatives."

Tod's voice faded, the drone became little more than a whisper. I'd failed to acknowledge the passage of a lot of years. Nearly thirty five to be exact, Tod was over eighty and I sure as hell wasn't twenty five anymore. His hands wavered slowly back and forth, the whispers were barely understandable. I leaned forward, "Gary, listen to me, The Black Robe Syndicate has set their strategy to take us over but, don't ever forget...Congress, our legislative branch of government as elected by the poor and the average people like you, and the smart assholes like me is still our *last* chance to hold on to this country's *fading* freedom."

These retrospections brought forth by uncovering the astonishing letter sent by the Supreme Court Clerks broke up as I was returned to the present by Powell's entering the door. He scarcely concealed his relief as he signed the substitution making Donna the attorney of record for Eddie. With piercing directness Bob quietly mentioned to Powell that we had inadvertently discovered the letter revealing his conspiratorial phone communications with the Clerks of the Supreme Court and the sabatoge of our Certiorari, no intelligible explanation was forthcoming from the lawyer. On our way out Bob spoke quietly to Florence, she went to a dark corner in a closet where Terrell had hidden the Certiorari's, the ones we thought had been sent to the Supreme Court hoping for a review and investigation. She handed the box to Bob.

On our return to Ventura Bob unleashed a bitter tirade of anger and disgust at Terrell's duplicity. It surprised me, I had seen DuPre upset several times but nothing like this, his anger wouldn't subside. The next day we returned to Inglewood, again Terrell silently signed a substitution of attorney, this time for me. Total responsibility for my case and Eddie's now lay heavy on tiny Donna's frail shoulders. I contemplated the Mafia man's quip, "How long do you think that poor little broad Donna is going to hold up against those gangsters?" The answer to that question wasn't long in coming.

CHAPTER 30

Right from the very beginning Cannizzaro's suit was trouble...big trouble. The evil wrath of Berenson and Nordman knew no bounds. Violently inflamed at the abhorrent temerity of such lowly citizens actually utilizing a Federal Court to defy their supreme powers they called in William Hair, their chief hatchet man, and issued a bitter, summary directive. "Destroy this dastardly lawsuit and every one of those people who oppose our authority, destroy them...NOW."

Judge Pregerson's Local Rules, specifically and cleverly contrived to circumvent the Federal Rules, were quickly brought into force by Hair and a woman attorney Tamar Stein, from the Pacht-Ross law firm who represented Metropolitan Development Company. Under the binding effect of their Local Rules, all sanity and resemblance of required Federal Court Procedure and Due Process of Law swiftly fled the scene. Their ensuing display of idiocy, corruption and chaos grew to such proportions that it became an incredibly farcical reality taking place within the jurisdiction of a U.S. Federal Court.

Eddie's lawsuit was assigned to District Court Judge Consuelo B. Marshall, she denied Berenson and Metro's Motion to Dismiss the case. Hair and Stein then invoked Local Rule 3.15, which *forces* the judge to *appoint* a magistrate to hear Discovery Motions. A million sub-rulings come under it. Rule 3.15.1 states Discovery Motions can *not* be filed until you first have meetings between defendants and plaintiffs counsel to work out all matters of Discovery. Local Rules

THERE'S A FISH IN THE COURTHOUSE 301

remove the proceedings from the District Court Judge. Magistrates are political flunkys appointed by the District Court judges, and are restricted in their duties and powers by Congress. However, under Pregerson's Local Rules the judges must pass sensitive lawsuits to a Magistrate. It is their specific job to completely muddle a case and to terrify lawyers and their clients so bad that by the time the judge gets the case back they are begging the court to quickly dismiss the case, or settle it under any conditions.

Before his lawsuit was filed Eddie had undergone major surgery for circulatory problems. Having suffered a severe setback he was given medication restricting him to bed, it precluded his appearance at the Deposition. Hair and Stein were so furious they threatened Donna with judicial discipline and outrageous sanctions if she didn't produce Eddie for Depositions at a new date.

Accompanied by doctors affidavits Donna filed a 'Motion For A Protective Order' for Eddie, but the Court Clerk refused the Motion saying that the exhibit numbers were at the top of the page instead of the bottom. Fixing it she *again* tried to file the Motion. The Clerk refused on another trumped up reason, Donna changed it, the Clerk *again* refused to file the Motion because *now* only sixteen days were left before the hearing date and Local Rules *required* twenty days. Due to their criminal, conspiratorial stone-walling Eddie's Motion For A Protective Order was *never* heard by the Court.

In accordance with Local Rule 3.15.1 Donna had been ordered to appear at two meetings of Counsel. Facing from five to six opposing lawyers Donna discovered that these counsel meetings more closely resembled a third degree with inquisitional tactic's. At one meeting of Counsels, a Local Rule 3.15.4 requirement, Paul Hamilton, with the firm of Pacht-Ross, representing Metro, dominated the meeting for over a solid hour continually threatening Donna. "You are liable for malicious prosecution in this state, you are jointly and severally liable with your client and all other persons involved in the suit." He then proceeded to quote Pregerson's Local Rules, "At a Local Rule 9 meeting you refused to sign Local Rule 3 stipulations. You are in willful violation of these Local Rules. An attorney may be subjected to appropriate disciplinary action. My client is outraged, he intends to prosecute each and every person who caused this lawsuit to be filed. You have no right as a lawyer to make charges without facts." Donna laid copies of Judge Berenson's rulings on the table. It was the Ruling that *destroyed* Ventura County's legal defense against the Metro lawsuit. The lawyers shoved the documents back at her, none of them dared acknowledge the existence of such clear cut evidence. Senselessly Hamilton persisted, "You have no facts...as a lawyer you can be prosecuted if you continue to pursue this lawsuit."

Donna shook them up, "There is also a document revealing that Mr. Nordman received $100,000.00 from Metropolitan. Besides Mr. Cannizzaro, two other witnesses have seen it."

Hamilton shot back, "There's not a witness in the world *anywhere* who can *testify* Ben Nordman got a hundred thousand dollars from Metropolitan Development Company, not a witness!" Twelve times he repetitiously continued his threats of penalties and prosecutions against Donna in rantings lasting over an hour. Finally he wound up his threats, "We *demand* that the case be Dismissed forthwith. If it's Dismissed forthwith our client will consider, but not yet commit to relieving all persons, including the Plaintiff Cannizzaro from liability. So, that is *our* settlement proposal, I will say nothing more, I have held the floor for quite a long time."

Donna's law experience was mostly in accident and compensation cases. Receiving threatening phone calls, having false affidavits filed against her and enduring third degrees by attorneys under guise of a legal procedure was a totally new and distressing experience that she'd never even dreamed existed. She'd always considered her oath taken upon becoming a lawyer to be a solemn, binding confirmation of her acceptance of the legal profession's ethics code, loyalty and obligation to a client being foremost in Donna's mind. Having been so suddenly subjugated by the 'Local Rules' and degenerate actions of the vicious opposing lawyers it had actually wounded her physical and mental vitality. Poisonous consequences from invisible traumas inflicted by the pernicious attacks upon herself and client had been silently absorbed, deeper and more painfully than she had realized.

Hanging around the halls of the new county building I waited two hours for Donna to emerge from their torture chamber. Alone and greatly outnumbered numerically, the tiny gladiator had faced her tormenters bravely at their required, Local Rule 3.15.1 Meeting of Counsel. As she exited the conference room I took her briefcase, it was so heavy she leaned like the Tower of Pisa. We met Bob in the foyer and went to Donna's car in the parking lot. It was noontime. The look on Donna's face prompted my concern, "You're very pale, let's go have lunch."

"No, really I'm fine," she insisted, "I have to return to my office." Donna drove away in her white Cadillac. Later that evening I went to Bob's office, he was just hanging up the phone.

"Crazy, plain crazy," he muttered.

"What is it Bob?"

Appearing stunned he stammered, "That was a friend of Donna's calling from a hospital."

"Hospital! What in hell happened?"

"All he knows is she was driving down the freeway not long after leaving us, she must have blacked out totally, doesn't remember a thing. She crashed into a cement pillar, demolishing her car."

"Lord, we better get to the hospital."

"No, her friend says there isn't anything we can do now, she has contusions and abrasions and struck her head on the steering wheel. He is going to call us again in the morning."

"It sounds damned suspicious to me."

"Yeh, I just don't know."

A few days after the accident Donna returned to work. Bob and I stopped by to check on her. Assuring us everything was fine she pulled up her sleeve baring her left arm, it was black and blue from elbow to shoulder, laughing she indicated yellowish spots edging the black bruises, "See, it's going away already."

"Donna," I watched her face, "Are you certain *something* didn't happen, could somebody have forced you off the road?" I watched her straining to think about what happened.

"I really don't believe so, it seemed like I just simply slipped off, you know, like when the nurse in the dentists office sticks a needle in your arm and says, 'Okay, count from one to ten,' and that's all you remember."

"How about at their meeting, did anyone give you coffee or coke or something else to drink before you left?"

"Yes," then she purposely *changed* the subject, saying, "You guys have to come up with the document that Eddie had as proof of the $100,000.00 payment from Metro to Nordman. I've agreed in accord with Hamilton's Local Rule 9 settlement demand, that Cannizzaro will dismiss the case if we don't locate that evidence."

"I don't know, Eddie returned all the files he had in the trunk of his car to people in the east. They say they can't find the document. Cannizzaro's hearing is coming up soon, are you certain you are up to handling it?"

"Oh sure," she nodded with positive assurance, "There won't be any problem."

"You know these people have *a lot to lose,* they aren't going to stop at anything."

"Oh please...don't worry...really I'm okay, I can handle it."

It was right after Cannizzaro's court hearing, Bob had just talked with Donna on the phone. He couldn't hide his utter dejection. "She was crying, in fact almost hysterical. Required by Pregerson's lousy Local Rules Consuelo Marshall appointed a Magistrate to take over the case. Donna said she had *never* appeared before such a vicious person in all her life. Magistrate Vanetta Tossopulos forced her into the untenable position of having to accept a tape recorded hearing instead of a required court reporter. Tossopulos told her there were no reporters available for over two weeks and was going to continue the case if she didn't agree. Ben Nordman's hatchet man Hair was there with a leering grin, anticipating Donna's expected degradation at the hands of a Magistrate, it was a set-up. Vendetta Tossopulos, a female Magistrate ranted and raised hell with Donna, raging right *flat out* that she would *not* put up with anybody who filed lawsuits against judges. Then she ruled...'there were no merits to the case.' And this was after Judge Marshall refused to Dismiss the case and gave Cannizzaro the Right to Amend."

"Well, after all Bob, this Tossopulos owes her phony job and title of Magistrate to the judges. If she *didn't cover-up* for them she sure as hell would not keep her prestigious title very long. Marshall was afraid to Dismiss the case so she has the Magistrate screw it all up first. Webster defines a Magistrate as nothing more than 'a minor official, such as a Justice of the Peace.'"

"That's right and Donna's discovering it the hard way. Tossopolus came on real hard, pouring it on she imposed $2,250.00 in penalties on Eddie, and $3,000.00 in sanctions against Powell. Then she hung $1,000.00 over Donna's head and threatened more to come, these were supposedly imposed because Donna failed to drag Eddie from his sick bed and force him to attend their Deposition."

"Jesus! Does Tossopulos actually have judicial authority to make all these rulings and decisions?"

"Hell no, under Federal Rules she can't rule on the merits of a case, nor can she impose or enforce sanctions or penalties. I did my best to explain all this to Donna, their tactics are scaring hell out of her, she's like petrified or mesmerized. She pleaded for me to help get her free from Cannizzaro's case."

I became sick over what Bob and I had let Donna in for. More and more I saw the significance of Bob's expoundings about the evil device of Magistrates and Pregerson's Local Rules, muddling cases and *scaring the living hell* out of attorneys and their clients. It's too much, the ordinary citizens could not possibly survive such terrible pressure put upon them by the Federal Court. Knowing the affinities of Wilshire Blvd. type lawyers toward perjury, corruption and other crimes, DuPre also felt deep responsibility for Donna's tormented predicament. Although he had fully realized those lawyers were as capable of crime as any hood on the street he'd *naively* banked on the strength of law and judges honesty to hold them in check. Not only had Bob over-valued the integrity of the law, he had dreadfully underestimated the *fathomless depths* of judicial chicanery.

Cannizzaro agreed it was not right to torture Donna further by not freeing her from responsibility, even though it meant being left without a lawyer and he'd have to proceed on his own. Under the stress Eddie's brittle health grew worse, he asked Bob to compose a letter to Judge Consuelo Marshall. He outlined the facts of being forced to release two lawyers because it was impossible to represent him under the vicious barrage of threats and intimidation thrown up by the lawyers and judges.

Magistrate Tossopulos's rantings and ravings at the hearing *now* loomed critically important. Asking to hear the tape recording Bob was astounded at an *incredible discovery* by court personnel, "The tape was unintelligible, *nothing* could be heard on it except static."

I said, "Hair and Tossopulos did one hell of a job at staging the hearing. They succeeded in scaring Donna to death, then destroyed all evidence of what actually took place. It is damn clear why they would *not* allow a court reporter to record that hearing." Wagging his head Bob concurred, an incredulous wave of shocked disbelief at the vitiated state of the Federal Courts swept across his face.

Tamar Stein, representing Metropolitan Corp. filed a 'Motion for Discovery Matter,' set for July 20, 1981, 10:00 a.m. in Tossopulos' court, No. J 1010. Stein also filed a 'Motion For Dismissal Of The Complaint' scheduled the same date and time in Judge Marshall's courtroom, No. 18. Utilizing their treacherous methods of muddling cases beyond repair, Stein's two Motions were seventy three pages of repeated railings, abuse and accusations. Stein accused, "Thirty years ago Cannizzaro was mob enforcer for the late Mafia King Pin Jack I. Dragna." She maintained that *because* of "Eddie's Sicilian nationality and supposed Mafia background the court should *deny* Eddie the right to file a lawsuit against such *prominent and noted* people as Judge Berenson, Ben Nordman and Rudy Schaefer."

Born in Sicily, Eddie was christened Gesualdo Michel Cannizzaro. He arrived in New York City at the age of eighteen months with his parents in 1924. He served four years in the U.S. Army, two in the South Pacific. As sergeant he was honorably discharged in 1946, and in contradiction to Stein's crazy vicious lies, Cannizzaro had never been arrested for Mafia activities or any other violation.

As a consequence of Stein's Motions, Cannizzaro was faced with insurmountable legal problems. Frustrated and deeply depressed at having no lawyer to defend him, a shroud of helpless defeat wrought havoc with his health. A million times DuPre and I had examined, dissected and denounced a morbidly diseased legal profession which corruptly and conspiratorially denies American citizens their right to legal representation.

Every day, Monday through Friday, lawyers swarm the courts, like honey bees in a hive, they suck and slaver the anus of the Presiding Judge. Pollinating each other they flit about, joyfully they swear, "If you aspire, as we all do to be illustrious, renowned lawyers we must never, never, represent or assist in any way a person who intends to sue a judge."

On Monday June 29, 1981, at Stein's orders, a secretary executed a 'Proof of Service by Mail,' she stated she had mailed copies of Stein's Motions to Cannizzaro. But with totally evil intent Stein did not actually mail them until Thursday July 2, 1981. This was right before the three day July 4th holiday when mail delivery would be jammed up.

Extremely ill, stripped of his attorneys when he finally received Stein's Motions, Cannizzaro was left with only four days to complete and file his answer in court. Eddie knew he was through. How could he possibly repel or expose her lies and accusations? The onslaught of overwhelming fury and frustration availed him nothing, there was no way out. Stein's tar and feather job had finished him.

Stein was low on the roster of the Pacht-Ross firm, but on this typical Pharisaical Beverly Hills day she visualized vast horizons of grandeur. Gazing confidently from her fifth floor Feejian cubicle in fabulous Century City, down on fascinating Wilshire Blvd., she was not disappointed. That old *legendary spell* of movieland's venerable, celebrated Boulevard struck her fancy, vivid dreams of adoring fans frenziedly applauding, praising her supreme, inestimable legal talent. Gleefully she contemplated Cannizzaro's fatal demise conjured up by her own delicate hands. Admiration for her own devilish cleverness thrilled her. Tamar Stein was never more certain of anything in her life, this case was her first class ticket to unprecedented recognition by Pacht-Ross.

The die was cast. DuPre knew Eddie could never get a lawyer to help him in ten thousand years. No Bar Association member would touch an untouchable like him with a ten foot pole. Eunuchs, these lousy bar members were nothing but a mess of friggin Eunuchs, not a whole man among them. Bob realized that within the whole United States, he was the *only* one who would help Eddie now, Dupre also had become aware that the vainglorious legal profession's wanton cowardice had expressly created this untouchable class of societal lepers. Untouchables of extreme caste.

Regardless of wealth, heritage, color or creed, if you attempt to sue a judge you instantly are an untouchable with the *certainty* of losing everything you ever had or could ever hope to have. DuPre was well aware of the hazards: severe penalties, extreme punishment lie in wait for a lawyer so foolish as to disregard the Bar's unwritten law. To aid or give succor to an untouchable was inviting disaster, exilement by the Association, not exile to a foreign country, but to *another world* entirely.

Born and raised in the Blue Ridge mountains of South Carolina, possessing a treasured membership in the Bar Association, Robert O. DuPre joined the FBI. He later became Executive Assistant to Senator Strom Thurmond during an era of congressional efforts to quietly stave off gains of Civil Rights for Racial Minorities. Under the Kennedy Administration DuPre became a Supervising Assistant United States Attorney in the Justice Department, investigating and prosecuting government corruption. DuPre was aware upon entering private practice that some clients could *never* win in court regardless of how right they were. Along the road he'd developed his vigorous convictions, the law was mandatorily required to serve *all* the people equally. Battling for his clients under this precept he consistently and painfully twisted the tails of corrupt, incompetent judges. He grew weary from the constant physical and mental drain, and futility of constantly struggling for such an elusive object as Justice.

Making arrangements with his remaining clients he wrote a letter of resignation to the Bar Association. Bob than traveled to California to escape Judicial inequity. But, the judges and lawyers whose tails he had scorched refused to accept his resignation. They had a much better idea, they wanted to make damn sure DuPre never haunted them again. Secretly setting up a disciplinary hearing they acted to permanently remove Bob's bar membership. Then rumors had it that Bob was returning to become a consultant to licensed lawyers. Such a frightening event could not be tolerated. The South Carolina State

Bar Association quickly pushed a law through that would punish any attorney who dared hire any person as a consultant who was not a member of their Bar.

Cannizaro's dire plight was specific proof of judges and attorneys compacting and combining in a conspiracy to destroy any citizen who sues a corrupt judge and his accomplices. Bob swore, "Sonofabitch, I am going to shuffle up a whole new deck of cards in this deadly game these judges are playing."

Bob was sure: A citizen could win in court even though stripped of his lawyers if he had experienced, dedicated legal assistance from competent people who could not be frightened off by vicious judges or the Bar. Hell yes an untouchable could win, a judge couldn't stop Bob from developing case strategy, researching and preparing legal documents and filing them. But he knew that no judges would ever let him as a *non-bar* member assist the unfortunate untouchables in the courtroom. Not one untouchable in a thousand had the vaguest idea how to protect himself in court. This was the precise situation the Black Robes had evilly orchestrated. Soon as the untouchables were stripped of legal assistance the judges could then destroy them and no one could do a thing about it. Any attempt to Appeal would be futile. Bob had come up with some good ideas of how to provide legal assistance and representation to untouchables in courtroom proceedings despite judges denial of their guaranteed Constitutional Rights. But for now that would have to wait...the pressing problem was to construct an 'Opposition' to Tamar Stein's overtly muddled 'Motions' and get it filed, only a few days remained.

Hour after hour Bob poured over the huge stack of court filings, studying, analyzing and re-analyzing. He'd long harbored suspicions that their method of operation based on muddling official records with reams of Motions and senseless filings could eventually destroy them, back-firing with a devastating exposure, because in effect they were actually deposing themselves.

Bob's innate patience and experience paid off. Slicing deep into such machinations laid bare their secrets. His minute scrutiny, and exacting probes of their records revealed startling evidence. In the small print of a 1974 Proxy Statement filed with the U.S. Securities Exchange Commission by the Metropolitan Corp., Bob discovered the incriminating evidence we needed. The firm of Pacht-Ross was paid $199,800.00 for legal fees. Out of this, $152,500.00 was listed as being paid in connection with the Judge Jerome Berenson 1974 zoning decision in favor of the Metropolitan Corporation.

Clarifying these facts DuPre laid it out plain. "This money paid out by the Pacht-Ross law firm in the Zoning Decision verifies the document you saw in Cannizzaro's possession, the one regarding the hundred thousand dollars paid to Nordman and Berenson for *fixing* the zoning in 1974. Now...here comes the *real* kicker, according to Metropolitan's Statement of Disclosure of 1974, N. Joseph Ross, of the Pacht-Ross firm owns thirty five thousand shares of Metro.. He also is a Director and the Secretary."

"Lord! What better way can there be to milk a corporation than by outrageous legal fees and pay-offs."

"That's right, almost one fifth of a million in lawyers fees in one year. That is besides N. Joseph Ross's sixty thousand as a Secretary and Director of the corporation. That was in 1974, seven years ago, who knows how many shares Ross has now and how much money he's skimmed off in phoney lawyers fees."

"This unravels a hell of a lot of mystery as to why Pacht-Ross is so desperate with Eddie. For one thing, they've obviously gotten to that Magistrate, Tossopulos. There seems to be no explanation why she'd endanger herself in felony crimes unless she's been paid off."

"Maybe she's been paid off, then again maybe she's taking orders from Judge Consuelo Marshall."

"Yeh, I see what you mean."

During the three day July Fourth holiday, Bob worked tirelessly. It was a tedious, demanding, mentally exhausting task, but he knew Eddie did not stand a chance if his answer wasn't filed before the deadline. Early Tuesday, July 7, 1981, the first day of court business after the Fourth, we met Eddie in Agoura. After examining the fifty seven pages of Bob's Memorandum of Opposition to Stein's Motion to Dismiss, Cannizzaro signed and dated the document in approval. In accord with his belief that court filings should be succinct, sticking strictly to the facts and law, Bob's Memorandum actually consisted of only seven pages. Fifty of the pages were photo copies of all the perjurious affidavits and documents of Stein, Hair and Hamilton, detailing their criminal obstruction of the Due Process of Law and Justice.

Leaving Eddie we headed for L.A., the documents had to be filed today at the latest. Bob drove while I studied his Memorandum. He said, "Let me point out a prime example of their talking too much. You recall when Hamilton *ranted* for two hours *threatening* Donna with what was going to happen to her if she didn't make Cannizzaro dismiss his case?"

"Of course I recall, that was at one of Judge Harry Pregerson's phony Local Rules meetings."

"Okay, go to page fifty one of the transcript, it's marked exhibit No. 6. Hamilton appeared to be enjoying himself, he was threatening Donna, now, quoting Hamilton, "There is not a witness in the world anywhere that can testify that the sum of $100,000.00 was paid to Ben Nordman or his firm by Metro Corp. *at any time,* not a witness! There is not a document that exists that will support that. Not one document anywhere in the world unless somebody has manufactured a document. *I tell you that! That is a fact!"*

"That guy Hamilton is kind of weird."

"There's more, turn to page thirty three of the evidence. Examine exhibit No. 5. Believe me, nobody manufactured that document. It is a verified copy of the Proxy Statement produced by Metropolitan Corp. and duly filed with the SEC in 1974. This Hamilton guy is a very cocky character alright, however his biggest mistake is in trying to be clever. Whether it can be proved that Nordman and Berenson got exactly a hundred grand right to the penny is not the issue. The overriding issue is, *did* Berenson and Nordman get a huge sum of money from Metro Corp. or Joseph Ross for the express purpose of *selling out* Ventura County and the taxpayers. Now, there's no way in hell Judge Marshall or Tossopulos can ignore this document, right there, read that."

Bob pointed to the spot with his forefinger. It read, "As a share holder, Secretary and Director of Metropolitan, N. Joseph Ross set it up for Metro Corp. to pay his law firm of Pacht-Ross, $199,000.00 supposedly legal fees for 1974. Of this sum, $152,500.00 represented legal fees in connection with a lawsuit, <u>Metropolitan Devel. Corp. v. The County Of Ventura.</u> The suit was settled in December 1974. Bob asked, "Do you get it now?"

"Of course, Ross and Nordman had worked out a deal. Ross gave Nordman and Berenson $152,500.00 and in December 1974 Judge Berenson ruled in *favor* of the Metropolitan Corp."

"You got that right, but then they proceeded further to cover-up the conspiracy. They were afraid there just might be some stupid ass around who would start screaming that the County should Appeal Berenson's decision. To *kill* any chances of this happening, Berenson and Nordman had John Conlon, Chairman of the Supervisors, set up a stipulation agreement between Ventura County and Metro Corp., which meant that there could be *no* Appeal. As a real estate broker in Agoura, Chairman Conlon *profited* highly money wise from the ensuing development and residential sales by Metropolitan Corp.."

In his Memorandum Bob meticulously detailed the perjury and obstructions of justice perpetrated by N. Joseph Ross and Nordman. Every violation was carefully defined and backed up by photo copies of documentary proof and clearly marked as exhibits. While Bob was filing the Memorandum I drove around the block waiting for him. On the drive home DuPre explained what he had in mind. "Actually your lawsuit and Eddie's both commenced as Civil cases, but digging deeper and deeper we have *uncovered* evidence and facts exposing many other crimes. Now they've involved themselves and others so deep in their attempt to cover-up that they have no way out."

"I know exactly what you're saying Bob, but what in hell good will it do going to Andrea Ordin, the Attorney General, in Los Angeles? She's married to Robert Ordin, a U.S. Commissioner. I've already had one very sad experience with her. Robert Ordin has been hand in glove with Judge Berenson, Nordman and Pregerson for years. They have defrauded people, cheated the taxpayers and stolen more money than you and I can count."

Bob hurried to say, "I am not even considering going to Andrea Ordin. What I'm thinking of is going back to Washington, D.C. to the Justice Department. They have a *Special Criminal Section* that handles Civil Rights violations, that *encompasses* judges who misuse and abuse their power against the people. The Kennedy's set up this Special Section in their administration, they realized the necessity of such an office *free* from influence and interference, *even* from the U.S. Attorney General himself. I may be back there two months. It will take a while to acquaint them with all the evidence and facts."

"It seems like our only hope, it's obvious that we are not getting anywhere on a Civil lawsuit basis. The judges, their clerks, the *entire* Federal Court menagerie is aligned to stop us."

"Yes, but the Memorandum I just filed should commence to open things up. I see no way Magistrate Tossopulos or Judge Consuelo Marshall can deny or ignore all this documented evidence."

"I sure hope so, today is July 7th and the hearing with Marshall is Monday July 20th." The next day Bob departed. Saturday, July 18th, Eddie phoned, he was screaming, "Gahrie, I got a letter, the judge *won't accept* the Memorandum."

"Take it easy, I'll be down soon as I can." It was three when I got to Denny's. "Jeez, calm down Ed, they can hear you all over town."

"God damn! What kind of horseshit am I getting into, you tell me to trust these courts, look what the hell they are doing to me. They file a bunch of lies and bullshit about me and when I answer them the judge orders that they won't even read my answer!"

"Okay okay, let me see what they've sent you." The letter was a hand printed thing on a piece of paper marked, 'Civil Minutes.' It looked *exactly* like one of Judge Pregerson's shithouse orders: No Attorneys Present For Plaintiff...No Attorneys Present For The Defendants...No Court Reporter Present...there was no name on it, only the initials of John Crenshaw, a Dep. Clerk, the letter stated that, "The Court would *not* approve of Cannizzaro acting as his own lawyer, therefore the Court would *not* allow the Memorandum to be filed. It would be placed in the Court file, but would *not* be used."

Good Lord! If I didn't get out of here quick I was going to start screaming louder than Eddie was, it was about to become one hell of a scene. Faking calm, I said, "Give me that letter, I expect a call from DuPre at anytime, I'll see what he says."

Eddie wasn't to be put off, he was mad, he knew something was radically wrong. "God Damn it, that hearing is coming up Monday morning, what are we going to do?"

"I've got to get back to Ventura in case Bob calls, come on, let's get out of here, I'll call you soon as I hear from him." Eddie stood in the parking lot glaring after me as I drove away. Damn, I didn't blame him a bit. First they *strip* him of lawyers, then when he tries to *defend himself,* the judge *orders* that he has to *keep* a terrified lawyer who *wants out* of the case frantically. Crenshaw, the Court Clerk, used the same rotten tricks as Stein. He had waited ten days before mailing this abortion to Cannizzaro. There wasn't *time* to do anything, even if there was *something* that could be done.

It began dawning on me, this was *proof* that Judge Marshall was part of their conspiracy...it was she who had *made* this pernicious order, that meant she'd read the Memorandum and *recognized* its danger, it could blast the top right off their whole cover-up scheme if it got into the record and was *heard.* It hadn't been part of their original strategy to force Donna back in as Eddie's attorney. It was the only subterfuge they could dream up to *keep the Memorandum from being heard* on Monday in Judge Marshall's courtroom.

Bob called from D.C. shortly after I returned home, he listened, he exclaimed, "Jeez...I *never* dreamed they'd pull something as hairy as this, it sure as hell goes to show I got back here to D.C. just in time. A massive investigation by the Justice Department is the *only* way in the world the *Judicial* corruption out there can be crushed."

"By God Bob they'd better get started soon."

"What we have to do is get hold of Donna quick, she's under the belief that she was relieved from the case. Gary, it's going to be up to you. There's damn little time left, but you have to contact Donna and make sure that she will be at the hearing Monday morning. She has to get Judge Marshall on record as to that Memorandum, one way or another. One more thing...take a copy of the Memorandum to Donna, tell her to *re-file* it immediately as Attorney of Record for Eddie. We have to get it *into* the record one way or another."

"Sonofabitch, you know those rotten bastards are running my ass off driving back and forth to Smogsville trying to keep up with their filthy tricks. How long can we hope to keep this up? We don't have the money or the influence they've got. Christ, I have been working fourteen and sixteen hours a day, seven days a week all these years trying to hold everything together."

"I understand, but this call is costing you money." Luckily I got Donna on the phone Sunday evening at her home. She was certain she had been relieved as Cannizzaro's lawyer, she hadn't received any notice from the court regarding this latest development, there was no requirement on her behalf to be there. I hated to ask her, I knew how bad she dreaded further involvement in Eddie's case. But Donna was a fine person, she agreed to be there the next morning. A rare lawyer for the times, Donna held unflinching, old fashioned loyalty toward her obligation to the legal profession.

Only two people had arrived in Consuelo Marshall's courtroom. I heard the clock ticking high up on the wall, Donna wasn't there, a young guy with a head of bushy hair in a black suit stood at a table near the judges bench. I asked, "Is the Metropolitan case scheduled for this courtroom?"

Before bushy hair replied, the other person hustled swiftly over. Tremulously he inquired, "Who are you, who do you represent?"

I looked at the smallish man in the blue suit. "I am here in behalf of a friend, and who are you?"

"I am Martin Zohn, Martin S. Zohn, I represent Pacht-Ross law firm." I wondered *why* in hell this guy was so nervous, sweat beads were popping out on his head where the hair line receded. I looked around the room, *where* was Tamar Stein, *why* was this Zohn here, *what in hell were they up to now?* Without any further conversation I left the room. Down the hall I saw Donna approaching.

"Hope I'm not late, what's going on?"

"I don't know, Stein didn't show." I pointed to the man in the blue suit, "That's Martin Zohn, he's here for Pacht-Ross." Going to the table she conversed with Zohn a few minutes. Observing, I thought, Donna might be getting back her spunk after having been so cruelly intimidated by these people. She'd struck a defiant, cocky fighting stance, hands on her hips, feet spread, now she shook her finger in Martin S. Zohn's face. Out in the hall when we had a little privacy Donna admitted, "I'll be damn if I could find out what is going on. This Zohn filed a bunch of papers this morning asking the court for an Exparte Order *relieving* them from having to *abide* by Pregerson's Local Rules. An Exparte Order is made by the judge in the absence of one of the parties. Crenshaw, the Clerk, told me Judge Marshall signed the Exparte Order relieving them from following the Local Rules."

"Does that mean *they don't* have to *abide* by Judge Pregerson's phony rules, *but we do?*"

"That's a very good question, but we *never* get to see a judge, all we ever get is half-assed information from some guy who says he is a court clerk. Anyway, Crenshaw says the case has been transferred by Judge Marshall back to Tossopulos who will hold a hearing at ten a.m next Thursday."

"It appears that Bob's Memorandum has *scared* hell out of them. The last thing Marshall can afford is to have that Memorandum in the record, she was *hiding* back there in her chambers just waiting, and if no one showed up to represent Cannizzaro she was going to pop out and Dismiss the case real fast. When you appeared in court this morning all Marshall could do was transfer it back to Tossopulos and let her *foul* it up some more."

Such contemptible, vicious judges were enough to make Godzilla puke. It would help nothing to get any madder than I already was. I suggested, "Let's go across Spring Street to the mall and have a cup of coffee. I brought a copy of the Memorandum, Bob wanted you to read it."

Going down the escalator Donna grabbed my arm, frightened, she whispered, "That man behind, he's following us, I am positive, I've been watching him for quite a while."

I shot a glance back, about six steps above us I saw The Angel. Not a large imposing man, he was slim, wiry like spring steel. A gray Van Dyke beard and narrow mustache stood out sharp against his darkly tanned face. The tight fitting gray sharkskin suit, white shirt and stiff collar with a thin black tie had created a more than slightly menacing apparition to Donna. Considering all the experiences she had *suffered* the last few weeks, bullying, threats, harassments and a mysterious car accident, it was enough to make even a brave man jumpy, much less an impressionable, young female lawyer. I had to smile, "Donna, that's our friend, Jimmy Angel. He keeps a vigilant, wary eye open for us."

"Oooh my, thank heavens," she sighed, relaxing her death grip on my arm. At the mall we located a table in a small patio. The Angel emerged from the cafe with three cups of coffee. Sipping her coffee, Donna remarked laughingly, "That was a mighty *short* hearing Judge Marshall just gave us, it's only ten fifteen right now." She'd become more self assured since leaving the Federal Building.

"Some things have happened that I haven't told you about Gary, I must tell you now."

"Let's have it Donna."

"Back in May I had a phone call from Hamilton, he's that hot shot lawyer from Pacht-Ross. I realize now he was trying to frighten me so bad I couldn't handle your case or Eddie's properly. Tauntingly he accused me of some real far out nebulous wrong doings. Hamilton smirked, 'How in hell did you get those clients? For Christ Sake, don't you know that Cannizzaro and Gary are dangerous people?' He also said he had a transcript of the Bar proceedings when they removed DuPre's license."

"Listen to me Donna, DuPre lost his Bar License *strictly* through political persecution, *not* because he'd ever done anything wrong. It was a lot like what is happening to *you* right now. Your phone call from Hamilton was two months ago. If the transcript Hamilton was popping off about had anything really detrimental to DuPre, believe me they would've done something about it before now. They have *nothing*, he was trying to scare you which obviously he did, or you would've told us about it when it happened. Pacht-Ross, Berenson and Nordman have spent thousands of dollars on private detectives trying to dig up something bad on Bob, Eddie and me. They found *nothing* because there *is nothing* bad to find. This Hamilton is just an old, tired yellow dog, a *hatchet man for big shot lawyers,* the same as William Hair. Donna, you've had the misfortune of bucking some of the *most vicious* lawyers around. I talked to DuPre in D.C. last night, he's made solid contact with two people in the Civil Rights Division of the Justice Department. They are fascinated by all this Machiavellian Judicial corruption in California. Bob is totally busy preparing documents for them to study, it's a tremendous job, there is so damn much to explain to them and to document. Incidentally Donna, the people in the Justice Department are well aware of that transcript Hamilton has about Robert and all the circumstances of his loss of membership in the South Carolina Bar Association. They aren't concerned about it in D.C., they know very well how *easy* you can become a victim of political intrigue."

Jimmy and I went into the cafe for more coffee to let her study the document. Donna's face reflected her zeal, "This Memorandum is great, right to the point and with hard hitting law. Alright, Judge Marshall has continued our hearing until Thursday in Magistrate Tossopulos's Court and since they are holding me as Eddie's lawyer of record, I'll file the Memorandum as such tomorrow. We will see if Magistrate Tossopulos can keep it out of the record. Lord, we've been talking almost two whole hours, it's five to twelve. Gary, there is something that is bugging me real bad. The last time I appeared in Tossopulos's Court she forced me to accept that tape recording machine routine, I intend to be prepared for her this time. On the way back to your car would you guys go by her courtroom to see if she is using a court reporter or a recording machine?"

"We're on our way, we will try to get there before she leaves for lunch. I'll call you tonight."

Dashing across Spring Street against the red signal Angel and I entered the Federal Building. Hurrying down the hall I peered into room J1001, we were too late, Vendetta Tossopulos was just leaving the bench and entering her chambers. Damn, I won't be able to get the information Donna wanted. The building was empty, the Civil Service employees had disappeared, gone to lunch. Absent mindedly leaning against the wall while Angel drank from a water fountain I watched a figure coming far down the deserted hall. I'll be damned, it was Martin S. Zohn. What in hell could he be doing here? Two hours have past since we left Marshall's courtroom, he should have been back in Beverly Hills by now.

Suddenly Zohn was wary, he recognized us, faltering he realized that it was too late to turn and run. His orders were irrevocable, a secret deal had already been made for a vitally important meet. He knew for his own sake he dare not fail, but these people in the hall watching him, *this wasn't supposed to happen,* after all, very powerful people, N. Joseph Ross and Nordman had assured him that *no one* would ever know his part in this conspiracy. Now, forced to brazen it out, a fresh batch of sweat popped out, shining on his bald head as he went by.

Angel and I stared at Zohn's retreating back as he limply slipped through the ordinarily *locked* hall door into Vendetta Tossopulos's chambers. "Angel do you realize what we've just witnessed, can you see what these crooked bastards are up to? They figured we would be miles up the highway, they were certain the coast would be clear. This guy Zohn is in Tossopulos's chambers right now conspiring with her to screw-up Eddie's case at the hearing on Thursday. Tomorow when they learn that Donna has re-filed Bob's Memorandum I want to see how Tossopulos will keep it out of the court record."

Abhorred with all the sordid intrigue that he had been wallowing around in since first entering the Federal building, Angel grunted, "Christ, these people, Marshall and Tossopulos are supposed to be judges...why should an American Citizen have to go through all this shit just trying to get a little justice...what in hell is their problem?"

"Now that is a mighty good question Angel. What in hell is their problem? Damn if that ain't the first question that should be asked of these corrupt Federal Judges at a Congressional investigation." I had a strong feeling that we would *not* be invited into Tossopulos's chamber along with Martin S. Zohn.

"Angel, we might as well head for Ventura." I finally got Donna on the phone about four p.m., she was upset, "Gary something damn strange is going on. I got a phone message from Tossopulos's clerk at two o'clock. He said that the Magistrate is *not* going to give us a hearing on Thursday, July 23. Tossopulos has cancelled the hearing and is going to take the case under submission in her chambers."

"I'll be damned, but it all figures." I gave it to her in detail, about catching Zohn sneaking into Tossopulos's chambers at noon. "Hell, you know what they were up to, they were rehearsing how they were going to screw-up Eddie's case at the hearing so bad that you won't be able to do a thing to stop them. Tossopulos must've been scared out of her wits when Zohn told her about Jimmy and me spotting him going into her chambers. She is aware that we know what they are up to. So now she isn't even going to give Eddie a hearing, she does *not* dare to."

Donna gasped as full implication of such vicious treachery by the judiciary struck her. I said, "Believe me, I understand perfectly how you feel. I know it's a very frightening situation for you but please, go ahead and file the Memorandum tomorrow, and be sure to get a copy of the filing stamped by the clerk as proof that it was filed, we just don't dare trust any of the goings on in that Federal Building." Weakly she assured me it would be filed. "Donna please don't worry, I'll be talking to Eddie and Bob tonight. I know they'll do everything in their power to get you released from the case."

I talked to Bob that night, he laughed uproariously at my story of Zohn's ludicrous, frightened attempt to *sneak* into the Magistrate's chambers. When told about Tossopulos's clerk calling Donna and cancelling Eddie's hearing Bob returned to dead seriousness. I could not mistake the swift, hard anger erupting in his voice. "Okay! God damn it, those crooked judges are holding the power now...it makes you sick to your stomach standing by helplessly watching them get away with their crimes. But Gary, believe me, their corrupt house of cards may already be commencing to crumble. I have made great strides at the Justice Department."

"Bob, I don't get it why Pacht-Ross suddenly starts using this guy Martin Zohn in place of Tamar Stein."

Snorting with disgust he rasped, "She's burned out like last years Fourth of July sky rocket. When we filed those documented charges of perjury against her, Pacht-Ross couldn't use her anymore. That's how those big law firms operate, there's only a couple big shots like N. Joseph Ross at the top who own the firm. All those other thirty or forty lawyers with their names in gold leaf on the door and letter head of the office stationary are flunkey's. I call them *throw-away* lawyers. Stein's through, they don't need her now, she'll be lucky if she isn't fired by Pacht-Ross. Now they send another flunky, Martin S. Zohn. He only has one job, if the judge asks him any pertinent questions he weasels, 'I'm sorry Your Honor, I'm new to the case, I can't answer that question.' See how they work it? Stein's stupid, she did all the dirty work thinking she'd be rewarded by Pacht-Ross like a celebrity. She didn't understand what an evil racket she'd entered. This guy Zohn is a bit smarter than Tamar. He knows how they are using him, that is why he was so nervous and sweaty. He is scared alright, but he has no choice if he wants to keep his name in gold leaf on the door at Pacht-Ross. Tamar Stein and Martin Zohn are just two among thousands."

"I still don't get it Bob."

"Well, they were probably law students at UCLA or Cal Berkely with high scholastic grades. Shysters like Pacht-Ross send out letters enticing these top-grade students to join *prestige* Beverly Hills firms like Pacht-Ross claims to be. They are thrilled at being chosen by a prestigious firm that took time to inquire as to their legal acumen before they've even graduated. Grabbing the bait these poor suckers are immediately innoculated as *life-time* clones of the big time law office psychosis, medically diagnosed as, Scam Lawyeritis Syndrome. Rapidly developing their own scams under Pacht-Ross tutelage they soon break away. Renting a Feejian suite they then send out letters to UCLA and Cal Berkely law students, soon *another* prestige law firm is born and is in action."

"Well Bob, since the judges won't give Eddie a hearing I predict it is just going to be another shithouse decision." Cannizzaro didn't have long to wait. Tossopulos's blood pressure was screaming, her *part* in the judicial chicanery had become far too hazardous to keep it up. Soon after her call to Donna, Tossopulos hurriedly bounced the case back to Judge Consuelo Marshall, who within days emulated Judge Pregerson. She Dismissed Eddie's suit...No Attorney Present For The Plaintiff, No Court Reporter Present, just another shithouse Dismissal. Marshall's only *stated* reason for the Dismissal was that she had "*Considered* The Papers."

Only days before Marshall's decision, Pregerson again Dismissed *my* case. Another Dismissal with, *No One Else Present*, Pregerson ruled my case was 'Res Judicata' in other words my suit had already been...'Tried and Adjudicated.'

His treachery was unbelievable, Pregerson always relied strongly on his *lifetime* appointment to the bench and his belief that *no one* could touch him no matter how corrupt he was. Again we faced the *eternal years,* waiting for an Appeal Court Decision. Jurisprudence, it's malevolent visage glared fierce, it had nothing but contempt for us, jeering at the despair created by intense pressures of financial and legal barriers imposed by vile perversion of the *law of the land.*

During DuPre's multitudinous hours of research and study at the Ventura County Law Library in regards to my lawsuit and Eddie's, he met Eve Kimball. A lady well in her seventies, she was obviously floundering hopelessly in legal mud up to her neck. DuPre with his vast sympathy for people mired in an on-slaught of legal distress lent a helping hand. Eve's nearly fatal transgression was that she'd dared to file a Pro-Per lawsuit charging a judge with corruption. Royce Lewellen, a Superior Court Judge of Santa Barbara County and his cohorts *without* legal jurisdiction had ruthlessly placed Eve's property under receivership. He then ordered the sheriff to confiscate Eve's bank account and Social Security checks, also a monthly check she received from her deceased husband's pension fund.

Prior to the court actions Eve was *stripped* of her attorney. By all State Bar standards she was now definitely an *untouchable*, yet the judge demanded that she hire legal counsel before again appearing in court. A lawyer, Arthur A. Garcia, agreed to represent Eve for a retainer of one thousand dollars, which she paid. At a subsequent court hearing Judge Lewellen ruled Eve in Contempt of Court for having failed to hand over the rental money from her properties to his court. In anger, the judge ordered her to jail. Succumbing to the shock of the harsh judicial decree Eve was stricken suddenly with a heart attack. She was carried to the hall on a stretcher and attended by para-medics. Staying in the courtroom, her attorney Garcia told the judge his client had *no objections* to her property being put in receivership, and her Social Security and pension checks confiscated. Hauled away to jail, fingerprinted and processed, Eve had another heart attack. She was transferred to the Santa Barbara County Jail hospital. After her release from jail, Garcia continued to conspire with the judge and his cohorts in harassing Eve into complying with the judge's *unlawful* demands to surrender her money and property to him. As her lawyer, Garcia demanded Eve's presence in court for numerous physically and mentally exhausting, senseless hearings. At one of them Judge Lewellen ordered that Eve was *not* to collect any rent money from her tenets, and was *forbidden* to even set foot upon her property. Though appallingly bewildered and frightened by the unbelievable judicial catastrophe descending upon her, Eve pluckily avowed before Judge Lewellen that, "You can put me in jail forever, but you *can not* stop me from fighting for my rights or my property while I'm still alive."

Bob was able to get Eve's checks returned after Judge Lewellen *admitted* under the pressure of proper law that he did *not* have any jurisdiction for his actions, however all the charges against him were Dismissed on the basis that *judges are immune* from their criminal acts even when *caught* red handed. Knowing it was senseless wasting more time and expense pursuing justice in the State Courts, DuPre assisted Eve in filing a Pro-Per Civil Rights Suit in Federal District Court. Lewellen and his accomplices were charged with, <u>Deprivation of Civil Rights Under the Color of Law, U.S.C. Sec. 1983, Civil Case No. CV 81-2391.</u>

Eve's new case was to be handled by Federal Judge Irving Hill. I recalled DuPre's consternation at the time, he had shaken his head with apprehension on learning that Hill was involved in Eve's suit. Curious I asked, "Why *such concern* over this judge Bob?"

"Hill wrote the Marguerite Shakespeare Decision." Momentarily Bob shuffled through stacks of papers on his desk. "Here it is, <u>Case No. 65-637 IH, back in July 1966.</u> Hill issued a particularly vindictive and abusive diatribe against a woman, Marguerite Shakespeare who as a Pro-Per sought justice in Federal Courts against conspiratorial acts of the State Court. Like Eve, she'd become embroiled in a real estate deal involving wealthy, influential people, she soon discovered the hard way just how powerful these influential persons were. She was put in jail for supposedly trespassing upon the real estate under litigation. Shakespeare was fingerprinted, processed and locked up. Having been previously *stripped of legal representation* she defended herself in Pro-Per before a jury of twelve citizens. They found her *innocent* of the *criminal charges* against her. Though being an elderly woman approaching her seventies she fought back. In Pro-Per she filed a suit in State Court against the judge and his co-conspirators. It was Dismissed on the basis that judges are immune from being sued for acts of criminally misusing Judicial Authority."

"It's the old story DuPre...Judicial Immunity, two very convenient words, protecting crooked judges from their multitudes of sins."

"That's true, American people have an ingrained sense of Judicial fairness: when standing before a judge they expect *one thing*, fair and impartial justice. People aren't stupid and they ain't ignorant either. For a long time now they have sensed a serious, frightening erosion of *integrity* and *morality* in the courts. The people simply won't stand for two kinds of justice, one for judges and another for themselves. There's going to be some kind of an explosion."

"I'd say the time is damn near."

"It'll be total chaos, because by then people will have abandoned *all hope* for justice through the courts. They'll take justice into their own hands. After all the ensuing chaos I don't believe we would *ever* be able to put our way of life back together."

"Go ahead Bob, tell me about Mrs. Shakespeare."

"Well, after being Dismissed in State Court she thought surely she would find a higher grade of justice in the Federal Court. It took a lot of effort on the part of a woman her age with no knowledge of Federal law or procedures, yet she managed to file a Pro-Per Civil Rights lawsuit in Federal Court. That is when she ran into Irving Hill. Needless to say, Hill Dismissed her case because a judge was involved. But, apparently he was not satisfied with just Dismissing Shakespeare's suit. Hill decided *something* must be done to *prevent* citizens in the *future* from filing Civil Rights cases in Federal Court against corrupt State Court Judges. Here is a photo copy of Hill's Dismissal of the Shakespeare suit. Listen carefully to this, it's Judge Irving Hill's *personal opinion* of an *American* seeking justice in the Federal Court:

'This action filed in Pro-Per, is a typical example of

the kind of action being filed with increasing frequency, under the provisions of the <u>Civil Rights Act of 1871, 42 U.S.C. Sec. 1981-1986.</u> Having once been defeated in the State Court proceedings and being unhappy and somewhat humiliated and frustrated by the results of such proceedings, these persons then lash out at judges, lawyers, witnesses, court functionaries, newspapers and anyone else within convenient range, terming all of them corruptly evil, charging them with perjury and conspiracy in a last desperate effort to re-litigate the issues on which they have once lost and are hoping to secure sizable damages to boot.'"

"Now Gary, here is my translation of the sum and substance of Judge Irving Hill's Dismissal Opinion. *No American citizen* has the *right* to lash out against *tyrannical* State Court Judges regardless of how corrupt and vicious their actions are, *No* American citizen has Civil Rights or *any* recourse in Federal Court against a State Judge once the Judge has *defeated* the Citizen in State Court Proceedings." Bob looked at me, "It's enough to scare hell out of the bravest." I had no answer. He went on, "This evilly *contrived* diatribe of Hill's has been used for over fifteen years as the *basis* to Dismiss Pro-Per Civil Rights actions against corrupt judges *solely* by means of ridicule and lambaste. Federal Judges are scornful, they know that not one out of a million has the vaguest knowledge or ability to proceed with an Appeal, and there's not a lawyer in the land who'll lift a finger to help them. Remember how County Counsel Schechter used Hill's invective against you and Eddie, and also Eve?"

While Bob was back east I couldn't shake the nightmare of Hill's evil hand in Shakespeare's case, I had to know more, locating her in L.A., we talked on the phone, she agreed to meet Tuesday, at one in the lobby of Beverly Hills Security Pacific Bank on Wilshire Blvd.

Well educated and traveled, the lady was quite interesting, in fact we talked nearly four hours. Recounting her *eons* of anguish in State Courts attempting to sue a corrupt judge she struck on an extremely significant recollection. During one of many courtroom appearances a State Court Judge had rebuked her arrogantly, "Mrs. Shakespeare, you do *not* really want to *sue* this judge, now do you?" Shortly after that her case against the State Court judge was *Dismissed.*

"I know these incidents took place almost fifteen years ago Mrs. Shakespeare, but can you remember the name of that judge?"

"Oh yes, I recall *very clearly,* it was Otto Kaus."

I too had *occasion to remember* that name, Otto Kaus. He was the State Appeal Court Judge who'd Dismissed my Appeal against Judge Jerome Berenson. He had treacherously changed *not only the facts,* but *the law as well* in my suit. Simultaneously in an attempt to cover-up his criminal and conspiratorial act Kaus had ordered that his decision to Dismiss the case was, "NOT TO BE PUBLISHED." Governor Jerry Brown recently compounded judicial sordidness by elevating the evil, corrupt Otto M. Kaus, to the California Supreme Court on a ludicrous basis. To quote Brown, *"Kaus' fine legal ability and judicial honesty."*

"Fortunately for us Mrs. Shakespeare, our law still allows us the right to have a jury, do you *realize* what one of those *tainted* judges would have done to you had you not *demanded* a jury?"

"Oh, but most definitely I know what they'd have done to me," she laughed, "Certainly a terribly dangerous criminal like me would still be behind bars."

Eddie, Eve and myself had all been maliciously Dismissed by the Federal District Court. Appeals must be filed. A staggering load of legal work faced Bob. I wished he would return from D.C. soon.

CHAPTER 31

Considerable wealth and prestige, also huge amounts of pretension reside in the fashionable Clearpoint neighborhood. Situated on the side of the hills the new community overlooks the City of Ventura and the Pacific Ocean a few miles in the distance. In the dark early morning hours of Friday March 14, 1980, Joan Taylor was wakened from a sound sleep by her huge dog who led her out the back door. The dog went swiftly to the side gate facing the neighbors home at 573 Highpoint Dr. and stood there, he didn't growl or whine, he just stared into the darkness. The eerie silence and the animal's strange behavior were scary. Shivers ran up Mrs. Taylor's back as chill mist infiltrating off the ocean grasped her with clammy hands. Obeying a quiet command the dog turned and followed, then halting he stared once again into the darkness engulfing the house next door before escorting his mistress back into their home. Nothing stirred in the Clearpoint community, but somewhere, somewhere out there in the darkness someone watched and waited.

On Sunday afternoon, March 16, 1980, the bludgeoned bodies of Lyman R. Smith and Charlene, his beautiful young wife were found murdered, lying in pools of blood in their bedroom. The bodies were covered with a sheet and a fire log suspected of being the murder weapon laid on the bed beside them. Smith's young son by a former marriage who lived nearby with his mother had arrived to mow the lawn and discovered the ghastly crime.

Emotional shock waves of fear were generated in the area by news of the killings. Neighbors reflected on the fact Smith was a leading candidate for appointment to a vacancy on the Superior Court by Governor Jerry Brown. Another influential resident of Clearpoint, Superior Court Judge Marvin Lewis had knocked on Smith's door Friday afternoon. There was no answer, the Judge later stated he'd wanted to speak to Smith regarding his pending appointment to the bench. Getting a warrant from Lewis, detectives entered the house. Dist. Atty. Bradbury arrived at the gruesome scene but didn't go in. A police official stated, "The victims had retired for the night and didn't know what hit them, a single blunt injury had been delivered to the head of each them, both victims were tied up when found."

A seven hour autopsy performed on both bodies by the County Coroner Ronald Kornblum, indicated that the Smiths had been dead since late Thursday night or very early Friday morning. A thorough medical exam brought forth a bizarre finding, they had been tied up alright, but not until after they were dead. Police found no evidence of any forced entry indicating a burglary, however, certain valuable things were missing giving rise to the theory that burglars had been surprised in the act, precipitating a double murder.

At two the following Friday afternoon nearly three hundred and fifty people arrived at Santa Paula Episcopal Church for Memorial services. Both bodies had been *ordered* cremated *immediately* after the autopsy. State and local government officials, lawyers and a host of friends and minor acquaintances were there. All pews, choir seats and the balcony were filled, the crowd overflowed the foyer and the aisles. In solemn respect for the dead and their grieving family the church was hushed, muted funereal music from an invisible source pervaded the room. Rev. Leonard Dixon eulogized Lyman R. and Charlene Smith, quoting from an old English cleric he intoned, "The death of a good person is like the putting out of a perfumed candle, the light is extinguished but the fragrance remains."

The double murder investigation by the Ventura P.D. intensified. They learned Smith was a prominent figure in county Democratic Party leadership, and very active in many civic organizations. Also Smith had become disastrously entangled in many business ventures. Three partners in a company, G.A.P. Development had approached Smith, they offered to let him buy into their operation. Harboring compulsive ambitions to make money and to profit in a variety of business undertakings the lawyer jumped at their offer. He simply asked, "You want a check?"

Joseph Alsip Jr. was a partner in G.A.P.. The first letter of his name supplied the A, letters G and P were the first letters in the names of the other two partners. G.A.P. Development Co. fell on hard times and the partners split up. Joseph Alsip Jr. was listed as a suspect, however, the police did not supply any information as to a possible motive.

Maverick International Airlines Inc., owned by Smith was formed to fly live cattle to Iran. For this venture he'd borrowed two and a half million dollars from a wealthy rancher, Aubrey Edward Sloan, better known as Bud or Haystack Sloan from his heavyweight boxing days. Despite a fiery temper, Sloan's wife says, "Haystack is a gentle man." The rancher was a good suspect because he had lost his huge investment in the defunct Maverick Airlines. He was forced to put up for sale his eighteen thousand acre spread in Mendocino County used as the collateral for the two and a half million. The immense sixty three year old Haystack said, "I'll fight, but I'd never sneak up on anyone." He expressed, "Deep affection for Lyman Smith," and would say nothing bad about him. But his attorney filed a lawsuit against Smith's estate for five and a half million dollars in general and punitive damages. Smith's oldest daughter was considered as a strong suspect by the police.

Judge Lewis' wife, Clair, described her friend Charlene Smith as a bubbly, popular person. The two women in the past had worked together as secretaries in the Municipal Court. A former Ventura County law officer who'd had a love affair with Charlene was also a prime suspect of the police. But *something* was wrong about all of this. I could feel it. What bothered me most was the suspects, they were all too damn pat. Such surface evidence invariably crops up in preliminary phases of a murder investigation. The detectives soon eliminated Smith's daughter and his wife's former lover as suspects.

Vehemently I was beset by a nagging question, *why* did they have to *kill both of them?* The answer had to be an essential part of a very complex motive for the crime. It wasn't logical that Alsip a partner in G.A.P., or Sloan, would take their grievance with Lyman Smith out on his wife in such a grisly manner. They could easily have set it up to kill him somewhere else and make it appear as an accident with less difficulty and risk. A hard line motive for Charlene's death at the hands of the two remaining suspects was *decidedly* missing. One thing I had discovered long ago, like the seekers of old buried pirate treasures had, if you want to unearth buried secrets you have to dig. I mean dig man...dig.

Smith was desperate for that appointment to the bench. It would be redemption, a salvation from the agonizing, goring horns of his disastrous financial dilemma, he was never a really top notch lawyer and as a businessman his acumen was non-existent. Rashly, Smith decided to put pressure on powerful people. He didn't really intend blackmail, but considering the circumstances he felt they *owed* him. His threats to expose the secret Empire's corrupt operations was to merely assure his speedy appointment to the bench. He knew these people had the power to arrange it with a snap of their fingers and Smith needed that position, right now without delay.

By threatening the Empire, the lawyer had just climaxed his long career of mistakes with one of the most serious blunders of his life, he had failed to accurately gage the enigmatic Empire's reaction to his threat. This time the error in Smith's judgement became fatal, it killed him and his wife. A killer had brought rope and a length of lead pipe, the job was not well planned, the assassin knew that, but it would have to do, the edict of death had been swiftly imposed for it dared not wait, not even a day.

Smith's threat presented an urgency demanding immediate action. Soundless as a shadow, the slayer reached the bedroom, he followed orders: deliver crunching lethal blows to the skulls of the sleeping victims with a pipe, tie their hands and feet with the rope, remove a few valuables and place a fire log on the bed as a decoy. Perhaps it would be mistaken as the deed of a random burglar.

Of the philosophy of *intuitions* and *instincts* I'm not sure, but of my *experience* and *knowledge* of crimes and events happening *far back in the past* and of their evil connections with the present I do know for certain. The bloody gangland style execution of the lawyer and his wife was *tied irrevocably* into the murderous Ventura County Government corruption. There was no mistaking it. Violent death, it was not something new, as a Gunners Mate in the Navy during WW11 it had happened right beside me, death and dismemberment was a thing you sort of expected and could even rationalize during wartime, there was no recourse, apparently it was legal. But bloody murder in civilized society is another matter, it is illegal, there are penalties involved. I remembered when I first became aware of the social distinction.

The lady who told me of Lagomarsino's threat at the White Bib meeting; it was a *connection*. She had called the next day to tell me Editor Judas Gius had been present, and she'd told me something else..."Right after you left here last night Gary, I made a phone call.

I told *someone* what you said about Lane Martin and the bag full of money to pay for that frame-up. They said, 'Don't worry, Martin will never spill his guts in a million years!'"

I asked who she had called but she refused to even say whether it was a man or woman. Two days after that phone call the Star Free Press headlines were big and black, "Lawyer and Wife Murdered!" I tried again, several times, but the lady would never reveal who she had called. But I learned later that she had been going with a judge.

CHAPTER 32

Aug. 1945, my ship sailed from the U.S. Navy Base at Tacloban, Samar Island in the Phillipines. Forty days later we passed through the Canal, then up the Gulf of Mexico to Mobile, Ala.. With thirty days traveling orders I took a train to New Orleans then to Frisco. There a new destroyer was due for a trial run, they needed gunners mates to test fire the main batteries of Five Inch-Thirty Eights. In ten days we pulled into San Pedro Harbor. After four years the war in the South Pacific had ended. With dress blues, white hat squared away and oxfords polished like a mirror, I stood on deck gazing out across the harbor watching proud fighting ships of the U.S. Navy tug listlessly at their anchor chains in calm waters.

The rousing sight of a mighty battle fleet sailing the high seas; expectations and excitement of shore liberty, drinking and carousing in strange far away ports; it was all over. I watched the white hats crowded on the ferry boat pass a hundred yards to the port headed for San Pedro, there'd be one hell of a big time at Shanghai Red's and the rest of the bars on Beacon Street tonight. Salty air off the bay whipped my neckerchief, sudden nostalgia, sad loneliness swept over me. All my possessions, my seabag and hammock were on my shoulder, saluting the ship's flag I went ashore. At the Naval Base, San Pedro, I was handed my honorable discharge as a Petty Officer Second Class.

I got a job in L.A. truck driving, but hell, I figured there must be

Author on deck watch duty - Sidney, Australia about December 1942.

Author on sky-watch duty, Noumea, New Caledonia about October 1942.

Author on left and member of gun crew cleaning gun, Noumea, New Caledonia.

something better around a bit more exciting and some action other than just battling noisy congested traffic. I took the written and oral examination and a physical agility test for the Los Angeles Police Department. February 1946, I started at the Academy. I liked it, the Department had real class, like the Navy. On my first day I arrived early. To get there I turned north from Sunset Boulevard's bustling morning traffic onto a side street into the Griffith Park area only a couple miles west of downtown L.A..

The street wound into a narrow, shady canyon. Suddenly I had a totally unexpected surprise, for an instant I thought I was somehow whisked to a tiny village in Old Mexico, slowing to five miles an hour I drove carefully through Chavez Ravine. Time had stood still here, women in colorful dresses walked along the road with wicker baskets on their heads. Small children playing happily darted among goats, chickens and dogs flocking the dusty, twisting road leading through the village. Chavez Ravine was mercifully hidden and protected from the frantic, raging city of L.A., surging around it only a few blocks distant. I left the tiny village behind as abruptly as I had entered it. The lane grew wider, ascending to the Academy buildings in a small meadow.

The days passed swiftly, filled with engrossing classroom studies and exhausting physical activities conducted by veteran policemen and tough drill instructors, most of them were ex-Marines. I swear they ran us cadets fifty miles a day over steep, rough trails through pine clad hills surrounding the drill grounds. Several hours each day were spent on a pistol range, it came easy, my experience with small arms in the Navy paid off.

For low grades or a lack of physical and mental aptitude a cadet faced an unceremonious expulsion from the Academy. The big day finally came, graduation from the Los Angeles Police Academy was an important event, relatives, friends and dignitaries filled the stands erected on grass at the edge of the drill grounds. Sam Browns and shoes were polished to a sheen, brass buttons and badges sparkled in bright sunlight like precious stones against the back drop of dark blue uniforms.

In cadence we paraded to a stirring military march by the Police Department Band, standing at rigid attention we were inspected, congratulated and reminded of our constant duty and responsibility to the public by Chief of Police, C.B. Horrall. In the locker room we changed clothes and packed our belongings, a sergeant handed each of us an envelope with orders for our new assignment.

It was luck, I was assigned to radio car patrol on morning watch at University Division. The lucky ones laughed at all the groaning as the majority of them found they had been assigned drab duties at City Jail and Pedestrian Intersection Control at smoggy downtown corners. After the ceremonies I drove into Chavez Ravine. I had a strange feeling I wouldn't pass through this quaint, tiny village again unless by some special circumstance.

I braked for the stop sign at Sunset Blvd., from this vantage point the moderate skyline of old Downtown L.A. was a few miles east. I had no thought or realization of the impending population explosion of post war L.A.. It would range from Orange County on the south to Ventura County on the north. Thousands of houses would cover all the beautiful orange and avocado groves, girders of steel creating monstrous skeletons for new banks, office buildings and department stores reached ever upward. Soon they'd violently burst the skyline of L.A..

The shoguns of progress were feverishly drawing plans for every type of new development conceivable or dreamable. County, state, city and federal governments teamed with brazen politicos spawned and profligate from all the easy money of WW11. They were a new breed, fast talking political and professional innovators of cyclopean financial projects they loudly proclaimed as being, "In the name of the public interest."

Soon giant caterpillars would gouge the earth, they would remove the useless tops of these hills. Chavez Ravine would be filled, then leveled with the excess dirt. On the large flat area, Dodger Stadium would be built. A strange monument, a multi-million dollar cement and steel head stone marking the grave of Chavez Ravine.

Three days later at eleven p.m., I reported on duty to Lt. A. J. Smith, Commander of the morning watch at the University Division Police Station. Roll call was at eleven thirty sharp. Lt. Smith with two sergeants read off the latest crime occurrences. I was assigned to radio car district 35, my partner was an old timer, walking toward the patrol car he laconically muttered, "You drive." The officers we relieved stared at Soderquist then me, they grimaced knowingly. I was puzzled, my partner ignored or appeared not to have noticed the by-play.

I was beginning to understand the pairs quasi-comical act. While patrolling streets, dark alleys and answering minor calls my partner constantly loaded his mouth with plug tobacco. Continually lowering and raising his window he spit. Tobacco juice sprayed all over the window of the rear door and ran down the side. Spluttering, "Car 35 to KGPL," was a disaster for the mike and dashboard. I considered maybe grabbing the mike before him, but thought better of it. His last name was Soderquist, it wasn't until the next day I learned his full name, Chew-to-bacca Soderquist.

A week later, the night-life action was slowing down. It was three a.m., our radio crackled, the sleepy voice of the woman dispatcher called out. "Car 35, go to 186 E. 47th Street, check unknown trouble." Soderquist acknowledged, "Car 35, Roger, Kay-Gee-Pee-EL." We were there in a few minutes. Parking the car, putting the keys in my pocket, I *quietly* shut the door in accordance with proper procedure for this type of call.

It was very still, no lights were on in the house, a street lamp in the middle of the block gave feeble help. Soderquist moved up the walk toward the front porch, taking a swift look around I followed. Suddenly halting he flashed his light on the sidewalk. What we saw wasn't just a few drops, it was a solid, unbroken trail of fresh blood. Cautiously we went up the steps to the porch, my light played on a huge black man sitting absolutely motionless in an old wicker chair, our beams froze. Lifeless, bulging eyes stared straight at us.

Buried to the hilt, the haft of a big butcher knife protruded from his chest. There was only a few small drops of blood in front of the chair, it was a startling, chilling sight. I wondered how in hell he had made it to the porch, there couldn't have been a drop of blood left in his body. Soderquist ordered, "Follow that trail of blood and see where it goes. I'll grab the mike and get homicide down here."

The trail went east on 47th, around the corner heading south on Main Street. It led to an all night cafe. A pool of blood was on the sidewalk in front of the door. It looked like he'd fallen down there. Stepping inside it was damn strange, there wasn't a drop of blood on the floor. A dozen customers sat at the counter, no one looked up. It appeared this guy had been stabbed outside and nobody heard or seen a thing. It was possible but I decided to look around anyway. At the rear of the dining room I could see into the kitchen, a cook and dish washer were busily occupied. When I entered the two gave no indication they were aware of my presence.

There seemed to be no evidence of a fight or anything unusual, about to leave something caught my eye, in a far corner the tip of a white towel hung over the edge of a large metal garbage container. It had a moist red stain. Walking over I jerked the cover off, it was chock full of towels, they were soaked with blood and dirt. Someone had used every towel in the joint wiping blood off the floor. Laying the lid on the can easy like, I looked at the two men. The scrawny old wino dish washer became doubly busy with his dirty dishes, but I knew he'd been watching me in the reflection of the grimy window above his sink.

Feigning indifference, the cook continued slicing tomatoes. Red spots spattering the front of his white shirt didn't look like tomato juice to me. A Filipino, he was larger than ordinary for his race. I noticed his powerful square wrists and swift dexterity with the razor edged knife as he laid over the thin slices of tomato. The wooden haft of the knife in his hand was identical to the one I'd just seen protruding from the chest of the dead black man. Under my scrutiny the Filipino's knuckles became white as he tightened his grip on the butcher knife, his sinewy arm tensed. He was a dozen feet away with the cutting table between us, but I had an awful suspicion the cook was capable of hurling that knife like a spear, right to its mark.

My hand moved to the butt of my gun. The cook's eyes flashed around the room, slowly his grip relaxed on the knife, he laid it on the table. Then carefully backing up to the wall he raised his hands. Christ...what a relief, I motioned for him to face the wall. Starting around the table to handcuff him I saw the real reason he'd changed his mind about using the big knife. Soderquist was standing in the doorway, his cocked thirty-eight aimed between the Filipino's eyes. Hands cuffed behind, I led the cook out while Homicide Detectives came hustling in. Not a customer looked up from his soup.

Despite my partner's indelicate chewing habit we got along good. I learned a lot the short time we worked together before he decided he'd retire. It came real sudden. One day he just up and said, "It's time to hang it up, if you stick around more than twenty five years you'll die on the job." The first of the month I switched to the night watch, Robert Forbes was my new partner. On this afternoon we'd wandered into the assembly room a little bit early for the 3:30 night watch roll call.

Behind a large table on an elevated platform in front of the room sat Lt. A. J. Smith, he also had switched to the night watch. The Lt. grabbed us immediately, "Okay you guys, we have an emergency," he thrust a set of car keys and a piece of paper in my hand, "Take this car, go to the address on that paper, pick up Officer Friday's wife and mother and take them as quickly as you can to Georgia Street Receiving Hospital. Friday has been shot, he's not expected to live."

Wheeling the car up to the front of Georgia, I used the mike to inform KGPL of arrival. Forbes helped the trembling women into the foyer where they took an elevator. Forbes would take good care of the ladies. I stayed downstairs to escape the scene of anguish and grief. Loud shouts of "Halt, halt," came from the staircase to the left of the front door, "Halt or I'll shoot," a man came racing down right at me. A detective at the top, gun in hand, shouted for him to halt. I jumped backward out of the line of fire, shots rang out. The body of the fleeing killer crashed to the bottom of the stairs, unmoving in the widening pool of blood just one step from my feet.

Friday was directing traffic at a downtown corner, he approached a car waiting for the signal to change, not knowing it was stolen or that the driver was armed and desperate. Leaping out, the car thief shot Friday at close range, running, he attempted to escape into the crowd but several traffic officers caught him. Detectives brought him to Georgia to see if Friday could identify him. Still conscious, Friday positively identified the gunman, he broke free, crashing down the stairs to his death. Friday's spine was shattered. He'd be paralyzed the rest of his life which could not be for long even with the best of medical help and attention.

I had been *introduced* to social murder and mayhem, a *palpable formula* of modern civilized behavior. I knew this routine of violence and death would never dimish and that intuition and instincts are just things rattling around in your head, but facts, cold hard facts are what you have to go by. And there are no facts to go by until *after* murder and mayhem has been committed. My partner Bob Forbes had no intuition of the tragic violence and murder that at this very moment stalked his family and himself.

We were on patrol, crisply the radio came to life ordering us to return to the station "Code two," that meant fast as we could without using our red light or siren. The sergeant stood in the parking lot waiting, leaning down to the window he said, "Forbes, your brother Colin and his partner have been wounded in a gun fight, he's at the Hollywood Receiving Hospital. Gary, drive Bob there then return." I left Bob at Hollywood Receiving. Returning to University Division I learned the facts of what had happened from the sergeant.

Det. Sgt. Forbes and his partner were hard on the trail of a thief, no ordinary thief, a daring criminal who stole hundreds of thousands of dollars of sophisticated electronic equipment. Colin learned where the equipment was being fenced in Hollywood Division and he was closing in. The burglar armed and dangerous, no novice with guns, got the drop on the detectives. He shot his way out. Colin was hit in the stomach, his partner in the arm. Colin suffered damage to vital organs, he'd live with pain and recurrent hospitalization the rest of his life. Later when captured the burglar-gunman was in possession of so many automatic guns that L.A. reporters called him 'Machine Gun Walker.' At his trial Walker was also found guilty of murdering Loren Roosevelt, a Highway Patrolman who had stopped him for a routine traffic violation.

Outside of his brother's nearly fatal shooting, Robert Forbes and his wife Despine were very happy. She was thrilled over a ceramics shop she'd opened on Wilshire Blvd., Bob helped in the store. One day her ex-husband, Mercouris, walked in and blasted away with an automatic pistol. Forbes and Despine died instantly of multiple gun shot wounds. During his trial for the murders, Mercouris became a wild man, screaming obscenities and threats he flailed out so violent that ordinary restraints were no avail. The judge ordered Mercouris shackled and locked in a special built sound proof cage made out of glass, through a speaker he could hear the proceedings. The gross scene of the wild man locked in glass added weird sensationalism to the deaths of two happy people.

I was no longer amazed at how swiftly your *future* could be over. At my request Lt. Smith reassigned me to a foot beat, Pico Street between Figueroa and Main. It was a rough neighborhood in those days but I felt like walking and thinking. Georgia Receiving was one block west of Figueroa, it got a lot of its business from the honkey tonk bars, cheap hotels and Tomaine Charleys. Olympic Stadium a few blocks south of Pico at 16th and Grand was on my beat, boxing and wrestling events were held two nights a week. A popular fight arena, it thrived with the skillful promotion of Cal Eaton. Many top notch boxers had taken their painful beginners lumps at the Olympic while nothing more than under-nourished kids harboring a burning desire for glory and money. Gangster Mickey Cohen, with his body guards and bail bondsman Abe Phillips was always there keeping a wary eye on his gambling actions. Harry Pregerson a law student, and several buddies exhibiting *due respect* hung close to the dapper Cohen. Anticipating the slightest command of his finger they'd all leap, vying to do his bidding, earning the prestige of his attention.

On my nights off Cal's wife Eileen hired me to work in uniform during fights. I got a real close *look* at Cohen's gambling operation, the set-ups, bettors odds and sometimes even what round the fight would be over. In their dressing rooms sulky fighters were pressured by scared managers, "Damn it man, do what you're told, it they tell you to take a dive in the fifth that's what you do, you ain't got any choice, because if you don't you know damn well what they'll do to you."

Then one day my name was on the transfer list, it was a surprise. I was ordered to report to the Metropolitan Division Headquarters at North Avenue 19, the old Lincoln Heights City Jail. Metro was a plain clothes unit working felony investigations that the uniformed divisions were not prepared to handle, teams could be sent instantly to any area in the city where a serious problem arose. It happened my first week at Metro, a rash of liquor store holdups with owners and clerks being slugged and shot in the process. Six of us were sent to Harbor Division, taking shotguns we staked out in back rooms of San Pedro liquor stores. On the second night we ended the specific problem. The holdup man, bold from a dozen successful jobs in less than a month in which he'd brutally sent people to the hospital and undertakers, made a serious mistake.

On my order, loud and clear, "Police Officer, drop your gun and raise your hands," the robber whirled, his pistol aimed ready to fire. He was blown clear through the store's plate glass window and his girlfriend, driver of the get-away car, ended up with a stretch in the State Pen.

This night things were calm. Sgt. Nichols said, "No use in you two hanging around headquarters just waiting for a crime to happen, go down to Old China Town and stir something up." We knew Nichol's thought he was being funny, he knew damned well two plain clothes paddy-guys wandering round China Town would stick out like sore thumbs. He was right, all we got were titters, snickers and sly looks. An old timer, Sgt. Nichol's understood these people well. His wife was a pretty, charming Chinese lady, also the daughter of a wealthy, respected merchant. Organized gambling down here was rife, but it was heavily worked by the Administrative Vice Detail.

It was drug traffic that intrigued me, we knew stupendous deals in narcotics were being transacted here in China Town. But how in hell could you get a lead into such furtive, silent dealings. Federal Bureau of Narcotics had sent their top Chinese agents out from New York City, but even they could not infiltrate or make a dent in the organization. Plain as the nose on our face we'd never stir anything up wandering around China Town on foot. After several nights we decided to try something different, at the police impound garage on Temple Street we grabbed a nondescript car, one that looked like everything else but a police vehicle.

Donning black leather jackets we simply parked at the curb and watched people. If you just sit long enough you'll spot some mighty strange things, pick pockets, derelicts scrounging for cigar butts in the gutter, a hustler throwing a pitch on a tourist. Across the street surreptitious lovers walked toward a parking lot, nervously glancing around they jumped in a car, then my entertainment was cut off by a big limousine pulling up along the curb, probably rich tourists. Idly watching I suddenly was interested, a pair of Mickey Cohen's goon boys had gotten out of the Limo, looking around to see everything was alright the hood on the sidewalk opened the door, the dapper gangster stepped out. I jabbed my partner, "Hey, take a gander at this, maybe things are going to get exciting after all."

"Yeah...maybe we'll find out Cohen has a yen for Chinese food."

"Well, have we got something better to do?" Mickey and his bodyguards entered the Pink Pagoda, China Town's most popular tourist restaurant. Leaving our car we sauntered across the street, the local people went about their business, they no longer showed any interest in us. Mingling with the throng of tourists we wanderd into a patio area, through a window we saw Cohen and his men sitting on stools at the counter. It was very strange, why would he do that instead of commanding plush booths where he could hold court putting on his usual Napoleon Bonaparte act?

Something was going down, Cohen hadn't come all the way from Beverly Hills to China Town *just* for a bowl of noodle soup. Melting in with tourists around a wishing well we tossed pennies into the well and kept an eye on the Mick. The handsome young Chinaman taking Cohen's order wore a spotless, white tailored shirt. During their conversation a man in a bright plaid sport coat and blue slacks approached. At a barely perceptible nod by the gangster the hood on his left moved over. The man took the vacated seat.

For several minutes the gangster, Plaid-coat and the waiter talked guardedly. It couldn't have been about food, Cohen and the man in plaid headed for the door closely followed by the two goons. I said, "We've stirred ourselves up something and it sure as hell ain't noodle soup, let's go."

Firing up our junker I whipped a fast U-turn in the middle of the street. The big black limo glided away from the curb, it was easy to stay with. Traffic was light but the Cad's driver meticulously obeyed traffic rules. Heading south to Manchester they hooked a left east, hitting Atlantic Blvd. they made a right, several blocks further they pulled up and parked in front of the South Gate Arena. The ticket taker, an old geezer in a seedy blue uniform, nervously saluted the group as they brushed past him.

Dashing to a window we got tickets, we weren't about to flash our LAPD badges in South Gate. Cohen was heading ringside, the main event was being announced. Abe Phillips, Mickey's bail bondsman, and Harry Pregerson holding down several empty seats in the front row, leaped to their feet at Cohen's arrival. Plaid-coat sat at his left and Pregerson on the right. The tag team of wrestlers began beating hell out of each other, the crowd roared. Deep in a discussion the three men showed no interest in the bloody battle.

Harry and Abe took off heading to the far side of the ring, Cohen and Plaid-coat moved up the aisle toward us. I handed my partner the car keys, "Go to the car and be ready to roll when I get there. I'm going to follow Pregerson and Phillips." Ducking out a side exit I went around to the parking lot. In a far corner I saw them meet with two men, they were big, like wrestlers. Only a few words were said then the two drove away in separate cars but not before I got the license numbers.

With motor running my partner urged, "Hurry up, Cohen's Cad is out of sight." Figuring Cohen would take Plaid-coat back where he met him we headed to China Town fast as we could, we didn't want to lose them, the way Cohen was treating this guy he must be damn important.

At China Town we saw the Cad parked at the curb ahead of us. On the sidewalk Plaid-coat was bent over talking to Cohen through the window, he took off walking toward the parking lot and the Cad began rolling. Bailing out I said, "Wait here, I'll follow the stranger." Not spooky, he went to a car in the lot and drove away, I wrote his license on my palm hoping it wasn't another Hertz rent-a-car with a phoney ID. By now we were convinced we'd hit on something big.

L.A. City Hall was a few blocks away. Criminal Records and the Warrant section were on the first floor. It was eleven thirty. At this time of night the place was humming, we found a desk with a phone not in use. DMV records revealed the cars at the Arena parking lot were registered to Nathan Turkebtahn and Sidney Bocarsky, the car driven by Plaid-coat was listed to Abraham Davidian. We decided we better talk with Sgt. Nichols before heading home, but we knew he wouldn't be at Lincoln Heights this late.

"Let's go over to Tang's," I suggested, "That's where we'll probably find him." Tang's, a Chinese bar and restaurant was several blocks from City Hall, the shadowy street with railroad tracks running in front attracted few tourists from nearby Union Depot, but inside, a noisy cocktail bar and crowded dining room belied its unfavorable exterior. The favorite haunt of the City Hall crowd, you never knew who you were sitting next to, it could be the Mayor's wife, or maybe his preferred secretary. The Oriental atmosphere was real, the place was a dead ringer for Singapore Charlie's joint in Manila.

Edging our way through a crush of drinkers four deep at the bar we spied Sgt. Nichols in a booth on the far side of the room, he was with Captains Donahoo and Chitwood, Commanders of Homicide and Narcotics Divisions. Catching the Sgt.'s eye, I hoped he would leave the table, instead he motioned for us to come over. "Sarge, we hate to bother you when you are busy but we'd like to talk with you a minute."

"Sure," he started to get up, Donahoo raised a huge hand.

"It's alright Nichols, you men sit down, let's hear what you've got to say." We remained standing, my partner indicated that he'd just as soon I did all the talking. Toying with his cigar, Capt. Chitwood sat back silent, Donahoo stared. Continuing with the story it didn't seem the Captains thought near as much of our *big deal* as we did. I began to feel like jumping ship, I could read their thoughts--'hell, Cohen was just picking up China Town gambling money and doing some book down at the Arena.'

I was beginning to maybe vision it the same way except---I knew Cohen *hated* wrestling---he'd never bet money on them in a million years. I hurried to get it over, we were wishing we were somewhere else. Rattling off the names of the men at the Arena parking lot I watched the Captains faces, apparently the names meant nothing. Edging away I said, "Oh yes Sarge, that guy Cohen dropped off in China Town was named Davidian." That got a response, Chitwood damned near bit his cigar in half springing to life.

"Abe Davidian! He's the biggest heroin dealer in the San Joaquin Valley. We've never been able to connect him with Mickey in any way. Damn, they must be working up something big alright. Nichols, your men did a hell of a job tonight."

The Sgt. grinned, he said, "You fellas wait for me outside, I'll be right with you."

Out on the street the fresh air was a life saver. Shortly Nichols appeared. "Capt. Chitwood is like ecstatic over what you guys came up with tonight. He's long suspicioned Cohen is just as involved in drugs as he is with gambling. This is the first possible break through he's ever got, he wants us to beat it down to the Pink Pagoda to see if I recognize the Chinese waiter Cohen and Davidian were talking to. I know most of them in China Town by sight."

Standing near the wishing well we again looked in the window of the restaurant. "That's him Sarge, the sharpy looking guy waiting on those two ladies."

He emitted a low whistle whispering, "Benny---Benny Wong, well what ya' know about that, he's young but one of the best smugglers in the country. Wait till Chitwood hears this. It's late, you guys go home, don't spread this around. Chitwood's Narco Dicks will take it over. But I'll tell you one thing, the Captain won't forget the work you've done on this."

It took months but LAPD Detectives and Federal Narcotic agents working in conjunction on the case finally nailed Davidian heading north to San Joaquin Valley with millions worth of narcotics. In a wild, shot punctuated car chase up Highway 99, Davidian was finally trapped and arrested near the Grapevine just past Gorman. Having no stomach for a long stretch in the pen he would cooperate. For certain guarantees against prosecution he was going to spill his guts.

Davidian was slated to be the star witness in a fantastic expose of the evil but extremely lucrative drug traffic. His testimony would be more than sufficient to incinerate the organization, not only gangster Mickey Cohen, but rich, powerful people in high mighty government positions would take a great fall. Davidian realized only too well the dangers of what he was about to do. The organization's penalty for a squealer was death. The Federal agents promised him protection. Not even the LAPD Detectives knew where he was stashed. Only a few top Feds and a handful of their Narco Agents assigned to guard him held this secret knowledge.

It was bright daylight in the quiet residential district in Fresno, California. Agents guarding the squealer *decided* since he was taking a peaceful afternoon nap it'd be okay to stroll to a nearby grocery store. Returning, they discovered someone had entered the house, gone *right* to the bedroom where Davidian was peacefully napping and blasted the star witness to his reward, in that *instant* the entire case was blown, right along with Davidian.

After a year at Metro I transferred back to University Division, it came about the time of the Elizabeth Short killing, reporters labeled it the "Black Dahlia Murder." A known Hollywood hooker, the body was found in Leimert Park district. My car was the second to arrive. It was a shocking sight, lying in a patch of weeds in a vacant lot the body was cut in half at the waist, completely drained of blood before being dumped, weird mutilations had been perpetrated on the body. A tattoo on her thigh was cut out like plugging a ripe watermelon and shoved into her privates which had been plucked of every hair, apparently using a pair of tweezers.

Homicide Captain Donahoo took command, nearly every man in University was put on overtime. Motels, apartment houses, hotels and businesses were searched in all out effort to find a clue to the location where the killing occurred. Donahoo had a suspect but not a shred of physical evidence backing it. After many days of intense search of buildings, laundry rooms, basement furnaces, knocking on doors and canvassing neighborhoods for leads nothing ever turned up. None of the victims clothing, jewelry or personal belongings nor bloody rags, bloodstains or knives were ever found. Capt. Donahoo was forced to release his suspect.

Back on night watch I was assigned my old foot beat again, Pico Street and the Olympic Stadium. I liked walking a beat, there was time to cogitate and quietly stand about once in awhile just taking in what was going on around you. About eleven, a jumping Friday night on Pico and Figueroa, I'd solved several beef's between jealous women and half gowed-up boyfriends. During one I got slugged in the ribs with a ten pound handbag wielded by a spindly little Oakie broad screaming I was taking sides with her boyfriend. Sam's Pawn Shop was dark, iron grates spread across the windows were locked. From the shadows of the doorway I had a good view of the street.

At the corner of Fig, the Four Aces bar loaded with cowboys was going full blast, doors wide open, a western band banging away could be heard a country mile. Across Pico at the Continental Bar and at Moran's they were coming and going, east of Moran's was a used car lot, something moved in the dark at the rear. Slipping across the street I weaved among the cars, suddenly I saw the car thief doing a hot-wire job, starting the motor he was ready to go.

In those days it was a *serious* crime, after the war cars were as hard to come by as gold bricks and twice the price. I knew he could have a knife or gun. The beam from my flashlight struck him in the eyes, he froze as I ordered, "Police Officer, stand fast or I'll shoot. Get out of the car, nice and easy. Now put your hands behind you." I snapped the cuffs on his left wrist.

He whined, "Don't do this to me, please, I just got outta' State Pen, I did three friggin' years, I can't stand going back. When I got caught stealing my first car I pleaded with the judge to let me join the Navy. I wanted to fight for my country but instead he sent me to the joint." I became careless, he whirled swinging the loose handcuff a hell of a crack to my ribs. Lord, same place that crazy broad hit me. Gasping for breath I watched the thief leap on a hood and to the top of an eight foot block wall, separating the car lot from the L.A. streetcar repair barns. Struggling to the top of the wall I saw him. Thirty feet away he raced down an aisle between two rows of big yellow streetcars parked over repair pits.

I couldn't miss, I'd done a lot of practicing at the range lately. A group of the guys had gotten to shooting cigarettes from each others mouths until Capt. Hayes heard about it. I yelled, warning, "Halt or I'll shoot." It would be just like shooting down a tunnel, the aisle was six feet wide, running right down the middle he wouldn't stop. The s.o.b was getting away with my cuffs, taking dead aim, squeezing the trigger soft and easy I could blow his head off. Hell, for just a lousy pair of handcuffs, a split second before firing I pulled a hair to the right. A dozen windows in one of the streetcars disintergrated with a crash, mechanics and clean-up crews dove head first into the pits. Lowering my gun I watched my handcuffs fly around the corner.

Several patrol cars arrived, we searched an hour but the thief had made his escape. I took a hell of a ribbing over it, one thing you just don't do is let some punk run off with your cuffs. A partner, Andy Drobatz, vactioning in Maine read the story in a local paper clear back there. Mailing a load of them back to Chick Macy, he pasted them all over the station house.

While I was at Metro Div. nothing had changed at the Olympic, Cohen and his entourage' regularly made their appearances. Taking down car licenses and asking an innocuous question here and there I *kept tabs* on strange faces Cohen made contact with.

Late 1948 I transferred to Hollywood Div. nearer to Tarzana in the San Fernando Valley where I'd moved. Staying on night watch I was assigned to a foot beat at Hollywood and Vine. Tinseltown had begun losing its glitter and glamour, occasionally you saw a genuine star stroll the boulevard or shop in the elite, but fading Broadway Department Store. Across from the Broadway on Vine the famous Brown Derby Restaurant was living in past glory along with Mike Lyman's. One by one the finer stores on Hollywood Boulevard were leaving. Ritzy Pig and Whistle next to the Egyptian Theatre where for years stars, producers and executives crammed down delicious banana splits and sodas, was looking down right shabby. The movie houses had turned to showing third rate horror films and pornos. With the evident perversion of the old time reverential awe for the

Hollywood scene, pimps, pillheads and fairies strolled the Boulevard with a new sense of proprietorship.

Forking up a fifteen dollar fine and ten for a shyster fee, hookers were out of jail faster than you could throw them in. Hell, what did whores care, they could make ten times that in one nights work. The enchantment of the Boulevard faded, soon there'd be no distinction between the slovenly disrepute of Pico and Main Street. Hollywood Vice working with State and Federal Narco agents were having field days chasing Scott Brady, Lawrence Tierney and Robert Mitchum around Hollywood's hills. Mitchum got his first real break, millions of dollars of free publicity made him a super star when they busted him amid cavortions at a wild pot and needle party in a hideout in Laurel Canyon. Bob Mitchum had no inkling how famous this *bust* would make him. Flowing crocodile tears when booked at Hollywood Station he moaned, "Christ, you guys are blasting my career. Have mercy, can't you give me a break. My God, I'm a budding star."

My beat included great places, celebrated Hollywood Palladium, Earl Carroll's Night Club, also CBS Television Studio's on Sunset Boulevard. But the most intriguing action was at Hollywood Legion Stadium on boxing night. A half block off Hollywood, between Vine and Gower, the Legion attracted lively, enthusiastic crowds from the movie world. Carnivorous starlets clawed and fought on their way to recognition and stardom in Tinseltown, they would do anything just to be seen at ringside with a Hollywood man about town.

With full retinue in attendance, gangster Mickey Cohen displayed his more expansive ringside manner at the classier Legion Stadium, extending a cosmopolitan galantry to the young starlets with their shimmering gowns split down the front to the navel. It was all very interesting. I *kept tabs* on Mickey and his Hollywood contacts same as I'd done at the Olympic.

Up on Franklin Ave. just off Vine, I'd spotted a Fancy Dan pimp operating a pad in a nice apartment house. In a new black Cad with white convertible top he'd park at the apartment around eight every night. Escorting his gorgeous little money-maker to her work-room he'd sit in the Cad playing the radio and counting her Johns while she slaved. Retrieving his hooker and her cash flow about midnight they would drive out Sunset Strip hitting a few bright spots before adjourning to their palatial pad above the Strip. This quiet night I watched a long haired but well dressed character stop at the Cad. After a short chat the pimp got out. Looking around the two walked to a dark spot, a deal of some kind was going down. They didn't see me until I grabbed the pimps arm, the bag of 'roaches' slipped from his limp fingers. Frightened, 'Long Hair' thrust his money back into his pocket. It was no big deal, tapping my baton on the hairy jerks chest I growled, "What are you hanging around for?" He left like a flash. After a closer look at the pimp I recognized him, he'd been a base viol player with a big time band. "What did you do, give up the music bit?"

He was jumpier than a mountain goat, "Huh, oh that, yeh, I gave it up. I have other things going now."

"Yeh, I can see that," looking down I said, "You've dropped your cigarettes."

He refused to look, "Oh no, they're not mine."

"You got more of them over in the Cad?"

"No, no, I don't mess with anything."

I picked up the plastic bag, "Let's go over to the car. You know if I call the Feds and they find any junk in your nice new Caddy...you know what they're gonna' do?"

"Oh my God, they'll confiscate it, my wife will just kill me."

"Is that your wife up in the pad?"

He was startled, "You know about her?"

I nodded, "All about her."

"Well, we're not actually married."

This guy knew his way around Hollywood, he'd be a good source of info if I worked it right. Grabbing his left wrist I pushed up his sleeve. He squirmed like a snake. "God damn it, hold still." I was in luck, fresh punctures in the crook of his elbow were oozing. "Okay, let's take a walk to the Gamewell."

"Where?"

"To the call box, I'm gonna' run you're ass in for marks and being under the influence."

"Oh my God, please, I got it from a rose bush, I was helping my mother trim some roses..."

"Oh horse shit."

"You got to listen, it's true." I pulled my handcuffs out. Shaking like a leaf he pleaded, "What do you want?" Please, I can tell you a lot of things."

"Do you know something worth my while? Something a lot better than what I've got on you right now?"

"Sure, sure."

"Well, hurry up, let's hear it."

"How about a couple guys stealing expensive cars and switching parts and repainting them? These guys are making nothin' but gobs of dough."

"Is that how you got this new Cadillac?" He looked like he was fainting.

"Oh my God no, I bought it straight from the dealer. I make my payments to General Motors Finance Co. every month."

"Alright, be calm, lets have some more dope on the car thieves." The pimp came up with the names of two ex-cons and a warehouse where the mechanic work and painting was being done.

"These guys are pros, they don't even steal the cars until they've got a buyer first."

"Okay, I'll give you a chance, if you are lying you know what I'm going to do to you."

"I'm not lying, I'm not lying."

"I'll see you later, " I walked off. Next afternoon before roll call began I went upstairs to the Dick's Bureau. I found Colin, "Sarge, I think I might have something good for you."

He retaliated with his dour look, "That's what I need, something good." I mentioned stolen expensive cars, Forbes jumped up, "Hold on a second," he waved his partner Sgt. Floyd Hubka to come over. Forbes groaned, "The last few months we've been going crazy with Mercedez Benz' and Porche's and fifty thousand dollar stolen autos. We haven't recovered a single one, the Captain is raising holy hell."

Hubka interrupted, "Go ahead Gary, we'll listen to anything."

"I have this guy who's coming up with a little info, I don't know how good it is but here are the names of two ex-cons and a location where they're changing the identities of expensive stolen cars."

Floyd said, "We will sure look into it." Back at roll call I felt a nagging. If that damned hype-pimp has handed me a line of his bull making a fool of me, I'm gonna' run his ass clear to hell and back.

A few days later Forbes called me to the Dick's Bureau. "Say, by golly, I've got to hand it to you, your man gave you some real good dope. We busted one of the biggest stolen car rings ever. Floyd will be at that warehouse cataloging automobile parts for a week. With the records we found we've recovered nearly a million bucks worth of cars."

"Great, I'm glad it panned out so good."

"About your informant, how about letting Floyd and me talk with him?"

"No can do Colin, sorry, he swears if I put his name out he will never turn another thing." Pimps and junk peddlers were about the best source of info there was, they knew everything that went on in town. I never pushed the Fancy Dan too hard but over the years he came up with great information.

My beat had been quiet. My own car was parked nearby. Calling the station from a box at Hollywood and Vine I signed off for the night. New freeway construction over Cahuenga Pass had messed up traffic. It was easier going over Laurel Canyon since moving to the valley. A few blocks west on Hollywood I turned up the canyon, nary a car this time of night. Then halfway up Laurel headlights flashed as a vehicle rounding sharp curves came down the grade. Slowing to less than fifteen miles I met it at a hairpin turn. The blue sedan was broadside in my bright headlights, faces of the occupants were lit up like actors on a movie set. Two Cohen hoods, Eli Lubin and Happy Meltzer were in front, I got a good look at the man in back. It didn't make sense, it was Jack Baumgartner, a Dep. Sheriff from Lennox and Gardena area. It was one a.m. when I got home, that afternoon in the paper, splashed across the front page was Sammy Rummel, a L.A. lawyer, shotgunned in his Laurel Canyon driveway during early a.m. hours. Eagerly I read, police believed it to be a Mafia killing. Underworld information had it that Rummel was muscling in on the gambling in Gardena.

I'll be, I'd wondered about Cohen's hoodlums being up in Laurel Canyon that morning, it was the only car I'd seen. Going down on the Valley side I could see for miles, there wasn't a thing moving. I made it early for roll call. Colin was busy at his desk, he said, "Grab a seat."

"What's with Rummel's killing?"

Forbes looked up, "Donahoo called me early this morning, Capt. Hamilton, Intelligence Commander, has Donahoo convinced it's a Mafia rub-out, another 'Bugsy Seigel' deal. They want all the info Hollywood Detectives can come up with."

"Okay, maybe I have something for you." Colin nodded, he drank from a beat-up brown stained coffee mug. I wondered, why did he continue to down that terrible black crap the trustees brewed in a huge pot down in the kitchen, after the doctors removed the lead from his belly along with his spleen and several yards of guts, they had ordered, "No more coffee and cigarettes." I told him what I had seen last night. Colin's eyebrows arched, he gave a whistle.

"Kee-rist, almost more luck than I can stand, I don't even want to put this over the phone. I'm on my way downtown right now to see Donahoo," he paused at the door, placing a hand on my shoulder he said, "For God's sake *do not* mention this to anybody, come see me here tomorrow afternoon."

The uniformed cops had lots of confidence in Det. Headquarter's ability. I was sure Donahoo and Hamilton would wrap this up quick. They would pick up Cohen and his hoods and get to the truth in jig time. Next afternoon I found Colin, he stared blankly out a window down at Wilcox Ave. Impatiently I pressed him, "Well, how about it, what's the latest poop?"

Forbes turned, he looked crestfallen, "Hell, I don't know what's going on downtown."

"What's that supposed to mean...you don't know what's going on?"

Forbes grunted, "It seems Hamilton is convinced for some reason it's a Mafia killing. He won't hear of anything else, he has Donahoo buffaloed."

"Mafia job my ass, Jesus, Colin those were Mickey Cohen's hoods up in Laurel Canyon. Lubin and Meltzer are *Jews*, they sure as hell ain't *Sicilians* and neither was the guy in the back seat."

"I know, I know."

"Well, what about it?"

"Hamilton says you probably were mistaken, you couldn't have got a good look at them in the dark."

A few weeks later Forbes hailed me on the steps of the station. "Hey Gary, about the Sammy Rummel hit. It appears Headquarter's is stymied on their big *Mafia* investigation." Colin's faint smile faded, he said, "I'll tell you something in confidence, you have to keep your mouth shut."

"Okay, whatever you say."

"I traced the shotgun used on Rummel, last time *anyone* ever saw it, it was locked up in a Sheriff Department Property Room with a tag on it *marked*, 'unable to locate owner.'" I understood the shrug of finality as Colin walked into the station.

During the years at Holywood Div. I developed a lot of valuable contacts and reliable informers. There's a big difference between a contact and an informant. On the street I heard rumbles about some real tough guys. Hoodlums known as, the 'Two Tonys,' were slapping hookers around, stealing their hard earned money. They'd knocked over a couple of gambling operations including Hymie's book. One night several months after Rummel's murder, the 'Two Tonys,' Tony Brancato and Tony Trombino were blasted into a bloody mess while they sat in a parked car on Ogden Dr. just north of Hollywood Blvd..

Their killers in the back seat suddenly opened fire, they pumped

On motor patrol - the author on the right and his partner

bullets into the 'Two Tonys' who were caught off guard in the front. Photos of the bullet riddled gangsters slumped in a bloody car were hot front page stuff. Hamilton picked up every Italian in Hollywood. Jimmy 'The Weasel' Fratianno was his favorite suspect, but in a few days he was forced to release him for lack of evidence.

The Orange Julius stand on Hollywood was one of my favorites, the coffee was hot and strong. Across the street by Musso-Franks Restaurant I watched the sharp looking sports car whip to the curb. A nattily dressed young driver ejected from a red Porche, sauntering over he said, "I've been looking for you along the Boulevard."

"How about a cup of coffee?"

"Naw, I'll have a fresh orange drink." In the past I'd done him a few small favors, we'd become friendly. A good looking, intelligent Sicilian stud he loved playing the Hollywood scene. Street wise, he had deep connections in the underworld, but he also had legitimate things going and stayed pretty clean.

I asked, "Something on your mind?" It was quite obvious he was stirred up about something.

"Ah, it's all these crazy damn newspapers with all the Mafia shit they're throwin' on the front page. Those God damn reporters don't know their ass from a hole in the ground, selling a lousy paper is all they care about." He was really steamed up, I just let him blow.

"That damn Capt. Hamilton is screwin' around with the 'Weasel,' doesn't he know that simple minded, lyin' son-of-a-bitch Fratianno hasn't the guts to point a gun at a mouse? He's just a two bit loud mouthed scammer and thief, the stupid kind of bastard that gives us Sicilians a bad name, he ain't even a Sicilian, he's 'Napolitan."

"Are you talking about the 'Two Tonys' deal?"

"Yeh, hell, Italians never had anything to do with that job. Those 'Two Tonys' were a pair of idiots, they thought they were so mean everybody was scared to death of them. They knocked over Cohen's gambling and bookmaking operations, slapped his whores around til they were scared so bad they couldn't even work. Hell, that's what got 'em blown-up, they were always poppin' off about how the Jews were scared shitless of them. Shit, it was two of Cohen's Jew hoods that blasted the morons. It's all wrong, I can't figure why Hamilton is making so much noise with all his Mafia crap, but I can tell you Cohen has connections that reach right to the top, not only LAPD, I mean the D.A., judges and newspapers."

"Why are you so certain it was not Italians?"

"Shit, there's no Italians in Hollywood with enough guts to do it, besides, they had no reason, the 'Two Tonys' weren't bothering any of them."

"Well, why don't you tell the Dicks?"

"Oh no, don't get me involved with them, they'll ask millions of questions about me."

"You got anything more substantial to go on besides what you've told me?"

"Sure, I heard two of Cohen's hoods talk about it the other night at the Melodie Room on the Strip. That's why I wanted to see you. These two pineapples bragged about how smooth it came off. From what was said they didn't do the shootin,' it was their job to lose the guns where they'd never be found."

"Did they say where they ditched them?"

The Siciian nodded, "Yeh, I know exactly where those irons are. Next day after the bump these two guys went out on a fishing boat off the Santa Monica Pier, they dumped them in about two miles of water."

"That's great."

"You said it, they did it good. But Cohen's got a whole cache of rifles, shotguns and pistols. After one is used to bump somebody off they drop it in the ocean, he has *connections* where he can replace it with any kind of gun he wants. They joked about how mad Cohen was a while back. According to them the boss jumped up and down flipping his lid like a wild man because one of his hoods panicked and left a shotgun at the scene of a killing."

"Did they say any more about this shotgun job?"

"No, I was in the next booth, when some broads showed up they changed the subject."

"It sounds like good info. I'll see it gets to the Dicks tomorrow."

Colin agreed, "Sure, I believe it. Cohen's behind the murders, but getting Hamilton to admit it is something else. He's real tight with the Attorney General in Sacramento, the politicians *like* this 'Mafia' propaganda. It gets them a hell of a lot of front page publicity."

"Well, if you think you'll be wasting your time don't bother telling Hamilton."

"Oh no, I'll give it to him. That way he can't ever say he was not told."

CHAPTER 33

In late 1954 I made the decision to leave L.A. and move about sixty miles north of Hollywood to Ventura. Scenic, the small town laid between rolling hills and the white capped Pacific Ocean. As a Det. Sgt. with the Ventura P.D., I worked everything from murder and rape to petty theft and mopery. Ventura Sheriff Headquarter's was just a few blocks away in the old County Courthouse.

Oxnard, a city several miles south across the Santa Clara River, was about Ventura's size. Working with Det. Sgt. Ed Patton, Oxnard P.D., and Sheriff Dept., Det. Sgt. Doug Paxton, we combined efforts and information. We knew just about everything moving in Ventura County. Narcotics weren't strictly an L.A. and Hollywood problem. We soon *pinpointed* the Oxnard area as a main distribution point of drug traffic on the entire west coast.

Ben Nordman's and Judge Jerome Berenson's law office was in Oxnard. Nordman was the Federal Commissioner and all Federal violators were arraigned and bail was set by Nordman. Around this time I got a *startling* surprise, Cohen's bail bondsman Abe Phillips was in real *tight* with Nordman and Berenson, they were conducting a brisk business bailing out prisoners. I asked Patton, "How long has this guy Phillips been operating up here?"

"Ever since Ben Nordman became Federal Commissioner, hell, Phillips and Nordman know *more* about the drug business than you and I'll probably ever know."

For some time before I came to Ventura, Capt. Robert King had been keeping his eye on Abe Phillips. He'd become suspicious after spotting Mickey Cohen and his hoods hanging around a night club Phillips had opened in town. King expressed concern about Cohen, "It worries me to beat hell about them being up here, I am certain they're expanding organized crime into Ventura County."

"You can bet your life they are Captain, they didn't send Phillips up here for nothing. Even with the military bases there isn't enough action around here for them to monkey with gambling and women. Abe wouldn't make any money bailing out whores. Its *narcotics,* and he's got *something* going real strong with Commissioner Nordman and Judge Berenson."

"Narcotics...that makes sense."

The following months we made a lot of small drug busts. Twisting small-time junkies we came up with some good informants, however these things took time, lots of time and work. We'd begun to put a few things together but it was frustrating as hell when we knew real heavy stuff was moving into the county. Covert routes of entry and distribution were *tightly* controlled by their organization, they were eluding us.

In the summer of 1958, I returned to L.A. as an Investigator with the D. A. Intelligence Section. Frank and I became partners. Years back we'd run across each other when I worked Metro. At that time Frank was operating undercover, the hoods called him 'The Polack.' He'd worked his way into the confidence of a top hood. Before his cover was accidently blown he'd developed contacts and expansive knowledge of underworld workings.

On one point Frank and I were in *strong accord,* the 'Big' money was in narcotics, illicit drugs and its related crimes were destroying the country. It was getting a lot worse fast, and harboring no false notions, we knew the drug traffic would *never* be dented until some real, high-powered people *behind* the scene were unmasked. In the following months we kept plenty busy. Ranging the county of L.A., working day and night, we busted a massive prostitution ring with headquarters in Alhambra. Under the guise of a physical therapist group they operated a flourishing business state wide.

Virgil Crabtree, head of the IRS Intelligence Unit and several of his agents were with us when we busted the therapist headquarters. Virgil's bureau coordinated simultaneous raids throughout the state. While still on the prostitution case, the wife of a socially prominent doctor was murdered. There were strange circumstances, a physical therapy gal who'd slipped us inside info on the hooker ring gave us a tip. Doc Finch and his secretary, Carol Tregoff were overwhelmed by love. Our source knew Carol when they worked as receptionists for other doctors. We located a tryst apartment in Alhambra where Doc and Carol had been having enthusiastic sessions at noon time. These were so successful they soon expanded from lunch to dinner, thence to weekends.

It wasn't only love, ambitious and avaricious Carol dearly coveted Mrs. Finch's social status and graceful way of life. Fueling and firing their motives the two lovebirds worked *diligently* to get themselves convicted of rubbing out the Doc's obsolete wife. Crime refused to rest.

At Rondelli's Italian restaurant on Ventura Blvd. in Studio City, Jack Whalen, 'The Enforcer,' got his brains blown out, right in the middle of the dining room during Pasta time. Everybody heard the shots, but, no one saw a thing. At that precise moment forty people were totally busy trying to keep their spaghetti on their fork.

'The Enforcer' was a real mean one, Frank and I called him by the name he liked best, 'Jack O'Hara.' He was the most formidable, feared man in Hollywood. For a percentage, O'Hara collected bad gambling debts, it was done simply by reputation. To collect a debt owed a bookie, Jack merely made a phone call to the unfortunate loser. "This is O'Hara, meet me at the Plymouth House tonight with those five big ones you owe Hymie's book, be there at nine."

After an ultimatum one of several things occurred, a smart debtor met O'Hara at the appointed time with five grand, thus preserving his teeth and credit rating with the book. There was no pardon, the deadbeat who did *not* show up at the appointed time but paid later would still suffer a broken arm or leg. O'Hara's reasoning was that this instilled not only honesty but promptness among his clients. But, a guy who took a powder, and Jack had to waste his valuable time looking for him, well, everyone in town knew that even after months in a hospital necessitating various orthopedic surgeries, the foolish bastard would still need a cane for the rest of his life.

We were in Hollywood, it was late but there was time for coffee before the bars closed. Frank said, "Let's hit the Formosa before we go home." I made a right off La Cienega and west on Santa Monica Blvd. The place was about half full, walking to the rear I saw Cohen in a booth with two goons, he nodded at us, the hoods were Italians in their late twenties, I'd never seen them before. With felt hats and heavy overcoats they glared war-like at everyone. Grabbing a booth we waited for coffee. "Frank, I wonder where in hell did that pair come from?"

"I heard Mickey imported a couple of tough guys from New York City to beef up his bodyguards, that must be them."

Peering over the cup, my eyes focused on O'Hara shouldering his way through the front door. His eyes were locked on Cohen. "Holy Jesus, I have a horrible suspicion all hell is about to bust loose."

"Yehhh," Frank agreed as he watched.

O'Hara aimed his huge finger growling, "Mickey how 'bout that God damned money you said you were gonna' bring me?" Cohen's eyeballs rolled in his head, lips flopped, no sound came out.

The bodyguards rose, calmly one said, "Mr. Cohen's busy, *do not disturb him.*"

Jack never took his eyes from Cohen, "Mickey, you're a welshing bastard, you owe seven big ones."

In a menacing Bronx accent the hood hissed, "I told you, do not disturb Mr. Cohen."

Frank snickered, "Lordy, this is going to be pitiful." Jack hit the mouthy one full in the chest, I was convinced he could blast harder than Marciano. I heard his ribs cave and cracking twenty feet away. The hood became a missile, flying backwards clear to the entrance before crashing to the floor, groaning something terrible he crawled out the door on hands and knees. Grasping the second bodyguard's overcoat in a grip like a deadly vice Jack O'Hara held him helpless. Crunching blows made jelly of the hoodlum, he kept screaming, "My God man, I'm Mafia...I'm Mafia...from the east...Christ, don't you know Mafia?" He shrieked, "Please, my God, *whatsa' matta'* you, you crazy?" Barely blubbering when 'The Enforcer' smashed his face with a sledge-hammer fist the hoodlum slid to the carpet.

Warmed up, Jack headed for a mortally terrified Cohen crouching in the booth. A man of few words, O'Hara had said all he intended to say to Cohen. The gangster chief was torn loose from the booth like a giant sea turtle brutally ripped from its protective shell, and was being bashed off a wall like a basketball when O'Hara suddenly tiring of the one sided game crashed a fist into Mickey's forehead. Bending over, 'The Enforcer' removed the gangster's wallet, taking the thick wad of bills he tossed the empty billfold on the quivering form and sauntered out the front door.

It was useless arresting O'Hara, underworld codes forbade Cohen from cooperating with the police in these matters. Those 'Overcoat Charlies,' grateful just to be alive would be on a jet plane halfway to

New York by noon. To save face Mickey would have to handle this in his own way.

Hollywood was loaded with young Italian hoods. They came from big cities in the east, New York, Cleveland, Pittsburgh, etc.. Like Ponce de Leon who feverishly sought the fabled Fountain of Youth, they searched for their mythical Mafia, The Family, talk of 'It' was crammed into their heads since birth. Like moths to a street light, they were drawn by an illusory tale of a *secret* 'West Coast Mafia Family.' Papers propagandized the 'Deeds of Mafiosos' like the Sica Brothers, John Roselli, Jimmy 'The Weasel' Fratianno, and Mafia *Godfather* symbol, Jack Dragna.

Soon after hitting the Hollywood scene they got a rude awakening, stark *reality*, there was no such thing as a Mafia *Organization*, the young punks had discovered that these *noted* Mafiosos were full of bullshit. Nothing but twobit scam artists, extortionists, back-stabbers fighting amongst themselves like hyenas scavenging on carrion, you'd starve to death hanging around them. They had no organization or money to put anyone on a payroll and let them lounge around while awaiting orders for exotic missions like in the movies. The Italian punks gravitated to Mickey Cohen, at least he had some ideas, and good contacts in Beverly Hills and Hollywood.

The would-be Mafiosos learned Hollywood was no different from the places they'd just left. To survive you latched onto a hooker, a good looking humper who could make enough bread to keep up the payments on your convertible Cad, sharp clothes and Sunset Strip apartment. Also one who'd tip you off on her rich Johns, the ones who were ripe to be blackmailed for a little steady cash each month. All it took was one colored picture snapped at the right instant with a Polaroid camera.

It wasn't long before these self-made Mafiosos were in the chips. It was the 'real-life' they dreamed of. Spending leisure days with the thoroughbreds at Santa Anita and Hollywood Park tracks they could afford the prestige of a 'line of credit' with Hymie's book operating out of the Melody Room on the Strip. Always they were mysterious about their 'real' income, after all...who wanted to be just another Hollywood pimp? It was much better for their ego and reputations as tough guys to *promote* the silhouette of a dangerous, mysterious Mafia brotherhood as their secret source of income. Hell, everyone seemed to find this Mafia apolog very easy to believe, why let useful fables die?

From the very beginning Cohen knew this particularly handsome young Dago would be a money maker for him. All the Hollywood hookers confided to Mickey that this Johnny Stompanato was the 'most' satiating sex performer on the Strip. Cohen eagerly set it up for Johnny to meet one of Hollywood's famous, most luscious movie actresses. Lana Turner, the gorgeous blonde star, jaded by common everyday Hollywood scenes was utterly captivated by Johnny's youth and manly Roman features. She became madly in love.

Johnny whispered exciting stories of daring Mafia exploits in the swooning Lana's ear while performing like a champ. A deluxe motel suite was most generously paid for by the chivalrous Cohen. Poor Lana, completely enthralled didn't have the slightest suspicion her every gasp, moan and groan, her shrill cries of ecstasy mingling with ravenous words screamed out amidst her splendorous sexual torture were being recorded. No, not even the vaguest thought entered her pretty head that hushed squeaks of bed springs and her whispered pleas, "more Johnny, more," were picked up by the super-sensitive microphone hid beneath the bed.

Cohen hadn't been wrong about Stompanato, "That Dago is going to make nothing but bread for me." As a starter two thousand discs of the recording were stamped out. They went over big in Beverly Hills and Hollywood. Cohen got fifty bucks a copy. At a Friars Club social, repartee was hilarious, up full volume, by unanimous request, they ran it again and again. Cohen, fair minded and not wanting to inhibit Johnny's sensitive libido, *never* mentioned the money.

The affair soon became a drag to the Dago. Wildly jealous, Lana created terrible scenes in public, but worse yet, she held back on his allowance, it was his 'flash around town money.' Johnny suffering from bad fits of temper roughed the actress up a few times. During a bitter quarrel at the star's home he ended up with a sharp butcher knife buried deep in his belly. Terrified, Johnny stared in disbelief at the haft. Blood gushing from his mouth, he collapsed on the kitchen floor. Watching the big red stain spreading across the linoleum he realized it was his life's blood. But he couldn't seem to make himself care, everything was a blur, something told him he was dead.

Sensational media exploitation of the bizarre melodrama created a big demand for Johnny and Lana's recording. According to some, it was one of the best performances she'd ever made. Ecstatically, Cohen ran off records by the thousands, like he'd always said, "That Johnny...he's a real money maker."

Things were going great for the Mick, these Dagos were natural lovers and extortionists, all he had to do was keep the punks in line.

Sammy Lo Cigno and Georgie Piscitelli had some very rich middle aged broads on the hook, the dough was pouring in. At the Melody Room, Sammy and Georgie each had their ten thousand buck line of credit with Hymie. The action was rolling smoothly until the West Hollywood Sheriff's Vice Squad busted Hymie, confiscating his tabs. Re-organizing, he called all his customers asking where they stood. The two sharpies knew they owed Hymie fifteen grand. With a spur of the moment brainstorm, Sammy said, "Well Hymie, you ain't too bad off, as of right now you only owe Georgie and me five hundred chips."

"Alright, you guys drop by the Melody Room this afternoon, I'll settle with you." Several days later Hymie's lawyer got an O.K. for him to see his bookie tabs held at the Sheriff's station. He was not long figuring out the trick they'd pulled on him. "God damn friggin' punks, I'm gonna' fix their asses good." Hymie got O'Hara on the phone, "Listen Jack, you can keep every God damn cent you collect, all I want is that you bust those punks in little pieces."

A rasping voice came back, "You got a deal Hymie."

The chiselers got the word straight from the horses mouth. "Be at the Plymouth House, nine tonight with fifteen grand. And also that five hundred dollars."

Scared out of their wits they ran to Cohen fast. "Mickey, we ain't got fifteen grand, not even five hundred, we went flat broke at the track today. Lord, just give us enough bread to get out of town, that God damn O'Hara will kill us."

Mickey's brain clicked like a yellow cab meter, lickety split. "Ah, I gotta' lot better idea, we're gonna' *bump off* that friggin' O'Hara, I've been laying for him a long time and this is our chance."

The two tough Mafiosos eyes bugged out at the thought of such an insane idea. Georgie stuttered, "My God Cohen, I ain't nuts, I'm not gonna' mess with O'Hara." Speechless, Lo Cigno's head wagged weakly in agreement.

"Hold on, you guys listen to me...this is our golden chance to kill that lunatic sonofabitch, I mean legal like."

Shakily Sammy queried, "Kill him...legal like?"

Mickey gagged, such stupidity, "Yeh! That's absolutely right. For Christ sake, don't you get it? Self defense...self defense! Every cop in town knows Jack's reputation, and everyone in Hollywood knows his intentions are to make basket cases of you guys...we can bump him and it'll be strictly self defense, we'll have a thousand witnesses, even the cops will have to back us up."

The two shot glances at each other, jeezz, what a hell of a happy thought, forever free of that crazy, stalking maniac. They yammered in concert..."Who's gonna' do it, where, how?"

"Alright, you guys get a motel room, hole up, then call and give me the number where I can reach you. Don't be calling any broads, stay out of sight til I get it all set up." Cohen was proud of himself, it was a hell of an idea, it couldn't go wrong. He'd get that friggin' Jack blasted and stay on the sidelines with a good alibi...also where it was safe. He got pistols from his arsenal, it'd be impossible to con them two punks into killing Jack even if he gave them sub-machine guns, so he got Joe Di Carlo and Roger Leonard to back them up. Four of them should be able to handle Jack.

From their hideout Cohen had Sammy call O'Hara and set up a meet, "Tell him you've got the money." Jack agreed, tonight at nine, the parking lot behind the Sportsmans Lodge at Coldwater Canyon and Ventura Blvd.. Mickey grinned, that's perfect, that parking lot is darker than a bat cave. He gave Sammy, Georgie and Joe each a gun, Roger Leonard had his own.

"Here's the way we're gonna' do it," Mickey explained, "Sammy and Georgie will stand out in the parking lot where O'Hara can see just the two of them. Joe and Roger will hide behind cars on each side. Soon as O'Hara gets within ten feet Sammy pulls his gun and lets him have it. Its got to look like self defense, not like a rub-out, so for Christs sake don't anybody else shoot unless something goes wrong. I'll be at Rondelli's having dinner where everyone can see me for an alibi. Sammy, after you blast Jack you go up to Santa Maria, get a motel room under a phony name. Call and let me know what name you're using and the phone number."

By now Sammy was scared shitless, he was having serious doubts about the whole scheme. "Damn Mickey, you know that O'Hara, if this don't work I could get mutilated."

"Stop your damn worrying, Joe and Roger will both be there. If something goes wrong, you all blast him. Don't forget Sammy, I've got all kinds of publicity set up. You're going to be a 'Big Man' in Hollywood. It'll be headlines, everybody'll know Sammy Lo Cigno as the *man* who bumped Jack O'Hara. Keep the gun so you can prove it was you who bumped O'Hara, the cops will want it for testing. It can't be traced to me, tell 'em you got it from some guy a long time ago, you don't remember his name." Cohen saw he was shaking like a leaf. "Sammy trust me, you ain't got a thing to worry about, you'll never do more than *one* day in jail. I'll have the best mouthpiece in town for you and Abe will bail you out. You guys don't forget, soon as Sammy bumps O'Hara he heads for Santa Maria, the rest of you meet me at Rondelli's. It's only a mile from the Sportsman, you can get there in minutes. Be at the parking lot by eight thirty, O'Hara might be a little early."

O'Hara was more than just a *little* early, he'd been parked up a side street since seven. Sitting in the dark of a huge elm, he patiently watched the dim lot for the two. His hard jaw dislocated in a wicked grin when he spied Mickey's four men drive into the lot at eight and group for the 'big kill.' Uh huh, just like he suspected. O'Hara was amused at their trick, he wasn't as stupid as they thought. For trying to pull this stunt he'd teach Mickey and those four assholes a lesson they'd *never* forget. Tasting the moment when he would lay his meat hooks on his quarry, O'Hara was immovable in the dark. With Indian like stoicism he waited, those idiots were gonna' lead him direct to Mickey. After an hour the ambushers could stand the nerve wracking tensions no longer. In a hurried conference they eagerly agreed that O'Hara was not going to show.

Tailing his would be slayers, Jack watched them enter Rondelli's. He waited ten minutes, letting them ease their tensions and feel safe. The dining room was warm, exquisite aromas wafted from steaming plates of hearty Italian food, they had a sense of euphoria. Seated around the large table the five conspirators relaxed as they poured the dark red vino. A sudden chilling fear pierced Mickey's brain. A grim specter, the 'Enforcer' had sprung up behind Georgie. Mickey saw it happen like in a slow motion movie, the giant hand smashed Georgie along side the head. Shattering his senses it sent him, chair and ravioli sprawling.

Paralysis numbed the rest. Stalking around the table Jack exulted at the terror frozen on his intended victims faces. The shot rang out, a black hole the size of a dime splotched Jack's forehead. He crashed to the floor like a giant Sequoia felled by a blow from a cyclopean axe. The gangster chief was real pissed that Jack should get bumped right in front of him. It looked exactly like what he *hadn't* wanted it to, a set-up involving himself. "Lo Cigno you get out of here, beat it to Santa Maria like we planned, call me tomorrow. The rest of you get lost and dump those guns, I gotta have time to think." Dashing through the kitchen and out a back door the hoods threw their guns in a trash barrel and beat it down the alley.

The cops found *three* guns in the garbage behind Rondelli's, but lab tests conclusively proved *none* of them was the murder weapon.

All fingerprints were wiped off and police were unable to trace any of the guns to an owner.

The heat was on. Cohen told the police Sammy fired the shot but it was in self defense. He said Sammy was in hiding but he would produce him in several days. With Mickey's furtive connections at L.A. TV stations, he set up secret arrangements for a live telecast interview of Sammy on Ventura Blvd. in Studio City. TV cameras rolled and reporters yammered a million questions. Lo Cigno in his overnight celebrity roll of the mysterious, 'Mafia tough guy hero,' preened while he confessed, "Yea, it was me alright, I knocked off 'The Enforcer,' that madman O'Hara."

Sammy caught on real quick to this acting scam. Hell, he figured he was every bit as talented as George Raft and besides, who in the hell had Raft ever bumped? The ambulance chaser Cohen hired for this production seized on his opportunity to impress the viewers and news reporters with typical legal circumlocution claiming, "Sammy's actions clearly were a *matter* of self defense."

The police had known nothing of Cohen's plan to make a circus of the murder investigation, in fact he'd guaranteed detectives the fugitive would turn himself in momentarily. Within minutes after the telecast hit the tube, the police arrived. Handcuffed, Sammy took a quick trip to Homicide, his acting career was washed up, from here on out it was for real.

It was a natural. Joe Busch a fiercely ambitious Dep. D.A. could taste the blood. It had everything exciting, a Hollywood underworld slaying with Mafia *involvement*. Joe dreamed of the publicity of the coming murder trial, his personal exposure on TV and newspapers. He saw it all now, plain as day, Joe Busch, competent, experienced, ferocious prosecutor of *Mafia* conspirators and murderers, the loyal guardian, custodian of the peoples safety and welfare, it set Busch's palpitations going crazy.

Abe Phillips couldn't get Lo Cigno out of jail, Busch had plugged the hole. Sammy was raising hell, "Damn it Cohen you promised I'd never do more than a day in jail. Christ, I'll do a year of dead time in this crummy hole just waiting for my trial."

"Hold on, they'll never convict you and you'll get a million bucks of beautiful publicity out of this trial, believe me, it'll be worth it to you. Hollywood'll never forget it was Sammy who bumped off that God damn maniac, just take it easy, a couple months in jail won't be so bad. Don't worry about a thing, I'll make your Cad payment and apartment rent. Trust me, you'll come out a 'big' man."

Characteristically, with vigilant fervor, Joe tackled preparation of the prosecution's case, not a stone was left unturned, he personally interviewed dozens of witnesses. Minutely evaluating statements he sorted out details, the physical evidence was reviewed and discussed interminably with detectives and lab technicians. On Joe's orders a floor plan of Rondelli's was drawn to scale on a four x eight piece of wood panel. On rollers, it could be wheeled around the courtroom with ease.

A diagram of the dining room placed the five gangsters in their respective chairs at the table, an X marked the spot where O'Hara stood when the diners heard the shot. From Lo Cigno's position he had a straight shot at Jack, but, so did one of the others. Though Busch had prepared what appeared to be a 'dead bang' case, Frank and I weren't convinced Sammy had killed O'Hara.

We met with Eddie Cannizzaro. Though now in the construction business he still had good Hollywood contacts. "I'm gonna' tell you guys something, and this is straight stuff. Last night I ran into Jack Sanzo a guy I know, he does a little bookin' just on his own, he isn't connected with anyone. Sanzo's a good friend of Sammy and thinks he didn't shoot O'Hara, he says Sammy's nuts for going along with this play, but Mickey has convinced him he's going to be a big man, he's eating it up. Sanzo says Mickey is *framing* Sammy to keep the heat off himself."

Pushing Eddie, Frank said, "But Sammy confessed, maybe he is changing his mind and has Sanzo spreading this story around trying to get him off the hook..."

"No...actually he told Sanzo to keep his mouth shut about it. But Sanzo doesn't trust Cohen, he thinks something should be done to help Sammy before it's too late."

I pointed out, "It's probably already too late even if we decided to do something. How can we *prove* he didn't do the shooting even if he'll cooperate with us?"

"Okay, after leaving Rondelli's Sammy called Sanzo telling him to come to a gas station at Laurel Canyon and Ventura Blvd.. He gave Sanzo a pistol and told him, 'This gun just killed Jack O'Hara, hide it where no one can find it, but where it'll be handy when I need it. I'm going to Santa Maria to hideout until Cohen *fixes* things.' Sanzo got scared about having it, he went up to Mulholland Dr. and threw it over an embankment into the brush."

Frank snorted, "Lord Eddie, there's miles of brush ten feet high along Mulholland, we'd never find a gun up there in fifty years."

"Sanzo knows right where he tossed it."

"What we have to do then is get with Sanzo and find the weapon, that'll be a starter."

"He won't show anyone where the gun is or tell who did it unless Sammy says okay."

"Eddie, all we can do right now is tell Busch about the situation and see what he thinks. In the meantime tell Sanzo we want to talk to him." We weren't sure how Joe would take this information, if it was true, Joe's case was out the window. At his desk in shirtsleeves he listened, I watched dark waves of purple suffuse Busch's round beefy face. I could see how he was taking it.

Eyeballs protruding slightly more than usual he leaped to his feet. "God damn it! These are just lousy rumors being spread around by Lo Cigno." Joe's voice grated like a dull knife on a dry grindstone. "He is getting scared because he knows damn good and well I am going to bust his phony self defense crap. Listen to me," Joe banged his desk, "Listen to me good, that was the *Mafia* around that table at Rondelli's." Busch strangled, then shouted, "Do you hear me, the *Mafia*, the God damn *Mafia* lying in wait for an execution."

Busch had been testing out his 'Mafia dogma' around the Hall of Justice for days. He was now to the stage of honing his courtroom technique, this was a preview, Frank grinned. "Okay Joe, be calm, we just want to keep you abreast of what's going on, no one knows anything about this except Gary and me, but Joe, it bothers us real bad, it's a loose end of your whole case. Admit it, the gun that shot Jack O'Hara is missing, why? Sammy confessed to the killing, what reason would he have for not producing it if he knows where it is? We have a feeling something is wrong, there's a possibility Mickey himself killed O'Hara." We saw it in a harsh tightening of his face, Joe didn't want to hear of that possibility.

Joe Busch, a fiery courtroom inquisitor, a dynamo, relentlessly he assaulted and destroyed Sammy's alibi of self defense, a masterful prosecution. Convicted of the murder, Sammy was going away for a long, long time. Before the trial we talked with Sanzo several times attempting to learn where he threw the gun but he refused to open up. "I can't talk unless Lo Cigno says ok." We hinted we might bust him for concealing evidence, but he still wouldn't budge.

After the trial we talked to Sanzo again. "Now that Sammy's been convicted maybe he will want to talk sense. Frank and I will go over to the County Jail tonight and see him." It was midnight when the jailer brought Sammy out to the small interview room. We'd picked a good time, the other prisoners wouldn't see Sammy talking to us. We introduced ourselves.

"Yeh, you're those guys from the D.A. that Sanzo told me about."

Frank started off, "Sammy, you've got yourself in a hell of a spot. You're about to go to the joint for quite a spell. Sanzo tells us you didn't kill O'Hara and Cohen tricked you to cover-up for himself. If there's any chance at all to get you off the spot you are gonna' have to cooperate with us fast because they're ready to ship you to State Pen. We can't run up there every five minutes to see you."

"I know, I just want out of this friggin' hole."

Frank went right to the point, "Sammy, tell me, did someone else kill O'Hara?"

"Yeh."

"Who was it?" Sammy hedged, we knew what he was conveying, it was the same old Mafia bull. He couldn't squeal, he was fettered, bound by, 'Omerta, The Mafiosa Code.' The conspiracy of silence doesn't permit cooperation with cops, but something besides Omerta plagued Sammy. Clearly he desperately wanted to unload the truth and get the hell out of that God damn jail but it had to be done so that it wouldn't pin the tag of 'squealer' on him. It was bad enough all the hookers, pimps, bookies and the rest of his bosom buddies in Hollywood would know he didn't wipe out O'Hara, it would ruin his reputation.

In the lock-up he was treated like a celebrity by the inmates, like Al Capone or something...they even gave him a private cell. What would happen when those guys found out he hadn't really bumped Jack and was nothing more than a shitty ass squealer? Jesus Christ, it could get him killed, if not here in the county jail, sure as hell in the State Pen. Frank said, "Sammy you've got justification to help yourself out of this jam. Do you know what that is?" The convicted killer indicated he did, he was grasping for the straw.

"Think about it, Cohen promised to take care of everything for you, but was *framing* you the whole time and laughing at you. You gave him money to keep up your car payment and the rent on your apartment."

"Yeh."

"Well he kept the dough. The landlord took all your clothes and sold them, on top of that Mickey's been banging your girlfriend. He took her to Vegas in your Caddy, he drove so fast out on the desert the convertible top tore off." The Italian froze. Frank poured it on, "Back in Hollywood he dumped your Cad on the street and let 'em reposess it. I sympathize with you Sammy, I realize you won't be a big man in Hollywood anymore, but at least you'll be out of prison. The way Cohen set you up, you got all the justification in the world to talk."

I took over, "Sammy, why do you think Cohen was so anxious to arrange that TV interview on the street and have you confess to the whole world?"

"Yeh, I know it was stupid. He figured once I'd confessed there was no way I'd ever get out of it."

"You've got that right. But, there is something else you probably don't know."

"What's that?"

"Well, he's pretty slick, the TV network gave him three grand to produce you, did he split the money with you?"

That shocked him, "Hell no, that sonofabitch ain't never given me nothin' since I been here except a pack of Luckies."

"That five grand from the insurance company you got for that car wreck, you gave Mickey the check to hold. We found out he got his sister to cash it, you know her, she runs that phony ice cream parlor out on San Vicente Blvd. in Brentwood. Mickey forged it and ran it through her business account."

Sammy shook his head, "Yeah I know that joint, it's another of Cohen's fronts, his sister's married to a guy named George Weiner."

"That's right, what the hell, you got all kinds of justification...why don't you tell us where the gun is and who shot O'Hara?"

He stared at the wall, "Let me think about it."

The next two weeks we visited Sammy several times, always late at night when the jail was quiet. Nothing seemed to bother him bad enough to start him unloading the truth. Not even Cohen tearing up his Cad or screwing his girl or losing his apartment and clothes and all his money Cohen stole. Talking desultorily with Sammy, we were just about to give up on him for the night when I happened to make a casual remark. "Sammy, it looks to me like this jail house chow is killing you."

Sammy's head jerked up, for the first time a spark flashed in his black lack-luster eyes. "How come you say that?"

"Shit, you're a skeleton. Your beautiful white teeth are turning a dingy yellow, by the time you get out of the pen they'll be nothing but brown snags flopping around in your shrunken gums."

Fidgeting he shrunk in his chair. Immediately spotting Sammy's agitation Frank chuckled, he added, "Yeah, the way you're going to look when you get out of the joint you'll be lucky to find a job in a shoe factory. There ain't no way you'll be able to latch onto a new cute little hooker and all those sweet little old widows with lots of dough ain't going to swoon all over your alligator Gucci's anymore. Yeah, you'll be old, you'll be all washed up."

I shoved the needle deep, "If you don't get out of here soon your whole career is going to be shot." There was silence. No jail house sounds echoed down the long aisles, it was like a morgue. Patiently we waited, we'd spent a lot of time on this case, a couple minutes more wouldn't hurt.

Sammy spoke, "Alright, like I said...I've been thinking about it. I have to get permission from my people in Cleveland. They've got to know how Mickey framed me and they'll decide if I can cooperate with you. It'll be best to have Cannizzaro contact them, they'll trust him."

After a month of phone calls Eddie finally got back a decision. "Sammy can cooperate with the authorities to help get out of jail. Cohen is a Jew, he is not one of our people, he framed Sammy and stole his money, Cohen should go to prison, he has tried to give the Italian people a bad name."

Sammy was trying to impose conditions on us to keep from being tagged a squealer. "That's the way it is, I can't show you where the gun is, Sanzo can, but he won't unless I tell him in person it's Ok."

"Fine Sammy, we'll bring Sanzo here, you can tell him yourself."

"No, don't bring him here to the jail, someone up here will figure out what's going on. Mickey has spies everywhere."

Frank was trying not to show annoyance, "Damn it Sammy, let's stop screwing around, maybe you don't know where the gun is, but you know who killed Jack and we want to know...right now."

"Frank you've got to understand, I've got this whole thing worked out in my head so no one can ever say I squealed." He held up his hand, "Please, just one minute. I don't have to say who shot O'Hara because when you find the gun 'it' will tell you."

"What are you talking about?"

"Just what I said, it'll be the *gun* who tells who shot Jack, not me. Get me out of jail so I can talk to Sanzo alone."

"Sammy, you are causing us one hell of a lot of grief. We've had to fight like hell getting special permission from Busch to even talk to you. He's not happy about this whole operation. In fact, he thinks we're crazy. As far as he is concerned he convicted you and you are guilty, he wants your ass sent up to the Pen. Sammy, we'll get back to you." Frank signaled the jailer to take Lo Cigno to his cell.

Virgil Crabtree from IRS Intelligence agreed to help us, he was in the Federal Building across from the Hall of Justice and the Jail. We'd spread word around the jail that Lo Cigno was called before a Federal Grand Jury about matters not connected to his case. We walked Sammy across the street and up an elevator to where Sanzo waited in Crabtree's office, emotionally the two Italians embraced each other. They moved to a far corner where excitedly they waved their arms and whispered in each others ears.

Frank gave them a few minutes then interrupted, "I hate to break up this family reunion, but we have things to do. Lo Cigno did you give Sanzo the word?"

"Sure, everything's okay. He'll show you where the gun is."

"Sanzo, in an hour you meet us at Coldwater and Ventura Blvd., you got it?" He nodded. Thanking Virgil we took Sammy back to the jail. When we got to the Valley, Sanzo was waiting.

From the back seat of our car he directed us. "Go up Coldwater and make a right at Mulholland." After about a block he instructed, "Pull across from that Spanish style house over on the left." Gazing around Jack said, "This is it, right here." Climbing out we stood on the edge of a steep bank, we saw San Fernando Valley far below us. Sanzo picked up a rock close to the size and weight of the gun he'd thrown away. "I threw it far as I could out in that direction just like this," he let the rock fly. "There were no lights on in that house over there but the moon was bright, I saw the gun fall in the brush down there, close to where the rock just landed."

It was getting late, we drove Sanzo back to his car. Frank and I made plans to be back early next morning, wearing old clothes. We could hardly wait to get our hands on that gun and hear what it had to tell us. That was the damndest brush I'd ever tangled with. Like ten foot high rolls of barbed wire springing loose, an impenetrable barricade, five solid days we fought that insane entanglement. One hundred and ten degree sweltering heat, snakes, giant lizards, pack rats and armies of damn bugs the eminent entomologists don't even know exist. The morning of the sixth day as we readied to enter the treacherous brush Frank got my attention. "Look here," he held up two thick, powerful hands, palms outward, they were deformed like from a severe case of arthritis. Attempting to straighten out those misshapen claws raw cracks opened, oozing fluid. "If we don't find that friggin' gun by noon today," Frank swore, "I'm going to strangle Sanzo and Sammy with my bloody bare hands."

My mood was even worse, an agonizing sharp pain stabbed at my twisted right knee, reminding me how I'd rolled down a twenty foot bank yesterday. "I'll tell you something Frank, I intend to kill those two lying bastards myself if we don't find it by noon."

At the beginning we had started where the rock fell then fanned out about seventy five feet. This morning we started over, searching deeper into the layers of mulch. Fortunately we discovered the gun at eleven fifty, ten minutes before our deadline. Deep in decayed brush it was hiding only a few feet from the starting point. Exposed to elements over a year there was little likelihood of prints. Even if a bullet from this gun matched the slug taken from O'Hara's head, it still wouldn't prove who'd pulled the trigger. According to what Sammy told us, "The gun will *tell* you who shot Jack," we knew the serial number was our only hope, jubilantly we put the gun gently in a shoe box. Washing up at a gas station we headed to the Bureau.

Teletypes went out for owner information on the pistol. There'd be nothing back until morning, we went home to soak in hot water and forget the bats. Fluttering and squeaking around our heads the bats had spooked us worse than all the slitherers and crawlers put together. Next morning it came, from Phoenix, Ariz. Our gun was bought at a hardware store, purchased by Roger Leonard!

The Mafia 'man' was brought to the interview room, Frank told him, "We found it, the gun's Leonard's."

Sammy's eyes gleamed, "See...I told you the truth, now, when are you guys gonna' spring me loose from this shithouse?"

"Not so fast Sammy, we got a long way to go. The gun is a good start, but we need lots more info before we can arrest Leonard, tell us what happened right after O'Hara was shot."

He grinned. "It was just like a friggin' Chinese fire drill. All the customers were trying to run out the front door at the same time."

"I can imagine, but how did you get Leonard's gun?"

"Well, in seconds the joint cleared out. Mickey locked the doors and said, 'We gotta' hurry, the cops will be coming, this is still self defense except O'Hara wasn't after Leonard, so Sammy, you *switch guns* with him.' Then Mickey told the other guys to scram out the back way and throw their guns in a trash barrel because they can't be traced. He told me to drive on up to Santa Maria just like we'd planned and call him the next day. Grabbing me, he ordered, 'On your way up the coast find a spot and throw that gun into the ocean because they can trace it to Roger.' I went out the front door and that is all there is to it, except my institution told me...I should hang on to the gun just in case."

I said, "Your what?"

"My institution, you know, something told me, that's why I called Sanzo and gave it to him to hide for me in case I needed it. Christ, I didn't know he was gonna' throw it away."

"You have to sit tight Sammy, we got lots to do. First, a talk with Joe." He listened but he didn't like it a bit. I reminded him, "You knew it Busch, we told Chief Thad Brown what we were working on and we'd turn the gun over to him if we found it, and you promised that that was the way we would do it."

Glaring at us, he growled, "I'll run my *own* lab tests on it, *do not* make a written report or mention the gun to anyone, and... you stay away from Thad Brown! I don't want you over there at all."

Frank asked, "What the hell goes on Joe?" He leaped up, a wave of purple exploded upward from his collar, his voice was no longer controlled. We knew this was no courtroom act, he was mad.

Joe screamed, "God damn, I convicted Sammy, he's a Mafia son of a bitch, and he's going to *stay* convicted!"

I knew better but I couldn't help it. "Mafia my ass Busch, whatsa Mafia, whatsa Mafia? Cohen and Roger Leonard are Jews, Christ, you could've convicted all five of 'em for conspiracy and murder."

"Jesus, son of a bitch," he roared, "get the hell out of here."

We went to work. Roger's brother Herbert, was a wealthy, very successful producer of TV films. Also he was one of Mickey's many influential contacts in Hollywood and Beverly Hills. It was Herbert Leonard who'd *set up* the TV production when Sammy conveniently confessed to killing O'Hara. His confession had *neatly* taken Cohen and Roger off the hook, something smelled really bad. We headed south on the Harbor Freeway to 74th St., driving west I found the number we wanted on the left, two doors from Hoover St..

A knock got no answer. A peek in a window told us Leonard had flown the coop, splitting up we checked with neighbors. Roger had not lived there too long, he was seen moving out a few hours before in a rush, we also gleaned he had a young son in a private school nearby. Dashing there we were too late, he'd just removed the kid from class under a pretext of an unexpected family problem. When the boy was enrolled, the school nurse had insisted on an alternate emergency address for her records. After a little finagling she came up with it, it was in San Diego. Heading to town Frank asked, "Are you thinking the same thing I am?"

"Without a doubt."

"Roger was tipped off his gun was found, also that we are looking for him."

"Right."

"It had to be somebody from the D.A.'s office."

"But he wasn't warned until late this morning otherwise he would not have sent the kid to school."

"So...are we going to Diego and talk with Roger?"

"Hell yes." But before we could go we got word that Roger was in a hospital for some sort of surgery on his brain. He *died* during the operation. Lo Cigno was quietly released from prison, but those soft touch days were gone forever for Sammy and Georgie. Piscitelli got his head blown off knocking over poker games in hotel rooms, and Lo Cigno got blasted hijacking trucks loaded with cigarettes, Sanzo died while undergoing heart surgery.

Several months after we'd found Leonard's gun the D.A.'s office turned it over to Thad Brown at L.A.P.D., just like Busch *promised* us he would. But it was in two pieces, the barrel was sawed off. The end of a great, 'Mafia *Organization*' prosecution.

CHAPTER 34

With diamond bright stars flashing in dark brown eyes, Mary had traveled to Hollywood just like a million other impassioned hopefuls before her. The Italian girl with long raven locks possessed all the enticing physical attributes for sudden discovery and stardom. Mary Mercadante was distressed very little at becoming a hooker instead of a star. With a genuine loathing she had watched those dedicated starlets claw their way up the ladder performing obscene, sick stunts in the name of fame. Kinky tricks Mary couldn't have forced herself to do for anyone. Just doing her own little thing she could hustle all the ready money she ever needed and she could sleep well into the afternoons.

Mary's psyche was touched, she'd been totally unable to resist the clean cut young fellow who told her he was a sailor wearing civies. His leave was up tomorrow, he'd have to hitch hike back to Frisco. Mary displayed a unique understanding, a tender heartedness that whores since time began are known to hold for special clients. She'd even offered to lower her going price. Mary was never so God damn mad in her entire life as she was when that friggin' slicker laid his LAPD badge on her. It was a hell of a dirty trick. That sonofabitch couldn't even have been twenty one, there wasn't any damned doubt about it, it was entrapment...nothing else but, furious, Mary decided to plead not guilty and fight.

She got a lawyer, Harry Weiss, Esq., that's when Mary's troubles really started. Weiss fell head over heels, asshole over teakettle in love with the gorgeous little whore. He had to do something about the situation, he must get her out of that degrading racket. How the thought of her with all those johns ripped him up. A different bum every damned night, it made him positively ill to his stomach. Weiss blamed the 'licentious Sunset Strip' as the seat of Mary's dissolute character. Her crummy 'Strip' friends were destroying her. All that could be changed, she only needed a different environment, a new approach. Weiss contemplated his compassionate, 'Good Samaritan' deed.

As Pygmalian the Cyprian sculptor had carved the statue of the maiden Galatea in ivory, Weiss would carve Mary's soiled flesh into that of an intellect, virtuous and loyal. Such a transformation would cleanse Mary of all her sins. She would be his own work of art. The lawyer got Mary a job with a good friend of his. Since she'd had no experience in office work it was a sort of on the job training. Abe Phillips Bail Bonds was on the third floor of an old building across from the Hall of Justice at Broadway and Temple. Laboriously she typed bail bond applications, filed documents and answered phones.

Mary did not particularly like the way Abe ogled and rubbed up next to her every chance he got. But hell, maybe that's what office work was like. Every evening at five sharp Weiss waited for her in front of the building. They'd then drive to the San Fernando Valley where they were shacked up.

The phone was jangling constantly, irritably she knew she wasn't getting any faster with that damned typewriter. It'd been a hell of a frustrating day. Phillips wouldn't leave her alone, he was grabbing at her ass all day long. Thank God, when she finished typing this last bail application it was time to leave. Concentrating on the lousy L.C. Smith, she was unaware Phillips stood directly behind her. Abe had been afflicted with this aggravating hard-on ever since Weiss asked him to let that little bitch work here.

He couldn't stand it any longer, his pants were unzipped and his pecker stuck out, hell, Weiss wouldn't care. She's just a cheap little Sunset Strip whore. Abe violently spun the swivel chair around, hair and all he savagely grabbed her by her ears. Stunned by the sudden attack and terrifying pain to her ears, Mary's lips parted to scream. But Abe was swift, he jammed his pecker in her mouth, viciously he tightened his ferocious grip. She thought her ears were being ripped loose as he flailed and thrusted frantically. In a brutal paroxysm of frenzied action Abe had an orgasm all over Mary's face. Weiss swung his car to the curb just as Mary came flying out screaming bloody murder. Flinging herself into his car she shrieked hysterically, "My face, that slimy no good sonofabitch, look at my face."

Despite her convulsions Harry got the general idea of what had happened. "Jesus Christ!" She sobbed, "Give me your handkerchief." Knowing his criminal law, Weiss vociferously protested, "No...no..., don't wipe it off, it's evidence." Totally wild with anger at Abe's vile attack on his girl, Weiss declared it an emergency as he screeched to a halt in the red zone at Police Headquarters. They dashed into the 'Glass House' as the building is known. A policewoman in uniform mercifully took over from Weiss.

Ushering Mary into a ladies room she calmed her with reassuring words, helping her wash her face and rearrange her hair. The towel the policelady used would be examined later for semen stains by the lab. A crime report was signed by Mercadante, the next day a felony warrant was issued for Abe. Mary's screams still echoed in the halls of the old building as the bail bondsman stealthily locked his office door. He sped out to San Vincente Boulevard where he holed up in a friends pad.

Talking so low on the phone I barely heard her, Mary said, "It is very important, please come out to the Valley, I must see you." In the past she'd given us real good info on dope. She hated junk, her best friend, a beautiful young girl died from an OD of cheap heroin crudely needled into a vein by her rotten pimp. It was three in the afternoon when I got to the coffee shop in Studio City. Mary's hand shook as she sipped. Calming she said, "When Cohen heard Phillips was held to answer at the preliminary hearing a couple days ago he flipped his lid. I know LAPD can handle Phillips, but Gary you and Frank have to do something about Cohen. He called yesterday, said I had to tell them to forget the whole thing and drop the charges."

"Did he threaten you?"

"Not then, but he called again this morning. He asked if I'd gone to the police like he'd told me to and took the heat off Abe. When I said no I hadn't, he started screaming and cursing and calling me names. He yelled, 'You do it now or I'll fix your damned ass so bad you will never be able to peddle it again,' he hung up. But he'll be calling me again tomorrow."

"Have you told Weiss about this?"

"He knows about the call yesterday. He was madder then hell, he doesn't know about this morning. I'm really scared, Cohen means it, but I don't care, I want Abe convicted. He has no right to do such a terrible thing like that to me and get away with it."

"The next time Cohen calls I want to record his threats. That is if Weiss has no objections."

"He won't object, I guarantee you, I have already straightened the son of a bitch out for getting me mixed up with that rotten pervert." Mary was brave about the whole thing, but understandably she was apprehensive, she knew she'd be in jeopardy soon as Cohen realized he could not intimidate her into dropping the charges.

I said, "We'll be at your place tonight about seven with recording equipment. Will you be there?"

"Absolutely, see you then."

We hooked the recorder to the phone. Next morning we dropped by, Mary was frightened to death.

"He called an hour ago, Weiss answered and Cohen threatened to *kill* both of us."

"Where's Weiss now?"

"That asshole took off like a rabbit."

Frank re-wound the tape and played it. Like a real gentleman the gangster came on slow and cool. "Okay Weiss, I have done my very best to be nice to that little dicksucker of yours but the dumb bitch won't listen to reason. Now I want you to take her down to LAPD and drop those charges against Abe...or else." Cohen's voice grew menacing, "I mean or else, do you understand me?"

Weiss came on like a wimp. "God Mickey, don't call Mary names like that. Please, I love her." At that Mickey lost his cool, suddenly he was screaming.

"Listen to me you stupid God damn Jew. She ain't nothin' but a worthless Dago slut, you do what I tell you...you make that whore take the heat off Abe."

"Mickey please, I've tried, I've done my best, she won't listen to..."

A raging Cohen chopped Weiss off. His voice shrill with menace, he screeched, "I'm gonna' *kill* 'er, I'm gonna *kill* both of ya." Cohen was screaming, "you put that bitch on the phone."

Mary's voice said, "Alright, I'm on the phone." There were more threats from Cohen. Desperate with fear she retaliated, yelling back her screaming became hysterical. Wildly, Mary was throwing names and places and incidents...Georgie Piscitelli...her pimp lover...Marilyn Monroe...uncontrollable she threatened Cohen, she yelled..."I know the damn lousy *scam* you are pulling on John Kennedy and Marilyn, same as Lana. Georgie told me all about it, and if you don't leave me alone I'm going to *blow* the whole friggin' works sky high."

Cohen cut her off, he wasn't fooling now, his voice was as deadly as I'd ever heard. "I'm gonna' *kill* you you cunt," the line went dead. Hearing her voice repeating everything she had said to Cohen made Mary turn white as a sheet.

I advised her, "Mary, you know you've got to get out of here, and I mean right now."

"Yes, I can stay with a friend in Hollywood. No one knows about her, not even Weiss. She's a straight one, I'll phone tonight and tell Harry I've moved out."

"Good, be damned sure to remain in that apartment out of sight. Cohen will have a lot of street people out looking for you."

"I know that, but it's his big shot connections downtown that scare me the most."

"Downtown? You thinking of somebody in particular, somebody you can actually name?"

"Hell yes!"

Frank carrying the recording equipment was standing by the door ready to leave but changed his mind. He told her, "Sit down on that couch for a minute Mary, let's hear about the people downtown."

She didn't hesitate, "A few years ago, when I first hit Hollywood I ran out of money, I mean totally broke, Louisa helped me out. At that time she was a madam working for Mickey Cohen, now she has a disco joint on Sunset Blvd.. A few weeks ago I dropped by just to say hello, it was early, she wasn't open yet but let me in. A guy was there, she called him Stan, he left when I arrived. Louisa was in a gay mood, she said things were going great. Cohen had introduced them and Stan fell for her. He is powerful in Sacramento and was helping her to get a liquor license for her disco."

Hesitating, Mary went on, "I probably shouldn't tell you guys the rest about Louisa, she's been a good friend, but I can't forget how Marcie died. I hate that rotten dope they are always shooting into their veins with those lousy needles." We nodded, Mary continued, "Louisa and Stan had just returned from a Mexican cruise on a big ocean liner, he had arranged for two staterooms with a connecting door, she had had a gorgeous dream trip. They *brought back* a suit case of Heroin."

Slowly Frank asked, "Mary, what was this Stan's last name?"

She was surprised..."Mosk...Judge Stanley Mosk, hell, I figured I was maybe telling you something you already knew."

"We knew Louisa was deep in dope traffic, but Mosk is something new." Before driving away in her sports car Mary promised us she'd play it safe, stay out of sight and call us tomorrow. We admitted to substantive cause for Mary's alarm regarding the gangster's big shot *connections.* What she'd just told us about Mosk put a lot of pieces into place.

It was only a few nights ago we'd followed two Cohen hoodlums leaving Louisa's disco joint. Dropping down to Wilshire they drove west through Beverly Hills and Westwood. Just over Santa Monica's city line they wheeled into the parking lot of Ben Blue's night club. It was packed, we got seats in the rear. Blue appeared on stage for his nightly act amid rousing applause, the audience sat down. A man wearing a business suit walked toward a reserved table near stage, he joined the two hoods. It was Martin 'Bud' Smith from Ventura County. I recognized him, he owned a popular restaurant and bar, The Colonial House in Oxnard.

The intrigue got heavier. Two men were tailing Smith, watching his 'meet' with Cohen's hoods. They were from Federal Narcotics, they took seats on the other side of the room, one headed for the men's room. Frank said, "I'm going to talk with Ray, find out what they're up to." Five minutes later he was back, whispering, he said, "Boy, you won't believe it, the Fed's have been interested in Smith a long time, they've documented him meeting with some of the top leaders in drug traffic. He owns a large boat docked at the Oxnard Harbor, he often puts to sea with a group of them."

"He is meeting a fine pair of hoods right now."

"Yeh, Ray was glad to see me, they didn't recognize the two guys Smith met. He wasn't very surprised when told they were Mickey's men." The audience applauded Blue's performance. Leaving the club the two we'd been tailing drove toward Hollywood. We were certain their night's mission was completed, so we broke it off. On the way home I was remembering a lot of things, more of the pieces.

When I was in Ventura, 'Bud' Smith was having a meteoric rise in the financial world, involvements in banking and gigantic real estate developments in Oxnard and Port Hueneme Harbor areas. It wasn't long after I returned to L.A. that the Ventura D.A. Roy Gustafson, commenced the sensational Ma Duncan murder trial. 'Ma' had hired two ex-cons, Moya and Maldonado to kill the wife of her son Frank, an attorney. A brutal murder, the victim a nurse was strangled and buried alive in a shallow grave near the site of Casitas Lake. The autopsy disclosed she'd sucked dirt into her lungs while desperately trying to breath as they buried her.

Bobbi, a hooker and good informant of Doug Paxton's and mine had been contacted by 'Ma' Ducan to help her hire some ex-cons to kill her daughter-in-law. She refused, later when hearing the nurse was missing she called me. I sent her to Lt. Bill Woodard, Chief of Det., Ventura Sheriff's Department. Within hours the Lt. had the two suspects, Moya and Maldonado in jail and had located the body of the nurse. Gustafson flamboyantly trying and convicting all three defendants, sent them to their death in the gas chamber.

Not long after the 'Ma Duncan' trial, Martin 'Bud' Smith hired Roy Gustafson to handle all the legal work for his enterprises. That had been surprising, the former D.A. had no experience or expertise in civil and real estate matters. With a snap I remembered another incident I'd had difficulty in understanding. That morning in Roy's office, his stubbornness, then his bitter anger at me for insisting he issue a Murder Complaint against Renzee Alemeda. Arrested for a traffic violation, Alemeda was transported to the County Hospital by a Highway Patrolman. With cuffs removed the prisoner grabbed the officer's gun from its holster. He shot and killed the patrolman. Other officers disarmed the killer. Gustafson rebuffed me from the very beginning with the weirdest legal conclusion I had ever heard. "Hell, I'm not going to issue a Murder Complaint in a case like this, it's obvious the guy is crazy or he'd never do such a thing like that." When I argued he got mad as hell, but Gustafson was adamant. The killer went to Atascadero Hospital.

Then even stranger was the fact that only weeks after Gustafson was hired by Smith he was appointed to the Superior Court, before he had served on the Superior Court, he was elevated to the Appeal Court. That was heavy political power, more than Smith had, there had to be someone extremely powerful behind Smith to finesse such a deal. The D.A. had to have performed one hell of an important service for whoever it was but I got the picture...Gustafson had little regard for safety of police officers, and no experience in real estate and civil law. But, he had 'high influence' and *deep* contacts within the D.A.'s office and the Atty. General's Office in Sacramento. Now he had 'high influence' in the Superior and Appellate Courts...that's what they wanted.

Frank and I watched Mary's little car disappear from view as it rounded the corner. We hurried back to town. We wanted the Dep. D.A. who was prosecuting Phillips to hear the tapes, but he was in court, we couldn't see him until tomorrow. Next morning Frank was on the phone when I arrived, his tone alerted me to the seriousness of the conversation. Frank's face was grim as he hung up.

"What goes on Frank?"

"That was Sgt. Jackson from LAPD, Mary's dead."

"What! Good Christ what happened?"

"She was killed in a car crash during the early morning hours on the Hollywood Freeway. There were no witnesses."

"No witnesses?"

"We can rule out narcotics, she hated it. Sgt. Jackson said there was no evidence of alcohol being involved. There was just no cause for the accident."

"Damn all hell anyway Frank, what was she doing driving around that hour of the morning? We told her to stay in that apartment out of sight."

"Somebody could have phoned and lured her out, who knows?"

"We both know...only *one* person could have found out where she was and got her to come out."

"Yeh, Piscitelli." Taking the tape we headed across Spring St. to the Hall of Justice. We wanted Joe to hear it and order a complete autopsy. Then we'd hit the street and grab Georgie. Busch refused to listen to the tape.

"Haven't got time fellas, hell, it was strictly a car accident. Anyway she's dead, can't do much to Cohen for threatening a dead woman." Like he wasn't really interested, Joe said, "But *leave the tape* maybe I'll listen to it later when I get time."

Frank did something strange, acting confused he slapped his coat pockets, "Hell, I didn't even bring it with me, it must be on my desk." Busch glared at him, we left. Walking back to our office Frank pulled the small box out of his pocket. "Gary, I got a sudden feeling if I had given this to Joe it would've ended up *exactly* like Roger Leonard's gun."

The Dep. D.A. prosecuting Abe went forward with the trial using testimony from the preliminary hearing, it was only for appearance sake, without Mary there to testify, Abe was found not guilty. Mary was dead, there was nothing we could do about it. It would be *many years* before I *put together* all the wild things and the names she had screamed at Cohen. Just a few months after Mary's death, Marilyn Monroe also met a mysterious death. Then only a few more months and President John Kennedy was dead.

We were spending a lot of overtime keeping our eye on Mickey Cohen. L.A. County Supervisors were on an austerity binge so the two or three extra hours a day we were kicking in were on us. One of our good sources had tipped us that Mickey was about to pull off a big narco deal, he was in heavy financial trouble but this junk deal would put him back in the chips. We had no real hopes of pinning Mary's death on Mickey, but if we could send him to the pen what did it matter whether it was for murder or cocaine.

A florist shop was Mickey's latest front. It was early afternoon, two hours had dragged by while we watched, only one person had bought flowers. Morning, noon, or night, you never knew when was the best time to watch. You just spent as much time as you could and hoped for the odds. Slouched under the steering wheel the hot summer day had me dozing off. With a start I jerked to attention. A man, Oriental, very sharp looking in a maroon and white polo shirt and gray slacks had appeared around the corner a half block away. He walked in the direction of the florist shop.

"Hey Frank look, do you see him...that Chinese guy walking down Vermont?"

"Yeh, what about him?"

"I've seen him some place before. Sure as hell, I'll bet he's going to see Mickey." Casually gazing around he entered the flower shop. I was excited, "Frank it's been a long time but I recognize that guy, it's Benny Wong, I'm sure of it. Years ago I watched him meet with Cohen and Davidian in Old Chinatown, we followed them to South Gate Arena where they met with Abe Phillips, Harry Pregerson and a couple of other guys. Capt. Chitwood said Benny was one of the best narcotic smugglers in the country."

"If you're right this could be the break we've been waiting for." I was getting jumpy, an hour went by and he still hadn't come out.

"Damn Frank, I hope he hasn't gone out the back door, he must have had a car parked somewhere, maybe he's long gone."

"Stop worrying, see, he's coming out now, and he didn't even buy a bouquet from Mickey." Benny got into a new dark green Mercury parked around the corner. Over our radio Frank ran a DMV on the plate, it belonged to a woman in Oxnard. Tailing the Merc north on the Ventura Freeway we played it safe, staying far enough back so Benny wouldn't spot us. In Oxnard he parked behind the Colonial House, going upstairs he entered Martin 'Bud' Smith's office.

From a nearby pay phone I got hold of Sgt. Ed Patton. He was there in a matter of minutes. Patton listened intently then said "I'll be damned, it fits right in. For some time now I've heard rumbles of a real big deal coming down, a load of heroin worth millions is supposedly coming into Port Hueneme Harbor, this could be it, I'm getting on it right away. I've got a good Mexican operator, a waiter

right here at the Colonial House."
"Good, we'll be in constant touch."
The next day at four I called Patton, he had news. "I've learned Wong works for 'Bud' Smith, he's supposed to be chief buyer for all restaurant supplies."
"I wonder if he was buying poppies from Cohen?"
Chuckling, Ed said, "I've got more good info, my operator Villa knows a Mexican from the Old Colonia district who is involved in this deal, he's a major pusher. Villa did time with him in Chino, he is in solid."
"Sounds good, I'll call tomorrow." In the following weeks Patton, Frank and I worked eighteen hours a day, we really wanted this one. We took a trusted operator to Oxnard to help Villa. Ed arranged a job for him at the Colonial House, they convinced the pusher they had wealthy purchasers in Hollywood for large amounts of dope, he agreed to cut them in on the action. Ed was pressing Villa hard to learn when the drugs were due, we knew it was soon and we had to be prepared.
The phone call from Ed was bad news, in fact it could not have been worse. "I'm sorry as hell Gary, I just blew the whole deal, but good, I had to arrest Benny Wong."
"Christ, what for?"
"Somehow the organization became suspicious of Villa, maybe he pushed too hard trying to learn when the stuff was coming...I don't know, anyway, Wong had orders to kill him, I couldn't let him do it. Benny was on his way to blast Villa when I grabbed him. He had a loaded gun so I booked him for being an ex-con with a concealed weapon. Nothing was said about narcotics to Benny but now the big guys won't take chances, they'll change plans. I sent your operator back to L.A. for his own safety and Villa is on his way to Mexico. Believe me, I'm sorry as hell about it..."
I interrupted, "Ed, naturally I'm disappointed as hell but you had no choice, it was all you could do. Frank and I'll be up to see you in a few days, we'll hash it over." I hung up, there wasn't anything to talk about really, we'd blown a big deal, but from experience I knew there would be *another* big one.

CHAPTER 35

It wasn't just some easy, snap conclusion that I had jumped to, it was cold sober absolute facts...it'd taken me over thirteen years to fathom the deep source of the evil working against me. It was a Jew conspiracy, right from the start, a crazy Jewish plot to destroy me. With aggravating insistence this ominous discovery had assailed my mind with tortured thoughts for years, it'd become a constant sick fear festering deep in the pit of my stomach. Why such a disastrous consternation set upon me I didn't know, it wasn't that I feared any physical danger or harm. It was a psychological thing, a complicated involvement of morals and social standards.

An unexplainable guilt complex about Jews kept striking me. Was I going to be castigated, accused of being nothing more than just a Jew-Hater or Jew-Baiter, or whatever they call people who happen to accuse Jews. It was causing a lack of confidence in myself, crazy doubts were aroused that maybe I'd been wrong, maybe I shouldn't have fought back so strenuously and harshly for my rights the way I had. Tormenting apprehensions were created upon discovery of the Jew conspiracy. Christians are vulnerable to an ingrained religious mania, forcing a bending over backwards within inner-most private recesses of their soul in a fearful *avoidance of being denounced* as, anti-Jewish, even by themselves.

Over and over I asked myself, what in the hell is the difference whether it be Jews, Italians, Black Muslims or Symbionese Army, if they are trying to destroy your rights there is not a damned thing wrong in fighting back. I could easily prove the evil conspiracy being perpetrated by Jewish judges, but the moment I made the charges public I knew their rabid revenge would label me as some kind of a fiend, prejudiced against Jews. Damn, how can you fight the Jews? You'll be damned if you do, but if you do *not* fight back they will destroy you.

Always they're ready for you, lying in wait to condemn, screaming, "Nazi Beasts, Neo Nazi, Ku Klux Klan, Anti-Semitic, Racist Pig and Holocaust." Lord, *no one* could survive this hail of bitter malignancy hurled upon them. You'll be melted down, consumed by their venom long before you ever reach the 'truth and merits' of the real issues. What's the answer? To escape such absurd, vitriolic accusations and a stigma of so called, Anti-Semitism which attaches to you like the criminal record of a sick rapist and murderer...do you abandon your fight for your rights and tail between your legs flee for safety? But it's already too late, there is nowhere safe to flee.

It started thirteen years ago. I knew the precise moment. When I had testified to county corruption to the Grand Jury exposing Judge Berenson and Nordman, Berenson had ordered the foreman of the jury to *kill* the investigation. At that very instant their personalized, coordinated Jewish vendetta against me was set into motion. What I knew was much too dangerous to their safety, they could *not* allow such a situation to exist. I must go. With uniform Jew disdain they proceeded with plans for my demise. They would sabotage my Civil Service hearing, I'd lose, be discredited, and anything further I said would fall on deaf ears. In disgrace I would take flight, nothing more would ever be heard from me.

They wasted little time. Prior to my hearing, Richard Wittenberg their law partner was sent to a meeting of the Ventura Employees Association. His job was to stop their giving me twenty five hundred dollars for help to get a lawyer. Later, Berenson made Wittenberg the County Administrator. Phillip Cohen, a lawyer from the County Counsel, was assigned as legal officer to the hearing. His first act of sabotage was making certain a court reporter was *not* present. This was done with the connivance of my lawyer. I was never told that a transcript of the proceeding was absolutely necessary.

Cohen's cunning stood out clear when he wrote a letter lying to the Board of Supervisors, he told them I had, "No right to a review of my hearing." Making this lie an official act, he signed it Phillip Cohen, Asst. County Counsel. Then Dorothy Schechter, the County

Counsel and Appeal Court Judge Otto Kaus, sabotaged my Pro-Per lawsuits. Kaus wrote a Decision wherein he *actually changed* the law and then ordered that it was 'NOT TO BE PUBLISHED.'

When I appealed to the State Supreme Court, it was a set up with Stanley Mosk and William P. Clark. They refused to hear my case. Clark was a law partner of Judge Jerome Berenson and Nordman. Mosk and Clark were criminally conspiring to take over the State Supreme Court but their treachery failed. Later when Gov. Reagan became President he appointed Clark to a high office in D.C., while Otto Kaus took Clark's place on the State Supreme Court.

I filed a Civil Rights Suit in the Federal Court in L.A., but Harry Pregerson insidiously took over and Dismissed it. The Appeal Court for the Ninth Circuit overturned Pregerson's Dismissal. Meantime Pregerson was appointed to the Federal Appeal Court. Now, as an Appeal Court Judge, he again took over. He overruled a three judge panel of the Appeal Court and again he Dismissed my case. Harry began his law career as an ambulance chaser hanging around Mickey Cohen, his specialty was making false claims for stolen jewelry and phony injury accident reports to the insurance companies.

One of the most ingenious tricks Harry learned from Mickey was how to cover-up his own crimes by blaming the Mafia. Mickey had developed this Mafia *scape-goat routine* to a science. A Pregerson scam involving Italians had backfired seriously. A lawyer and close associate of Harry's, Stephen R. Reinhardt had set it up for Harry to receive a Gauguin painting worth half a million bucks...for this he agreed to 'fix' an up coming trial involving reputed Mafiosos, Louis Tom Dragna, Dominick Brooklier and Sam Sciortino, the Dagos had been indicted by a Federal Organized Crime Strike Force for alleged extortion of Jew pornographers and bookmakers, also for supposedly rubbing out an Italian, Frank 'The Bomp' Bompensiero. A Stephen Reinhardt operator, Joseph Hauser, a two time Federally convicted Labor Insurance swindler and con-man was making long distance calls to Carlos Marcello in New Orleans, setting-up delivery of the Gauguin to Pregerson, when the FBI who'd been routinely bugging Carlos's phone, digging into Labor Union Insurance bribes in New Orleans, accidently picked up their conversation.

Trapped in a vise, Hauser an accomplished liar *didn't* tell the FBI about Reinhardt's and Pregerson's conspiracy to 'fix' the case for the valuable painting. The Feds indicted Marcello and Phillip Rizzuto in New Orleans along with the Italians in L.A. for attempting to bribe Federal Judge Harry Pregerson. We contacted the U.S. Prosecutor

James Henderson in L.A., DuPre and I advised him of Pregerson's criminal activities and that he wanted that Gauguin so bad he had refused to remove himself from the case. Henderson chopped us off, refusing to hear the facts he stated, "Judge Harry Pregerson is *not* involved in anyway in the bribery."

We told Henderson *we knew* that he'd *had* to file a secret affidavit against Pregerson to get him off the case, the prosecutor slammed his office door in our face. Covering-up, Pregerson told reporters, "I am not involved in the bribery and I do not even like paintings." But two months after the FBI pressured Pregerson about their discovery of the bribe, Henderson's affidavit forced Pregerson to withdraw off the case. Pregerson was in a real nasty position. He had guaranteed the Italians to 'fix' the case, but they knew now he would screw them to save himself.

Harry Pregerson had never forgot the teachings of Mickey Cohen his old mentor, *"Blame it on the Mafia."* From his mighty sanctuary in Federal Chambers, Harry adorned in his Black Robes and Regal Pomp, flayed these evil people. "I find Sciortino's alleged conduct and the conduct of the others so 'personally offensive' that I could not in 'good conscience' continue to preside impartially over this criminal trial." After Pregerson's Judicial indictment of the Italians appeared in the newspapers and on TV they were found guilty of trying to bribe a Federal Judge, but not guilty of killing 'The Bomp.'

With his nimble mind, Harry's accomplice Stephen Reinhardt was conjuring a big scam with Al Davis, owner of the Oakland Raiders. Reinhardt instigated a move of the Raiders to L.A.. As a member of the Coliseum Commission he schemed, stealing millions in attorney fees from taxpayers. Pregerson kept it alive by bludgeoning lawyers from the National Football League in his chambers behind locked doors. When it was all over, Judge Pregerson and Reinhardt *owned* the Raiders with Davis as a front.

Slick operators, Pregerson and Reinhardt curried the insipience of President Carter. Convincing him they could deliver the Jew vote in the coming election, Carter promptly appointed them to the Federal Appeal Court. Police Chief Darryl Gates had Intelligence files with enough evidence of Hauser's and Reinhardt's criminal activities to put Reinhardt in the state pen instead of on the Federal Court. The Chief's Intelligence squad had also dug up astounding evidence that Russia was systematically immigrating Jew criminals like Hauser into America to sabotage the U.S. government. Always a sharp operator, Reinhardt had arranged to get himself appointed to the L.A. Police

Dept. Commission, and Hauser was controlled by Henderson, the Strike Force Prosecutor. With Reinhardt's and Pregerson's political power their criminal history and activities were covered-up during the investigation and their judicial appointments were approved.

A belated dawn was breaking, shafts of brilliant sunlight sliced into the smog of dullness blanketing my brain. Of course, how the hell had I forgotten so easy? Tod...my old friend Tod had laid it out for me. He couldn't have made it clearer, I remembered his words. "A new power is taking over our government, a sect, spreading their sinister, malignant fever." Tod displaying wariness had said, "At my age and no longer foolhardy, I've no desire to aggravate them." Tod called them "The Black Robe Syndicate." he was close, however they weren't a syndicate, they were a *family.* A virulent 'Criminal Family.' Similar to, but far more tightly woven than the Sicilian Black Hand Mafia Family, they were the Jewish Black Robe Mishpucka Family. The Mafia demanded fealty, allegedly sworn to secret blood-oaths. With the Mishpucka such oaths weren't necessary, Jews were tightly welded by millenniums of years of inbred racial chains. Credentials to be a member of the select cabal of the 'Mishpucka' are that you be a 'Jew from Russia' and you wear the Black Robes of the U.S. Judiciary. Other Jew judges can be lesser members, but Jews from Russia are 'The Elite.' More powerful in matters of life and death than any over-lord of the Black Hand Mafia ever envisioned himself becoming.

The Black Robe Mishpucka's rulings are absolute, backed by the might of America. Their ruthless, evil judicial decisions are protected by their decree of 'Judicial Immunity.' They do *not* allow themselves to be sued or restrained. While they waged a relentless vendetta to destroy me over the past thirteen years their names burned intense in my memory:

Richard Wittenberg, the County Administrator, a Russian Jew, born in New York, a partner of Berenson and Nordman.

Phillip Cohen, the Assistant County Counsel, a Jew born in Russia.

Dorothy Schechter, the County Counsel.

Jerome Berenson, the Presiding Judge of Ventura County.

Ben Nordman, former Federal Commissioner.

Otto Kaus, a State Supreme Court Judge, born in Russia.

Stanley Moskowitz, aka Stan Mosk, State Supreme Court Judge.

Harry Pregerson, a Federal Appeals Court Judge, both parents born in Russia.

Stephen Reinhardt, Federal Appeals Court Judge.

Joseph Hauser, convicted swindler, operator for Pregerson and Reinhardt. Born in Russia.

Judas Gius, Editor of Star Free Press, father a Jew from Russia, fled his country to keep from serving in the army in their time of need.

Marvin Sosna, Editor of the Thousand Oaks Chronicle, conspired with Gius to cover-up criminal activities of Mishpucka Judges and to censor information vital to the public in their newspapers.

Darkly subservient to this evil power, all Jews readily respond and perform to the Mishpucka's will and commands without questioning. Those entrenched in government office are geared to throw up road blocks on instant notice. Two employees, Ron Vogelbaum, Planning and Zoning, and Steve Solomon, Health Dept., acting under their secret orders from the Mishpucka sent false accusations to a state agency to sabotage my application for a beer license. The flagrant lies of supposed zoning violations on my property and their threats that they were going to "prosecute me to the fullest extent of the law" for numerous county ordinance violations were extremely vicious. There were *never* any violations and they *never* filed any charges against me however they prevented me from getting the license.

Exerting every ounce of strength and finances I could muster to fight their treacherous evil I ran for County Supervisor. I must have been doing pretty good, at least good enough to worry hell out of the Mishpucka because they went to work on me again. Two days before election, Geraine Jacobson, a clerk in the County Clerks office and a reporter named Gregg Solkovits cooked up a vitriolic story which they planted in the Camarillo Daily News and other county papers. According to them, I was a real bad character, not a person that you should vote for. They claimed I owed the County about two hundred dollars for many years and refused to pay.

According to Jacobson, "The Board of Supervisors were going to take me to court to recover the money." She added, "I'm just waiting the go ahead from the County Clerk, Robert L. Hamm, to file the complaint." But they never did. The Santa Paula Daily Chronicle in a commendable effort to keep their readers informed of candidates abilities decided to print their picture and statements just before the election. At the time I didn't stop to think this was possibly another trick of the Mishpucka. Jesus, you hate to be paranoid and suspect all our *fine* old American heritage, particularly American newspaper traditions and their precious values of 'honesty and integrity.'

The paper's offer sounded like a good deal. For weeks I'd been campaigning hard contacting voters. They'd been eating up the facts and evidence I'd provided them proving corruption and malfeasance in county government. The people knew *something* was very wrong. The unemployment rate was the highest in years yet politicians were giving themselves increases at the same time that they closed schools and libraries and took away the old folks tiny supplemental checks. Voters and taxpayers wanted *somebody* in office who'd put a *stop* to the corruption.

As they said they would, the Santa Paula Daily Chronicle printed the pictures and statements of all the candidates, that is all of them except me. They left mine out. In apology for this minor dereliction and to *prove* their honesty they said they'd print my statement and picture, however it would not be on the street until *after* the election. With an added touch of derision they placed the wrong name under the picture. No doubt about it, I'd got a lesson. Hell, the American people have to be absolutely nuts if they think they are ever going to get a choice! I thought about that a lot!

Well, alright...maybe the people are nuts, but they're not imbeciles. That's why one of these days *no one* will show up to vote. I'd lost the election. Jacobson and Solkovits had done a first-class job. Aided and abetted by the newspapers they'd successfully eliminated me as any danger to the Mishpucka. Deep in the dark crevices of governmental office, Jacobson, Solkovits, Vogelbaum, Solomon, and Lord knows how many more Jews lie in wait. Sneering and with *unyielding* hatred they will eliminate the next American patriot to appear on the scene as they have *all* the others. Eagerly, they accept the coveted praise lavished upon them by the cruel Mishpucka in salute for their service and loyalty.

By now I was able to comprehend the Black Robe Mishpucka and how their tremendous sources of power flowed to them through their insidious usurpation of the Judicial System. Sure, I had figured them out, but still hadn't totally rid myself of incomprehensible stirrings of guilt and a reluctance that plagued my every thought of fighting back against Jews...even though fully aware of their malicious vendetta to destroy me.

Unexpected, by the barest of chance and fortune an extraordinary document fell into my hands. It was written by The Anti-Defamation League of the B'nai B'rith, their Pacific Southwest Regional Office, Los Angeles, Calif.. Like a magic wand this document's malevolence banished *all* my mental blocks and *all* reluctance of a Christian to fight back against Jews. The ADL document was an instrument of extortion and intimidation. It was the *name* of their game.

Turn of the century extortion, the protection racket as attributed to the Black Hand Mafia was a crude operation, they collected a fee from businesses for phony protection service. If you didn't pay your insurance fee they simply tossed a pineapple through your window and blew the joint up. The Italian extortion racket is still the same basic operation of violence.

Mishpucka extortion and protection racket is highly sophisticated. The organization consists of possibly as many as a thousand or more small sub-groups all wired into the Anti-Defamation League of B'nai B'rith which is the power-arm of the Mishpucka, always these groups use deceiving official sounding titles, such as:

Committees, Coalitions, Congregations, Leagues, Federations, Congress, Unions, Foundations, Councils, Conferences, Authorities, etc.. To name a few typical B'nai B'rith sub-groups:

Jewish Life Issues (Committee)
National Urban (Coalition)
Jewish Defense (League)
American Civil Liberties (Union)
(Conference) of Presidents of Major American Jewish Organizations
(Union) of American Hebrew (Congregations)
Anerican Jewish (Committee)
Jewish (Federated Council) of Greater Los Angeles
American Jewish (Congress)

Each of the myriad sub-groups has but *one* function, to provoke and aggravate every incident that in even the remotest of ways could be propagandized as being Anti-Jewish, thus structuring a hysterical, so-called criminal act of, so-called Anti-Semitism.

In an East Los Angeles Jewish Cemetery headstones and markers were toppled, instantly, like in an early warning system the myrios sub-groups swung into action. Jew psychiatrists, Jew politicians, Jew TV producers and editorialists, Jew lawyers and Rabbis. Across the nation they screamed wild vitriolic accusations from their roof tops, "Anti-Semitism, resurgence of Nazi holocaust, Ku Klux Klan and Neo Nazis, etc., involved in desecration of Jewish Cemetery."

False accusations of anti-semitism were screeched to a hysterical pitch by Jewish genius' of deceit and psychological warfare, and Jews called for all Christians to renounce these despicable acts. However, working quietly and diligently on this alleged case of anti-semitism

Sheriffs Detectives quickly solved it. Five fifteen year old Mexican boys in a gang initiation had dared each other to enter the spooky graveyard at night and topple the headstones. Anti-semitism never entered into their minds, they didn't know a Jew from a Mongolian. Convicted on felony charges of 'malicious mischief,' one of the boys was sentenced to six years in the California Youth Authority.

Seigfried Halbreich, a board member of the ADL in Beverly Hills, is a top B'nai B'rith psychological propagandist. He spreads phony personal horror tales to young school children even though admitting he has never been within five miles of so-called Nazi gas chambers. Halbreich also promotes the "Diary of Anne Frank," which has been proven a hoax. It was written with a type of pen not made until long after the diary was allegedly composed. If school children are to be subjected to Halbreich's Nazi horror tales he should at the same time be required to tell them of present day atrocities committed by Jews against Lebanese women and children.

An eye witness to Jew terrorism, Times Staff Writer Charles T. Powers wrote from Beirut, Lebanon, "Five remaining members of an Arab family of fifteen were lying on the floor in the basement of a hospital. Two little girls about seven or eight years old lay speechless between the equally speechless mother and two old men. Rumpled sheets were pulled up from the girls feet which were scorched with phosphorus as if acid had eaten into their flesh. They were wounded when their brothers, sisters and uncles were killed last Sunday while the Jews bombed and shelled West Beirut for fourteen hours. Now the attacks were on again. Berbir Hospital by eleven a.m. had taken two direct hits already. There was no one in West Beirut Wednesday who doubted that the Israeli's were either coming into the heart of the city or that they would bomb and shell it to pieces."

The ADL constantly attacks Americans. Extorting apologies, cash and concessions with their threats of 'spray-painting' them with foul accusations of Anti-Semitism if they attempt to reveal the powerful, cunning, Jewish control over Congressmen. Rep. Paul N. McCloskey, candidate for the U.S. Senate was mercilessly assaulted by the ADL for stating, "The Jew Lobby is the most powerful lobby in America today. It has completely unbalanced our foreign policy. And also our Defense Dept. cannot contend with the Jew Lobby in Wash., D.C."

Rep. John Anderson, had three times sponsored a Constitutional Amendment in Congress to declare the country, "A Christian State." Assailed by Jews at a packed synagogue, Anderson, as a candidate for U.S. President, groveled before their power, he cried, "I made a mistake, it's that simple, please believe me, I won't do it again."

James Watt, with his reputation as a 'hard-case' Secretary of the Interior, meekly apologized to a Jewish group for an innocuous letter he'd written to Ambassador Moshe Arens of Israel. Kenneth Bialkin, the National Chairman of the ADL of B'nai B'rith crowed, "After our press release by the ADL criticizing his letter, Mr. James Watt has apologized to the Jews for his indiscretion with great sincerity."

During a stormy argument over the constitutionality of voluntary school prayers which Senator Metzenbaum, Ohio, opposes, Senator Ernest Hollings, S. Carolina, under heavy pressure by Metzenbaum, finally, and with utter exasperation gave up, "I yield the floor to the Senator from the B'nai 'B'rith." Angrily, Metzenbaum demanded his apology. Hollings quickly cringed, "I apologize, I am not throwing it off onto your Jewish faith, I said it only in fun." Sen. Hollings knew it was not just for fun when he accused Metzenbaum of representing the B'nai B'rith instead of America. But he didn't dare stick to his guns and face the ruinous, evil wrath of the B'nai B'rith. To force Hollings and other Congressmen to stay in line, David Brody, Wash., D.C., agent for the B'nai B'rith, issued another ADL press release, castigating Hollings for his revealing statement.

June 8, 1967 the U.S.S. Liberty, an Intelligence ship sailing in the Mediterranean was suddenly attacked by Israeli torpedo boats and jet bombers for more than three hours. Napalm, incendiary and high explosive bombs and torpedoes blasted and ripped the Liberty apart. The Liberty and its life rafts were strafed with machine gun fire by the Jewish boats and fighter planes, its decks ran red with the crews blood. Almost every sailor on the Liberty was either killed or badly wounded. Later, the Israelis claimed they thought the Liberty was an enemy Egyptian ship and they had attacked for only a few minutes before they discovered their mistake and withdrew.

Lt. James M. Ennes Jr., Intelligence Officer on the ship during the attack, has since written a book, 'Assault On The U.S.S. Liberty.' The Lt. states the Israelis have lied about their attack. Egypt never had a vessel that resembled or could even remotely be mistaken for the Liberty, which was clearly marked and flying the American flag. The attack occurred not only for a few minutes as Israel claimed but for hours. They feared that the Intelligence ship had detected their plans to invade Syria the following day. They didn't want the U.S. to discover their plot because they'd be forced to halt their imminent invasion.

Orders from the Jewish High Command were direct and concise.

"Sink the U.S.S. Liberty...there must be *no* survivors." The Israeli Task Force 'sneak attack' ran against a serious problem. One that's confronted America's foes for over two hundred years. With proud and stirring American Naval fighting tradition the lightly armed old ship's crew stood fast, they *refused* to go down. The truth about the attack was politically covered-up. Fourteen years later Lt. Ennes and the remaining survivors of the U.S.S. Liberty have become engaged in another bitter, desperate fight, a battle for a Senate Investigation into the wanton murder of U.S. sailors.

Inconceivably they find they are embattled with the *same* vicious enemy who murdered their shipmates. After reviewing *irrefutable evidence* of the unmerciful *sneak* attack, Senator Adlai Stevenson, Illinois, was convinced of the flagitious crime of the Israelis, and he moved to call for a full Senate probe of the attack. But four months later Stevenson regretfully informed Lt. Ennes and the other Liberty survivors, "A Senate investigation into the ship's attack will *never* be allowed to be conducted because our U.S. Congressmen are fearfully intimidated by a powerful Jew Lobby which takes its orders *directly* from within Israel."

State Senator David Roberti, Pres. Pro-Tem, Beverly Hills, Calif. uses his political influence in press releases boasting that, "Jews are sacred," he states, "It is verboten, authoritatively prohibited to say anything derogatory about Jews because of memory of the holocaust, where six million Jews were killed by Nazis during WW11." Roberti became carried away with his diatribe, "This will *prohibit* Christians from conjuring up 'medieval memories' of when the Jews devoured Christians blood."

Presidential Counselor Edwin Meese and William Wilson, Envoy to the Vatican, have been under a fierce attack from the ADL for their charges that the ACLU is, "Part of a nationwide criminal lobby supported by organized crime." Their accusations are true, however common sense should tell Meese and Wilson that, Norman Dorsen, Stanley Scheinbaum, and Ira Glasser, heads of the ACLU could not possibly be members of the Italian Mafia. Hell, they're top members of the Jewish Mishpucka. Meese and Wilson are on the right track about crime but they just can't seem to get the correct definitions of 'organized crime' in their heads. The Mafia and Mishpucka are two altogether *separate* crime families with a wide variance of ideology and goals.

The important difference is that the so-called Mafia is a loosely knit group of Italian criminals. They're loyal to the United States in the sense of having no *conscious* intent to destroy America. But the Mishpucka is a secret, *racist* organization, a criminal *blood-line* that owes allegiance to the Family alone. Their sworn declaration, their evil goal is subjugation of *all* people and total control of the world's power and wealth. Focusing on the B'nai B'rith's document I read and reread it. Their allegations and veiled threats in the crude letter left no doubt of its real intent. It was clever, heavy handed extortion laced with phony racial and religious implications and accusations. It was *intimidation Mishpucka style,* much more *ingenious* than a Mafia pineapple tossed through your window.

The gist of the letter was based on a complaint made by a Jewish waitress working at a large restaurant. Her supervisor allegedly made a statement within her hearing that he "Hated Jews." He apologized, but she complained that, "He showed no remorse or regret over the comment." The letter demanded prompt disciplinary action against the supervisor, 'Fire the sonofabitch.' The unmistakable 'blackmail intent' of the message was summed-up in one sentence where B'nai B'rith reminded the Italian restaurant owner of the "demographics of his clientele."

In the heart of a rich Jew neighborhood the restaurant depended totally on its Jewish clientele. With Jewish pickets on the sidewalk in front of the business screaming, "Anti-Semitic," the B'nai B'rith could break the owner in a week. The makeup of B'nai B'rith stationary in itself is a menacing bludgeon, it left no doubt of the powerful force breathing down your neck. The left margin, from top to bottom is a list of over forty powerful Jewish judges, Rabbis, lawyers, newspaper editorialists, TV directors, etc.:

The Honorable Robert Feinerman
Irwin Levin
Frieda Lowitz
Charles Goldring
Kaygey Kash
Irwin Weinberg
Moe Kudler
Maxwell Greenberg
Burton Levison
Kenneth Bialkin
Morton Pinz
Hyman Haves, etc. etc..

The letter was signed Harvey B. Schechter, Regional Director. Below Schechter's name was the *kicker,* it said..."Remember ADL," in other words "do *not* forget your contribution."

Two psychological propaganda 'avenues' combine to produce an infectious virus, a mysterious malady, the Christian Guilt Complex. The first avenue of propaganda is so-called Anti-Semitism, according to Jews this includes it all, *everything* from whispering a derogatory remark about a Jew, on up to the alleged holocaust. The next avenue is even more soul searing from a religious viewpoint, words that Jews chant ceaselessly, "Jews are Gods Chosen People."

This 'Chosen People,' dogma is a very ingenious 'mixed metaphor' that Jews use like word-games small children play. The catch to the clever word-game is simple. Like the child's game, it consists merely of twisting the meaning of what they know is false into a deceptive half-truth. This syndrome of propaganda germs results in a crippling disease, very devastating, creating a vast, unexplainable moral guilt among Christians. "Jews are Gods Chosen People." The explanation of the Jews claim to 'Gods Favor' came to light in an extraordinary manner. It occurred in L.A. while Dr. Walter White of the Western Front Christian Organization interviewed Harold Rosenthal, one of Senator Jacob Javits Chief Aides on Jewish Affairs.

Dr. White asked, "What makes you believe Jews are Gods Chosen People?"

Rosenthal hedged, "Sen. Javits could better answer that." White pressed on, under the momentary stress Rosenthal suddenly blurted, "I'll tell you something few Jews will admit. We worship a different God than you, we worship Lucifer, we are *his* chosen people." After this terrible blunder Rosenthal was ordered to return to Tel Aviv, Israel. Shortly after this incredible slip of the tongue, Rosenthal was executed, gangland style by the Jews.

The deadly microbes spewing forth from the Jews psychological warfare factory withered, dissolving when exposed by this revelation. They fled into thin air like a haunted house apparition flushed from the mind by the light of truth. Miraculously, I was freed from their insanity, the *guilt complex* from Christians supposedly picking on the Jews that had affected my common sense was dead. How had I been so stupid to be taken in by such childish propaganda?

Analyzing the weird phenomena sensibly, I realized the infestation of propaganda germs became possible only because of centuries of the Jews *wild screams* of persecution. Their scheming whines were dinned into the ears of Christians from before kindergarten. Then suddenly confronted with a powerful Jewish propaganda machine it appeared to be a reality. Never had I really given their Anti-Semitic thing much thought. I'd known and was friendly socially with many Jew lawyers for years and had sat in the Masonic Lodge with them. To me they'd seemed just like anyone else. Thinking back I didn't recall any of them ever having mentioned being persecuted.

Until my sudden realization I was the target of a Jew vendetta the subject was very distant in my mind if there at all. My curiosity was aroused. I had to know more about Jews, for months I studied and researched deep into their ways. One of the documents I found was a study of Bedouins in Israel, it was extremely critical of the Israeli government. It likened their acts against Arabs as harsher than Nazi treatment of Jews before WW11. I gave the study full credence, it fortunately had been written by Yoav Peled, a Jew himself.

An Israeli citizen, Peled was a Ph. D candidate in Political Science at UCLA. He described the Bedouins as "Loyal, peaceful citizens who've lived on their land for generations. Their land has been *taken away* and given to Jew settlements and used for military bases. They are concentrated into areas under military control and can't leave an area without a permit. The Israeli Government has organized what they call the Green Patrol to do their rough stuff. The Green Patrol was *patterned* after the Nazi's Brown Shirt Sturmabteilung, Storm Troops.

Bedouins are shifted from one place to another so that they can't claim ownership by possession of any particular property. They aren't given any water for cultivation, even when their plots are adjacent to irrigated Jewish-owned fields. Under their Likud Party, the Israeli Government has taken on a brutal form.

Ali Abu-Sulb has lived with his family on lands for sixty years and has his documents to prove it. Early one morning the Jewish Green Patrol, 'Storm Troopers' showed up. Loading the family's tent and possessions on trucks they dumped them forty miles away damaging their tent and meager possessions. The Ali Abu-Sulbs without their tent huddled among the bushes for protection from the desert sun and cold nights. Their Green Patrol functions as a para-military force to *harass* and *intimidate* the Bedouins. They *destroy* the houses and sheds for violation of building permits and zoning laws set up by the Jewish Government. Herds of sheep and goats dwindle for the lack of grazing lands which have been seized by the Green Patrol. The mainstay of the Bedouin economy has been virtually destroyed. The Jewish Government passed a law enabling them to confiscate twenty thousand acres of Bedouin land without going through *any* judicial channels and without allowing Bedouins 'recourse' to the courts."

The Jews wanton disregard for boundaries of other countries is difficult to believe. Bombing an atomic plant in Iraq which was not yet completed the Israelis in a military press release stated they had totally destroyed the installation because in 'their belief' it could be a future danger to them. If the U.S. had taken action on this same *far out* premise it could have destroyed Russia many years ago with a sneak attack, long before they'd developed the ability to retaliate with nuclear weapons.

In Israel's latest military invasion of another country they used the excuse they had to destroy the Palestine Liberation Organization in Lebanon. With a murderous irresponsibility the Jews leveled villages and towns killing thousands upon thousands of women and children. Beirut was literally destroyed.

Menachem Begin, the *blood thirsty* organizer of the early Jewish terrorist Stern Gang, is now a leader of all the Israeli Government's atrocities. Begin's power over life and death drives him to ever more dangerous doctrines. He threatens the world that, "As far as he is concerned Anti-Semitism is no longer an internal affair of all other countries." Begin asserts his right to, "Intervene to protect the Jews wherever they are."

France's former Prime Minister, Pierre Mendes-France, a very widely respected Jew has stated, "Begin is totally irresponsible, a *mad dog fanatic* and what he is doing is a tragedy for the world and his own people will suffer." Begin's Stern Gang was ruthless and active constantly. About the time they murdered Count Folke Bernadotte, U.N. Peace Negotiator, they destroyed an Arab town. Begin brought the bodies of his victims, men, women and children, to Jerusalem. Proudly boasting of his bloody deeds, Begin displayed them before Prime Minister Ben Gurion and throngs of Jews.

The WW11 horror stories from Germany had their first beginnings as nothing more than another of the *endless* Jewish scams to gain financial reparations from the suckers through sympathy. Their wild stories were so successful the scam spread like wild-fire. Soon they were reporting entire families wiped out. The scam soon became *big business,* known as, 'The Holocaust.' At first it was quite believable because of mass confusion during the liberation at the end of WW11. Many years later the true facts of their wild stories are starting to reveal the Holocaust for the massive racket it actually is.

The Nazi's had done nothing more than intern suspected enemies of their nation, precisely as the U.S. did when rounding up Japanese on the West Coast in 1942, after Pearl Harbor. Thousands of Jews are now contacting relatives still alive long after they had reported each other being killed in the Holocaust.

Manya Kornblit and husband Majir, now U.S. citizens discovered that her brother, Harry Nagelsztajn is alive and a wealthy building contractor living in England. Perpetrating and magnifying these false horror tales over forty years, the B'nai B'rith uses them incessantly in their psychiatric-propaganda warfare against the Christians.

In his 1981 report on Organized Crime, Calif. Atty. Gen. George Deukmejian, revealed the existence of Israeli Organized Crime. He stated, "The Jews are *competitors* of the Mafia. They are involved in drug smuggling and specialize in narcotics dealing." In January 1981, fifty two U.S. hostages were released from Iran's imprisonment for over a year. The one receiving the most attention as a hero was forty seven year old Jerry Plotkin. L.A. Councilmen Joel Wachs and Zev Yaroslavsky honored Plotkin on his return to Los Angeles. He was driven to City Hall in a gold limousine bearing a giant yellow ribbon mounted on its hood. Unlike the other hostages the *hero's* reason for being in Iran was very obscure. LAPD and FBI records disclosed his criminal record of narcotics smuggling went back twenty four years to 1957. Police authorities suspected he was in Iran to negotiate a huge cocaine deal when he was seized by the Iranians along with the U.S. Government employees.

If police suspicions were correct, the big drug deal was the most important negotiation Plotkin had ever been entrusted with. Being snatched up along with the Embassy people by the Iranians was just more of his miserable bad luck. Then again, perhaps it was not just misfortune. Why had Plotkin been at the Embassy? Maybe that was his contact. Always a small time hood hanging around the likes of Charlie Rosenfeld, Sammy Weinstein and Jerry Stein, a two bit bail bondsman it looked as if Plotkin had blown his one real chance to make the big time.

L.A. Councilmen Wachs, Yaroslavsky and Marvin Braude stirred up media propaganda to camouflage Plotkin's Iran trip as that of a legitimate U.S. businessman. Among experienced investigators this cover-up threw strong suspicion on the Mishpucka councilmen who'd duped Mayor Tom Bradley into declaring February 4, 1981 as Jerry Plotkin Day. The councilmen were already deep into another deal that would be one of the Mishpucka's biggest single scores yet.

It was a revenue bond deal that would make the two hundred and fifty million dollar Ventura County Courthouse scam look pale. A four and a half billion dollar nuclear power plant was proposed to be built in Palo Verde, Ariz.. The bonds supposedly will be repaid by revenue from the plant. Due to lawsuits by the Pima Indians, local farmers and City of Phoenix, the power plant might never be built. A California Taxpayers Organization, "The Alliance For Survival" filed a lawsuit to prevent sale of bonds based on fraud by the L.A. City Council's *illegal* adoption of a bond issue.

Lawyers for the taxpayers group argued to the court that the bond issue was a criminal fraud being perpetrated on taxpayers. Despite all the facts and evidence *exposing* this fraud, L.A. Superior Court Judge Leon Savitch ruled against the taxpayers. This allowed a block of bonds worth five hundred and forty million to be sold a few days later by the Southern California Public Powers Authority, another Mishpucka corporation set up same as their phony Public Facilities Corp. in Ventura.

When analyzed, the revenue bond scam is a simple scenario. All it takes is a corrupt Board of Supervisors or City Council, but most important, a Black Robe Mishpucka Judge to Dismiss any lawsuits filed by irate people. The phony Public Powers Authority then sells the entire block of bonds to a Mishpucka bank which sells the bonds in small lots. The Public Powers Authority presently has four and a half billion dollars of citizens money to play with and the taxpayers have forty years to pay back the four and a half billion plus interest.

Danger of exposure for the Mishpucka is far more inherent in the revenue bond scam than in narcotic deals. All legislative actions and declarations are documented. Collection of the payments themselves by the Southern California Public Powers Authority is a *continuing* conspiracy to defraud the public. Strange enough, as time passes the part played by *each* conspirator involved becomes more evident, take the acts of Mishpucka Judge Savitch when he wiped out a taxpayers lawsuit, it could hardly be more obvious. However it merely displays Mishpucka arrogance, their belief that their Black Robes cannot be touched.

Begin's threat to interfere by force into other countries internal affairs is not an idle threat, his agents provocateur operate around the world. In the U.S., Irving Rubin, a Begin gangster has set up a militant organization, the Jewish Defense League. Training pre-teen Jew boys and girls, he turns out professionals for para-military duty. They are taught the fine art of killing as they enthusiastically chop apart human silhouettes with their sub-machine guns. Rubin boasts that police leave the JDL alone because it would be *Anti-Semitic* to interfere with his guns.

The exact size and composition of JDL's arsenal is a mystery, but they have Ruger Mini-14's, an easy to conceal version of the M-14, a standard weapon of the U.S. Forces in Vietnam. There has also been seen a variety of other weapons, Bk 91, M-14 rifles, shot guns and Ingram Model 10 counter-insurgency weapons. Many handguns are in their arsenal, 38 cal. and .357 magnum revolvers and 45 cal. army pistols.

Born in North Africa, Dina Mizrahi now lives in L.A., a thirteen year old Jewish girl, Mizrahi received weapon training from the JDL along with sixteen year old John and his younger brother Eric. Her grimace became a wide satisfied grin as she coolly squeezed off three rounds from a 38 cal. revolver into the heart of a human silhouette. Sixteen year old John helped his baby faced brother Eric shoulder a powerful semi-automatic Bk 91, a civilian version of West Germany's Army G3 assault rifle. John helped Eric absorb the weapon's sharp recoil as he began eagerly blasting away at the neat row of human silhouettes.

Irv Rubin's predilection for murder and mayhem was very evident when he offered "a cash bounty of five hundred dollars to any Jew who kills, maims or seriously injures any member of the American Nazi Party." He added, "If they bring us their ears we'll make it one thousand." After his offer was made at a well publicized JDL speech, Rubin was prosecuted for solicitation of murder, but was found not guilty, all it took for a not guilty verdict was to get one Jew on the jury. To Rubin anyone who is not a Jew is a Nazi. To make Rubin's plans for murder and mayhem easier, the Mayor of San Francisco, Diane Feinstein and Congresswoman Bobbi Fiedler are pushing laws to take handguns away from honest citizens. For many years Fiedler has been a close confidant of Menachem Begin.

Unlike the macho Italian Mafia, the Jew Mishpucka has always known the value of women members to their organization. The most powerful political female Mishpucka in California's judiciary is Judge Joan Dempsey Klein. Gov. Jerry Brown appointed her to Presiding Justice of Division Three, Second District Court of Appeal, in L.A.. Speaking before members of the Women Lawyers of Ventura, Judge Klein exhorted them to secure judicial positions. An avowed racist, the Mishpucka Judge directed fiery intensity to three female Jewish lawyers, J. Koehn, M. Kleinman, and L. Freedman, inciting them to pack the courts with Mishpucka judges. During meetings of female lawyers throughout California the Judge incessantly vents her wrath against Christian Churches that stress moral values.

It was over twenty years ago, I'd witnessed a dire warning of Ms. Joan Dempsey Klein's evil racist temperament. At the time I hadn't recognized it for what it really was, but my disgust for her perverted abuse of the American Judicial System had kept my memory of the incident vivid. A friend of mine was studying law and had need of a typewriter. Having a wife and three small children to support he'd been searching for one at a reasonable price. I'd warned Lin to stay away from Main Street pawn shops but he located a machine he was certain would do the job and the price was right. Mr. Ginsberg the pawn shop owner assured Lin it was a fine typewriter, he had, "Just tuned it all up, it runs like a new Rolls Royce no less." Furthermore the pawn broker gave his *personal* guarantee, claiming that his word as his bond was sufficient. As a law student versed in such matters Lin demanded a written guarantee. His *word* not being immediately accepted the pawn-man affected an injured pose. But not wanting to lose a sale he reluctantly put his words in writing. Lin was satisfied, positive that the law would protect and safe guard his interests. That evening as Lin typed papers for his next day's class the Rolls Royce just kinda' like disintegrated from under his fingertips.

Lapsing into unintelligible gabble, pawn broker Ginsberg threw up his hands walking away when Lin mentioned his written guarantee. Judicial remedy was the only recourse left. Trusting Due Process of Law to settle the problem fairly, Lin filed a complaint in the Small Claims Court, he asked me to be a witness. It was almost noon, we were the only ones there. Lin was starting to explain his typewriter deal when suddenly Judge Klein's visage became fierce, her arms swooping furiously out from her body like huge wings she appeared to be launching off her bench. Bursting with anger she hissed, "You mean to say that you have come into *my* courtroom with such sham accusations demeaning this honest businessman, accusing him of a dishonest deal with no proof whatsoever?"

Lin waved his paper, the signed guarantee, "Your Honor, I......."

Judge Klein cut him off, "The Court refuses to listen to anymore of these accusations...the Court rules in Mr. Ginsberg's favor, Case Dismissed." It had not been necessary for Ginsberg to utter a word. He scurried from the room.

It was pretty rank, the Judge must have something going with that pawn broker or else she's plain nuts. My snap deduction of Klein's behavior wasn't even close, it went much deeper, but back in those days I didn't even suspect the *real* truth. Lin was Chinese, a more honest and loyal American could not be found. I knew him well. He had served as a Marine Lt. in the South Pacific and was one hell of a regular guy. The whole thing was a hard blow to Lin's perspective on the study of law. Leaving the court Lin carried Ginsberg's busted Rolls Royce, he had brought it to show to the judge. Clutching the worthless piece of paper with Ginsberg's signature written on it his shoulders drooped as he mumbled, "Jesus Christ, Jesus Christ."

Out on the street I said the only helpful thing I could think of, "Damn it Lin, I warned you to stay away from those friggin' Main Street pawn joints."

It would be years, in fact, not *until* the events of the present that I would understand the *real* truth of Judge Klein's *terrible fury* with Lin. Her profane Judicial act was simple, basic for the Mishpucka. Lin was Chinese, Ginsberg was Jew. For Joan Dempsey Klein there could be only *one* judicial decision possible.

Murder and mutilation...the Mafia or the Mishpucka...hell, there's no difference. In Mafia disputes over gambling and narcotics bodies are dismembered, stuffed in barrels and dumped into the ocean. In Mishpucka disputes over narcotics and money, bodies are disposed of the same way. Jew cocaine dealers Esther and Ele Ruven were killed in a downtown L.A. hotel. Pieces of their bodies were thrown into a trash bin. Police arrested two Israeli drug smugglers, Joseph Zakaria, and Jehuda Avital. Convicted, they were sent to prison for the grisley killings.

In San Fernando Valley, Sol and Elaine Salomon, along with their son and daughter mysteriously vanished from their blood splattered four bedroom home. Salomon an Israeli, was an associate of known Mishpuckas. Twenty five grams of hashish was found in the house. In the daughter's bedroom a section of blood soaked carpet was cut out. Strangely, in the hotel room where the Ruven's were killed and dismembered a piece of blood soaked carpet had also been cut out, used to carry away the bodies. International drug traffic is an evil place to survive.

CHAPTER 36

Immortalized by Henry Wadsworth Longfellow in his story of Paul Revere's Ride, 'Old North Church, Boston, Mass.,' is a living symbol of our freedoms inherited from our Colonial Americana. Its plebeian staunchness and dignity is a memorial, a tribute to our forefathers. Their courage and faith over two hundred years ago gave Americans their liberty. The fragile spire rising above the bell tower received no hint from the blue sky and warm sun that it was winter. In hushed, respectful huddles the large assembly of people tarried outside.

It was noon, as if obeying an invisible command, the groups were breaking up, moving into the church. My old partner Frank had been struck with a massive heart attack, he died within a few hours. When talking with his wife Ginny on the phone that night she told me, "His brain and body were terribly damaged by the attack, had he survived he'd have been hopelessly crippled." Knowing it was far beyond our power to change things we concurred, it was more merciful this way, over so quick. Somehow we felt Frank would have agreed.

Services were at Forest Lawn Memorial Park, Hollywood Hills, California, not Boston, Mass., this accounted for the bright February day. The Old North Church we were entering was the exact replica of the beloved, 'Old North' of Boston. Nestling among the green hills and the pines of the cemetery the church cast a subtle emanation, a warm feeling of Colonial New England.

Frank and I had worked as partners a long time, over seven years.

It was sixteen years since I left the L.A. District Attorney's Bureau of Investigation and moved to Ventura. We'd gotten together only a few times for coffee since. On the way to Hollywood, DuPre and I picked up Cannizzaro at Denny's in Agoura. Next stop was Cables Restaurant in Woodland Hills, we met Marty Philpot, Supervising agent with the Intelligence Section of the IRS, and one of his agents. There was plenty of time so we talked over coffee.

A few weeks ago I had talked to Marty mentioning my problems with the Santa Barbara ABC office. Also I'd learned the agent who was handling my application received secret orders to deny the beer license. Marty exclaimed, "Hell, beer license's only run a few bucks, every food place on the highway gets one if they apply."

"Yeh, I know, everyone except me."

"It would be *very interesting* to learn who has that *kind of power* over ABC, I'll do some checking, we'll discuss it next time I see you."

A waitress filled our cups, she moved away, Marty spoke, "About our conversation, I called agent Huntington in Santa Barbara."

"What happened?"

"Well, he convinced me of one thing. Something damn strange is going on."

"What did he say?"

"When I asked him a couple questions about your case he told me to go screw myself."

"You're kidding?"

"Nope, that's what he said and hung up on me."

"Well, it's somebody *damned powerful* giving them orders if they feel that confident."

"Yeh, and you can bet that those people know by now that IRS Intelligence has made an inquiry." Marty changed the subject, "We better get going, don't want to be late for the funeral." He offered us a ride, "I've got a big station wagon, we can all fit in."

Frank's friends were many. Inside the church I saw millionaires, judges, movie people, law enforcement officers from all agencies and just plain street people. They'd all known Frank, they'd come to pay respect to a man they knew as a good cop. But one very special long time friend wouldn't be here. Audie Murphy was killed in a plane accident several years ago. But still, subconsciously I looked around expecting to see his reassuring presence. He was a friend Frank had really missed. The services were over but some people remained to talk. I saw a guy who was an investigator for the D.A. when I knew him years ago, now he was a Judge. Most of the guys had done real good for themselves over the years. One hell of a lot better than I had, the way things were going for me there was damn little future. I walked over to where Philpot and Cannizzaro were talking with a heavy set man near the station wagon. Marty introduced us, "Gary, meet John Babcock, he's a program director for Channel Seven TV. We are going to meet with Babcock and some others at the Smoke House Restaurant on Barham Road for a drink."

A Maitre'D arranged for an alcove in the lounge, fourteen of us crowded in. Drinks flowed, lots of old memories were dredged up and rehashed. Frank's unusual detective talents along with his witty dry humor gave occasion for many brisk stories, reminiscing went back many years. Frank had pulled a million funny little stunts, but one I had to tell.

"Big time Hollywood operator, Benny opened a real classy, plush joint on Sunset Strip. Benny always came on real friendly to us, but it was plain he didn't like Frank and me coming around, intimating that we seemed to cause his 'big spending' clientele to become very nervous. A profuse, gushing welcome was Benny's trademark. He'd say, 'It's a tradition, you know, kinda' like a Continental style, they love it.' Benny's joint was jumping, his arms waving in extravagant flourishes he danced over to greet us. His splendid tailored tux was enhanced with a perfect, tiny white carnation. Accompanying Benny this night was another guy, also in a tux and a white carnation.

He was big, I mean this character was huge. Benny looked like Mickey Rooney next to Mike Magurski. Young and handsome, lots of black curls adorned his head, unsmiling he was strictly business. Muscles in his arms writhed, ready to burst his tuxedo. Frank with his hint of insult easily detectable deliberately goaded, 'Who's this guy Benny, your keeper?'

Benny's expression was pained, 'This is my associate, he just came out from Cleveland. Frank I would like you to meet Arthur.' The big guy thrust out a hand, it looked more like a ham. The two clasped hands, suddenly a vein in Arthur's neck swelled, bulging out around his collar. A gleam flashed in Benny's eyes. I knew what was in his mind. He planned to have this ape bust up Frank's hand. Humiliate him so bad when he fell to his knees crying uncle before the crowd maybe we'd never return. Benny would laugh it off, just an innocent prank, you know, 'Gee'z Frank, I'm sorry, Arthur is just a growing boy, he don't know his own strength, ha, ha.'

Frank kept on talking to Benny like nothing was wrong. Arthur's face turned blood red, his mouth fell open, gurgling, the muscleman slowly went to his knees, his left arm jerked helplessly. Speechless, his eyes implored Frank who was talking unconcerned to Benny who was staring in astonishment at Arthur's weird performance. I knew Frank was making bone meal of Arthur's right hand. When younger, Frank worked long hard hours at a steel mill forge. He'd developed incredible strength in his right hand with a grip like a hydrolic press operating under tons of pressure, no one knew it better than me, I'd tested his grip once and only to a certain point. Expecting Arthur to let out a blood curdling scream any second I headed for the door. I heard Frank say, 'It's been very nice meeting you Arthur.' Glancing back I saw Frank release Arthur's mashed hand and follow me out. On his knees, watering eyes rolling up, Benny's associate appeared to be deep in prayers."

While stories and cocktails flowed I grabbed a chance to talk with John Babcock. It was a golden opportunity, if I could get a television program like 'Sixty Minutes or Twenty Twenty' digging into judicial corruption in Ventura and L.A. we could *bust* it wide open. Babcock showed a keen interest in the subject, he suggested, 'Let's meet next week at my office, we can go into the details.'

"That's great, I'll bring along some files for you to look at." The impromptu wake for Frank at the Smoke House finally ended, and Marty drove us back to Cables where I'd left my car, Cannizzaro, DuPre and I returned to Ventura.

American Broadcasting Company facilities were located between Hollywood and L.A. in what used to be a movie studio. Built many years ago, the design was early Californian. The time worn sound stages were surrounded by residential neighborhoods, the jumble of buildings and parking lots were spread over several acres. Cradling an intercom phone the guard at the gate said, "Okay, Mr. Babcock's secretary says for you to come on over to his office." He pointed at a white stucco building fifty yards away, "Just ask anybody in there for directions." The place was a labyrinth of halls and tiny rooms. I mentioned Babcock's name to a group gathered by a water cooler. A trim messenger girl spoke up, "I'm going that way, follow me."

She led off, deftly flitting through a maze of passages and around corners. Never, not even in Hollywood had I seen jeans jammed on so tight, how in hell can she sit down? I was trying to figure it out when we reached John's door. It was open, from its looks his office must be a prototype for harried TV news execs. Program schedules, news clippings, old manuscripts...a million scraps of paper scribbled with notes cluttered up the desk in the small room. Babcock nodded, he indicated a coffee maker and styrofoam cups in a corner.

Despite phones ringing and aides popping in and out with vital communiques John was a good listener. His comments assured me he'd absorbed everything I told him. Hours of conversation slipped by when an assistant beckoned John outside. Sitting so long my legs were cramped. Moving around the room I looked at collections of pictures covering the walls, mementos of 'On the spot' news events he had covered as a reporter. I recognized Ma Duncan at her trial. Crime accomplices Moya and Maldonado sat with her in court, that was over twenty years ago. Babcock was in the business a long time, lots of experience. I was sure of his ability to put it all together on film. John returned. I said, "I see you covered Ma Duncan's trial."

"Yes, I stayed in Ventura during most of it. I made friends with many lawmen and reporters. It could be a help. I keep in contact by seeing them whenever I go up there." I knew Cannizzaro was giving info on his own case to Babcock involving Pregerson and Berenson's judicial corruption. There was no lack of evidence for John to lock his teeth into. On my next visit to Babcock one of Marty Philpot's IRS Intelligence agents arrived. John phoned for lunch reservations. The Tail of The Cock on Los Feliz Dr. was a popular watering hole for Hollywood 'TV Intelligentsia.' Judicial lawlessness remained our topic of discussion. We readily agreed rampant *judicial depravity* is destroying our government and country's way of life faster than the murderous crime waves on the street. Corruption in itself is a *base* instigator of crime.

Judicial rot is no longer hidden. More and more honest citizens are gored by fierce frustrations, a gnawing fear of losing everything they have worked for their entire life. The sight of American Justice collapsing before their eyes is a *nightmare* that goads even the most docile of citizens into committing criminal acts they otherwise would never contemplate. Racked by intense fears and panic they cry out, "I'm gonna' get mine now, before it's too late, judges are stealing us blind, if they can get away with it, so can I."

When considering their frantic reasoning, justification for such a tumultuous clamor becomes plausible. 'What in hell's the difference, I might as well steal everything I can get my hands on, the country is going to hell anyway.'

A few days later, supposedly for making sure he had all the facts, John met Eddie, Bob and me at Denny's in Agoura. Eating a grilled cheese I half listened to them briefing John on the latest evidence. With a jolt my mind came to attention, there was something wrong.

Having survived more than a dozen nightmarish years of fighting off the Black Robe Mishpucka, I'd developed a sub-conscious receptor. It was fine tuned to pick up the faintest wave of betrayal moving in the air. Something started an old song going around and around in my head, the record refused to quit. Irked by its insistence I began to heed the words, dah dee dah, I've got that ooohld feeling, da dee da da. Wide awake I focused on John, he was saying, "I've assigned investigative reporters to Ventura to begin putting a story together. In a few days I'll send a camera crew up there to start interviewing you and a lot of other people on the subject of Judicial Corruption."

Automatically the record player switched to another song, one that was very popular during WW11. The lyrics seemed to carry a special warning, dah da dee da dah da, "It seems to me I've heard that song before, it's from an old fah-miliar score," dah dah dee da dah dah. I looked at Bob and Eddie, they both seemed pleased, convinced of John's sincerity. I guess they hadn't received any negative vibrations. Maybe my receptor was becoming over sensitive, well, I could wait a couple more days and see what happens with John's promises.

Tuesday Babcock sent us word, "Meet me and a crew at Denny's parking lot in Agoura, nine sharp tomorrow morning." A reporter assigned to conduct the interview and a technician and camera lady arrived but John didn't show. Something must have come up at the studio to delay him. Everyone crowded into the motorhome we had provided, while the soundman readied his equipment the interviewer tuned up his vocal cords by asking Eddie a few innocuous questions about the Mafia. Flipping switches up and down on equipment the technician announced, "Okay, we're ready to roll."

The lens zoomed in on Eddie, the reporter began the interview by pressing him with 'Mafia' questions in depth. Puzzled, Eddie broke it off, "Hey, hold it, Babcock sent you people out here to investigate crooked judges, what gives with all this 'Mafioso, Jimmy the Weasel Fratianno' horseshit, what kind of a routine is this anyway?"

The reporter turned hostile, "I don't know anything about crooked judges. The only orders I got from Babcock was to get an interview from you on the 'Real Mafia.' You know, like who was the Mafioso who really killed that big time gambler Les Bruneman in the Roost Cafe on West Temple back in October 1937. A guy, Pete Pianezzi was convicted of the murder but he's now making a big stink trying to get a pardon from the Governor. He's eighty, but still screaming he's innocent. Fratianno's been spilling his guts to the Feds, he says it was Frank 'The Bomp' Bompensiero and Leo 'The Lip' Moceri that shot Bruneman."

Hot under the collar Eddie screamed, "Oh yeah, that Goddamn 'Weasel' is a crazy liar, he'll tell those Feds anything he thinks they want to hear, what the hell gives with John? What's he trying to pull on us anyway?"

Bob turned to Cannizzaro, "No use jumping on these guys Eddie, they're just following orders. It's obvious somebody's scared hell out of John. He knows what they'll do to him if he doesn't forget about the judicial corruption, that's why he didn't show up today." Without another word the TV crew packed their equipment, they left within seconds. Babcock was pulling that same old cover-up the Mishpucka always used. It was his job to keep that Mafioso crap going. Keep it in the headlines and on TV, don't let the public *ever* forget it. It was plenty discouraging, but at least I was sure of one thing, my senses hadn't been over reacting last week when they warned me, "It's still the same old story, da dah dee dah dee dah."

Bruneman was killed ten years before Fratianno ever hit L. A.. The 'Weasel' had admitted that he supposedly heard it from another member of the Mafia, who'd heard it from another member of the Mafia, that another member had done the shooting. Mickey Cohen, the young east L.A. hood figured that rubbing out Bruneman, a Jew bookmaker, would be his *big move* to take over all gambling in town. Being triggerman would firmly establish Cohen as top gang boss of L. A.. One of his first murders, it was also when he learned one of his most valuable lessons..."Let the Mafia take the blame."

An eye witness, Elaine Huddle, wife of the cafe owner described the killer as "Short and stocky, he hypnotized me with his cold, steely eyes, I will never forget them." But at the trial Huddle was asked by the Prosecutor, "Do you see those eyes in court here today?"

She answered, "Yes sir, over there, that's the man," she pointed at Pianezzi, who was over six feet tall and skinny. Two other suspects were accused of being with Pianezzi at the time. The charges were dropped when it was learned one of them had been working in an airplane factory in Alaska and the other had been in jail in Frisco with pneumonia. The steely eyed, short and stocky Cohen laughed with surprise and relief when Pianezzi was convicted of the murder and sent to prison. "Holy shit, these people will believe anything, all you have to do is tell 'em *The Mafia' did it.*"

I discovered why Babcock finked out on the investigation, he had had no choice. The wealthiest, most powerful people in TV and the news media had met for three days in Ojai Valley. Their purpose was mapping out strategy and battle plans against what they saw as the most dangerous threat to them, 'The Moral Majority.' Citizens across the country were banding together to do something about the blatant sex, sick pornography and narcotics glamorized on television. Religious groups and non-religious organizations like the Coalition for Better TV were advocating consumer boycott of the products of sponsors of offensive shows. The Apalachin meeting of the so-called Italian Mafia Dons was a kindergarten event compared to the Ojai meeting of the powerful Jew Mishpucka members who control TV and the newspapers.

A list of their names was like reading a Tel Aviv phone book:
G. Eckstein;
Mel Shavelson, Pres. of the Writers Guild of America;
Producers, B. Yorkin, Norman Lear, W. Froug, NBC Entertainment;
Alfred Schneider, V. Pres. of ABC;
D. Wolper, Producer;
A. Dershowitz, Harvard Law School Professor;
J. Greenfield, Political Commentator;
Multi-millionaire advertising sponsors of objectionable programs were in attendance:
R. Goldstein, V. Pres. of Proctor and Gamble;
Marvin Koslow, V. Pres. of Bristol Myers Co.;

I was amazed that Babcock had survived the venom of their fury considering that at first he had actually contemplated working with us in a TV expose of the savage Black Robe Mishpucka. A tip-off on the Mishpucka's secret battle plans of using their force of TV power was the malevolence of Betty Friedan's presence at the Ojai meet. She claimed to be a 'womens activist' but her looks were deceiving. It seemed the last thing in the world that possibly could happen to Friedan would be to get pregnant. Not even artificial insemination appeared a feasible substitute. Regardless, she was a co-founder of the National Abortion Rights Action League. As a hatchet woman for the B'nai B'rith, Friedan's orders were to create *volatile political situations* by *inciting* the sensitive issue of abortion and using it to foment *riotous dissension, disruption and choas* within the United States Government.

In Betty, the Mishpucka picked a perfect agent for the abortion mission. Since conception she was plagued by the curse of her own genes. Through out her life Betty had been jealously and hatefully rankled by any natural beauty or happiness shown by more fortunate women. Inner fury and angers demanding avengement she became a zealous architect of clever pro-abortion propaganda. Skillfully she drew plans that enraged religious opponents of abortion. Hollow but slick slogans such as, "Pro-choice" and "Right to my own body," were spawned by Betty's pregnant brain. As battle cries justifying abortion they were constantly pounded into the publics mind nationwide by Mishpucka newspapers and TV media.

The Abortion Action League was another of the Mishpucka's evil schemes dedicated to destroying the Constitution. There is nothing new in conspiratorial plans to decimate a government's power prior to inflicting a fatal blow. In 1184 B.C. it was the Trojan Horse, in WW11 it was the Fifth Column. Not content in controlling the three major TV networks the Mishpucka established a separate Jewish TV network operating from L.A. and New York City, coast to coast the channels broadcast propaganda material for the Jews. A powerful, politically motivated organization, The United Teachers Union of L.A. backs the network.

I'd known for some time Mishpuckas had *infiltrated* every strata and facet of American life, both public and private. However, I was startled when discovering that Judy Solkovits, the President of the L. A. United Teachers Union was the wife of Gregg Solkovits. That was the guy from the Camarillo Daily News who wrote lies about me in the paper before the election. I didn't need a ton of bricks to fall on my head to convince me *we were dead* so far as getting any help from TV networks. It was scary as hell, no matter what direction I desperately twisted and turned, the deadly Mishpucka's agents were there. It was like they were inhuman.

By using religious sermons on TV, Jerry Falwell, the Evangelist Baptist Preacher from Lynchburg, Va., had drawn forth millions of Christians and extracted billions of dollars in donations. Evolving as a strident off-shoot of Falwell's vast congregation the Moral Majority had established a newly found, very lucrative political clout for the Evangelist. But swift, rigid action planned at the Ojai Meet quickly forstalled any danger the emerging Moral Majority presented.

Tough Mishpuckas quickly convinced Falwell his religious empire would shrivel, and quickly collapse *without* his TV time which they controlled. The Reverend made a deal, Moral Majority would form a Political Action Committee, PAC, its stated purpose was raising funds for anti-abortion, but it would also finance pro-Israeli political candidates. Mishpucka genius was diabolical, unbelievably devious, they *now* controlled the antagonists on *both* sides of the issue, with

Friedan's National Abortion Rights Action League on one side, and the Moral Majority's anti-abortion PAC on the other.

The Mishpucka was stirring the pot satanically, they could care less whether a woman got an abortion or not, their objective was to *divide* the country, sow and spread confusion, hate and chaos in the government. The Moral Majority with their donations to PAC was *financing* both pro-abortion and anti-abortion plus the Pro-Israeli politicians who are scheming to destroy the U.S. It was insanity, the witless Christians were *financing* their own destruction.

The presence of Judas Gius with the Mishpuckas at the Ojai Meet signified that newspapers were just as disastrous a scene for us as was the TV media. Editors for Scripps papers in Ventura had their reporters under control, severe censoring kept all evidence of the Mishpucka corruption under wrap. Misleading stories, mealy-mouth editorials and cleverly altered facts were a main diet concocted by Judas Gius. Even so DuPre and I were not about to just quit, we'd come up with another idea. Maybe the big newspapers in L.A. were not so tightly controlled by the Mishpucka as they were in Ventura.

At Frank's funeral, when talking with Babcock we'd also met Bill Farr, a reporter with the L. A. Times. We decided to contact him, it was worth a chance, what in hell did we have to lose? Certain events involving Farr led us to believe maybe he had the personal character and experience to help us expose the Black Robe Mishpucka. These events occurred during Charlie Manson's trial. Before their arrest for the Tate-La Bianco murders, Manson's Family had laid plans to kill a number of Hollywood stars, among them was Frank Sinatra. Dep. D. A., Vincent Bugliosi, the Prosecutor, had this kill list in his possession but for legal reasons it couldn't be admitted as evidence. Somehow Farr got the list and wrote the story. The judge demanded to know who gave it to him. Having given his word Farr refused to tell. Four lawyers involved in the trial were suspected by the judge who repeatedly ordered Farr to reveal the name of the lawyer who had leaked the list. Enraged by Farr's refusal the judge held him in contempt of court, ordering him to jail until he decided to confess. Bill spent considerable time in jail, he knew the judge would disbar the lawyer if he talked. Farr didn't weaken, he kept his word not to reveal his source. Bob and I concluded Farr was the caliber of news reporter we needed, one who'd stick by his guns.

I remembered Charlie Manson and his women. I'd never forget. It was a few months before Richard E. Fish, alias Richard E. Erwin, fired me. I had been working out of the Public Defender's Office in the Camarillo Courthouse. Driving a beat up rusty old bus, Manson and his family had worked their way south down the coast. A Dep. Sheriff spotted the bus parked with many small, unbelievably filthy naked children playing perilously close to the edge of the highway. Their mothers were arrested for child neglect. About eleven in the morning while his women were appearing before the judge, Charlie and I talked out in the hall, his voice was low and controlled, but wild, trapped animal eyes flashing with enraged defiance betrayed murderous horrors smoldering beneath a tissue paper surface.

Released by the judge, Manson's wives and kids filed aboard the grimy bus. Each woman aligned herself by a window, several held up naked babies, others flattened bare breasts against the dirty glass panes. Ghostly faces stared from the windows as drug ravaged brains vibrated sinisterly through the air. Charlie floated his crazy bus away from the curb heading out of town, I felt big relief. I knew they were one hell of a bloody calamity just waiting for a place to happen.

Our first meeting with Bill Farr was encouraging, it bolstered our lagging spirits when he agreed that, "An investigation into judicial corruption will make a great story for the Times." In the following weeks we had a series of talks with the newsman, our last meet was at Denny's Restaurant in Newbury Park. After lunch it wasn't busy, DuPre, Eddie and I chose an upholstered booth in the dining room, Farr arrived the same time as the coffee.

Sliding over Bob said, "Well Bill, everything going good I hope."

"Real good, I got an interview with Judge Berenson tomorrow. He claims he's eager to clear up the accusations of corruption you guys are making about him and his partner, Nordman."

"Indeed yes, that is good news," Bob added, "I'd sure like to be able to ask the good judge a few questions myself. I'm really amazed Berenson agreed to the interview. I just don't see how he dares talk to someone from a *free* press."

"Well, no one from the front office has said anything to me about it. Yesterday I drove our cameraman to Oxnard, he took pictures of the houses where Nordman and Berenson have lived next door to each other more than thirty years. I'm laying the ground work, you know, showing how close these guys really are. From what I've dug up already it's quite evident they're a hell of a lot tighter than just two former law partners."

"You better believe they are."

"As a starting point I want Judge Berenson to *explain* just *why* he killed that Grand Jury investigation and what's his *connections* with the Public Facilities Corporation, from there I'll go right down the line."

Eddie handed Farr some papers, "You should acquaint yourself with this info before talking with Berenson. It is evidence outlining his and Ben Nordman's conspiracy with the Pacht-Ross law firm in Century City. It lays out the entire plot, exactly how they pulled off the whole job with phony zoning and court decisions enabling them to develop the two thousand acres in Agoura."

Farr picked the papers up, "It's getting late, I'd like to beat that heavy freeway traffic back to L.A., I'll read this tonight Eddie when I get home."

Eager to learn what Farr had accomplished with Berenson, Bob reached him on the phone in L.A. the next evening. Bill apologized, "I am really sorry fellas' but I won't be able to go ahead with that investigation. I didn't get to Oxnard to interview Berenson because something very important turned up. When I got back to L.A. after talking to you there was a message for me at the news desk. It was a flash from William French Smith, the U.S. Attorney General. He wants me to be his Press Secretary, I am flying to Washington, D.C. tomorrow morning to see him."

That was the last we ever heard of Farr's big L.A. Times expose on judicial corruption. Soon afterward Bob was in D.C. on business. He stopped by the office of Lars Nelson, Bureau Chief for the New York Daily News, also Larry Mc Quillen a San Francisco Examiner reporter was there. In a casual conversation DuPre mentioned Bill's offer to become the A.G.'s Press Secretary. A surprised Mc Quillen blurted out, "Are you kidding, where'd you get that story Bob?"

Nelson echoed, "How in hell did that ever get started? That post was never offered to Farr, fact is someone else has it all sewed up." Suddenly Farr's tale had taken on strange dimensions. It would bear some checking.

On returning from the east Bob and Eddie made a trip to L.A.. They contacted a Times reporter, a friend of Cannizzaro's who shed very interesting light on the matter, it focused back over ten years to the Manson trial when the judge was tossing Farr in jail for refusing to reveal his source of info. At that time William French Smith was a lawyer for the L.A. Times, also Counselor and personal friend of Gov. Ronald Reagan. As house-attorney for the Times, Smith was eating the newspaper alive with outrageous fees claiming they were necessary to keep Bill from jail. Subsequently the Times refused to spend any more money for Bill's legal defense leaving him out on a shaky limb. Crushed by mounting pressures Farr had no choice, he signed a note indebting himself to the powerful lawyer for thousands of dollars. This explained the reporter's predicament, but...what was the connection between French Smith and Judge Berenson?

Digging deep we learned Nordman made numerous calls to D.C. soon after Bill contacted Judge Berenson for the interview, the calls went direct to their law partner William P. Clark, National Security Advisor for Pres. Reagan. It wasn't hard to figure out why Bill Farr was called to D.C., but *who* back there had threatened him, giving orders to knock off his investigation into Judge Jerome Berenson's corruption? Was it French Smith or William P. Clark, or had they *both* ganged up to tighten the thumb screws on Farr?

By now the Mishpucka was thoroughly alarmed, realizing that just *one* bold, unrestrained reporter could strip away their facade, their entire evil mask of secrecy. They had stopped Farr's investigation of the Mishpucka, but now something else had gone awry, it happened when hostages from the American Embassy in Iran were released.

On that day an L.A. paper printed an expose of Jerry Plotkin, the only private citizen of the fifty two hostages. Two reporters dug up info that Plotkin was under investigation and close scrutiny by police and Federal Narcotics agents before going to Iran. A story by Adam Dawson and Arnie Friedman, L.A. Daily News reporters was hitting dangerously close to important operators of the Mishpucka narcotics *pipeline*. In a frantic effort to cover-up Plotkin's narcotic smuggling record the Mishpucka posed him as a legitimate U.S. businessman and *hero,* this farcical ploy didn't fool too many, the heat generated by the expose was sparking an explosion. Inquisitive reporters were a nemesis, a menace that the Mishpucka *would not* tolerate.

These investigative reporters and their role in gathering news had to be destroyed. Reporters had a code of honor, they couldn't reveal a confidential source of information. Aware of this the Mishpucka devised a clever plan. It was simple...they would trick the reporters into destroying themselves with their own code of honor.

Plotkin activated their scheme by filing a $ 60,000,000.00 libel suit against the newsmen, L.A. Daily News, and its owner the Tribune Co. of Chicago. Leading them into the *ambush,* a Mishpucka Judge, Sara K. Radin, ordered the newsmen to reveal *all* the names of their sources of information. Standing firmly by their code of ethics they refused. Radin couldn't conceal her contempt, they were fools. With inborn deceit she *black-jacked* them, ordering a Default Judgement of sixty million against the newsmen and Daily News. The reporters had followed the Judas goat into a trap, precisely as the Mishpucka planned. Such a court order could financially destroy any newspaper or publication in the United States.

Terrorized by Radin the frightened President of the Daily News, J. Scott Schmidt panicked. Ordering his reporters to disclose their informants, he filed placating documents in Judge Sara Radin's court. Editors nationwide reacted with stunned disbelief to the Daily News demand on reporters to betray the identity of their sources, which could easily get their informant killed. Referring to Radin's order, Gene Roberts, Exec. Editor of the Philadelphia Inquirer, exclaimed emotionally, "Good God, I am appalled." Members of the National Reporters Committee for the Freedom of the Press objected, "The protection of confidential sources is a fundamental principle *without which* American Journalism can not function effectively."

L.A. reporters protested such suppression of the news media. A letter was drafted by a committee made up of Bill Farr, L.A. Times, Linda Breakstone, L.A. Examiner, John Marelius, Daily News, Jeffry Kaye, KCET-TV, and Bill Stout, KNXT-TV. Farr said in the letter, "The reporters have been ordered to break a sacred commandment." I wondered, did his conscience remind him of the newsman's sacred trust he had been forced to break in Washington, D.C.?

Publishers of the nation's news events saw the handwriting on the wall. Restrained by this powerful judicial coercion, they didn't dare provoke more Black Robe vengeance. They must keep the reporters under *strict control,* thus, newspapers in the U.S. had been effectively censored.

A noted television commentator and journalist, Walter Cronkite, was given an honorary degree at Loyola University. While speaking at the ceremony he criticized the *censorship* and *control* of the news media. Cronkite asserted, "Washington, D.C. and the foreign news should have greater depth. Serious things that we should be trying to communicate are buried." He hit harder, *"The majority of American people are not even adequately informed enough to intelligently exercise their Constitutional Rights."* Cronkite then forcefully emphasized the message with a succinct declaration, "TV newscasts *fail* the American public." A stern warning from a man who knows that being denied all access to the truth, America is doomed.

TV programming is under the Mishpucka's control. On the regular channels their sit-com propaganda is slick, subtly obtrusive. Closely intertwined is a separate Jewish TV network system, it employs far more aggressive tactics. Operated from New York City by Jessica

Savitch it is controlled in the west by Leon Savitch, the judge who'd ordered L.A. taxpayers to pay four and a half billion to the *Southern California Power Authority,* a phony Mishpucka corporate setup who's biggest problem is in laundering the *enormous* sums stolen by their crime empire. One way is through the *myriads* of phony corporations they've set up. The separate Jewish TV network and its propaganda mill is operated by their *Corporation for Public Broadcasting.*

Ages and ages ago the world's wickedness began. Satan offered the Jews the secret of acquiring great wealth and political power, but in return they must accept him as their leader. Upon the acceptance of his evil contract Satan impregnated into Jews a primordial, bestial lust for gold and power. It was their *inexorable curse* struck with the mark of Cain, the evil ways established by Satan worked fine for the Jews. As the years passed they became wealthier and more powerful. Then Jesus Christ, son of God, the Savior appeared. Entering into the Jews Temples he toppled their idols of gold and denounced the evils of murder and usury.

Raging at this intrusion into their lucrative, well organized rackets the Jews screamed for Satan's protection. Obeying Satan's order of covert intrigue and vicious lies they conspired to kill Christ. For gold, the Savior was betrayed, the Jews perpetrated their ultimate crime. On Mount Calvary, blood flowing from hands and feet cruelly spiked to the wooden cross, Christ was crucified. A sight that can *never* be forgotten or forgiven, except by God himself, father of Jesus Christ. Upon his death the Jews were stricken suddenly, not by remorse but by uncertainty. They'd been enticed by Satan's sly words, "Seize the wealth of the world, steal, kill and lie. Sate yourselves lavishly, fear no spiritual punishment for 'believe me,' there is *no* here-after, you have *no soul,* when you *die* you are *dead.* This is the secret of your power. Now go, propagate, teach your off-spring in *our ways* to perpetuate themselves as possessors of all wealth." A psychalgiac dread smote the Jews, they'd been tricked. Satan had said, *"When you die you are dead."* Though they could control the wealth of the universe, shadowy, brooding wings of death constantly hovered over the Jews while Christians had eternal life in the here-after.

They realized they had made a bad deal, a Jews death was *final,* there was *nothing* after death. The Jews were terrified, a maddening jealousy engulfed them. Raging, they screamed that Satan *must* give them life after death. But he could *not,* he did *not* have that power. In covert attempts to gain life after death, the Jews joined Christian congregations. They even ate pork trying to prove their assimilation, it would not work. As devotees of Satan they could not comprehend faith in Jesus. How could Jews ask Christ for eternal life? They had killed him. Idolatrous rituals of the Jewish Temples were conducted by High Priests. They presided over offerings and human sacrifices in worship of their idols of gold.

Per ancient accords with Satan the Temples had become extremely lucrative. Their success comprised a simple, uncomplicated racket involving only the *basics* of money and power. It was the Crucifixion of Christ that undid all the simplicity of their evil. With the advent of the hypothesis of life eternal, great confusion and turmoil spread among Jews. A new value had been perceived, their rapacious traits demanded that they possess it. This was a dangerous turn of events for Satan, he became very frightened of losing his followers, thus his power.

Satan knew the Christians source of strength was derived from their faith, their lasting faith in God and His promise of salvation through the Savior, Jesus Christ. Tortured with the furies of madness Satan swore with vengeance, he would destroy their faith. No vestige of it would escape the wrath of his flames of hell, then he became calm, Satan schemed.

After the Crucifixion of Jesus, High Priests of the Jewish Temples were called Rabbis. Satan ordered Rabbi Juda to write new laws that Jews have to obey. Teachings of the Pentateuch, the first five books of the Bible were ignored, proceeding with instructions from Satan's special source Juda *contrived* the 'Mishna.' The Mishna became the *absolute law* that *all* Jews must study and follow in criminal, political, civil, religious and family matters. After this accomplishment Rabbi Juda was known as, The Holy, and *all* Rabbis became spiritual heads of their communities. Presiding over mysterious idolatries, oblations and sacrifices the Rabbis were the *authoritative* teachers of Satan's law, the Mishna, an evil diagram of ruthless sabotage, intimidation and terror.

Satan was positive, the Mishna would wreck utter havoc with the orderly processes of the sovereignty of Christian states. Their *judicial* and *legislative* systems would *crumble* under the Mishna's cunning chaos. Financial institutions would *fail,* the *entire global monetary and economic structure would collapse.* The Christians governments would become *paralyzed,* and their world demolished. Overwhelmed by chaos, poverty and degradation the Christians way of life would become a cruel shambles churning within a slaughter house. When all hope was gone, their faith would die, signifying the end.

The Jews were dispatched to wander across the face of the earth. Invading every country they formed communes within their borders, then connected them around the world with their secret system of communications. Their tightly knit communes were a *bloodline* that could *not* be penetrated by outsiders, an enigma of morbid hate that Christians have *never* understood. Satan and his followers were now ready to launch their major assault. Deadly germs of confusion and disorder were spread, the fatal disease of chaos would *penetrate the heart* of the Christian governments. Soon the world would belong to Satan, through the Rabbis constant teachings of the Mishna to the Jews never ending offspring they would create '*a form* of eternal life.' Nearly two thousand years have passed since the events of Satan's evil plot signaled *the beginning of the end, the end of the world,* the prophecy of Armageddon...

All of the mighty battles fought upon the great plains of Esdraelon put together could never equal the approaching cataclysmic clash in space...the inevitable, *final conflict* between the forces of good and evil. Be it Faith in Christ the Savior, or the Mishna, the sacred law of the Jews, only *one* could survive.

During months of research and study I'd learned a lot about the Jews. But very soon I was about to learn one hell of a lot more, the hard way. By six every morning I was at my place of business in Oak View, I restocked and did the janitor work, at eight I was ready to lock up and leave. The day bartender wouldn't arrive until ten. The last thing I always did was carry the trash out to a big metal bin on the parking lot. A few weeks ago while doing this I'd spotted a large four door sedan lurking behind the American Legion building fifty yards away, just the hood stuck out. It was there every morning like clockwork and stayed until after I dumped the trash. It was the fire department, they had been sicked on me again. I knew I was in for more harassment but why in hell would they be watching me dump trash? All I could figure was they were looking for any little thing to dream up some kind of a violation to put on me, it bothered hell out of me, I could feel their crap coming, but what could I do?

It was a small news article planted deep in the Star Free Press a few months ago that had triggered this latest affair. The typical, sly handiwork of Editor Judas Gius in the article had caught my eye. By now I was expert at recognizing it. He was up to something, it was his come-on, the subtle priming of an *unwary* publics mind. It stated that, "Supervisor John Flynn of Oxnard is part of a group organized to urge Gov. J. Brown to appoint Judge Jerome Berenson to a newly created State Appeal Court position." The article's intent tipped me off, I knew what Gius was up to, a major Star Free Press campaign to give Berenson *more* judicial power would soon hit the street.

Sure enough, three days later Gius wrote a full scale impassioned editorial urging Gov. J. Brown to appoint Berenson to the new court. On a take-off from his first tiny, introductory news article, Gius now swore that the entire population was clamoring with praise for Judge Berenson. Gius was a bunco, but I had to admit he was talented, he could put more lies onto one page than Vladimir Illich Lenin.

To quote Gius, "I most heartily join the grass root movement that arose spontaneously in Berenson's behalf." I gagged, what grass roots movement? Spontaneous my ass...that shyster Berenson couldn't get grass roots with a shovel. Gius continued his fourth estate betrayal of the public trust with his drivel, "Judge Jerome Berenson's career in the law has been most impressive. His firm leadership of a vastly over burdened court system has been extremely productive." A burst of anger shook me. Productive! I shouted, *productive* of what, a crazy chaos? Gius' damnable deceptions and lies he put upon the people were as terrible as Berenson's corruption. The vomit spewed as he persisted with his sick editorial, "In personally resolving many issues without any trial and in expediting other matters on court calendars, Judge Jerome Berenson's genius has shown bright and effectively. He is, as I've written before, both the spirit and the anchor of the court establishment at our Hall of Justice," etc. I puked, but something he had said spurred my thoughts.

Several times I went back over the last section of his editorial. It was there...he'd committed a grave over sight, Gius' arrogance had taken him too far. Authoritatively he'd exposed the modus operandi of the Black Robe Mishpucka affirming what I'd suspected for some time. Gius had said of Berenson, "In *personally* resolving many issues *without* a trial!" Those few words revealed it all..."*Personally resolving issues without a trial.*"

It was *Mishna,* the Jew law of chaos, the Black Robe Mishpucka Judges, Berenson, Pregerson, Klein, Kaus, Mosk, Canter, all of them, "PERSONALLY RESOLVING WITHOUT A TRIAL." It was Judas Gius describing their shithouse decisions, *no* merits considered, *no* attorneys present for either side, *no* recorder, *no* court reporter, *no* one present, only the BLACK ROBE MISHPUCKA. I felt better, I wasn't just taking a paranoia out on some poor hapless Jew, what I'd suspicioned was real, a frightening reality. Two days after Gius' sick editorial it again became necessary for him to perform. This time he needed the front page of the Star Free Press in his attempts to mask Berenson's corruption. The Metropolitan Development Corp. case was breaking, irrefutable evidence of Berenson and Nordman's fraud was coming to light. Proof was found in Federal records, specifically U.S. Securities Exchange Commission records and Ventura County Superior Court documents, also in Metro's corporate records.

Gius was jumping around desperate, like a three legged cat on a red hot tin roof, it became more and more impossible by the minute to make Judge Berenson and Nordman look honest. Metropolitan Corp. and the twenty seven hundred acres in Agoura belonged to old Ben Weingart, a real estate developer tycoon. Ben owned hotels in L.A. and many other enterprises. Buying farm land between L.A. and Long Beach he had developed the entire City of Lakewood.

Reliable sources conservatively estimated Ben was worth between five and seven hundred million. Weingart was declared to be senile by his lawyers, the *Pacht-Ross* law firm from Beverly Hills. Locked in a room with no phone and around the clock guards to stop friends from contacting him, Weingart's Metro Corp. and the Agoura land mysteriously turned up in the hands of Pacht-Ross. Two months later Berenson made the zoning decision on the Agoura land in favor of Pacht-Ross. Kept in guarded captivity and out of touch with friends for several years, Weingart died.

L.A. County Coroner Thomas Noguchi determined Weingart had been administered an overdose of narcotics...it was murder. Then the Coroner's troubles began, he was fired. Judge Berenson had become maniacal when he learned I'd been allowed to walk into the Superior Court Clerk's office and research the entire Metro Corp. files. He knew it was a hell of a can of worms. It was dawning on him harshly, there was over twenty five years of Mispucka corruption stashed in those Superior Court files, right out in the open for anybody to see. He'd been stupid, he had endangered the security of the Mishpucka, he'd pulled off so many crooked deals he couldn't begin to remember them. He'd never be able to search out all the incriminating files, his brain screamed with agony, 'Holy Juda,' acrid moisture poured from his eyes and nose, sshheesh...he was responsible to the Mishpucka, he raged, Holy Juda! Who the hell let that sonofabitch go through 'our' records? He swore, "There is going to be no more of it, it is going to stop," bilious fluid choking him, Berenson cried out, "It has got to stop right now."

About this same time Berenson and Nordman were hard at work on another of their perverted scams, a bill in Legislature for fifteen more Appellate Court Judges, costing taxpayers multi-millions. The State Treasury was already going broke. The Treasurer didn't even have the funds to mail out the Civil Service Employees checks. State Senator Omer Rains, bag-man for Judge Berenson was handling the 'new judge' operation, it was going very well. Governor Jerry Brown already had his booty in his pocket along with his list of Mishpucka judges to appoint. Berenson of course would be Presiding Judge of the new Appellate Court. Kee-rist! It was no different from twenty five years ago. Frank and I had taken moving pictures from behind a screened alcove in a fancy hotel where Jerry Brown's old man Pat, and his buddy 'Big Daddy' Jesse Unruh were selling State Savings and Loan Charters. They went for a hundred grand a copy.

Sen. Rains more than made up for a sad lack of legal ability with his sad lack of morals. He was a hand operated crank, shoving new bills into a hopper fast as Berenson and Nordman's secretaries could type them. Besides their new judge deal Berenson had come up with three more sick bills for Rains to push through, and they were also emergencies. Their bills were extraordinarily designed, they had to immediately stop my frightful depredations into the 'Civil Rights' of the Mishpucka.

Number two bill drawn by Berenson and Nordman and introduced by Rains, would remove elected officials in charge of Superior Court records, and the County Recorder. Jurisdiction of all Court Records and the powers of the Recorder would be lodged in the hands of the Presiding Judge of the Superior Court, nobody but...Judge Jerome Berenson himself!

Number three would reduce jurors from twelve to six, hastening the time when there will *no* jury at all, a plot they've already started by simply calling minor violations of the law infractions, which does *not* allow an arrested person the right to a jury.

The fourth bill would put a stop to Pro-Per lawsuits against judges. It would empower a judge to rule that a Pro-Per lawsuit was a sham regardless of its merits and empower judges to levy such tremendous fines and sanctions against citizens they'd lose everything they had. Naturally law abiding citizens couldn't jeopardize their family, home and future against these awesome *punitive* powers of ruthless judges. Without the Pro-Per right to represent and defend themselves from injustice the only alternative left to the citizens, though totally gutless and un-American was to swallow their pride, erase from their minds those silly ideas about rights to The Due Process Of Law.

Senator Omer Rains' bill to appoint fifteen new Appellate Court

THERE'S A FISH IN THE COURTHOUSE 419

Justices passed and was signed into law by the Legislators, a totally irresponsible act: we *needed* more Appellate Judges like we *needed* another hole in our heads. It cost millions of bucks, at a time when politicians were closing schools and libraries and blaming Howard Jarvis's Prop. 13. I knew Berenson had it already cut and dried and paid for with Gov. Jerry Brown, he'd be Presiding Judge of the new three panel Justice Appellate Division based in Santa Barbara.

I also knew I was going to *stop* Berenson, one way or another. It took almost two weeks, I put together a file with facts and evidence detailing Judge Berenson's unsavory, corrupt career as the Presiding Judge of Ventura County the past twenty years. I mailed the package to Republican State Senator Ed Davis, former Chief of Police of Los Angeles. Republicans put searing heat on Gov. Jerry Brown. If this evidence of corruption involving a Democrat Judge was publicized it would make one hell of a scandal.

J. Brown had his own *political future* to consider, he was already under a heavy pressure created by his insane *judicial* appointments. Further complicating matters it was his father, *former Governor Pat Brown* who had appointed this crook to Superior Court in the first place. Berenson wanted that Appellate position more than anything else in the world, it was a fetish, he had connived for it for years, it belonged to him, no one else. Gov. J. Brown called Judge Berenson personally, with extreme regrets he told him it would be impossible to appoint him. When the noted jurist discovered I was the cause of his terrible misfortune, he became a wild man.

Berenson had retained power because *no* other lawyer *dared* run against him. At one point we put heavy pressure on the Supervisors to place Judge Berenson's name on a ballot even though no lawyer ran against him. This way the voters could reject him, but Berenson quickly killed our effort to de-robe him. This took place about seven years ago during a short period of time when members of the Grand Jury were picked from the voters register and not by Berenson.

A committee of Grand Jurors, Vice Chairperson Mrs. Marjorie Hudson, Santa Paula, Mrs. Pat Riewer, Simi Valley and Mrs. Vilate Stewart, Ventura had proposed a law to place incumbent judges on the ballot when no lawyer filed to run against them. The ladies had made an appointment to discuss this matter with the Supervisors at eleven a.m.. But Richard Wittenberg, the County Legislative Analyst and also Judge Berenson and Nordman's partner, *sneaked* in ahead of the ladies and pressured the Supervisors into *not* passing the law. Upon their arrival the Jurors were flabbergasted when told by the

Supervisors that they'd already unanimously rejected their proposed law and they had no intentions of discussing the matter any further with them. Mrs. Hudson vigorously argued for a reconsideration, but Supervisor Ralph 'Hooter' Bennett, Ojai, gave the ladies the final 'hoot' and it was all over.

After Gov. Jerry Brown's bitter message Judge Berenson salved his gaping wound with the knowledge he was still Presiding Judge of the County Superior Court, no one could take that away from him. But a strange thing happened, without any doing of mine. A terrible disaster again befell Judge Berenson, his luck clearly had run out. A deadly bolt of lightening had struck from the blue. William Hinkle, a Deputy District Attorney decided to run against Judge Berenson. Hinkle had personally run up against some of his corruption, he felt that strong action must be taken to restore judicial integrity.

With this latest catastrophe Berenson came unhinged, he ranted and raved, now he'd be *forced* to campaign to retain his judgeship, knowing damn well that I was ready to drop a ton of his corruption right down his neck. Something very funny flashed through my mind, I wondered, did Gov. J. Brown feel sorry for Judge Berenson, would he give him back his hundred grand? Berenson had one chance left, with Judas Gius' help he would make Hinkle wish to God he'd never even thought of running against him.

Day after day Star Free Press letters and editorials depicted Bill Hinkle as a lawyer of low ethic and moral scruples who was nothing more than a selfish job seeker. Publicly ostracized by brother lawyers, angry, nasty phone calls were made to his wife at home. But worst of all were the 'Honey Bees.' For years the 'Honey Bees' had busily buzzed about the anus of the 'Great Judge.' Unbelievably riled, they became furious at the very thought of losing their source of nectar. Highly incited the 'Bees' wrote letters to Gius who eagerly printed the ridiculous statements and accusations in the Star Free Press.

Ira Goldenring's strong forte was driving his divorce clients into chaotic legal entanglements, then hit them with five to ten thousand dollar fees. If they could not pay up, he eagerly took mortgages on their homes and threatened to foreclose. In a letter to Editor Gius he said, "It's sad indeed that Presiding Superior Court Judge Jerome Berenson, in his twentieth year of service to this County, has been forced from his judgeship by the unkind aspirations of a Dep. D.A.. I don't understand why the District Atty. didn't counsel Mr. William Hinkle that his actions are most inappropriate."

Richard A. Regnier was an old time 'Honey Bee.' I harked back to the murder trial of William Clinger. Regnier had been present at the secret polygraph of Clinger's girlfriend Didi Casto when she'd revealed that another man was with Clinger when the bartender was killed. Regnier and Mr. Fish criminally violated a direct court order prohibiting anyone from talking to Castro. She was the major witness testifying in a capitol murder case, yet Berenson, Presiding judge of the Superior Court allowed his 'Honey Bees' to keep buzzing busily around the hive.

In Judge Berenson's behalf lawyer Regnier authored a real jewel, "The ill conceived last minute opposition to Judge Jerome Berenson is another glaring example of the unfairness of a Dep. District Atty. opportunist trying to unseat a *'magnificent specimen'* of a trial Judge and human being at Judge Berenson's personal expense. Those of us who know Judge Jerome Berenson support his re-election effort for *one reason only:* to get the best man for the job, favoritism is neither sought, expected, nor suggested. Voters should not assist selfish job seekers who crave to advance themselves at the expense of this excellent judge. Ventura County needs to retain Judge Berenson."

Another Honey Bee, W. E. Patterson, raised hell with Hinkle in a letter to Judas, "It is difficult to convey the depth of our collective affection and respect for Judge Jerome Berenson and our outrage at the manner of Mr. Hinkle's actions."

Committing the felony of attempting to bribe a judicial candidate to quit, another Honey Bee lawyer went so far in his letter to state, "He'd gladly give Mr. Hinkle back the $632.27 he had paid for his filing fee if Hinkle would quit and not run against Judge Berenson." Despite a concentrated attack of letters, news articles, editorials and nasty telephone calls battering him, Hinkle wouldn't quit.

Judge Berenson was furious, he wouldn't dare campaign and face the accusations and evidence of his corruption in office. He had no alternative but to announce his retirement. There were more reasons why he *dared not* run, if Berenson lost he couldn't sit on the bench as a retired judge. This was *critical,* he had many multi-million dollar cases still hanging fire that were so steeped in chaos and corruption that he must personally stay on top of it. And if he retired the filing period would be extended allowing others to run against Hinkle. It would prevent him from automatically getting the judgeship the same way Berenson himself had gotten it for the last twenty years.

When Berenson announced his sorrowful, reluctant retirement the Honey Bee letters and editorials recommenced, but in another vein. Now they barely concealed an out-right hatred, accusing Hinkle of terrible, unforgivable misdeeds. He had destroyed Berenson's judicial future, his lifetime desire to be elevated in stature. Now the Honey Bees swarmed, waiting for a new Presiding Judge to be selected.

Soon after sending my information to Sen. Davis I got word that a so-called respectable Ventura law firm was hopping mad at one of Berenson's shocking, degenerate courtroom operations. Benton, Orr, Duval and Buckingham represented Argo Petroleum Corp. who were defendants in a lawsuit. At a hearing Berenson made a proper ruling in Argo's favor, but when the lawyers left the courtroom he *changed* his ruling and destroyed the court records documenting his orignal decision. The *plaintiff's lawyer* was Berenson's law partner Nordman. Benton was mad as hell, he and his partners threatened to take the matter to the Judicial Council, but they were only blowing smoke, they knew Judge Berenson controlled the Judicial Council, it would be putting their necks in a noose if they tried to expose him.

Looking in the Superior Court index I found the case, Lenora F. Harth, Plaintiff v. Argo Petroleum Corp. It was originally filed May 27, 1977. I went to the counter giving the case number to a clerk. In a few minutes she returned, "I'm very sorry, that file is unavailable."

"How come? That case is over six years old and it's never come to trial." Nervously she looked around at the other girls hoping for a little support, but no one looked up from their desks.

I repeated, "Can I see that file, you know it is a matter of public record and I have a right to see it."

She flared, "I know that but the judge keeps it *locked up* in his desk."

I stammered, "Oh, I see...well I guess if the Judge has it what can you do." She was relieved as I started moving away from the counter. I turned back, "Oh, just one more thing, I know some of the Judges personally, can you tell me which one has the file?"

Hesitating, she answered, "Yes, Judge Berenson has it."

I'd figured that, but I wanted to hear her say it. "Thank you very much." Berenson had been unable to pass his law whereby he'd take control of the County Clerks office and Superior Court records, but he was doing a good job of it regardless. I went down to the lobby, a patio was between the Courts building and Administration building a hundred feet away. Heading there I passed the large fountain in the center of the patio. It had to be the ugliest, most useless excuse for a fountain I ever saw, a pile of river rock cemented together with pipes four to six inches in diameter sticking up. Ominously the metal cylinders three to four feet long looked like burned out rocket tubes and mortars from WW11. My God, Judge Berenson and Nordman's Public Facilities Corp. stole $250,000,000.00 from the taxpayers for this place. Architecture of the drab buildings with the cheap desert tan paint resembled pictures I'd seen of buildings in Tel Aviv.

Maybe they'd gotten a good buy on some used plans. The County Center was just a hunk of cement in comparison to the old Spanish Courthouse in Santa Barbara, just thirty minutes north up the coast. Its picturesque tile roofs, thick white stucco walls and huge beams were incomparable, graceful arches and small balconies created cool, pleasant alcoves. Green lawns and ferns with small fountains under the protective canopy of immense, ancient oaks were friendly, maybe that was it, this place sure as hell wasn't friendly.

In the trial index I'd found plaintiffs other than Lenora F. Harth. I wanted to get a lead on the names, the voter registry was always a good place to start. The Registrars Office was in the basement of the Administration Building. On a wide flight of stairs and on down the long hallway the chintzy gray carpet was wearing thin. Through open double doors there was a counter, I went to the left to go around it just like always. Record books were kept back in the rear on shelves aligned against a wall. A voice growled, "Hold it, where do you think you are going?"

It was Geraine Jacobson, she had leaped from her desk directly behind the counter. "I'm going back to check some records."

"No you aren't. You can't go back, a new law's been passed and the public is not allowed in here."

"What law?"

Snapping her lips she gloated, "A new law was just passed and if you don't like it you'll have to complain to an Assemblyman." I saw her lunch spread out on the desk. I'd bet a buck she hadn't left there since the new law was passed, not even to the toilet, she had orders. From morning to night she'd waited, eagerly anticipating when she could tell me I would *never* be allowed to get back to those records again.

I didn't even want to talk with Jacobson much less argue with her, there was no use. By now Judge Berenson was aware I'd been to the Superior Court records looking for the Argo file. There were better ways to get what I wanted. It would take a little longer and I'd have to ask a few favors. When I got the info back I was surprised. I had expected it to be rank, but if all the cases Berenson had locked up were this fetid, the *stench* in his chambers must be *unbearable*. The plaintiffs were Arthur L. Martin, Bonnie Lee Martin, Mary Aidlin and Joseph W. Aidlin and several other trustees of the C.R. Price Testamentary Trust.

Martin was a lawyer, his wife Bonnie Lee Martin was a Superior Court Judge in Los Angeles, their attorney was Berenson's partner Ben Nordman. These Mishpuckas had twisted and turned the Argo Corp. every way but loose for over five years but didn't dare bring the case to trial. Judge Berenson knew their phony case would never stand up before a jury and they would lose. Argo held out knowing if it was not brought to trial it would be dismissed when the statute of limitations ran out. What the crooked Judge Berenson did next was unbelievable. To prevent dismissal of the case he kept it locked in his desk well over a year while making daily findings and signing them under Judicial oath swearing that, *"No judge was available to hear the case."* It was an incredible fraud and extortion. After more than six and one half years Argo Corp. was forced to give up. With their oil production cut in half and unable to drill more wells they faced financial ruin. Admitting no guilt to the fraudulent allegations Argo agreed to pay an out of court settlement giving the Mishpucka $2,000,000.00. What Argo didn't know was they'd been doublecrossed by their own basic attorneys, the most prestigious law firm of Ball, Hunt, Hart, Brown and Baerwitz. These shysters had cleverly farmed the suit out to Benton's law firm in a move to slough off the scent of chicanery from themselves. Former Governor Pat Brown was the *Brown* in the firm of Ball, Hunt, Hart, Brown and Baerwitz.

As Governor, Pat Brown had *appointed* Berenson to the Superior Court years before. They were *long-time* conspirators and schemers. Coordinating the fraud with Berenson and Nordman, Brown *furlined* their pockets by buying up Argo Corp. stock which they had caused to plummet. They knew it would sky-rocket soon as Argo went back into full production. Then later in further manipulations they'd force Argo into bankruptcy and take over the corporation.

In a million years Carlo Marcello, an alleged Mafioso King and supposedly with unlimited influence and power could *never* have put together this extortion plot and got away with it like the Mishpucka had. He would've turned green with envy of their organization if he knew how the Black Robe Mishpucka pulled it off. In New Orleans, the Mafioso was involved in one of his *old-time, out-moded* Labor Union health insurance scams with a Beverly Hills swindler, Joseph Hauser, when they were nabbed by the FBI. The con-man was also running scams with a Mishpucka lawyer in L.A., Steven Reinhardt. Knowing Reinhardt was in tight with Judge Harry Pregerson, Hauser went to Reinhardt for help.

Hauser, an intermediary knew Carlo owned a valuable Gauguin and through Reinhardt, Judge Pregerson had agreed to fix the Labor Union charges for the painting. Hauser was relaying it long distance to Marcello in New Orleans when an FBI tap on the phone picked up their conversation. The Bureau could have nailed Pregerson and Reinhardt as well as Carlo if they'd waited till the painting had been delivered, instead, they told Pregerson about the intercepted phone conversation. The crooked judge denied knowing anything about a painting. He claimed Hauser and Marcello must have been planning to bribe him but he had never been approached.

But Hauser knew Pregerson and the lawyer had previously made inquiries of the European Art Mart. They'd determined the painting was valued at over one hundred thousand dollars. It seemed strange that FBI agents would tell Pregerson about the phone call and tip him off when it was their duty to determine if a bribe to fix a case was already accepted. But maybe not so strange when realizing that the director of the bureau was Wm. H. Webster, an ex-federal judge.

The awful fiasco Carlo found himself embroiled in was his first dealing with a Black Robe Mishpucka and it was a hell of a sad one. Found guilty of insurance fraud in the New Orleans State Court, he was then brought to L.A. and tried in a federal court. Found guilty of attempting to bribe Judge Harry Pregerson, top Mafioso Carlo Marcello went to the Federal Penitentiary. The dumb s.o.b. still has not figured out what in the hell happened to him. Mishpucka Judge Pregerson was *elevated* to Federal Appeal Court and the Mishpucka shyster Steven Reinhardt was *appointed* to the same court by Pres. Carter. Hauser under oath at Reinhardt's confirmation hearing gave evidence as to their under-world connections and criminal activities. Joseph Hauser is a federal protected witness but no one can figure out if he is hidden to *protect* him from Mafia revenge, or to prevent him from *exposing* the Mishpucka.

However, hiding Hauser was a necessity, Federal Appeal Court Judges Pregerson and Reinhardt couldn't have him running around squealing about secret European appraisals of the Gauguin painting. Especially since it was made *before* the FBI tapped the conversation between Hauser and Carlo. A painting worth only a hundred grand did not seem like a lot for a federal judge to jeopardize himself by *fixing* a case but the judge seemed to go more for volume business, vacant lots, nearly new cars, etc., etc..

For a measly five grand Pregerson *fixed* another case, a special deal for his old law school buddy. The Oxnard attorney drove to a popular Japanese restaurant in downtown L.A. and met Pregerson. With the five big ones in his hand Harry was as good as his word, the *fix* was in without a hitch.

A grand retirement dinner with special guests and entertainment was planned for Jerome Berenson's exodus as a judge. A crowd, four hundred people came to Martin 'Bud' Smith's Lobster Trap Bar and Restaurant at Oxnard Harbor. The entertainment theme was quite familiar, a satirical skit with Jewish judges *masquerading* as Italian Mafioso characters. Judge Marvin Lewis, a partner of Berenson and Nordman was a highlight of the program appearing as a Mafiosa in a black coat and hat. He was introduced as, Don, Sonny Linquini, Dean of the Torquemada Institute of Judicial Oppression in Sicily. Barbarous in black coat, hat and makeup, the skinny Jew judge was grotesque. Mimicking a phony Italian accent he mouthed his slickly designed denigrating insinuations that it was the Sicilians and their Mafia who had created organized crime and was responsible for all judicial oppression raging throughout the world.

I pondered the Jews hypocrisy, did they really believe everyone was fooled? I knew they thought it was clever...keep attention away from the Mishpucka...*never* let anyone know of its existance...focus the spotlight on a scape-goat...the Mafia. It was an old Jewish scam, Aaron, the first Jewish High Priest invented the scape-goat. Heaping *all* the sins of the Jews upon the head of a *scape-goat,* he had turned it loose upon the world.

There were no mass demonstrations or Letters to the Editor from raging Italians screaming about the 'black-slanderous, anti-Italian' devious insinuations of these Jew judges and lawyers. The rancorous propaganda was spread among members of the Bar unrebutted...but reverse the role...if in front of four hundred members of the Bar an Italian judge had masqueraded as Rabbi Izzy Goldblatz, Dean of the Tel Aviv Institute of Judicial Oppression and Arab Decimation while aping the whining voice of a Russian Jew all hell would have broken out. Sky high headlines in the Star Free Press would have screamed, 'Anti-Semitism rampages in Ventura County Bar Association.' Judas Gius' tales of German atrocities in WW11 and alarming predictions of a new holocaust in the making would bulge the newspaper.

Upon this dire anti-Jew outbreak the Temple Rabbis would order overwhelming retaliatory actions by millions of Jews. Mayor Diane Feinstein, lawyer Goria Allred, and Congresswoman Bobbi Fiedler, would go stark raving berserk at such rampant *anti-semitisim*, they'd demand that the FBI be fully mobilized to act. Betty Friedan would offer free birth control pills and advice to all Catholic women from Ventura County. Jewish Defense League General Irving Rubin, on receiving his emergency orders from the B'nai B'rith would deploy a machine gun platoon to Ventura, immediately declaring his bounty of five hundred dollars for a severed ear of any Christian who looks askance at a Jew, and one thousand dollars for a matched pair.

CHAPTER 37

So...one lousy crooked Mishpucka judge, Jerome Berenson was forced to retire and prevented from being Presiding Judge of a new Appeal Court. So what! It was no victory. We hadn't gained an inch toward an honest, fair judicial system. In fact we had been hurled backwards...way back. Instead of rotting in a jail cell, the conspirator now sat as a retired Superior Court Judge, still perpetrating his Argo Petroleum type extortions, and devastating the legal rights of honest citizens with his malevolent depredations.

Bill SB 137 creating the *new* Appeal Court was the destructive force. Architected by the Mishpucka and *greased* through Legislature by Omer Rains, it was a 'judicial bubonic plague' California would never recover from. Actually opinions were generally divided about whether Omer Rains was a duplicitous traitor lining his pockets with gold, or in more probability just a dangerous simpleton. However, it didn't matter, the Mishpucka plot had been successful in engineering a gigantic state wide *judicial shuffle,* geared to rip and shred any and all opposition to their ferocious seizure of the judgeships.

Alert to this sinister manifestation, a group of patriotic citizens in San Francisco filed a lawsuit to prevent Gov. Jerry Brown from appointing the eighteen judges to the Appellate Court. Lawyer Paul Haerle represented taxpayers Richard Wall, Richard J. Hazlewood and Sue C. Woods in Superior Court, they alleged the State Supreme Court had unconstitutionally cleared the way letting lame-duck Gov.

J. Brown make the appointments and that the positions were totally unnecessary, and a despotic waste of taxpayers money.

Judge J. Pfotenhauer hearing arguments from both sides issued emergency orders prohibiting Brown from making the appointments. But, the restraining order was *swiftly overruled* by the Black Robe Mishpucka. With his outrageous midnight hour appointments Gov. Jerry Brown inflicted upon the citizenry of California his dread gift of cancer cells, he made dozens on dozens of Mishpuckas judges as well as the eighteen on the new Appeal Court.

Until now things were under control, the Mishpuckas tentative plans were to make Judge Charles Mc Grath the Presiding Judge of Superior Court when Berenson moved up. A partner of Berenson and Nordman, Mc Grath would follow orders and not being a Jew, they'd use him to camouflage Mishpucka activities. Things changed, with Berenson forced to retire and their patsy governor gone they were leery of Mc Grath. They wanted their *'Bloodline.'* Mishpucka Larry Storch, a New York Jew Brown appointed to Superior Court five years ago became Presiding Judge, and Judge Steven J. Stone, also appointed several years back now took over as Presiding Judge of the new Appeal Court, the spot Berenson was slated for.

Berenson now sitting as a retired judge squeezed $2,000,000.00 from Argo Petroleum and hammered them with other harsh terms. Presiding Judge Storch then put his stamp of official power on the extortion scam. Approving retired Judge Berenson's corrupt order, he announced with majestic force, "This matter is now concluded."

The name Steven J. Stone sounded like an All American hero quarterback from the midwest, Ohio, Kansas. But Hymie Blitzberg, alias Steven J. Stone was born in Russia. As presiding judge of the new Appeal Court he was now a top ranking Mishpucka controlling three counties, Ventura, Santa Barbara, and San Luis Obispo, ruling them with an iron fist. Stranger than fiction and *worse*, Hymie's twin brother is another Black Robe Mishpucka, a swiftly rising Superior Court judge in Northern California.

Not to be addressed simply as Judge, Hymie is now a 'Justice.' He'll have two associate justices. His staff consists of five attorneys, two to assist Hymie and one each for his associates, with a fifth to exclusively handle immediate court order requests. Each justice has a private secretary. There will be four court clerks, one receptionist and several file clerks. Bill 137 specified the headquarter's for the court was to be in Santa Barbara, a geographical center, however, Hymie Blitzberg immediately ordered it moved to Ventura County.

A minuscule news item in the star Free Press glossed over the movement. Knowing that anything like this that Gius printed for the Mishpukcas was a cover-up and hid something much more devious, I felt it wouldn't hurt to take a look. Completing my bank business before noon I walked north on Victoria to the courthouse. It wasn't hard to determine there was plenty vacant space in the government buildings to house the three justices and staffs. Replete law library facilities were available and no rent or utilities to pay. The taxpayers were already paying through the nose to Berenson and Nordman's Public Facilities Corp. for the building lease. Several questions shot through my mind. Why was this Justice Stone moving the court, *why* was he leasing thousands of square feet in a building only a couple hundred yards from free rent?

Long ago I'd solved the Black Robe Mishpucka's M.O., all I had to do anymore was sit down and think a minute about a motive, it took two seconds, MONEY, there had to be a pile of money in this for the Mishpucka. Lord, what else did these scum ever think of and it was always the taxpayers who paid. In the next hour I did a little leg work, it told me quite a bit about Justice Stone's office building at 1280 Victoria Ave..

It was built by Raider Construction Co. for Ventura Enterprises Co., both were at 7334 Topanga Canyon Blvd., San Fernando Valley. By three in the afternoon I dropped off Ventura Freeway stopping for a signal at Topanga Canyon. Going north on Topanga I glanced to my left up on the hill where Judge Pregerson lived. Prestigious, it overlooked the entire valley. Several blocks farther on I parked at 7334 Topanga Canyon Blvd.. In room 203 I located the Raider Co. and Ventura Enterprises, it was the law offices of Theodore Stein, Jr. and R. Hirschman, two Mishpucka accomplices of Justice Steven J. Stone. I wasn't surprised, not even a little bit...it couldn't be any other way. For the Mishpucka to pull off this swindle on the people it involved corruption of key Ventura politicians, but what was new about that? It was depressing as hell, was the *whole world* nothing but one great big giant shitty scam? I wanted to dig more but other matters sidetracked me, anyway, there was no rush, Blitzberg, Stein and Hirschman would never change, they'd still be stealing taxpayers money when I got back to them.

His last days in office Governor Jerry Brown appointed so many Mishpucka judges no one could keep track. In Frisco he appointed Jack Berman, ex-husband of Mayor Diane Feinstein to the Superior Court. Sidney Feinberg already a judge and Jerome Cohen, a private lawyer, were elevated to Appeal Court, but Gov-elect Deukmejian blocked these last two appointments...for this he was lambasted in State Supreme Court chambers by Sidney Feinberg in a long abusive tirade. Sidney received a standing ovation from a stacked crowd of Mishpuckas including the newly appointed Supreme Court Justice Joseph R. Grodinsky, aka Joe Grodin, who applauded and stood up in respect for Feinberg's sick spectacle.

In Ventura, Brown made Kenneth R. Yegansky, aka Yegan, and Steven Hintzlestein, aka Hintz, Municipal Court judges. To Superior Court he appointed Steven Z. Perrenowsky, aka Perren, from the law firm of Gitterman, Hourigan, Grossman, Finestone and Perren. To the Appeal Court Brown appointed Hymie Blitzberg, aka Steven Stone, as the Presiding Justice.

But there was a *notable* non-Mishpucka appointment to Ventura Superior Court, Melinda Ann Johnson, called Mindy by her friends, an attractive face, but very thin. Within that frail body stormed fiery ambition, the mountain peak, the top of the heap in the judicial and legal world, and beyond. After all, she had become the first female judge of Ventura Superior Court, she could easily be the first female President of the U.S.. Luck accompanied her driving ambitions, but luck is nothing more than a knack for being in the right place at the right time and Mindy had a knack. Superior Court judges require a minimum of ten years as a lawyer. At thirty five, with ten years and several days experience Mindy mounted the Superior Court bench.

A text book definition lists politics sinlessly as, "The Science of Civil Government," but a veteran politician understands the vicious turmoil of politics as being, an *infinite* evil plotting of intrigue for advantage and survival. Brown was on his way out, in eight years he had made more enemies than he dared think of. The advantage had been his, now his thoughts turned to survival. After he was out of power he'd need someone he could trust to cover his tracks. To his dismay Republican Atty. Gen. Deukmejian, would surely become the next governor. Even more worrisome was Assist. Dep. Atty. General, George Nicholson, he had filed to run for Atty. General. Appearing honest, incorruptible and fearless he attacked the all powerful State Bar Assoc. for being taken over by corrupt judges and lawyers.

Brown wanted L.A. Dist. Atty. John Van De Kamp to be Atty. General. Van De Kamp had more than fully qualified his skill and willingness at concealing homicidal crimes of rich, influential people for a price. Covering up the murders of movie idol Marilyn Monroe and billionaire Ben Weingart were two of Van De Kamp's toughest accomplishments, but he succeeded. There is one fatal drawback to such evil political intrigue, an old Irish maxim, "Murder Will Out," haunts all those who dare to defy its tenets.

Purportedly, Michael Bradbury, the Ventura D.A. was what they call a solid Republican. He supported Pres. Ronald Reagan, Robert Lagomarsino, William P. Clark, and George Deukmejian, etc., like any good staunch Republican politician should. But, Bradbury had created a sticky problem. One of his female Dep. D.A.'s leaned on him heavy, it was her perfume. Anyway, Bradbury was sending her husband also a Deputy D.A. on out of town assignments, giving the two a chance to get better acquainted. She wanted to be a Superior Court judge more than anything she could think of. Michael gave it lots of thought. Democrat Van De Kamp was opposing Nicholson for Atty. Gen.. Bradbury conjured a devious trade, he'd support Van De Kamp, if he would get Gov. Brown to appoint his female deputy to a Superior Court Judge, it was a deal.

Bradbury's influence in Ventura and the surrounding counties assisted Van De Kamp to win. Gov. Brown was pleased, he felt safe now that Van De Kamp was in, his forked tracks would be covered. On New Years eve Mindy got a call at home, Gov. J. Brown's voice filled her with joy, "You are now a Superior Court judge." There was little time left before Deukmejian's take over, she must be sworn in fast, within hours Judge Berenson swore Mindy in. So, Bradbury, the good Republican had helped a Democrat become Attorney General so that Mindy, a Democrat, could become a Superior Court judge. So, was that *too much* for the mother of his child to ask of him?

Soon afterwards Judge Mindy threw out charges of subornation of perjury against a convicted molester of two small girls. Mindy's emotions had run high, her breathing was effected as she appraised the animal manliness of the molester. She ruled, "This defendant is so charming, and so manipulative that it could be difficult to convict him, Case is Dismissed." Michael Bradbury refused to re-file charges against the child molester. Perhaps Mindy isn't all bad, however her purulent ambitions directly affects the health, safety and welfare of all California citizens.

John Van De Kamp, a *ready for hire* politician, a cover-up artist deluxe, became Attorney Gen. and George Nicholson, a man who'd demonstrated a comprehension of official corruption and apparently intended to deal such conspirators a serious blow was defeated. So, politics are, "The *Science* of Civil Government."

CHAPTER 38

The big sedan still staked-out every morning behind the Legion Hall. I had a friend drive by it, he knew the driver, it was Inspector Schierenbeck from the Bureau of Fire Prevention. Soon after I had noticed Schierenbeck watching my place, firemen began to come in looking around. One morning after the bartender opened up I went there to talk with him. Standing in the middle of the room near the pool table were two firemen. The big, puffy one was Schierenbeck. Waving a pen in his hand he commanded loud with acid disdain in his voice, "Hey you, come over here and sign this." I looked at him, he was putting on a show for the young fireman, teaching him, like, "Just watch me, I'll show you how to handle people like this guy."

Aiming a pen at me then toward his clipboard he blustered, "We discovered an extension cord on your premises, you gotta' sign this promise to appear in court." An extension cord! Lord, this had to be it, I knew what they were up to, I also knew it was only a beginning. Sure as hell, I was about to learn a lot more about the Jews.

My unwelcome incursions into the corruption of the Black Robe Mishpucka had hurt Berenson more than I'd realized. The Family blamed his incompetence for letting me force chinks in the armor of fiercely protected secrecy. Harsh criticism from higher up impugned Berenson's cunning as a Family leader. He never dreamed he'd be demoted to nothing more prestigious than just sitting as a retired judge. It was torture, Berenson's life blood fed on adulation. Praise from the Honey Bees and Judas Gius' editorials were his comet in the sky, raining shafts of brilliance, spotlighting what he c107E*persona* described as his, "Long and *honorable* career as a *noted* Jurist." Now, before his horrified eyes the comet had gone dark, flaming out in a total eclipse. In fits of terrible rage and anguish at his ignominious fate his skull nearly split in half from unbearable pressure. His fury exploded wildly with uncontrollable hatred. It was all my doings, for all these years. In his whole life no one had ever opposed his force or dared resist his schemes, no one, no one except me.

The violation Schierenbeck came up with was what the judges with evil ingenuity were now calling *infractions,* as such, people don't have a right to a jury. Judges are disposing of rights to a jury fast as they can. They say it hinders their ability, their *discretion* to "Dispose of cases expeditiously." I was aware of what expeditiously meant and if I got before a judge without a jury I wouldn't stand a chance. Not only that, this Schierenbeck could come up with some kind of a new phony infraction every day of the week. It could go on *forever.* The Inspector's face had gotten redder. Jabbing toward me with his pen he growled, "You are gonna' sign this or I am going straight down to the courthouse and get a warrant for your arrest." I shook my head, stomping toward the front door Schierenbeck fired a parting shot, "I am on my way downtown right now."

It seemed this was the best way, at least he would have to file a complaint with the D. A. and have a judge sign a warrant. That way I'd get a jury. The incident was nearly forgotten when two days later right after lunch I answered a knock on my door at home. A Deputy Sheriff in uniform greeted me, "Hi Gary, could I talk to you outside for a minute?"

Recognizing him, I figured why not, if he has a warrant I might as well get it over with. "Sure," suddenly a strange feeling hit me as I stepped out. I looked to my left, several feet away pressed close to the wall was another deputy, lurking behind him was Schierenbeck. On my right a fireman stood close to the wall, another was stationed behind the hood of my truck about nine feet away. Twenty feet over at the side entrance to the bar I saw a sixth fireman and could see still another behind him. Lord! Seven uniformed men surrounding my door, I was leery, were they working this thing up into some kind of a felony against me...maybe they intended provoking some sort of a serious incident or violence? It just didn't make any sense. I asked the deputy, "What gives? You have a warrant for me?"

He spoke slow, "Well...no...we haven't."

I queried, "What's with all the man power?"

"These firemen say the day before yesterday you refused to sign their citation to appear in court."

"Yes, it's nothing but trumped up charges, political harassment."

"Well, if you don't sign you'll be arrested and taken to jail."

"Are you deputies arresting me?"

"No," he pointed at Schierenbeck, "The man from Fire Protection is, we're just going to transport you to jail." For emphasis he pulled out handcuffs. It was beginning to make even less sense, why seven men just to ask me if I'd sign?

Along with the handcuff by-play the fireman crouching behind the hood of my pickup began yakking angrily, "Why don't you sign it, by law you are required to."

I asked, "Who are you?"

"I am Captain Spykerman from the Bureau of Fire Prevention." I'd never heard of the guy before but he sure was mad at me, like it was personal. I sensed he had *hard-line* orders from higher-up. Spouting off about his knowledge of the law he kept insisting I had to sign. I was thinking about all this fast as I could, I asked myself, why didn't they get a warrant like Schierenbeck threatened? They wouldn't have to go through all this. Why did they want me to *sign* so bad, why was it so important they needed such a *big raiding party*, seven men with a Fire Captain in charge? If this loud mouth jerk Spykerman was trying to stir me up he was doing a damn good job, his over-bearing arrogance was hard to take.

It had gone far enough. I didn't know if I was falling into their web or not but I made a decision, I knew *I had to have a jury*. I told the deputy, "I'm not going to sign."

He motioned, "Turn around, I'm going to cuff you."

"Hey, for Christ sake, that isn't necessary, I'm not a criminal." He insisted, snapping his cuffs on behind my back he ordered me to walk to the parking lot on the other side of the bar. So many police, firemen, and vehicles surrounding the building sparked a carnival of curiosity, everyone in town saw the handcuffs, it was broad daylight.

Opening the back door of a black and white the deputy ordered, "Okay, get in." Heavy wire mesh separated the front from rear, and no handles on doors or windows. Spykerman, Schierenbeck and the two deputies having moved away from the car were carrying on a big conference. Spykerman seemed in charge. Firemen were running in and out the open doors of the bar. Forced to sit there like a damned caged monkey in a zoo, the crowd gawked, lips moving excitedly they whispered, "Did you see that, Gary had handcuffs on, my God, what in the world do you suppose he did?"

Humiliating was not the word, it was sickening. I fought like hell to keep my temper. They'd been pretty smart, if I'd signed I would have to appear before the judge without a jury. I would be at their mercy, the judge would find me guilty and I'd be sentenced to jail, if I refused to sign they'd make a spectacle of me before a crowd, then they'd take me to jail, but this way I had a chance with a jury.

Later, the bartender who had watched the whole scene told me, "It was like an old time police raid in the movies, they came rushing in all three doors scaring hell out of me. One of them was shouting, 'Where's Gary?' When I said you weren't here, they dashed out the doors and ran over to your house and surrounded the front door. It was crazy, just like a three ring circus."

In jail a deputy making out my arrest report recommended I be released on my own recognizance, the reason, "I was a nice guy." It meant I'd be out in an hour, but, an ominous *directive* came from higher up, it ordered, "Deny him release on his O R, set bail at two thousand dollars." Fingerprinted, I was then mugged with a number on my chest. The information was sent to Criminal Record Bureaus of the FBI in Wash., D.C. and State CII in Sacramento, Ca.. I now had a criminal record...a number...it would *never* go away. The next routine was a shower and dousing with bug spray. Given jail clothes I was put in a small cell with a derelict who couldn't speak English. After a couple hours we were taken out and given blankets, a guard led us through a security check area and headed for the cell blocks. Another deputy approached, pointing a finger at me he said, "Follow me." Ending up in another four by four cell I was given my clothes and told I'd be released on my own recognizance. I sat silent for an hour waiting, wondering, why had they changed their minds? It was getting dark outside when I was finally turned free, it had taken over eight hours. To get released on my O R, it was necessary to agree to appear in court two weeks later.

On the specified date, July 8, at eight fifteen a.m. I appeared in Municipal Court Division 11, my name was called, I stepped forward prepared to plead not guilty and demand a jury trial. I was taken by surprise. Judge Robert J. Soares smiled, friendly, like he liked me. He said, "The charges against you have been rejected. You are free to go as you please." The bailiff handed me a piece of paper, in the hallway I looked at it, a pre-arraignment docket, my case had been *rejected* yesterday by Dep. D. A. Charles S. Cacciatore. Strange, all this 'you are free to go' shit didn't really make me feel any better. Something was *wrong*...more was coming...like a roaring freight train blasting through a pitch black night it was *coming* at me. I couldn't see it, but the tracks were humming...a message of danger vibrated the soles of my feet.

A month and a half *later*, on the morning of August 17, a letter arrived in my mailbox, it was postmarked July 23....twenty five days *before* I got it. Written by Michael Bradbury the D. A., and dated July 23, it said that a criminal complaint had been issued against me and I was to appear in Municipal Court, August 6, eight thirty a.m.. If I failed to appear a warrant would be issued for my arrest. It was more dirty tricks. According to the letter I was *due* in court eleven days ago. By now they had a warrant out for me, Failure to Appear, there would be no bail, this time I'd never get out. Now I knew why they had rejected the extension cord violation. Bradbury knew my arrest was illegal, but if he could toss me in jail for *failure to appear* in court it would make me look like a bad guy with no respect for the law. Lord! They could be on the way right now with another of their raids. I had to move fast if I didn't want to end up in jail.

Jumping in my car I headed for the courthouse where a clerk put me on calendar for the next day August 18, at eight thirty. I left in a hurry. Somebody had that warrant in his hand and was looking for me. It made no difference whether I was on the calendar or not. If they found me before morning I would be back in jail again and looking more like a bad guy all the time.

I swung by the Ventura post office, a postal inspector examining the envelope with an expert eye agreed, "There is something mighty strange indeed, this envelope was postmarked here on July 23, but it would be delivered to your mailbox by the Oak View Branch. If they had lost or misplaced the letter that long, twenty five days, the Oak View office would have put their branch postmark on before they delivered it today." There was another thing I had to verify to be sure I was right...somebody had *removed* the letter from my box and *held* it for twenty five days until a warrant was issued for me, then put it back in the mailbox.

Cruising Oak View, I found the mail carrier. I asked if she had put the letter in my box today. She looked at it, "No, I'd remember if I had. All I left for you was a few throw-away advertisements." I drove up a winding road to Lake Casitas Dam, Look-Out Point was deserted. Scrutinizing the envelope and letter I paid more attention to details. Bradbury's letter was dated July 23, and the envelope was postmarked the same day, in his letter he said he'd filed a complaint against me on the previous day, July 22, and attached a copy of the complaint. There was no Municipal Court file number on the letter, however, the complaint was stamped and signed by the Court Clerk and a Court File No. 38204 affixed thereto on July 28. That was five days *after* the letter was *mailed* in Ventura on July 23.

That meant...Bradbury's complaint *'could not'* have been inside the envelope when it was mailed on July 23! Whoever removed the letter had carefully opened it and inserted the complaint on July 28, *'five days after'* the letter was postmarked. They then *held* it up until August 17, when the warrant was issued for me. At that time they had put the letter back in my mailbox. Something else was also very wrong, during the big raid Dep. Sheriff Davis told me that Inspector Schierenbeck from the Bureau of Fire Prevention was arresting me and that he was only transporting me to the jail. That was June 24, but a full thirty five days *later,* Davis for some reason got busy and made a crime report against me. It was officially filed, stamped and signed by a Municipal Court Clerk on July 28. All this proved one thing, Bradbury *lied* on July 23 when he wrote and mailed his letter stating he had filed a complaint against me in Municipal Court. He didn't even have a crime report from the Sheriff to base a complaint on until five days *after* he'd mailed the letter. *It was a terrible game they were playing with peoples lives.*

My mailbox was on the street, several neighbors boxes were next to it. Bolted on four by four posts they were a height where anyone could easily pull up and remove a letter without attracting attention. Watching from my house when a car drove up in front of the boxes you couldn't tell which one they opened. Mine was about a hundred yards away but only a few feet from where Schierenbeck had been staked-out behind the Legion. Also, he drove back and forth on the street many times a day.

How far Judge Berenson would go with this insanity I couldn't even guess. Across Lake Casitas it was sparkling blue and serene in the sun. God, if my brain could only be so peaceful, just for a while. Next day, August 18, I was in court, I pled not guilty and demanded a jury trial. Judge Soares set it for September 28. I asked about the bench warrant he'd issued against me. I held Bradbury's letter up in my hand, "Judge, I want you to look at this evidence, it's *proof* that these people are lying and trying to frame me," I moved toward him.

He threw his hands in the air, "NO, NO, I don't want to see it, I have *recalled* the warrant."

THERE'S A FISH IN THE COURTHOUSE   439

"I want to make certain of that."

"Oh, yes, yes, certainly, I have *recalled* the warrant."

I'd bandied with too many cowardly liars in my day, the judge was *lying,* he knew what was going on. Eight days later proof of this came in my mail. A letter from the Court Clerk, it threatened that, "If I did not come immediately to the court and post $250.00 bail I would be arrested." Forty miles round trip, a whole day shot, fast as the law allowed I drove to the courthouse. I told the clerk that eight days ago Judge Soares stated twice on the record that he'd recalled the warrant. She checked, "Oh yes, Judge Soares has recalled it."

"Where's the warrant now, who has it?"

Slowly thumbing through the file she shrugged, "It's not in here, it must have been just a *little* mistake of some kind."

That night DuPre called from D.C., I gave him a quick rundown on what had happened. "My God, you can't go to court before those people, you won't stand a chance!"

"Yeh, I already figured that out all by myself." The phone was silent, "Hey Bob, you there?"

"Yeh, I'm here, I am thinking." Pretty soon he said, "Tomorrow morning get to the law library. Look up section 1443, Civil Rights Cases and make a copy of it. What we've got to do is file a petition for removal of your case from Ventura Municipal Court to the U.S. Dist. Court. I'll explain this to you later tomorrow night when I call. Right now I've got something else to tell you. A week ago I mailed a letter to Chief Judge James R. Browning, U.S. Court of Appeal, Ninth Circuit in San Francisco, putting him on notice that as Chief Judge of this circuit he was notified officially of the corrupt conduct of Judge Harry Pregerson with his violations of the rights of litigants before both the Appellate and District Court."

"Yes, you sent me a copy of that letter."

"Well, Browning's no cleaner then Harry Pregerson, he sent me an evasive answer, something about how he did not have power or authority to do anything about Pregerson. Here in D.C. I have been reading records of a Congressional hearing where Browning testified before a Senate Committee, he's been lying to them. Believe me, he is not too brilliant, he slipped up really bad by mentioning that he and William Webster, a *former* federal judge who is now Director of the FBI, are very close. Moreover, Webster's been putting the *fix* on some cases for Browning. I'm copying his testimony. Soon I plan on making contact with Sen. Strom Thurmond, Chairman of the U.S. Senate Committee on the Judiciary. You may recall I told you I was

Executive Secretary and a Legislative Assistant to Thurmond before I left the government."

"Yes, I remember."

"I'm hoping he'll do something if we give him the ammunition."

"Good Lord, so do I."

"Alright then, you get a copy of that section, 1443, and I'll call you tomorrow night."

In Wash., D.C., it was seven thirty p.m., three hours later than here. DuPre's call should come any moment. I sat back and read the copy of section 1443 I'd got earlier in the day. It was encouraging. It stated, "Any of the following Civil actions or criminal prosecutions, commenced in a State Court may be removed by the defendant to the District Court of the United States for the District and Division embracing the place wherein it is pending:

1. Against any person who is denied or cannot enforce in the courts of such State a right under any law providing for the equal civil rights of citizens of the U.S., or of all persons within the jurisdiction thereof:

2. For any act *(under color of law)* providing for equal rights, or for refusing to do any act on the ground that it would be inconsistent with such law."

While endeavoring to comprehend the meaning and powers of these words my thoughts drifted, trailing back and forth across the last four years. When I first met Bob his resolute confidence in the Federal Laws and procedure bolstered my outlook for the possibility of judicial justice. But, underneath I'd never been able to forget the bitter experiences. Harsh years, struggling for justice in a merciless, steaming jungle of corruption that was the State Courts. I could not shake a deep down rangling distrust of the Federal Court, they could not possibly be any different, the *same* crime family, the Mishpucka controls them. I had mentioned this to DuPre but he'd rejected my fears as an insult to the vast integrity of attorneys and judges on the federal level.

Bob enjoyed accrediting my miserable experiences with judicial depravity in State Courts as the result of what he called, "A sordid phenomena of loose, fornicating morals indigenous of California and which could never happen in South Carolina." The way he said it his animosity was toward California, as if the word California itself was to blame, and responsible for all corruption in the state. For some far-fetched, abnormal reason Bob was blaming all his own personal problems on California, even though his misfortunes took place in

South Carolina. He was just like a small kid in this respect. It was a weird unfairness. Spitefully Bob vented his accusations everytime he could. Hell, the word California wasn't to blame for anything. It was so stupid, the senseless aspersions pissed me off, but I decided to wait, be patient and observe the results of the vaunted integrity of DuPre's Federal Courts.

Studying Judge Harry Pregerson's first dubious actions and inane rulings Bob was shocked. But he refused to believe Pregerson was crooked. He swore, "It had to be stupidity or inexperience, or maybe a mistake Pregerson would swiftly remedy soon as it was brought to his attention." Gradually Bob became aware that it was no mistake. Finally after four years of bashing out his brains against that judicial stone-wall he was convinced. The District Court, Court of Appeals and Chief Judge of the Ninth Circuit were guilty not only of stupidity and ignorance of Federal Rules and Procedure, they were corrupt, dead-bang *gangsters* wearing Black Robes. Bob had become terribly depressed by the futility of fighting the judicial stone-wall, it was a frustration that ate you up. He took to wandering aimlessly around the country, he had no money, Eddie and I sent him what we could, it kept him from starving.

Bob was a talker, he would talk with anybody, Legionaires on a convention in Rochester, a black guy with one leg peddling pencils on a wintry freezing corner in Akron, or on a foray into plush Dean Witter emporiums of stocks and bonds in Chicago. He soon learned by himself, the stone-wall wasn't just in California, it was *everywhere* across the land. The last few years Bob and I'd desperately scoured our minds and searched our souls for a formula to destroy judicial corruption, we'd even thought of forming an organization of citizens powerful enough to destroy the stone-wall. Like an American Rights Association, citizens demanding Due Process of Law, it might work, it was an idea, but not feasible, even with unlimited funds there was not enough time left to organize, the Black Robe Mishpucka already has America *coming apart* at the seams. Action was needed fast.

The phony *Local Rules* and *Magistrates* are the stones and mortar used by Mishpuckas to construct and cement their stone-wall. This implacable barrier to justice deprives citizens of the most valuable Civil Right of all. The *inalienable* right of individuals to go to court and have the *merits* of their case determined by a jury. But why...*why* in hell should we have to organize an American Rights Association or have to *contemplate* demonstrations, sit-ins, riots or revolution? All that ground has been well traveled by American Patriots in the past, more than two hundred years ago the people created just such an organization, U.S. Congress, the elected representatives of the people. Congress has the power, it is their *bounden duty* to abolish the virulent *Local Rules* and *Magistrates*. Thus the stone-wall would disintegrate, Due Process of Law would be returned to the Federal Courts. Any judge refusing to adhere to the U.S. Federal Rules and Procedure would be known as being either corrupt or stupid. After three out-right incidents of failing to follow the rules they would be *expeditiously removed* from the bench. Stupid or corrupt, it matters not which category, one is just as dangerous as the other when you consider that lives and futures of American citizens are at stake.

With hunger and bitter frustration stalking the country, Ronald Reagan's Presidential Counselor, Edwin Meese stated to the press, "Hunger does not exist in America, most people go to soup kitchens simply to avoid spending money." Reagan's National Security Advisor Wm. P. Clark knows far better, he understands those bitter hatreds and deep frustration, the underlying fear rampant among the people. Secretly Clark is aware that *riots* and *bloody violence* are imminent. Clark knows all these things because it is he and his superiors, the Black Robe Mishpucka who have instigated, engineered and prodded the situation to a deadly point of no return.

Clark knows the *raging onslaught* is coming. They've opened the flood gates of our borders and seaports, hordes of *provocateurs* and *felons* pour in. He's taken steps to protect himself and family from the bloody chaos. Furtively Clark has set up a heavy caliber machine gun in his house covering all approaches. His murderous weapon is military ordnance, stolen in a burglary of a National Guard Armory.

As a Gunners Mate in the Navy I was acquainted with 50 caliber and twenty millimeter machine guns. I knew the damage they were capable of, they could chew up a car and its occupants like a ragdoll, just the thought of it made me shiver. This Clark must be insane, a *madman* to rig up such a scheme.

The jangling phone broke my thoughts, it was DuPre, "Yes Bob, I've got a copy of section 1443 right here in my hand."

"Okay, what you do is write up a synopsis of what has happened, start clear back at the 1969 Grand Jury, outline everything showing that it's *impossible* for you to get a *fair* trial in Ventura. Make copies of all documents proving this and include them. Get right on it, it's a lot of work, it should be filed soon as possible."

"I'll start first thing in the morning and thanks for your help."

"I'll call every other day because you'll run into snags."

"I'm sure of that."

"No use running up a phone bill, I'll talk to you later." Bob was right, it was a hell of a mess of work, tedious digging into reams of old files and material for dates and facts. He called every other day to check if I was on the right track. Fortunately I'd just completed the Petition except for typing it up when Bob said, "Something very important has come up, I finally contacted Senator Thurmond. He's very interested in both your case and Eddie's. I'd like you to make a complete copy of both files and send them to Strom. He wrote to me acknowledging he'd received my info about Judge Browning. In his letter he *promised* he'd have a member of his Committee Staff review it. Can you do this right away? It's mighty important."

"Of course, it's good as done. Sounds like we might be getting somewhere at last."

"Yeh, my God, let's hope so, I hate to interfere with your work on the Petition Removal."

"No, I'm through except for the final touches."

"I'm mailing a copy of Thurmond's letter to you to put in your files for future reference."

In four days everything was ready for Thurmond. Copies of the files Bob asked for and the Petition To Remove my criminal case, the *Extension Cord Trial*, from State Court to Federal Court. Inside the package I placed a special, sealed envelope, written in red ink, 'Confidential and Private, for Senator Thurmond only.' I didn't want his staff to read it. I wanted the Senator's unexpurgated, personal reaction to the info about William P. Clark's machine gun and his extremely close ties with Pres. Reagan. It began back in the mid 60's when Reagan was preparing to run for Gov. of California. Berenson and Nordman shrewdly realized Reagan might win. They already had Gov. Pat Brown in their pocket however they planned ahead. They had William P. Clark switch from a Democrat to Republican. With clever manipulation and duplicity they wheedled him into Reagan's Gubernatorial Campaign Committee.

The Mishpucka spent millions of dollars bringing Clark carefully up the political path, California Superior Court Judge, Appeal Court Judge, State Supreme Court Justice, National Security Advisor and Secretary of the Interior. The Mishpucka knew Ron Reagan would be re-elected in 1984, but the *scheme* was that he'd never finish his second term, his health would fail. In 1987 or early 1988 Clark would be installed as President of the United States just as easy as Lyndon B. Johnson took over when President Kennedy was assassinated and as smoothly as Gerald Ford replaced Nixon. Both occurred during a dreadful state of national emergency. As incumbent, Wm. P. Clark would easily be elected in 1988. The Mishpucka would then control *both* the Judicial and Executive branches of government. Congress would dissolve in a rabble of weaklings. Wielding the mighty power of the United States Military establishment the Mishpucka will rule the planet, outer space and beyond.

Not wanting to make a mistake and costly delay by mailing the package to a wrong address I called D.C. information. Thurmond's office phone was area 202-224-4934. A lady answered, I explained who I was. "Oh yes, the Senator told me he was expecting some files from his former associate Mr. DuPre." She was very pleasant, "I am Sally Rogers, the Senator's secretary."

"Fine Sally, I would like your exact mailing address, I'm going to mail the package today."

"Alright, use this address, it'll come direct to me; Senator Strom Thurmond, 2226 Dirksen, Senate Office Building, Washington, D.C., 20510. Put att: Sally Rogers on it, I'll make sure the Senator gets it immediately."

"That's great, thank you Sally."

The following day I left early for the long drive to L. A. to file my Petition. At the Federal Courthouse a deputy clerk, a tall blond woman looked my papers over, then she looked me over, then she fingered some papers on the counter to her right. From beneath the counter she brought out a long sheet of paper, an official form, the insignia at the top left corner said, "Seal of the U.S. District Court, Central District of California." Swiftly the clerk scratched some X's on the form. Still with no facial expression she shoved the form and Petition For Removal back at me. Under the seal I read the large printed words, they were underlined, "Your Document Is Returned Herewith For The Reasons Checked Below."

She had checked off six Local Rules as the reason to refuse my Petition. Local Rule 32 demanded I put up a bond of $500.00. Other Local Rules she had marked were, No.2, No.4, No.4b, No.4e, No.41. A notation at the bottom informed me, "To get a copy of the Local Rules go to the L. A. Daily Journal, 210 S. Spring St., Los Angeles, California, 90012. Local Rule No.4b said, "No documents other than exhibits shall be in type smaller than Pica size, with not more than 10 typed characters per inch." My God...there are hundreds of damn Local Rules that can be *indiscriminately* and *maliciously* evoked. The strategy is simple, delay and obfuscation, frustrate the people, force them to miss their court appearances and deadlines on Motions and Answers until the case is Dismissed, or the Statute of Limitations runs out. Suddenly you're in another category, the *original issue* and *merits* are lost in the stink of judicial effluvia. You spend insane time at the law library desperately searching for a means to get your case in court. Every time you appear before a judge you see and feel his hidden smirk, you are a *beggar*. You know what he is thinking, he's laughing, "Shit, this poor dumb bastard will never live long enough to ever get his case before a jury."

Judge Harry Pregerson laughs, conjuring up new Local Rules, sabotaging the people, he thrills, sensations whip through his body, the evil pleasures of his Black Robes, *"I'm a Federal Judge for life. They can't touch me."*

That night I talked with DuPre, "Bob, I don't know what in hell to do. There isn't time to revise and retype my Petition and worst of all I don't have five hundred dollars."

"God, I know, it's crazy, all that stuff is pure harassment. But, they have given themselves away, that bond is *only* on Civil Matters, there's no bond for removal of criminal cases. They know that... it's damned deliberate, calculated sabotage, without a doubt, they've red tagged your name. Lord! It makes me gag," there was a pause, "Ok, when you go to court here is what you should do. Tell the judge you want to make a Motion. If he allows it then give him a copy of the Petition and ask for a sixty day continuance to file it. You got that?"

"Yes, I understand, and Monday morning Bob, I'm going to call Sen. Thurmond. Maybe I can talk to the guy on his Committee Staff. Surely there must be something that can be done about all this."

A girl answered my phone call, "I would like to speak with Sally Rogers please."

"She is out to lunch. I'm Ann Land, can I help you?"

"Yes, I mailed the Senator a package last week from California."

"Oh, it arrived this morning. Sally put it on the Senator's desk." Just as pleasant as Sally, Ann said, "I am also one of his secretaries. If you will call back tomorrow I am certain we'll have an indication as to whom the Senator will have review your documents."

The next day Sally answered, she recognized my voice. "Oh yes, how are you?"

"Just fine. Sally I'm very anxious to contact the person appointed to review my files."

"Oh, oh yes," she faltered, "Well, they're in Senator Thurmond's hands, however, to my knowledge he has not yet selected any person to examine them." With Sally's first quavering words I knew it, I had detected her shock, they *always* reacted the same. The Senator had gotten my secret letter. Sally heard the explosion behind the closed door. "Good God, why did they have to send this to me, what in the world am I suppose to do, damn it to hell. How can I advise Reagan about a damn machine gun and Clark, his National Security Advisor wanting to *shoot* Niggers and Mexicans." Thurmond's fierce outbreak of anguish made Sally shiver spasmodically, icy chills stabbed at her. She couldn't hear all the words screamed beyond the door but she knew it had something to do with me and the package I sent.

Sally's shocked voice told me all I wanted to know. I'd just been advised of Senator Thurmond's *unexpurgated reaction.* There would be no review now, the file and my letter would be buried forever, the Senator prayed, *"Buried forever."*

Trying to sound like it wasn't too important I asked, "Sally would you do me a little favor? Write me a letter acknowledging that the Senator received my package, just something for my records."

Her words quickened, "Why, why do you want a letter? I already told you on the phone, the Senator received your package and has read it, and you have your return receipt from the Post Office. Isn't that enough?" Sally's voice became tinged with defensive suspicion, thinking perhaps she'd already said too much for her own good.

"I know Sally, but I'd appreciate just a short note verifying the Senator read my...."

She interrupted, "You already have my word on the phone, that should be good enough."

I didn't press it. "Alright and thank you." I hung up, there'd be nothing more from Sally. Several days later I called Ann Land. She reacted identical to Sally. That night I told Bob, "We can forget it, there will be *no* help from Senator Strom Thurmond or his Senate Judiciary Committee."

Eight thirty a.m. on September 28, I was in Municipal Court, the judge was A. Gutierrez, he nodded when I asked to make a Motion. I handed him a copy of the Petition for Removal, "Your Honor, I'd like a sixty day continuance in which to refile this Petition in Federal Court. I've been informed the Federal Clerk was mistaken, there is *no* bond requirement of $500.00 in criminal cases." Gutierrez stared at it, surprised, he plainly didn't know what to do. His *orders* hadn't prepared him for such a problem. Hastily stuttering, "There'll be a recess," the judge dashed for his chambers and made an emergency phone call.

I watched as the group of Deputy D.A.'s arrived in their private elevator at the end of the hallway just outside the courtroom. They rushed into Gutierrez's chambers. As the defendant I had the right to be in on the discussion and determination but they wouldn't allow me to come in. When I tried to, a Dep. D.A. said no and the bailiff held up his hand to stop me. It was a long wait, two hours later they called me back into the courtroom. Gutierrez asked me, "Would you like to 'plead guilty' to the charges and ask for probation?"

"No Judge, I'd like a continuance for the purpose of refiling my Petition for Removal to the Federal Court." A mighty protector of *minorities*, Gutierrez didn't know what to do, I was not a *minority*. He recessed again and rushed into his chambers, more Dep. D.A.'s tailed him. I wondered...if the District Attorney was influencing the judge and *telling* him what to do, why didn't I have the right to be there and if I do have the right...*how* do I go about getting it? I had no lawyer to represent me, I was Pro-Per, it was late afternoon when Gutierrez returned. Attorneys with cases scheduled to be heard had congregated with curiosity, wondering what was going on. Obviously my Motion to Remove my case to the Federal Court had thrown a monkey wrench into the courts *predestined* procedure.

The bailiff motioned me up to the lawyers table. The courtroom was silent, expecting. With head down, staring at his feet, Gutierrez said something. I couldn't make it out, "Sorry Your Honor I can't hear you." Not looking up he mumbled. Trying to understand him I moved forward, the lawyers were also straining to hear him.

Bill Hinkle, a Dep. D.A., sitting closest to the bench grasped my sleeve. Pulling me forward he whispered, "Judge Gutierrez says he's *denying* your Motion for a continuance, and transferring you to the Presiding Judge, John Hunter."

I whispered, "Why is Gutierrez acting so damn strange?" At that Hinkle froze. Hearing a whispering amongst the lawyers I followed their gaze toward the bench. Etched on Gutierrez's face was a limp look of immense relief. I understood it's significance, obviously he'd been released from further involvement in whatever sinister acts of wickedness they were plotting but, whatever had upset him so bad it sure as hell wasn't good for me, it must be a mighty evil operation if they have decided the Presiding Judge must handle it.

Going down the hall to Hunter's courtroom I puzzled, was Judge Berenson directing their every move in this abortion...was he telling them exactly how he wanted it handled...or was he leaving Bradbury, the D.A. to his own devices? I wished I knew what had transpired in

Gutierrez' chambers. Worried as hell, I wondered, how far are they going to carry this insane extension cord crap? The courtroom was empty, I walked in, that was the cue, back-stage they must have been watching through a peep-hole, it was a play, theatrical drama played on a high school auditorium stage, done by the numbers, One, Two, Three. Emerging from the wings the bailiff took his post beside his desk...the clerk seated herself primly...the Judge swirling majestically amid his black robes swooped to his throne.

They had carefully rehearsed their script in Gutierrez' chambers. I wasn't a member of the cast, I wouldn't know how the script read till after it was played. I was the prey in their extravaganza. In one breath the bailiff announced, "Court in session the Honorable Judge John Hunter presiding be seated." The bailiff sat down. On Hunter's left and a foot lower, the clerk nervously toyed with a tape recorder like she actually intended to record something, but knowing better, Hunter paid no attention. Not looking up he monotoned, "We will continue the trial two days for the purpose of getting a jury panel." Swooshing his black robe he vanished into the stage wings...by the number, Two...the bailiff, Three...the clerk, they disappeared.

I looked around, the room was empty, it was a strange feeling. I asked out loud, why? *Why* this two day delay, supposedly for the purpose of getting a jury panel? It was still early in the day, plenty of time to get a panel up here and begin jury selection, why not get the show on the road? Half a dozen times today I had wandered by the jury room. It was full of people sitting, smoking, drinking coffee, snacking on cafeteria food, waiting, waiting impatiently to be called for duty.

On my way to the parking lot I again strolled by the jury room. I stopped...suddenly my mind was revolving. Good Lord! The jury room was still *full,* the same people sitting there, now tired looking, staring, still waiting to be called for duty. A chill raced up and down my spine, the truth snapped at me! A jury had been available and ready to go all the time! Time...Time...hell, that was it. That's what they needed the two day continuance for, time...*time* to *fix* a panel of jurors.

In the parking lot I sat in the car, staring at nothing, sick with the dread knowledge I didn't have a ghost of a chance in court. A million questions crashed on me, mashing and squeezing. Why was I so dangerous to them that they didn't dare stake their chances on an honest jury, what in the hell could possibly make them take such extraordinary, hazardous risks as to *fix* a whole jury panel? It wasn't just what I was doing to them now, there was more to it than that, there had to be, I could feel it. I had had this weird feeling before, deadly secrets from the past. A secret so *monstrous* it could *destroy* the entire Black Robe Mishpucka. I thrashed my memory, Geez, so much had happened since 1946, it was *something* that they knew I knew, but I had not put it together yet. They didn't dare let me win my case, they had to completely discredit me, make me look like an idiot so that no one would ever believe me again. Damn, why can't I remember! It was there, hidden, *locked* for years in a recess of my memory. It was the key, the breakthrough, it would scalpel out the whole rotten, cancerous Black Robe Mishpucka scheme. I wondered, how did they intend to *fix* the jury?

Slowly I returned to my surroundings. The sun was dropping, dawdling with the tips of the tall fir trees lining Victoria Ave.. In the past the thick row of pines served as a windbreak from prevailing ocean breezes buffeting the west boundary of the citrus ranch...now the County Government Center.

Two mornings later as ordered, I arrived in the courtroom. The jury panel was already there sitting in the spectator seats. A young deputy D.A. stood at the lawyers table preparing for action. One, Two...the clerk and judge took their place, Three...the bailiff recited, "Court in session, the Honorable Judge John Hunter presiding be seated."

Judge Hunter was raring for action, in a big rush he ordered the clerk, "Call the jurors."

The clerk read from her list, "William Tice." I watched him walk toward the jury box, I bet myself a dollar, that will be their foreman, their enforcer. Without hesitation he went directly to the foreman's seat. Like a well rehearsed Oakland Raider's offense team leaving their huddle, the rest of the jurors in close formation filed into the jury box.

The jurors were asked, "Are any of you a fireman, a volunteer fireman or closely related to firemen or county personnel? All the hands in the jury box went up. Turning around I saw the remaining members of the panel, all of their hands were in the air. The huge knot in my stomach grew, spreading its torment as my suspicions of the two day continuance were verified, that's what they've been up to the last two days, setting up a *sure-thing* jury. I'd been positive they were monkeying with the jury but until now I hadn't figured out how they intended to do it. To *stack* a whole jury panel with a *single group-type* of people whose *thinking* and *prejudices* all ran down the same isolated one way track took a tremendous amount of effort. It would be necessary to exhaustively scrutinize the files and records and analyze backgrounds of hundreds of prospective jurors, and it would have to be performed in utmost secrecy.

There was only one person with access to those files and with the capability of handling such a project that Judge Hunter would trust to do it, James G. Fox, the Municipal Court Clerk, who was appointed by the judges. If he wanted his job he'd do *exactly* as he was told, and that was precisely what Jimmy Fox had been doing for years. I'd noticed the last few months every time Fox saw me in the courthouse he had come up to me with a big smile and glad hand.

I studied the jurors. It was useless for me to play like a lawyer and start eliminating prejudiced jurors. They'd only be replaced by more of the same from the panel. And I sure as hell wasn't going to get anywhere making a big uproar complaining about a *stacked* jury to Judge Hunter. How far would I get appealing to Judge Berenson in Superior Court, and on up the line, Hymie Blitzberg, alias Steven Stone, in the State Appellate Court and Stanley Moskovich, Joseph Grodinsky, Otto Kausinsky, etc., in the State Supreme Court, and then to Harry Pregerson and Stephen Reinhardt in Federal Appeal Court.

A raging knot of hopelessness in my chest spread its paralyzing, burning fluid throught out my limbs, a terrible hatred seethed in my brain. I had to hold my temper. God, was I in America?

Judge Hunter pushed, "Do you accept the jury?"

Deputy D.A. Kevin Mc Gee said, "Yes your Honor."

I thought, what in hell else can I do. I just nodded, that seemed to satisfy Hunter and he began talking to the jury. I was looking at some documents I'd brought when with a start I took heed of what he was saying. "Ladies and gentlemen, I realize that you may think this court is going to extreme lengths for just a little old extension cord, but...after all, there's a morals violation involved here and this is serious." Good Lord! What is he talking about, a morals violation. What the hell is Judge Hunter trying to do? The clerk was clacking her recorder, pulling and pushing a tape in and out. There'd never be a coherent recording to make a transcript even if I did want to file an Appeal, it was hard to believe.

I looked at Mc Gee, maybe his boss Bradbury hadn't fully clued him in on this abortion, he appeared momentarily shocked. Even so he was smart enough for his own good to keep his mouth shut. The D.A., Mc Gee shuffled a pile of papers like he hadn't heard Hunter or the clacking recorder. I thanked God I'd decided to put the small recorder in my briefcase. I looked in, it was running, I wasn't stupid enough to believe Judge Hunter would ever let the tape be played. But I was *sure*...one day the proper time would come.

I glanced apprehensively at the jurors, two gray haired guys in the back row glared at me, both had sons who were members of the Fire Protection Bureau. Their wrathful eyes never blinked. I was a criminal, a morals violator, I had shamelessly defied the will of the Protection Bureau. Two ladies in the front row stared with faces of stone, they were firemens wives. A retired school teacher's thoughts were all over her face, plainly written, I was a bad boy, I had to be taught a lesson. Counting an alternate juror, thirteen pairs of hostile eyes were glued on me.

Mc Gee called his first prosecution witness. A fireman I did not recognize being present when I was arrested. He must be one of the two stationed in the bar. Under questioning the fireman established that indeed, "I observed an extension cord in the Hill Top Bar."

It was my turn to ask the questions, "You state you observed an extension cord?"

He was emphatic, "Yes, I did."

"Do you know which end of the cord is the male end?"

"Yes."

"Was it plugged in?"

"I don't know."

"Alright, what was the other end connected to?"

"I don't know."

"Did you arrest me for this violation?"

"No."

"Are you a fireman?"

"Yes."

"What unit are you assigned to?"

"I am assigned to the Fire Protection Bureau."

"As such what are your specific duties?"

"I go around looking for extension cords."

I said, "No further questions."

Mc Gee called another fireman to the stand who testified he'd also seen an extension cord in the Hill Top Bar.

When I questioned him he answered same as the first fireman. He didn't know if it was plugged in the wall or if there was anything on the other end. I continued to question, "Are you assigned to the Fire Protection Bureau?"

"Yes."
"What is the code section for an extension cord violation?"
"I don't know."
"Do you understand that to be in violation of that section it is necessary that I was 'maintaining' an extension cord?"
"Yes."
"If that extension cord was not plugged in and nothing was on the other end does that constitute maintaining an extension cord?"
"I don't know."
"Are you acquainted with the laws of arrest?"
"No."
"Do you have the power to arrest people?"
Judge Hunter broke in quickly, "All firemen are police officers." He glared at me, the room became silent. Obviously he didn't want me to continue this line of questioning, but also he didn't want to come right out and say it.

I continued my questions, "Alright, if you are a 'police officer' what is an infraction?"
"I don't know."
"What is a misdemeanor?"
"I don't know."
"Do you know what the difference is between a misdemeanor and a felony?"
"No."
"Do you know who arrested me?"
"No."
Hunter interrupted, "That is far enough with those questions."

Going to my seat I stole a glance at the jury. Lord, if they were hostile at the beginning, they were now seething. Hell, I hadn't been trying to belittle firemen. I had always believed like everyone else, firemen were heros, risking their lives climbing tall ladders to save old people, women and kids from fiery, collapsing buildings, fighting terrible forest fires, saving homes and property, their rescue squads prying hurt victims from horribly smashed cars and bringing small children back to life from the bottom of swimming pools. But that's what they are, firemen, not policemen.

Mc Gee called Capt. Spykerman to the stand, he testified he'd never seen an extension cord but related the incident that took place when he had surrounded my door with firemen and deputy sheriffs. Mc Gee said, "Your witness."

I asked Spykerman, "Were you in charge of the raid on my place of business and at my home?"

"That's right."

"From what I understand you took this police action based on information from Inspector Schierenbeck from your Fire Protection Bureau."

"That's right."

"But you were in charge and it was you who laid out the raid?"

"That is correct, I planned, coordinated, and directed the whole operation."

"Now, if I understand you right, you assembled four firemen and two armed deputy sheriffs at the fire station, counting yourself that is seven. You briefed them where all the entrances were located at my property, diagraming how the raiding party should dash through the doors simultaneously, and if I wasn't there they should rush to my house surrounding the front door?"

"Yes, that's right." Capt. Spykerman was entertaining himself by throwing big smiles at the jurors. He was enjoying his importance, gloating and laughing at my distress.

I asked, "Weren't you actually acting on secret orders given to you by someone else?" The Captain's smile vanished. I caught the split second flash of fear in his eyes as they darted toward Mc Gee. The Deputy D.A. didn't bat an eye. Spykerman was on his own, he faltered. I repeated, "Did some one 'high up' give you clandestine orders to pull this police raid?"

He recovered, "Nope. It was all my idea." However his grin had deserted.

"Were you the one who arrested me?"

"No."

"Well, who arrested me?"

"It was Inspector Schierenbeck."

"Is he here today to testify?"

"No, he is not here. The Inspector was sent *out of state* on Fire Prevention Bureau business." It struck Spykerman as being funny, he grinned.

I said, "No further questions."

In closing his case Mc Gee made an impassioned speech to the jury demanding that I be convicted. There wasn't any question of my guilt, I had maintained an extension cord. It was the juries duty to convict me. They should allow no thoughts of pity for me to enter their mind which would deter them from this duty. Pity..! Who was asking for pity. That was the last damn thing I needed, pity. I didn't know why I bothered, but I got up and said a few words to the jury, maybe I was hoping for a miracle. I looked at the jurors, their faces were hard, the eyes harder, I went back to my chair.

Judge Hunter began reading instructions to the jury, the usual stuff. Suddenly his voice pitch changed. There was an intensity, his words were *not* to be mistaken. Hunter was *issuing an order* from the court. The drama of the stage production heightened. "Probably this case of an extension cord seems to be so trivial that it is ridiculous but there are morals violations involved. It is your bounden duty to give this your utmost attention."

Morals violations! This is crazy. Hunter wants to bury me with an extension cord twisted, knotted and cutting into my juggler. The clacking with the tape ceased as Hunter's jury instructions ended. The jury filed out to deliberate. They were out just long enough for coffee and a cigarette. Back in their seats Foreman Tice announced, "We find the defendant guilty as charged Your Honor."

Hunter was pleased, congratulating the jurors, he said, "You've done a good job, jury dismissed." Then he directed his words at me, "Sentencing will be two weeks from now, the guilty party will remain free on his O R." The clacking was over, with a final yank the clerk removed the tape from the recording machine, she took it with her. ONE...TWO...THREE...the judge, clerk and the bailiff faded away into the wings backstage, the extravaganza was finis. No, not quite finis.

Tice, the enforcer, walked toward me. They had one last act of derision to perform, he said, "Well, I will tell you, even though you knew you were guilty you did it the American way, you had a jury." Grinning he marched from the courtroom, the jurors in his wake. It was their final finale. That day...the day of the extravaganza, I didn't have to swear an oath to *remember* it. That day I'd *never* forget.

Opening my briefcase to shove some papers in I saw the small recorder still going. I switched it off, what the hell good was it, no one would ever listen to it, what court of justice was there to appeal to? The drive home was long, depressing didn't begin to describe it. I was a lousy convicted criminal, it galled so bad I couldn't stand it. Giant claws tore at the pit of my stomach. No one in my family had ever been arrested, jailed or convicted of anything. That had always been of great importance to me. I was the first one. They'd stolen something from me, something vital. For twelve terrible years their friggin' Mishpucka insanity had been carried on, it was putrid. The stench grew worse each second. Vengeance blocked everything from my mind, a reckless son of a bitchin' scream for revenge rampaged with my temper, God damn if there wasn't going to be the damndest bloody violence all over the friggin' place. I had had all of it I could take, just sitting there, meekly letting them beat me to death while I hoped for friggin' *non-existent* judicial justice. Screw 'em, nothing was left but revenge, violent, swift and hard.

Through this maelstrom of terrible hatred a small ray of light sifted into my senses, a dab of reasoning spread some control. No, not violence, that was Kamikaze thinking, it wasn't the answer. The sudden shaft of reasoning did not serve to make me happy...violence against the Mishpucka would give me one hell of a pleasure. But I knew it was not the right way. All my life I had abided by the law, and respected it. I wouldn't let them drive me into doing something foolish. But I swore, I would be damned, I was going to smash the Black Robe Mishpuckas God damned evil. Within the boundaries of the law, I was going to destroy it and I sure as hell didn't intend to spend another thirteen years of my life doing it.

My wife did not sleep that night, she cried till morning. It was impossible for her to conceive or to believe what was happening to us, to our lives. She could never break a law of any kind. I recalled, it was in 1947, I'd taught her to drive, in thirty five years she'd never gotten a traffic ticket, not even for parking, no accidents, not even a fender bender. She couldn't understand, it was incomprehensible, how had we come to this frightening, grim, debased state of being. Harsh pangs of guilt reproached me. I could have avoided all this misery, I hadn't considered her health and happiness, it would have been so easy to just leave town, like certain people had advised, but I was too stubborn to leave. But if I'd left town would I have been any better off than I am right now, or would she?

We wouldn't have prospered under that black cloud. The passing of every year would have created a blacker and blacker prison cell, an inescapable cage of torture. A stifling, mounting anger and guilt at having run away and doing nothing till too late would have been a craven bitter shriveling into dust. I couldn't have died under those terms. It still had not been fair to her the way I was trying to do it, but Lord, was there any other way? I knew she could not take much more of this insane struggle, hell, it was not a fight, it was just plain murder. They were shaming us from the face of the earth.

I could do nothing except wait for sentencing, wait and worry. Night after night with no sleep I sweated it out. If I was sent to jail we'd lose everything we had. I put in fourteen, fifteen hours every day, seven days a week, all hours of the day and night, fixing broken equipment, all the janitor work, stopping fights and arguments. My wife couldn't keep the place going, she'd end up in a hospital if she tried.

It was noon, I had just returned from the bank. The bartender motioned me to come to the back room. He was scared, in a hushed voice he said, "Two firemen just left, they were here over an hour going all over the place, into everything," his hands shook.

"Were they in uniform?"

"Yeh, they were wearing gray shirts and badges, one said he was a Captain something or other from the Protection Bureau."

"Was it Captain Spykerman?"

"That sounds like it."

"Gray shirts from the *Protection Bureau.* What did they want?"

"That Spykerman guy left this paper, he said to give it to you."

It was a sheet of lined paper hand written with a long list of new violations Spykerman claimed he had found, even the Yale locks on the doors were illegal according to Spykerman. The following day, October 15, I appeared before Judge Hunter for sentencing for the criminal act of having an extension cord. Deputy D.A. Mc Gee was there. I showed him the large cardboard box full of wires. "Look at this, Spykerman forced me to tear out the wires and speakers from the jukebox and telephone wire the phone company installed. They are strictly legal and have nothing to do with the Protection Bureau. He wrote a letter to the Building and Safety Dept. demanding they make a complete inspection of my property. It's nothing but damn harassment by this Protection Bureau, right from the start." Mc Gee looked at the speakers and wire. He would not say a word. He just shook his head.

Judge Hunter announced, "I've received information from Capt. Spykerman about *new* violations he himself has found. He has asked the Building and Safety Dept. to conduct a complete inspection of the said property. I'll wait for their report before imposing sentence. You are hereby ordered to return to this court a week from today, nine a.m., for further proceedings."

I'd been right, there was to be *no end* to it. It made me sick to my stomach. Several mornings later I again had just returned from Ventura, again a look on the bartender's face warned me, there was more trouble. I followed him to the back room. Peering around like the walls had ears he whispered, "Jesus Christ, the *Gray Shirts* were here again, there was another guy with them, they didn't say a word to me, they went all through the place. Behind the bar, everywhere. The safe door was open just a crack, they rummaged through it, and smack in front of all the customers they screwed lamp fixtures right off the wall. That Captain Spyker gave orders to the others, and was giving me the evil look, I mean bad." The employee was badly shook up. "Hey Gary, I've been bartending a long time, I've been around but believe me I ain't never run up against anything like this, they didn't show a warrant or nothing."

"Listen, you did real good, don't worry. They aren't after you."

The handwriting on the wall was vivid, a blood red. They were trying to shut us down, my blood turned to ice, we'd lose everything. I had no right to jeopardize my wife's life further. Her health was poor, during the thirteen years of all this insanity she had undergone ten kidney operations and had to have one removed. After working hard, looking to the future all our lives we'd end up as derelicts and it was my fault. There were no savings, I'd used every dollar we had to fight this thing, there was no money for doctor bills and medicine, even Medicare was cut off. I had brought terrible disaster down. All those years she had been deprived of everything normal. Only one vacation during all that time, three days on the Colorado River in a camper. We never stopped worrying about the place all the time we were gone. I was scared, for the first time I felt real fear, a fear of the future, penniless, destitute, incapable of taking care of my wife. The bitter humiliation, responsibility for losing all family reputation. A worthless bum, shunned, and avoided by everyone. I'd brought all of it upon both of us, a failure, a nothing and nowhere to go. Over and over it drummed, I couldn't tear it from my brain, thinking only made it worse. There was only one way out, I would have to beg, no matter if the thought made me puke...something had to be salvaged. I'd tell them I would quit fighting them and leave town for good. I'd become a beggar, crawling, but I knew it wouldn't work.

It would be funny to them, a big joke. They'd laugh. Hell, why would they make a deal with me, but I had no choice. I didn't want my wife to know what I intended. That night after she went to bed I wrote a letter to Judge Hunter. It was short, "If he would stay the proceedings I would dispose of our property as fast as possible for anything I could get, and leave town." A beggar and coward, my legs felt weak as I walked down to the Post Office that night and mailed the letter.

I received no answer, six days later at nine a.m. I was sentenced. Hunter ordered that I correct all the violations Spykerman claimed he had found, also the ones supposedly discovered by the building inspector. I'd have to get a building permit. All work would have to be done by a licensed contractor. Hunter gave me only ninety days to complete the work, have it inspected and show proof to the court that it was done.

None of the work was necessary, but I knew it would cost five or six thousand dollars which I also knew I didn't have. I was fined a hundred and fifty dollars, it had to be paid at once. It was all pure harassment. Judge John Hunter continued talking, suddenly the real picture came into sharp focus, Judge Hunter had gotten down to the marrow. "You are ordered to be on probation to the court for two years, obey all laws, City, County, State and Federal. If not, you'll be in violation of probation. You'll consent to *searches* of your person, vehicles, residence and any other property *anytime* you are ordered to do so by a peace officer, probation officer or inspector, also to report any changes of address to this court. Now, you will sign this form agreeing to these terms as a condition of being released from custody." Hunter handed the papers down to the bailiff. I signed the form taking the copy he handed back. If I wanted to stay out of jail did I have a choice?

By studying Hunter's 'Conditions of Release,' I had a good idea what they were after. With nothing more than a phony charge of an extension cord they'd stretched me tortuously over the rack, tighter than the hide of an old skinned jack rabbit. They could tighten the screws anytime they wanted, with those code violations hanging over the property I couldn't even give it away. There was no guarantee that even after spending thousands of dollars with a contractor the *Protection Bureau* would not start the same old shit all over again, what would stop them?

They could search me, my home, vehicles or any other property I owned, at will. Suddenly it dawned, all my files, my documents and evidence I'd laboriously compiled over the years proving Black Robe Mishpucka corruption. They had to be moved fast to a safe place.

The *Gray Shirts* were sworn police officers, *a separate political police force,* operating as a *'Protection Bureau,'* never trained in law enforcement, unprincipled, unrestrained by prescribed police rules and procedures. Regular police are powerless, they can not stop the *Protection Bureau* anymore then the FBI could be controlled by the Salvation Army. The *Gray Shirts* are accountable only to the Black Robe Mishpucka. *Unified* throughout the state the *Protection Bureau* maintains files, keeping personalized records on all business people and their places of business. These intelligence files are stored in computer banks, electronic brains available to all counties.

Invariably a businessman is totally unaware that because of some business activity or political infraction he commits against them he has become a mortal enemy of the Black Robe Mishpucka. When the *Protection Bureau* pushes a button the electronic brain obeys, it reveals the person has businesses in other counties. Very easily the *Gray Shirts* discover this person has extension cords in other places as well as Ventura. Suddenly he finds himself arrested and in court with so many problems he'll be lucky if he survives. Administering a death blow, the coup de grace, Judas Gius in his Star Free Press makes it public, "Indeed, this businessman is a first-rate scoundrel, it appears very obvious he is conducting these outrageous violations throughout California."

Building their power base the *Gray Shirts* will soon claim they can be far more effective if armed. They'll need interrogation rooms and holding cells at *Protection Bureau* headquarters. Supervisors and City Councilmen ominously passed a new law, "Requiring owners of apartments, motels, hotels and houses to install smoke detectors."

The regular police know they can not enter the homes of people without their permission, they would not even attempt it, but *Gray Shirts* can. With this law Capt. Spykerman and Insp. Schierenbeck can enter a home on a pretext of looking for a smoke detector, once inside they can cite every kind of a so-called code violation they can think of. Later returning with a building inspector and supposedly looking for more code violations they will search for pistols, rifles, shotguns, ammunition re-loaders etc., listing everything, binoculars, knives, souvenir swords etc. etc.. This intelligence info will be fed to the computer banks of the *Protection Bureau* electronic brain for use against all enemies of the Black Robe Mishpucka.

Mayor Dianne Feinstein, Queen of Aids in San Francisco, is the chief designer of legislation taking away citizens guns. She aims one day to be President of the United States. With powerful political pressure from Mishpuckas like Frisco's Feinstein, the U.S. Supreme Court ruled that local politicians can pass laws prohibiting people from owning or having guns in their homes, guns will be confiscated and violators arrested. Irving Rubin, a *racist gangster* and leader of the furtive Jewish Defense League, threatens to slice the ears off of Christians. But Mayor Dianne Feinstein's gun laws do not prohibit Mishpucka maniacs like Rubin from stockpiling a secret arsenal of machine guns and small arms. Nor do Feinstein's laws stop political lunatics like National Security Director Wm. P. Clark from arming himself with a heavy caliber military machine gun and plotting evil cabalas to, "Kill niggers and Mexicans" to incite riots, revolution and insurrection against the U.S. so the Mishpucka could take over.

Secret police...political intriguers...counter-parts to the Russian KGB Secret Police, *the Gray Shirts* operate under the deceptive title of the *Protection Bureau.* They obey the sinister orders of the Black Robe Mishpucka.

Three times I ran for the office of Supervisor. The Mishpucka wasn't afraid I might win, not while they had Robert L. Hamm, the versatile County Clerk, rippling the keys on that electronic voting computer. Like Liberace tinkling the ivories on his piano, Hamm could make whatever name he wanted come out. What enraged the Mishpucka most was my screaming at those public political forums about their conspiracies and exposing all their damned corruption. They wanted it stopped before the people started thinking about it and maybe putting two and two together.

They had put the stops to me but good, it'd be useless for me to try to run, being on probation I didn't know if I could even file. The two years ran clear through to the next election. Undoubtedly they had some trick, a law or ordinance stashed away they could invoke to stop me from filing. Even if they did not, Judas Gius would hold field day in the Star Free Press telling voters what a real bad guy I was. But worse yet, he could prove it, I was a convicted criminal on probation, who in hell would believe anything a guy like me says?

After four years in office, Supervisor Maggie Erickson was now, according to Judas Gius, "A Seasoned Politician." A quick learner, Maggie had discovered a powerful secret, the easiest way to stay in office was making sure no one ran against you. Backing her clear to the hilt Judas gleefully reported in his paper, "Maggie receives an overwhelming, fantastic mandate from all the people to keep her in office."

With just two political unknowns filing to run against her Maggie received several hundred thousand dollars for her fund. According to her, "The exact amount was hardly worth mentioning. Just a few fond land developers, financiers, and rich oil men expressing their deep gratitude and admiration for her *extraordinary* civic mindedness during the last four years." Maggie was more than seasoned. Since she wouldn't have to run much of a campaign it obviously was just plain old damn foolishness to put all that lovely money in a silly old campaign chest, how in hell would she ever get it out? However, on second thought, probably it would look better to put a little of it in, maybe about forty grand. Yeh, report only about ten percent of the dough, that should do it. Politicians, elections, money, dirty tricks, intrigue, its heaviness hung over the county, oppressive, menacing. Electric currents surged through the air, a powerful evil, unseen, but people could feel it, they didn't know its source, only that interfering could be dangerous. In Ojai not *one* person filed to run against the incumbents for a seat on the City Council, people had backed away. In Ventura's Court system nine new judges were recently appointed by out-going Gov. Jerry Brown, they were up for election. However, not a *single* lawyer had the *courage* to run against an appointee, the judges and politicians were home free.

Trumpeting in his editorials, Judas Guis proclaimed, "Citizens and lawyers of Ventura County are just so happy and content with our politicians and judges that not even 'remotely' do they want to contemplate a change." It was crazy, it appeared Judas would never stop *lying*, the guy was diseased. There were lawyers in the county who wanted to be a judge so bad they'd sacrifice their wife and kids on a bloody alter just to wrap themselves in that damn Black Robe. Lawyers with money, lots of money to campaign, willing to put up anything, *almost* anything that is except their *own* ass. The lawyers backed away, not a *single one* in the county *filed* to run for judge.

My mind raced to another problem, getting the repairs done on my building before the deadline. At the last minute two contractors who'd agreed to do the work mysteriously backed out. One became so frightened he refused to even talk to me. I got lucky, I found a contractor who was about to go bankrupt, his reaction was, "Hell, I will do it for you, those courthouse people don't scare me anymore, the bastards can't do a damn thing more to me than they've done already." The work was completed and inspected just ahead of the deadline. But more perilous than the Great Sword of Death hanging over the head of Damocles was the *treacherous* probation, two years yet, hanging over my head by a hair. I knew I didn't dare close my eyes. Not even God knew their next evil move.

CHAPTER 39

My errands in East Ventura being done, I thought of something else. Oxnard was only a few miles away, there was a person there I wanted to see. A lawyer, Jerry Palmer was helping the Concerned Citizens in the Ojai Valley with environmental matters. No fee was involved, just as a friend, mainly because the other side weighed so heavy with attorneys and political influence. I was keeping track of what was going on. It was a very sensitive situation, one hell of a lot of money was about to pass hands. If Palmer stepped on the toes of certain people he was going to be in big trouble.

Going over the new Victoria Ave. bridge and Santa Clara River I made a left on Gonzales Road then right on A Street going south. For no real reason I pulled to the curb. Like always my eyes were drawn to 625 North A Street, to that strange, alien structure on the corner, the 'Bat Cave,' it was perhaps three or even five stories high. There was no rational way to be certain, like the expressionless face of a sheer stone cliff there were no windows. Portentous, forbidding it was the den of Judge Berenson and his partner, Ben Nordman.

Driving slowly by I heard it, low, an unearthly whispering sound floating from a small entry in the front of the stone cliff at 625 No. A Street. A sinister swishing noise, a whir of a million bats deep in the blackest bowels of a cavern, membranous wings fluttered insanely through the dark rabidly seeking a victim and his life's blood. Jerry's office was three blocks farther south. I parked in front. The instant

I walked in I was warned. The silence hung heavy in the room, like death warmed over. Fear pierced the air, wariness clamped steely fingers on me, sweeping my eyes around the waiting room I saw no one. Jerry's office door was shut, nothing appeared out of the way, on the surface things seemed normal, except my old friend *'intuition'* told me it wasn't. Two secretaries sat at desks in an alcove. I looked at them, they appeared dazed, thunderstruck. Their lips were tight, their eyes attempting to shut out all evil. Dutifully one girl smiled, it was more of a grimace. She spoke from habit, "Good morning, can I help you?"

"Yes, I'd like to see Mr. Palmer for a moment." At Jerry's name her eyes grew large. Whatever had happened the secretaries were badly unnerved by it.

Stammering she murmured, "Oh, Mr. Palmer is not in his office now," she dared a quick, fearful look at his door.

It wouldn't do to probe so I said, "Well, that's alright, I'll give him a ring later today, thank you." At the front door I shot a glance backward, trance like, hands limp the girls stared down at the silent typewriters. Puzzling about it on the way back along the beach road I was giving Palmer's apparent crises lots of thought, the two scared secretaries had had a genuine, full blown nightmare, I didn't doubt that a second. My intuition would never have kicked up the way it had, not with just a possibility of some every day type of occurrence like Jerry having a heart attack or car wreck. Something damn bad was going on, Jerry was in trouble for sure. I admitted I hadn't seen the Mishpucka, but they had been there alright, I'd sensed it.

Trouble, good Lord, *trouble,* is that all I'm ever going to know? A sea breeze blew gently in the window, I looked out towards the Channel Islands, all nature's beauty right before me and all I could see was trouble. I had to ease up on my poor brain. I tried guessing which of Mother Nature's gifts to mankind was the most beautiful, that extraordinary crystal blue sky, the dazzling white stretches of sand delicately edged with silken lace crocheted by foamy surf, or was it the ocean's deep, mysterious changing moods? Today it was masquerading as a calm, emerald green jewel. But, I found it was impossible to second rate any of the wonders of Mother Nature, I quit trying.

There was another kind of nature, human nature, riven by all its rotten deformed greeds, hates, and lusts for evil power. This ugly, dominant *genetic madness* in human nature was destined to destroy all of Mother Nature, and consequently the human race. It was sad, but I shrugged, what the devil could I do about it, it was inevitable. A million suppositions about what possibly happened were whizzing around in my mind, totally disjointed, however, like the mysterious, unknown ingredients to make up a nuclear bomb they still had to fit somehow. They were after Palmer, I knew this would happen, he'd brought the Mishpucka terror down on himself. A number of times I'd warned him, trying to convince Jerry that the vicious Mishpucka actually existed and were deadly to their enemies. He'd say, "Hell, I'm not seeking public office or acclaim, why would anybody come after me?" He chuckled, politely refusing to believe such a thing as the Mishpucka could exist or thrive in our democracy.

Jerry was confident, even if it did exist, nothing like that could touch him, he had the Bar Association, the Judicial Council and the collective brainpower of all the attorneys themselves behind him. It was ridiculous, entirely impossible for such crazy things to happen. True, Palmer wasn't seeking public office or notoriety in Ojai. He'd bought eighty acres in the foothills between the north end of Lake Casitas and the mountains of Los Padres National Forest. Calling it 'The Ranch,' he'd spent lots of time and money improving the land and buildings. Several hundred citizens in the Ojai Valley formed a group calling themselves the CPO, Citizens to Protect the Ojai.

Palmer, a ranch owner but not a member of the CPO identified with them in concern for 'air and water quality' in the Valley. His activity with the CPO was nothing more than his earnest desire to assist them with legal knowledge and experience. The CPO weren't died-in-the-wool, wild eyed environmentalists like the news media tried to characterize them, the group had no specific overall quarrel with industry or oil production per se, nor did Palmer. It was only that they recognized the peculiar geographical structure of the tiny mountain locked valley and an inherent danger of ruinous air, water, and sewage pollution. Judge Berenson and Nordman's hammerman, lawyer William Hair was plotting behind the scene to set up zoning changes on the three thousand acre Matilija Ranch just northeast of Lake Casitas. The scam was to break it down from ten and twenty acre residential-rancho parcels to tract size lots.

That would mean as many as four or five thousand new houses. Lawyer James Loebl the Mayor of Ojai was part of the conspiracy with Hair, the same 'two hoods' who had set up the secret contract with the Ventura River County Water District that gave Kay Haley the rights to most of the water in Lake Casitas. At that time Loebl was the Mayor as well as the private lawyer representing the Water

District, it had been easy for him to pull it off. This time, with the Matilija Ranch zoning change, their big problem was lack of sewage facilities.

The County Planning Department at that time had been denying individual homeowners a permit to build on an additional bathroom because of dire problems of overloaded sewage plants. The Meiners Oaks Sanitary District was over their capacity, and so was the Oak View Sanitation District. As it happened, lawyer Hair represented the OVSD and not just by chance they'd appointed Jack De Long as a Director. He manipulated devious plans designed by Loebl and Hair to let them hook into the OVSD. Supervisor Ken Mac Donald then ram-rodded the zoning change through. The corruption was so outrageously blatant that the citizens called Mac Donald an outright crook when they met him on the street.

Mac Donald was hard, he laughed. He didn't really give a damn what people thought. His payoff by the Mishpucka was big enough he could retire forever. But before retiring he gratefully took care of Jack De Long, he fixed him up with a good paying job with the County.

Jerry Palmer helped the citizens to *understand* the complicated legal *deviousness* of Mayor Loebl and Lawyer Hair. In the ensuing city hall fracas they had come close to busting up their conspiracy. For his efforts Jerry brought himself under the wrathful eye of the Mishpucka. He was a dangerous meddler, they wouldn't forget him. Ojai Valley had been a hidden paradise, Shangri-la. So beautiful it was the locale chosen to film James Hilton's novel, Lost Horizon. Regrettably Shangri-la was filling with smog. Carbon monoxide from cars and petroleum vapor emissions from oil wells and the refinery at the mouth of the Valley were a proximate cause of the smog that would eventually make the valley unlivable.

The gas refinery was built by Shell Oil along the Ventura River. Running water was necessary for the operation, unfortunately it was just below the entrance to the Valley. But it was back in those good old days when no one thought about such inconsequential things as air pollution or what direction the wind always blew. Logistically and financially the plant became impractical for Shell to operate, so they shut it down. A group of local entrepreneurs decided to buy up and reactivate the old refinery. The new company was called Petrochem. There would be strident opposition to their plan from the CPO but Petrochem's lawyer William Peck and his law partner Mayor Loebl could handle them easily.

Petrochem wasn't just a loose, under financed harum-scarum oil scam devised by a few quick-buck artists. It was an important step in a precise, long range, secret *Master Plan*. Billions of dollars and unbelievable power were at stake. Only a small select group knew of the enormous pool of oil lying shallow beneath the Valley floor and of other great pools in the National Forest immediately surrounding it. Before the turn of the century, two companies, Phoenix Oil and Ojai Oil, drilled exploratory wells in the Valley and forest land. The discovery of *vast* pools of black gold was circumspectly charted into *confidential* files. In May 1981 Chevron paid the U.S. Government one and a fifth billion dollars for off-shore tracts in Santa Barbara Channel, an area approximately Ojai Valley's size and there was no guarantee oil was there, that was a hint of the fabulous worth of the Ojai and Los Padres oil fields. During 1983 thirty million barrels of oil came out of Santa Barbara Channel. Ojai Valley produced only one and a half million barrels. By 1990 in the Channel they will be producing one hundred and eighty million barrels of crude a year. Transmitted into gallons this amounts to around nine billion gallons. To tank-truck the same amount out of Ojai and Los Padres Forest would require one million and two thousand truck and trailer loads per year. Bumper to bumper that's a procession of more than eleven thousand, three hundred and fifty miles.

Obviously oil could not be trucked to Petrochem, and there was another problem. The obsolete refinery with its inadequate storage tank farm couldn't handle such an enormous increase of crude oil. But nothing would be allowed to deter them, too much money was involved. Nine billion gallons of crude oil was worth four and a half billion dollars. After refining it would be worth eight billion dollars and another two billion on reaching the market. Ten billion dollars a year. For that kind of money they'd burn their mother at the stake and laugh at her scream. It required a major pipeline and a massive expansion of the refinery and tank farm. Incredibly a fourteen inch pipeline was laid from one end of the valley to the other and never aroused curiosity or suspicion and the newspapers were quiet.

Expert manipulators of political chicanery and trickery, Dorothy Schechter, a County Counsel and Richard Wittenberg, the County Administrator, both high ranking Mishpuckas handled intricate legal details of easements and rights of way on highway and county roads with consummate stealth. Strangely, near the mouth of the Valley a smaller pipe angled away from the main line. Going across Ventura River then up a narrow winding road toward Casitas Dam it veered up to Haley's ranch. Residents along the road were told by the job foreman that it was a Southern California Gas Co. pipeline but they couldn't hook up to it as it was a *special* line. It became stranger by the second. If the main line was taking crude down through the Ojai Valley to the refinery how in hell could the smaller line jutting out of it carry natural gas back the other direction to the Haley Ranch? Why did she need a six inch natural gas line? There were only two possibilities, Haley planned to either subdivide, or drill for oil and pump it down the small line to the main pipe to the refinery. While running for governor, Duekmejian and Dist. Atty., Bradbury spent a lot of time at Haley's Ranch. Duekmejian received a huge sum for his assurance he'd do away with the Coastal Commission and it was Bradbury's job to keep *everything* covered-up. The tiny community of La Conchita on the coast just north of Ventura is about twenty miles by highway from the Haley Ranch, but as the crow flies across the hills it's only a short ways. I'd heard Kay Haley was building a pipeline across the hills to La Conchita and there were plans to drill oil there by Energetics of Ventura Co., the Coastal Commission was against it but what could they do? Duekmejian already had a payoff and orders from Haley to wipe out the Commission.

And something else big was in the wind. Congressman Robert Lagomarsino, son of Emilio 'Red' Lagomarsino, had been setting up ground work for some kind of a mineral and oil activity in the Los Padres National Forest for years. Huge deposits of minerals are in the mountains where mining interests wolfishly want to strip-mine them. They promised to put back all the dirt the way it was before they started.

Petrochem applied to the Planning Dept. for a permit for a two hundred million dollar expansion of their plant. CPO was fighting them every inch of the way. Further complicating matters the Mills Grammer School was directly in the path of their expansion plans. As *chance* would have it Mayor James Loebl's *law partner* William Peck was a School Board member, people wondered why he wanted on the Board, he was not married and had no children. About that time a series of giant flare ups occurred at the Petrochem refinery. Roaring flames shot high in the air, alarms sounded, the frightened teachers abandoned the school herding terrified kids up the road. The vision of an oil plant going up in flames and fiery explosions of huge storage tanks was enough to scare hell out of anybody.

One morning about ten I was driving on the freeway passing the refinery. Suddenly bolts of flame burst from tall stacks blasting into the sky. Pulling over I watched. The teachers and children dashed from the schoolhouse in fear of their lives. I would've gone to check the buildings to see if everybody was out, but there was no need to. The whole terrifying scene had been contrived, they could make the flames shoot out anytime they wanted. But the teachers and parents had had enough. Soon afterward the grammer school was put up for sale. MAI appraisers valued the property at two and one half million dollars but it was sold to a mysterious group for eight hundred and eighty five thousand dollars. Two lady members of the School Board *protested* the extremely low sale price vigorously but were quickly overruled.

Mayor Loebl's law partner William Peck was then appointed to the Superior Court Bench and summarily Dismissed the CPO's suit against Petrochem...Supervisor Erickson okayed multi-million dollar expansion plans for the refinery...County Counsel Dorothy Schechter and County Administrator Richard Wittenberg drew up a *"New Oil Ordinance."* Guided by Maggie it quickly passed. With this new law Victor Husbands, Director of the County Environmental Resource Agency had the sole power to issue oil drilling permits.

It was now an Administrative function, as such the people no longer had a voice in the matter. They wouldn't even know a permit was issued till drilling was well under way, and there'd be no trucks roaring and snarling the highway. The oil would be flowing swiftly through pipelines underground, out of sight. Maggie had become a *'very seasoned'* politician, she was raking in more money than she'd ever dreamed of. She smiled to herself, yes it was easy.

Mayor Loebl and Judge Peck had personal scams working, just like Berenson and Nordman did when they extorted the two million bucks from Argo Oil Co.. Mishpuckas are allowed to work side-line scams so long as they don't conflict with any of their 'Master Plans.' An out of town developer had bought some expensive commercially zoned acreage in the Ojai city limits. His plans were to construct a shopping center with a Safeway and TGY store as major tenants, but not being a Mishpucka he became fair game. The Mayor sabotaged him with the City Council and Planning Dept. and he was denied a building permit.

His only recourse was to sue the City of Ojai. The developer's attorney, another Mishpucka, Phillip Drescher, received a large sum of money for filing the lawsuit but Mayor Loebl's partner, Judge Peck quickly dismissed the suit. The scenario gets heavier. Drescher made another large sum when he filed an Appeal, then his partner,

Justice Blitzberg, aka Steven Stone ruled in favor of the developer. Then it became Mayor Loebl's turn, the City appealed against that ruling and over the years Drescher takes loads of money from the developer, then he brings in Judge Berenson for the final bleeding. This is what the Black Robe Mishpucka calls, "Giving you, *your day in court.*" When it's all over the valuable piece of property will still be developed, the only difference will be that now Mayor Loebl and Judge Peck own it. Mayor Loebl has already picked the spot where the new Post Office is to be built on it.

Since Loebl, the attorney for Casitas Municipal Water District conspired with Judge Berenson and Nordman to syphon water from Lake Casitas there had become a very severe shortage. The city of Ventura wanted more Casitas water because of their expansion, and environmentalists want more water released in the river below the dam to preserve fish and wild life. Loebl has to keep all the water in the lake he can to conceal what's being stolen by Haley's Ranch.

Environmentalists, Friends of the River, sued the Casitas Water District. Mayor Loebl makes money supposedly for representing the District's interest. A Mishpucka attorney, Phillip Seymour, makes money for representing the Friends of the River, they appear before Mishpucka Judge Joe Hadden who then rules in *favor* of Loebl who says, "I'm very pleased with the decision." Lawyer Seymour says, "It isn't over yet...I'll appeal." While waiting for Appeal Court Justice Hymie Blitzberg's ruling Mayor Loebl keeps on taking money from the Water District and lawyer Seymour keeps on taking more money from the Friends. Meanwhile Haley keeps on stealing all the water, and meanwhile District Attorney Michael Bradbury covers it all up. Everywhere, it's the same.

In the City of Oxnard embattled citizens were fighting to stave off the corrupt juggernaut of *Redevelopment.* The City Councilmen *also* make up the *'five members'* of the Redevelopment Agency. One Councilwoman, Dorothy Maronowsky, aka Maron, with her husband and other Mishpuckas were forming a new bank. They wanted the *best* location in downtown Oxnard to build it. The City Council *voted* to take-over the property of forty landowners. Walking into another room, they *convened* as the 'Redevelopment Agency' and *approved* their *own* plan. The name Dorothy Maron was familiar, I recalled years ago she'd been involved in framing Supervisor Robinson. To prevent their land from being *stolen* the owners filed suit against the City Councilmen and the Redevelopment Agency.

Judge Peck dismissed the landowners suit and they Appealed his decision. As part of their routine, Justice Hymie Blitzberg and his two Mishpucka Associate Justices, Abbe and Gilbert, swiftly Denied the citizens Appeal. Then the Mishpuckas decided they'd teach the people a lesson for fighting to save their land. They filed a lawsuit charging the citizens with...'Malicious Prosecution.' During a court hearing while under heavy pressure from the citizens attorney, the Mishpuckas lawyer could give *no* cause of action for their lawsuit or why it shouldn't be dismissed. Judge Peck asked several times, "Give me cause for your lawsuit." Getting no answer Judge Peck pleaded, "Speak up...give me *anything*, just some kind of a reason so I won't have to dismiss the case." The lawyer was unable to answer. Angry, Peck gave up on him, "Alright, I'm still *not* going to dismiss the case. I'm taking it under advisement." Alone in his chambers a few days later Judge Peck made his ruling, the suit *would not* be dismissed.

The peoples land was being stolen in a scam and Judge Peck still would not dismiss the lawsuit. It was more Black Robe Mishpucka evil to harass the people with a vicious, frivolous lawsuit.

In the Ojai Valley and Los Padres National Forest, Emilo 'Red' Lagomarsino and his son Congressman Robert J., own and control most of the mineral and oil rights, the New Oil Ordinance was vital to their plans. It had cost big bucks getting Supervisor Erickson to punch through the new law, but real soon it would pay off fabulous dividends. The way was paved...everything was laid out perfect, the two hundred million dollar expansion plan of Petrochem, a pipeline across the Ojai Valley, and the New Ordinance. The Lagomarsinos had the National Forest lined up, Gov. Duekmejian was set to wipe out the Coastal Commission. William P. Clark, former Nat'l Security Director, who'd been eased in as Secretary of Interior, would open the Nat'l Forest lands to a great, black gold stampede.

At Clark's confirmation hearing, Senator Strom Thurmond,(R), South Carolina, displayed his cowardice. Betraying his *sworn duty* to the people he covered-up Clark's Mishpucka conspiracy, despite glib coolness, the Senator underneath was on pins and needles. All it'd take was just one person to bring up that fool Clark's damn threat, "To kill Niggers and Mexicans with his friggin' stolen machine gun." Lord, his diarrhea was about to be totally uncontrollable, but he was lucky, if anyone here in D.C. knew of Clark's threats they kept their silence.

With President Reagan frequently flying to his California ranch, his trusted, close confidants, Clark and Lagomarsino accompany him. The intimate stratospheric privacy of Air Force One affords a rare, most advantageous access to the President's ear. After several hours of flight and conversation they arrive at the Point Mugu Naval Air Station on the Ventura Coast. Like Reagan, his two close associates own huge California ranches. Copter crews on alert stand by to fly them from the Base to their ultimate destinations.

William P. Clark, Secretary of Interior, former law partner of Judge Berenson and Nordman, is one of the top Mishpucka agents planted in the government. Congressman Robert J. Lagomarsino, is one of the top, Real Mafia, representatives from the West Coast.

Back in '46, Harry Pregerson was busily kissing Mickey Cohen's ass, convulsing with eagerness to run errands at the snap of Cohen's finger. But Harry's devious brain was clicking slyly, his ferret eyes missed nothing. Intently he'd observed the covert guile of the small cadre of Jew judges Cohen had put together for his private use. He was intrigued, but perplexed by the amount of genuine respect the judges got as individuals, especially when everyone from court clerks and cops on down knew that they were corrupt.

Harry was shrewd, there had to be something of importance, of great strategic value in this strange giving of respect. It annoyed him, the full significance was unclear. It wasn't too long before his nimble brain picked it apart, it seemed there was a mental delineation in this matter of respect. The Black Robe was a *symbol* of Justice, the respect shown by the people was for the *Robe alone,* not its wearer. Harry was angered by it, "Who gives a shit if they don't respect the wearer, they are all stupid, the *wearer* of the Robe wields the power, screw their respect, just give me the friggin' robe," suddenly Harry screamed, "Juda! That's it, Juda, not just one robe, give me all the robes, Juda." Pregerson was shook to his roots, his wildest delusions whirled before his eyes, a kaleidoscope revolving insanely. As a boy on City Terrace, looking down on the sprawling city of Los Angeles, even his dreams were braggarts. Day and night his fantasies fondled him, convincing him he'd be the most powerful man to ever set foot in that city, and now, Juda, he knew the secret, he knew just how to do it. It was so simple, it danced in his head, he mouthed it, "When all the Robes are mine, when all of the wearers of Black Robes are Jews, Great Juda, the Black Robe Mishpucka, *nothing* can stop it." Exulting ferociously he roared, "I'll be the master of all America's mighty strength. With it I'll control the world."

'Red' Lagomarsino's Mafia, the Black Hand, over fifty years ago had slipped quietly underground. With the ending of prohibition the lush, wild days of bootlegging were gone. The underlings and dregs were thus left without leaders or brains. Instinctively they fell into gambling, prostitution, drugs and the labor and protection rackets. Unlike the Real Mafia who had become invisible they relished the limelight and garish, tough mobster reputations heaped on them by cops and reporters. This was the self proclaimed Mafia that young Italian hoods were *rushing* to Hollywood to pattern themselves after. Hollywood's portrayal and the *glamorization* of this breed of scum *created* the image that's now believed by the American public to be, The Mafia.

The Real Mafia is something else. Prohibition, adoption of the 18th Amendment of the Constitution declared in effect Jan. 16, 1920 and Repealed in 1933 precipitated thirteen years of wild, alcoholic capers. Fortunes were amassed overnight, billions of dollars with no income taxes. The Lagomarsinos were in the right place and at the right time. They owned a bank, vineyards, wineries and distilleries. Of great importance were their underworld contacts for distributing alcohol reaching farther north than Sacramento.

The Ventura County coast became the focal point of smuggling. Stretches of lonely beaches and marshes at river mouths where tides came in regularly were ideal. On dark moonless nights rafts loaded with liquid contraband were floated in on the surf by the scores. The barrels of alcohol were trucked to isolated barns and out-buildings deep in the county where they were diluted, bottled and packaged. By sun up the booze would be packed in innocent looking passenger cars and on its way to the big cities.

From Ventura, highways led north to Frisco and south to Los Angeles. A lesser known road wound over Los Padres mountains to Bakersfield and to Fresno in San Joaquin Valley. Soon a problem developed. They'd become bloated with money. Lagomarsinos threw the fortunes of their small bank in with A.P. Gianini's Bank of Italy. Across California Italian families owning vineyards and wineries did the same. In the midst of the country's great depression when banks everywhere were closing their doors, Bank of Italy was bursting with cash. They scooped up failing banks across the state. They knew the fantastic money making days of Prohibition would not last forever. Their banks had far outgrown the limited ethnic value of the name, Bank of Italy.

In September of 1930 with the Lagomarsinos at the helm of the Ventura Branch of the Bank of Italy, they took over First National Bank of Ventura and the Home Savings Bank of Ventura. President Gianini of Transamerica Corp. met with the Italian families. It was agreed, Bank of Italy, Transamerica Corp. and the banks that were taken over would now become the Bank of America National Trust and Savings. B of A became one of the largest banking institutes in the world, and A.P. Gianini did not do it by pushing an apple cart around the streets of Frisco.

With unlimited capitol, Lagomarsinos bought up farm and citrus lands, commercial property in towns, and real estate and investment companies and tied up oil and mineral rights of huge areas. Repeal of Prohibition created massive confusion in Sacramento. New laws were legislated governing sales of alcoholic products. No one knew the liquor business like the Real Mafia, and also no one had more money to spread in the right places in Sacramento.

Unperturbed, the Real Mafia never for a moment lost control of the transition from bootlegging to a state licensed operation. Their integration into the government was smoothly handled. An Alcohol Beverage Control Department was set up and a Real Mafia member became Director, the licenses for liquor stores, bars, distilleries and territories were cut up. Lagomarsinos got distributorship for several counties along with exclusive right for Seagrams, Calverts and other top brands. The Real Mafia became a formidable behind the scenes organization *controlling* the ABC, Attorney General, County District Attorneys and Senators and Assemblymen throughout the state. For years 'Big Bill' Bonnelli's roughshod reign as Director of ABC was so viciously corrupt that not even the Real Mafia could cover up for him.

The Black Robe Mishpucka leaped at the chance to replace Big Bill with one of their own. Probing the power of the Real Mafia they issued felony warrants for Bonnelli. The Real Mafia's political power was great but they *soon* discoverd they could *not* force a Mishpucka judge to recall the warrants. Fleeing, Bonnelli hid out in Mexico to escape prosecution. Wrathful, the Real Mafia set up a deal for him to retire as a California State Employee. Each month his retirement check was mailed to him in Mexico.

During this battle for power the Real Mafia managed to hold on to control of ABC. In 1933 when the Real Mafia had created their government within the government, all the angles were covered...they thought. But they had under-estimated the extraordinary powers of the judicial system, not that they hadn't given it any thought. They owned a judge here and there and when necessary they were always able to buy another, still they'd missed a bet. The incredibly cunning Master Plot of the Mishpucka to *take over* the *entire* judicial system had never occurred to them.

For many years the Black Robe Mishpucka and the Real Mafia built their secret organizations. Penetrating and submerging within government offices they became more powerfully entrenched every second of the day. Committing corrupt, treacherous acts behind the scenes the evil Crime Families were each determined to be the 'Sole Genius of Supremacy.' But *always* it was America and the innocent people who suffered and paid the price for Mafia and Mishpucka depravity. Loyal Americans and their families were being destroyed for no reason other than having gotten in their way. Their pattern was Political and Judicial violence...pitting people against people and government agency against government agency, spreading mistrust and suspicion. The interlacing threads of murder and assassination wove deeply through the pattern.

In 1969 when Martin had offered me thirty five grand to help him frame Robinson and Reiman I went to the Grand Jury. Instead of them investigating corruption, I got myself crushed, right between the Black Robe Mishpucka and the Real Mafia, it took me nearly nine years to find out they really existed. During the next few years I learned enough about the hidden terrors of Political and Judicial murder and mayhem that nuclear bombs didn't worry me anymore.

Red Lagomarsino owned the Ventura Realty Co. which owned most of Ventura City surrounding the old courthouse. Berenson and Nordman had tied up all the property around their proposed new courthouse site. The new government center was the lure. Billions of dollars of new development and investment would take place and the older parts of the city would die. Their decline and death was simply part of the sinisterly calculated evolution master-planned by the Mishpucka. When the buildings and land values had *deteriorated sufficiently* for their purpose, the Mishpucka City Council steals it from the owners under the guise of Redevelopment. It is then sold cheap to Beverly Hills developers who build billion dollar shopping centers.

To Emilio Lagomarsino this attack on his domain was just like back in Prohibition, the old days with a rival mob muscling in on his territory. The only difference was that now he'd let the law handle it. Highly incensed at their war-like, sneak attack to take over the Real Mafia's good thing, Red filed a suit to prohibit the Mishpucka from relocating the old courthouse. It was a good lawsuit with real merit. But all that Judge Berenson had to do to *finish* them off was to utter his routine words, "Case Dismissed." The Real Mafia had learned the desolate futility of filing any appeals against Black Robe Mishpucka Judicial power. They suffered the same mental tortures as did the down trodden citizens, massive frustration, the damnable hopeless frustrations of being 'denied' the right of Due Process of Law, being refused access to the courts and a jury. But unlike the good citizens who *refused* to go out-side the frame work of the law the Real Mafia was geared to take matters into their own hands. Filled with a terrible anger they retaliated against the Black Robe Mishpucka.

It was at the height of the vicious, invisible conflict between the Crime Families that I'd gone to the Grand Jury. I had a time bomb, when the evidence of political corruption and crimes I had given to them came out it would destroy the two Families with a big blast. Instead, the Grand Jury investigation was *killed* and the Real Mafia and the Mishpucka Families *combined forces* to wipe me out. There I stood, a damn pigeon, *dead center* in the battlefield, clutching my friggin' time bomb.

Bodies lie gross on the battlefield and the war continues. I knew I had been lucky as hell to survive as long as I had. But in my wild, unorthodox flailings I'd contrived a lot of strange, unexpected legal moves...things neither Crime Family anticipated. I'd dumped loads of their own crap right back down their necks. My odious thrashings touched off fierce bickering amongst the two Families. They fought over *who* was guiltiest of stupidity, bitterly accusing each other of bungling the job of getting rid of me they dredged up a much more caustic possibility...*who* would take the big fall when everything went wrong?

With this they became desperate, their ravings were hysterical. County Counsel Dorothy Schechter was very frightened, screaming like a stuck sow, Juda! "What is the matter with Gary, why won't he accept his dismissal? Judges Berenson and Pregerson are both such noted, *prestigious* Judges, Juda!...why's he allowed to do this to me?" This fighting amongst themselves was fine with me, it slowed them down, giving me a breathing spell. Each time I got a little smarter or at least became better educated. In the last twelve years of tortured, 'on the job training' I had picked up enough credits for my diploma, majoring in **HOW TO SURVIVE POLITICAL AND JUDICIAL MURDER AND MAYHEM,** without cum laude.

Back at Palmer's law office the scent of the 'unseen menace' had been overpowering, suspended in air. So virulent it could mean only one thing. I'd sensed it, it wasn't just the Mafia, *both* families had been there. Lord, the Families were combining against Jerry. It had to be damn critical to bring them both down on him. I knew he was helping the CPO who were a thorn in the side of the Real Mafia's oil plans. They'd been *secretly promoting* a movement to incorporate Ojai Valley into one *valley-wide* city and govern it under a General Law Charter, this way they could control it. At a meeting discussing future government, Palmer had infuriated the Real Mafia. He had spoken out in opposition to their power scheme using a frightening illustration, the politically strife ridden General Law City of Oxnard. Jerry pointed out how easily the citizens could lose all control of the city's destination to corrupt special interest forces under this type of rule. He suggested they should consider a Charter City as a definite advantage to the citizens in retaining a firm grip on city operations. At the moment I was not sure what they'd done to Jerry, but I was amazed something terrible hadn't happened before now.

Everything was nervous, even the air, tensely the Mishpucka and Mafia Crime Families awaited that momentous, far reaching event, the Presidential Election, November 8, 1984. Re-election of Reagan was absolutely imperative. He could not lose, he didn't dare. Both Crime Families had invested billions in a sequel of Reagan's Reign, and the ultimate *take-over* by William P. Clark. With Sen. Thurmond *covering-up* for him Clark was confirmed as Secretary of the Interior. However, through a back door I was able to get this evidence about Clark to a woman very close to Reagan, the President was extremely upset, particularly about the machine gun. After a brief talk with his new Secretary of Interior, the President decided Clark should quietly leave D.C.. The word was spread, Clark had suddenly become very homesick for his ranch in California.

I'd *broke up* their schemes. With Clark out of power it had torn up *master plans* of both the Mishpucka and Real Mafia. Who would be designated to take his place I could only surmise. The Real Mafia was well aware the CPO was capable of wrecking their carefully laid plans in Ojai Valley and Los Padres National Forest. And there was Palmer, right out in the open exhorting the CPO to do it, unaware the Families were furious at his actions and wanted him destroyed.

I'd heard of guys waving a red flag in front of a mad bull, but this wasn't play. I doubted if Jerry even got a cup of coffee for his effort. Since I had left his office my brain was spinning in a million directions. A red light flashed, the signal a block ahead at Harbor and Seaward had changed, it's flashing returned me to the present. I swung a quick left into the Thriftimart shopping center. The Star

Free Press might be in the racks by now, I had a weird feeling I was going to read about Palmer.

Front page, there it was, bold letters..."Three prominent county men were arrested on charges of *bribery,* and *conspiracy* to bribe a Sheriff's Department official and the Board of Supervisors." So this was how they were going to do it. Nothing had changed. Good old Judas Gius the Editor, *another frame-up* like Sup. Robinson thirteen years ago, it was a *carbon copy.* I wondered, was the price to frame a guy still thirty five grand or had it gone up with the cost of living index? I read, "Attorney Palmer was arrested along with two of his clients, Willard Laskey the former owner of the Chevrolet dealership in Ojai and Roscoe Morris a Santa Paula car dealer and a former official of the Peace Corps.. Two other men are being sought in Las Vegas in connection with the alleged bribery attempt."

A shocked Palmer told reporters, "These people came to me to form a corporation and to negotiate a lease for them, it was just a business deal." The story continued on page two. "The arrests culminated a two and a half month investigation which began Jan. 29, 1982 when an alleged attempt was made to bribe Lt. Vince France of the Sheriff's Department. Laskey allegedly offered France thirty five thousand dollars if he would grease the skids in the Sheriff's Department and D.A.'s office, and buy a vote or two on the Board of Supervisors." My God...thirty five grand, exactly the same amount Martin offered to me thirteen years ago, it had to be more than just *weird coincidence.* "The money was to be given to France to motivate him to *pressure* the Supervisors into re-issuing a gambling license for the Pass Club, a club on the outskirts of the City Of Simi Valley."

I paused, thinking. No wonder I'd sensed the dark, malevolent presence of the Crime Families in Jerry's office. He's been marked for a fate *worse* than destruction, damn, Jerry had refused to believe how corrupt the judges were. More than once I'd done my best to clue him in about interfering with the Real Mafia and their oil deal. And now, somehow he's gotten himself involved in the Black Robe Mishpuckas gambling operations for the entire west coast. I was very surprised they hadn't rubbed him out like lawyer Lyman Smith and his wife Charlene for getting in the way.

Larry Storch, a Bloodline Mishpucka from New York, picked to replace Jerome Berenson as Presiding Judge of the Superior Court, handled the *judicial end* of the *frame-up.* He issued arrest and search warrants, and sent five Deputy Sheriffs to Jerry's office. Storch's warrants did not comply with the Evidence Code, he had failed to appoint a Master to be present as required. A Master is necessary to be sure only files pertaining to the specific case are removed. All the brutal tricks of judicial exacerbation are known and used by the Black Robe Mishpucka. Without a Master being there the deputies took just about everything in Palmer's office. When he asked them to return his files the officers denied they had them. Later on this worked an unbelievable hardship on Jerry. Then Jerry and his two clients were handcuffed and booked at the County Jail. Palmer was fortunate, the Crime Families were not going to kill him, all they intended to do was give him a *one-way* ticket to the State Pen and *disbar* him for life, Jerry would *never* meddle again.

I knew all about the Pass Club gambling license, it was a Black Robe Mishpucka Master Plan. It had been cooking several years, it was impossible that Palmer was involved in it. In 1958, Supervisors passed an ordinance, "No new gambling licenses were to be issued and owners of existing card rooms were prohibited from selling or transferring their licenses and upon their death the license expired with them." In March 1980 the owner of the Pass Club died.

Under the county ordinance the Club should have been closed immediately. Anticipating this event the Mishpucka had devised a Master Plan, it was set in motion upon the owners death. Mishpucka Judge Larry Storch would let Carol Garziano, the daughter of the deceased owner, keep the club open. They didn't want to stop a flow of millions of dollars from the Club that they could get their hands on. Carl Ward, Jr. was the Garziano's lawyer. He was also the law partner of Judge Berenson and Ben Nordman. As such, he was chief of all Mishpucka gambling operations in the western states.

Ward, Jr. was the son of Carl Ward, who as Mayor of Oxnard back in the good old days had supplied Berenson and Nordman with instant zoning and permits to build huge tracts of homes. They were extremely successful in the construction racket while other builders continually suffered severe setbacks and financial loses created by City Hall dirty tricks and rejections of permits.

Mayor Carl Ward, Sr. described his *cleverness* in guaranteeing success for one person and financial *suicide* for another as, "Civil Ambidexterity, an inherited gift." Prospering within the Mishpucka organization Ward, Sr. sent Ward, Jr. to law school. Becoming a law partner of Berenson and Nordman, Ward, Jr. with his *'inherent'* gift rose fast in the organization. He was soon a top boss of Mishpucka gambling operations.

Mishpucka Master Plans are usually relatively simplistic. First step; with Ward, Jr. holding a position of trust and confidence as the Garzianos lawyer the Mishpucka would smoothly take-over the Pass Club. Ward, Jr. *feigned* a lawsuit in behalf of the Garzianos asking that the supervisors *re-issue* a license for the club in Carol's name. For months while using the guise of legal fees and costs, Ward, Jr. stripped Garzianos of large sums derived from the card room.

Aug. 1981, after a year and a half of toying with the Garzianos, Judge Storch dismissed the case ordering the Pass Club closed. Next step; Ward, Jr. filed a *sham* appeal to Storch's decision, it drained more money from Garzianos. Step three; The appeal was denied on September 1, 1982. Garzianos did not appeal to the State Supreme Court. All recourse to the Courts regarding re-issue of a gambling license was now dead, res-adjudicata.

Implacably Garzianos were cleaned of hundreds of thousands in sham legal fees. Ludicrously they'd financed their own demise. Step one had now been successfully completed. Step two, the wheels were synchronized and already in motion. Surreptitiously along the way Ward, Jr. formed a corporation, 'Pass Club Properties Inc..' Under a corporate cover, obscure behind Carl Ward, Jr. lurked Berenson, Nordman and another Mishpucka, Marvin Lewisinsky, aka, Marvin Lewis, a Superior Court Judge. The Black Robe Mishpucka had no intention of bluntly attempting to *re-issue* a license for the card club in county territory. It could create a precedent for others to follow and cause out-cry and furor against gambling. Their Plan was much smoother, it involved the boundary line of the City of Simi Valley only a short distance from the Pass Club. Secretively, the powerful county politician had spread pay-offs to the greedy City Councilmen. Without fanfare the Pass Club was to be quietly *strip-annexed* into the City of Simi Valley and a *new* license under City control would be issued to Pass Club Properties Inc.

A few weeks before Jerry's arrest I had received a call from a friend, his connections for inside info on political intrigue in Simi were excellent. He said, "An angry, half hysterical lady called saying a man was involving her corruptly in the Pass Club license and that they were trying to steal the Club."

"By any chance did she mention this guys name?"

He chuckled, "I was hoping you'd ask that, because this is going to grab you. She said it was Jim Dougherty, the County Supervisor."

"That grabs me, indeed it does!" It was against the rules to quiz a man about his source of information, but I gave it a whirl. "You wouldn't consider telling me the ladies name?"

He hesitated, "I wish I could...but you know how it is." Then he threw in a hint, "She's a lady with a heavy foreign accent."

Gambling ties of the Mishpucka are wide spread. The Pan Card Club in Filmore, the east end of the county was their operation. In San Fernando, a city across the L.A. county line, Ward, Jr. was slyly setting up councilmen to open a new club there.

Charges of Jerry's alleged involvement in the Pass Club license was screwy as hell. It just didn't make any sense, the more I thought about it the screwier it got. The Mishpucka was out to destroy him, that much I was sure of. But why in the hell would they involve and jeopardize their own very carefully laid multi-million dollar Master Plans with all this destructive, messy publicity unless...unless it was something they couldn't control, unless maybe they'd had no choice. That must be it, they had no choice. It aggravated me to beat hell, more and more pieces were falling in place, but still not enough to come up with the big answer.

What was happening with Palmer was connected with what was happening to me all these years. I felt it strong, my suspicions had been growing, *someone* very close, *someone* I was confiding in was one of *them*, a Real Mafia or Mishpucka. It had to be that way, they always knew too much about what I knew. Like right from the start in 1969, when I went to Chief Al Jalaty in Port Hueneme, and Mal King, Chief Investigator for the District Attorney.

If as things appeared, the Pass Club scam was *out of control*, the Mishpucka could be vulnerable. This could be my big break, the one I had been waiting for. What I discovered in Simi turned out to be even more than I hoped. The Mishpucka hadn't only lost control of their Master Plan, they'd come unglued. They had been *blasted* by one of those crazy, totally unpredictable occurrences that lie-in-wait to countermine even the most perfect of evil plans. The Mishpucka was entrapped in a maddening Watergate, with all the elements of a nuclear explosion. A chain reaction of exposure that could destroy them was present. All I needed was a little luck, a tiny spark to set it off.

I had learned that in 1981 Laskey was going down the tube fast. His auto agency in Ojai had failed, financially he was busted. To top it all off he had fierce marital problems and was losing his home in a divorce. If that wasn't enough, he'd had brain surgery. Fifty seven, he was broke, sick and depressed. Palmer, his lawyer, was trying to help him with his problems. In late 1981 Laskey read in the paper how the Pass Club was being closed. Early in January '82, he had a brainstorm, a gambling joint, just what he needed, like in Vegas, all that sweet, easy money rolling in, it'd solve his problems instantly.

Without Jerry knowing it Laskey went to Simi and talked to the Garzianos about buying the Club. They explained about the license and their legal problems. Coming on like a big shot Laskey scoffed, "Don't worry about getting the license *re-issued*, we've got that all wired." Tossing officials names around like confetti Laskey bragged grandiosely, "Listen to me, Jim Dougherty has the supervisors in his pocket and the Sheriff is okaying it, the money is already spread. Jim is working it through Ken Mac Donald, you know, Mac Donald used to be a supervisor, before that he was a State Assemblyman, and Dougherty was his right hand man. Those two are close, ve-ry, ve-ry close." Laskey held up two crossed fingers, "I mean close, just like that. Don't worry Dougherty knows how to work it. My lawyer, Jerry Palmer is handling the legal work, everything's set to go, all I want to know from you is what do you want for this joint?" When Laskey left, the Garzianos were speechless.

After thinking about what Laskey had said their astonishment quickly turned to rage as the enormity of his proposition sunk in. They bounced it back and forth off each other, "Good Lord," Carol exclaimed, "Ward's taken us for everything we've got. Hundreds of thousands of dollars and we're all *washed up* in court, *finished*, and he's known it all the time. There wasn't a chance we could win that Appeal, and never was, it was a set-up. From the beginning, Ward, Berenson, Nordman and Storch, they've planned it all." Carol was emphatic, "We've been suckered, framed by people claiming to be friends." Furiously she spat it out, "That damn Dougherty has been cozying up to us and all the time he's planning to screw us and so has Jalaty." Tears of helpless rage filled her eyes, "Damn it to hell, the bastards, they're all screwing us, but they will not get away with it. I'll stop them one way or another."

Carol grabbed the phone screaming, threatening to expose them all with every newspaper and TV in the country before she finished. Ward, Jr. and Jim Dougherty were ready to jump out the window. Dougherty lapsed into a *full* politicians panic. Calling Ward, Jr. and Al Jalaty he cried, "Good God, if this comes out I'll be ruined, my reputation. Oh Lord!...you've got to do something quick. I am being accused of something I didn't do. I told the Garzianos I don't even know this guy Laskey, or his lawyer Jerry Palmer, or anything about re-issuing a license." Dougherty experienced a momentary surge of pride in himself as he realized he was *actually* telling the truth, he really didn't know anything about re-issuing the county license. That hadn't been their plan at all, their scheme was to strip annex..."Oh Lord, who in hell is Laskey and this Palmer?" Jalaty calmed Ward and Dougherty down.

"Ward you get to Simi quick, talk with the Garzianos, explain, convince them you have no connection with Laskey or Palmer, no one is going to 're-issue' those people a county license." Jalaty told Ward, "It is Palmer, that damn lawyer who is the brains behind this. He has been stirring up trouble in Ojai with the CPO crowd. Red Lagomarsino has been after me for months to do something about him. I don't know what Palmer's game is, but the time has come to put a stop to him. You cool the Garzianos down before they louse things up beyond fixing, and tell Dougherty for God sakes to stop his crying all over the place."

At that point I would not have bet one plugged nickel on how much longer Jerry would be breathing. But...before anything could happen, Laskey went into his *second* crazy act. It set the stage for the whole show. January 29, 1982 Laskey approached Sheriff's Lt. Vince France about using his influence to re-issue a county license for the Pass Club. He offered France thousands if he'd, "Grease the skids with the Sheriff and D.A., and also buy a few votes with the Supervisors." The Lt. knew Laskey well, all his misfortunes, the car agency failure, his divorce and disturbed mental condition. France just let him ramble on, he felt pity. Hell, if Laskey was in his right mind he should know an obscure Sheriff's Lt. didn't have that kind of downtown influence.

After Laskey left his office Lt. France mulled it over. That was dangerous talk, even though he is batty, I better play it safe, go by the rules, write a memo. France figured all he would ever get back for his trouble was a brief acknowledgement, probably in a couple weeks. Routing his memo to Sheriff Jalaty, he erased the incident from his mind. When Jalaty read the memo the burning question of what to do with that troublesome Palmer was solved and Mal King agreed, it was a natural...Palmer had played right into their hands. They'd nail him for bribing a Lt., the D.A., and the Supervisors. It was a stroke of purest luck. His arrest would solve several of their most serious problems simultaneously.

Most urgent of all it would lull Garzianos, prove to them that Ward, Jr. and Dougherty had no connection whatever with Palmer or Laskey. And it would put an end to Palmer stirring up the CPO, that would make 'Red' happy as hell. When they were finished with

Palmer he was going to be a bleeding, suffering, *horrible example* to all the lawyers. They would *never* forget who was running Ventura County. The Lt. was surprised and a bit perturbed by the urgency of the *emergency* order summoning him to report *immediately* to Jalaty and King at County Center Headquarters.

Learning that the meeting was about Laskey he became amazed at the seriousness and credibility both officials were attaching to his conversation with the mentally disturbed Laskey. But, what in the hell...if this was the way they wanted it...France became cagey, just listening, they made it clear. "We're going to screw this guy Palmer right to the wall, but good." France was wishing he wasn't hearing this but the next words brought him around. "Lt. France, if you use your head and pull this operation off you'll be well rewarded." The possibility of the mission failing was never mentioned, that wasn't necessary. As the two pairs of steely eyes locked on France a chill shot through him at the thought of his screwing up such a *big-time* political intrigue. In their grim faces he had read the lurid details of his future if he should fail.

To nail the lawyer, Jalaty and King knew they'd need far more evidence than what they had. Sheriff's Detectives, and Dist. Atty. Investigators were assigned to Lt. France's command. Microphones, cameras, undercover radio cars, recording apparatus, vans specially outfitted and sophisticated surveillance equipment became available to him. He was told, "Requisition anything you need, this operation is top priority, we want it wrapped up damn fast. It's in your hands, your responsibility, one more thing, stay away from Garzianos and Dougherty, Carl Ward, Jr. is handling that end of it."

At this juncture, during the first days of Feb. 1982 when France got his explicit orders, Jerry knew absolutely nothing about the Pass Club. Outside of representing Laskey with his divorce and defunct car agency Palmer had no idea of Laskey's brainstorm to become a big-time gambler. Wasting little time France wired himself and his telephone. The first thing was to get Laskey on a tape implicating Palmer in a 'conspiracy' with the Pass Club. He invited Laskey into his office, a hidden mike was going. France became a thespian, for over twenty minutes he stuffed Laskey with double talk about how he was a mean, crooked cop on the take.

"Sure Laskey, just trust me...for thirty five big ones I'll fix it, I'll get that gambling license re-issued for you."

"That's good, very good."

Eager to bring Palmer's name into the picture Lt. France asked,

"Laskey, besides your lawyer Palmer, who else did you mention the Pass Club license to?"

"Palmer? No...no...he doesn't know from nothin, he doesn't know I've talked to you or Garzianos. I intend to discuss the legal matters with him later."

France was shook, "Now wait a minute," he waved his hand in front of Laskey, "Hold on, I've got to get this straight. You say you talked to the Garzianos about re-issuing the license?"

"Yeh, besides you they are they only ones I have talked to."

"Did you mention Palmer's name?"

"Sure. I told them Palmer was my lawyer and he was handling the legal end of things."

"But you told me Palmer knows nothing about any of this."

"He doesn't." Laskey gave the Lt. a sly wink, "Look, you know how that goes when you're talking to people. They are much more impressed when you mention a lawyer...so I just dropped Palmer's name on them."

"Was that the only time you dropped his name?"

"Uh huh, except for the other day, when I first talked to you."

"What other names did you drop on Garzianos?"

"Just Ken Mac Donald and Supervisor Jim Dougherty...hell, you know it as well as I do how crooked they are, shit, they're good for anything if there'a buck in it."

France was convinced Laskey was telling him the truth, Palmer knew nothing of the Pass Club license. His brain was flipping. Good Lord, what in hell have I got myself into. In my memo to Al Jalaty I named Palmer but not Dougherty. Hell, I couldn't have mentioned Jim Dougherty because I didn't even know about him...but King and Jalaty knew...they ordered me to stay away from Dougherty. There was only one way for them to find out about him, from Garzianos. It means in some way Jalaty and King are connected with them and with Ward, Jr. in gambling and they're trying to put it on Palmer.

Vince was trembling. He couldn't control it, geez, anyone with half a brain listening to this tape could figure it out same as I have. He was being used to nail Palmer, maybe even *he* was being set-up. But he was in too deep now, they'd never let him back out, he was sick to his stomach. France thought for a second then said, "Laskey, I'm sorry, I remembered some very pressing matters I must wrap up today. If you don't mind let's continue with this conversation in the morning. Just give me a call before you come in." France watched Laskey wobble out of his office. Sucking a deep breath he held it, hoping to slow his pounding heart. His hands shook so his fingers could barely slip the tape out of the recorder. Pulling a desk drawer out he shoved the tape beneath a batch of loose papers in the back. Vince mumbled, "They are *using* me to *frame* Palmer, I don't know what kind of reward they've got in mind for me but I'm going to be damn lucky if I get out of this in one piece. The tape might come in handy before its all over." He locked the drawer.

Next morning in his office, before switching on the concealed recorder, the Lt. prompted Laskey. He wanted this tape to be right. "Listen carefully, this is extremely important, I do *not* want you to mention anything to Palmer about me or what we're doing. Do you understand?" Solemnly Laskey nodded. "If you go to him about your divorce or Chevy agency problems be very careful you don't make a slip. If you do it could blow this whole deal, is that clear?" The Lt. was doggedly repetitious, "Tell your attorney absolutely *nothing*...not until I say we are ready."

Rolling his eyes Laskey nodded, whispering, "I understand." He didn't see the furtive movement of the tape recorder being started. France got the ball rolling.

"Everything is looking good Laskey, I talked to some 'influential friends' last night, it is very possible we can get the license for the card club re-issued."

Laskey grinned, "That's good news, real good."

France poured it on, "I have to see some money up front, you know what I mean, real soon."

"No problem with that. I got a couple buddies from Las Vegas, they want to cut themselves in on this deal, they'll put up the dough when ever we want."

"The two guys from Vegas, what's their names?"

"Buzzie Rivkin and Yummie Phillips."

"Vegas eh, sound like a couple real operators."

"Sharp guys alright. Originally from Chicago, they know all the angles," he smirked, "You know what I mean."

"Chicago eh, I get it, but keep them away from Palmer till I say so. I'll tell you when we are ready for him, don't forget it."

"Okay, okay, don't worry Captain, I got you the first time."

France met with Buzzie and Yummie. In the weeks following he led them into all kinds of conversations designed to implicate and incriminate themselves in a bribery conspiracy. France was getting it all on a secret tape, and at the same time a crew of detectives were taking pictures from a van every time they had a meet. It was one hell of a production, like Abbot and Costello. France just hoped it would stand up in court. He thought of Buzzie and Yummie. Lord, those two were something right of Damon Runyon, they talked in a weird Las Vegas jargon. But if they were hardened gamblers he was an orangutan. He had checked, neither one of them had a criminal record. Just a couple old geezers Laskey dug up...God knows where and I'm afraid to ask him. Buzzie was almost seventy, he couldn't sit still five minutes without pissing his pants.

France's nerves became raw. It was hard setting up a deal like this to nail Palmer. Not like simply driving by a liquor store, seeing people inside with their hands stuck in the air, that's an easy one. You just pull over and wait until the robber comes out and you nab him with the goods. You have everything you need to nail him. A victim, witnesses, evidence and a *guilty* party to a robbery. France muttered, what in hell have I got here for a bribery. Laskey a dingy old goat who started the whole thing with a crazy song and dance to the Garzianos and Buzzie and Yummie, two more old goats I have to repeat the scenario to twenty times every time I see them. And they still do not understand what it is all about. I don't think they even realize they are supposed to be doing something wrong. Then there's me, I'm a Lt. they are are supposed to be bribing. Lord, this is a *bribery,* a big *conspiracy?* Who are the witnesses, where's the evidence, who is guilty, who in hell is the victim? His head was like a pincushion, needles jabbing everywhere. For almost two months he'd been screwing around with recordings and pictures of the three old clowns. He couldn't stall Sheriff Jalaty or King any longer. If he was going to nail Palmer he'd have to manufacture something and quick.

France called Laskey to his office, "Alright we're ready to make our move, it's time for you to see your lawyer Jerry Palmer. We'll start this off real easy on him. I don't want anything said about me, or pay-offs or bribes. We've got to prime him first, you know what I mean?" Laskey nodded. "What you do is tell him you already have the license for the Pass Club, you want him to set up a corporation for you, Buzzie and Yummie, you got that? Remember, that is all you do the first time. Later on you'll introduce Buzzie and Yummie to Palmer and I will come into the picture."

On March 17, '82 Laskey went to Palmer's office and he agreed to form a corporation for Laskey and his two associates. Five days later Laskey revealed to Palmer he did not *really* have a license but, "Lt. France was going to help him get it and France might even put it in his own name. "The lawyer had had no experience in applying for gambling licenses but the part about the Lt. putting it in his own name seemed mighty strange. Knowing that Carl Ward, Jr. was the Garzianos lawyer Palmer made an appointment to talk with him.

Having no idea of the tangled criminal intrigue surrounding the Pass Club license Jerry was getting sucked in further every minute. France installed a concealed mike on Ward, Jr. then with Palmer's naivete of gambling laws and procedure, Ward, Jr. led him into an inane conversation that could be construed as being almost anything besides what it really was. Becoming more suspicious he did some legal research regarding the re-issuing of the license. He concluded it couldn't be done and that Lt. France was a crook conning Laskey and those other two jokers out of some money. Palmer told Laskey what he thought of the whole set-up, he advised Laskey, Buzzie and Yummie to get the hell out of it.

Laskey repeated this to Lt. France who cursed Palmer wildly for screwing up his plans. Then with a sudden thought he felt relieved. Hell, this might be a good chance for me to check out of this mess before it backfires all over me. France reported to Jalaty and King that Palmer was uncooperative and was not going for their scheme. He suggested that they drop Laskey and the whole operation. Their reaction was unexpected, they became furious, "You get Palmer or else....you've been six weeks now, too much time has been wasted, you were told this was urgent."

Lt. France was in quicksand up to his eyeballs. He would have to make his move fast, deliver Palmer or he was in big trouble. But things were getting worse, Buzzie and Yummie took Palmer's advice and backed out. Vince jumped Laskey, "Damn it, you have to come up with the front money, the whole deal is blowing up." Laskey then conned another sucker into the web, Roscoe Morris, a car dealer in Santa Paula. This poor guy understood even less of what was going on than Buzzie or Yummie had. Palmer strongly advised Laskey to get the hell out of the deal but he refused to give up. He was still convinced France could get him the license.

With Laskey refusing to take his advice Palmer wanted him to get another lawyer. Jerry called the Bar Association several times. He was told that under Section 6068 of the Business and Profession Code that he couldn't drop his client and he could not breach the confidentiality of a client by reporting the matter to the authorities. If he did so he would be subject to disbarment. Jerry was now stuck with Laskey, but so was Lt. France. Later the three of them held a meeting at Maxie's Bar in Oak View. Palmer didn't suspect that the deputy was wired, he was convinced he was a crooked cop trying to take Laskey for some dough.

At a remote table they talked over three hours. Oddly the Lt. brought up the deaths of Lyman Smith and his wife. Joseph Alsip was one of the first suspects but he wasn't arrested for the double murder until more then a year and a half later. France dwelled on the gory, bloody details of the bludgeonings. Then very strangely he revealed confidentially to Palmer, "The District Attorney Bradbury and Sheriff Jalaty both *knew* that Alsip was innocent but were going ahead with the trial anyway." Very peculiarly Lt.France stressed one point, "If Alsip was *innocent* then the *real* killer was still stalking the streets, free to *kill* again." When the tape of this conversation was played at Jerry's trial the part about the murders was missing. The tape had been tampered with, obviously it had been cut and spliced and re-spliced.

Palmer had reached a definite conclusion, this thing with the Lt. was the craziest affair he'd ever gotten into. He needed a lawyer as bad as Laskey or any of the others. But before he could talk to one his office was raided and he was charged with Conspiracy to Bribe Lt. France, the D.A. and the Supervisors. It was a few weeks after his arrest when Jerry called me, "Gary, I have to see you right away, it's important as hell."

"Where are you calling from?"

"I'm at a phone booth in Oxnard."

"Can you come to Oak View?"

"I'll be there in twenty minutes."

"Alright meet me at Cuddles Restaurant."

Along with urgency in Jerry's voice I'd sensed fear. He entered Cuddles and came over to my booth, a big man about six three and two ten. Worry and anger were etched on his face. He slid the small cassette across the table. "That's a recording of threatening phone calls, the yellow s.o.b's are threatening to kill me and my girlfriend and harm my children and grandkids. I want you to keep it in case anything happens to me. Other then you I don't know a damn soul who has guts enough to do anything with it if I get killed." On the white strip on top I wrote in my initials and the date and slipped it in my pocket. His voice was taut, "I got the first call at my office at seven twenty five the morning of March 26. A man said, 'Do what Lt. France wants you to do, or you and your girlfriend will *get* what Charlene and Lyman got.' I didn't recognize the voice and it didn't seem like he was disguising it."

"Maybe it's Laskey, he wants that license awful bad."

"No, he reeled off an address of my children in Redondo Beach and Carson, in L.A. County. Laskey is goofy enough to pull a stunt like this, but he doesn't even know I have children much less where they live. This guy means business...I can tell by the way he talks. In two calls he threatened me with the same that Lyman and Charlene got, in the others he threatened harm to my family. I've moved to the ranch and keep my rifle handy. I sleep in a different place every night, mostly under the trees with my dogs. They would raise hell if anyone comes sneaking around." Jerry's voice rumbled with anger, "Hell, I'll fight anybody face to face if I have to. How do you defend yourself against the kind of sleazy scum who sneaks up on you when you're asleep and caves your head in."

I promised Palmer, "I'll keep the recordings in a safe place, but do me a favor, write all this down and sign it, if something should happen to you it will back up the recordings."

"Good idea, I will do it this evening." Shaking hands he left. To Jerry it wasn't going to make any difference who would be the judge in his case. Against the Mishpucka he wouldn't stand a chance, even so Marvin Lewis was a particularly *vicious* choice. Lewis was a law partner of Judge Berenson and Nordman as well as Carl Ward, Jr. who'd be testifying against him. Despite the extremely harsh pretrial newspaper treatment he had suffered at the hands of Editor Judas Gius, Lewis denied Jerry a change of venue.

Ward had taken the witness stand. During a recess I met Jerry in the hallway outside the courtroom, we had a quick nervous talk. "Jerry, I've been sitting there in the courtroom listening to all this shit just like the jury has, I can tell you for sure, Ward is crucifying you. But what the jury *doesn't know* is that at the same time he is covering up and concealing his own guilt. It is imperative that you subpoena Supervisor James Dougherty and Garzianos. You've got to expose their whole gambling operation so the jury can *figure out* that it is this God damn Ward and Berenson and Nordman who are involved in the Pass Club license conspiracy and not you."

Jerry hesitated. I knew what he was doing, he was thinking like a lawyer, conjuring up a million insurmountable legal technicalities why it could not be done. But his real problem was he was afraid of making enemies. "I'll just be making them madder at me if I try to get rough."

"Jerry, these crooks are already your enemies, you think you're going to win friends and influence these people by smiling at them?"

The lawyer had become confused by his immersion into such a mess. He vacillated, "But we can't make them talk. You know that Dougherty will never tell the truth, anyway we can not impeach our own witnesses."

"Why in the hell not? If they lie, impeach them, what difference does it make? Just get them up there on the stand, you can squeeze enough out of them that the jury will get the picture."

"No I don't see how we can do it, besides Lewis would never let us put them on." There was no use to argue, it was Palmer's choice. He just couldn't get it in his head, he was in a fight to the finish, his entire future. He still had far out visions he was going to come out alright in the end. But the Mafia and Mishpucka despise the weak and timid, they do *not* deal in *sympathy* and *mercy*, and certainly not with someone they have already doomed.

"Alright, just do one thing, have Judge Lewis order that Ward is to remain on call so you can haul him back for further questioning." I had a definite reason for wanting Ward back on the stand. We'd fallen into some luck, the good kind for a change. A sharp reporter, James Long, with the Oregonian in Portland had been probing deep into a large gambling operation in that city. He'd dug up evidence that a millionaire California lawyer, Carl Ward, Jr. was head of the ring. A phony church had been set up as a front, the Church of the Conceptual Truth. A crew of Vegas gamblers that Ward brought in were running the huge operation. They claimed to be Ministers of the Church, running a religious and charitable cause.

While vacationing in California, Long happened to read in the local paper about Carl Ward, Jr. testifying against Jerry in the Pass Club case. Suspicious of Ward's motives he called Palmer. Excited with new hope, Jerry called me. "The newsreporter's going to run an expose on the gambling in Portland and unfold Ward's involvment. Hell, that'll bring 'em all in. Berenson, Nordman and Judge Marvin Lewis who's their law partner and who just happens to be the Judge crucifying me in a damn kangaroo trial."

"I understand all those things Jerry, I agree what they're doing to you is so damned outrageous it's unthinkable, but I am afraid a news article way up in Oregon isn't going to help. There is no way in the world Lewis will allow something like that to get to the Jury." Jerry was crestfallen, I had thrown a bucket of cold water. I knew exactly how he felt, I changed my tone, "Don't give up all hope, we will think of something." Trying to keep him from becoming totally discouraged I remarked off-handedly, "You know, if the police were to raid the gambling operations and Ward was arrested then Long's news story would carry some real weight, it might do the trick."

Jerry leaped at the thought, "My God, do you think it could be worked?"

The minute I said it I wished I hadn't, it was giving Jerry false hopes. I used to have good contacts, retired cops up in Oregon but now they spent all their time fishing. I didn't see or hear from any of them very often but after opening up my big mouth I'd have to make a try. "Jerry, I'll see what I can do, but no promises, you have to understand that." I phoned an old buddy, born in Medford, Mac had over forty years in law enforcement and private investigations. His dad was an Oregon lawman before WW1. McMahon knew just about everyone up there. I told him the story, he gave me the same answer I had given Jerry, "No promises, but I'll see what I can do."

It wasn't even five a.m. yet, moonlight came shining through the window, my phone was ringing off the hook, it was Mac in Medford, the delight he took at rousting me out so early was thinly concealed, "Hope I didn't wake you up, ha, ha."

"Just a little, what's the matter with you?"

"I thought you'd want to hear this. A couple hours ago Portland Police, the State Attorney Office and County Dist. Atty. combined raided Ward's phony church and his gambling operation. They were booked for illegal gambling, in a few days the Attorney General will file charges against Ward and the others under RICO. That is the State Racketeering Influence and Corrupt Organization Act."

"By golly Mac that was fast action. It's only a week since I called you."

"Sometimes that's the way it goes."

"Thanks, some day maybe I can return a favor."

"The papers will hit the street soon, I'll send you copies. This is Sunday morning so I'll mail them to you first thing tomorrow."

Jerry and his attorney took the Oregonian's front page story to Judge Lewis in his chambers. The other defendants, their attorneys and the prosecutor were there. Lewis was furious when confronted with the expose of their gambling ring. The revelation of millions of dollars being funneled to his partners, Judge Jerome Berenson and Ben Nordman and to several of their corporations turned his neck turkey red. Judge Lewis adamantly refused to call Ward back to the stand for more questioning, meanwhile, Ward did a disappearing act before Palmer could subpoena him.

A juror, Constance Weeks, had Lewis very upset, she wasn't in awe of him as he felt she should be. One time he barely controlled his temper when she spoke out at a serious mistake in judgement he made. He feared her acuteness had pierced the flimsy shell of their case against Palmer, it was a possibility the jurors might appoint her foreman. The Judge hadn't forgotten his position in the Mishpucka would be in jeopardy if Palmer was found not guilty. Lewis started a campaign of denigration against the juror. In his chambers, in the presence of defendants and lawyers he called her flakey. Ultimately Weeks was forced from the jury, an alternate, Bert Seiderman was installed. A Mishpucka, Seiderman by strange odds became foreman of the jury. With the jurors well in hand Lewis clamped his death squeeze on the witnesses.

Jerry's lawyer put Yummy Phillips on the stand. He could verify Jerry had never been a part of their conspiracy to bribe Lt. France. But on the stand he took the fifth amendment, refusing to testify on the grounds it might incriminate him. It was ludicrous, he'd already pled guilty and made a probation file detailing his involvement. But Phillips still had a problem, he hadn't been sentenced yet and they spelled it out to him, if he cleared Palmer with his testimony Judge Lewis would shoot him to the Pen instead of giving him probation.

Laskey, the idiot who started the whole mess also was promised probation. He penned a letter to the Probation Department stating that Palmer had *not* been a member of their conspiracy, but Lewis wouldn't let the letter into the trial. Laskey, terrified of the Judge fled to Cicero, Illinois failing to appear as a witness.

Just as the case was about to go to the jury, Editor Judas Gius planted vicious lies in the Star Free Press, so slanted against Jerry anyone reading it would've convicted him on the spot. Judge Lewis denied Palmer's lawyer's Motion to poll the jurors to determine if they had read the article and he refused to poll them himself.

Lewis allowed all the D.A.'s instructions to the jury but *denied* Palmer's defense instructions outlining Outrageous Conduct by the Government. Jerry was charged with five felony counts, the jury had dismissed four of them and seriously suspected 'entrapment' in the fifth. But with no instructions to interpret Outrageous Government Conduct, the jurors found Palmer guilty of one count...'Conspiracy to Commit Bribery.'

France got his promised reward, from obscure Lt. in Ojai, the Sheriff promoted him to Commander and brought him 'downtown.' But even so, for some lurking, undefinable reason France didn't feel secure. While cleaning out his desk he found a cassette, it was that revealing first tape he'd made with Laskey. Fingering the recording he glanced at a waste basket a moment then placed it in his pocket. Hell, it might still come in handy.

Jerry was ruined, his license, ranch, law practice, everything was gone. Judge Marvin Lewis magnanimously let him remain out of jail while preparing an Appeal. That was a macabre joke, the only place left to Appeal was to the 'Black Robe Mishpucka'...Hymie Blitzberg, alias Steven Stone, Presiding Justice of the Ventura Appeal Court. When that was denied, his last chance to Appeal was to Black Robe Mishpucka, Moskovitz, Grodinsky and Kausinsky-the State Supreme Court. The cruel combined evil power of the Mafia and Mishpucka had crushed Jerry, but the Commander wasn't finished with him yet. Palmer had given him some damn scary, sleepless nights. Vince had a desire for personal revenge. He sued Palmer for fifteen thousand dollars and punitive damages, claiming that Jerry had, 'Invaded his Privacy,' by inquiring into his integrity.

At the outset Palmer was informed by the Bar Association he could *not* disassociate himself from Laskey. If he did not represent and protect his client properly he could be disbarred. He had given this premise a lot of thought, considering what Jerry knew up until then he'd become convinced France was a crook, and that he could never come up with a license for the Pass Club like he'd promised Laskey. Boiling it down...France was a con-man taking Jerry's client for money. It being his bounden duty to protect his client's interests he decided to learn more about Lt. France, he hired a private eye. Unnerved by what Palmer found out about him France claimed it was an invasion of his privacy. France knew that filing the lawsuit would be dangerous, it could open the door for Palmer to drag out a pile of his dirty linen in a trial. But the Commander had figured it out so there was not going to be a trial. That's why he had hired the notorious shyster James Farley.

A direct descendant from Shakespeare's Shylock, the avaricious Jewish usurer in Merchant of Venice, Farley prepared to extract the last pound of flesh from Palmer's body for payment. When served with the suit Jerry answered it as required. By then he'd closed his office, his new address was a P.O. box in Oxnard. This number was typed in as the mailing address on his Answer To The Complaint, which was then dutifully filed with the Municipal Court Clerk.

What followed was pure, unadulterated Mishna, the 'Jew Law' of Chaos, Corruption and Conspiracy. James Farley and James Fox, the Municipal Court Clerk, conspiratorially sent all their letters and the 'Notice Of The Trial Date' to Jerry's old address instead of the P.O. box. When the documents and Notice were returned as being undeliverable, Farley and Fox destroyed them. Farley and his client the Commander then appeared on the trial date before Mishpucka Judge Kenneth Yegan.

Unaware of a trial date Palmer didn't appear. Farley swore on his oath that he and Fox had notified Palmer by mail. "He received it because it was not returned." That's all Judge Yegan needed, he ordered, "Palmer is in default," then issued a judgement against him and Fox recorded it. Accordingly Palmer had received 'Due Process Of Law,' he had had *his day* in court...

The frightful annihilation of Jerry was killing two birds with one stone, he would never again interfere with the Mishpucka or Mafia schemes. Second, every lawyer in Ventura county was aware of the butchery in detail, etched into their brains, awe stricken, on-looking lawyers stared in numbed shock at the scene. Sitting high, an eerie caricature, the spindly form of Judge Lewis wrapped tightly in his Mishpucka Black Robes, was jerking a giant electric switch...on and off, on and off, his lips moving slackly in unison. Palmer sitting in a chair in the center of the room reacted to the heavy jolts, his body writhed, tortured nerves jerking and quivering spasmodically with terrible agony. In horror the lawyers watched wisps of smoke rising from invisible electrodes screwed in the unfortunate Palmer's head. Before their very eyes a brother lawyer was being fried, sacrificed, a human barbeque. Terrified they knew that it could happen to each and every one of them if they should forget their place, but they'd 'never' forget!

Not long afterward there was an election. Although there are a thousand attorneys in the county, not 'one' *filed* to run against nine *un-elected* Mishpucka judges who had just recently been appointed. No, the lawyers 'would never' *forget* their place. They had received the word.

CHAPTER 40

All conditions of the escrow had been properly performed and completed by both parties. Recordation of the documents with the Ventura County Recorder officially closed escrow, by law the escrow holder was, 'Now bound to deliver the Deed to the buyer and hand the purchase money to the seller.' On close of the escrow the Trust Deed then belonged to me, it belonged in my possession. However the escrow company refused to give it to me, instead, they handed the Trust Deed and the purchase money to the seller.

With my Deed in his hand the seller wielded the whip. He filed a fraudulent foreclosure against my property and demanded a large sum of money. To keep from losing my property it was necessary to pay the ransom plus outrageous costs and fees to the 'Trust Deed Services Co.' to cure their spurious foreclosure. A few months later the seller repeated his extortion scam. Again I was forced to pay a huge sum for costs and fees to cure their rigged foreclosure. It was clear, these crooks could continue the scam forever, as long as they had my Deed. I filed a lawsuit in Federal Court under Civil Rights Section 1983 trying to put a stop to the fraud and recover my Trust Deed, but a Mishpucka Magistrate, Ralph Geffensky, aka Geffen, recommended to District Court that they dismiss it.

Another Mishpucka, District Court Judge Edward Rafeedie then dismissed my lawsuit ruling that his decision was predicated on the, 'Non-judicial Foreclosure Law' and as such that law allows peoples property to be taken by private interests without the owner having any right to go to court. Rafeedie rammed his ruling home stating, "The only legal rights the property owner has is to pay the amount demanded by Trust Deed Services Co., plus costs and fees or they will suffer the loss of their property."

I soon learned, T.D. Services Company was tied in with judges, loan companies, escrow companies, title insurance companies, and trustee officials, etc. etc., in one great big kick-back and fee splitting racket. With guarantees of massive kick-backs the T.D. Services Co. incites loan and escrow companies to file spurious foreclosures. In a criminal conspiracy of kick-backs and a complicated, clever system of laundering stolen and extorted property titles, T.D. Services Co. is the propelling force behind ninety five percent of all foreclosure action in California. Scrutinizing the malignant array of Black Robe Mishpuckas depraved scams, their multi-billion dollar, 'Non-judicial Foreclosure' racket is one of the most vicious, ruthless schemes they have devised.

Before Geffensky and Rafeedie even dismissed my Civil Rights Suit, T.D. Services Co. had phonied up a buyer and commenced a 'sham foreclosure' sale. They maintain a catalog of shysters in every county who eagerly fight to make a quick buck. They are part of the mechanism in 'laundering' stolen titles. In my case they used a local electric contractor, John E. Taft. Trying to force me off my property the fraudulent buyer served me with a Three Day Notice To Vacate. When I refused to abandon my property, Mishpucka lawyer Stanley Cohen filed suit for Unlawful Detainer in Municipal Court. At this stage of the scam the phony buyers go to extreme methods to scare the owner into abandoning his property in panic. The same day of the sham foreclosure Taft sent goons who prowled the yard looking in the windows and climbing up on the roof.

Bob DuPre was staying there while helping me fend off the mass of deadly judicial tricks the Mafia and Mishpucka were burying me under. The goons succeeded in shaking up Bob considerably. One of Taft's conspirators, Harrison Rubbish Co., dropped a huge steel dumpster about twelve feet by thirty and ten feet high in my front yard. Big dump trucks from Taft Electric loaded with rubbish from construction jobs crashed the junk into the dumpster strewing trash around the yard. The ear splitting, nerve racking events went on all hours of the day and night. When the dumpster was full they piled it higher with old broken down davenports and chairs. The eye sore was left in the front yard for neighbors and passers by to view with scorn as harassment and humiliation to me. Every few days they'd bring in a huge diesel rig and remove the over-loaded dumpster and replace it with a new one. The routine with the dump trucks would commence all over again. Taft's goons had been nailing signs on the front door. They threatened to break in and throw my belongings in the dumpster if I didn't move out.

Taft was coming on hard, with bolt cutters one of his hoodlums cut a lock and chain off a gate. He chopped the wires in the meter box and jerked out fuse blocks, cutting off the water he prowled the building peering into the windows. It was the last straw, thoroughly frightened DuPre packed and fled in panic, for where he didn't say. It was a tough blow. I was left without any source of legal assistance whatsoever. Things looked dark, it was a hell of a spot to be in, but there was no way I was going to give up. It meant I'd have to fight harder and work longer.

I deliberately killed a half hour loitering in the main lobby until only one minute remained before I was due in court. I entered the elevator, in five seconds I emerged on the next level. I spotted him, vulpine, scurrying toward me through the throngs of people. Jimmy Fox displayed a big smile, the one he was programed to flash when pretending he'd unexpectedly spied me. He thrust out a hand, "Well hi there Gary, what you doing wandering around the courthouse?" With a pat on my shoulder, his 'surprised to see me act' was superb. His sincerity nearly got to me, except I knew my stall in the lobby had made him sweat. For half an hour, immobile, hiding in a corner of the hallway, fighting a nervous tic Jimmy tensed for the instant I walked out the elevator. Fox was a perfectionist, his stage walk-on must be faultless, never overdone. Cocking his head to one side he eyed the papers in my hand. "Oh, I see you're due in Judge Hintz's court." Like he was eager to help, he pointed, "That's his courtroom right over there, I have to say, you're lucky indeed." He confided, "I happen to know Steven Hintz is a very sharp judge, he is really on top of the law." His voice had become silkier, "Believe me, you can't go wrong."

Getting my hand back from Fox I headed toward the courtroom brooding, probing what the clerk just said, 'on top of the law,' yeh, with Geffensky screwing up my Civil Rights case, Fox soaping me up here in the hallway and just inside were more Mishpuckas, lawyer Stanley Cohen, and Judge Hintzlestein *laying-in-wait* for me. On top of the law, yeah, I believe you Fox. It was depressing. I pushed my way through the heavy doors, Judge Hintzlestein, alias Hintz, was slouching towards the bench. With the big black oblong mustache perverting his lip he evidently figured he looked like Groucho.

Without Bob's help it took days of desperate, frantic research at the law library preparing for this hearing, all my other business and responsibilities were forced to take a back seat. With no money and even less time it was always nervous touch and go.

First of all Taft didn't even have a Deed or Title to my property, which meant his phony Eviction Notice and lawyer Cohen's sham, Unlawful Detainer was no good. All the trespassing and malicious harassment Taft had committed against me were criminal violations, perpetrated with felonious, conspiratorial intent to scare and force me into abandoning my property. But I knew it was stupid to think Judge Hintzlestein or the D.A. would do anything about it.

In Unlawful Detainer procedure the California Civil Code grants Municipal Courts jurisdiction of fifteen thousand dollars only. My equity was far greater then that and case law very clearly placed the jurisdiction in Superior Court. In Morrissey v. Morrissey 1983, 191 CAL 782-784, "The true rule is; if the issue of the Title or Right of Possession is so involved that it must be decided in order to determine the case, the Superior Court had original jurisdiction whether the involution may be said to be merely incidental or not."

In Asuncion v. Superior Court, 1980 108 CAL APP. 3d 141, the Appeal Court ruled in no uncertain terms, "The property owners are entitled to defend the eviction action based on their claims of fraud and related causes which they asserted; Therefore the action necessarily exceeded the jurisdiction of Municipal Court and could not be tried there."

California Code of Civil Procedure and State Court Of Appeal were explicit, Hintzlestein *'did not'* have jurisdiction. I filed a Motion to transfer my case to the Superior Court but he refused. Hintz and Cohen both knew Municipal Court lacked jurisdiction. They had to move fast. Amending his suit Cohen added a fictitious defendant. I again filed a Motion to force Hintz to transfer my case to Superior Court. To stall me off he gave me five days specifically to file proof that my equity was over fifteen thousand dollars.

On the fourth day I went to the Municipal Court to file proof. I got a shock, Fox, the clerk had issued orders that I could *not* file my documents. A clerk brought the court file out, she said, "I can *not* let you file *anything,* you are in Default."

"I'm in Default! What are you talking about, Hintz gave me five days to file these documents and tomorrow's the fifth day."

"According to the court's record you *did not* answer the Amended Complaint."

"The hell I didn't. I've got my stamped copy and receipt for the fee I paid. Not only that, the last time I was in court Hintz had my answer right in his hand. He was reading it when he ordered that I had five days to file these papers."

"Yes, but this other party Stanley Cohen named in his Amended Complaint *didn't* answer, they have filed the Default against him."

"Cohen is a God damned slimy liar, there is no other party, that is a *phony* name he's manufactured." Loathing for sick Mishpucka scum like Fox, Cohen and Hintz choked me, I couldn't talk.

"Well I'm sorry, it's Mr. Fox's orders, I can *not* file your papers." There was no use arguing, Hintz and Cohen had planned the whole thing. They knew that without jurisdiction Hintz *didn't* dare issue a Court Order for an Unlawful Detainer, so they were going to do it this way. Damn 'em to hell anyway. As it stood now, Stanley Cohen had a Writ of Execution issued by James Fox, the clerk, not against me but against the phony name Cohen had manufactured. Fox and Cohen then took the spurious Writ to the Sheriff and got a Notice to Vacate against the fictitious name Cohen had phonied up. It was neither signed nor dated. One of Taft's goons nailed the Notice on the front door. The phony piece of paper could never have held up with an *honest* judge.

I considered staying there and making an issue of it, make them force me out. I felt certain the minute a responsible deputy sheriff examined the bogus Notice he would never enforce it. However on second thought this would be a dangerous chance to take, much too risky with them holding that damned probation over my head. All they'd have to do was say I was breaking the law, any law, and I'd be in violation of probation. Then I'd find myself in jail. I couldn't afford such a confrontation even though I was right. Obviously I'd get the worst of it, they'd label me a willful, deliberate offender of the law. This was exactly what they wanted to pin on me. I intended to stay strictly within the law no matter how galling it was knowing the law meant nothing to those people.

I figured it would be a waste of time, however, I wrote a protest to Hintz. Outlining what Cohen and Fox had pulled I asked that he rectify the situation and order the documents to be filed as he had originally ordered. I was surprised twelve days later when a letter came from Hintzlestein, on reading it I quickly understood why he felt it so imperative to reply. Clearly, the fraud they'd committed to get the phony Writ and Notice to Vacate had them apprehensive as hell. With arrogance typical of the Mishpucka they underestimated their quarry, they had been certain I'd never figure out their clever chicanery. The letter was a cover-up, a *sly* attempt with which they still hoped to mislead me.

Very carefully Hintz sidestepped mentioning the phony person Cohen had insidiously written into his Amended Complaint. He now maintained that it was me who was in Default, he claimed I hadn't filed an answer. Hintzlestein wrote, "I am not positive but I believe the reason that you were not allowed to file an answer was because you were technically in Default. On August 25, 1983 I gave you five days to answer, you apparently did not file an answer within the five days." Hintz was lying, the truth was that four days later, on August 29, 1983 I had indeed filed an answer.

As proof a clerk had stamped and certified my copy. And for the fourteen dollar filing fee I was given receipt, No. 37755, printed out by their computer cash register. Furthermore, eleven days later, at nine a.m., September 8, Hintz sat in court with that very document in his hand that he now claimed I had not filed. It had challenged Hintz's jurisdiction of the case and he had ordered, "You have five days to file an answer as pertains specifically to your equity in the property and the lack of jurisdiction by Municipal Court." I learned that Cohen and Fox had *already* arranged for the Writ of Execution and had gotten their Notice To Vacate *earlier* that morning *before* I even got to court.

With a straight face the *lying* Hintz had sat there and given me five days to answer. He knew he was safe, Fox, the Municipal Court Clerk was never going to let me file an answer. Gathered in the evil Mishpucka Sanctum of Hintz's Judicial Chambers the trio inspired by their *hatred* for Christians laughed uproariously. The spectacle of me sleepless, burning up five days and nights laboriously typing all those documents that I'd never be able to file amused them greatly. The papers I had dutifully and respectfully prepared under a court order lay spread upon the table along with Hintz's letter. I glared at the worthless papers and the small tape recorder beside them.

Overcome with friggin' anger I'd forgotten about the recorder. I pushed the starter button, there was a whirring, then Hintz's voice clearly audible on the morning of Sept. 8, from the bench. He was reading the document out loud, the one I filed on Aug. 29, the one he *now* claimed in his letter I never filed. The voice was giving me five days to file documents regarding the Municipal Courts lack of jurisdiction in my case. The recording and letter was absolute proof of that sick son of a bitch Hintzlestein's lies. This was a big relief, I hadn't been dreaming it or going nuts like I was beginning to think. If you listened to those treacherous scum too long you could easily make the mistake of believing them. Thank God I'd taken along the recorder, I placed the letter and tape in a safe place.

Mired in the treacherous depths of Mishna chaos the Mishpucka had stupidly revealed their connivery and even more witless they'd attached their signatures to the conspiracy.

Rabbi Judas' transformation of the barbarous Temple Priests to supposedly becoming scholarly Rabbis in Synagogues had assuredly been a superficial operation. In fact, blood sacrifices of Christians by the 'Priests of Satan' had *never* stopped. Menachem Begin, the most murderous 'Jew terrorist' of all times spread death and terror among the leaders of nations throughout the world. Kidnapping two British soldiers from a street he hung them without legal cause or a trial. Begin bombed a hotel into a mass of rubble, murdering over a hundred innocent people just to show Great Britain his terroristic capability for insane violence and death. Jews had accused a French politician of anti-semitism, it so enraged Begin that he ordered his Jew assassins' from Israel to take revenge upon him. A Frenchman answering a knock on his door was met by a blast of vitriolic acid striking him in the face. The hideous, ravaging fluid ate his eyes out of his head. The *only* crime the innocent eighty year old man had committed against Jews was the misfortune of having the identical name of the man Begin ordered destroyed.

Rabbi Meir Kahane, born in the U.S., was a fiery admirer and student of Begin's heinous evil. Kahane created the vicious Jewish Defense League in America, bringing together a gang of fanatical, blood thirsty degenerates backed up by a huge arsenal of automatic weapons. Then Rabbi Kahane became an elected official of Israel, a foreign country. A member of Israeli's Parliament he still claimed U.S. citizenship and the right of entry into America at will for his traitorous schemes. In many treasonous attacks Rabbi Meir Kahane arrogantly sabotaged and terrorized voters and American Electoral process during a Presidential election. It was for a sinister purpose of fomenting riots and revolution. Kahane's attacks in the United States followed precisely his violent modus operandi in Israel where he had stridently called for *denial* of voting rights to *all* citizens not of Jew descent. It is the basis, the Master Plan for setting up a Pure Jewish State for Mishpucka power and International spread of the

Mishna, their Jew law of chaos, corruption and conspiracy.

Back in the early 1950's two of Mickey Cohen's henchmem came to Ventura County to coordinate future gangland operations. These bail bondsmen brothers, Abe and Hymie Phillips were closely allied with Federal Judge Harry Pregerson in L.A. and Commissioner Ben Nordman and Judge Jerome Berenson in Ventura. During Begin's many visits to Hollywood and Beverly Hills he and Cohen were up to something. Cohen was making big noises how he was promoting Hollywood stars to perform in a gigantic benefit to raise money for guns for Israel. In the darkest hours of a night in 1959 the National Guard Armory in Oxnard was raided. This was at a time when the Jews needed guns for their terrorism program badly.

Contributions and the benefit performances by stars were raising millions of dollars. But the huge sums of money never got further than Cohen's and Begin's possession, nor did the guns stolen from the Armory. Hidden in secret arsenals they were to be used by the JDL. The machine gun mounted in the house of National Security Director Wm. P. Clark was stolen during the raid. I wondered if his partners Judge Berenson and Commissioner Nordman had more of them concealed in the 'bat-cave,' the strange, windowless building at 625 North A. St.. And there was Clark's sinister avowal, "When the revolution and chaos begins we are going to kill all of those friggin' Niggers and Mexicans, mow 'em down like dogs."

To spark their revolution, unemployment, hunger, drugs, crime, all means of provocation would be used to pressure and torch lethal frustrations. Blacks, Mexicans and Asians provoked and baited into marches and protests sinisterly fanned to violence by provocateurs would be misled and inflamed by a treacherous Mishpucka.

Conspiratorially, American borders and ports had been left wide open to hordes of illegal Mexicans, Asians, and Jews from Russia by Black Robe Mishpucka court rulings. These *uncontrollable* criminal masses would be a deciding factor.

In the following cataclysmic chaos, total destruction of the U.S. Constitution will occur. Black Robe Mishpuckas wielding dictatorial judicial power will *take over* with their evil Mishna, the Jew law, the Law of the Temple Priests. At the time of the Jews covenant with Satan, they knew it was a monumental blunder. It caused a massive inferiority complex, this low quality syndrome developed aggressive behavioral patterns becoming innate in their racial character. This brought forth their weird fetish, a *need* for a scape-goat in all their plots. Always in the Jews plots their strategy and propaganda must provide for a scape-goat. *Always* there must be somebody else who was responsible, someone besides themselves who precipitated the holocaust. This time they'd point the finger of guilt for their chaos in all directions. At Blacks, the Ku Klux Klan, neo Nazis, Southern Baptists, Moral Majority, Eastern States Catholics, everywhere but at Jews and Black Robe Mishpuckas...

Even the raid of Oxnard's Armory, the Star Free Press concocted a story and *blamed* it on, "Insurgent Mexicans in Baja, California." Furiously the Jews worked at fomenting serious trouble between the U.S. and Arab nations. Deftly they planted fabricated evidence and rumors into our intelligence community that Arabs were sending a squad of specially trained assassins to the capitol to kill President Reagan. One hell of an uproar ensued, the papers and TV were full of it. American border crossings were alerted to be on the lookout for the black haired, swarthy Arab killers.

Extra guards armed to the teeth were posted in forests along the Canadian borders. Every precaution was taken, Canadian Mounted Police, the FBI and CIA were alerted. Even Pres. Reagan's *sharpest* Intelligence advisors fell for it. Israeli's agents provocateur grinned as the Arabs futilely protested their innocence of the plot.

For many years the Black Robe Mishpucka had *slyly* made crucial court rulings, implementing laws that singularly signaled no notable deleterious impact in any one certain area. However, combined and interlocking, these legal rulings formed a *deadly pattern* designed to undermine and destroy the principal banking system of the Bank Of America and the off-shoot banks created by old Italian families in California. These institutes were the power bases for the Italian land owners, a monetary safe-guard and protector of their immense land holdings and business empire. With the collapse of the banks they'd no longer be a politically powerful, integral organization. Already Bank of America and its satellites are reeling from the sabotage of the Black Robe Mishpuckas judicial attacks. Their total destruction will occur during the Master-planned chaos.

It was a colossal jigsaw puzzle, thousands of pieces of all sizes, trying to come together in my head. Presidential candidates, Dem. Gary Hart, Walter Mondale along with Jesse Jackson publicly spoke out against the Jews demands that the U.S. assist them to move the Israeli capitol from Tel Aviv to Jerusalem. With the top candidates rebuff of this obvious scheme to usurp Arab Holy Lands the shrieks of Anti-Semitism blasting from the Rabbis and the Synagogues was earsplitting. Across the nation Jewish news editorialists hot-penned accusations and innuendo's of Anti-Semitism, TV networks wailed acrimonious threats that the "Jewish Community in the U.S. would *cut off* all their votes and their *financial* support to the Democrats." Clamoring and gnashing teeth the Jews stridently black-jacked Hart, Mondale and Reverend Jesse Jackson with insane accusations and aspersions of Holocaustic tendencies.

It was the *same* old Jew propaganda horseshit, but it frightened holy hell out of Mondale and Hart. Swiftly they crawled on hands and knees into the Synagogues packed with thousands of glowering Jews watching as they groveled. Begging forgiveness, Mondale and Hart swore upon their honors, "Never again would they ever take a stand *against* Israeli *demands,* because they now realized it would be, Anti-Semitic to do so." Only Jesse Jackson remained standing, easily he'd seen the Jews demands to move Israel's capitol to Jerusalem as nothing more than what it was, a ploy, an Israeli scheme to critically involve U.S. Military Forces in a conspiracy to inflame a Holy War they themselves had started by invading Lebanon. It would instigate a *conflagration* engulfing the oil producing Arab countries that the Jews had coveted so many years. Perhaps Mondale and Hart were astute enough to see through the scheme as Jackson had, if this was true, then it made the two politicians disavowal of America's vital interests all the *more* cowardly and traitorous.

Jesse Jackson had refused to knuckle down to the Jews screams. I knew what his refusal to creep servilely into the Synagogues would cost him, the Jews would rip his flesh like jackals tearing the carcass of a still breathing buffalo. Along the hectic trail of the Presidential campaign Jackson made a slip of the lip. In front of a newsman he called New York City, "Hymie Town." Jews pounced on this, Rabbis screamed, in unison every Jew in the country screamed, newspapers and TV shouted out, "Jackson is guilty of terrible Anti-Semitism, he calls Jews, "Hymie." At first it merely amounted to what street-wise people cynically sneer at as, "A big FBI case," but the Jews shrieks escalated it to a full blown 'International incident.'

Rabbis en masse shrilly demanded that Jackson be "Thrown out of the Democratic Party and forbidden to speak at the Democratic Presidential Convention being held in San Francisco." Jetting from Israel, evil Rabbi Meir Kahane came to stir and enrage Jews against Jackson and the Blacks. Fanning the *flames* of riots and revolution the media interviewed old Jewish men and women on the streets of the ghettos in Beverly Hills and Palm Springs. Their stories of Anti-Semitism were spine chilling. They could *not* remember any *specific* facts of how they managed it but each and everyone of them *swore* they'd escaped right out of the flaming jaws of the furnaces of death during WW11 in Germany. "Oh yes, oy yoy yoy! This Jesse Jackson is a bad man, very bad, he should be stamped out. I am tellink you, I'm knowing all about the holocaust."

They raised hell with Jackson because he wouldn't repudiate his friendship with Louis Farrakhan, a Black religious leader based in Chicago. Farrakhan was a true example of Black frustrations ready to explode under a relentless provocation of being denied the Due Process of Law. It came on me suddenly, some of the pieces of the puzzle caroming around my head like marbles in a pinball machine began dropping into their slots. I was seeing it happen right before my eyes. Farrakhan was being *baited* and *set-up* by newspaper and TV media, whipped into a frenzy of anger by the deliberate goading lies and insinuations spread by Mishpucka propaganda machines.

I knew that if the Blacks let themselves be enraged to the point of being swept into demonstrations and physical confrontations with the Jews it would be a bloody slaughter. Farrakhan and his followers had no arsenals of machine guns or ammo. They were no match for Rabbi Kahane's JDL with their fire-power and their repositories of arms and munitions. Jackson was smart enough not to let them goad and lead him into doing something foolish. He apologized for saying "Hymie." But it didn't really make any difference, apologies weren't what the Jews were after. They had never intended to give Jackson their *so-called* Jewish vote or any *financial* aid in the first place. The real purpose for their vitriolic screaming was to make Jackson look like some kind of ogre...discredit him and fragment the new political power base he was awakening. No question, the Jews had cremated Jesse deep in a cesspool of their venomous, Anti-Semitic bullshit.

Obviously Pres. Reagan was going to be re-elected in November 1984. But regardless, Reagan, Mondale or Jackson, it wouldn't make any difference. The Due Process of Law would still remain nothing more than a memory. Property rights and personal possessions were nothing more than *passing fantasies* to be taken away by the wave of a Black Robe Mishpuckas hand. Faced with such a foreboding crisis the White people would begin to glean what Black people long ago had learned by heart. They understood Civil Rights Law as the last hope for survival as free men and women.

Slowly as Whites began to *comprehend,* a roaring tornado swept across the land, an infectious wind brought a horrifying realization. Their freedom was being buried, the ostrich act wouldn't do, as their heads popped from the sand a piercing light opened their eyes. The rich, the poor, the Intelligentsia, all discovered something they had never felt as being worthy of any *great consideration* before now, the *significance* of the Civil Rights Laws. There came *monumental* White acknowledgement, slightly humble with this discovery that their own existence, in fact their *own survival* was as *dependent* on Civil Rights Laws as was the Blacks. The sum total of mans progression toward freedom was made possible only by, Due Process of Law, without it governments are *obsolete,* and *free* enterprise dies.

During Reagan's second term the crushing of the peoples rights to Due Process of Law by the Black Robe Mishpucka will become the most explosive crisis ever to strike the *life-line* of the nation. Not since the dread issue of slavery set off the chaotic, bloody Civil War a hundred twenty four years ago had such evil depravity threatened to destroy America.

Access to the courts and Due Process of Law is not complex or mystifying, it means just one thing, simply, a trial under the law of the U.S. Constitution with a fair jury and an honest judge. Never at anytime should the Civil Rights Laws of America ever be remotely confused with the Mishpuckas mockery of justice, their *treasonous,* so-called Civil Liberties Union. American citizens Civil Rights and the poisonous Civil Liberties are two different things altogether.

I realized I had less chance of getting justice from Hintz than a snail trying to cross the Ventura Freeway during rush hour. He had *no jurisdiction* in the spurious Unlawful Detainer suit lawyer Stanley Cohen had filed against me but he was never going to let go of it. If I didn't file a suit in Superior Court it was going to be all over, my property would be gone, the futility of it all was just overwhelming. It was fifteen God damn years, I thought about it, that's a hundred and eighty months, seven hundred and eighty weeks, My God...five thousand four hundred and seventy four days of hellish *insane* Black Robe Mishpucka bullshit. They were never, ever going to let me in court with a fair jury. They'd done a good job of scaring hell out of DuPre and running him off, I'd heard nothing from him since. I had no source of legal advice, not even someone to discuss it with.

There wasn't a *single* lawyer in the U.S. with a license issued by the Bar Association that would stick his neck out for the likes of me for any amount. I was in a class, an *untouchable*. I felt the sting of a bitter hatred, all those phony *self-heralded* Sir Lancelots of the Bar parading their buffoon morals and ethics, if only they didn't mouth off about it all the time, and the worst diarrhea of all, the one about their *dedication* to the noble and great traditions of the high calling of the law. I'd never forget, at my Civil Service Hearing, the sinister rasping of Fish crying out his grotesque pretenses of "*devotion* to his high calling."

Without having to listen to their hypocritical deceit perhaps my utter disgust wouldn't have burned so intense against the miserable poltroons as I watched them wiggle and slither into their worm-like holes when I asked for legal representation. More than a month of toiling aggravation day and night, piece by piece, I put it together. Finally the lawsuit was filed in Superior Court, August 23, 1983, in Pro-per, Case No. 80986.

During my struggles with every word and sentence I continually asked myself why, *why* in hell do I bother with all this agony? I am only delaying the inevitable, that damnable Black Robe Mishpuckas barbarous, "Dismissed With Prejudice." In this perilous situation it would take a lot more than just hope, however, an embryo of a plan, a strategy had long been forming. From the very beginning my suits were based on Code Sections and Legal Precedents as cited in law books. This was the prescribed normal procedure to go into court and settle a dispute. But, if the courts were *normal* all this bullshit would never have started in the first place. Normal...the key word in a nut shell. Never, at no time had I ever been dealing with a *Normal Judiciary.* Well, this time the Black Robe Mishpucka was not going to be dealing with a Normal Lawsuit. The Black Robe Mishpuckas M.O. was rabid chaos. That was exactly what I intended to drop on them, chaos...*chaos* galore!

Mishpuckas revel in smashing weak and helpless victims, but I'd noticed something very significant. Their cruelty was steeped heavy in cowardice. Like a school yard bully, when the Mishpuckas caught an unexpected retaliatory smack in the mouth they'd always react in confusion, losing their control. Step by step, all the way I was going to smack them right in the mouth with such *paralyzing fear* of being *exposed* they would lose all restraint. I was sure what they would do when I struck back.

In their ungovernable rage a demonic fury would sweep aside all caution. With brutal contempt they'd break a thousand laws in their mad, satanic desperation to annihilate me. Their tyrannical actions would swath a wide trail, easy to trace. Their judicial chicanery, inch by inch would all be documented, the resulting evidence and proof being undeniable. I had to force the invisible, sinister Leader of the Black Robes out in the open. I had to know, *who* was this shadowy fanatic who's *unearthly* evil plotted to overpower our government, to imprison and manacle the people with monstrous chains of slavery.

Across the country it was happening, Mishna *chaos* was striking everywhere. Lashing out from the *Metropolis* to the *smallest towns* it was *crushing* Due Process of Law. The people were trying to fight back the only lawful way they knew how, hire an attorney and go to court, but this recourse had broken down to a pitiful hoax, a Danse Macabre. One of the Mishpuckas fetid trails I was following had led me north to Monterey County's Courthouse where I had rummaged through some very interesting records. Returning down Highway 101 I decided to take a cut off, Lompoc, a small town was about twenty miles west near the ocean, not far from the Vandenberg Air Base in Santa Barbara County. Eve Kimball lived there, the plucky little old lady was almost eighty now. She was still fighting with every breath left in her frail body to save her possessions, all the treasured things she had worked so hard for during her life.

Eve made coffee while I looked at her latest documents from the courts. Though no longer amazed at the rot in the courts, I read in disbelief. What this Mishpucka Judge Canter was doing to Eve was shameful, sickening. Gov. Jerry Brown in one of his last vengeful, morbid acts had appointed this anthropoid lawyer Zel Canter to the Superior Court Bench.

Time was short, I stayed only an hour, from Lompoc to Hwy 101 a narrow blacktop road wound through rolling hills. It was the time of year, deep green of spring's new grass spread a luxuriant blanket across the country. Peaceful grazing cattle dotted the hills as far as the eye could reach. My mind was torn from the beauty, Eve's quiet words would not fade, "Tomorrow I am going into the hospital for a cancer test, if they show a malignancy I will have to stay there." Her documents filled my thoughts, she had filed four separate lawsuits. In one case she had ten days to answer a Motion but Judge Canter Dismissed her in only five days.

Sec. 437c, Civil Code Procedure provides *Due Process* protection, it gives *ten days* to file an answer, it makes *no provision* for a judge to shorten time. It is backed by numerous Supreme Court Decisions. It was only one instance of Canter's evil Mishna chaos. Calling Eve's suits, "Frivolous," he Dismissed them all and imposed sanctions of five hundred dollars on her. In a direct violation of Supreme Court Decisions and Statutes Canter ordered her to pay thirteen thousand dollars in fees to the defendants lawyers. Eve's only recourse to Zel Canter's Mishna insanity was an even *more* frightening development

THERE'S A FISH IN THE COURTHOUSE   509

to contemplate. It was just a 'higher degree' of Mishna chaos. The next step was to the Appeal Court...Justice Hymie Blitzberg, alias Steven Stone and his two accomplices, Abbe and Gilbert.

Hell, before reading any of Eve's papers I easily predicted what Blitzberg would do. Upholding Canter's chaos Hymie malevolently retaliated further against Eve for *daring* to use the Appeal Process to defend herself against the Black Robe Mishpucka. Venomously labeling Eve's Appeal, "Frivolous," he imposed further sanctions of five hundred dollars for filing it, then ordered his vicious decision was "NOT TO BE PUBLISHED." The three 'Justices' had blasted U.S. Constitutional Due Process of Law into a rubble as ruthlessly as their brother terrorist Menachem Begin had dynamited the King David Hotel into steely shards of death while his innocent victims were still inside.

The Not To Be Published crap was the *same routine* Pregerson and all the rest of the Black Robe Mishpucka had used against me. Since then I had researched into it. It was one of the Mishpuckas most cunning and destructive weapons. When the evil Black Robe Mishpucka orders that one of their wildly chaotic rulings is Not To Be Published it's for a specific reason. It keeps the atrocity of their chicanery from being printed in Law Digests where the treachery of their misdeed would be exposed. The masked, nightmarish laws that they fabricate and impose wiping out existing Codes and Precedents cannot be challenged in courts of law or brought to light. The Black Robe Mishpuckas can destroy *any* lawsuit...big or little...insignificant citizens...or giant corporations, it doesn't matter, they *all* fall to the Mishna Chaos. All the Mishpucka has to do is put their black mark on their insidious works, "NOT TO BE PUBLISHED."

Each degree of the Appeal process dominated by the Mishpucka becomes more menacing, even Godzilla would be terrified. Snared in the *nightmare* of Mishna Chaos, Eve's last recourse in search of justice was an Appeal to State Supreme Court, to Moskovitz, alias Mosk, Kausinsky, alias Kaus, Grodinsky, alias Grodin, etc. etc. etc..

From that point on Eve would be facing the grinding, exhausting, everlasting mental and physical torture along with financial ruin that is inevitably brought about by the *'endless wait.'* After months, even years, whatever time lapse fits the Black Robe Mishpuckas purposes best the Supreme Court will eventually mail Eve a twenty two cent postcard. Unsigned, in small print, she'll be informed, "We Refuse To Hear Your Case." For Eve it would be all over, they would steal everything she had. Not even the stout courage of the little old lady could hold up. The frightful scourge of the Mishna's Chaos is more than mere flesh and blood can withstand.

Refusal of the U.S. and State Supreme Courts to hear a case and write and sign a Decision for all to read is a high treasonous crime. This portentous, Black Robe Mishpucka crime by Supreme Courts means but one thing. The Appellate Divisions of the Judicial System have become the High Court of the Land. The U.S. Judicial System, once proud, world renowned and respected for meticulous fairness is a pus-filled *scam*, a giant Black Robe Mishpucka racket, operating under the same precepts of the Black Hand Mafia. Yet, Mishpucka *Judicial crimes* menace much deeper than the Mafias gangsterism, per se, gambling, union pension fund fraud, loan sharking, extortion, narcotics and prostitution. The Mishpucka gangsterism portends a malevolence *far greater* than the Mafias theft of billions of dollars that are *countable*. How can you count the monetary loss of Judicial Due Process of Law?

How are *Rights* to be equated? Do they come in *units* like dollars so you can count them? Like the *Right* to breathe...the *Right* to walk down the street without fear...the *Right* to ambition and a desire to pursue success and happiness? Are *Rights* nothing more than little green paper units like dollars? Are units worth one dollar each or two dollars? How in the world do you add up the loss of *Rights*?

American Justice, its frail body created by the power of thought, fed only by a delicate spinal cord through which flows the vital gray matter nourishing Judicial Orderliness. Triggered by the Mishpuckas traitorous *Racial* Poliomyelitis Hypodermic piercing directly into its veins, the body of the American Justice System atrophies. A paralysis of extinction spreads as deadly injections of Mishna Chaos corrupts and consumes the gray matter.

Under fraudulent guise and touting themselves as "Appeal Court Specialists," Mishpucka attorneys strip 'desperate for justice' clients out of fortunes. Their *pitch* is what they call "Writing a Brief to the Supreme Court." The lawyers know from the start their client is a loser. All he will ever get for his money and prayers is a twenty two cent postcard saying, "We Refuse To Hear Your Case." On the other side of the lawsuit the Black Robe Mishpuckas are busy taking their massive cut, *millions* flowing into *billions,* like the Mishpucka Judges Jerome Berenson and Bonnie Martin extorted all the millions from Argo Oil Company.

When necessary in more complicated matters requiring urgency the Mishpucka for expedience sake will deign to 'split their cut' with lawyers on the other side. Judges *combine* and *compact* in conspiracy with the attorneys to defraud their clients, thus giant corporations are consumed. Like Ben Weingart and his billion dollar holdings, his Fed Mart Corp. he founded, hotels, construction and development companies and thousands of acres of choice undeveloped land ready for tracts of houses and shopping centers. The corporation's assets were devoured, *enigmatically* swallowed, poured into the secret glut of the Black Robe Mishpuckas untold multitudes of frauds.

Locked deep in mysterious Temples of Holy Juda, impenetrable dark fanatically guards the monstrous secrets of the Mishpuckas far flung International Financial Empire. The insatiable greed, hidden from sight in shadowy catacombs stirs violently, mixing explosively with maniacal hatreds and hubris screaming out for a *blood sacrifice* of their enemies, "This time we will not fail, Christ must be killed, forever."

I wasn't the only one who had become aware of the Black Robe Mishpuckas treasonous corruption. Leonard M. Friedman, a retired Associate Justice of the State Court of Appeal on his own knowledge and experience firmly concurred with my uncovering of Mishpucka Judicial gangsterism. With a blast he accused Hymie Blitzberg, aka Steven Stone, of being, "A disaster for the state's system of Justice and the Courts of Appeal of becoming a form which threatens long term injury to the state's body of Case Law." Friedman proceeded to *denounce* "The Appellate structure as a Judicial Tower of Babel."

Friedman had written and protested vociferously to California's State Bar about judicial corruption. But hell, he'd been an Appeal Court Judge himself, he should know that was useless, the Bar was an *integral* part of the Mishpuckas Organization.

His accusations and facts amazingly paralleled and backed what I'd already discovered. Friedman pinpointed it definitively when he declared, "Stare Decisis requires that all the lower courts adhere to Precedents established by State Supreme Court. The Calif. Supreme Court serves as the law-unifying consistency producing mechanism in the system. Article 6 & 12; CAL. Rules of Court 29(a)."

Startlingly the Justice had *indicted* the Black Robe Mishpuckas treason by using almost identically my own words. He accused, "The Appellate Divisions are out of control and in all but a tiny fraction of lawsuits the *Appellate Divisions* are in fact, Courts of last Resort." Friedman forgot to mention that the *tiny fraction* of lawsuits that the Supreme Court chose to hear were *choice suits* from which they took their own massive cut. With further revelation he explicitly described the Mishna, the Jew Law of Chaos, Corruption and Conspiracy. The former Justice declared, "Each years flood of *unreviewed* Appellate Decisions will deposit a new layer of discordant precedents, lawyers and trial judges shoveling through this detritus in search of clear cut Case Law will find only *Confusion, Conflict* and *Incoherence.*"

Justice Friedman was explicit in revealing the Mishna Chaos, and knowing what I did about the Mishpuckas I found it *impossible* to explain even in my own mind *why* he would do it. *Why* would a Jew Judge expose the Mishpucka, his own people? It was a new twist, the only answers I could come up with was supposition, preposition and an empty space in the puzzle. It was one of those missing pieces.

Everywhere it was the same thing, the Mishpuckas were on the move, *attack* and *destroy,* Americanism was being jerked out of the soil by the root.

A local Ventura businessman Ray Ellison, was doing his best to expose the corrupt mayor of the city, a Mishpucka lawyer, Dennis Orrock. As an attorney Orrock advised and encouraged a group of businessmen to invest money in a venture. Ellison was one of them. An inventor, Harold William Johnson, was perfecting the proto-type of an automated packaging machine. Orrock claimed it was a sure thing to be a huge success, a top money maker; the investors should hurry to get in on the ground floor because all the inventor needed was some money up-front to finish it. Orrock formed a corporation to promote and market the machine....the businessmen put up their money...the machine wouldn't work...the investors lost their money. To their chagrin they discovered that the inventor was a convicted con-man from Santa Barbara. He had bilked investors up there for half a million dollars with the same scam.

Then the roof caved in. To the grievous disgust and outrage of the businessmen they dug up evidence that Orrock had known about the phony inventors criminal record and scam all the time. In fact, he'd known long before he ever proposed forming the corporation to market the invention. Obviously the Mayor had conspired at great length to keep this knowledge from his clients who had put up the dough. Ellison having placed his faith in the lawyer was seething, not so much because of the money he'd lost, it was the principle of the damn thing, like having a mayor of the city who was an out and out slippery crook. Ellison got another stinging lesson, going to the City Council meetings trying to get those 'self-proclaimed' civic minded servants of the people to remove a crooked Mayor from office was like running full speed, head down into a spike studded stone wall.

I knew that Bradbury the D.A., wouldn't investigate the corrupt Mayor. Ellison became just another helpless, frustrated taxpayer but, there was one thing about him, he hadn't even started to fight yet. He had a huge truck and on its large bright aluminum sides Ellison swished dozens of cans of spray paint. In bursts of rainbow colors, purple, yellow, green, red and polka dot he spelled out his indignant message. He called the Mayor everything, everything that is, but an honest man. At the curb of busy Thompson Blvd, Ellison parked the wild spectacle in front of his office. It was a strategic vantage point, across the boulevard was a well strolled park with a traffic light on the corner, it controlled an approach to the freeway. People entering the on-ramp gawked in astonishment at Mayor Orrock's nightmare. Laughing and hooting they *spread the message* of the intellectual and moral spectacle to every city for miles. Mayor Orrock was horrified. It was an unbelievable, shocking development, he'd never dreamed of such a terrible thing happening.

Orrock knew Ellison was upset at being screwed, but the Mayor's Mishpucka mentality assured him that after the harsh stone-walling Ellison got from the City Council he would give up. Publicly Orrock was taking a hell of a beating from Ellison's charges. Not daring to let it go on, he offered to air the matter at a public forum. Ellison agreed and City Council appointed a committee of three volunteers. Appearing in the Star Free Press the names picked by the Council to conduct a *fair* hearing fanned a bad smell I had sniffed from the beginning. It would be a set-up, contrived, a carefully orchestrated white-wash, what else could it be? It was impossible to conceive the Mishpucka Mayor jeopardizing himself to exposure at any hearing if he didn't have it tightly wired up.

One of the three chosen was Ray Charles, it was years past but I'd never forgotten Charles. At that time he was an assistant to Al Palmer, manager of the Public Employees Assoc.. Al had arranged to get twenty five hundred dollars from the Employees Association for legal assistance at my Civil Service Hearing. When Charles had recommended Dean Pic'l as an attorney to defend me I didn't know there was a connection between the two. It was later on I'd learned that Ray and Pic'l had been partners in a Hollywood public relations operation that went bust, they were in hock to their eyeballs.

They split my defense money and after my hearing Pic'l wouldn't answer my desperate phone calls. Ray then lied to me about trying to get Pic'l on the phone and driving to Covina attempting to find him. Not changing his thieving ways Pic'l was convicted a few years later of defrauding and stealing from clients. Presently he is sitting in prison contemplating his belly button and disbarment until 1992.

Like Pic'l, Ray had never really changed his M.O., he had merely grown more crafty. Using his influence in the Employees Association to clever advantage, he had risen in status. Recognizing his unique talents, the Board of Supervisors appointed him to the Civil Service Commission. These were impressive credentials, making for a solid, imposing, *leading citizen-type*. But Ray had not arrived at his high, important status through a fidelity and compassion for insignificant, lowly members of the Employees Association.

Ron Harrington, attorney and former Ventura City Councilman, and close associate of Orrock, was also chosen. Another lawyer, Jay Johnson, husband of Judge Mindy Johnson, was the last member of the trio picked by City Council. Jay, the cuckold husband of Judge Mindy would do exactly what the Judge or D.A. Bradbury told him. The set-up stunk worse every second, checking around town through close sources I confirmed my suspicions, my smeller was right. The civic minded trio were bought and paid for, lock, stock and barrel, but, there was more to it than just whitewashing Orrock.

The trios orders were to seize every opportunity to make Ellison look like an idiot. Judas Gius would stir it up in the Star Free Press using his snide editorials, slanted articles and a campaign of phony Letters to the Editor. The letters would be artfully designed to make it seem most citizens disapproved of Ellison's efforts to harm their *great* Mayor.

Thinking about it all I figured it wouldn't be fair if Ellison wasn't aware of the three civic minded citizens and what he was up against with the Mayor's conspiracy. Meeting at Ellison's office I clued him in. He was shocked and particularly dismayed at Gius and the Star Free Press's part in the conspiracy but was determined it would not stop him from exposing the crooked Mayor.

Orrock's hearing began at eight p.m. in the old Courthouse, now called the new City Hall. Harrington acted in the capacity of a judge in a trial. Ellison produced a stunning witness, one Orrock and the trio never counted on dealing with. His story threw them completely off stride, Marvin Branch was a realtor at the Hope Ranch in Santa Barbara. Along with several wealthy businessmen he was defrauded of nearly half a million dollars by Harold W. Johnson, the con-man. Obtaining a judgement of over three hundred and twelve thousand dollars, Branch was trying to collect it. Learning the con-man was doing business with Orrock's law firm in Ventura, he mailed copies of Johnson's record to Orrock. Getting no response he made long distance phone calls to Orrock's office and explained the situation. To make sure they understood Branch even drove to Orrock's office and left copies of the documents.

This event had taken place two years *before* Ellison ever became involved with Mayor Orrock and lost his money. The realtor's clear cut testimony and evidence had Orrock squirming. He spewed out the craziest lies, denials and protests imaginable before the packed room and the rolling TV cameras. There was an embarrassed hush, everyone there recalled when Ellison first made his accusations to the Council. Mayor Orrock had *sworn* vigorously, "On my honor, my mother's honor, on a stack of bibles, for God's sake, on a stack of anything, so help me...I knew absolutely nothing of that Johnson's criminal record until *after* Ellison put up his money. Believe me, I was as totally surprised as everybody to learn about it."

Apprehensive, nerves tingling, the trio of *civic minded* citizens sat stone-faced, frozen, if Orrock hadn't been positive they'd been paid off and irrevocably geared for his whitewash he would have snatched his bulging briefcase in panic and fled full speed for International Airport.

My aisle seat was in the rear row. Mayor Orrock was bewailing his innocence, desperately he twisted and turned to evade the hound dogs of truth snapping his baggy pants. Unobtrusively a lady entered the room, hesitantly she moved along the back row pausing behind my seat, leaning over she asked, "Which one of the men up there is Mr. Ellison?" I pointed, she nodded and walked to the front of the room. With the touch on his arm Ellison turned, silently the woman handed him a small folded piece of paper. The eyes from the whole room glued on her as she swiftly walked toward the exit. Orrock's eyes bulged, hands grabbed the edge of the table so tight his fingers turned white. He couldn't stand the thought of more surprises, then he was struck with another horrifying possibility. Great Juda...maybe *his trio* couldn't stand another surprise either! Following a hunch I went to the parking lot, the woman was getting in a car, writing the license number on my palm I went back to the hearing room. While gone my choice aisle seat was taken, I leaned against the wall at the rear of the room. The Mayor was still squirming, trying to shore-up his sick act with bad alibi's. He carried on like a man who just could not stop talking even though he knew he should.

Thinking of Branch's testimony something rang odd, sticking in my mind it troubled me. I chewed some more on what he had said,

"Right after Johnson's arrest and hearings in Santa Barbara he left the area." Why had this caught my attention? It seemed a natural enough impulse to want to get away from that area. But he had not gone far, under orders Johnson traveled straight to a lawyers office in Ventura where he commenced his same old scam again. Branch had mentioned a name, Canter, only once had he said the name but my memory tugging hard on the rope started bells ringing loud and clear. My God, he was talking about Zel Canter, the judge! Now it was making sense, no longer was it puzzling why the con-man went directly to lawyer Orrock in Ventura.

There was a connection...there had to be...in a conspiracy there's always a connection of one kind or another, either people or events coupling an evil intent. The con-man was capable of pulling in a lot of money. He was being protected, used, that is where Canter fit in. I knew I would be making a trip soon.

The documents I found in Santa Barbara Court records couldn't have more clearly set out the diorama. It was simpler to follow than a Super Bowl game-plan laid out by coach Bill Walsh *after* already winning the game. All it took was a couple short passes here and a couple runs there. Amazed I analyzed the Mishpuckas game-plan. It was in 1972, six years *before* Ellison was ever involved, Zel Canter was the Deputy D.A. handling the prosecution of Harold Johnson, the con-man.

The diagram led me play by play. Canter had filed five counts of Penal Code Section 487.1 on Johnson, then he hauled him before a judge and made a Motion that, "In the interest of justice four counts should be Dismissed." Johnson then pled guilty to a single count of Sec. 487.1, Grand Theft. At that point in the game the con-man was officially guilty of having swindled and salted away more than half a million dollars but....

The Judge; suspended *pronouncement* of judgement for three years.

The Judge; released him with *no* jail time.

The Judge; ordered *no* restitution to be made to the victims.

The Judge; ordered that Johnson's cash bail was to be *exonerated* and returned to him.

The con waltzed out the door a *'free man'*...except for one little thing...Canter now had a *'steel vice,'* a squeeze on him. At any given moment in the next three years if he didn't perform like a monkey on a stick he could be jerked back in front of the Judge and carted off to state prison.

Canter a Dep. D.A. made about a thousand bucks a month, but soon after these events he sported a couple hundred grand. Quitting the District Attorney's office and at top dollar, Canter bought into a prestige law firm, simultaneously he became owner of an expensive home and a new *expansive* life style, he was on the move. Operating from his prestigious law firm and without ever appearing on a ballot Zel became a powerful Superior Court Judge.

For Canter's vicious *judicial crimes* against the people, (one being the helpless little old lady Eve Kimball) he is accountable to no one except Hymie Blitzberg who *rules* the tri-counties. I spent some time nosing around Santa Maria and Solvang in the north part of Santa Barbara County. In courtrooms attorneys on both sides of the fence discernibly hovered under shrouds of tension and apprehension. To ask them questions about anything but the most innocuous subjects brought on strange behavior, a sudden seizure of nerves and weird reactions. But around town I picked up pretty good info from less inhibited citizens. They related their hatred and genuine fear of the local judicial power.

Returning south on 101 I slipped off at the Gaviota rest area to hit a pay phone. I reached Marvin Branch, after clearing my reason for the call he decided we'd have a talk. The basketball player sized realtor invited me to come to his office in his home at Hope Ranch, he gave me directions. Leaving a narrow blacktop road I headed up a long white cement drive. It ended in a patio parking area behind the rambling ranch style house. Roaring ferociously, two huge dogs furiously surrounded the car. At Branch's appearance and command they quieted. He said, "We've had several burglaries recently but since I got the dogs they've stopped."

"I can easily understand why."

He smiled, "Come into my office." It was bright and comfortable, several hours of talk passed quickly. Branch had tried diligently to collect his large judgement against Johnson. He explained, "That's why I contacted Orrock in Ventura." Hesitating for a moment, like maybe he feared I'd never believe what he was about to say, he then slowly and methodically went on, "I found a valuable asset belonging to Johnson and wanted to file a lien on it." Again he paused, "You just might have trouble believing this, but my attorney said I should *not* file a lien, in fact he advised me strongly *against* it. He wouldn't give any reason and when I insisted he adamantly refused to do it for me."

I reassured Branch, "Not only do I *believe* what you are saying, I understand it very well. More times than I can possibly remember I have experienced that same incredible thing with lawyers. In your instance it is most likely he wasn't as much a crooked lawyer as he was a very frightened one."

Branch's eyes lit up, "That's exactly the feeling I got. You don't know how relieved I am to hear you affirm my own conclusions. I'd begun to think maybe I was getting paranoid."

"No, you aren't paranoid, you are on the right track."

The tip of his yellow pencil tapped nervously on his desk, "Well, if that's the case we evidently are agreeing that this opens the door to much deeper suspicions and cause for alarm."

"Yes I'm afraid so." I mentioned a few alarming things that had happened to me, it served to loosen his reticence some, he began to open up.

"For sometime now I've had a strange premonition, although I can't prove it I know I'm right. The burglaries here are part of this thing."

I had been thinking along the same lines. "It's very possible they think you have something here, documents or evidence that exposes them. But it doesn't make any sense that it would be the con-man's doings, he has no motive. It's ten years and you haven't been able to squeeze any money out of him yet. I'm sure that after all this time a crook like him isn't afraid of anything you could do to him now."

Branch was doing some profound brooding. I said, "If you think about it the people really hurting are Orrock and Canter. When the Mayor set up that phony hearing he didn't realize you'd show up. With the hornets nest Ellison is stirring, Canter without a doubt is scared to death he will be tied in with the whole rotten operation. If the D.A. was honest an investigation could send them to the pen."

Staring out a window at the ocean, Branch deliberated, mostly to himself he commented, "We are looking at very evil motives aren't we?"

"Are you thinking its somebody else?"

"No, that's it, there are no other possibilities I can think of." He weighed his words, "A mayor and a judge, very powerful people." A strained perplexity pinched his face, "I have to ask you something," he took a deep breath, "Do you think they'd send a hit man to kill me?" His concern was startling, I sensed that this wasn't just a loose hypothetical question, something that jagged nerves conjured up, he was not the type.

There was no need holding back the truth, "Sure they are, these people are capable of killing anyone who gets in their way."

Without hesitation Branch blurted it out, "They've already done it...they sent a man to kill me."

I was taken aback. "Are you absolutely certain of this?"

"Positive, there's no mistake. A man called me on the phone, he tried to lure me away from my house on a pretext real estate deal. I can't explain why I knew it was a ruse, I just knew, it was like I felt something evil coming right out of my telephone. Anyway, I agreed to meet him at a location in Santa Barbara but instead I called the police."

Good Lord, I prayed this wasn't some kind of wild tale leading to nothing. "Did they catch him?" I was holding my breath, his answer was even better than I had hoped for.

"Yes, the police grabbed him, they found evidence linking him to these people. In his pocket was a pay-off check, he even admitted he was sent." I could hardly believe my ears, this was a fantastic break. It could start a chain reaction, break things wide open. It struck me, the full impact of what he had said, the hit man was from another state. That meant there were phone calls, messages, contacts made across state lines in a 'Conspiracy to Kill.' A killer had agreed to a contract, received payment and crossed state lines to California for the purpose of committing murder.

It was heavy Federal Civil Rights violations, the FBI could hardly get out of making a full scale investigation. Eagerly I asked Branch, "What stage is it in now, is the Santa Barbara D.A. investigating? Is he going to take it to the Grand Jury, have the Feds been notified?"

He was a bit bewildered, "I'm not sure, I think the police are still holding him, but so far as I know they haven't done anything more." He shook his head, "I haven't seen or heard from them since." The words were a sledgehammer to the pit of my stomach, it was the old sinking sensation. In the excitement of this extraordinary news I had screwed up. Damn, what's wrong with me, hadn't I learned anything yet? The Mishpucka was never going to let an investigation of this get off the ground. No news reporter or editor would ever print this story. Out at my car we shook hands, Branch's dogs stood immobile, down in the mouth, it was strange, it was like they knew their job was useless, just a lot of noise.

Slowing, I came up to the red signal. For some reason my gaze was compelled upward to the mountains just ahead. Huge and close they seemed to be irresistibly closing in, pressing Santa Barbara into the sea. Up there at the top was Pres. Reagan's Ranch. From those regal heights Ronald Reagan and his guests, William P. Clark and Robert Lagomarsino, two of his most trusted political buddies stared down upon the whole scape. Clark was Reagan's National Security Director, his strings were pulled by Mishpuckas Judge Berenson and Nordman from Oxnard. Security Director Clark knew that race riots were being *deliberately* antagonized and fueled by the Mishpuckas across the land. Preparing for his *own* personal and family's safety the *maniac* mounted the murderous fifty caliber machine gun in his house. Cong. Lagomarsino is controlled by his politically powerful, wealthy father, Emillo 'Red' Lagomarsino.

Fifteen years ago, while Governor, Reagan had been notified of what was going on. He'd received my registered letter *detailing* the corruption being committed by Judge Berenson, Nordman and 'Red' Lagomarsino. But in covering-up for his 'two buddies' and all their criminal associates Reagan had *refused* to take action to uphold his sworn duty and obligation to the people. Lagomarsino at that time a State Senator, *sabotaged* my evidence of corruption to Reagan in behalf of the Mafia, and Clark, a judge appointed by Gov. Reagan, *manipulated* Reagan to cover-up for the Mishpucka.

Gov. Reagan sent me his answer in a letter, "I am sorry, there is *nothing* I can do, but I sincerely hope you can finally get an attorney to help you." Reagan had *desperately* wanted the massive, unlimited financial and political backing that *both* the Mafia and Mishpucka could provide for his future plans to become President. That's when the Black Hand Mafia and the Black Robe Mishpucka had seen the value and tremendous safe guards of combining forces, they'd both have an *inside* track, the confidential ear of the most powerful man in the world, President Ronald Reagan of the United States.

It was later when I tried to get a beer license for my restaurant that Cong. Lagomarsino ordered the ABC agent in Santa Barbara to deny my application. Then I filed a Federal suit. The congressman was furious. He got George Duekmejian, State Attorney General to assign an *entire corps* of lawyers and investigators to my case. They were shipped all the way from Sacramento to L.A. just to *make sure* I didn't get a lousy beer license.

They did a good job. I recalled how the Federal Judge, *'learned'* Manny Real was primed so strong he Dismissed my case before my lawyer Powell could get his first name out of his mouth. Also, how cocky and insolent the ABC agent was when the Intelligence agent from IRS asked him, "What the hell is going on?" The ABC agent's attitude was now obvious, with forces like Cong. Lagomarsino and top Mafia, 'Red' Lagomarsino protecting him he could easily afford to flaunt his arrogance.

Horns honked behind me, the light was green, I slid into heavy south bound traffic on 101. One last quick look to my left, my eyes swept across ridges and clefts to the top of the mountain where 'his' ranch was. Mean looking thunderous clouds, gray and black scudded sullenly along the peaks like sinister, sleepless out-riders on patrol. They glowered down at me, it was ominous.

In Ventura it was *happening,* just like I'd told Ellison before the Mayor's hearing ever started. The three *civic minded* citizens avidly were earning their pay-off. In their, 'report' to the City Council the trio painted Orrock lily white, and scourged Ellison for having made a mountain out of a 'little old molehill.' Never failing his part, Judas Gius engraved Ellison's epigraph using the *cutting tools* of his trade, malicious editorials, misleading articles and those oh-so-cute, deadly Letters to the Editor.

There was nowhere left to go. Ellison was now an *untouchable,* with no standing, left to feebly pound on the cold stone wall. For the Mishpucka it had been a precarious moment with Ellison hurling his corruption charges against Mayor Orrock, their top agent planted in Ventura's government. The dangers presented by the possibility of a run-away investigation of Orrock's flagitious criminality had posed a serious threat. It could *easily* have *wised* the people up to what was really going on. All of their intricate scams they are normally able to ram through so easy with *power-play* conspiracies in redevelopments, zoning, bond issues, etc. etc., had all been on hang-fire.

But the *committee of three,* those fine, Civic minded citizens, so very carefully hand-picked by the City Council were proof of the old axiom, "I am going to get me the finest judge that *money* can buy." Harrington, Johnson and Charles had put the wily Mishpucka Mayor back in business, and with that sweet-money jingling in their pockets their conscience bothered them not.

Mayor Orrock was back on top, riding a tall horse. At the ritzy Harbor Town Marina Resort Hotel he delivered a momentous State of the City Address to a huge audience. This affair of great prestige was the Mishpuckas *Greater* Ventura Chamber of Commerce annual membership banquet. On the Star Free Press front page, Judas Gius dramatized Orrock's speech. His glorious Mayoral accomplishments overflowed clear to the fifth page. Calling the prior months, "A year of prosperity and achievement," Orrock talked of "Projects he hoped to achieve the coming year." The Mayor *specifically* mentioned the, "development of the eighty acre Montalvo Mound," owned by Ben Nordman and Judge Berenson. The acres are on Victoria just south of the new Government Center which also belongs to Nordman and Berenson 'via' their Public Facilities Corporation. The Mayor was specific, "Nordman's Bank of A. Levy's plans are to construct their new headquarters complex on an eight acre section of the Mound." Exulting, the Mayor declared, "It will be another major step in our *establishing* the area around the Government Center as the *Financial Center* of Ventura County." Levy's new headquarters were estimated at seventy million dollars. Its site would comprise only one tenth of the Mound's area. On the assumption of their estimate the eighty acres was valued at seven hundred million to a billion dollars.

Paying only a couple million originally for the Mound, Berenson and Nordman's conspiratorial use of the fraudulent Public Facilities Corporation in building their Government Center had increased its value a thousand fold. But, the really incredibly clever part was the insidious masterful way in which they had *manipulated* and *tricked* taxpayers into paying for the whole thing.

Deviously Orrock paddled amid precarious rapids of his, "Great Year of prosperity and achievement." The Mayor boasted, "Millions of dollars of new industrial and commercial construction are adding dynamic revenues to our city coffers," however, Orrock neglected to *mention* one thing. A high percent of the speculatory buildings stood empty and under the threats of foreclosure and bankruptcy, but the Mishpuckas had their answer for that, "Sell them to the taxpayers, those stupid people don't know the difference anyway."

At 4651 Telephone Rd. stands a large cement and glass industrial commercial structure in the heart of the City Council's illusory and unneeded newly zoned area. It was vacant over a year, in fact, ever since it was built. The building was constructed by Mishpucka scam artists, a faction setting themselves up as the, "Ventura Group Seven Associates." Installing a huge sign in front they fallaciously dubbed their scam the, "Ventura Research Center Building." Just a shell the structure cost two point four million dollars. Saul Kay, a Mishpucka *front-man* for the Group Seven Associates arranged a phony *inflated* appraisal of five million dollars. Discounting the appraisal a lousy two hundred thousand dollars, Saul then gave the taxpayers a *'good deal,'* selling it to them for only four point eight million dollars.

The Mishpuckas had made a fast two point four million dollars, double their money. However, only a shell, it would cost taxpayers another two million to finish, and God knows whose pocket those millions would end up in. Overall the scam cost the taxpayers more than six point eight million dollars to move a few small departments into the new building a few miles from where the employees could have been housed in the existing Government Center.

Slyly, County Administrator Richard Wittenberg and City Mayor Orrock greased their fraud machinery. In the Star Free Press one of Wittenberg's stooge's smooth-coated the scam. His voice whispering confidingly to the taxpayers he stated, "Economically this just makes sense, the County is getting a *'good deal'* in paying only four point eight million for a building with an *appraisal* of five million." Later another Wittenberg flunky made statements in Gius' paper conning the people, "We just happened to stumble onto this deal, we saw it was an *opportunity* to make a good buy." Saul Kay added his two bits worth in the Star Free Press, with muted sarcasm he congratulated the taxpayers for their good fortune, he told them "It's a real *'good deal,'* the building is equipped with a beautiful *atrium* in the center." I wasn't sure about atrium, the dictionary called it, A cavity, sac or any opening affording bacterial infection, a court or a hall, and also a cemetery. With little ado and even less discussion the supervisors passed this *'good deal'* through *before* the taxpayers even knew what was happening. Smooth and adroit, P. Pedroff, a Mishpucka *overseer* of the County Budget and Administrative Services manipulated the finances for the purchase. The whole deal between buyer and seller took less than two weeks. Yes, the lily white Mayor Orrock was back in business.

From the car license jotted on my palm I'd traced the source of the mysterious note delivered to Ellison the night of the hearing. A young woman had been watching with an intense interest to Mayor Orrock on the local TV station programed for the hearing. She was appalled at the clumsy transparency of Dennis Orrock's *arrogant* lies with which he was attempting to cover his corruption. It was as if he didn't give a damn whether anybody believed him or not. Switching her shocked gaze to the smug faces of the three *civic minded* citizens she knew it was true, Harrington and the other two were bribed to whitewash the Mayor. Revulsion swept over her. As treacherous as the Mayor's thievery was, even *more* appalling was the committee's traitorous sell-out of the people. Harrington *himself* had told her of the bribery during a dinner date. Affable and enjoying her company after several drinks the lawyer couldn't contain his self-importance. This was *'big-time'* and he was an *insider,* he boasted, "Ellison hasn't a ghost of a chance in the hearing, he is way out of his class. Don't think for one minute a *sharp* operator like Mayor Orrock would risk his precious body in the open like that if he didn't have things under control. Hell, the committee has already been *paid off.*" Harrington took delight at the incredulous look on her face. He chuckled, "It's the truth, this thing is in the bag, Ellison is just spinning his wheels. There's no way he's going to win."

She punched the TV off, what the lady had in mind took strength of character. It could be horribly embarrassing, even dangerous, but she knew it must be done, right now, tonight. She knew it would be plain foolish prancing into the hearing in full view of Harrington. A girlfriend offered to deliver the message, Harrington wouldn't know her. The friend felt a little weak, her legs trembled as she walked to the front. TV crews focused upon the lady approaching Ellison, she handed him the small piece of paper. There was no faltering as she hurried from the room. But what was their next move...who could Ellison or her report their knowledge and evidence of this criminal bribery and abject corruption to?

The question loomed more grotesque each moment. The District Atty., Michael Bradbury, a tool of *both* the Mishpucka and Mafia would *never* listen to them. The Grand Jury ruled by the Black Robe Mishpucka would riptide them under with betrayal. The poor lady would be in danger, lose her job, and be crucified by Judas Gius in his Star Free Press. They'd make her look and feel like something much less than human. Conscientiously she had dutifully reported a serious crime to the proper authorities, what more could she do?

Orrock was deep in *another* sinister Mishpucka plot. He and law partner Randy Siple represented Jaime Font, owner of a waterfront restaurant and bar in Santa Barbara and the Scotch and Sirloin Bar fronting on Ventura Harbor. The six acre parcel was also occupied by a boat yard and sportfishing dock, extremely valuable real estate. Flying his helicopter Jaime Font commuted between the businesses. On Sept. 4, 1983 the aircraft mysteriously crashed into the ocean off the Rincon area and Font was killed. The autopsy, according to the Ventura Coroner's Office disclosed no trace of drugs or alcohol. A National Transportation Safety Board official said he could find no evidence of mechanical failure. Font, forty two, was a trained pilot of helicopters in the Army and flew in Vietnam.

The NTSB vaguely speculated that, "Font had possibly suffered spatial disorientation which could have led to improper handling of the helicopter." However, *immediately* upon his death Orrock came forth with a will, supposedly Font had had him and Siple draw it up and he'd signed it in their office. According to its date the signing took place on February 2, 1983 a few months before the fatal crash. Two men James A. Johnston and Wayne Troxell signed the will and stated they had witnessed Font sign it. It was a *very odd* will, Font had *cut off* his daughter and other heirs making Siple and Johnston the all-powerful Executors of his estate.

Contested strongly by the daughter, the will was the subject of a hearing in front of Judge Larry Storch. Three nationally recognized handwriting experts, John J. Harris, 523 W. Sixth St., L.A., Lawrence Moute, Supervising Investigator for the Questioned Document Unit of the L.A. District Attorney's Bureau of Investigation, and James Fraser, La Habra, testified the signature on the will was *not* Jaime Font's. Ventura D. A., Michael Bradbury investigated the case, and after a short period without taking it to the Grand Jury, Bradbury *killed* the investigation, he announced in the Star Free Press that, "There was *insufficient evidence* to prosecute."

Mishpucka Judge Larry Storch again took over, in the probate proceedings he ordered that two men, Larry Stone and James Hardy would take title to the property in Santa Barbara. No appraisal was made and the sale price was ridiculously low, no down payment was required and the monthly payments Storch approved did not even cover the interest. Storch called this, "A *good deal,* and that to safe guard the estate it was all above board, an *arms length* transaction."

Font's prime six acres viewing Ventura Harbor entrance and the Channel Islands was worth well over five million. With no appraisal, Storch ordered title transferred to a mysterious front man who was darkly financed by Berenson and Nordman's Bank of A. Levy. Same as Santa Barbara, the Ventura Harbor property was disposed of at a ridiculous low price. Another of Judge Storch's *"good deals* at arms length." The Port District Commission who controlled Font's lease contract agreed unanimously to the duplicitous orders of Storch's transaction. But then of course, they'd all been appointed by Mayor Orrock. With a law implemented by the Mayor himself he could fire them with a flick of his finger if they didn't perform.

Mayor Orrock's top barracuda among these self-exalting political fish was Commissioner William Crew. So valuable an operator was Bill Crew that Orrock put up fifty thousand to have him elected to the Ventura City Council, seated there he'd be of even *greater* value to Orrock. The fifty grand went to a top official of a mobile home association controlling a block of votes that could muscle in anyone he wanted. Orrock replaced Bill Crew on the Port Commission by appointing Richard Hambleton, another Orrock toady. Checking at the County Clerk's office I found that only a *small* part of the Font Estate records were filed. Probate Court decisions by Judge Storch for the last two years were missing. According to the clerks, "They were *locked up* by the judge."

Despite being unable to see the estate's file I picked up another sinister trail that lead deep into dark tunnels of the two evil Crime Families power structure *within* the courthouse. James A. Johnston claiming to be a witness to Font signing his will in Orrock's office, was the husband of Catherine E. Johnston, Treasurer, Tax Collector and Public Administrator of Ventura. She held this position through *powerful connections* with the Lagomarsinos.

CHAPTER 41

It was an *implacable monotony* of Mishpucka and Mafia treachery and corruption, in cadence, *everywhere* it was the same. All the cities were hooked in together like a *huge wheel.* The spokes led directly to the *hub,* to the Black Robe Mishpuckas at Government Center. Across the Santa Clara river in Oxnard, a Mishpucka Councilwoman Dorothy Maronowsky, aka Maron, a counter part of Mayor Orrock was busier than hell *setting up* her Mishpucka scams. She had a big one going, the *biggest* one ever in Oxnard. A redevelopment scheme, nearly two hundred million bucks worth. Always the Mishpucka uses grandiose, hoodwinking titles. Maron called her scam "The Plaza de las Palmas."

Her redevelopment scheme would *wipe out* more than eighty two buildings, taking seven whole city blocks of the downtown area. The underlying and motivating catalyst of the entire intrigue was a new bank Maron and her husband were forming. A towering black glass building would anchor the *'commercial structures'* and Maron's bank would dominate the *'financial structure'* of the Plaza de las Palmas' scene. The City Council is the Supreme Redevelopment Authority, when dealing in redevelopment they merely *adjourn* as the Council and quickly *re-convene* as the Redevelopment Agency, that's *'hard'* to beat. The Planning Commission...Redevelopment Commission and Zoning Commission, etc. etc., all are handpicked and appointed by the Council, that makes it *'impossible'* to beat. Maron was positive, nothing could stop her Redevelopment.

There were fifty to sixty property owners, most of them old time residents of Mexican descent, they'd be easy marks. Maron's dictum was scornful, "They'll take *whatever* the Agency *gives* them or else." Anyone opposing the Plaza or bank would be crushed, obliterated as mercilessly as the giant caterpillars she was sending would bulldoze away their buildings.

But for the Mishpuckas there continually lurks those rebellious fundamental *units*, 'people and nature,' incomprehensibly rising up against their mentality. Roy Lockwood, veteran foe and caustic critic of the Oxnard Council's thievery joined with property owners in a group called Citizens for Oxnard. Roy wasn't just an irresponsible gadfly pestering the good councilmen as the Mishpucka and media tagged him. He was a retired Senior Fire Chief of the Aero Space Defense Command at Oxnard Air Force Base. Roy, born in Oxnard in 1921, graduated from Oxnard High School. From 1942 to 1946 he served with the U.S. Army in the English and European Theater of Operations. Roy's insight into *rampant* civic corruption and his deep seated hatred for the political rot simply would not allow him to sit idly by watching it destroy the country. It wasn't like WW11, in this war he had only a few weapons to fight with, unfortunately none of them were money or political clout. In that respect Roy was only an ordinary, every day citizen.

He'd been fighting the crooks hand to hand, eye to eye in close combat, experience from battling their *vicious power* was learned the bitter hard way. First the Citizens for Oxnard filed a lawsuit against Councilwoman Maron and the city, they then attacked the Council's corruption strategically from several other directions. Maron had set up a new city tax and rammed its passage through the Council even though the city had not conducted an audit of their finances in over three years.

At Council meetings Roy asked questions and demanded answers, "How in the world can the Council possibly justify *new* tax when you don't even know how much money you have...and *why* do you refuse to conduct an audit and give the information to the taxpayers?" Roy hadn't yet got a real good handle on Mishpucka thinking, but Maron was about to clue him in. The City Council was discussing a three hundred thousand dollar HUD loan. Federal strings attached and other inherent hazards of the loan made it a real bad deal. Financial catastrophes and lawsuits happening in other cities involved in these grants made it clear that Oxnard would lose money before it was all over. Four Council members turned thumbs down but Maron's greed couldn't stand the thought of all that easy money just sitting there ready for them to snatch. She yowled, "For God sake *grab it,* it's a pot of gold."

The Citizens for Oxnard used every weapon possible to muster. They passed petitions for a recall, they soon had more than enough signatures to put it on the ballot. Suddenly the City Council found themselves on the defensive, but the Mishpucka using full control over the press, their powerful influence forced it into a drawn out bitter struggle. Then a hard blow befell the people, Judge William Peck 'Dismissed' their lawsuit, it came as no surprise. The Citizens had known from experience this was how the Black Robe Mishpucka would try to finish them. Not giving up they filed an appeal of the dismissal with the Appellate Court.

Presiding Justice Blitzberg merely whipped up a little Mishna, the Jew Law of Chaos, Corruption and Conspiracy and Dismissed their appeal. To bury the entire matter Blitzberg decreed his treasonous Mishna judicial action was "NOT TO BE PUBLISHED." Yes indeed, the Black Robe Mishpucka had the evil power to slaughter peoples rights to DUE PROCESS OF LAW and they'd *never* cease doing it. Even so they hadn't yet *succeeded* in slaughtering their soul. Fighting with all their might the Citizens had halted the *conspiracy* to defraud them of their property, putting the heat on they had killed Maron's redevelopment and bank scam. The Mishpuckas were stunned, their mortifying defeat by the people had finally sunk in.

This was an unbelievable repulse of their power scheme. A shaft of foreboding split their mind, always the Mishpuckas had suffered from a terrible panic when the people rose against them. They were maddened, swarming with fierce hatred the Mishpucka rage swiftly turned maniacal. Fuming with deadly curses Maron conjured up the wrath of the Black Robe Mishpucka to destroy these insolent people with a blood thirsty lesson, a condemnation so chilling they'd never again dare try anything so bold. She swore, "The people responsible for this will be *punished* relentlessly." Initiating her vengeance threat Maron filed a *vicious* harassment suit for five million dollars against Lockwood and the Citizens for Oxnard. Her irrational and meritless charges claimed the property owners "Maliciously prosecuted her in that they had fought to *'protect'* their land from her redevelopment and her bank."

A hearing was set, William Peck was the judge. I wanted to catch the action first hand since Peck also had my case. It had been only a few days prior that he'd ordered me to amend my lawsuit. Sitting near Lockwood, watching the proceedings, I was fascinated by Peck's judicial contortions. The word *atrocious* simply didn't do him justice. Comedian Joey Cappo's hilarious *'Idiot Judge'* act at old Ace Cane's in Hollywood during the war was never as funny as Peck's routine. Remembering how we rolled in the aisles at Joey's inane jokes and mime I nearly burst out laughing. I caught myself in time, this was no joke, Peck was dead serious, he was out to *destroy* these people.

The attorney for Lockwood and the Citizens made a 'Motion To Dismiss' Maron's lawsuit for 'Lack Of Cause.' Peck had no intention of dismissing the lawsuit regardless of its malevolent meritlessness, but, he was having a serious problem prompting Maron's lawyer to say the right thing. Aggravated beyond endurance Peck's bald pate glistened with sweat, his incessant drone was bullying. Pushing the attorney to the brink Peck did his utmost to impel him to come up with something...anything remotely resembling a "Cause Of Action." Just any old thing would keep Maron's suit alive. Frustrated out of his skin, now almost begging, Peck continued harassing the hapless attorney. "Now...once again counselor...I am asking you...give me a 'Cause Of Action,' speak up...just one cause," Peck wheezed, *"Give me* just one cause, I need *something* to go on...*anything!"* Hunching forward he glowered at the lawyer, any second now he was going to start cursing the poor guy.

Concentrating fiercely with his papers Maron's lawyer searched desperately for that *'non-existent'* Cause Of Action. Slowly turning the pages one after another, solemnly wagging his head from side to side he could not answer. The Citizens lawyer addressed the court. His Motion To Dismiss Maron's suit was strong, solidly backed up by law. Any *'honest judge'* would have dismissed Maron's case and headed for the shower hours ago. Judge Peck's enraged eyes jumped from Maron's tongue-tied lawyer, shifting wildly his venomous glare transfixed me. I knew the sickness, having witnessed the Black Robe Mishpuckas *'mental'* incapacity before, their inability to cope when confronted head on with solid facts and law. Then as though he was not aware that the Citizens lawyer was even talking, Peck broke in vacuously, "I have absolutely *no use* for people who maliciously file lawsuits." Surprised, nonplussed, the attorney stammered, "Are you referring to me?"

Like in a stupor Peck said, "No." Mystified the lawyer looked at Roy and Marie White in the front row. Marie was a defendant in the lawsuit and founder of a Sacramento group, Citizen Advocates.

She'd been helping Oxnard property owners in their bitter struggle against Redevelopment. With his finger pointed at Roy and Marie the attorney asked, "Then if its not me you are referring to, is it my clients sitting there?"

Peck answered, "No, I do not mean them." Only three of us were in the front row, I was sitting between Roy and Marie. With Judge Peck's red, anger-bloated visage glaring at me there was damn little doubt left in my mind who he was referring to. In his weird mental derangement the Black Robe Mishpucka was blaming me for what was happening to him, his fierce stare locked on me. Raging hatred grated in Peck's voice, "I am referring to 'people' who file malicious *pro-per suits* against legal forclosures and 'muck up' the courts with their filings," his voice trailed to a mumble.

Tension gripped the room, the air was leaden with Black Robe Mishpucka rancor. In some way Peck returned himself back to the case on hand. He had forsaken the idea that Maron's lawyer could ever find a Cause of Action against the Citizens. His surliness easy to detect, Peck said, "I have decided to take the Motion To Dismiss under submission in my chambers."

My purpose in coming to the hearing was to see the Black Robe Mishpucka perform first hand, I was seeing it! Several days later, all by himself in his chambers the judge dreamed up a Cause Of Action *'somewhere'* in Maron's complaint. With this amazing discovery he then 'Denied' the Citizens Motion To Dismiss Maron's malignant, meritless lawsuit. Maron had called the shot, the Mishpuckas would wreck *'full vengeance'* upon the Citizens. There's an old saying, "Out of all the bad there always comes a little good." I had to believe this, Peck's weird outburst had given him away, it told me something of utmost importance. My Pro-Per lawsuit was perfect, it was gouging painfully into their depravity.

If it wasn't hurting them Peck would be sneering at me instead of raving madly. It was his job to cover-up Cohen's and Hintzlestein's insane criminal acts to conceal their judicial corruption. No wonder the Mishpucka had such hatred for citizens who, "Mucked them up with their Pro-Per lawsuits." Attorneys owing their lives to the bar association would never have put them in such a terrible position as this. I knew that Peck ordering me to 'amend' my complaint was a Mishna trick. If I started chopping my suit up with amendments I'd be admitting there was something wrong with it. That would spring the door wide open for their Mishna chaos to start. It would drag on forever, finally ending up with my lawsuit ripped and torn beyond all possible recognition or repair.

At my next hearing Peck did not show up, another Black Robe Mishpucka, Joe Hadden was there. It was a *set-up*, they were putting on their Mutt and Jeff routine. Hadden was being the nice guy, he'd make it more palatable, I'd easily swallow whatever it was they had trumped up. Hadden was smiling at me, like maybe he was a friend. Strange but as always in their prearranged 'perfidious episodes' the courtroom was empty, they didn't like any witnesses. Widening his brotherly smile Hadden commented pleasantly, "Well, I see you did not amend your complaint."

I stood there waiting while he fumbled with papers. Looking up he cajoled, "Perhaps you didn't have enough time, would you like an extension?" I didn't answer. Almost undetectable his smile thinned. "Well, I think you should amend it, would you like two more weeks?" Slowly and only once, I shook my head no. The brotherliness died in a flash of anger, the act was over, he became taunting, "Do you want more than two weeks? What would you do if I gave you four weeks, would you amend it, what is it you want?"

I told him what I wanted..."I want a jury of twelve people so I can go to court and win my case."

That broke the camel's back, Hadden flipped his lid worse than Peck had. Clenched fists struck the bench, he catapulted half out of his chair screaming..."You ain't *never* going to get in court, do you hear me...*never*...there's no way *you* are ever going to get to trial." The guy was coming unglued, Jesus! I had seriously underestimated how desparate they were for me to amend my complaint. He yelled, "CASE DISMISSED." As I left he was still shouting, "DISMISSED."

I knew they would do it, they'd had no choice, like Hadden said, they could *never* allow me to go to trial. Alright, the Mishpucka had Dismissed me, but one thing was impossible for them to change, my case, it was still the original lawsuit just like I had filed it. One day they would be forced to face it, it and all the others right from the beginning. I got myself the hell out of the government center.

A few days later I received a notice from the court, a copy of an "Order of Dismissal With Prejudice." Odd, it was signed by Peck not Hadden, I wondered about that. At the bottom of the page a rubber stamp had imprinted a typical Mishpucka harassment, it said, "You owe costs in the amount of," then hand written in was, "$433.00 to the defendants." In his order the only defendants Peck had dismissed were those being represented by Stanley Cohen. During the last five months while Peck had stalled off with Cohen's Demurrer crap the

other defendants had failed to file an answer, they were in Default. The clock said eleven a.m. when I walked in the clerks office on Tues. Jan. 24, 1984. Properly typed, dated and signed by me, I laid the 'Request To Enter Default,' on the counter. The clerk looked at it. I waited for the reaction I was certain would come next. The lady stiffened, grasping the papers she turned and headed for the small office a dozen steps behind her and disappeared. My eyes following remained riveted on the door. A lady, actually just her head, came visible around the corner, peering out, eye-balling me balefully she ducked back. The clerk returned, at a row of file cabinets she jerked out drawers and riffled through manila folders without removing or reading them. Dropping all pretense she became openly hostile, "I can't file your Default," then muttered something about maybe one defendant was not served correctly.
"Oh no, he was served correctly."
"I said I *won't* file it."
"Well file the rest of them."
Testily she shot back, "No, I am *not* going to file any of them."
An argument would get me nowhere. I said, "Is it permissible for me to ask your name?" From a drawer she grabbed a rubber stamp, banging it on a scrap of paper she shoved it at me. I read her name, plainly Janice Rhoades held people such as me as inferior, a subject of derision and contempt, she had dismissed me from her presence. Walking parallel to the long counter, I made a right around a corner out of her sight. In the hallway I made another right, moving swiftly about forty feet there was another door, through it I could see back into the room.

Janice hadn't moved, she stared at the spot where I disappeared from sight. Satisfied I was gone she went to her desk and picked up a phone, dialing she cupped her hands holding it close to her mouth. Her message was secretive, intended for the ears of one person only. Flicking her eyes to the sides to make sure nobody overheard she made a report.

The long process of appealing Peck's Dismissal required I file a notice of my *'Intention To Appeal,'* it meant going to the courthouse. I was in a small room, only four paces from where I'd encountered Rhoades yesterday. While the Appeal Clerk was preparing the forms and filing fee receipt, my gaze combed the area behind the counter where Janice held forth. She was not there. Another girl, obviously with less experience waited on the people at the counter. Rhoades' continued absence seemed a mite strange. She was gone too long for a coffee break and it was too early for lunch.

Dark suspicion dogged me, I knew county employees were prone to taking an extra day off on Monday or Friday giving them a three day holiday. But this was Wednesday, they seldom used up a special day off in the middle of the week unless they became sick or had an urgent errand to run. The full impact struck suddenly, I remembered Rhoades' *furtive* phone call yesterday when she thought I had left, now her tell-tale absence. Sure enough, she had a damned important errand today, I would stake my life on it, not only was Janice gone so was my lawsuit. The Appeal Clerk got my attention, "Here's your receipt," I read the amount and date, Wed. Jan. 25, 1984. Slipping it in my pocket I went over to the young clerk at Rhoades counter and asked for my case file. Searching the shelf where it belonged a perplexed look came over her face. Returning she said sheepishly, "I can't seem to find it."

I suggested, "Maybe Janice Rhoades can tell you where it is, she had the file yesterday."

"Janice isn't here today." Dealing with the Black Robe Mishpucka it surely would be a hell of an advantage if I remained in a constant alert of full blown paranoia. I calmed down, I wanted to pinpoint my suspicions with fact and certainty.

"Would you mind checking Rhoades' desk, I'd like very much to see the file this morning if it's at all possible. I only need to see it a moment."

Searching diligently she was unable to unearth my file in Rhoades desk. She was apologetic, "Gee, I'm awful sorry about this, it is very unusual. I guess you will have to wait and ask Janice when she gets back."

"Thanks, you were very helpful." She'd been far more help then she realized. I wasn't mistaken, Rhoades was gone, so was my file. I was sure I knew where both were. A few phone calls to Oxnard, then a long distance call to Newport Beach. With some brain-picking double talk and pretexts I verified what my wild-eyed paranoia was screaming. Rhoades and my case file were at lawyer Stanley Cohen's office in Oxnard. Madly she and Cohen's secretary duplicated and sorted everything to *make* copies of a 'Demurrer' for the defendants who were in Default.

Early next morning, Thursday Jan. 26, Rhoades was back at her desk. She exulted, no one had even noticed her absence. My file was back in its place, and the prestigious law firm of Davidson, Matsen and Strouse, 4000 McArthur Blvd., Suite 600, Newport Beach, Calif., now had a 'Demurrer' to my Complaint officially filed with Ventura Superior Court Clerk's Office. Their client, the politically powerful and extremely wealthy Commercial Credit Corp., now called Control Data Business Centers Incorp., was no longer in Default.

It wasn't til the following day, Friday that copies of the Demurrer were hand delivered to the lawyers in Newport Beach. A secretary, Yvonne Vidal signed Harold W. Davidson's name on the document dating it Jan. 27, 1984. That same day she signed a Proof Of Service mailing it at a Newport Beach Post Office. I got it the first week of Feb. 1984. It was just a 'twenty eight page copy' of Cohen's original Demurrer to my Complaint.

They included copies of three Civil Rights suits that I'd filed in Federal Court which had no bearing on this case whatsoever. Only the cover page and other slight changes were made to coincide with the names of the defendants. In their phrenetic haste created by the Default crisis Janice filed attorney Davidson's Demurrer in Ventura Superior Court Records 'a day' *before* he could possibly have signed it. My anger nearly broke loose, but I held it back, if I wasn't careful I'd blow everything. All the preparations, all my evidence compiled and guarded so conscientiously during all those tormented years of documenting Black Robe Mishpucka Judicial 'insanity' could be lost. I had to stick rigidly to my plan. Anyway, the time for my plan had come. Beyond a doubt this last Mishna dementia crescendoed their chaos and corruption to a final degree. I was ready to take the first step, it was time to strike back, yet burdensome recriminations hung on...the fear of insouciantly violating the law of my country haunted my thoughts.

I didn't want to be made an outlaw or outcast, nor did I want to give an impression I'd developed contempt for the law while in wild pursuit of my rights. It was a mighty narrow line to walk, closing my eyes I gave it thought. It was complicated, a matter of justification, but a decision had to be made. In a civilized society justification for your actions is necessary. When *'stone-walled'* from justice to a point of abject frustration, to a point where vague, dangerous, embryonic broodings of revolution and violence begin to rear ugly heads, then for the sake of civility do you simply roll over and 'quietly die' like most?...or do you continue to writhe in terrible cerebral struggles of moral right and wrong? In a dismal lonely search for Due Process of Law where you're reduced to *begging* for miracles of judicial justice so you will not be forced into some fringe area way of getting it is repugnant. Is there justification in forth-rightly taking action against a *'corrupt judicial system'* that has gone beyond the endurance of the common sense of reasonable men in a civilized society? The answer would have to wait. It would take a jury of twelve honest people and an honest judge under the laws of the United States Constitution to make that determination.

Right now it was time to act, I had no intention of wasting more of my valuable time in foolish hope of dubious, *'non-existent'* judicial justice. My Appeal was to be invoked as part of an over-all plan, one that had long germinated piece meal in my head. A strategy, the *first* phase of fighting back. Realization that a momentous appointment with fate finally had arrived became more intense knowing that my hands no longer were shackled. Contemplation of freely swinging my fists into a vicious, treasonous enemy that had had me hanging on the ropes, pounding me to death for years shot powerful adrenaline roaring through my veins. A sobering thought jolted my exultation. I knew I couldn't finish off the fiendish Mishpucka by myself. The *next* stage would take the shocked fury, the indomitable rise of the people to put the final torch of destruction to Mishpucka madness.

One thing for sure, my plan better work. If not there was *nothing* left between America and total ruin by the Black Robe Mishpucka. The first step in my Appeal strategy was entitled, "Opening Brief Of Plaintiff And Appellant From the Judgement Of The Superior Court Of California, Ventura County, William Peck, Judge." The Plaintiff and Appellant, that was me. By judicial decree the front page of this omnibus must be a green color. Confronting Peck perversely was his major problem of *'covering-up'* the forged, phony title to my property Cohen had brought to the court. Neither of the *'two signers'* of the bogus title were officers of the corporation as required by law, also the corporate seal was missing. Beginning the Brief I threw in case law, <u>Major Blakeny Corp. v. Jenkins, 121 CA 2d 325, 263 P2d 655,</u> a Supreme Court ruling, "Where the Seal is *absent* from a Corporate Deed the 'burden of proof' is on the party relying on the Deed to *establish* the authority of Corporate Agents or Officers executing it."

No amount of U.S. Constitutional Law could *ever* dislodge Hymie Blitzberg's Mishna, 'the Jew Law,' not even a little bit. But what I was going to throw into the Brief next would explode their minds, it was a shocking effrontery. Using the Court Records as a vehicle to document treasonous Mispucka usurpation of our American judicial system would hurl them into rages, spasms of mouth frothing. Rabid anger would incite them viciously like *'mindless piranha'* attracted by blood.

With capitol letters and words underscored I attacked the Black Robe Mishpucka at the heart of their evil, secret Racist Conspiracy: "THE PLAINTIFF IS A VICTIM OF RACIAL PREJUDICE, DISCRIMINATION AND HATRED BY A, 'RACIST JEW JUDICIARY' WHO OPERATE UNDER THE MISHNA, (THE JEW LAW OF CHAOS, CORRUPTION AND CONSPIRACY), INSTEAD OF THE UNITED STATES OF AMERICA CONSTITUTIONAL LAW."

Next I entered a small segment of evidence from my files marking it, 'Exhibit A.' The authoritative documents laid bare the terroristic, violent racist persecution committed against helpless humans under the malignant leadership of Israel's evil madman Menachem Begin and his cohorts. An Israeli Jew, Yoav Peled who is a Ph.D candidate in Political Science at UCLA recently spent many months studying Arabs in the Negev. Peled told all about it:

"Ali Abu-Sulb, an Arab, lived with his family near the Israeli town of Dimona. He tills the land and supplements his income by working in town. His family has lived in the area for generations, and he has documents proving that they have lived there for at least sixty years. Jacques Amir, Mayor of Dimona and member of Israel's Parliament wants to build a sports center on their property. The Abu-Sulbs were told to leave their place of residence, they refused. One morning a government Green Patrol showed up and loaded the family's tents and all their possessions on trucks and dumped them in the desert 'twenty miles' away. The Abu-Sulbs vegetable garden, and some of their meager possessions 'were destroyed' in the process. When I visited the family *three weeks later* they were still living near Dimona *without* their tents huddled among the bushes for 'protection' from the desert sun and cold nights."

Israeli Government's Green Patrol is a twin of the Nazi Brown Shirts of pre-WW11 Germany, it is a *diseased depravity* that Jews in their pharisaic hypocrisy viperishly condemn and hang the Nazis for.

"The Arabs are 'loyal, peaceful citizens,' they pay taxes and serve as volunteers in Israel's Army. Although they are citizens they cannot leave an area without a permit. The 'Israeli Land Authority' leases land to the Arabs for cultivation for one year at a time but they are refused water for cultivation even where their plots are 'adjacent' to irrigated Jewish owned fields. Since the Likud Party took power the 'violence against Arabs' had picked up momentum and taken on a brutal form; the Green Patrol functions as a paramilitary force to harass and intimidate the Arabs. Houses and sheds are destroyed for violating building permit and zoning laws. Herds of sheep and goats already dwindling because of lack of grazing land have been seized by the Green Patrol for allegedly violating laws regulating the size and movement of herds, so that this mainstay of the Arab economy has been virtually destroyed. But the final blow came when the Jew Parliament passed a new law that allows the Israeli Government to confiscate Arab owned land without going through judicial channels and without allowing Arabs *recourse* to the courts. The Government is presently confiscating twenty thousand acres in Tel el Malakh, an area with 'eight thousand' Arab inhabitants who under the *Jew Law do not* have the right to Due Process of Law in the courts. So far the Arabs have been remarkably calm and have not engaged in any acts of hostility against the Israel Government. Traveling among them in recent months I often heard 'vows of resistance' and their 'defiant' statements to the effect that, 'we are not going to submit peacefully any longer.' So...the Israeli Government has already succeeded in turning a peaceful, loyal minority into an alienated, angry one. What the effects will be on the next generation...those who grow up under conditions of poverty and deprivation only the future will tell."

Digesting what Peled said prompted the intense question, *why* was he doing this? Once again I was experiencing a strange, minute sense of mystery...of being unable to understand the motive. It resembled the incident where retired Judge Leonard Friedman, a Jewish Judge had excoriated the corruption of the Black Robe Mishpucka. Yoav Peled was an Israeli Jew. Yet he was flaying the Jewish Green Patrol and revealing Israeli and its 'leader' Menachem Begin, as no saner and *no less* 'guilty' than Hitler's Brown Shirts. It was crazy, certainly Yoav didn't think it would make him a hero in the Jewish ghettos of Beverly Hills or Palm Springs. And surely he didn't think that Simon Wiesenthal, the Jew claiming to be a legendary "Nazi hunter and the decrier of racist atrocities" would ever investigate Irving Rubin the 'demented leader' of Rabbi Meir Kahane's Jewish Defense League.

Or that Simon Wiesenthal would investigate or expose the *'vicious racism'* of the Green Patrol. There was another simpler possibility however remote. It could mean there were Jews who didn't approve of the Mishpuckas evil conspiracies. That was an assumption, I didn't know the answer, it still remained nothing more than a mysterious empty space in a giant jigsaw puzzle. But one thing I did know, the Mishna, Jew Law of chaos, corruption and conspiracy operated as one and the same in America and in Israel. In America we have no more *right* to our land or future than the Arab, Ali Abu-Sulb and his family have in Israel.

Due Process of Law had been crushed, destroyed. It's a matter of common knowledge and open discussion that the System of Justice is collapsing in America. What people have not yet comprehended is the causation, that it is the *'rot'* of the Mishna, the Jew Law that's causing the collapse. But meanwhile, underneath, buried from sight, U.S. Constitutional law as originally set out is as good as ever, just waiting to be activated. This brings to bear the time of an arduous decision, are we justified in rising up and sweeping the 'Mishna, the Jew Law' trash from our shores? I thought of the time the little old lady, Eve Kimball 'tearfully described' the situation as well as could be done with just a few words, "Judge Zel Canter's muggings from the bench are as criminal in every respect as muggings on the street, and much more devastating to his victims."

I had stumbled and struggled a long time with my strong beliefs surrounding the necessity of just cause and moral justification before citizens could take such serious action. With strange timing Patrick Buchanan in his syndicated column broached the very same question boldly, "In America...vigilante Justice...at what point in the collapse of a System of Justice is an individual morally entitled to take the law into his own hands?" Buchanan related the true story of a crime, I put it in my brief as the Exhibit following Yoav Peled's. This crime intricately involved Justice and Punishment. Most important the case grasped and clarified the National mood and temper of the citizens regarding Due Process of Law.

Through this case the people overwhelmingly answered the vital, pressing question of 'moral justification' to take over. It was a 'sad story' of a little ten year old girl. Buchanan wrote, "In Buffalo over July Fourth Holiday, Willie Williams returned home and found his daughter missing. For hours, he agonized over her disappearance. When in the early morning hours she returned wrapped only in a pillowcase and gave her father details of her attack, and describing her attacker, Williams and neighbors headed for a nearby housing project. There they seized the assailant, beat, castrated and knifed him almost to death. The assailant who had had some *fifty previous* arrests on charges ranging from robbery to rape etc., was out on bail having paid two hundred and fifty dollars for his freedom while he *awaited trial* for an almost identical attack on a fifteen year old girl. The reaction to Williams *'personally avenging'* the sexual assault on his daughter was almost universal support. Cops came to Williams' cell congratulating him. Checks poured in for his defense, neighbors set up a fund for the local hero. People phoned congratulations in from all over the country. Americans who had heard about Williams cheered him, because through his hand, one of our enemies got what he deserved when he deserved it."

The electric 'mood and temper' of people across the nation was evident. The brittle crust of the Mishna, Jew Law, burying the U.S. Constitutional Law was closer to cracking wide open with unchecked citizen outrage than anyone had realized. The naked point was clear, the 'rapist and the mugger on the street' and *'Mishpucka gangsters on the bench,'* there was no difference, they were both vicious, sworn enemies of the people. As Eve had noted, "Judge Canter's muggings from the bench are as 'criminal' in every respect as muggings on the street, but much more devastating to its victims."

At the closing of my brief I again set out the astounding facts: "THE PLAINTIFF IS A VICTIM OF RACIAL PREJUDICE, DISCRIMINATION AND HATRED BY A, 'RACIST JEW JUDICIARY' WHO OPERATE UNDER THE MISHNA, (THE JEW LAW OF CHAOS, CORRUPTION AND CONSPIRACY), INSTEAD OF UNITED STATES OF AMERICA CONSTITUTIONAL LAW."

Finally it was completed, May 19, 1984 I filed my Opening Brief with Hymie Blitzberg's Appeal Court in the Mishpuckas building at 1280 So. Victoria Ave., Ventura, Calif.. On June 14, 1984 Stanley Cohen filed his answer, the 'Respondent's Brief.' Very impatiently I had waited for a month. Quickly reading it, slowing down only when I saw that Cohen spurred by 'terrible anger' had rashly gobbled the bait. Lord, my *Opening Brief* had set them wild. Hyper-furied, Cohen screamed hysterical, "The dignity and authority of the court must be vindicated...the only way to accomplish this is to find the Appellant 'guilty of contempt' and to 'punish him' severely."

An overwhelming awareness of disaster assailed Stanley Cohen. He knew his and Hymie Blitzberg's Mishna was on trial, he writhed to escape. Juda...swift action, total vindication was *necessary* to cover the Black Robe Mishpuckas crimes. Deep panicking fears provoked by this sickening realization spurred lawyer Cohen to wild, fanatical tirades. Repetitiously he demanded that I be *"Severely punished* for my contemptuous frivolity." Racked by frightened psychotic fetishes to cover-up, he depravedly cried, "Only by *discrediting* him, only by his being *'jailed and severely punished'* by the Court can the integrity of the Court be *vindicated."*

Cohen's invective was a blunder, whether due to his stupidity or

THERE'S A FISH IN THE COURTHOUSE   541

arrogance mattered not. His incredible *admission* of the Court's guilt of treasonous crimes was saliently clarified by his 'acknowledgement of a desparate urgency' to cover it up. My strategy had worked, an occasion to rejoice. Still I read the Brief minutely, there had to be more. Most carefully my tactics had been designed to draw Cohen into a specific, critical mistake. I was sure it would be there, then I saw the words I hoped for. As I'd thought, Cohen's mental capacity was incapable of passing up what he'd consider an ideal opportunity to denigrate and denounce me and my Constitutional Rights. With eyes open he'd walked right into it, bringing up pertinent facts and evidence, allegations I'd made in my Civil Rights suits. In an absurd, clumsy attempt to cover-up and wipe out 'truth' and revealing facts lawyer Cohen disparaged them as..."Scandalous, bigoted, paranoid accusations regarding the asserted conspiracy to deprive 'Appellant' of his Constitutional Rights."

A dramatic, foolish mistake, his inveterate lack of 'legal acumen,' opened the door for me to reassert and affirm the entire Mishpucka Conspiracy, clear back to the *beginning*, to the time when Mishpucka Judge Jerome Berenson had *killed* the 'Grand Jury investigation' and Mafia Boss Emilio Lagomarsino *framed* my Civil Service hearing.

Locked in the dank evil labyrinth of judicial deceit it now became my turn to make the next move. They called it the, "Reply Brief of the Plaintiff and Appellant." Starting at the beginning I wrote all of it down. Hell, the Mishpuckas name calling didn't break my bones, but I was damn sick of that same old 'reviling crap' from scum like Stanley Cohen and Dorothy Schechter. Not yet had the Mishpuckas dared to hurl their most vicious, *favorite* thunderbolt at me, that crap where they scream, "Anti-Semitic," they knew how bad their absurd propaganda and lies would back fire on them.

Perhaps like they said..."I was scandalous and contemptuous," and who wouldn't be a little paranoid after more than fifteen long years of withstanding their treacherous judicial lunacy. But bigoted I did not think I was. Funk and Wagnall's Practical Standard Dictionary defines 'bigoted,' "Adjective, stubbornly attached to a creed, party, system or opinion." My only stubborn opinion was my 'Right to Due Process of Law under the Constitution of the U.S. of America.' I'd never belonged to any *clandestine* organizations such as B'nai B'rith, Nazis, Jewish Defense League, Ku Klux Klan, Civil Liberties Union, Sandanistas or Communists etc.. A member of the American Legion and the Veterans of Foreign Wars I'm a loyal, law abiding American Citizen.

Yes indeed, I was damn sick and tired of their name calling and corruption and treason. Constantly during ensuing years I'd come up with new info and evidence of gangsterism and treason perpetrated by the Black Robe Mishpucka. I incorporated the new material along with the rest in my Reply Brief. After nearly ten years of trying I'd nearly given up hope of ever seeing the closely guarded records of the Ventura County Public Facilities Corp.. Then in Sacramento a contact came through, she'd managed to get some copies from the office of the Secretary of State.

Their 'Articles of Incorporation' claimed "The Corporation was organized by a group of *public spirited citizens* for the sole purpose of constructing a new courthouse as a 'civic venture in behalf' of the people. As a non-profit organization, the Corporation is irrevocably dedicated to charitable purposes." The Mishpuckas crazy lies were a mockery, a circumvention of the wishes of the people who'd already twice, soundly voted down a bond issue to build a new courthouse.

The documents revealed someone in the *'non-profit'* organization had made over sixty five *separate* trips to Los Angeles, Beverly Hills, Palm Springs, Sherman Oaks, Culver City, Hollywood, Playa del Rey, and Glendale, where they opened up individual passbook accounts at American S&L, Fidelity Federal S&L, Central Bank of Glendale, Great Western S&L, First Los Angeles Bank, Coast Federal S&L, Home S&L, Transworld Bank, Gibraltar S&L, Financial Federation Inc., JCB Trust Savings, California Federal S&L and Home Federal S&L. The non-governmental investment passbook accounts, totaling $23,437,480.72 were spread among out of county financial institutes as a diversionary tactic necessary to conceal duplicate payments and huge kickbacks from contractors. Local bank employees would have quickly spotted the subterfuge and begun leaking the scam.

Also among the documents were sheets of paper called *Financial Transaction Charts,* pages of devious, conflicting bookkeeping figures that were unable to *hide the fact* that the Mishpuckas were siphoning off millions more than was coming in. The nearest thing I saw to an official examination of the corporations financial records was a letter written Aug. 15, 1977, that was seven years ago. Norman R. Hawkes, the County Auditor Controller prepared financial statements for the PFC. Obviously leery of the whole operation he had written:

"Gentlemen: The accompanying financial statements prepared on a modified cash basis, were *'not audited'* and accordingly *'we do not'* express an opinion on them."

In Portland, Oregon, when the authorities busted up the gambling

Seated left to right, Mrs. Liston, Sonny Liston. Standing left to right Marty Denkin, a District Attorney Investigator and fight referee, Artie Aragon, top boxer and Champion contender and the author.

The Las Vegas Mishpuckas were setting up a scam wherein Liston would take a dive and Cassius Clay (Mohammed Ali) would win. Clay was unaware of the plot to fix the fight. Mishpuckas were threatening dire physical harm and death to Liston's family if he didn't go along. The author, a member of the L.A. District Attorney Bureau of Investigation, Criminal Intelligence Unit was conducting an investigation into the Mishpuckas underworld control of the fight racket.

Left to right, Marty Denkin, Cassius Clay (Mohammed Ali), a Mishpucka fight promoter and Artie Aragon. The night of the fight between Ali and Archie Moore which Ali won a festive party was held at a downtown Los Angeles hotel for sports writers.
The big bash was to promote an upcoming match between Ali and Sonny Liston. The young Cassius Clay was being brought along slowly to become the next Heavy weight Champion.

operations of Berenson and Nordman's phony church it caved in a cesspool of Mishpuckas secrets. Their church scam operated under the same motto as their PFC, they claimed "Irrevocable Dedication to Charitable purposes." Despite this *'sworn devotion'* to charity, all the money was funnelled to Berenson and Nordman's law firm, then completed its laundering process through Bank Of A. Levy. These millions were used to secretly *power-finance* their political hacks and *buy* judgeships for Mishpucka lawyers.

Carl E. Ward, Jr. was the top man, he set up and ran Berenson and Nordman's gambling operations. Michael H. Wallace, rancher and businessman from Paso Robles was a close associate of William P. Clark, Reagan's right hand man and National Security Director, now Secretary of the Interior. Owner of the Wallace Machinery Co. of Oxnard for years Wallace was deeply involved with Carl Ward's gambling empire in California and Oregon. In 1979 and '80, Wallace mounted a force strong enough to become Reagan's new, *sensational* National Campaign Finance Director in charge of his fund raising. He'd replaced Lyn Nofziger, another powerful, well known financial manipulator of contributions.

Oregon's Asst. Atty. General Timothy M. Wood took depositions from Ward and Wallace under the penalty of perjury for the state's pending racketeering case against them. Sticking to their story of an "Irrevocable *dedication* to charitable purposes," both denied they had "Received any gambling profits, and that if they had they would have donated it to charity." When contacted in L.A., Hazel M. Richardson, Dep. Regional Coordinator for Reagan's 1984 re-election campaign reluctantly admitted that, "Wallace was *heavily* involved in the 1980 campaign, but she claimed, "He wasn't on the '84 Presidential Staff." Neither Richardson nor Reagan's National Campaign Headquarters in Wash., D.C. would give further details of Michael Wallace's role in the 1980 campaign.

Democrat Mun. Court Judge Steven Hintzlestein, aka Hintz, was appointed by Democrat Gov. Jerry Brown during his infamous last minute orgasm in 1982. Now a Superior Court position was open in Ventura but a Republican, George Deukmejian was Governor. Hintz changed his party affiliation from Democrat to Republican...denying the 'switch' had anything to do with the Superior Court opening, he declared, "I changed to reflect my philosophy, it was just a matter of my registration being in line with my philosophies." Combining with his philosophies, Hintz' wife is an influential Republican, her mother is an influential partner in the political consulting firm of Reagan's veteran fund-raiser and financial aide Lyn Nofziger.

Michael Wallace was too hot to handle and was eased from the scene, Nofziger returned more powerful than even before. Standard Mishpucka judicial appointment arrangements were made, Nofziger gave the Governor $200,000.00. One hundred grand was to appoint Hintz to Ventura Superior Court, the second hundred was to install a Mishpucka in the opening left by Hintz's elevation.

It was the chance I'd waited for, Deukmejian wasn't a Mishpucka but for dough he'd play along. I was anxious to see how far he would back the crooks if he got a blast from a blow-torch. I mailed a large manilla envelope with a copy of my Brief. A separate letter enclosed I marked for the Governor's eyes only. It vehemently protested his schemes to appoint scum like Hintz whose character qualified him as nothing more than an ambulance chasing shyster from the Bronx. More to the point I reminded Deukmejian of his secret agreement, the huge sums of money he'd taken from Hoffman's to supply water from northern Calif. to Lake Casitas.

The volume of water Deukmejian agreed to send was strangely the *'exact amount'* Hoffman's were stealing from the lake. The water thefts had already cost taxpayers millions of dollars. The missive was sent by registered mail, a receipt came back, proof that Deukmejian received it. He didn't answer, not even a twenty two cent postcard thanking me for my concern. Despite not answering, his reaction of dropping Hintz like a red-hot potato told me what I wanted to know. In an about-face of strategy the Governor was suddenly impelled to seek an altogether different public image. Installing another person in the Superior Court opening he then appointed Herbert Curtis, a Democrat and first Black man to Ventura County Municipal Court.

Deukmejian's reaction hadn't quite told me everything, a bit of the puzzle remained. Like Gov. Jerry Brown with Judge Berenson's hundred grand payoff, did the Duke *keep* the two hundred thousand after his double cross?

On the last page of my Brief I repeated my accusation of "Racial Prejudice, Discrimination and Hate by the Racist Jew Judiciary." I filed it July 3, 1984. On September 18, '84, Appeal Court Presiding Justice Hymie Blitzberg, aka Steven Stone, Dismissed my Appeal. I had predicted it, right down to the big capitol letters underlined on both the front and back pages ordering that his decision was "NOT TO BE PUBLISHED." The judicial order was seven pages of inane Black Robe Mishpucka double talk. Hymie ruled that *all* the judges involved had, "Taken *Judicial* Notice" of the *phony* Trustee's Deed from the foreclosure sale and they had judged it as legitimate. Then the Appeal Court wrote..."Although we are *not sure*, there *appeared* to be an *uncertainty* of *some kind*, or *something*, or *other.*" So based on their Judicially proclaimed *'uncertainty'* they Dismissed me. Good Lord, no wonder these scum didn't want their sick shit "Published."

I still had one last chance to scream for Due Process of Law, a 'Petition for Rehearing.' Of course I knew it was senseless, this time I would be lucky to get a postcard, but anyway, I went to work on it. As a matter of procedure I repeated the process of adding case law. But by now the *original* issue was a corpse, sucked into a suffocating deadly quicksand swamp of the Mishna's chaos. Absolutely nothing of sense remained, the issue now had become solely that the Black Robe Mishpucka had *treasonously* seized control of the U.S. Judicial System. Most terrifying of all there's no recourse, *no place left to go.* My Petition now had but one useful purpose, expose and document the Mishpucka, it had to shine the *same* harsh, glaring spotlight of *'recognition* and *identification'* on Black Robe Mishpuckas that law enforcement and the media always put on the Black Hand Mafia. For instance, Mishpucka reporter J. Goldman, L.A. Times, gleefully wrote about the..."Latest U.S. indictment and arrest of five top New York Mafia bosses." He published their pictures and with headlines he 'ridiculously propagandized' them as being "Godfathers Belonging to the Ruling Council of Organized Crime," Anthony Salerno, Phillip Rastelli, Paul Castellano, Anthony (Tony Ducks) Corallo and Genaro Langella.

FBI Director William Webster crowed vainly, "This indictment is 'historic.' It exposes the *'structure and leadership of organized crime'* on a scale never done before." The Director traveled to New York City personally to make the 'announcement' of the arrests and take charge of publicity. Cleverly he covered-up, hiding the existence of the treacherous Mishpucka. With an adroit propagandist deceit he assured America, "With the arrests of these Mafiosos we are taking out the top players."

In its structure the hierarchy of the Mishpucka is similar to the Mafia which has its genera of Godfathers, Consiglieres, Capos, and lowly Soldiers.

As Presiding Judge of an Appeal Court District, Hymie Blitzberg, alias Steven Stone, is the 'highest ranking' Mishpucka controlling the 'Crime Family' in three counties, Santa Barbara, San Luis Obispo and Ventura. Stone's status as a Mishpucka leader is comparable to Mafioso Frank (Funzi) Tieri, the top Boss of the New York City's

Genovese Family. Superior Court 'Judges Larry Storch and Jerome Berenson' of Ventura are comparable to the Mafia classification of capos, such as Charlie (Bats) Battaglio, and John (Frankie) Carbo. Although he is a Superior Court Judge, Zel Canter's 'low hair line' mentality locks him into the comparable rank with Mafioso, Johnny (Peanuts) Tranelone, a lowly soldier.

I prepared mug shots, a rogues gallery of the two Crime Families illustrating similar hierarchies and structure. I entered the mugs of the Black Hand Mafias 'Italians' and Black Robe Mishpuckas 'Jews' as Exhibits A and B in the Petition For Rehearing and filed it.

Federal Judge Irving Kaufman, one of the most ruthless, vicious, 'high ranking' Mishpuckas was named to head Pres. Reagan's new Crime Commission to crackdown on organized crime. Senator Strom Thurmond, Chairman of the Senate Judiciary Committee, who had *covered-up* for William P. Clark, National Security Dir., was also a member. After two years of directing the crime commission, Judge Kaufman announced, "We have uncovered new criminal organization networks emerging in U.S. cities in drugs, gambling, prostitution, and extortion. The operations are highly structured and disciplined. They operate virtually unnoticed by the American public." He emphasized gravely, "These crime groups must be stopped." Then dramatically he identified the new crime groups he'd uncovered. "One syndicate is known as the Chinese Triad Societies, based in Hong Kong, another, the Japanese Jakuza, operates out of Tokyo. Both groups function much like the Mafia." *Not once* did Kaufman mention the Mishpucka or the fact that a Jew Crime Family existed or that the Black Robe Mishpucka was annihilating the United States. Chairman Kaufman is an expert at exposing and fighting the Mafia, the Jakuza and the Triad, but no U.S. agency exists that can protect the people from the Black Robe Mishpucka...not even the FBI, its director Federal Judge William Webster is one of them.

Judge Irving Kaufman's 'evil tentacles' of treasonous acts spread *deep* into stygian depths of the past. Over thirty five years ago Chm. Kaufman was the Mishpuckas *designated* Judge 'presiding' over the spy trial and *death sentence* of Julius and Ethel Rosenberg for theft of atomic secrets, allegedly for Russia. In a cunning courtroom farce where the *judge, prosecutor* and *defense lawyer* were all Jews, Judge Kaufman wielded total mastery, the charade proceeded exactly as he directed. American patriotism against communists was running high, and Kaufman's evil subtlety left no question of his desire for a *guilty verdict* when he allowed no Jews to be on the jury. I recalled Irving

Rubin's trial for the crime of offering *cash bounties* to maim or kill Christians. All it had taken to find him *Not Guilty* was one Jew on the jury. This time the Black Robe Mishpuckas plan was different, it was to be a verdict of Guilty, a Mishpucka *rub-out*, but insidiously America would be *blamed*, accused of murder.

The Rosenbergs were dead, right from the start. A sinister, evil necessity required their execution, their tongues had to be silenced forever. Supposedly it was a simple case of spying, the Rosenbergs were dyed in the wool communists, traitors who'd stolen American atomic secrets for Russia. But here it breaks down...the Rosenbergs were Jews, in Russia Jews were stridently screaming that the Russian government was committing persecution and holocaust against them. It conjured up a burning question, why...*why* in the world would the Rosenbergs risk their lives to steal atom bomb secrets for a Russian government that was torturing and killing Jews?

The truth was startling and bizarre, Mishpuckas control Russia's government, it was into *their* hands that the atomic secrets had been delivered. Alleged persecution of Jews by the Russian government was a *massive* Mishpucka propaganda. Psychological warfare, lies for the world to hear and made to believe that Jews are forever being persecuted by some-body...some-where...at all times...for no reason other than they are Jews.

Russian people have no more control over their government than Americans have of theirs. The Mishpucka rules the worlds two most powerful governments, to maintain this evil control and manipulation of the *entire globe* the Mishpuckas have to keep the ordinary citizens of these two giants continually at each others throat. The threat of this fierce enmity and its constant churning of global turmoil created by a terrifying specter of two behemoths starting a nuclear war is an ever present holocaustic nightmare. It shrouds the *entire world* but it must be kept this way for the Mishpucka to exist.

Ordinary people of both countries must never be allowed to come together where 'common sense' might tell them neither wants war or bloodshed anymore than the other, in this event the malignant power of the Mishpucka would evaporate...gone like a puff of smoke in a gale. The Rosenbergs would never be given a 'chance' to answer the explosive question. Judge Kaufman's terrible Mishpucka duty was to make sure the Rosenbergs lips were sealed forever, the executions were *strategic*, serving *more* than *one* purpose. He felt positive that it would satisfy American hatred for communism, Kaufman was even *more certain* that for a Jew judge to sentence two Jew spies to death

548 THERE'S A FISH IN THE COURTHOUSE

would be the quintessential proof that he was a loyal American. His unrelenting stance against the Rosenbergs treason would *insure* him a deep cover no one would challenge or suspect. A mole that could *penetrate* far into America's intelligence community, walking among prominent government officials and traveling within *select* circles.

For years U.S. Intelligence agents puzzled over strong suspicions that Israel as well as Russia had atomic weapons in huge amounts secretly stock-piled. But massive Mishpucka propaganda proclaiming an implacable 'hatred between Russia and Israel' forced them into an uncomfortable, compromising assumption that if Israel had these weapons they had developed them on their own.

It was sixty seven years ago, 1918 when the Mishpucka took over Russia. Nikolai Lenin, a Jew, seized control of the shaky Kerensky Republic. Leon Bronstein, a Jew, aka Leon Trotsky, in New York City in 1918 recruited, financed, and trained a cadre of murderous, cut throat Jew gangsters and shipped them to Russia. Using Trotsky's ferocious, blood thirsty New York hoods, Lenin overthrew Kerensky. He then appointed these Jew thugs to high office within the Russian government and ruled with an iron fist until his death in 1924. The Russian people became known as Communists, but it was the Secret Mishpucka hierarchy that ruled the government. During forty seven years from Lenin's takeover in 1918 to '65 it is well documented that the Mishpucka government tortured and killed over seventy million people and enslaved over a billion others. From 1965 to the present the Iron Curtain closed down so tight in protecting the Mishpucka that it's impossible to estimate how many innocent people have died at their hands. This bloody *record* of Mishpucka terror far outstrips the claim of a holocaust horror the Jews have made against Nazis in Germany during WW11.

Universally, peoples minds have been mesmerized by Mishpucka propaganda to accept a false concept of a close 'affinity and alliance' between Karl Marx' Marxism and Nikolai Lenin's Bolsheviki. It's the greatest misleading political plot ever propagated. Their 'propaganda was stretched' to its capacity to cover-up the fact that Karl Marx a Jew, was actually rabidly Anti-Semitic.

Descended from a *long line* of Rabbis on both sides Karl's father was converted and baptized a Lutheran a year before Karl was born. At twenty five, Karl Marx married a Christian and wrote a treatise, "On The Jewish Question." It was almost a *classic* Anti-Semitic tract. Marx asked a series of questions and gave his answers. "What is the profane basis of Judaism?...practical need and self interest. What is the *worldly cult* of the Jew?...Huckstering." In Funk and Wagnal a huckster is, "A mean, venal fellow, a petty trickster." In Marx' third question, "What is his worldly God?...Money!" He answered, "The God of the Jews has been secularized, it has become the God of this World. The bill of exchange is the *real* God of the Jew."

Marx maintained that the Jews had corrupted the entire world, "By acquiring the power of money, and turning money itself into a World Power." His cure for this 'Jewish evil' was, "In emancipating itself from huckstering and money, and thus, from real and practical Judaism, our age would emancipate itself." Emphasizing a vehement Anti-Semitism Marx wrote a letter to his German friend, Friedrich Engels. He claimed as proven, a 'statement' made by Egyptian Priest Manetho about 280 BC, "The Jews were a race of lepers and rootless people without a country."

Marx and Engels often discussed their notion that Jews were an inferior race. In 1849 Friedrich Engels wrote in the Neue Rheinische Zietung, Marx' newspaper, "The next World War will result in the disappearance from the *face of the earth*, not only reactionary classes and dynasties, but also of entire reactionary peoples and that too, is a step forward." Engels saw Marx' Anti-Semitism as, "A sufficient warrant for genocide." In another article, Marx deals with the Jewish archetype, the *'usurer,'* he recites a lengthy, violent quotation from Luther. "A usurer is a double dyed thief and a murderer. Since we break on the wheel and behead highwaymen, murderers and housebreakers, how much more ought we to break on the wheel, kill, hunt down, curse and behead all usurers."

All the writings and theory's expounded by Marx evolving to what is known as Marxism is grounded entirely in the idea that, "The Jews God is money and Jews have corrupted the *whole world* by acquiring the Power of money, thus World Control." The role of Marxism was the destruction of the fiendish Jewish World Conspiracy. Nikolai was but thirteen years old when Karl Marx died, there was *no* connection between the two whatsoever. Lenin a revolutionary and leader of the Bolsheviki had become a student of Marxism, it was perfect for his use except for one thing, the role of Marxism no longer would be to *destroy* the Jewish World Conspiracy. Under Lenin, a consummate Jew, Marxism's role would *now* be the total *destruction* of American Capitalism. Russians would be called Communists and Americans Capitalists. The Mishpucka would keep them at each others throats forever. Perceiving the dangers of what he called Anti-Semitism to the Jews God, money, Lenin took *savage* steps against his enemies, he conducted pogroms against the Bourgeoisie on a huge scale.

Bourgeoisie to Lenin meant, "Any and all *non-Jews* who owned property." In bloody, inhuman pogroms Lenin murdered millions of people, not on the basis of 'individual' guilt...but *merely* membership in a condemned group.

A big problem has sprung up enmeshing the Mishpuckas. Their propaganda *promoting* an alleged Nazi holocaust of 'six million Jews' has sprung such serious flaws and gaping holes that world-wide many strongly question its authenticity. I did a lot of researching, especially pictures of Jew prisoners in April and May of '45 when liberated by American troops. Except for their shaved heads from delousing they seemed well fed and warmly clothed. All were smiling, with mouths opened wide I particularly noticed their good teeth. Comparing their general good physical condition with 'haunting' pictures of America's Bataan Death March survivors in Japanese prisons I was sick. One hundred and eighty pound men reduced to eighty pound bags of skin and bones with arms and legs missing. After four years of captivity, brutality and starving, their pitiful smiles at being saved revealed few teeth except for rotten snags. Pictures of captured German soldiers in Russia at the war's close showed evidence that Jews in the prison camps surely were better fed than they were.

A certain desperation was being taken on by the Mishpucka with their *insistent* attempt to force the people into, 'Remembrance of the Holocaust.' Jew pressure and influence enabled them to pass a law in Canada jailing anyone expressing an opinion that the Holocaust never happened. In Toronto, Ernst Zundel was convicted and faces two years in jail and heavy fines for what Jews call, "Spreading false news." He printed a pamphlet entitled, "Did Six Million Really Die?" Helen Smolack, the Mishpucka chairman of the Canadian Holocaust Remembrance Association brought the charges against Zundel.

In L.A., student editors of a community college newspaper face being shut down by District Trustees because of articles questioning the Holocaust. The Editor-in-chief of the Hawk at Harbor College says, "He will 'sue' the Trustees if they try to shut down the paper." Reporter Joe Fields had written an article calling accused Nazi war criminal, Andrija Artukovic a *Croation hero* and urged the American government to refuse to deport him to Yugoslavia. Fields said, "Irv Rubin, Pres. of the JDL, came to the paper threatening me but I'll not be intimidated by Rubin and I am now more determined than ever to continue."

Mishpucka desperation to bolster Holocaust propaganda neared a frenzied pitch. Controlling the Department of Justice they set up the Office of Special Investigations. Neal Sherbinsky, alias Sher, a crazed Mishpucka fanatic was appointed Chief of Investigations to conduct witch hunts for Nazi war criminals. John Demjanjuk, 63 year old retired auto worker was accused of being a "Nazi concentration camp beast" by Sher and his Mishpucka associate Stephen Trottsky, alias Trott. They declared that Demjanjuk "Trained at the infamous Trawnicki Camp for guards to be used at Sobibor Treblinka killing centers. Also he had exhibited cruelty and an *unexplained* hatred for Jews, and was known as Ivan the Terrible." Demjanjuk's lawyer said his client was never at Trawnicki, Sobibor or Treblinka. He is not Ivan the Terrible, he's a naturalized citizen *stripped* of his citizenship *without* Due Process of Law. Demjanjuk's lawyer demanded a civil trial in 'open court' to face accusers and challenge false statements made against him. Instead Sher *set up* a hearing with an immigration panel. They ruled, "Since we believe him to be a Nazi war criminal he should be deported to Russia or to Israel." There he will survive about as long as as an ice cube in the Sahara.

A self proclaimed Nazi Hunter, Simon Wiesenthal, a conspirator with Sher and Trott issued a document accusing Ivan Stebelskyi, a U.S. naturalized citizen of being a Nazi war criminal in Poland and a member of an SS Division that collaborated in killing Jews.

Stebelskyi, outraged, claimed he had been a merchant during the war. He'd never served with the Germans, and had in fact saved the lives of two Jew employees. After a search the two were located, one in Australia sent affidavits confirming Stebelskyi. The other died in Haifa in 1982, but two brothers and his son confirmed his gratitude and regard for Stebelskyi. In New York two Ukranians were located who confirmed they'd been business partners with him in Boryslaw during the Nazi's occupation and agreed to testify. Stebelskyi wrote to Simon Weisenthal, *The Great Nazi Hunter*, demanding to see his evidence. Simon refused to reply.

Arthur L. Rudolph, close friend of Werner Von Braun, father of the Saturn 5 Rocket that propelled American astronauts to the moon in 1969, came to the United States after WW11 with other German rocket experts. Rudolph became a loyal U.S. citizen and worked for years with NASA on the space program. He received acclamation as Chief Coordinator of the Saturn 5 Program. Sher, Director of The Office of Special Investigation accused Rudolph of WW11 crimes. With absolutely *no* specifics or evidence Sher stated, "When Rudolph worked on the German rocket project during the war, the conditions of slave labor were gruesome by all accounts." Neal Sher threatened Rudolph, "If he did *not* leave the country *voluntarily* he'd be *stripped* of his citizenship and deported." In West Germany a spokesman for the Central Agency for the Prosecution of War Crimes said it has *no* evidence that Rudolph while working on the German rocket program had ever abused any prisoners. The German Agency contacted Sher advising him they'd prosecute Rudolph if he'd send evidence he was responsible for inhumane treatment of workers at the rocket factory. Sher would not answer. Although Rudolph is still a U.S. citizen he's never been prosecuted for any crime but can't return because Sher, the Mishpucka Chief of Special Investigations will not let him.

For 35 years Valeria Trifa served as Archbishop of the Romanian Orthodox Church. Residing in Grass Lake, Michigan, Trifa now 70, was highly visible as Archbishop. A certificate from police authorities of the county stated, "The files disclosed *no* criminal record, warrants or criminal process outstanding for Trifa." Sher had accused that in Romania during the war, "Trifa used his position as an editor of the newspaper Libertatea to spread propaganda inciting Anti-Semitism with crude caricatures and comments." *Without* Due Process of Law he was deported. Of Sher's punitive victory over Trifa for supposedly making crude caricatures and comments about Jews, Sher boasted, "This 'war criminal' left America because the U.S. had exposed him." Mishpucka Elie Wiesel, head of still another of the '*countless* Jew organizations,' The U.S. Holocaust Memorial Council applauded the deportation of Valeria Trifa with exultation. "This signals once again that there's no room for such war criminals in our midst."

CHAPTER 42

Always the trail led back to Hollywood. The brutal killing of a beautiful whore created one hell of a problem for the Mishpuckas. Bludgeoned to death while asleep, Vicki Morgan was a mistress of Alfred Bloomingdale a rich Hollywood Mishpucka and a Presidential confidant to Reagan. Robert Steinberg, the original attorney for the alleged killer Marvin Pancoast, attempted to make contact with Pres. Reagan offering audio-video tapes of Bloomingdale and government officials engaging in *sadomasochistic* sex parties with Vicki. Steinberg told administration officials, "If Reagan didn't want the tapes," which he said, "If released, constituted a *high risk* to the U.S. Natl Security, he will destroy them." Steinberg told United Press International that, "There are a number of people in the tapes shown engaging in sexual acts." In addition to Vicki and Bloomingdale he identified the other individuals as, "Friends of Bloomingdale reaching *all the way* to the head of the country." But he made it clear that he was not indicating President Reagan was on the tape. The film ran about an hour and appeared to have been made within the past several years.

At CBS News, Steinberg 'went further' by saying the individuals were a *businessman,* three government *appointees* and one *elected* official. He said that shortly after getting the tapes he viewed them with an attorney and *someone* from the Justice Department, but he refused to name them. Suddenly Steinberg became scared and wildly inconsistent, he told detectives he no longer had the tapes...they had been stolen from his office. The defendant, Pancoast, also told his new lawyer Arthur Barens that there were sex tapes, both audio and video that were *very* embarrassing to the Reagan Administration.

At his murder trial Pancoast's lawyer Barens subpoenaed the FBI and CIA for any sex tapes on which Edwin Meese, Attorney General Designate, or other government officials might appear. The defense repudiated the prosecutions tape recorded confession as, "An illusion brought on by Pancoast's masochistic urge to take blame for crimes of others." They maintained that, "Vicki was murdered by someone other than Marvin Pancoast, someone who wanted her dead because of *compromising* material she possessed about some very influential, and powerful people. An agent for the 'real killer' might even have hypnotized Pancoast into believing he had killed Vicki."

But Judge David Horowitz refused to allow any of the sex tapes information to be heard by the jury. The Mishpucka judge said, "This is just a simple case of Pancoast caving Vicki Morgan's head in with a baseball bat and confessing. That is all they need to know." Like the Rosenbergs, Pancoast was a sacrifice to protect the Mishpucka.

Judge Horowitz was a Jew, the *prosecutor* Stanley Weisberg, was a Jew, the *defense* lawyer, Arthur Barens was a Jew, *defense* witness, lawyer Robert Steinberg was a Jew, and his *lawyer,* Leonard Levine, was a Jew, the *courtroom charade* proceeded precisely as Black Robe Mishpucka Judge David Horowitz directed.

Shortly after Pancoast was found guilty a phone call came from Hollywood. It was LeFleur, I picked up on the nervous quiver in her voice, for 'The Flower' to lose her cool something must be upsetting her damn bad. "Gary," she shouted, rambling on swiftly, "I've got to tell you this, no one else would understand. Good Lord, every pimp and hooker in town is scared half to death and you'd better believe Steinberg is too. He screwed up really good when he blabbed about those video tapes, then he double blew it when he *lied* about them being stolen. He's still got 'em stashed out, that's to keep him from getting killed like Vicki."

"Flower, relax, slow down a little. I figure you are talking about Vicki Morgan's murder."

"Lord what else, Vicki was a dear friend. She was one of my girls for a while and believe me...those video tapes are for real. She was counting *real big* on them in case Alfred backed out on his *promises* to take care of her financially the rest of her life. She was extremely depressed over having to do all those shitty things Alfred wanted her to do, especially for his kinky *big-shot* friends."

"Well, they are certainly burning Meese. It seems mighty strange his name is the only one that they've brought out."

"That's the work of Marvin's lawyer Arthur Barens, he's covering up for the 'big guy' that's on the tape. All those attorneys made a lot of noise just to make their defense of Marvin *'look good.'* They knew Horowitz wasn't about to let any of those sex orgies in the trial, and about Meese, they don't like him anyway."

"One hell of a crazy situation, Hollywood hasn't changed a bit. Flower, tell me, who is the big-guy you're talking about?"

With a catch in her voice, only calmer and much slower she said, "Weinberger."

That threw me, "Weinberger! Casper Weinberger? The Secretary of Defense...is that who you mean?"

"You've got it right."

"Good Lord, is that why Steinberg was screaming about National Security being threatened?"

"I suppose so."

Damn, bells rang, Weinberger...somewhere in the past, it tied in. A big piece of the puzzle dropped right out of the sky into its slot. A bunch more of the pieces were hovering around, circling to land but I couldn't concentrate on it now. It would have to wait till later.

Flower was saying, "A lot of hookers were into this thing, Alfred Bloomingdale's orgies weren't exactly a *secret* on the strip. But when the pimps heard about those video tapes and the Mafia being mixed up in it they damn near died of fright. The pimps grabbed all their hookers and split for Vegas, Phoenix and wherever, until this blows over."

"How does the Mafia come into it?"

"Bugliosi, hell you know...that lawyer, Vincent Bugliosi, he's got big Mafia connections in the East, Chicago and New York."

"So, how does that.... Flower cut in.

"Look, this whole thing's crazy right from the beginning, everyone on the strip knows Marvin didn't kill Vicki. He is a fruitcake, he'd confess to anything if you talked to him right. You notice Barens did not put him on the stand to testify, they wouldn't *dare* to, he would blow the lid clear off this friggin' town. Marvin has mental problems coming out his ears and I'll tell you...*nobody* 'knew' this better than Bugliosi, he's known him for years. Back when Bugliosi was a D.A., Marvin confessed to the Manson Family Murders."

"I agree Vicki's tapes were a hell of a motive to get her killed, far more plausible than any reasons Pancoast appeared to have. You got some good ideas?"

"A real good one, I think Marvin stole Vicki's tapes long enough for the Mafia to run off a copy, then they went to D.C. where they got a bag full of money for it. The *big-guy* found out that Vicki still had the original, but Steinberg got hold of it first and ran off more copies which he is holding on to for dear life. Not too many people on the Strip think Marvin will ever get out of prison alive."

"Flower, I've got to think about all this awhile, and I mean a lot longer than five minutes. Hollywood hasn't *changed* a bit has it?"

"Hollywood's Hollywood, and it will *always* be."

"You've got that right. I'll come down soon, meantime I wouldn't even talk about this in my sleep if I were you."

In L.A. Federal Court, Neal Sher, Justice Dept. Chief of War Crimes Investigations and Stephen Trott were pressing their *insane* Mishpucka chaos and Holocaust propaganda. They were extraditing 85 year old Croatian, Andrya Artukovic to Yugoslavia on allegations of war crimes. Held prisoner during the proceedings, Artukovic was legally blind and confined to a wheelchair suffering a variety of heart and brain problems, Alzheimers and Parkinson Disease, aneurysm and brain atrophy. After being arrested he suffered strokes partly paralyzing his face. Mishpucka prosecutor, Assist. U.S. Atty., David Nimmea, hired *another* Mishpucka, psychiatrist Saul J. Faerstein, he testified that Andrya was competent to be extradited. Nimmea then claimed, "It is clear Artukovic should return to Yugoslavia to face war crimes."

Artukovic's attorney was a Jew, G. B. Fleischman, it was shaping up to be another courtroom charade, with Artukovic as a sacrifice to Mishpucka propaganda. But something very mysterious was brewing, Fleischman seemed genuinely trying to help Andrya, his stance was clear, "When I took the case I assumed Andrya was probably guilty, but even so I would still defend him. I'm an experienced extradition lawyer and been a Civil Rights lawyer a long time. I am *convinced* Artukovic's Civil Rights have been destroyed and he needs the best lawyer he can get. I take a position you *can't do this* to an old man in America, and in the process of this extradition procedure I have come to believe he is *innocent* of the Yugoslavian charges."

What occurred next was even more strange than the Yoav Peled and Judge Leonard Friedman incidents. Suddenly truth burst forth like Fourth of July rockets lighting the sky with a shocking proof, it verified my accusations of being a victim of Black Robe Michpucka racist hate. As a result of Fleischman's decision to defend Artukovic, he received unbelievable cruel treatment and threats of death at the hands of Jews. Terrifying phone calls threatening to blow up his car when he started it if he defended Artukovic were stark reality.

Armand Grant, owner of Southern California Atty. Services was Fleischman's process server 23 years, being a Jew, Grant *abandoned* him. Refusing to serve anymore papers he said, "It is not in the best interests of my company to continue our business relationship..."

Fleischman also lost his Jew clients who accused him of being a 'Renegade Jew.' Irving Rubin, head of the JDL, backed by three Jew thugs came to Fleischman's Hollywood condominium and threatened him. They had to be removed from the building by security guards. Simon Wiesenthal's Center for Holocaustic Studies made harassing calls and Rabbi Abraham Cooper urged *all* Jews to call Fleischman expressing their outrage against him. Hundreds of wild, milling Jews showed up at the court proceedings to harass Fleischman, screaming "Pig and traitor," they spit in his face.

Several members of the JDL were arrested. U.S. Marshalls had to escort Fleischman to his car. Rubin knew the *demonstrations must* be kept alive and going in the papers and TV. From the courthouse steps he screamed his ridiculous and insane threats, "Artukovic, your days are numbered." The 85 year old mentally incapacitated man did not even know what was going on. Some of the Jews were arrested, others took a live pig to Fleischman's office where they continued to raise hell. But there were far deeper, *more sinister* reasons for the ruckus than just the fact that Fleischman was a Jew representing an alleged Nazi war criminal. He'd made an *authoritatively prohibited* statement, "I believe Artukovic is *innocent.*" Judah...! If Fleischman was to prove that Artukovic hadn't killed any Jews at all much less 700,000 it could be disastrous...it could presage *total collapse* of the entire Holocaust propaganda.

Desperately Rabbi Abraham Cooper tried to *force* Fleischman to drop Artukovic and extradite him as swiftly as possible so he could be disposed of. In ultimate hypocrisy Rabbi Cooper made clear the *partition* that Jews must keep between themselves and the country they happen to be living in. Cooper ruled, "Every defendant has their right to counsel, but, people in the *Jewish community* are outraged that a Jew would take this case, it is inappropriate for a Jew to be Artukovic's lawyer." Then in an amazing response G. B. Fleischman castigated Rabbi Cooper and the Jews. He informed them, "I am an American lawyer first and a Jewish lawyer second...if these people cannot understand that, then there is not much I can really do about it. I have given up explaining it to them." Genuine desperation, sad fear and dread seeped from Fleischman's bitter, disgusted words. His astonishing, startling statement had torn away the cloak of mystery surrounding the Peled, Friedman incidents. They were trying to warn brother Jews, awaken them to the terrible inevitable self-destruction they were bringing down upon themselves.

It went back to Marxism...150 years ago, Engles wrote in Marx' newspaper, "The next World War will result in a disappearance from the *face of the earth* not only of reactionary classes and dynasties but also of entire reactionary people. And that also is a step forward," thus Engels saw Marxism as a, "sufficient warrant for genocide."

Intelligent Jews like Fleischman, Friedman and Peled knew if the Jews did not emancipate themselves from the sinister Jewish World Conspiracy they were doomed. With the nearly total disaster they'd brought on themselves in WW11, Engels prophecy had almost come true. But the Jews could *never* free themselves from huckstering or usury, or the World Conspiracy. The Mishna locked them into their binding contract with Satan, and they were close, very close to their goal, their great triumph, World Mastery.

The Israeli's top guarded *secret*, Operation Responsa Project, was just completed, a universal closed system of instant Communication. A 'global electronic computer,' its mysterious spidery network ran to chief synagogues in every country in the world. They felt the power emanating from it, it was unthinkable that the Mishpucka could fail. Certainly a few Jewish renegades...traitorous pigs like Fleischman, Peled, and Friedman could never stop them. Based at the Bar Ilan University in Tel Aviv the massive computer was 'sanctified' by the Rabbis with a cover of innocence, supposedly *'scholarly research'* of Jewish Heritage.

Back to ancient times Jew lawyers wrote to Rabbis for rulings in keeping with the Jewish Law. The Rabbis would respond in writing, these volumes of questions and answers were called the *Responsa*. Through the ages 500,000 questions and answers...fifty million words of *'rabbinical judgements'* were penned in Hebrew by Rabbis on legal questions from 10th century Yemen to 20th century Brooklyn. These judgements and laws have been encased in the *database* of Responsa. All the laws governing Jewish life day to day came from Rabbinical rulings, now from the Rabbi computer. Throughout the world Jewish lawyers and judges are hooked into Responsa.

The Mishna, *Jew Law,* had taken over. This is well documented where the Israeli government *confiscates Arabs deeded land* and they have no legal recourse in court. Locked into the Rabbi computer the Responsa network sends forth its evil Mishna throughout the world, a *death grip* on the jugular vein of freedom. But more unexpected incidents plaguing the Mishpuckas plans were occurring. Fleischman had shocked them when he shouted to the world, "I'm an American lawyer *first* and Jew lawyer *second*, if people cannot understand that, there's not much I can really do about it...I have given up explaining myself to most people." Fleischman was threatened with violence by Irv Rubin and his JDL thugs. He should give serious thought about starting up his car.

A vile incident across town from Hollywood bore this out. George Ashley, a retired history teacher, had made comments in class that the Holocaust never happened. A bomb exploded early one morning directly under a bedroom where a 20 year old son was asleep. The demented Irving Rubin denied to reporters that the JDL planted the bomb but added, "I certainly have no trouble believing this incident took place, I can't shed one tear because it is too bad he didn't die in the blast." Irv's wife, Sherry, a sweet Jewish thing told L.A. Times, "We are a nice Jewish Organization, we certainly did not bomb his home. But it's too damn bad Mr. Ashley was not blown up." All this hatred, mayhem and death *directed* at people who do not think just exactly as the Jews *want* them to think...this from people screaming from roof tops every day of their lives about being persecuted.

Relentless with their propaganda several of the myriads of Jewish Organizations who continually *'scream'* persecution and Holocaust gathered in Camarillo, the east part of Ventura, *protesting* Violations of Human Rights in Russia. Mishpuckas, Miriam Wise and Merrill Alpert just returned from there. They will speak to the Natl Council of Jewish Women, etc., etc., about persecution of Jews in Russia.

In Wash. D.C., Max Kampelman, a Mishpucka lawyer who could not be trusted to negotiate a traffic citation for a client was sent to Europe on behalf of the U.S. to conduct *nuclear arms reduction* talks with Russian Mishpuckas. Kampelman's aide, Mishpucka, Maynard Glitman a Foreign Service Operator went with him.

In Israel, Jacques Amir, a member of Parliament and the Mayor of Dimona did not want Ali Abu-Sulbs and other Arabs lands for a sport center as he had claimed. Secretly the Jews were building the world's largest underground nuclear weapons factory near Dimona. Soon Israel's secret, *deadly silos* bordering the southern shores of the Mediterranean, and nuclear armed, will be capable of destroying all of Europe. Jew spies and traitors in America have stolen U.S. Naval

Codes and Operational plans including submarine movements and underwater defenses. The Mediterranean Fleet could be destroyed in only a matter of hours. Blowing up the U.S.S. Liberty proved that the Jews had *no compunction* against destroying our ships and killing U.S. sailors. Casper Weinberger, Sec. of Defense and his treasonous aide Richard Perle were in Spain and Europe *sabotaging* the strength and potency of U.S. Air bases. *Perle was caught* in D.C. handing vital *U.S. Military secrets* to top Israel Officials. But Stephen Trott, Assist. Atty. General in the Justice Dept. covered it up. With Israeli nuclear warheads aimed at its heart Europe will be a captive hostage.

Scores of scholarly Rabbinical communications *supposedly* dealing with Jewish Heritage Studies shot from Bar Ilam University in Tel Aviv to the Rabbi Responsa stations *worldwide.* Even if suspected by U.S. Intelligence, the code hidden in the messages was impenetrable. Mysterious scrabblings of Hebrew and Semitic dialect interwoven in Talmudic ramblings mixed up with computer ciphers and codes was impossible to unscramble unless you were a Rabbi. Preserving strict security they intermittently float phony test messages and flyers that immediately reflect in the Responsa if their code is tampered with or breached. Network *traffic* to the synagogues in Central and South America and to Eastern European countries was exceptionally heavy during negotiations between Mishpucka Kampelman from the U.S. and the Mishpuckas from Russia. Military and political upheavals in these target areas flared on alarming scales, each specific crises had a direct bearing on the level and intensity of the U.S. and European arms negotiations, all of it heightening the *power* and *scope* of the Mishpuckas *global manipulations.*

Back in Geneva, with Kampelman and Glitman's agreement with Russian Mishpuckas on arms reduction, U.S. and Russia will become second class nations. The Israeli's conspiracy of *world conquest* and control is very near.

Upon finishing my Petition For Rehearing I again repeated my accusation and charge against the Black Robe Mishpucka:

"THE PLAINTIFF IS A VICTIM OF RACIAL PREJUDICE, DISCRIMINATION AND HATRED BY A, 'RACIST JEW JUDICIARY' WHO OPERATE UNDER THE MISHNA, (THE JEW LAW OF CHAOS, CORRUPTION AND CONSPIRACY), INSTEAD OF UNITED STATES OF AMERICA CONSTITUTIONAL LAW."

A few days later my twenty two cent postcard *arrived* from Hymie Blitzberg, aka Steven Stone, *Denying* my Petition For A Rehearing.

It was the end of the line, Due Process of Law was *dead*. For fifteen years I had fought and struggled...done everything in my power that could possibly be *required* of American citizens to get justice through the courts. Now it was established beyond all doubt...*every* avenue of legal and judicial recourse had been *totally exhausted*. Continuing on with an appeal to the State Supreme Court would not only be *useless* it would be degrading, and cost thousands of dollars, plus the wasted time. Judges Moskovich, Grodinsky and Kausinsky would only laugh when they mailed me their twenty two cent postcard.

Still I knew I was getting to them, an attempt was made to blow up my pickup parked a few feet from my house by torching the fuel tank. A deputy from the crime lab said, "You're lucky the tank was full of gas instead of fumes otherwise it would have gone up like a Roman candle." What the Mishpucka pulled next got to me about as bad as anything they'd done yet. The day of June 5, 1984 I went to vote in the Presidential Primary, but they couldn't find my name on the list. The ladies at the poll had known me for years, they couldn't understand what was wrong. They suggested maybe I'd been changed to the other polling place in Oak View, but I wasn't on that roster either. One of the ladies offered to call the courthouse. She talked to a clerk in the Voter Registrars Office. Hanging up she pondered, "That's strange, I don't know what to tell you."

"What did she say?"

"Well Cheryl, a clerk, went through the files. She can't locate any record you were ever registered." I wondered what in hell was going on now. Being helpful she said, "You can fill out these special forms, that will allow you to vote." It came all at once, *'allow me to vote,'* of course, they didn't care if I filled out special forms and voted. One little vote either way didn't bother them. The point was they hadn't wanted me to run for office...so they fixed it. They'd been scared to death I was going to campaign against Maggie Erickson for County Supervisor and scream about all their corruption. They weren't sure the probation crap they put on me would stop me so they destroyed my registration. They'd had no way of knowing I'd already decided not to run because of the friggin' probation hanging over me.

Not wanting to lose my temper in front of the lady I said, "Thank you, I appreciate it but I think I'll come back later and vote. I had to get away and think. They had destroyed my right to Due Process of Law, now they had destroyed my right to run for public office. They could take it away any time they wanted, as easy as just pulling my registration out of file and flushing it down the toilet and what could

I do about it. My head was ready to bust, my blood pressure must be two thousand. Suddenly the pressure left, my head felt shrunk, like one of those decapitated South American Indian heads on a stick. I felt nothing, I had nothing, hell, was I a citizen...what was I?...for the first time since getting out of the Navy I didn't vote. I didn't bother going back, I didn't have the heart.

A week later I stopped at the Registrar of Voters Office. Geraine Jacobson, the vicious Mishpucka who'd sabotaged my campaign four years ago had gone to another county down south, Santa Ana or San Bernadino, where she was setting up the same Mishpucka operation. Myron Kampfer had taken over but was on a break. A clerk, Clara Trom waited on me. She was Stanley Trom's mother, the lawyer who was picked to replace Woody Deem the District Attorney they'd run out of the county. Though I had always been polite and courteous to Clara she was very nervous. I knew she was aware of what they were doing to me and was part of it, today she was even *more* fidgety than usual. Since they'd passed *their* new law that the public couldn't have access to voter records it was necessary to tell her what I wanted.

"Mrs. Trom I want to see my voter registration file please."

Looking through the files she soon returned. "I am sorry but you don't seem to be in there."

I said, "That's amazing. Can you possibly tell me why?"

She nodded and went to a computer. Pecking away, Clara threw furtive glances in my direction. I knew Clara desperately hoped I'd get disgusted and walk off. After considerable time at this game she finally returned. "Yes I found out what happened, in December 1982 we destroyed your file. We had sent you sample ballots, they were returned marked no such address. *There's a law,* if the sample ballots come back we destroy your records." I was burning, I had to cool it.

"Mrs. Trom, I've lived at that address for years and you know it. If you sent those ballots I would have gotten them." Clara shrugged. "You say you destroyed my registration in December 1982. That's a year and a half ago, now I want you to read this." From my pocket I took a receipt showing I'd voted six months ago which meant my registration was in file up until then. She backed away like it would burn her at the touch. I couldn't help it, "Mrs. Trom you are lying, I know what you did, the filing period for supervisor was February 1 to March 9 of this year. You pulled my registration out just before February 1 so I *couldn't* run for office, but you messed up when you *forgot* to put it back after March 9th." Clara almost fainted.

Back at my car I collapsed on the seat, waves of hatred drowned me. My probation was almost up, I'd planned to run for supervisor once more before I was too old, but they could stop me at any time they wanted. What could I do, sue them? That was a *laugh,* complain to District Attorney Bradbury, their cover-up man? That was even a bigger joke. This time it was different, I couldn't make the hatred go away. I was sick to death of the Mafia and the Mishpucka. Sick of the damn Jew Law and being ruled by a bunch of God damn friggin' Russian Jew gangsters like Harry Pregerson, Hymie Blitzberg, and Otto Kausinsky. Sick of their damn screaming about Anti-Semitism and Holocaust. Jesus Christ, I didn't want to feel this way. It was a hatred so bad I hated it.

I *understood now* why Arabs were reacting with such malice, what did they have to lose? The Jew Law had taken away their land, their rights, leaving them *without* legal recourse. In the *terrible* Shatila and Sabra refugee camps in Beirut where these people were herded like animals the Pro-Israeli forces were massacring the terrified civilians. Men, women and children were shot indiscriminately and grenades were thrown among wounded gathered at local hospitals. At a White House reception when asked about *reports of the slaughter* of Arabs, the President was unconcerned, "I do not know anything more than what's in the news." Secretary of State George Shultz wouldn't even comment on the massacre.

The Jews had just compounded more *bitter hatred* against themselves. Regardless of how many Arabs the Jews slaughtered, Arabs would *never* stop fighting for their land and rights. These things were sacred, it was a Holy war. In America it had already started, I could hear the *degenerate,* animal screams of the JDL and Irv Rubin and his wife, that sweet Jewish thing Sherry Rubin screeching out, "Blast them, blast them to bits, blow them up. I can't shed a tear for them, let 'em die, die." The Rubins were not referring *only* to Arabs, they meant American Christians and Jews like Fleischman, Friedman and Peled, anybody who opposed their schemes. My anger was great but to retaliate violently against their violence would plunge Americans into the same disaster facing the Arabs. Anybody trying to fight back would be branded an outlaw, not a patriot. The Mishpucka held all the cards. They'd seized the Judicial System and the Mishpuckas in the Justice and State Department *controlled* the FBI and Pentagon. It wasn't time to move yet, I must stick to my plan no matter what the provocation, it was the only hope, and it was slim...damn slim.

CHAPTER 43

    The jangling phone sounded same as always...unconcernedly it gave no indication of its important message. It was from Hollywood, an old friend, he'd worked federal intelligence while I was with the D.A. Bureau of Investigation. Retired from the Feds, he was now a private-eye with an office on Sunset Strip. We exchanged greetings trying to recall the last time we saw each other. Agreeing it must be more than twenty years he said, "I'll get to the point, there is a guy, Anthony Summers, running around Hollywood, says he is an author with the British Broadcasting Corp. in England. He's come up with a supposition that Marilyn Monroe did *not* commit suicide, she was murdered. Summers wants to research it and write a book, so he's been hitting up on the L.A.P.D., Feds and D.A. Intelligence for any information about Marilyn. Everybody told him the same thing, he should talk with you and Frank, you were the only ones who really knew what was going on in Hollywood in those days. He discovered Frank was dead and he couldn't find you, but someone sent him to me. I told him I could probably contact you. What I want to know is will you talk to him? If so I'll give him your number."
    "Sure, do that. Tell him don't give it to anyone else. Next time I'm down I'll give you a buzz, we'll have a drink."
    "Okay, but don't go in any of those joints unless you check with me first. It ain't like it use to be, there's more friggin' hype-weirdos in Hollywood then the cuckoos nest, and believe me, most of them

are damn dangerous."

This strange timing of Anthony Summers interest in Marilyn's death seemed almost occult. For sometime my thoughts mysteriously had been returning and picking around certain *related incidents* that happened years ago. I couldn't put my finger on what was triggering these flash backs, but now this quest of Summers about Monroe. I had never given much credence to the supernatural but sure as hell this was something I couldn't figure, mysterious forces were working. I felt the invisible hand putting a small, key piece of the puzzle in place, I had to play off it.

After the author's call we met in Ventura, a bar and grill, The King and I on east Main Street. Summers was easy to get on with, intently I listened, "I'd spent several years of exhaustive research of Pres. Kennedy's assassination for my book, Conspiracy, copyrighted in 1980. During that period of investigation I came upon events and facts pointing out strong *connections* between Marilyn and Kennedy. These strange, very unusal circumstances caused me to suspect she may have been a victim of murder, not suicide." With a hesitant look he asked, "Do you think I'm looney?"

"Of course not, Frank and I were sure Marilyn was murdered." My mind was suddenly racing back exactly where it had been picking around in the past, I thought about what I was recalling. I couldn't see that it would interfere with or harm my plans if I told him a few things. "It is quite long and involved Tony, but I'll help you if I can. Marilyn was as mixed up a poor woman as you can find. I'm talking about emotionally, much worse than Lana Turner was when Johnny Stompanato was screwing around with her. You see, Johnny, Sammy Lo Cigno, Georgie Piscitelli and Joe Di Carlo worked for Mickey Cohen. There was also Roger Leonard, but he was just a fat little Jewish boy not a Latin Lover like the Italians, he just hung around Mickey kind of like a lackey. Cohen had Piscitelli hitting on Marilyn *same* as Stompanato set up Lana Turner in the motel with the sex bit...cameras and tape recorders. Georgie was Mary Mercadante's pimp and she was jealous and madder than hell at him for screwing around with Marilyn. She threatened to not hustle for him anymore, that's when she took up with lawyer Harry Weiss, but she didn't give a shit about Harry, she was in love with Georgie. Mary was telling Frank and me all about her troubles, she wanted us to bash Georgie around, threaten him with being busted if he didn't stay away from Cohen and Abe Phillips. Mary was so mad she didn't even care if we removed a couple of his front teeth. She had an idea Marilyn might not think Georgie was so cute without them."

Tony said, "Sounds like they lived a rough life in those days."

"Yeah, that's when Mary told us the really weird stuff. She was still messing around with Georgie only Weiss didn't know it, she'd promised him not to hustle anymore. Piscitelli was trying to convince Mercadante his relation with Monroe was purely platonic, anyway, he wanted to drop Monroe because she was going crazy. Every time he asked her about John Kennedy she would throw a fit screaming she didn't know anything about politics. Georgie told Cohen he had had enough of Marilyn, anyway she wasn't even interested in sex, it was a waste of time and money trying to get her in a motel. Cohen got madder then hell, he ordered Georgie to stick with Marilyn and pour drinks or pills down her, whatever it took to learn what John Kennedy intended doing about financing Israel. The gangster Cohen and Begin were furious over Kennedy's plans to give billions to the Peace Corp. and South American and African countries."

I gave Tony a rundown about Abe assaulting Mary and Cohen's threats to kill her. "It's very possible she got killed for *more* reasons than just because she wouldn't drop her case against Abe. She had shot off her mouth about Georgie telling her Cohen was *squeezing* Marilyn for info about President Kennedy."

Summers had an astounded look on his face. He said, "Did you make intelligence reports on this to the L.A. District Attorney?"

"Yes. Frank and I made reports to the Chief of the Bureau of Investigation."

"Would the D.A. still have them?"

"I am sure all those records were destroyed, it's a long time ago you know."

He was insistent, "If I asked for those reports do you think they might find them?"

"No, that's impossible, when we filed our reports we didn't sign them, Intelligence agents used code names, only the Chief knew who they were. However it's very possible the files were stolen. Someone might still have them...I didn't actually see them destroyed."

He stared at me strangely. "Do you have any of them?"

"No, I don't have them."

The author took a different tack. "I had a talk with a specialist regarding methods of administering fatal doses of medicine or pills to unsuspecting victims."

"Well I can tell you, Piscitelli was fully capable of it. He could get pills down Marilyn a dozen different ways. He could have killed

Mary also, he was the only one I know of who could've conned her out of hiding. But it would have been on Cohen's orders, he could've given Georgie money, or threatened to kill him, either way Georgie would do what Cohen told him."

Summers was taking notes so I said, "Write down these names I give you so you won't forget them. Joe Di Carlo, he's the only one still alive who was at the table in Rondelli's when they shot O'Hara. Di Carlo was a pal of Georgie's, he knew all about what they were up to with Marilyn. I'm talking about the scam Georgie was working on Marilyn, like Stompanato worked on Lana Turner, the motel bit and recordings, the part with John Kennedy came later." I gave him the madam's name who furnished the whores for the party at Peter Lawford's Malibu beach house. "There are all kinds of stories about Marilyn and John Kennedy knowing each other for years, but that's a lot of bull. The first time John ever met Marilyn was the night of the Democratic Convention in L.A. in '60." Then I figured I'd give Tony a hint, a lead that maybe later on would soak in and he'd pick up the trail on his own. That is if he got to *really* digging into this.

"It was Joey Bishop who came up with the idea of a wild party for Kennedy, he talked Lawford into it and set up the deal with the madam. Joey *himself* arranged to have Marilyn there knowing that Kennedy would be taken by the Monroe sex appeal. Joey was a Jew and real tight with Cohen, and at that time the Rabbis were pushing them hard as hell to squeeze every bit of dough they could get *out of Hollywood* for Israel. Menachem was spending more time hanging around Cohen in Hollywood than in Israel. He *desperately* wanted to know what Kennedy's plan was for Israel if he became president. Cohen figured if they duked Marilyn into Kennedy, Piscitelli could *manipulate* her to tell them everything Kennedy told her. Also they would work a squeeze if a romance blossomed. Mickey's girlfriend Candy Barr, was making a lot of trips *back and forth* between Jack Ruby in Dallas and Cohen and Begin in Beverly Hills."

Summers who was scribbling notes fast looked up with surprise, "Are you positive Ruby and Cohen were associated?"

"Sure! I saw them together in L.A. way back in '46. Ruby was there again in '47, I talked to him."

A look of disbelief came over Summers face, he said, "When I investigated President Kennedy's assassination I checked into Ruby's background thoroughly. He could not have been in L.A. then. They had *nothing* in the FBI files about him being there."

"Excuse my language Tony, but I don't give a shit what *wasn't* in the FBI files. The summer of '46 I was working patrol at University Division, the morning watch, midnight to eight a.m. The Inglewood Police Department was short handed during Hollywood Race Track season so they used to pay LAPD officers extra to help them direct traffic. I worked the corner of Prairie Ave. and Manchester. Every day just before the races began Cohen's black limousine pulled up at the signal. He knew me from when I walked the beat at the Olympic fight stadium. I put on a little show for him, blowing a loud blast on my whistle I'd hold my arms out and bring all the traffic to a dead halt. Slowly I'd motion my arm for his chauffeur to make a left from Manchester to Prairie. Mickey's driver and bodyguard team, Hooky Rothman and Eli Lubin made the turn real slow stopping when they got to me. I'd lean over looking into the back seat and give Mickey a little salute. Wearing his soft brim felt hat, Cohen never cracked a smile, just a nod, tough like Edward G. Robinson in the movies. I took a good look at the guy with him, about the same size, a snappy dresser like Cohen and an identical felt hat. I never saw him before but I figured he must be important, Cohen never let his hoods sit in the back with him. I gave Cohen the celebrity treatment all through the track season. It was on the last or next to last day, I don't recall, anyway, Hooky stopped the Cad right beside me. Cohen rolled the window down and held his hand out with something in it, 'Here, this is for you.' I said forget it...I don't want anything...'Come on, take it, it ain't money...it's nothing...see,' he waved the scrap of white paper between his thumb and index finger. I took it and motioned him on. When traffic died down we locked our gear in the trunk of the car and put on a sport jacket. We'd get inside the track before the first race. There was about six hours to kill before we had to be back to the corner. I usually took six bucks and bought two dollar tickets. If I was lucky and picked up a winner sometimes I could hold out clear to the sixth race. I pulled a five and a one out of my pocket and the piece of paper came with them. I saw that it had the numbers from one to eight and a nag's name after each number. At the bottom was written, *'bet each race to win.'* All I could lose was six bucks, so I bet the first three races, just like the piece of paper said. I was slightly amazed when all three were winners, they weren't favorites so they paid real good. Suddenly I had a pocket full of money. I slipped two bucks in my pocket so I could start all over in case the luck changed, then I bet the whole bundle on the fourth. It won. I got excited and parlayed the whole pocket full on the fifth, *it won*...I couldn't believe it. Closing my eyes I parlayed on the sixth, then the seventh, holding about two grand I got chicken. I was too smart for their game, I was being set-up to *lose it all* on the eighth, the last race, and it would be all gone. So I only bet ten bucks and it happened just like I figured. Coming down the stretch neck and neck all the way my horse lost. I headed for the intersection, traffic was starting to get heavy. Going through the gate into the parking lot I heard the loudspeaker blare excitedly. 'Everybody hold your tickets. Hold your tickets everybody on the eighth race, it's a *photo finish,* judges will decide the winner.' I froze in my tracks, right then I knew *my horse would win.* The loud speakers sputtered and crackled. The judges had decided, my horse was the winner. Can you imagine, if I'd bet the whole wad, I'd have almost twenty grand...then I realized...good Lord, sure as hell Cohen made millions today, his dough was probably scattered around with every book in the country. Mickey gave me that list just showing off what a *big man* he really was."

Summers had listened in silence, skeptically he asked, "Are you saying it was Ruby in the back seat of the Cadillac with Cohen?"

"Yes, it was Jack Ruby alright." His skepticism was still showing.

"How did you determine that?"

"Well...it was over a year later when I learned who he was. In late summer of '47 I was transferred downtown to the Metropolitan Felony Squad, *plain clothes.* One night my partner and I were driving around Old China Town. It was a quiet evening, parking the car we moseyed along the east side of Main Street down toward Sixth, after a few blocks we wandered into Harry's Place. Harry wasn't around, it was like a morgue. A dapper guy in a suit looked us over, smiling, 'You guys like a drink...on me.' No thanks, where's Harry tonight? 'He's on a trip, I'm his friend. I'm managing the joint for him while he's gone.' I said, we're from Metro. 'Yeh, I knew you were cops, my name is Jack Ruby. I just came out from Chicago to get with Harry. Since the war is over the West Coast is dead, so's Chicago, we are moving operations to New Orleans and Miami. That's where *all the action* will be from now on, between the States and Cuba. Harry is there now looking around.' Jack Ruby was the guy *I saw* with Cohen at the track. Strangely he seemed to have no qualms whatever about talking, he rambled on just like we were old buddies. His light beige suit cost as much as my pay check for a year and Jack fluttered his right hand so you couldn't miss the gold ring with its ruby setting at least half an inch square."

Summers was scribbling fast. I paused to let him catch up. He asked, "Did you ever see Ruby again?"

"I'm coming to that...over four years during the war Harry's Bar was packed with sailors and marines, from six a.m till closing at two a.m.. It was only a few blocks from Union Station, the Greyhound Bus Terminal and Pacific Electric Red Car Depot at Sixth and Main which ran to the Navy Base at San Pedro and ships at Long Beach. There was lots of action in those days. Just as many farm girls from the midwest got off trains and busses looking for excitement as did servicemen. Champagne parties were Harry's specialty, cheap crap with his own label. He got twenty to fifty bucks a fifth, whatever the traffic would bear. 'B' girls were all over everybodys lap, after those harpies squeezed all the cash from the drunken sailors and marines, huge bouncers threw them out the back door into an alley and fresh ones were ushered in the front. Believe me I know, it so happens I went out the back door a couple times. An old wino told us how he worked for Harry during the war boxing the empty wine bottles and hauling them to the dump early in the morning. Harry was smart, he didn't want city trashmen to see how many bottles he went through and maybe give City Hall big shots strange ideas about muscling in. There was never less than a hundred cases a day. Harry was making so many millions he bought up a whole string of ponies, also a small training track. Then he and Cohen made more millions *fixing* races. Cohen had grabbed control of wire services on the West Coast and they worked more tricks than a monkey on a stick. Ruby was right, the bar was dead, a couple sailors in the corner with two of Harry's veteran harpies egging them on and two winos at the bar was all the action. Taverns all over the county were closing for lack of business. In late afternoon I'd been stopping in a little bar down in University Division where I lived. I wore old work clothes, Max the proprietor, thought I was a truck driver. It was a quiet neighborhood type joint, the Red Devil, on the corner of Vernon and Hoover. This afternoon Max was behind the bar and there were very few customers. I gave him a big song and dance about going home to clean up because at night I went down to the Union, I was going to be an official of the local. I hinted I knew the Union was crooked and run by hoods but that was okay with me because I wanted to make dough just like all of them, Max ate it up. He said he'd just come from Chicago and hinted darkly about how the boys back east gave him the money and sent him to L.A. to locate a nice quiet little joint where he could set up *headquarters* for Southern California gambling and girls. The way Max came on I figured he was bullshitting me about as bad as I was him. The more he talked the less it sounded like bull. 'The big guys in Chicago, Cincinnati and Los Angeles have gotten together. They are taking a *billion dollars* down to Miami and New Orleans to set up the biggest gambling operation in Cuba there ever was.'"

Tony broke in, "How does Ruby come into this?"

"Hold on, I'm coming to it. Max told me, 'I am just a small cog in L.A. for *wire service* connecting the race track circuit around the country. Hell, if you want to make bets or for the guys down at the Union Hall and the truck company, I'll do you a favor, I can cover it right here, any amount you want.' In the next weeks I made a few small bets with Max just to keep up the bullshit. One afternoon the place was empty, Max was wiping off the bar mumbling something, I held a heavy glass mug to my mouth to drink. Somebody entered, looking in the mirror I nearly broke my front teeth on the mug, my God, Cohen and Ruby were walking right at me. Max stiffened like a broom handle. Their eyes weren't adjusted to the dark but when they got close Ruby did a double take. Cohen was cool, with a poker face he gave his Al Capone nod of recognition. They continued to a booth in the rear, Max followed. After huddling a few seconds Max turned to me, his eyes bulged with fright. I sauntered out the front door. Around the corner on Vernon I saw Cohen's limo parked with the hoods in the front seat. I'll be damned, Max hadn't been kidding at all. Right now I'd hate to be him trying to explain *me* to Cohen. That was in '47, I never saw Ruby again. A few days later I stopped by to see how Max would take it. He almost killed himself running behind the bar to his office in the back. Max wouldn't be telling me anything more about the *big guys* so I departed.

Later I learned that Harry sold everything he had in California and moved to Miami, Ruby went with him. I can tell you Tony that the..." (I was about to say the Mishpucka) but quickly thinking better of it I said, "The Organization took a fortune down there for their *Cuban operation* in 1946 and 1947, equivalent now days to ten billion dollars."

I'd decided it wouldn't be too smart to mention the Mishpucka to Tony. I didn't know too much about him, anyway I didn't think he was ready to digest it. I was sure he'd understand if I said *Mafia* but I knew he'd ask a million curious and likely antagonistic questions about the *Mishpucka*, next thing he'd be mumbling Anti-Semitic. I knew even less about the BBC, if Summers got his pay check from the Mishpucka like John Babcock with ABC TV, I'd just be stirring up unnecessary trouble. Tony kept on writing notes so I drank my beer and waited.

With deep thought he said, "To dwell on Monroe, this Piscitelli was involved with her like Lana was with this Stompanato fellow and Mickey Cohen was their boss?"

"Absolutely."

"And Marilyn was very closely associated with JFK and all his Hollywood chums?"

"Right, but you have to remember, these events took place over a period of several years, from late '58 to '62 when Marilyn died."

"Yes, President Kennedy was assassinated just a little more than one year later. I have become more and more convinced, the deaths are inextricably tied together."

"I agree with that. In those days Cohen had no idea how close Frank and I were getting to him. We had an operator, a little Jewish guy, Henry Jacobs. He'd managed to get in serious trouble with the law and was about to do some time in jail, we had helped him out." A waitress came over, while Tony ordered beer I began thinking of Hank. A real likeable guy, we became friends, but he was lazier than hell. He fought continually with his wife over getting a job, she was always kicking him out. Hank was intrigued with detective mysticism. He didn't consider prowling around the Hollywood scene at all hours of the day and night as being work.

Constantly hanging around our office he plagued us to let him operate some cases. Henry was shrewd, he had a strange quality of importance no one seemed to challenge. He could approach wealthy, arrogant bankers in plush offices or a wily madam in a whorehouse, it made no difference, he would come out with the damndest info you could imagine. The most important part of all, Henry never lied to us about the facts of what he had learned or ever exaggerated a situation making himself appear more important. He played it like we were all three partners. Several times we thought for sure we'd got Henry killed. When we worked that state wide masseuse parlor whorehouse case we sent him into their headquarters in Alhambra, where they kept master records. Wiring Henry we staked out down the street with recording equipment in a van painted as a plumbing truck.

Hank had been in a few times and became acquainted with the madam and some of the girls. Now we wanted some conversation on tape for evidence. The metal van was hotter than hell. Other then a few words when he first went in, there wasn't a sound from Hank's mike for nearly an hour. There was a possibilty they had found the bug on him, he might be in danger. We'd almost decided to bust in which would blow the whole case. There was a chance we were in a dead spot. We decided to drive around the block trying to pick up sound. We spotted Hank staggering down the side street completely dazed. He had a big cardboard container, one of those flat kind you put record albums in. We got him in the van.

"Hank, are you okay?" He looked like he'd been run through a giant laundromat, he was all bloated out of shape, red as a lobster. "What in the world happened?"

Mumbling he said, "My God...I couldn't go through that again, please, don't ever send me in there again. It was Myrna, the madam, she fell in love with me...she loves me. Myrna wouldn't let any of the other girls touch me, she pulled my clothes off."

"Did Myrna find the bug?"

He croaked, "No, I wadded my coat up and threw it on a chair in the corner."

"That explains why we couldn't hear any sound."

Myrna was blonde with a thick Swedish accent, at least 6'2", two hundred and thirty pounds. Hank was 5'5", a hundred thirty pounds. He went on, "Myrna jerked my clothes off, threw me on a table and began squeezing me. God, her hands were like a gorilla's. Music was playing loud, she kept asking if I liked the Blue Danube, I told her yes, yes I love it. Even the lights were blue, the whole damn room was blue. She kept saying, 'Henry, I love you, you like Blue Danube, I give it to you.' Near the table there was a small stand with a little brazier gadget with a candle under it heating up a container. Myrna flipped me on my stomach spreading my legs, man you don't know how scared I was. She shoved a funnel in my rear and took the little container and started pouring hot oil up my ass, I almost went crazy but I became so weak I couldn't even scream. She climbed up on the table on top of me. I thought I was going out of my mind. She stood up on me with her bare feet, there was some kind of a trapeze thing bolted to the ceiling. Hanging from it she screamed at the top of her voice the Blue Danube and Henry I love you with a terrible screech while mashing me with her feet. I must have passed out, I was naked on the table when I came to, it was absolutely quiet, the blue lights were gone. I managed to struggle into my clothes. Returning Myrna said, 'Henry, I love you, you love Blue Danube I give it to you. You keep it and never forget me.' Throwing me out a door into an alley she said, 'You come and see me soon.' I don't remember leaving the alley."

"Well Henry, you've still got your passport to return," I pointed at his record album.

He gave me a dour look, "You can forget it, no way..." Henry's seriousness did it, Frank and I laughed so hard I had to pull the van over to the curb. Henry got mad, then he couldn't help himself, he bust out laughing. But Hank had guts, one night three hoods jumped Frank and me in a dive on Santa Monica Blvd., they were mean and we where having one hell of a time. Henry was at a table with some people and wasn't supposed to know us. Running over he leaped on the back of the biggest and meanest of the three. We got handcuffs on two but before we could help Hank the big bastard was smacking him around like a rag. He was trying to kill Hank. Frank got there before me. I shuddered from the sound, it was the first time I ever saw Frank sap anybody so hard, it was over in a second.

We took Hank to Hollywood Receiving Hospital, they bandaged him up, but he wouldn't stay. We drove him home, next day he was alright. His wife cornered us pleading we should make Hank settle down. She had a good job, a nice apartment and took good care of him when he was there. She wanted them to be like other married people. I got Hank an easy job, from nine to five in a drug store on Hollywood near Highland Ave.. They furnished a car, all he had to do was deliver medicine and stay home at night out of trouble. But Hank couldn't stand it without excitement. He got to taking pills to calm his nerves at home so he wouldn't start an argument, one night Henry dropped one pill too many and died.

The waitress was leaving, Tony said, "Sorry to interrupt, where were we?"

"Talking about Hank. Frank and I had been watching Mickey Cohen from a distance, we knew he was up to *something* out of the ordinary. He was spending a lot of time with a weird looking little guy at the Beverly Wilshire Hotel's drug store lunch counter. What got our curiosity most was Mickey seemed to be taking orders from the stranger. Painting a new logo on our surveillance van we parked it close to the hotel. The Village Florist sign fit in much better in prestigious Beverly Hills than Ace Plumbing. We got *pictures* with our telescopic lens of Mickey and his *mysterious* friend. We picked up on his name, it was Menachem Begin.

We gave Henry money for a hotel room. His suits were pressed and he had a whole box of new white shirts. He looked more like a multimillionaire movie mogul than Metro-Goldwyn and Mayer. He understood Yiddish which Mickey and Begin were using. They were not the least bit uneasy when Henry sat next to them at the lunch counter reading the Examiner sport sheet racing news. Scribbling on small pieces of paper and mumbling to himself seemed to indicate to Mickey and Begin he was above suspicion. Henry reported to us that the two in a deep discussion were very excited, there was a lot of talk about Cuba and military operations and the Kennedys.

One night they discussed plans to meet the next evening in the restaurant...then they'd drive somewhere for a *secret* talk with very *important* people. That night I parked the florist van a block west of the Beverly Wilshire Hotel. Henry was in the hotel and Frank was across Wilshire where he watched the entrance. If Cohen and Begin started to leave Henry was to come out and give Frank a high sign. Everything was going good, getting the signal Frank was returning to where I waited on the street corner.

Suddenly all hell broke loose. A car speeding east didn't stop at the red light, crashing broadside into a motor officer. Running into the intersection I halted traffic, laying on its side the motorcycle was roaring and jumping with its throttle wide open. I cut it off and used the mike to call for help. The officer's gun skidded down the street, Frank ran after it. We'd forgotten about Hank till I saw him coming from the hotel. Within seconds radio cars arrived, showing my badge to an officer I told him we'd come to the station and make a report as soon as possible. Jumping into the van we forced our way through the curious crowd that had gathered. I headed for the hotel, we were lucky, Cohen's limo was just pulling from the curb going east. Henry was jumping around excited and jabbering, 'We really got something going, just don't lose 'em for God's sake. I wouldn't miss this for a million bucks. Mickey sounded like a politician, they were going on about *wars* and billion dollar *appropriations* and cursing JFK about his *crazy* Peace Corps and *wasting* money.'

We made a left on La Cienega following them to Sunset where we made a right. Not too far the Cad went left on Marmont, Frank said, 'We got a problem, its a dead end street.' It narrowed down to an alley, suddenly we were right on top of the limo turning into a parking area in front of a house. Another vehicle was already there. I read the plate number to Frank who'd ducked out of sight in the back of the van. Another hundred yards and I was in a cul de sac. It was so small it took about seven jogs back and forth to turn around, then we got out of there.

The next day we checked it out, the house belonged to Melvin Belli and the car was Casper Weinberger's. Naturally we did a hell of a lot of wondering as to why Belli and Weinberger were meeting with a couple cutthroats like Cohen and Begin. And just as curious, shortly after this, Candy Barr, Cohen's girlfriend showed up at the Beverly Wilshire and Henry saw Begin making trips up to her room. He commented everything must have been successful because Begin always came back with a smile. Belli also made trips returning with a smile."

Tony and I talked over four hours. I suggested that Cannizzaro might help with information on Monroe and I would introduce him. A few days later we met Eddie in Agoura, but he was in one of his strange Sicilian moods and wouldn't talk, we left him in Denny's. In the parking lot I asked Tony if he'd let me have a copy of his book Conspiracy but he didn't have one with him. He had become visibly upset when I wouldn't answer any of his questions about the Crime Organization. I hadn't mentioned the Mishpucka, I had no idea what Tony might do with it. At this stage of the game it could come down on me like mountains of molten lava. I had only told him it was an extremely powerful, very *secret* criminal organization, much more so than the Mafia. Summers said angrily, "It would have been better if you'd told me nothing rather than just enough to arouse my curiosity so bad."

"Tony, I've told you *far more* than I ever told anybody and I've given you names and leads. If you follow through it will be possible for you to discover everything on your own. That way it will be far easier for you to understand than me telling you." With no further words Summers tromped on the gas, he shot from the parking lot. In Ventura I stopped at the public library on Main St., they didn't have Summers book Conspiracy but they had a book he'd written several years before, The File On The Tsar. A big handsomely printed hard cover, I checked it out. Across the street at a book store I ordered a copy of Conspiracy, the clerk said it'd take about three weeks. I wanted to learn the kind of investigative writer Tony really was.

File On The Tsar was about the sinister mystery *surrounding* the time, place and manner of the end of the Imperial Family of Russia. The version accepted *by the world* was the massacre of Tsar Nicholas II, Tsarina Alexandra, and their five children in a room in the cellar of Ipatiev House in Ekaterinburg, a Siberian city. They were held prisoner by the Bolshevik Revolution leader Nikolai Lenin and Leon Bronstein, alias Trotsky. The death room was a nightmare scene of carnage with bullet and bayonet holes scattered all over the blood spattered walls and floor. There were witnesses to sounds of muffled volleys followed by individual gun shots coming from the cellar room of the prison house at midnight on July 16, 1918. The following day there were eye witnesses to the horrible blood drenched room. But not one witness was ever found who had actually seen the Romanov Families dead bodies, nor were they ever seen again dead or alive.

I read until early morning, with scant sleep I continued the next day until I'd finished. File On The Tsar was 416 pages with pictures and index. It was incredible. Summers had documented a Mishpucka diagram of diabolically clever false evidence, lies, bogus documents, innuendo and sly trails leading *away* from the guilty culprits, creating *scapegoats* to their horrendous premeditated crime. I was astounded, it was a *fantastic outline* exposing the Mishpuckas modus operandi, total Mishpucka chaos as I had already come to know it.

Summers had conducted a skillful and exhaustive investigation except for an amazing omission. The most *important* part of all, the *motive* behind the entire affair. I couldn't believe it, the motive was glaringly clear, I remembered that strange song and the first time I had heard it. "Money, money, money." There was one fact that could *not possibly* be ignored. Tsar Nicholas II was incredibly wealthy, the richest man in the world. A staff of fifteen thousand people and the Crown property worth over ten billion pounds. At the present day it is comparatively equivalent to at least six hundred billion dollars, an astronomical fortune.

Lenin and Bronstein, aka Trotsky, the Mishpucka revolutionary leaders were in a terrible need of money to *finance* their war. They had all the canon fodder needed, millions and millions of peasants. Money was all they needed, and Lenin would *never* have massacred the Romanov hostages in a senseless, murderous rage and lost that fortune, not even considering that the Romanov Family had *hung* his elder brother for conspiring in a bomb plot against the Tsar. Lenin would let the murderous rage come later, *after* the *massive fortune* was safely in his hands. During that period Lenin and Trotsky were taking *good care* of the Imperial Family. They knew the Tsar would *never* cooperate in transferring the Crown fortune if the Tsarina or his children were harmed. The Tsar must be *convinced* he would be allowed to keep a small fortune and be guaranteed safe asylum in a friendly country.

Lenin did not trust the Russian peasants or even high ranking Russian Bolsheviks to conduct his *most secret* mission. The only ones he trusted were the vicious Mishpuckas Trotsky imported from New York. They had performed expertly in *routing* Kerensky's Provisional Government, and were in *command positions* in Lenin's Bolsheviki hierarchy. Now he offered them grand cuts of the world's greatest fortune for their services. In Ekaterinburg this cabal of Mishpuckas took control over the inner areas of the prison, where later, *Yiddish scribblings* were observed on the walls. The Russian guards who were unable to read or write Yiddish had been transferred to the outside perimeters of the prison. Fakement of a bloody massacre scene was carried out successfully. The Imperial Family was spirited from the Ipatiev House in disguise. Upon news of the murders the oppressed Russian peasants became satisfied *vengeance* had been accomplished, and power of the Royal Family was dead forever. The Tsar and his family were transported to a new, extremely secret, closely guarded location near Moscow where Lenin and Trotsky had *personal control* over the *financial intricacies* of the fortune's transfer.

Soon afterwards Germany surrendered. Nikolai Lenin sent his hardened Mishpucka *agents* to Europe and every country around the world. Powerful governmental, industrial and financial factions were secretly contacted and were presented with *authentic documents*. The instruments bearing specific instructions and orders of transfer were prepared by a Mishpucka, Dimitri Rubenstein, Tsar Nicholas' Chief Banker, they bore the Tsar's signature and his Imperial Seal. These conspirators were offered *special incentives* for their cooperation and silence in the transfer of the worlds most fabulous fortune. Though ultra secret, this transfer of vast reaches of real estate, diamond and ore mines, International Corporate assets, railroads and tons of gold bullion etc., left trails a mile wide. Elephant *tracks* in the snow that an experienced investigative reporter backed by all the resources of BBC could not miss. It was a cause for *considerable* wonderment.

With the Crown fortune in his hands Lenin didn't dare free the Romanov family. Millions of Russian peasants would be outraged, conceivably they'd revolt when learning how Lenin and Trotsky had deceived them. But worse, the *transfer* of the Crown fortune would be revealed and peasants would be asking stupid questions like, *what* happened to it? As it stood, the Tsar, Tsarina and their five children were officially dead, victims of a bloody massacre, it would have to remain that way. It was then that Lenin's *premeditated* murderous madness burst forth. The Mishpucka then *committed* as cold blooded and horrible a mass *political assassination* of a Royal family that was ever perpetrated in the world's history.

Then forty five years later, another horrifying *political execution*. In public, the *assassination* of the President of the United States on television.

CHAPTER 44

On a street in Dallas, Texas, several shots rang out. President Kennedy riding in an open car said, "My God, I've been hit," a few seconds, then came more gun fire. The President's head exploded in a spray of brain tissue, blood and bone. The President's wife Jackie was heard to cry out, "Jack...they have killed my husband," then, "I have his brains in my hand." This, Mrs. Kennedy repeated time and time again.

Officially, the Warren Commission concluded, "One man, Lee Harvey Oswald murdered John F. Kennedy. The *lone sniper* had lain in wait and picked off his victim with two accurate rifle shots. There had been *no* conspiracy." This was an *official* edict, like the Russian Royal Family, the version that *had* to be *accepted* by the people of the United States and world wide. But in truth there was conspiracy upon conspiracy...and conspiracy to *double cross* a conspiracy.

Harvey Oswald did *not* kill President Kennedy. Frank and I had learned this *shortly after* the gruesome crime took place. The Sheriff of Dallas County, Bill Decker, was a good friend of Audie Murphy, he occasionally came to town on official business. They loved to go to the L.A. Police Academy and eat at the restaurant. On Decker's trips I'd arrange to reserve a booth, which wasn't always easy. Only a couple weeks after the assassination...Audie, Frank, Decker and I were having lunch, naturally there was but one subject on the tip of our tongues.

We were all skilled in firearms, Audie and Decker particularly were experts with hunting rifles and scopes. We had little difficulty coming to our *unanimous* conclusion, considering the existing factors it was virtually *impossible* for Oswald to make those shots with that rifle. It was basic, there had to be someone else shooting, with this concurrence Decker leaned forward slightly, gazing around the table at us his voice tempered, "I have another much stronger reason for knowing Oswald *never* shot JFK. There's a man in Dallas I've known a long time, he knows the *entire truth* about Oswald's involvement. He's scared to death to go to the Dallas PD or FBI. There's been a terrible *double cross* somewhere and everybody is scared shitless of everyone else. You would never believe all the accusations and *crazy* suspicions heaped on law enforcement in Texas by imbeciles in D.C. and the chaos it has created. This man feels that it's his duty to tell someone what he knows in case something happens to him. I realize it isn't in your jurisdiction, but that makes it even better. God only knows how this will turn out so you guys get something straight right now. There was *never* any conspiracy in my Sheriff's Dept. involving the assassination nor in the Dallas PD. I've known all these people too long...I would have known it...believe me, something as crazy as this I'd feel it in my bones." Bill's words threw a somber pall over lunch. After moments of silence Bill said, "I'll be in L.A. on business a few more days, when I return to Dallas if this guy wants to talk to you I'll give Audie a call and set something up."

A week later we got a call, drop by Murphy's office at Universal Studio. Audie loved excitement, his grin gave him away. "Hey, you guys want to take a trip?" We nodded silently never knowing what to expect. This caused his grin to widen, Audie never believed in long explanations, it was his military training, on a battlefield you didn't have time, you had to be sharp enough to figure it out fast. "Okay, tomorrow morning be at Burbank Airport at six forty five sharp. We are meeting Decker and his friend in Ruidoso at noon."

It had been convenient for Decker to arrange a meeting about halfway to Dallas. Audie had some sort of race horse deals going in New Mexico. He always lost so much money on them we tried never to mention his horse fiascos. He had a favorite story he dropped on people foolish enough to quiry him as to how his ponies were doing. "Oh well, I plain lost my shirt the last three years in a row on those stupid nags, but geez, this last year was fabulous."

Invariably they'd exclaim, "That's great, how much did you win?"

"Win," he'd shout, "Win hell, I broke even."

Staring out a small window of the two engine plane I'd become absorbed by the wild snowy mountains and desert we zoomed over. Everything was forgotten till suddenly we began losing altitude. Bill was waiting at the dirt airstrip in his Sheriff's car. Out of the plane I realized it was dead winter, the wind was blowing, it was freezing cold. Audie neglected to mention this, it didn't seem to bother him. Decker explained, "John is waiting for us in town." Little more was said until we parked at the cafe and went inside. Shaking hands we settled in a large leather booth. John was middle aged, a large man, serious. From his speech and bearing I felt he had spent years as an officer in the military. We didn't ask and he didn't say.

Concealing any nervousness or tension he seemed eager to tell what he knew. Decker and John had already had lunch, we ordered the house specialty, steaming bowls of chili beans and soda crackers with lots of butter. We ate and John talked. It wasn't a rambling or memorized dissertation broken with pauses to think and review for likely mistakes. It came out smooth and positive like an experience etched in the mind, needing no prompting because it was there fresh in his brain, it had been a job, a duty he'd been personally involved in and had performed. Amazing and harrowing as was John's tale of intrigue there were few interruptions.

Decker's friend began, "First and most important I must qualify Lee Harvey Oswald, he was *none* of the criminal things he's accused of. He was an *agent* of the U.S. government acting under *the specific* orders of E. Howard Hunt. The *true facts* of the assassination as far as I know them are so fantastically shocking if I tried to force them out in the open I'd surely end up in the same graveyard as Oswald, or committed to an insane asylum, buried so deep *no one* would ever hear of me again. Hunt is a patriot, a Super Patriot, he understood and feared the *danger* of Castro's Cuba as a communist fortress only a few miles from our shore better than anyone. He had worked and labored on the invasion of Cuba by the exiles like a man possessed. When the Bay of Pigs became a terrible, embarrassing fiasco, he like others in CIA blamed President Kennedy. But deep in his soul and in fairness he realized the blame was not Kennedy's although he'd officially taken the brunt upon his own shoulders. The failure was a combination of errors, outrageous misjudgments, and bad luck.

But Cuba's danger to the U.S. grew in intensity as its ties with Moscow became obvious. Dreaming up fantastic schemes Hunt had devised extraordinary methods of assassinating Castro, poison pills in coffee, poison in his food at his favorite cafe, exploding cigars, all dismal failures, then Hunt's festering frustration conceived what has become the most *bizarre* political assassination intrigue of all time. His scheme was to *inflame* the American people against Castro and *stir patriotism* to a boiling point not felt *since* the bombing of Pearl Harbor. Enraged Americans would demand that our military invade Cuba and wipe out the two-bit dictator for his barbarous *attempt* to assassinate President Kennedy."

John read our incredulous looks. "Oh yes..! There was to be an *attempt* on the life of President Kennedy so *realistic* that its failure would be looked upon as nothing less than a miracle. The footprints would lead *directly* to Castro's doorstep, a trail the rankest amateur couldn't lose. Very unfortunate for Oswald he fit the bill perfect for Hunt's operation. He'd worked for Military Intelligence for several years with considerable success. It started when he was a Marine at Japan's Atsugi Air Base a few miles south of Tokyo. An Intelligence Officer recognizing Oswald's possibilities had asked him to assist in making a connection he was trying to establish. The young Marine was not only surprised but very pleased with the assignment, which was a beautiful Japanese hostess at the Queen Bee Club a popular bar in Tokyo. Because of a natural proclivity for Intelligence liaison his role escalated increasingly to more important assignments. The Russian defection incident was *part* of Military Intelligence grooming of Oswald for a *deep cover* of communist affiliation. That was before Hunt had chosen him for his *Assassination Mission.* He was inducted into the dark, mysterious, clandestine secrets of the CIA, ending in an ignoble death.

The Cuban exiles in New Orleans and Miami were seething. In early 1963 Oswald was dropped right into a *boiling cauldron* in New Orleans. His instructions were to establish himself as a disgruntled ex-Marine and Commie adherent, a zealous left-winger. Joining the Pro-Castro, Fair Play for Cuba organization he got himself arrested to accentuate his activities and profile and to top this off Hunt and General Edwin Walker, a recognized leader of the ultra-conservative right wing, faked a shooting attempt on Walkers life. It was blamed on Oswald to add a dangerous, *sinister touch* to his character which would be needed later."

John smiled at Frank who's head was wagging, he said, "I know exactly what you are thinking Frank and it gets worse. At first Hunt did not tell Oswald what his exact mission was, except it was of the *highest* National Security priority. He was instructed to give his wife absolutely *no hint* whatsoever of his secret government connections.

Hunt did not trust her, in fact, he was paranoid about Marina being a Russian spy. It was only two months before the *Fake Assassination* when Hunt gave Oswald the rifle, explaining his part in the scheme. Oswald was to fire *three shots* from his rifle *in the air,* then abandon it and the empty cartridges at the scene. He was to quickly leave the building for a rendezvous with agents who would transport him to a secret destination where he'd remain in hiding until after Cuba was invaded by the United States. A *fake trail* to Mexico City ending at the Cuban Embassy would lead investigators to think he had fled to Cuba. The *belief* that Castro planned the assassination of President Kennedy and the assassin was being *harbored* under his protection in Cuba would stir the Americans to a feverish pitch of anger, like, 'Remember the Maine,' the battleship blown up in Havana harbor in 1898. It *started* the Spanish American War. Oswald was shocked and not a little frightened, however Hunt convinced him that he could be saving the United States from destruction by nuclear rockets being planted in Cuba by Russia. He confided to Oswald that JFK had *not* been made aware of their plan, that was for the sake of authenticity of his reactions. But it was approved and *sanctioned* by *high ranking members* of the cabinet. Hunt assured him, after U.S. Forces overran Cuba and exposed the Russians nuclear missiles, President Kennedy would forgive them for their precipitant actions. He would perceive them as American heros. Oswald could come in out of the cold and live as an *ordinary citizen* with his family, which desire he'd indicated a number of times. On first blush Oswald was extremely leery of the feasibility of Hunt's plan. But commencing to see and feel the power and confidence of people behind the mission he joined eagerly. His orders were to leave a trail that could be *easily followed,* yet not so overly obvious as to bring down suspicion. And specifically the most critical part was the *moment* of firing the rifle. It must be *instantly clear* to the crowd and security people in the street as to the *location and source* of the shots. Success of the operation depended entirely upon police *quickly* finding the rifle and the *clues.* The hysteria and excited press and TV announcers *picking up the scent* would trumpet a bloodhound *hue and cry* following the trail right to Fidel Castro's doorstep."

Audie mused, "Sounds exactly like a *Hollywood script."*

"Yes, but by standards it was a basic plan. Of course all covert operations have inherent danger and are subject to break downs, but *my God,* this was no break down or neglect of performance, or even bad luck. What has happened is *incomprehensible.* It cannot be that the Mafia or Cuban exiles have done it, there is no motive, they had already been given *inside tips* that an operation was underway that would return them to Cuba. It would've been *totally stupid* for them to interfere. Anyway, even Oswald wasn't told the route to take for his rendezvous until the *last minute,* so *how* could they possibly know where he was? Only a few of Hunt's most trusted men knew all his plans down to the last detail. It is impossible to believe any of them is a traitor. Still it is clear, *who ever* killed the President *had* to know all the minute details to pull it off the way they did. Something very frightening, horribly sinister had *interposed* Hunt's mission. He and his men are petrified, they conceive this as not just murder, they've been drawn into *treason.* The mysterious assassins then intercepted Oswald before he reached his rendezvous. Certainly they were about to kill him when the police officer *happened* upon the scene, they did not dare be caught with Oswald so they shot the officer. During the shooting Oswald ran and hid in a theatre, he was captured minutes later. It had to happen that way, I know, Oswald would *never* have shot an officer under any circumstances, I'm positive."

From his pocket John removed a *manila envelope,* business size, about 4x10, it was thick, he pushed it over to me, the flap was glued. Strangely it was further secured by red sealing wax about the size of a quarter with a thumbprint impression, a procedure police used to protect vital evidence from being tainted before it reached the court. I saw it was perfectly plain, no writing, I passed it over to Frank.

John said, "Inside are *irrefutable* documents, evidence verifying what I have just told you."

There was silence around the table, then Decker said, "We have to get rolling back to Dallas, it's a long haul." They shook hands and left. Audie had rented an auto to take us to the plane. On the way we stopped at some horse stables, Audie talked with some people a minute then we returned to the airstrip. Back at Burbank Airport Frank handed the envelope to Audie and asked him to put it in his safe with other things he was keeping for us.

Driving to our office *Frank and I agreed* that the murder of JFK was an evil whirlpool so dangerous it could destroy Dallas. We had no business sticking our noses in, we *remembered* Big Bill McKesson threatening what he would do to us if we even thought of going near Malibu the night that JFK was at the party. We weren't sure he was kidding with his threat to kill us. Now if McKesson heard about this, if he didn't murder us, there was a damn good chance someone else would. The frightening part was that *no one* knew who that someone else was...it was impossible to defend against.

It was only a few days, Frank and I got a hurry up call to come by Audie's office, this time there was no grin. He'd received many urgent calls from Bill Decker. Audie explained, "Hunt and his agents have regrouped from their horrified panic, they've sprung back into action. Hunt's machinations and connection with Oswald had to be *covered-up* at all costs. Bill says Military Intelligence, FBI, and the CIA were terrified. If their secret schemes were to be *exposed* they'd be rooted out in an eruption of calamitous national anger. In their *nightmares* all they can see is a firing squad. In fact they've solemnly declared that National Security is at stake. That's their *justification* for a *cover-up* at any cost. John told Decker he had made a horrible mistake by talking to us and giving us that envelope in a moment of panic, he wants it back *immediately*. I don't know if I made a terrible blunder or not, I said the first thing coming to my mind. I told Bill we'd destroyed it on the flight back to Burbank, over the desert we had torn it into little pieces and let them fly out the pilot's window. Bill repeated this to John, he told Bill if we were lying and still had it we would all be destroyed. Decker says for our own good we had better believe this." Frank and I figured Audie made the best move he could when he said the envelope was destroyed.

Then we watched the plot unfolding as the powerful, *politically contrived* Warren Commission covered-up the heinous assassination of JFK under orders of the new President, Lyndon B. Johnson. We could easily guess our fate if we interfered. Some months later I left the District Attorney Bureau of Investigation in L.A., and took the job as Chief Investigator for the Public Defender in Ventura County.

Just as the clerk in the book store had said it would, Summers book, Conspiracy arrived three weeks later. Like File on the Tsar, it was excellently put together. Diligent and *definitively researched* with integrity, it was 648 pages of itemized sources of information and a name index. In future years it obviously would be of great historical research value, it would also drive people insane, the *who* and *what* responsible for JFK's assassination was a *labyrinth* of conspiratorial chaos. I hadn't voted for JFK, at that time strong personal feelings had prevented it, but these had begun to change. Upon his death an awesome feeling of terrible loneliness, a *fear for America* swept over me. Momentarily in Conspiracy, its author had arrived right at the veritable *point of truth* when he speculated, "Perhaps some terrible *unfaceable embarrassment* of involvement rather than a murderous intent had forced United States Intelligence to *cover-up* their part in the assassination."

Instead of rooting into this involvement Summers succumbed to the Mishpuckas devious, false evidence and rumor trails concluding that those *guilty of the assassination* fell into one of *three groups,* the Mafia...Anti-Castro Cubans...or a U.S. Intelligence Agency. Helping Tony down this road of *misinformation* was Mishpucka, Aron Kohn. In '78 as the Director of the New Orleans Crime Commission, Kohn *lied* to Tony, he deceivingly described Carlos Marcello as, "The most powerful single *organized crime* figure in the Southern United States, the head of the Mafia or Cosa Nostra in this area." Kohn also told him Jack Ruby's friend Harold Tannenbaum, was manager of five of Marcello's biggest money making joints on Bourbon Street, but he'd *reversed* it, actually it was Marcello and the Italians who *worked for* Harold Tannenbaum and top Mishpucka Meyer Lansky. When the Mishpucka took more than a *billion dollars* to Miami right after the war, it was Lansky's brains and wizardry that put the Mishpuckas *in command* of gambling, prostitution, narcotics and political corruption in the New Orleans, Havana, and Miami area. Marcello couldn't put two and two together much less Lansky's empire. Without Lansky's patronage Carlos could never have risen higher than a two-bit street thug. He was a *front man* designed to take a rap for the Mishpucka. The fact he'd become personally rich and notorious was merely for their convenience. Hunt and Oswald salvaging their senses from the *paralyzing shock* of the Kennedy murder most certainly had identical thoughts, *'I've been framed.'* A double-cross of fantastic dimensions. The consequences were too devastating, far too terrifying to grasp, it was the end for them.

By my knowing that *none* of the *three suspects* Tony had named were guilty, hundreds of rumors and *false trails* in his book *instantly* became extraneous. Then in relation with the *real assassins* the first and most *important clue* found was the well publicized Magic Bullet, a *dead give-away.* A bullet was found on a stretcher carrying either President Kennedy or Governor Connally into the hospital. Warren's Commission would have the *public believe* that the Magic Bullet in its travels *had,* pierced JFK's back...coursed through the front of his neck...went on to strike Connally in the back...then pierced his lung, severed a vein, artery and nerve, broke the right fifth rib, destroying five inches of bone and emerged from Connally's right chest...it then plunged into the back of his right forearm and broke a thick bone, the distal end of the radius and came out the other side of the wrist, finally ending up by striking Connally's left leg. After doing all this damage it was still in *pristine* condition, without distortion when it was discovered on the stretcher. Thus amid derision and skepticism it was dubbed, "The Magic Bullet."

Ballistics experts were positive that the Magic Bullet came from Oswald's rifle. They were correct, but it had not *returned* from the sky where Oswald had fired it then *miraculously fell* on the stretcher at the hospital to be found. It had been very carefully planted there. Regardless of Hunt's convictions that his closest agents were beyond suspicion, *one of them* was a spy, a mole in deep, deep, cover...

Hunt's scheme of a *phony assassination* was monitored from the beginning by an insidious enemy. At some point after the rifle was first received it was test fired, they had to be sure the cheap weapon would fire at the crucial moment. During the test firing into cotton a perfect bullet was *quietly* palmed, the enemy knew when the time came their own bullet destined to kill JFK would be shattered with no ballistics identification being possible.

The mole pocketed the test bullet, passing it to a confederate who could get near enough during the confusion to plant it. Thus the trail would lead directly back to Lee Oswald and his rifle. When the shots in Dealy Plaza rang out Jack Ruby had a perfect alibi. He was in the advertising department of the Dallas Morning News talking to people that knew him. Amid ensuing excitement and confusion Ruby quietly slipped away to complete the assignment that he'd been paid for. He was to park on a quiet tree lined residential street where he would intercept and kill Oswald *before* he could make his rendezvous with Hunt's men.

His killing would be blamed on one of the *three* suspect groups, the Mafia, the Cubans or an American Intelligence Agency. Myriads of crisscrossing trails of rumor and suspicion already were carefully circulated *pinpointing* these suspects, Mishpucka *chaos* was in effect. But fate now, as it had in the past, dealt a horrifying blow to the evil Mishpuckas schemes. It came in the form of an entirely unexpected policeman doing an *observant* job on patrol just as it should be done.

When the astounding message of shots fired at the President's motorcade was broadcast over the police radio the Mishpucka was certain all patrol cars would *converge* on Dealy Plaza. But the Dallas police didn't panic and stuck to *good patrol procedure.* At 12:44 p.m., fourteen minutes after Kennedy was shot they broadcast a suspect's description, "White male, about 30 years, 165 pounds, slender build," it fit Oswald. One minute later at 12:45 p.m., Officer J.D. Tippet, in a radio car was ordered to the Oak Cliff area and was instructed to

"Remain at large for any emergency."

Oswald came walking down the street toward him, Ruby stepped from his car. He was at the instant of pulling his gun to kill Oswald when unexpectedly Officer Tippet came up. He'd spotted Oswald's close resemblance to the broadcast. Observant, the officer kept his eyes watchfully on Oswald's movements. But suddenly and startlingly he placed Ruby, *seeing them together* the officer's eyebrows shot up with comprehension and alarm. Ruby spotting this panicked. God, if he got arrested *with Oswald* it was all over, a hand on the gun under his coat prepared to kill Oswald flew up. He fired repeatedly at the officer. Then fleeing in terror, leaping into his car in mortal fear he sped away.

At 1:16, forty five minutes after the shots in Dealy Plaza there came the call from a citizen using Tippet's car radio, "We've had a shooting here, it's a police officer, somebody's shot him." The most reliable witnesses to the officer's murder were Mrs. Aquilla Clemons and Frank Wright, both lived on Tenth Street. Mrs. Clemons stated, "I saw *two men* near the policeman's car just before the shots. The man with the gun was short and chunky, kind of heavy build, wearing khaki and a white shirt," a description *fitting Ruby,* "the second man was thin and tall," *it fit Oswald.* "The chunky man with the gun ran off in one direction, the second man in another."

Mr. Wright heard the shots in his front room, he said, "Stepping out my front door I caught sight of Officer Tippet in time to see him roll over once then lie still. I saw a man of medium height wearing a long coat that ended just above his hands, he ran around the police car fast as he could and jumped in a little old gray coupe, he drove away very fast." Within three minutes radio cars and an ambulance arrived. Four empty casings were found on the ground *ejected* from an automatic pistol.

Sgt. Gerald Hill, an officer with many years of army experience and police work behind him *recognized* that the shells were ejected from an *automatic pistol,* he radioed this information immediately to headquarters. At the *same time* he ordered Officer J.M. Poe to mark the casings with his initials to record the chain of evidence. Another patrol officer radioed in, "I have an eyeball witness to the suspect in the shooting, he's a white male armed with a dark finish *automatic pistol.*" When arrested only minutes later in a theater Oswald carried a *revolver* which *does not* eject its shells. No one in their right mind would conceive that fleeing from a murder scene, and expecting the killers next bullets to strike him in the back, Oswald would dally to *eject* shells from his revolver and drop them on the ground before he ran. What was to have been a nice *clean-cut* execution with no clue to the killer had suddenly become *a fiasco,* an unbelievable mess. An officer killed and Oswald in jail where he could talk and *blow-up* the Mishpuckas entire operation. And *somewhere* in Dallas, holed up in his Command Post, E. Howard Hunt was cursing...sweating...going crazy, no matter how he squirmed *it came out the same,* Lee Harvey Oswald was a double agent, he'd been double crossed.

In his cell at the Dallas police station Oswald could only scream, "I did not kill anyone, *I'm a patsy."* Back at the Carousel, Jack Ruby was a mental case, fearfully he reported the debacle. One of his *first* long distance calls was to a contact man, Jack Gruber in Hollywood, Mickey Cohen's associate. They were so enraged with Ruby's fiasco that if they hadn't still needed him they'd have butchered him. His new orders were to get into the jail where Oswald was and kill him immediately. They laid out the reason he was to give for killing him, Ruby was to claim that, "He had become so mentally distraught over this lousy commie shooting the President and the thought of his poor wife and children suffering that he had become temporarily insane." He must stick with that and nothing else. He would become a *'hero'* for having killed this traitor and be back on the street in only a few days.

Strangely, the *'hero'* bit was the *same words* Cohen used when he conned Sammy Lo Cigno into taking the blame for Jack O'Hara's murder. Ruby *disposed* of the automatic pistol he had been supplied with to kill Oswald but instead had used to kill Tippet. Pocketing his own 38 revolver he'd purchased legally a few years before, he started prowling the police station waiting for a chance to finish off Oswald. It came two days later. In the basement of the Dallas City Hall, Ruby shot and killed Oswald.

At the time JFK was killed Ruby had himself a perfect alibi, but wasn't covered at the time Tippet was shot. The description by eye witnesses of the killer fit Ruby so close, the Mishpuckas decided he needed an alibi. Seth Kantor, a White House Corespondent provided it. At Parkland Hospital where Kennedy was taken only a handful of reporters were allowed in. Kantor claimed that just before entering, Ruby tugged on his sleeve asking him if he thought he should close the Carousel until further notice out of respect for Pres. Kennedy. Kantor told him it was a good idea and hurried on into the hospital. This was the *exact moment* Tippet was shot, the *perfect alibi.* Kantor had known Ruby from four years previous while a news reporter in

Dallas. Even more disturbing, Seth Kantor also was *connected* with Oswald, Candy Barr, and Melvin Belli, and even *more* coincidental, he was one of the very few outsiders let into the hospital area where the Magic Bullet was planted. But strangest of all, Ruby *denied* going to Parkland Hospital and repudiated Kantor's alibi for the officer's death. Kantor was stuck with this *sinister* embarrassment which not even the Warren Commission was able to swallow.

An unseen airtight skin protecting the *real assassination* scheme by the Mishpuckas had been pinpricked. I knew they had committed the two murders in Dallas on November 22, 1963, still it just didn't make sense, the most necessary element, that important ingredient, a motive...was missing. *More than once* Oswald had openly professed genuine admiration and liking for JFK and his family.

As for Tony's *three* prime suspects, the Mafia, Cuban exiles, and a United States Intelligence Agency there was no logical motive, and the Mishpuckas deep mole had monitored Hunt's *Fake Assassination* operation all the way and had approved. As with Summers suspects, the Mishpucka had *no reason* to interfere, if Hunt's plan succeeded, the Mishpucka and Mafia would both regain their bases for criminal activities in Havana, the Cuban exiles would return to their homes and U.S. Intelligence would be satisfied by the removal of Russia's nuclear missile threats from our shores.

But suddenly, about two months *before* Kennedy's visit to Dallas everything changed. Something deeply affecting the Mishpuckas had occurred, it was then that their own *Real Assassination* plans were put into effect. In Dallas strange events began to happen that later would point at Lee Oswald as the assassin. In one instance a person resembling Oswald and giving his name as such went to a gun shop, he wanted three holes drilled for the telescopic sight mounting on a rifle. But Oswald's rifle found at the Texas School Book Depository needed only *two* holes. This was one instance, the book Conspiracy had documented a whirlwind of Mishpucka conspiratorial chaos left to be *found after* the assassination. The sinister clues and trails lead direct to and incriminated Oswald of the assassination. But Oswald would not be alive to defend himself or refute this evidence.

Ruby had been in *serious* financial difficulties, his night club was months in arrears on rent. IRS was on his back for over $50,000 in unpaid taxes. Suddenly Ruby who'd long lived out of his hip pocket was waving around *huge sums of money*, he began using a safe in his office which he talked about embedding in concrete. Ruby's part in the conspiracy was to simply, at a *specific* time and place, fill Oswald full of lead. Learning that Ruby's contact man in Hollywood was an associate of Mickey Cohen's, I began to *generate* a startling, shocking picture of some very powerful people who were involved. But it was crazy, they had no motive.

Page by page I had worked my way into Conspiracy and Tony's remarkable documentary of Mishpucka chaos with its dark abyss of crooked, manufactured trails leading to Miami, New Orleans and to Marcello and Cubans and U.S. Intelligence Agents. Then amazingly, Chapter 21...with monstrous comprehension the motive for the *real assassination* catapulted before my eyes. New Orleans, Miami and all the other *chaos* trails were blotted out. Tony had dug deep, probably deeper than he realized. Lord, like Audie said, it was a *Hollywood scenario*, I was amazed, reading on was like slowly twisting the dial on a very complex camera, bringing it to an ultimate focus.

My blood curdled with the terrible irony of it, it was diabolical. President Kennedy, the dynamic, vital young leader of the greatest country on earth, holding out such *bright hopes* to everyone was shot, murdered because of one word, *PEACE*. It was known to only a very few trusted aides, JFK had been on the verge of *negotiating* World Peace. His life was forfeited for his interference into the Mishpuckas unspeakable, insensate *greed*, money....billions on billions, cold, cold money, money, money, money.

Chapter 21 had brought the lens to a fine focus. In Hollywood, Gruber, the man Ruby called *minutes after* shooting Tippet...that was the connection, where the orders issued forth. Not long before JFK was killed, the conversation Henry Jacob's had overheard between Cohen and Begin at the Beverly Wilshire Hotel, Henry had become terribly excited, he had felt it, he knew he was on to *something big*. Frank and I were amused at his exuberant rantings in the van. We'd kidded him, but we knew Henry was no novice with his imagination running wild. I remembered his exact words, "Mickey was sounding real important, like he's going in for *big politics*, he cursed Kennedy and his Peace Corp, and his wasting millions on two-bit countries in Africa and South America." What really chilled me now was *recalling* Hank's vivid description of their aroused, *excited conversation* about "War and Peace and the *catastrophic* possibilities of *losing* all their multi-billion dollar defense appropriations." We'd tailed Cohen and Begin to Belli's house above Sunset Boulevard for their *meeting* with a mysterious guest, Casper Weinberger. To Frank and I this incident had meant *intelligence information* of obvious value because of Begin the *terrorist's* presence. But hell, it was to be *more* than twenty years before it began to add up.

We didn't know Weinberger was head man of a giant corporate colossus with powerful *tentacles* around the globe. The corporation was constructing billions of dollars of U.S. military installations in Europe, the Mediterranean, and in South East Asia because of overt threats of war. Until Conspiracy, Chapter 21, I had not known that the biggest threat in the world to Weinberger's billions was the news of President Kennedy's *negotiations* of World Peace.

With the killing of Kennedy all thought and hope of Peace was instantly destroyed. shattered along with the lives, limbs and minds of thousands of America's young men caught up in the premeditated insanity of Viet Nam's holocaust. And now fantastically, more then two decades later, Casper Weinberger is the Secretary of Defense, demanding billions upon billions for his corporation to build military installations. And this in the face of tragic losses of young lives and the *abandonment* of billions of dollars of equipment and bases in the fiasco of Viet Nam. At the same time Casper Weinberger sinisterly attempts to demoralize United States military strength and morale by undermining the servicemens traditional pension plan.

In Wash., D.C. just *prior* to JFK's trip to Dallas, a White House Correspondent, Seth Kantor obtained the latest information of the Presidential motorcade routes. Through inside D.C. informants and sources Kantor was one of the *first* to learn of the *secret* Peace talks Kennedy was setting up with Fidel Castro. Besides *knowing* Belli and Cohen who were at the Hollywood meeting and Jack Ruby, Oswald and Candy Barr in Dallas, he knew Weinberger in D.C.. Kantor was *tied in* full circle.

Belli was Ruby's lawyer, he refused to put him on the stand for fear he'd lose control of his mouth and reveal why he shot Oswald. Babbling, "I've been *used* for a purpose," Ruby was frightened nearly to death by the Mishpucka about what *would happen* if he broke and spilled his guts that the *assassination of the President* was a Jew plot. They'd put all the blame on him for endangering their master plan with his failure to *kill Oswald the first time.* Ruby was told, "It would mean the torture of his family and of Jews in the streets, there could be a *total extermination* of the Jews if the *truth came out."* Terrorized by the Mishpucka threats, he ranted on about his Jewish origins and how, "The Jews would be killed by the millions because of what he had done."

Four days after John F. Kennedy's funeral, Lyndon B. Johnson, now President, *summoned* Chief Justice Warren to the White House.

Melodramatically he informed Warren that it was his National duty to head a "Commission of Inquiry" into the murder of JFK. Johnson told him, "If certain *dangerous facts* were *not* concealed it could cost forty million lives." Then commenced one of the most lurid, official, governmental *cover-ups* of all time. Over the years it has grown into a *national disgrace*. Public demand for the *true* facts of the murder of the popular John F. Kennedy has burgeoned and multiplied out of government control.

At one point Ruby was *ready* to talk, he stated, "The murder of JFK was an act of *over-throwing* the government," then even more electrifying he declared, "I know *who* had President Kennedy killed." In person, Ruby told Chief Justice Earl Warren that his life was in danger and if he'd arrange to get him to D.C. under his protection, he would talk. Repeatedly, *eight times* in all, Oswald's killer *begged* Warren to arrange his transfer to D.C., the Justice refused.

Several times when pressured, President Lyndon Johnson had invoked secrecy in the name of National Security. The purpose was to cover-up, *first*, the *Phony Assassination* by Hunt, and *second* the *Real Assassination* committed by the Mishpucka. Hunt's wild scheme had created the lunatic effect of positioning JFK as the target in a shooting gallery. Johnson's National Security fears were tied to the Real Assassination scheme. If it was revealed to the public that JFK was assassinated by the Jews it could ignite a *Holy War*, forty million Jews in America could be exterminated, *precisely* as Ruby fearfully predicted, "Jews will be killed by the millions *because* of what I have done."

To Christians, white and black, President JFK's murder would be *tantamount* to the *second* Crucifixion of Jesus Christ. This time it was a *high powered bullet* exploding his head in a halo of blood, bone and brains. Not like nailing his hands and feet to the Cross, but still the *second killing of Christ*. President Johnson feared a populace out of control, gone mad...riots...revolution...a fearful Holy War, so the decision was made, America and the world were not entitled to the truth.

Conspiracy, Chapter 21, page 419, "On September 17, 1963, with nine weeks left until Pres. Kennedy's Dallas trip, an American and an African met over coffee at United Nations Headquarters in New York. Seydou Diallo, a little known diplomat was an Ambassador, the Guinean Envoy to Cuba. As his American contact he'd selected Ambassador William Attwood, Special Advisor to the United States Delegation at the UN. Diallo knew and trusted Wm. Attwood as the former American Ambassador to Guinea. Diallo was aware Attwood had met Castro and was also on close personal terms with Kennedy. Diallo's *urgent message* was that after three years of confrontation Castro wanted to reach some sort of an understanding with the U.S.. He was especially unhappy about the way Cuba was becoming tied to Russia and was looking for some way out. Just *two days later* on September 19, Kennedy gave *secret* approval to tentative talks with Castro, he selected Ambassador Attwood to handle it. Robert, JFK's brother, was very concerned with the secrecy of the matter and was bothered about the *possibility* of a leak. But Peace was on the move, a hot-line telephone link between the White House and Kremlin had been opened, a symbol of determination to bring the superpowers into closer touch on sensitive issues."

Soon Pres. Kennedy and Kruschev would sign a nuclear test ban treaty, and JFK had projected the return of a thousand troops from Viet Nam, the first stage of a withdrawal that was to bring all U.S. personnel home within two years. Kennedy's quest for World Peace was taking shape. But Robert Kennedy's great concern for leaks in the proposed Castro, Cuban peace talks was *real.* In a *few weeks* his brother's assassination would shatter all hope for peace and security around the world for years to come. The eventful facts of the White House intrigue during the *few weeks prior* to JFK's death as related in Chapter 21 were of over powering interest. Of equal importance in Conspiracy, Chapter 20, entitled, "Double Image In Dallas," were the motivating clues *pointing directly* at the Mishpucka.

CHAPTER 45

The bloody murders of prominent lawyer Lyman Smith and his wife Charlene was a *festering* sore for Dist. Atty. Michael Bradbury. Now nearly two years since that dark night of the sensational killings and still public clamor *refused* to die down. Bradbury received orders from the Black Robe Mishpuckas to end *growing rumors* of sinister goings-on behind the executions. The case had to be *officially* closed, soon...one way or another a *scape-goat* must be found. On November 20, 1981, Joseph Alsip was arrested and charged with two counts of first degree murder. Bradbury was primed to demand the ultimate penalty, death. Such *finality* should quell all of those nasty rumors. Going for the kill the servile D.A. assigned his ace prosecutor Peter Kossoris to the case. Eleven years previous Kossoris had made his mark with the Mishpucka. They had given approval of his efficiency and hardness in the *prosecution and conviction* of Supervisor Robbie Robinson.

Without physical evidence, the D.A. based his entire prosecution on statements of a minister he had dug up. Donald Mikel, ordained minister of Ventura's Missionary Church was an Associate Pastor in charge of family marriage counseling. Two months after the murders Alsip and his wife had visited Pastor Mikel in a counseling session. At that time nothing was said about the deaths. A week later Alsip returned alone for more counseling. According to Mikel during their conversation the suspect alluded several times to having knowledge of the murders. Fortunately, after much struggling to get a lawyer Alsip finally got Dick Hanawalt.

After doing a background investigation of Kossoris' star witness, Pastor Mikel, Hanawalt laid for them at the preliminary hearing. To the stand he called S.R. Mc Dill, professional therapist, one of only a few counselors in the state licensed to assess the abilities of other counselors. Knowing Mikel personally he had this to say about him, "As to Mikel's honesty and veracity he has tendencies which would *compromise* his statements *to the point* that I'd have to question the truth and honesty of his word. In cases where there was an ounce of drama, or intrigue or excitement, Pastor Mikel would add two and two and get seven."

Under Hanawalt's expert cross examination Mikel went off the deep end. He claimed that since he'd counseled Alsip, "My own life has become in danger. One evening while walking on Victoria Ave. this old type car pulled in front of me with one wheel coming over the curb, three men were inside, one came out and he warned me to keep my mouth shut about what I knew about the Smith case. I can only describe him as a Caucasian, I did not get the license. Another time while walking in the afternoon a man with a withered arm came over a stone wall at me muttering something unintelligible. And also I received numerous threatening phone calls warning me repeatedly to keep silent or suffer dire consequences. Once the only sound on the line was a gun shot." Detectives put a recorder on the Pastor's phone to trap and record these calls but there were none.

Hanawalt had learned that a few years before in Indiana, Mikel was involved in an identical incident where he'd supposedly helped police investigate a crime. He told police *several gunmen* approached his car, it was a close call because he had been able to avoid them only by gunning the engine of his car and escaping. On the stand he related still another occasion when he and his family were in danger. He had sneaked a police officer into his house in a laundry bag to protect him. After questioning Mikel very close about all his alleged threats on the street and over the phone, Hanawalt told the court, "We are talking here about a pathological case of paranoia, Pastor Mikel suffers from a psychosis with *definite* paranoid characteristics."

At this time the judge called a halt of Mikel's testimony. In an unusual and surprise move, Hanawalt called Alsip to the stand. He denied *ever* making any admissions of being involved in the murders. Also he testified that while in custody he had cooperatively signed a release to let police question the Pastor regarding their confidential conversations as he had no fear of anything he had told Mikel.

With no physical evidence to go on and just one witness of the Pastor's caliber, the judge held Alsip to *answer* to a double murder, under the *penalty of death.* But the D.A. knew he had no chance to convict Alsip, sending him to death and closing the case, he had to drop the charges. His hope for a clear cut *burial* of the *real* motive for the murders had failed. Then, Bradbury still desperately trying to close the case with Joe Alsip as the guilty party, claimed in the Star Free Press, *he knew* that Alsip had murdered the prominent Ventura attorney and his wife, but he just didn't have quite enough evidence to try him. This then would in effect be the recorded, *official verdict* solving the murder of Lyman and Charlene Smith. Bradbury's *Star Free Press conviction* of Joseph Alsip would have to be accepted by the people.

But the Smiths trail of death was far more devious and crooked than Dist. Atty. Bradbury revealed. Three years before his murder, Smith formed a corporation, Maverick International Airlines. It was the world's largest shipper of live cattle by air, flying them to Iran. Smith's two Boeing 707's flying out of Stewart Airport in Newburgh, New York to the middle east could carry 100,000 lbs. of dairy cattle per load. On return flights Lyman's 707's sometimes brought back miscellaneous cargos, auto parts and shoes from Italy or flowers and vegetables from Israel, however *something else* was also coming back on the 707's *not* on the manifest. Lyman was unaware of millions of bucks of cocaine being smuggled in the mostly empty cargo jets. For a year and a half the cattle shipping venture worked, then, the Shah of Iran was toppled, losing control of his government he was run out of the country. With the close of Tehran Airport, Maverick Airlines hit upon bad times. Payroll checks bounced, employees were laid off, investors failed to come through with money and one of the 707's was repossessed.

For the attorney it was a desperate time fighting to salvage the airline. It meant endless trips to the east coast, three and four days at a time, which soon became periods of weeks. Working night and day he put in hundreds of hours. His young wife resented the airline thing because he was gone so much. She'd reverted back to an old lover and was carrying on a heavy affair. Smith was going mad with frustration, it seemed hopeless, corporate withholding taxes hadn't been paid for eight months. Over a quarter of a million dollars was owed, soon the IRS would be breathing down his neck.

Delving deep into minute details of immensely costly employee operations Smith began to wonder and think about the unprofitable return flights from the Middle East. Why hadn't greater effort been put into bringing back larger pay loads? The question was put to an employee with some back pay due. Apparently of a mind that Smith was *part* of the cocaine operations it elicited an insolent retort. "Shit, how much *more* valuable cargo do you want to carry?"

At first the lawyer was puzzled but shrewd in some instances he ferreted out the drug smuggling operation. Shocked out of his wits he couldn't believe it. His own law partner, Steven Stone, a Superior Court Judge was the *brains* behind a multimillion dollar cocaine ring. They had been using his jets to bring it back, making millions while he went broke trying to pay for fuel. Lots of things began falling into place. He'd wondered about the odd kinship Stone had with William Morgan Hetrick, the owner of an airplane repair company at Santa Paula airport. He had seen Hetrick fly in and out of Stewart Airport picking up the stuff and taking it to California. Another judge, Larry Storch was just as friendly with Hetrick as was Stone and Storch had his own plane flying in and out of Santa Paula Airport.

Shock was replaced by anger, a rage such as Lyman Smith had never known. They had ruthlessly jeopardized his entire future, his life. If Feds had discovered the cocaine on his 707's he would be the fall guy, ending up in prison. It was unbelievable, all the time while they watched him going broke they had continued to use him. While he agonized over a pending financial ruin and loss of his reputation and suffered tortures of the damned with a growing estrangement of his wife, they didn't care a damn about any of these things. Revenge swept across his mind, but clinging to a bit of shrewdness he realized that was a loser, he had a better way, and they *owed* him. The only way out of his dilemma was to *become a judge.* Stone and Storch had the power, there were two openings. They could do it with a flick of a finger. With the prestige of the Robes he could work his way out of his financial problems and best of all Charlene would *never* dream of deserting him, not while he was clothed in Black Robes with their elegance reflecting glitteringly on her own ego and social aspiration. It was the answer to everything.

Smith was no coward, just a little nervous, but the confrontation with his partner Judge Steven J. Stone was not near as harrowing or threatening as he'd feared. It was as if Stone had expected it. When he dropped the cocaine smuggling bomb right in the judge's lap he didn't flick an eyelash. Instead, he assured Smith he was as good as wearing a Black Robe right now. Lyman was elated. Later it nagged him, not once had Stone given indication of remorse or any feeling for having placed him in such dire jeopardy. Smith could see these were cruel people. He suffered many moments of uneasy feelings of danger but shrugged them off, so what, what could they do about it, he had the goods on them.

In the following days things with Maverick Airlines deteriorated rapidly, Smith was worried sick, he had not heard a word about his judicial appointment. He became convinced that Stone was tricking him...stalling...in desperation Lyman poured heat on them, he took Hetrick to Judge Richard Heaton who also was a pilot owning a four place Beechcraft hangered at the Santa Paula Airport. In privacy of Heaton's chambers the three exchanged loud, fierce words.

Many times in the 1950's while on patrol during early morning hours I would find lawyer Heaton crapped out in doorways on Main Street. He was a terrible alcoholic but a hell of a nice guy. Dusting him off I would dump his body in the back seat and take him home. A knock on the door brought his worried wife in seconds, dragging him in she would whisper an embarrassed "Thank you." Dick and I became friends.

In 1956 the governor appointed Heaton to the Municipal Court, he never took *another* drink. In '66 he was appointed to the Superior Court. It was late in '79, maybe December, not long after Smith had taken Hetrick to *Heaton's chambers,* I was threading my way through the crowded courthouse hall, I felt a touch on my arm, it was Judge Heaton. The strange deep seriousness I saw on his face startled me, then he smiled. "Gary it's real good to see you." I felt his sincerity and started to answer, he interrupted, "My God, I've felt so terrible about the part I played against you in that awful thing with attorney Paul Caruso. It was me who gave it away to Berenson."

"Yes, I know, but judge that's almost ten years ago."

"Yes...yes...years ago, but we were friends, I stabbed you in the back, you've got to understand, I *owed* them, but I know how they've tried to destroy you." The way he was almost jabbering it out sudden suspicion struck me, Lord, is he hitting the jug again? His face was pinched and ashen and his body shook but it wasn't booze, this was different. Something was *unnerving* him terrible, it was *confusion* and *fear* I saw written on his face.

"I've returned to God, He is everything, I have been a terrible, hurtful sinner in the past but I have seen the wonders of the Lord Almighty, our Savior. I have *returned* to a *true Christian,* I am in His hands forev...," stiffening, his words chopped off, his eyes stared over my shoulder, I turned. Thirty feet down the hallway Berenson stood motionless, watching us, his face was a *clouded mask*, dark with rage. Turning quickly he disappeared into the crowd. When I looked back Judge Heaton had also disappeared.

Only a matter of weeks later, Lyman Smith and Charlene were savagely bludgeoned to death in their bed. Then, only a few more weeks, Judge Heaton with his wife took off on a flight from Santa Paula Airport in their Beechcraft Debonair. Over the desert, close to Winslow, Arizona, something happened to the controls. The plane *suddenly* flipped over plunging straight down, burying itself six inches into the pavement of a Winslow Street. Debris was scattered for a block, both the Heatons were killed instantly. The Winslow Airport control tower reported that no emergency transmission was received, *supposedly* they ran out of gas. If so, Heaton would reasonably have had time to glide and use the radio, but it happened too fast, there was no warning. Heaton had filed flight plans, known as one of the most cautious of fliers he would *never* have run out of gas, he could never understand people who took chances.

Lawyer Smith and Judge Heaton were *dead*, their wives also had appointments with death, they knew *too much* to be allowed to live and talk. Three more deaths were involved. Shortly after Supervisor Robinson's bribery conviction, William Wilcox, his wife and another man took off from a Ventura County airport. They'd been involved in the frame-up of Robinson and the Ventura Chief of Police. High above a Mexican desert south of San Diego their plane inexplicably ran out of gas. Crashing in the desert all three were killed.

William Morgan Hetrick was multi-talented, not only an expert pilot of small planes, he flew four engine propeller jobs and jets. A top mechanic and *inventor* of many interesting gadgets he spent his weekends at Santa Paula airport tinkering with engines. Hetrick was capable of designing and installing a small sophisticated instrument that at a pre-set time could destroy the controls of an airplane and be undetectable during examination of the wreck. The Mishpucka had never been able to control their deadly enemy, *fate*. Just a few months *after* the Smith and Heaton deaths, Hetrick was *busted* along with John De Lorean, a wealthy car manufacturer, in a federal drug sting. Hetrick had smuggled in 220 lbs. of cocaine valued at twenty four million dollars. De Lorean was arrested in a hotel at the L.A. International Airport and Hetrick shortly afterward was picked up in Hollywood. There followed a spectacular, sensational newspaper and TV trial, De Lorean was found innocent. Hetrick wasn't allowed to testify, he had disappeared. The Mishpucka *controlled* Justice Dept. had hid him out. He knew too many answers, he'd *never* be allowed to talk to anyone.

The Smiths *were killed* Thursday night, the bodies weren't found until 2 p.m. Sunday, almost three days later, the Mishpucka became apprehensive. Perhaps one of the victims had not been finished off, Judah, if they had gasped dying words into a recorder, or scribbled a last-second death message...they could not chance this. On Friday night, one day after the bludgeoning, Black Robe Mishpucka Marvin Lewisinsky, aka Lewis, was at the Smiths door. It was imperative the Mishpucka know if anything had gone wrong. Later on, realizing his fingerprints were on the doorknob Lewis told officers, "I live up the street from Lyman, we are friends. I just went there to ask if he had gotten any word on his judicial appointment."

The police saw nothing suspicious about Lewis' explanation but I *knew* he had *lied.* He had been forced into making a slip, he knew damn well Smith had not received any word. His lie whirled through my brain triggering something, recollection of another sinister event, the same explicit words..."Have you gotten any word on your *judicial appointment?"* I had heard Lewis say those very same words before, it was a long time ago, I dredged my memory.

I had become acquainted with lawyer Hugh Gallagher about the same time I met Judge Heaton, the mid-fifties. As a Detective Sgt. I took crime reports to the Dist. Atty. to be reviewed for complaints, Gallagher was a Dep. D.A., he left there to go into private practice in Santa Paula. The incident I was *remembering* occurred years later, about January 1970. I pinpointed it, again, like my strange talk with Judge Heaton, I was in the hall of the courthouse, I was talking with Gallagher. I congratulated him, the word going around the grapevine was that Hugh was in line any moment for a *judicial appointment.* Now ten years later, they were saying Lyman Smith was about to be *appointed* any minute. It was *weird,* Gallagher *was also* a law partner of Hymie Blitzberg, aka Steven Stone, in Santa Paula *just like* Lyman Smith. While Hugh and I talked, Judge Marvin Lewis walked up to us. Greeting Hugh effusively and pumping his hand Lewis pointedly ignored me, I had just lost my Civil Service hearing a few days prior. Smiling heartily at Galllagher, Lewis said, "How is everything going, have you gotten any word on your *judicial appointment?"* That was all the conversation I'd heard, I quietly moved on down the hall. A short time later Gallagher was *dead.* As my recollection grew clearer I thought, Lord, Lewis' *solicitous words* were actually arrogant barbs, barely concealing the Black Robe Mishpukcas derisive contempt for fools, a mocking, grotesque *kiss of death!* If so, they were damned powerful words because the same time Hugh Gallagher died, Judge Phillip West died with him. Superior Court Judge West was up for re-election. Three other judges were also running, West was the only one who drew opposition. Strangely, Municipal Court Judge Robert Shaw had chosen to run against him.

Everybody agreed it was Shaw's prerogative to run, but among attorneys and county employees there was much tittering and even laughter at Shaw. Why in hell would a little known Municipal Court Judge be spending all that money trying to beat the popular, honest and fair Judge West. The consensus around the courthouse was that Shaw didn't stand the proverbial snowballs chance in the Sahara. It prompted an odd comment from a veteran news reporter, "Well, all I can think of is Shaw sure as hell must know *something* the rest of us don't."

About eleven a.m. Saturday April 11, 1970, West and Gallagher set sail from Ventura in West's twenty one foot sloop for Anacapa Island about twelve miles on the western horizon. There was another crew member, Douglas Deihl, twenty seven, experienced scuba diver. He was also deputy marshall of Judge Shaw's Municipal Court. Next morning about nine, Deihl was picked up by fishermen from a rocky Anacapa Island beach. He reported to the Coast Guard that Judge West and Gallagher had disappeared in the ocean, he was stranded on the island all night. Deihl related a quite amazing account, "After leaving at eleven a.m. strong winds came up, by three thirty we were only halfway to the island. Then high winds dismasted the boat. We went to Frenchy's cove at Anacapa Island and tried to anchor but it wouldn't hold. We tried to get the outboard going, it wouldn't start, then a huge wave threw the boat on the rocks. I made it ashore, the others floated right by me but I was unable to help them, that's the last I saw of them."

Deihl's account of the missing judge and lawyer rang phony, one thing in particular made no sense at all. After more than four hours of sailing and they were only *halfway* there when wind tore the mast out, why in hell didn't they use the motor to return to the mainland instead of continuing on to the island? And it didn't make sense to leave the sail up while it ripped out the mast. The Coast Guard had reported winds of thirty four m.p.h. at the time.

It was in 1980, shortly after the Smiths were killed when Judge Lewis electrifyingly *tied in* their murders with the *deaths* of West and

Gallagher. Doing more checking I discovered the Deihls had gotten a divorce almost ten years before. In fact, it was soon after the boat wreck, Douglas began drinking heavy, becoming abusive and mean. I figured Patricia Deihl might talk to me. In trying to find her I got a shock, she was dead. All that my source of information knew was that shortly after the deaths of West and Gallagher she had suffered a sudden asthma attack. At a hospital she had died. Everything was piling up. I went to county records, the death certificate and autopsy report should tell me something, this time I *really* got a shock, about twenty thousand volts, there was *no* death certificate. I checked both her married and maiden name, *no record* of her death was filed in the county records.

Not long *after* Judge Phillip West was *lost at sea* the Black Robe Mishpucka judicially *declared* him dead and Robert Shaw became a Superior Court Judge. Missing death certificate and autopsy reports on Patricia Deihl bothered hell out of me. It necessitated a person with high official power to keep it from being recorded. Somebody with police authority, the D.A. could hold it out using any number of excuses. Mal King was the Chief Investigator for the Dist. Attorney, he could do it. He was a close buddy of Deihl's, also they both were strangely associated with Judge Shaw. But what was the motive, was Patricia killed for the same reason as Heaton's and Smith's wives? Had she known too much to live?

Before becoming a Municipal Court Judge, Shaw was in private practice. King ran errands for him. Wearing his sheriff's uniform off duty, he would serve legal papers for Shaw. The uniform intimidated people into signing and making statements damaging to themselves. On first hearing this from people I'd contacted I refused to believe it. Not the honest, dedicated law enforcement officer I knew. King would never stoop so low. But it came from several different sources not connected in anyway. King was a climber, I had known that. He managed to get sent to the prestigious, FBI Police School and also other institutes that issue impressive, gold seal embossed diplomas.

King was ambitious alright, he had a gross of those little papers hanging on his wall, framed and under glass to prove it. Through the years I'd become aware King liked to take credit for solving a lot of sensational cases he had never investigated. The Ma Duncan case in 1958 was one he *particularly* liked to have people believe he'd solved. One of my informants had broken the case at the very beginning. A few years before, Sgt. Doug Paxton, a Sheriff's Detective and I had busted a gal in Ventura for hustling, a minor beef, but after that she contacted us when she got good information.

This time it was a homicide. When Bobbi contacted me on this one I was back in L.A. with the Dist. Atty.'s Bureau of Investigation. The murder wasn't in my jurisdiction so I called Lt. Bill Woodard, Chief of Sheriff's detectives in Ventura. Woodard was an old timer, a go-getter, after getting with my informant, Bill and one of his men, Ray Higgins had the two suspects in jail and their confessions within hours. Mal King was just getting started in law enforcement, he was a court bailiff running errands for attorney Shaw. His penchant for snatching recognition and building up his ego hadn't bothered me or Paxton or Det. Sgt. Ed Patton from the Oxnard PD.. We had always worked our cases in conjunction, in those days Ventura County law enforcement was a small community, everybody knew who was out there doing the work. King's career was fostered and promoted by Judas Gius, Mishpucka Editor of the Star Free Press, whose utility reporter and cover-up man, Bob Holt gave King a big boost at every opportunity.

For thirty four years Bob Holt worked at the Star Free Press, supposedly as an investigative reporter. *Not once* did he initiate an investigation into civic corruption. In fact, *never* at anytime had he followed a clue leading to local corruption, and there'd been plenty of leads shoved right under his nose. Sitting in a courtroom during a murder trial taking notes on scraps of paper so he can write a few lines for the evening paper, then going to San Quentin to watch Ma Duncan and her hired killers, Luis Moya and Augustine Maldanado die strapped to a chair in the gas chamber, then writing sensational words of their squirmings, this didn't make an investigative reporter. But never has the Star Free Press ever helped the people to ferret out corruption and treasonous filth inhabiting the courthouse and city hall which is the bounden duty of a free press. Just the opposite, under Gius' orders they join the crooks to act against the people.

On Holt's retirement, Star Free Press Editor Gius praised him, "Bob Holt has become a legend in his own time. He is the kind of reporter every Editor wants on his staff...possessed of a keen news sense, an able interviewer, diligent digger of facts, a fast, accurate and often brilliant writer. But it will be Bob Holt, the man, who will be most missed in our newsroom, his integrity, cheerfulness, helpfulness to junior reporters, and fabulous store of knowledge and quick recall of people and events in *Ventura County* in his thirty four years at the Star Free Press."

But regardless of Gius' soul-stirring *glorious accolades* conferred upon Holt, his dashing investigative reporter, the facts were still the same. During all those years, all thirty four of them, Holt never *once* exhibited a moral consciousness of a newsreporter's duty or concern for the protection of the country or the people. Bob Holt's tribute, if any, should have been shorter and more to the point...'Here was a guy whose conscience and ardor was just a wee bit weaker than his concern for his paycheck.'

Shortly *after* Robert Shaw was sworn in as Superior Court Judge replacing the dead Judge Phillip West he was called as a prosecution witness in the trial of Robbie Robinson. Dist. Atty., Woody Deem, sent Mal King to hold an investigative interview of Shaw before he testified against Robinson. It was becoming one hell of a mess, the Mafia and Mishpucka *war* over the *multimillion dollar scam* to move the courthouse had crossed them up so bad it was *impossible* to keep the stories straight. Prosecutor Pete Kossoris while questioning Shaw on the witness stand had caught him in an outright, glaring lie.

Kossoris didn't pick up on the dangerous *reverse* ramifications of *Shaw's lie* at first. Plunging ahead in the exhilaration of a *chase* he twisted the wretched Judge into making more mistakes. Popping his killer question Pete skewered the Superior Court Judge to the wall, "Why are you deliberately *withholding* vital evidence in this case?"

Trapped and in a frightened rage Shaw screamed, "Because...Mal King never *asked* me that question."

Astounded, the ace prosecutor *suddenly realized,* Good Lord, he was about to break the trial wide open, but in the wrong direction, he'd nearly *exposed* their conspiracy to frame Robinson. Quickly he back-pedaled, agilely his questions switched to another subject and assumed a different, quieter tone. That's when Pete's ability earned the grateful *respect and trust* of the Mishpucka, and it was also when he got his reputation as an *ace* prosecutor.

After the Robinson trial things got politically rough for Deem. King *abandoned* him, appointed to a prestigious new job he became Mishpucka Judge Jerome Berenson's right hand man. The California Criminal Justice System had become a treasure chest of gold, filled by the endless flow of taxpayers money from the Federal Omnibus Safe Streets Act. Judge Jerome Berenson was *top man* in California's Criminal Justice System. King's new job in the organization was to *siphon* millions of dollars from the *treasure chest.* All he had to do was use his imagination, come up with *novelty ideas* in police work. According to Berenson's propaganda, King's new, unusual concepts will, "Stop crime and make streets safer for the citizens." Mal called his novelties, *'innovations.'* A master of the treasure chest frolic, he *dreamed up* ideas that would pop the eyeballs of master Detective Inspector Clouseau with envy. *Unaccountable* millions of dollars were sucked from the treasure chest into Berenson and Nordman's *Public Facilities Corp.* through Mal King's ingenious deceptions instead of going into new jail construction where it was supposed to. Eventually even an endless flow of taxpayers money into the treasure chest had to dry up under the *merciless assault* from the Mishpucka, so Judge Berenson fazed it out. Mal King returned as Chief Investigator for Michael Bradbury the District Attorney, their years of depredations and corruption had to be kept *tightly confined* within their control.

It was 1969, sixteen long years ago when I went to Al Jalaty and Mal King, honest policemen...my friends...I trusted them...I needed help. I told them of the corruption I'd come upon. They promised to help but it wasn't that way at all. The Grand Jury investigation into governmental gangsterism was *killed* by Judge Berenson. Mal didn't tell me about this until I squeezed it out of him. I was cut adrift in a hellish black sea of endless treachery, betrayal and hopelessness. Unsuspecting, I had walked straight into the lair of the Black Robe Mishpucka, into its jagged steel jaws. I'd had no inkling in the world such a deadly, mephitic beast even existed. But somehow I managed to hang in, survive its vicious blood thirsty attack, though admittedly just barely, and very painfully. However, neither had the Black Robe Mishpucka escaped free of injury. I'd ripped and gashed pieces and chunks out of its fetid body.

CHAPTER 46

Fitting those sixteen years of accumulated bits and pieces into proper sequence seemed hopeless, there was a million combinations and possibilities. Pieces of all shapes and sizes drifted in and out of my brain testing and checking my recollection while I tried to fit and refit them in their niche, but it never was the right piece. Amazingly I discovered that *perseverance and luck* were one word. Logically but wrongly I'd transfixed my target on 1969, sixteen years ago, the year they'd *killed* the Grand Jury investigation...no wonder the bits and pieces refused to fit, the beginning was way back, 1947, thirty eight years ago...that night my partner and I *tailed* Mickey Cohen's long shiny black Cad from Old China Town to the fight stadium, where we watched that mysterious *meeting* of the six powerful Mishpuckas at the South Gate Arena.

Cohen and Abraham Davidian walked down to ringside meeting Harry Pregerson and Abe Phillips. I remembered the faces of those four hoods, harsh in glaring overhead lights from the ring. Davidian and Cohen returned to the limo. I followed Pregerson and Phillips to the parking lot where they made contact with two men, a pair of *shadowy figures* among the cars in a far dark corner. I couldn't see their faces but I got the license plates as they left. Sidney Bocarsky and Nathan Turkebtahn were the two who'd waited, skulking in the deep shadows.

Partly completed the puzzle now revealed to me, it was one of the six hoods at the wrestling matches who had become the Leader, a homicidal maniac whose evil ambition was behind the treasonous, despicable Black Robe Mishpucka. He had created a Frankenstein monster, an octopus enslaving the lives of every person on earth. I knew eventually, like the monster had slain its creator and destroyed itself, the Black Robe Mishpucka would do the same, but if I waited for that to happen it would be far too late, because first its atrocities would destroy America.

In 1947 Cohen was a tough, hard boiled *gang leader,* keeping his small cabal of corrupt Jew judges in hand. Even so, his errand boy, law student Harry Pregerson was having fantasies, it was his original idea, *all* judges would be Jews, their power would become fantastic. Because of this I had for a long time *believed* it was Pregerson who'd taken over and become 'Leader' of the Black Robe Mishpucka. But soon I learned Harry was full of wild visions of glory, most of them extremely dangerous, he sure as hell was no mastermind, his mental qualification was basically an ambulance chasing type. Although very wealthy and powerful already from his arrogant, criminal abuse and misuse of the Black Robe, Harry still could not resist *fixing* a case if a lawyer was to slip him a grand. While a law student his struggling classmates *marveled* at the roll of bills he carried around. Cohen was very generous to Harry for all the little jobs and errands he willingly performed and the law student was dependable, he stuck real tight to Mickey. Pregerson had big dreams alright, but it had to be one of the others with more brains who had taken over.

Sid Bocarsky was not a brain either, mainly Harry's handyman, he manipulated real estate deeds and titles that Harry furtively and corruptly acquired. Sid would put the property in his name, like the beach property in Ventura. Harry and Sid were successful hoodlums financially, they performed well under explicit orders from their new leader.

Abe Phillips handled bail bond problems. He knew every rapist, gangster, holdup man, and burglar in the country. The two who had burglarized Oxnard's National Guard Armory were arrested by the FBI but the weapons weren't recovered, they had disappeared into Cohen's secret arms cache, all except one, the fifty caliber machine gun in William P. Clark's house. After Mickey went to prison all the guns in his possession were transferred to the JDL and Irv Rubin's arsenal. Phillips was cagey, a sly hood, but his sex maniac proclivities removed him from the mastermind class.

Later Cohen's power over the gang weakened. He'd outlived his usefulness as the Leader, his gangster shenanigans, and high profile in newspapers was outmoded, a distinct danger to the *sophisticated* plans of the new Leader. Mickey was betrayed by his old errand boy Harry Pregerson who'd *become a judge.* With Black Robe Mishpucka *protection* pulled out from under him Cohen was tried and convicted of income tax violations and sent to prison. Behind cold, steel bars, Cohen suffered the same traumas that broke his gangster pal Jack Ruby, it needled him into serious slips of the lip. In vengeful rage, Mickey screamed he was going to, "Write a book...I'll expose every God damn thing and everybody, I don't give a shit *who* gets burned."

It was hard to believe that federal prison authorities would let insane inmates run loose with pieces of leadpipe in their hands. But *sure enough,* one of these poor, irresponsible nuts sneaked up behind Mickey and bent the leadpipe right over his head, caving it in quite badly. Prison doctors operated on Cohen's brain and saved his life, they gave Mickey a financial settlement and released him on parole. But *after* the operation Cohen couldn't seem to *put it together* about who and what it had been he wanted to write about. That part of his brain was in a mayonnaise jar back in prison. It made no difference, he didn't live long afterward anyway.

Davidian was ready to spill the *secret* narcotic operations of the Mishpucka, but while under *protection* of the federal agents his brain functions, like Cohen's were interfered with, he also had suffered an over dose of lead administered under force.

It was a process of *elimination,* Pregerson, Phillips and Bocarsky didn't have brains to *mastermind* the *complex* Black Robe Mishpucka and Cohen and Davidian were dead. Only one of the six remained, Nathan Turkebtahn. A surge of excitement, eagerness, after all those years...I was close...if I could force the Leader...the mastermind out into the open...the Black Robe Mishpucka could be destroyed.

Sidney Bocarsky and Nathan Turkebtahn had been but shadowy figures in the dark parking lot, I couldn't see their faces. Although Bocarsky *altered* the spelling of his name slightly he was easy to find. Now all I had to do was find the last man, Turkebtahn. But it wasn't that easy. I was doomed to *bitter* disappointment, hellish frustration. After that meeting in the parking lot not even the shadow that had been Turkebtahn appeared to have existed...there was nothing. For weeks I *checked records:* births, marriages, divorces, deaths, lawsuits, criminal and civil, property records, taxes, any of these events would have been recorded. Even now, many years later they should still be a matter of record...but there was nothing.

I realized that in a burst of hope and zeal I had made a serious blunder. Aware that several of the *final pieces* of the puzzle were still missing I'd stupidly allowed myself to *anticipate* a situation. Equating in terms of the *non-genius* talents of people like Pregerson, Phillips and Bocarsky I had allowed myself to become over confident, it was dangerous. I grossly *underestimated* the evil intellect and treacherous talents of Turkebtahn, in that one sighting he'd been a mere shadow, but I knew that dark form was a man, not a phantom or apparition vaporizing into the blackness of a night without a trace whatsoever. There was only *one way* a person could vanish so completely in such a mysterious manner.

Turkebtahn had changed his name...moving to a new location he'd assumed an entirely *new identity* within a completely different social stratum. How did he accomplish it...who was Nathan now? I wondered about that strange meeting at the arena. The conversation they had had in the parking lot consumed only seconds, was it that Turkebtahn had *received* orders or had he been *giving* them?

My position I knew was clearly more terrifying than ever before, in a hundred ways I'd revealed, in fact advertised to the Black Robe Mishpucka Leader that I was getting near, on his trail, he knew I'd destroy him if possible. He could strike back from any direction, I was sitting under a 'friggin spotlight...trying to fight a *shadow*. Lord, who had this Turkebtahn been...who in hell was he now...was he a super-international hit-man, an evil specter commanding millions for his deadly services of *assassinating world leaders* and creating chaos? Was he a deep mole in the CIA or the FBI...a high ranking official in the justice or state department...maybe a powerful federal judge or United States Senator?

Morbidly I realized that Nathan Turkebtahn *the shadow,* could be anyone...Casper Weinberger, Secretary of Defense, Menachem Begin, the murdering international terrorist, or Henry Kissinger, the influential Jew who oddly always got appointed by the presidents to supposedly negotiate foreign affairs for the U.S., hell, it could even be Melvin Belli, but careful consideration eliminated this possibility. Belli was in the same wretched classification as Pregerson, Phillips and Bocarsky. But I couldn't dismiss Belli completely, something was hidden there that I was trying to grasp. He'd always involved himself deep in machinations trying to *manipulate* law enforcement. I began stumbling on a memory, it triggered a powerful explosion, wildly its shock penetrated my senses, damn! manipulating Law Enforcement, the implications were startling, so far reaching I scarcely believed it.

THERE'S A FISH IN THE COURTHOUSE   611

A man, high in Peace Officer organizations...one who'd managed to gain unbelievable stature through certain political and judicial power and news media backing. All city, county, state and federal criminal justice systems and their files and record facilities would be at such a man's command, a tremendous, strategic position. On the surface, an impressive, manly configuration of good...but hidden, there was a dark soul consumed by malignant evil bent on the *destruction* of our United States Constitution, to replace it with the Mishna, the Jew law of chaos, conspiracy and corruption.

The incident rocking my memory returned in full. About eleven years ago, Al Jalaty was running for sheriff, wanting my backing and support he sent Sheriff Captain Reed Hunt, an old mutual friend to my store to throw a little, 'old buddy' pressure on me. "What we are aiming to do Gary, is win this election at the primary...save us a long expensive campaign, Jalaty can do it if we all stick together...get out there and pitch."

I'd never forgot how Al Jalaty and King helped bury me when Judge Berenson *killed* the Grand Jury. Sending Hunt around wanting me to help him become sheriff pissed me off. I didn't want to stir up anything with Hunt because my situation was precarious, but hell I figured I'll *aggravate* them just a little bit, "Well Reed, I was thinking that maybe I might run for sheriff myself." Jeeze, I wasn't expecting the violent reaction, Hunt, enormously fat around the belly sprang out of the chair, his face puffed and became blood red. I realized I'd hit on the real reason for Reed being here, Jalaty wanted to know if I intended to run.

I had stirred the pot far worse than I'd wanted...obviously this was a very touchy subject. Jalaty feared what I might *reveal* during a campaign. Before I could tell Reed I was only joking and cool him down he came on strong. Wheezing, he exhorted, "You've known Al a long time, you know he is strong for good law enforcement, he will make one hell of a good sheriff, he's a regular guy and sure as hell no pussywillow either." Reed had built up a hell of a head of steam, exploding like a safety valve that had held too long. I couldn't tell if the pressure was fired by fear or anger. He blurted out, "I'll tell you something very God damn few people know. A long time ago Jalaty was a professional wrestler, a tough mean man...he was *known* as the Terrible Turk."

Reed stopped shouting suddenly, breaking it off like he realized he had said far too much. We stared at each other in silence a little amazed at the heat that had generated. I said, "Hell Reed, I was just bugging you a little."

"Then you don't intend to run?"

"No."

"Does that mean you will back Al, I mean come out public and say it?"

"Yeah, I'll say it." Reed appeared satisfied, he put his hand out. After he left I just sat there, it was weird, a strange incident. Yes, I'd known Al quite a while, but only in law enforcement, I knew nothing of his past before that. It had been a *blank* except he claimed he was in the Navy. I knew nothing about his being a professional wrestler called the Terrible Turk. Reed's story seemed to stir a vague name recollection of some kind, that was all and it was soon forgotten. But now my brain was burning, Al Jalaty had been a wrestler known as The Terrible Turk. In late '47, almost thirty nine years ago Nathan Turkebtahn, a *shadow* on the parking lot of the South Gate Arena disappeared, never to be heard of again. A man named Turkebtahn, *what* in hell would they call him?...Turk...his nickname just naturally would be Turk...a wrestler...The Terrible Turk! Had he assumed the name Al Jalaty and moved to another location becoming a member of a completely different social stratum, law enforcement?

If Jalaty *was* Turkebtahn, one of Mickey Cohen's old gangster mob, I had sure as hell been in the den of the beast, in the jaws of death. Had Al somehow *learned* of our meeting with Sheriff Decker and John? A few years after President Kennedy was murdered I had introduced my partner Frank and Audie to Jalaty when he was the Police Chief of Port Hueneme. Audie was quite impressed with his *eminence* in law enforcement. Could Audie have possibly confided to Jalaty about our trip to Ruidoso and the *envelope* with the seal on it...and also the other documents Frank and I gave Audie to keep in his safe? If Jalaty indeed was Nathan Turkebtahn it meant a million frightening possibilities, just thinking about it was insanity.

During this same period of time I'd discovered something else. Jalaty was real tight with a Russian born Mishpucka, Louie Lewis, from New York City. He was *tied in* with Fred Marlinsky, alias Fred Marlow. They'd cooked up a *scam* with the Oxnard City Council to fill in an old oil field chemical waste dump, then they'd rezone it to residential development. Jalaty and Lewis had bought an old World War II government housing project in San Pedro. They planned on loading the buildings on barges and towing them to Port Hueneme and relocate them on the old dump. Running into legal snags in San Pedro, Al and Lewis went to Judge Pregerson who put a *'fix'* in. For this, Marlow and Lewis deeded Judge Pregerson *two* very valuable *lots* in the Oxnard Shores development across Harbor Blvd. from the waste dump. Harry definitely didn't want lots in what they called the Dunes Development. It would be twenty years *before* residents of the Dunes learned about the cancer causing chemicals (benzene, xylene and toluene) beneath their houses. They filed a lawsuit, but they'd never accomplish anything except handing over a fortune to lawyers, they were up against the Black Robe Mishpucka, right up the line to Federal Appeal Court Judge Harry Pregerson.

The insidious power that Pregerson wields over the Oxnard City Council is flagrantly evident. Harry and his partner Federal Appeal Court Judge Stephen Reinhardt, owners of the Raiders, moved their football team's training facilities to Oxnard, their *scam* included the construction of a hotel to house the players but Oxnard's Planning Commission denied the project.

The Council swiftly rushed in and *overruled* the Commissioners who *quickly reversed* their action and approved the zoning to comply with the Raiders. The project called the River Ridge Radisson Hotel was built next to a municipal golf course which is on an old landfill. Deadly explosive methane gas from the dump seeps under the hotel creating a disastrous situation. The Ventura Grand Jury investigated "the questionable urgency of the hotel project" and stated in a report that "such a departure from customary planning practices *undermines* the basic governmental system upon which citizens rely." A required environmental impact study and report were *never* conducted but the Black Robe Mishpucka will never allow the Grand Jury investigation to get off the ground.

The Mishpucka is eating America alive, sabotage and espionage are directed right from Israel. Giant corporations and great United States financial institutes are falling under their rapacious appetite. On Wall Street the greedy treasonous swindlers are stealing billions from the *life blood* of American economy. Appearing before a senate committee, Felix Rohatyn, an investment banker cried out his fears of a vicious backlash against Jews. Top Jew figures in the stocks and bond business held private meetings, the *topic* was, "their fears that because so *many* of the men caught *stealing* and about to be indicted were Jews that it could cause decided anti-semitism."

But Mishpucka A.M. Rosenthal, with New York Times News Service wrote, "There's *no need* for Jews on *Wall Street* to feel called upon to *explain* the number of *Jews* involved." A.M. Rosenthal would have Americans believe that there is *no* conspiracy of *greed* among

Jews and if anyone *dares* suggest such a thing they'll suffer the Jews anti-Semitic treatment. But it *never* stops, in New York a Mishpucka lawyer, Israil G. Grossman was indicted by a Federal Grand Jury on twelve counts of securities fraud and twelve for mail fraud. He was associated with the law firm of Kramer, Levin, Nessen, Kamin and Frankel. In L.A. the SEC filed charges that Mishpuckas, Robert A. Gutstein, Jacob 'Jack' Rubenstein, Steven Dulyea, Lawrence 'Eddie' Ruben, aka Edward Pollack, and Jerome Feinstein, all of California, and Herbert Stone of New York and David Siegal of Florida were running a *sham* company. They operated a scheme, a *massive* market *manipulation* driving up their scam company stocks from seventy five cents a share to over nine dollars. Ludicrously the SEC officials are *trying* to obtain a *court* order to prohibit these thieves from breaking the security laws in the future.

The ramifications of Sheriff Al Jalaty being Nathan Turkebtahn, a hoodlum with *international connections* were staggering, much too frightening to contemplate. Jalaty claimed he was born in Lebanon. Politicians and police authorities in high office traveled all the way from North Africa to see him. *Why* would a sheriff of a small county north of L.A. attract such *note-worthy* visitors? Jalaty had a by-pass heart operation and took a physical disability retirement, but in an unprecedented move the supervisors made him Sheriff Emeritus of Ventura County with an office, secretary and phone in the Sheriff's Department.

Al had to keep this power to protect the Mishpucka corruption. The supervisors elevated Under-Sheriff John Gillespie to Sheriff, a puppet on strings, flipping on the orders of the Sheriff Emeritus. It was crazy, but even so it all coincided perfect, and this time I would make no mistakes, there'd be no anticipating, every damn last piece of the puzzle would be locked tightly in place before I acted. Was Al Jalaty the Leader, the evil mastermind of the Mishpucka? It plagued me, I knew where *the answer* was hidden, while searching the official records I'd overlooked something, but the clue was there in L.A. and Hollywood, buried deep in its past with the Hollywood people.

Daylight the next morning I headed south, prepared for a long search, long enough to locate certain records and Hollywood people, that's if they were still alive. Most of them I hadn't seen or talked to in over twenty five years. Gliding off the freeway I dropped down to Broadway and Temple. L.A. was in the middle of a scorching heat wave, only ten and already a sweltering ninety degrees, it would be an ordeal, but I found the documents *and* the people. It had taken more than two weeks to put it all together, now I knew the Leader, the assassin, the Mishpucka mastermind. My long search had bared a devastating secret, its *revelation* would *inflame* the Christian world, setting religion against religion, Church against Synagogue, nation against nation, it would *force* the masses to *choose sides* in a conflict as profound as the Crucifixion... A Jihad, a Holy War...a Holy War of such *magnitude* it would engulf the world.

CHAPTER 47

For weeks *after* my L.A. and Hollywood expedition I worked on the complicated project of *collating a succession* of murderous events crisscrossing many years. Then Anthony Summers vivid volumes of Marilyn Monroe's Secret Lives hit all the book stores. Flogging dark secrets leading up to her death, Tony christened his book 'Goddess.' His story propelled readers to one *incredible,* inevitable conclusion, John and Bobby Kennedy had a real and volatile motive to murder Marilyn, and that Bobby was with her the night she was killed. Only two reasons could possibly motivate Summers to such an incredibly irresponsible hearsay indictment of the Kennedys for murder: egoic monetary desire to *create* a Hollywood sensation, or more sinister, hard, dirty politics. Whichever, Summers was wrong. For the sake of justice and the Kennedys *place* in American history and *legend* I was glad I knew the true story. At our first meeting I gave Summers the names of three people, they were a key that could open a door to a mysterious room of untouched secrets.

One, *the madam* who furnished the girls for the party at Malibu; Two, Joey Bishop, *the Mishpucka* who under Cohen's orders hired the ladies from the madam and *orchestrated* the plot for Marilyn and John Kennedy both to be at Lawford's beach house party. John had many times expressed a desire to meet her, Marilyn was to be a big, exciting Hollywood *surprise* that night for JFK. Three, Joe Di Carlo, the *last hood* still alive who was sitting at the table in Rondelli's the

THERE'S A FISH IN THE COURTHOUSE 617

night they killed Jack O'Hara. Lo Cigno, Stompanato, Piscitelli and Di Carlo were buddies, Mickey Cohen's 'Italian Boys,' the ones he was putting onto sex stars like Lana Turner to blackmail them. Joe Di Carlo knew all about Piscitelli's orders to get Marilyn in motels to make recordings of her having sex, also that Mary had found out from Piscitelli about Begin and Cohen's scheme for Georgie to feed Monroe drugs and liquor and pick her brain about Pres. Kennedy's plans. To Georgie this was a top level operation, he could not help boasting about it to Mercadante.

On the night of Monroe's death it was Georgie who was in her bedroom between ten and eleven, *not* Bobby Kennedy as Summers suggests. Marilyn's house companion, Eunice Murray was aware of Piscitelli's presence but stayed in her room, she knew he was a hood and was very frightened of him. When he left, Mrs. Murray checked Marilyn, finding her unconscious Eunice *immediately* telephoned Dr. Greenson, Monroe's psychiatrist who then contacted Arthur Jacobs her agent. The two arrived before midnight, almost simultaneously, an ambulance was called and Marilyn was taken away, but Greenson and Jacobs riding with her saw she was dead. They returned Marilyn to her home and let it *appear* to be a *simple overdose*. Milton Rudin, her attorney, who had just arrived and Jacobs called Freddie O'tash to take care of certain details, like covering-up the ambulance trip. Right from the *very beginning* Marilyn had been totally surrounded by Mishpuckas. Summers named lots of them in 'Goddess,' doctors, lawyers, agents, acting coaches, directors, producers and newspaper reporters. During those years she was indiscriminately supplied with narcotics from doctors like Greenson, and Hyman Engleberg. Using drugs they had *manipulated and controlled* her ruthlessly. For nearly four hours the Mishpuckas prowled Marilyn's home, stage setting a scene before calling police.

Inexplicably, Tony, an experienced investigative reporter, didn't even *mention* the exclusive Hollywood madam or Joey Bishop or Joe Di Carlo in Goddess. The madam could pinpoint Joey Bishop's part in paying for the whores and duking Monroe into JFK. Di Carlo was the last of Cohen's hoods still alive *who knew* about the plans Cohen and Begin had implemented to use Marilyn as a dupe to break into the *circle* of presidential and national security secrets.

Numerous times before his book came out Tony had asked me to appear on a TV show promoting 'Goddess.' During these phone conversations I repeatedly asked if he'd contacted any of the three people whose names I'd given him, Tony was evasive. It was during his last call that I pinned him down. He confided that he had talked with Joey Bishop. Strangely, Summers voice dropped to a whisper as though fearing he might be overheard. "Joey admitted to me that it was him who had made all the arrangements to sneak John Kennedy out of the L.A. convention and for a helicopter to *whisk him* to meet Marilyn at Lawford's beach house party.

I was amazed that Joey would reveal this, I asked what else he told him but Summers would say no more. This bit of info explained a mystery puzzling Frank and me for many years. When we left the convention Kennedy was still there. Driving swiftly to Lawford's in Malibu we were surprised when we peered over a wall and saw John Kennedy *already there* in a change of clothes and a glass in his hand. Bishop's timing in the plot was perfect, he waltzed Marilyn into the party for the big surprise only moments after Kennedy arrived. Why in hell had Tony left Joey *out of 'Goddess'?* Sifting through the chaos had he *discovered* like I had tried to clue him in...a *far more* sinister *crime family* than the Mafia was involved and that this diametrically opposed his *indictment* of the Kennedys?

There was another strange event, *shortly* after meeting Summers a call came from New York City, "I'm Ed Tivnan, a writer, I've been commissioned to write a book about Menachem Begin. There are a lot of rumors afloat that Begin was *tied in with activities* of notorious American gangsters. My book's *purpose* is to deny, dispel and silence the accusations of Begin's criminal associations with them." Curious, I asked how he got my name and unlisted number. "Just yesterday I had lunch with Tony Summers here in New York, he mentioned you and your partner's surveillance of Begin and the west coast gangster Mickey Cohen many years ago."

"That's right." It seemed to jar Tivnan when I mentioned I was writing a book about it. He tried hard to pin me down when it might be coming out. An alarm jangled but it didn't make sense until after I'd read Goddess, the indictment of the Kennedys. Edward 'Teddy,' was the last of Joe Kennedy's sons. Did the Mishpucka fear Edward would run for president? Bobby Kennedy once with heated emotion publicly declared, "The *only way* to become powerful enough to learn who *really* killed my brother John is to become the president." This declaration made it clear that Bobby did *not* believe Oswald killed the President. Not long afterward when it appeared Bobby Kennedy might indeed become the next president, he was also killed.

Tony's book linked John and Bobby with Marilyn as lovers, also suspects in her mysterious death. It generated enough melodramatic notoriety for 'Teddy's' enemies to destroy any presidential chances he may have had through vicious and wild media propaganda.

It all went back to Mary Mercadante. In her fit of anger at Abe Phillips for his insane attack and Cohen's phone threats to kill her, Mary had reacted by *screaming* at Cohen, "I know *all about* what you have Georgie doing to Marilyn and I'm going to *tell her* if you don't leave me alone," the next day Mary was dead. Frank and I took the tapes of Cohen's *death threats,* statements by witnesses and a written report to Joe Busch, a deputy District Attorney. At the time we had trusted him. We wanted Busch to order a full autopsy on Mary for drugs, which we knew she *never touched,* but Joe had backed us right out the door. A few years later he became the District Attorney.

Monroe and Mercadante were old friends. Many times they had reminisced and giggled over their sharing some kinky, wealthy tricks in the tough, harsh days while trying to get a start in Tinseltown. It was sad, two little orphans, a couple of poor, terribly mixed up little broads lost in the dark forests of Hollywood, begging the world for a little happiness. Not many months after Mary was killed, Marilyn was also dead. She too had *discovered* how Piscitelli and Cohen were using her, like Mary she'd wildly screamed threats of exposing them. And just prior to her death Monroe tried *desperately* to contact the Kennedy brothers on the telephone *to warn* them, but unsuccessfully. Not many months *after* Marilyn's death President John F. Kennedy was dead.

Shortly after Goddess hit the street I discovered that Summers book about Monroe at *its inception* had plans for a TV documentary. This revealed that Ed Tivnan's part was an investigator building up the story for a TV scenario. After reading Goddess and viewing the *TV sensation* I realized it had been prudent to refuse Summers offer to appear on it. The few things he attributed to our conversation on page two thirty four were twisted, totally missing the point.

Ed Tivnan's chief source of information for their documentary was Freddie O'tash, without any equal, the most conniving, thieving, lying shamus the Hollywood scene ever experienced. Yet the girls on the Strip, cocktail waitresses, struggling starlets, secretaries, whores and addicts loved him. They furnished Freddie with all the *latest info* about everything moving in Tinseltown. O'tash's rogue life style was the *inspiration* for the popular private-eye TV series, 77 Sunset Strip, with *Freddie's headquarters* at Dino's Restaurant on Sunset. With his girls shoveling him the latest goodies on *'whom was screwing whom,'* O'tash was the prime source of info for Confidential Magazine, the most lurid *tell-all* Hollywood publication of its time. He was making nothing but money, his hand was in everything, but Freddie's scam of sticking race horses in the rump with *needles full of dope* blew up. He'd done *real good* with some beat-up Tiajuana nags he'd imported until he got greedy. Freddie figured if a *little* dope made them run fast, a *whole lot* would make them fly. One of his longshots with too much juice charged like lightning from the gate and dropped dead in a hundred yards. The District Attorney busted him. A jockey and a trainer involved were testifying against him, I remembered how mad Freddie was, he threatened to blow their heads off with a shotgun. Frank and I had to hide and guard the witnesses in a hotel room. Freddie was convicted but it didn't slow him down.

One of O'tash's men installed the tape in the motel room where Lana Turner and Stompanato had cavorted, Cohen had ordered the job and O'tash made a bundle. In a *duplicate operation* Marilyn and Georgie were recorded in bed in a motel, another of O'tash's sound technicians did the wiring, this was early 1960, several months *before* Marilyn first met JFK. It was this *successful* recording operation that spawned Cohen and Begin's *evil inspiration* to throw John Kennedy and Monroe together and bug them. With Georgie in a position to manipulate Marilyn and pick her brain it was a hell of a scheme. In the underworld rumors fly *far and fast*. Hoffa had heard the rumors about a romance and wire tap conversations between John Kennedy and Marilyn. *Desperately* he'd wanted something on both John and Bobby to halt their devastating prosecution of his Teamsters Union. Jimmy Hoffa sent *his* trusted wiretapper, Bernard Spindel out to the west coast to talk with O'tash. Freddie lied, he convinced Spindel he had the JFK and Marilyn situation under control.

As an introductory offer to *whet* their appetite Fred let Spindel hear the Marilyn and Piscitelli motel tape. He made a copy for him to take back to Hoffa. Freddie told Spindel that *soon* he would have *tapes* of Kennedy and Marilyn. He got a *bundle* from Hoffa but that one tape *was all* the Union leader *ever got* except fabrications from Freddie to keep the money coming. Once Hoffa boasted, "I have a *tape* of John and Bobby Kennedy which is so terribly filthy and nasty my people wanted me to expose them, but I put it away and said the hell with it," he declared, "I wouldn't embarrass his wife and family." But this was just a *bluff,* Hoffa was *referring to* the introductory offer O'tash had sent him and wishing to God it was one of the Kennedys instead of Georgie with Marilyn. If Jimmy Hoffa, an alley fighter if there ever was one, had been in possession of a tape with either of

THERE'S A FISH IN THE COURTHOUSE 621

the Kennedys and Marilyn having sex he'd have *screamed* the lurid details from the *rooftops* of every one of the Teamsters Union Halls in the country.

O'tash *never* had a bug in Lawford's beach house or Marilyn's like he told Tony. But he had worked desperately to get something, *anything* that would sound authentic to *back up* all his crazy lies. He had told Hoffa *one thing* and Cohen *another*. Siphoning money from both of them Freddie had begun to sweat. His lies and rumors had spread, *crossing and recrossing* over lines they ran like wild fire from Hollywood to Wash., D.C.. Freddie's wild stories *spooked* the whole government, the FBI, CIA, Justice Department, State Department, and Welfare Department. If Cohen and Hoffa discovered the truth, Freddie knew he was a dead race horse. For weeks Frank and I had watched O'tash and wiretapper John Danoff, out in Malibu. Danoff was there every morning by six, Freddie would arrive shortly after. We knew O'tash was desperate, there was hardly any calamity could roust the chubby boy out of bed before three in the afternoon. From our vantage point with binoculars we watched Danoff. Disguised in his telephone lineman outfit, he'd park his van by a telephone pole a short ways from Lawford's beach house. Spending days climbing that slivery, creosote pole, he'd hang there like a monkey on a stick. O'tash would arrive moments later in his black El Dorado. Standing near the pole waving his arms and shouting obscenities he exhorted Danoff to get hooked into Lawford's line. Danoff never did find it. O'tash was frantic, he'd taken *a lot* of dough from Cohen and Hoffa, he'd have to make up a *lot more* lies for them, very convincing lies.

Now many years later, here they were, Freddie O'tash and John Danoff on the tube. It was the TV documentary that Ed Tivnan had *concocted* about John and Bobby Kennedy and Marilyn. Knowing the statute of limitations had long expired they allowed their avaricious imaginations to run hog wild. The more sensational their story the more dough they would get. I listened to Danoff lying, "In 1961 the O'tash-Danoff team had succeeded in wiring the rooms of Marilyn's apartment and Peter Lawford's beach house. The *bug* at the Lawford house transmitted conversation between the President and Marilyn and unmistakable sounds of lovemaking...you know...you could hear the *bed squeaking.*" According to Danoff his main part was sitting in a van monitoring sound equipment.

During his investigative research for Goddess, Tony interviewed O'tash several times. On the first occasion he'd taken his wife along. Summers knocked on the door, it opened, there stood O'tash stark ass naked, a big grin on his face. It seemed strange that Tony would believe him, he knew Freddie was weird.

Goddess and the TV documentary had its desired effect. After it was aired, Senator Edward 'Teddy' Kennedy capitulated to their threat, he announced, "I will *not* be a candidate for presidency in '88, it would be far too much to put my family through." The Mishpuckas evil propaganda machine had eliminated a possible candidate from the scene, one the Mishpuckas believed was a menace to them.

More big black headlines, "Peter John Milano...alleged leader of La Cosa Nostra in Southern California along with fifteen others was arrested after indictment by a Federal Grand Jury under the Federal Racketeer Influenced Corrupt Organization statute." U.S. Attorney, Robert Bonner said, "The main body of La Cosa Nostra in L.A. has been severely gutted." Richard Bretzing, Special Agent in charge of the FBI's L.A. office claims that, "We have dealt La Cosa Nostra a decapitating blow." U.S. Atty. General Edwin Meese III, released his statement in L.A.. He called it, "The biggest organized crime case on the west coast in a decade. This indictment and the others to follow will involve as defendants virtually all of those who the government charges make up the membership of La Cosa Nostra in L.A."

The whole thing was insane...what's the Mafia...? So they had a bunch of Italian names...it sounded real good, but they *all worked* for the Mishpucka. Jimmy Caci, aka, Bobby Milano, was one of Cohen's boys, he worked for the Mishpuckas along with Piscitelli, Lo Cigno, Stompanato and Joe Di Carlo...they *all* worked for the Mishpucka. Singer Keely Smith was in the *same category* as Marilyn Monroe and Lana Turner. Under Cohen's orders Caci was setting-up Keely for the motel sex recording bit, instead he found it *more useful* to marry her because Keely could duke him into the *entertainment* world. One night shortly after Marilyn's death Frank and I grabbed Di Carlo on the Strip. He told us he and Caci *had orders* from Cohen to con the singer into putting a fortune in a phony company supposedly making Italian food, they intended to take her one way or another.

The U.S. Justice Dept. Organized Crime Strike Force continued using the *same* old M.O...the Mishpucka was merely sacrificing more stupid Italians as scape-goats to cover-up their own crimes. United States Intelligence agents, damn good men are relegated to obscure positions, their experience and knowledge ignored while *all* United States agencies plan operations with *insidious* intelligence supplied by treacherous Israeli agents.

America was *set-up*, the entire Iran arms fiasco was urged by an

Israeli official, David Kimche. This prime instigator of United States *involvement* in the *insanity* was subpoenaed before a Special Grand Jury. The Israeli leaders protested strenuously, under their pressure U.S. Dist. Judge Aubrey Robinson, Jr. *ruled* that Kimche didn't have to testify. His decision will preclude the U.S. from ever questioning Kimche about Israel's role in setting-up the Iran arms deal. Melvin Rishe, an overbearing Mishpucka lawyer *representing Israel* told U.S. Investigators, "The Israeli government was *not* required to make *any* guarantees to return Kimche from Israel to testify." Israeli Cabinet Secretary, Elyakim Rubinstein flaunted his arrogance in a Jerusalem radio interview that they would cooperate *only* through diplomatic channels and not by coercion in court, Rubinstein *warned* Lawrence E. Walsh, U.S. Special Prosecutor in the Iran-Contra scandal that, "Mr. Walsh, if you try for too much...you will get nothing."

CHAPTER 48

Out the window on my left the concrete landing strip appeared to be sliding backwards, the deep rumbling of the powerful jet engines became a whine as we climbed over the Pacific. Gracefully sweeping back over L.A. the plane headed east, across from me the two ladies with great excitement whispered. They were on their way, the most dramatic mission of their lives, destination, Washington, D.C.

By summer of 1987 I'd completed my tremendous task, hundreds of pages, a recordation of *all the events* since 1946. The story of evil, murderous people, their vile acts *paralleled* the insidious inheritance of their ancestors, they who'd *manipulated* the craven Crucifixion at Golgotha, near Jerusalem.

My manuscript was printed in book form, the ladies would hand deliver to *each* of the *one hundred* United States Senators a copy. At the same time these representatives of the people would be handed a petition, an ultimatum demanding a sweeping Senate investigation of the Black Robe Mishpucka.

It was strange how the *purpose* of my petition to the U.S. Senate *paralleled* the intent of the Declaration of Independence only two hundred and eleven years ago on July 4, 1776. In history class I had memorized certain parts of it:

> "We hold these truths to be self-evident, that all
> men are created equal, that they are endowed by
> their Creator with certain unalienable rights, that

among these are, life, liberty and the pursuit of happiness. That to secure these rights, governments are instituted among men, deriving their just powers from the consent of the governed, that whenever any form of government becomes destructive of these ends, it is the right of the people to alter or to abolish it and to institute new government, laying its foundation on such principles and organizing its powers in such form, as to them shall seem most likely to effect their safety and happiness. Prudence, indeed, will dictate that governments long established should not be changed for light and transient causes and accordingly all experience hath shown that mankind are more disposed to suffer, while evils are sufferable, than to right themselves by abolishing the forms to which they are accustomed. But when a long train of abuses and usurpations, pursuing invariably the same object evinces a design to reduce them under absolute despotism, it is their right, it is their duty, to throw off such government, and to provide new guards for their future security. In every stage of these oppressions we have petitioned for redress in the most humble terms: our repeated petitions have been answered only by repeated injury."

Most certainly I do *not* advocate overthrowing the Constitution or altering it in the *slightest* but only restoring its power and blessings to the people by destroying its usurpers.

The Senators first step is to instantly *remove* all Magistrates, and rescind the Federal Judges political power to *appoint* them. All Local Rules and the *political* power of Federal Judges to promulgate them would be revoked, the Federal Judges would be strictly *required* to adhere to and operate under the U.S. Federal Rules. Any *failure* of Judges to follow the U.S. Rules would be *cause* for instant *removal* from the bench.

Also to be revoked would be the power of judges to *cover-up* their corruption and treason by ordering that their decisions were, "NOT TO BE PUBLISHED." These revocations are within the immediate power and jurisdiction and *responsibility* of the Senate. Their austere enforcement must be put into effect at once. These requirements are the preliminary steps *absolutely necessary* to restore America to the sanity and security of Due Process of Law under the United States Constitution.

I wasn't stupid enough to believe that the hard-knot of *treasonous* Senators would take any action in behalf of the people. Neither did I have any hope the *corrupt* or the simply *cowardly* ones would take any action. The petition was for the purpose of *documenting* the fact that all the Senators were indeed given every opportunity to act as their duty commands, a chance to become honest, true Americans. If the Senators disavow their solemn trust as elected representatives the conscience of the people will be fully *justified* in taking over.

Somebody once said, "Extremism in the *defense* of liberty is no vice." But this time *legal and moral justification* to remove corrupt politicians will *empower the people* to use whatever reasonable force necessary. The amazing secrets and documents I'd uncovered during the last seventeen years have been put in a secure place. Since the ruthless murder of JFK, the official track record of Congress clearly reveals their *double-dealing cover-ups* and merciless destruction of witnesses and evidence. In the event of the Senators almost certain treasonous rejection of the petition, all documents and evidence will then become the property of, and will be handed over to the people. I hoped to God it wouldn't be *necessary* for the people to take over, it could lead to *chaos and destruction* of our country. The *Mishpucka* is forcing us to a *final* decision, the identical desperate situation that *forced* the people of Germany in 1933 to take over. Certainly among those one hundred men in the capitol there are a few with strength, wisdom and loyalty who will step forward in the dire emergency and lead, to bring the country back to its senses and to safety.

Such hopes were pipe-dreams, nausea welled up to join a thump in my chest. The jet was landing, the Senators would soon have the book and petition in their hands. It was *frightening*, the one hundred were so deeply *enmeshed* in the shadowy, *sinister webs* of Mishpucka domination and conspiracy that I knew they could not function. For years Senator Alan Cranston had been slipping into Century City to pick up his bundle...hundreds of thousands from Lew Wasserman, a high level Mishpucka in Hollywood. Wasserman owns Cranston from top to bottom, and California's other Senator Pete Wilson had just made an initial trip to Wasserman and the Hollywood fountain that spews out the green stuff.

For many years, *too many* to remember, Ronald Reagan's puppet strings have been greased and *manipulated* by Wasserman. Another powerful *Hollywood* Mishpucka, Jack Valenti, was President Lyndon

Johnson's aide, he is *now* Pres. Reagan's advisor. It was Valenti who frightened Johnson into *covering-up* the assassination of President Kennedy because, "Forty million people would be killed if the *truth* was revealed."

Time for America is swiftly running out, the Mishpucka is nearing their goal of total *worldwide* domination. The ultimate climax could possibly come even before President Reagan's term is up in 1988. The Responsa in Tel Aviv has accelerated their coded messages of Mishna. The Jew Law of chaos, corruption and conspiracy is being sent out to their synagogues everywhere on the globe, coordinating the Mishpuckas funnelling of arms to maniacal criminals in the far corners of Earth, North Ireland, Lebanon, Nicaragua, South Africa, India etc., Israeli *agents provocateur* everywhere stir violence, riots, bombings, assassations, *eruptions* of fiery terrorism. Death was being stepped up all over the place, the Mishpucka, an evil organization so *almighty* that it could murder the President of the United States with impunity fears nothing.

Through their synagogues and Mishpucka psychologists *stationed* in the U.S. Military Academies the Responsa has gained *access* and infiltrated the Officer Corps. The unbelievably murderous attack on the lightly armed U.S.S. Liberty and cold blooded murder of United States sailors by Jews is *direct evidence* of their inborn murderous nature. Under their merciless attacks of fiery napalm and torpedoes by *Israeli* jet fighters and torpedo boats the Liberty sent an *SOS*. The radio calls to the Fleet urgently pleading for help were *treasonously* mis-routed to such distant stations as Ethiopia and Greece. Finally, Jet fighters were launched from the carrier U.S.S. America. Racing to defend the Liberty they were *suddenly ordered* to break off from their rescue mission and return immediately to the carrier, leaving the crew of the U.S.S. Liberty to its fate, this treasonous command issued direct from D.C. Next appeared the Mishpuckas mysterious power over Congress to *cover-up* their *sinister* acts. Then their ability to suppress the book, Assault On The U.S.S. Liberty, written by Lt. James Ennes a member of the crew. Wielding their evil power over the newspapers and TV media they *suppressed* scheduled talk shows and appearances by Lt. Ennes.

Systematically the South African government is being *destroyed* by riots and killings stirred by secret Mishpucka agents. Like the Arabs rich oilfields, South Africa's productive diamond mines are fiercely coveted by the Mishpucka, they are *prime targets*. Around the world Pretoria's financial structure is subverted by the fiendish Mishpucka screaming for trade and economic sanctions against them. A *massive plot* to crucify Pretoria by wiping out millions in trade and monetary investments with the city of Los Angeles is *underway* by Councilman Joel Wachs. All over the world in financial centers the *pattern* is the same.

L. A. City Councilman Joel Wachs screeches out his *concern* for black people in a country six thousand miles distant. His *motives* are sinister, in Watts, a black ghetto several blocks south of City Hall, Wachs does nothing for them. A vicious AIDS driven homo, Wachs is wed to another Mishpucka councilman. Out of his *closet,* Joel is insolent, he flaunts his life-style. Thereby hangs the tail, a group of ten Harvard University scientists working at New England Regional Primate Research Center, in Southborough, Mass., discovered under their electron microscopes a virus in blood cells of Rhesus monkeys identical to human AIDS. With identical *deadliness* it kills monkeys and humans. With their microscopes laying bare the *killer* virus, the scientists note: "Rhesus monkeys dying from the immune-deficiency syndrome formerly lived in group cages where both heterosexual and homosexual relations and the eating of feces and spraying of urine were frequent." The scientists were *appalled,* reluctant to admit that the world *faced an epidemic,* millions of corpses laying in the streets. Not even the terrible *bubonic plague* of the middle ages matched the terror of this. They had discovered that *gays weren't gay,* they were shit-eaters, a deadly mass incubator, spreaders of a killer virus, for which there is no cure.

Chaos..! Chaos..! From every conceivable direction the American industry is being attacked and destroyed by the international trade conspiracy. Dancing to the Mishpuckas tugs on his strings, President Reagan cons the people, "Low priced *imported* shoes are saving the American people millions of dollars." This clever glib coming while our American factories close and thousands of people are put out of work. Israeli made shoes have captured over seventy percent of the U.S. market because Israeli can make shoes cheaper, Reagan sends them billions of U.S. *taxpayers dollars* to do it. Reagan commits even *more deadly* chaotic insanity with his nomination of Mishpucka, Alex Kozinsky to a lifetime appointment to the Federal Appeals Court in San Francisco. A thirty five year old Jew born in Russia, Kozinsky *mysteriously* became a lawyer for President Reagan and a law clerk to Chief Justice Warren Burger. This treasonous Mishpucka actually ghost-wrote *critical decisions* that were made by the Chief Justice of the United States.

THERE'S A FISH IN THE COURTHOUSE 629

Absurdly, Kozinsky became Chief Judge of the U.S. Claims Court, and there, the treasonous *agent provocateur* sabotaged and thwarted criminal investigations into military waste and procurement frauds. He then *conspired* to destroy the federal employees who'd exposed frauds against the U.S. Because of Kozinsky's *treasonous acts* against America, two watch-dog groups and the Government Accountability Project along with the Federal employees demanded that the Senate investigate into this *Israeli saboteur's* corruption and treason.

Former Dep. Special Counsel of the United States Claims Court, Jessie James, accused Kozinsky of making *outright*, absolute lies and statements to the Judiciary Committee at his confirmation hearing, May 17, 1985. But all this had no effect, understandably, *the head* of the Judiciary Committee is the *traitorous* Senator Strom Thurmond who covered-up the machine gun crime for Pres. Reagan's National Security Director, William P. Clark. Then Senator Thurmond aided and abetted by two *cowardly* Senators on the committee ramrodded through Pres. Reagan's appointment of Alex Kozinsky, a treasonous Mishpucka from Russia.

Senators Paul Simon (Illinois), and Dennis De Concini (Arizona), *admitted* their betrayal of America to the news media: Simon stated, "Frankly I feel some *un-ease* with this nomination, but I do not have a basis to vote against it." And De Concini stated, "After all of those accusations made against him I feel some uneasiness about this Alex Kozinsky," Then attempting to cover his *betrayal*, De Concini came on with some sick slop, "I hope that Kozinsky will hear these words and that he will *moderate* his temperament and manners that he has exhibited in the past." Lord, *what more* had the Senators needed!

The Mishpucka strategy *never* changes. Gov. Duekmejian's Annual Report to the Legislature regarding Organized Crime in California is a lengthy document prepared by Attorney General Van de Kamp's Bureau of Organized Crime and Civil Intelligence. The report uses the same old worn out Mishpucka propaganda they used on Carlos Marcello, they called him, "The King of the New Orleans Mafia." All they need is an Italian name, this time it's a half-assed bookmaker, Peter John Milano. In the report, Milano is labeled, "The new Boss of Southern California's Crime Family." The dumb dago *loves* all the notoriety, eating it up he *plays* the part just like Marlin Brando. But in the Report there is *not a hint* of the Mishpucka Crime Family.

The Mishpucka chaos nears its peak, assassinations, terrorism and death around the globe, governments on the *brink* of collapse, world bank catastrophes, and AIDS, an *uncontrollable* deadly plague, chaos, deadly chaos.

The people have been run, harried like the hare by the hounds, but trapped against a stone wall with *no place* left to run even the hare comes out fighting. And this time the hare has *recognized* his enemy, the Jews can manufacture *no scape-goat* to crouch behind, they have brought their evil down upon themselves.

As Jack Ruby *babbled* under duress of his *horrible guilt,* "Jews will die by the millions, they will be killed in the streets." And President Lyndon Johnson *had known the truth,* he had stated, "Forty million people will die if the truth is *revealed.*" There were forty million Jews in America.

Only the United States Senate led by the Constitution is powerful enough to save America. Of one hundred Senators, the treasonous, corrupt and cowardly will *desert* their country. The small group that remains will have to *stand fast.* If not, the people will have *no choice,* they will take over. The mighty war will be engaged, a Jihad.....a Holy War to end Holy Wars.....a deadly, *bitter struggle* to the End.....

INDEX   631

Aaron, 426, Jewish high priest
Abbe, Judge, 470
Abbott & Costello, 97, 486
Abu-Sulb, Ali, 392, 537-8, 559
Abortion Action League, 407,
   Mishpucka plot
Ackerd, Robert, 35-7
Aidlin, Mary, 423, trustee, C.R. Price
   testamentary trust
Aidlin, Joseph, 424, trustee, C.R. Price
   testamentary trust
AIDS, 628-9
Alcohol Beverage Control (ABC)
   148-50, 152, 260-3, 266-70, 400,
   473, 520
Alemeda, Renzee, 375, murderer
Alliance For Survival, 395, California
   taxpayer assoc.
Allred, Gloria, 426, lawyer
Alpert, Merrill, 559
Alsip, Joseph, Jr., 326, 488,
   595-7, murder suspect
American Broadcasting Co., (ABC)
   402, 571
American Civil Liberties Union,
   140, 389, 506, 541
American Legion, 415, 433, 438,
   541
American Patriots, 441
American Rights Assoc., 441
Americanism, 512
Amir, Jacques, 537, mayor of
   Dimona, 559
Anathema Maranatha, 259,
   a dreadful curse
Anderson, Federal Judge, 270,
   272, 275
Anderson, John, 387,
   U.S. Congressman
Andrews, Judge, 86
Angel, Jim, 314-7
Anti-Defamation League of The
   B'nai B'rith, (ADL) 385-90,
   members, 394, 406, 427, 541
Anti-Semetic, 387, 391, 541, 549
Apalachin Meeting, 406, Mafia Dons
Appeal Brief, 230-1, Ninth Circuit
Arabs Holy Lands, 503
Arens, Moshe, 388, Israeli
   Ambassador
Argo Petroleum Corp., 422-4,
   428-9, 468, 510
Armeggedon, 415, end of the
   world

Armstrong, Bill, 59, 60
Arthur, 401-2, muscleman
Artukovic, Andrija, 550,
   Croatian hero, 556-7
Ashby, Herb, 27-8, 96, 98, 127
Ashley, George, 559
Assassination Mission, (fake)
   582-3, 587-90, 593
Assassination, (real) 590, 592,
   593, Jew plot
Assault On The U.S.S. Liberty,
   627, book by Lt. James M.
   Ennes
Asuncion v. Superior Court, 498
Atsugi Airbase, Japan, 582
Attwood, William, 593-4
   U.S. Ambassador
Avital, Jehuda, 398

B Girls, 570
Babcock, John, ABC-TV,
   Channel 7, 401-6, 408, 571
Baker, Judge, 86
Ball, Hunt, Hart, Brown &
   Baerwitz, law firm, 424
Ballots, 180, 197, 419, 421, 461,
   494, terrorizing lawyers, 517
Bank of A. Levy, 97, 147, 174-7,
   181, 197, 522, 525, 543
Bank of America Natl. Trust &
   Savings, 473, 503
Bank of Italy, 472-3
Bar Ilan University, 558, 560
Barens, Arthur, 554-5, lawyer
Barham, Barbara, 131
Barr, Candy, 567, Mickey Cohen's
   girlfriend, 576, 590, 592
Bat Cave, Oxnard, 462, 502
Bataan, Death march, 550
Battaglia, Charlie, 546, Mafia
Battson, Dr., 9-11, 17, 32
Baumgartner, Jack, 346, Deputy
   Sheriff
Bedouins, 392, in Israel
Begin, Menachem, terrorist Stern
   gang, 393, 395-96, 501-03, 509,
   537-8, 566-7, 574-6, 591, 610,
   617-8, 620
Belli, Melvin, 575, lawyer, 219-20,
   576, 590-2, 610
Bello, Joey, 286
Bennett, Ralph, (Hoot) 145,
   155-7, 159-62, 248, 252-3, 420

632 INDEX

Benny, 401-2 Sunset Strip operator
Benton, Orr, Duval & Buckingham 422, law firm
Berbir, Hospital, 387
Berenson, Judge Jerome, 119-24, 126-7, 138-9, 142, 144, 146-8, 154, 156, 164, 167, 172-9, 185-94, 196-8, 201, 207, 209, 211, 213-5, 217, 222-3, 227-30, 232-3, 236-8, 240-1, 246, 249-51, 255-6, 258, 260, 262, 264, 268, 270, 272, 276-8, 281, 285, 288-91, court log jams, millions of taxpayers dollars, 292-3, 296-7, 300-1, 305, 308-11, 315, 323, 350-1, 381, 383, 403, 409-11, 415-8, 420-4, 426, 428-30, 432-3, 438, 443, 447, 450, 464, 468-9, 471, 474-5, 477-9, 489-91, 502, 510, 520, 522, 525, 541, 543-4, 546, 599, 600, 605-6, 611
Berman, Judge Jack, 430, ex-husband of Diane Feinstein
Bernadotte, Count Volke, 393, U.N. Peace Negotiator
Betty, 77, 79
Beverly Hills Developers, 474
Beverly Wilshire Hotel, 574-6, 591
Bialkin, Kenneth, 388 (ADL) National Chairman
Bishop, Joey, 567, Comedian 616-8
Black Muslims, 379
Black Hand Mafia Family (Sicilian) 383, 386, 471, 510, 520, 545-6
Black Robe Mishpucka Family, (Jew) 383, 395, 404, 406, 408, 412, 416, 424-5, 429-30, 433, 441-2, 449, 455, 458-60, 469-71, master of America 473-5, 477-9, 493, 496, 502, 505-7, 509-11, 520, 524, 527, 529-32, 534-8, 540, 542, 544-7, 556, 560, 595, 601-3, 606, 608-10, 613, 624
Black Robe Syndicate, 298-9, 308, 383
Blais, DeWitt (Red), 40-1, 50-2, 74, 120-2, 144
Blitzberg, Hymie, 429-31, see Steven Stone, 450, 469-70, 493, 509, 511, 517, 529, 536, 540, 544-5, 560, 563, 598-9, 601
Blodgett, Lila, 91
Bloomingdale, Alfred, 553-5, President Reagan's buddy,
Blue's, Ben, 374, nightclub
Bobbi, 374, informant 604
Bocarsky, Sidney, 226-7, 229, 338, 607-10
Bolsheviki, 548, Lenin
Bompensiero, Frank, 381-2, The Bomp 404
Bonaparte, Napoleon, 337
Bonnelli, William, 473, (Big Bill)
Bonner, Robert, 622, U.S. Atty.
Bourgeoisie, 550, non-jew
Bowling, County Bldg. Insp., 205
Boyd, David Lerrel, 110, 116-7, 125
Boyd, Thomas C., 97, Civil Service Commissioner, 109, Pres. Bank of A. Levy, 110, 117, 122, 125, 167, 176-7, 281
Bradbury, Michael, 207-10, Asst. Dist. Atty., 262, 289, 325, 432, 437-8, 447, 450, 467, 469, 482, 488, 513-4, 524-5, 563, 595, 597, 606
Bradley, Thomas, 394, L.A. Mayor
Brady, Scott, 343, actor
Brancato, Tony, 347, one of the Two Tonys
Branch, Marvin, 514, realtor, 515-8, 519 hitman
Brando, Marlin, 629 actor
Braude, Marvin, 396, L.A. city councilman
Bravo, Joe, 156
Bretzing, Richard, 622, FBI
British Broadcasting Corp., (BBC), 564, 571, 578
Broadway Dept. Store, 342
Brody, David, 388, B'nai B'rith agent
Brogett, Lylia, 91
Bronstein, Leon, 548, aka Leon Trotsky
Brooklier, Dominick, 381
Brotherton, Claire, 3, 5, 7, 8, 21-2, 24-7, 31, 43, 51, 68-72, 83, 87, 96, 102, 133
Brown Derby Restaurant, 342
Brown, Gov. Jerry, 197, 323, 325, 396, 415-6, 418-20, 428-32, 461, 508, 543-4
Brown, Gov. Pat, 197, 418-9, 424, 443
Brown, Thad, 75-6, 79, 367-8, Det. Chief, LAPD
Browning, Judge James R., 246, 439, Congressional Hearing, 443
Bruneman, Les, 404-5, gangster

INDEX 633

Buchanon, Patrick, 539, vigilante
Bugliosi, Vincent, 408, L.A. Dep. Dist. Atty., 555
Burger, Chief Justice Warren, 628
Burleson, Robert, 245, arson investigator
Busch, Joseph, 359-61, L.A. Dist. Atty., 364, 367, 376, 619

Cabaret, 172
Cable's Restaurant, 291, 400, 402
Cacciatore, Charles, 436, Dep. D.A.
California Criminal Justice Comm., 256-7, 270, 605
California State Atty. Gen., 119, 144, 154, 349, 375, 473
California State Bar Assoc., 84-6, 94, 99, 121, 125, 127, 144, 180, 196, 307-8, 431, 464, 487, 493, 506, Sir Lancelots, 531
California State Treasury, 418, going broke
Camarillo Daily News, 257-8, 384, 407
Campbell, Clyde, 234-6, chm. of MWD, 234-6
Canadian Mounted Police, 503
Cane, Ace, 530, Hollywood bar
Cannizzaro, Eddie, 285, Siciliano Mafia, 286-93, money collector, 299-309, 311-9, memorandum, 322-23, 360-1, 364, 400-5, 409-10, 576
Capitalist, 549
Cappo, Joey, 530, idiot judge act
Captain's Table Restaurant, 1
Carbo, John, 546, Mafia
Carousel Club, 589, (Dallas)
Carter, Jimmie, 201, 273, President, 382, 425
Caruso, Paul, 134, lawyer, 137, 139, 179, 599
Casitas Mun. Water Dist., (CMWD) 232-4, pipeline, 236, 464, 469
Castro, Didi, 30-3, 35, 37-41, 44, 46, 51-3, 55, 60, 62, 73-4, 94, 120, 421
Castro, Fiedel, 581-3, 592, 594
Cavin, Laura, 295, Judge Marshall's law clerk
Century City, 306
Certiorari, 274, 294-5, 299
Chamber of Commerce, 521, Ventura
Chapter 20; 594, double image in Dallas

Chapter 21; 591, countdown to conspiracy, 592-4
Charles, Ray, 81, Asst. Mgr. Emp. Assoc., 108-10, 118, 121, 158-9, 513-4, 521
Chase, Eileen, 83, 97
Chavez, Ravine, 330-1
Chevron Oil Co., 466
Chinese Triads Society, 546, gangsters
Chirp, Wilhelmina, 60-1
Chitwood, Capt., 339-40, LAPD Narcotics Div., 377
Chosen People, 391
Christians, 391, guilt complex
Christian State, 387
Church of The Conceptual Truth, 490
CBS Television Studio, 343, 553
CIA, 503, 554, 581-2, 610, 621
Citizen Justice Assoc., 180
Citizens For Oxnard, 528-31
Citizens To Protect The Ojai, (CPO) 464-8, 476, 482
City Of Thousand Oaks, 291
City Of Ventura, 176, 182-3
City Terrace, 471, East L.A.
Civil Rights Law, 196, 199
Civil War, 506
Clark, William P., 174, Pres. Reagan's Natl. Security Advisor, 296, Secy. Of Interior, 298, 381, 401, 432, 442-3, machine gun, 446, 'Shoot Niggers & Mexicans,' 460, 470-1, 476, 502, 520, 543, 546, 608, 629
Clark, William Petit, 174
Clear Point, 324, High Point Dr.
Cleaver, Kenneth, 33-4, 36-7, 41-2, 44, 46-8, 50, 75, 96-101, 103, 131, 133
Cleck, Milam, 248
Clemons, Aquilla, 588
Clinger, William, 30-7, 41-2, 44, 46, 48, 51-2, 54-5, 74, 88, 421
Clinton, Paul, 7, 64-5, 69, 71, 102
Clouseau, Inspector, 606
Coalition For Better TV, 460
Coastal Commission, 467
Cocaine, 597-8
Cohen, Jerome, 430, lawyer
Cohen, Mickey, 226, gangster, 227, 335, 337-40, 324-3, 346-64, 366-7, 371-4, 376-8, 381-2, 405, 471, 502, 565-71, 574-6, 589, 591-2, 607-9, 612, 616-7, Italian boys, 618-22
Cohen, Phillip, 96, County Counsel, 98, 102, 108, 212-4, 280-1, 380, 383

634   INDEX

Cohen, Stanley, 496-500, ambulance chaser, 531-2, 534-6, 540-1
Cole, Carl, 147
Cole, Joan, 147-8
Coliseum Commission, 382
Colonial House Restaurant, Oxnard, 374, 377-8
Commercial Credit Corp., 535, same as Control Data Business Centers Inc.
Communists, 198, 541, 546-49
Compton, Robert L., 292-3, lawyer in Nordman ofc.
Confidential Magazine, 225, 619
Conlon, John, 287, County Sup., 288, new ordinance, 290, 310
Connally, Gov. John, 586
Conspiracy, 591, book
Constitution, 119, 199, 279, 502, 506, 509, 539, 540-1, 611, 625-6, 630
Cooper, Rabbi Abraham, 557
Cooper, Ofc., Ray, 111-16
Cormany, Ralph, 177, 235
County Recorder & Tax Coll., 173
Crabtree, Virgil, 351, IRS Intell., 365
Cranston, Sen. Alan, 626, Century City
Crenshaw, John, 312, U.S. Dep. Clerk, 314
Crew, Bill, 525, Ventura councilman
Crime Commission, 546
Criminial Records, 436, FBI-CII
Cronkite, Walter, 412, commentator
Crucifixion, 593, 624
Cuba, 581, Bay of Pigs, 583, 586, 594
Cuban Exiles, 582, 587, 591
Cuban Operation, 571
Cuddles Restaurant, 488
Curtis, Herbert, 544, Black Judge

Dallas Morning News, 587
Damocles, 461, Sword of Death
Danks, Donna M., 276, atty., 277-8, 281-3, 293-4, 296, 299, 301-5, 309-10, 312, memorandum, 313-19
Danoff, John, 621, wire tapper
Davidian, Abraham, 338, plaid coat, 339-40, drug dealer, 377, 607, 609
Davis, Al, 382
Davis, Anthony, 192
Davis, Ed, 419, Ca. state sen.-former LAPD Chief, 422
Davis, Dep. Sheriff, 438
Davidson, Harold W., 535, lawyer

Davidson, Matsen, & Strouse, 534, law firm
Dawson, Adam, 411, reporter
Deadly plague, 628-9, AIDS
Dealy Plaza, 587-8
Deane, Richard H., 275, clerk U.S. Court of Appeal, 9th Circuit Frisco, 295
Decker, Bill, 579, Dallas Sheriff, 580-1, 584-5, 612
Declaration of Independence, 624
De Concini, Sen. Dennis, 629
Deem, Woodruff, 2, 8-10, 17, 32-3, 36-41, 43-53, 61, 63, 88-91, 94, 103, 119-20, 141, 163, 179, 188, 211, 562, 605
Deihl, Douglas, 602-3
Deihl, Patrica, 603
De Long, Jack, 155, 252-4, 258, 465
De Lorean, John, 600, cocaine bust
Demjanjuk, John, 551, accused by Mishpucka
Democratic Convention, 567, Los Angeles 1960
Denny, 36
Denny's Restaurant, 286, 288-9, 293, 311, 400, 403-4
Department of Motor Vehicles, 338
De Sanno, Capt. Ventura Sheriff, 151, birds and the bees, 206-7
Deukmejian, George, 270, State Atty. Gen., 271, 394, Israeli organized crime, 431, The Great Defender Of Law and Order, 432, 467, 470, 520, 534, 544, 629, Gov.'s Organized Crime Report
Diallo, Seydou, 593-4
Di Carlo, Joe, 357, 565, 567, 616-7, 622
Dillon, Robert, 34-7, 41-6, 48, 50, 53, 74, 88, 101, 103-4, 108
Dino's Club, 219-20, 225, 619
Dixon, James E., 135-8
Dixon, Rev. Leonard, 325
Dodd, Bruce, 8, 10, 17, 107
Dodd, Mrs., 11, 107
Dodger Stadium, 331
Donahoo, Capt., 339, LAPD Homocide, 341, 346-7
Donlon, David J., 144-8, 150
Dorsen, Norman, 389, ACLU
Dougherty, James, 479, County Sup., 481-4, 489-90
Doyle, 104

INDEX   635

Dragna, Jack, 226, 285, 305, 354, alleged Godfather
Dragna, Louis Tom, 381
Dragon Lady, 76-8
Dreever, Hugh, 24-5
Drescher, Phillip, 486, lawyer, 469
Drobatz, Ofc. Andy, 112, 342
Dulyea, Steven, 614
Duncan, Frank, 374, lawyer
Duncan, Ma, 374-5 murderess, 403, 603-4
Dunes Development, 613
Dunham, Harrison, 20-3, 25, 27, 61-8, 72-5, 84-6, 90, 94, 98=9, 106, 108, 110, 119, 121, 123, 125-7, 129, 134, 147-8, 156, 173, 176, 184
Dunham, Mrs., 85
Du Pre, Robert O., 196-8, 201-2, 207, 209-18, 221-4, 228-30, 240-4, 252, 261-69, 271-85, 289-96, 299, 302-7, S. Carolina Bar Assn., 309-10, 312, 314-5, Justice Dept., 316-21, two kinds of justice, 322-3, 382, 400, 402, 404-5, 408-10, 439-45, 496-8, 506

Eagle, Danny, 77-80
Eagle, Tommy, 77-9
Earl Carrol's Nightclub, 343
Eaton, Cal, 335
Eaton, Eileen, 335
Egyptian Theater, 342
Ekaterinburg, 576-8
Elections, Judicial, 197, 421, 461, 494, lessons to lawyers, 501
Ellison, Ray, 512-6, 518, 521, 523-4
Embrecht, Charles, 228, state assemblyman
Energetics of Ventura, 467
Engels, Friedrich, 549, writer, 558
Engleberg, Hyman, 617, Doctor
Ennes, Lt. James M., Jr. 388-9, author of Assault On The U.S.S. Liberty, 627
Erickson, Maggie, 460, Ventura Sup., 468, seasoned politician, 470, 561
Erwin, Mrs., 411
Erwin, Richard E., 3-5, 7-11, 17-8, 20-4, 26, 29-44, 46, 50-4, 59, 61-2, 64, 68, 70-5, 81-3, 86-90, 91-2, real name Richard E. Fish, 94-5, 100-04, 106-09, 119, 144
Esdraelon, 415, Great Plains of

Eskin, George, 31, 61, 63, 89-91, 94, 179, 211, extension cord case, 443, 448, 450-1, 454, 458
European Art Mart, 425, Gauguin painting

Faerstein, Saul J., 556
Falwell, Jerry, 407, preacher
Farley, James, 158-60, 493-4, shylock
Farr, Bill, 408-12, reporter
Farrakhan, Louis, 505, Black Religious leader
FBI, 150, 198, 286, 307, 381-2, 394, 425, 427, 439, 458, 503-04, big FBI case, 519, 545-6, 554, 567-8, 580, 585, 603, 608, 610, 621
Fed Mart, 511
Federal Bureau of Narcotics, 336, 340, 343-4, 374, 411
Federal Court Rules, 242-4, 273-4, 282, 295, 300, 304, 440, 442
Federal Judicial System, 298-9
Federal Omnibus Safe Streets Act, 174-9, 256, 605
Federal Organized Crime Strike Force, 381-3
Feejian, 306, 309
Feinberg, Judge Sidney, 430-1
Feinstein, Diane, 396, Frisco Mayor, 426, 459
Feinstein, Jerome, 614,
Festerling, Capt., 240, Ventura Fire Captain
Fiedler, Bobbi, Congresswoman, 396, 426
Fields, Joe, 550
Fifth Column, 407, WW11
File On The Tsar, 576-7, 585
Finch, Dr., 352
Finch, Mrs., 352
Fire Protection Bureau, 433, 435, Grey Shirts, 453, 456
First Natl Bank of Ventura, 472
Fish, Richard E., 91, aka Richard E. Erwin, 95-9, 106-8, 110, 121-3, 126, 129, 131, 133, 135, 137, 140, 142, 144, 147-9, 158-9, 163, 167, 173, 176, 229, 280, 408, 421, 507
Fitzsimmons, Dave, 59-60, 67-8
Fleischman, G. B., 556, lawyer, 557-9, 563
Florence, 'Flo,' 292-4
Flynn, John, 415, Ventura County Sup.

Font, Jaime, 524, Scotch & Sirloin restaurant owner, 525-6
Forbes, Det. Sgt. Colin, 334-7, 349
Forbes, Despine, 335
Forbes, Robert, 333-5
Ford, Pres. Gerald, 444
Forest Lawn Memorial Park, 399, Hollywood Hills Park, Old North Church
Formosa Restaurant, 352, 360
Four Aces Bar, 341
Fourt, Judge Walter, 166-9, 171
France, Lt. Vince, 477, 483-8, 492-3
Frank, 75-80, 351-3, 361-7, 372-8, 399-402, 408, 418, 564-6, 572, 574-5, 579, 582, 584-5, 591, 612, 618-22
Frank, Anne, 387, diary
Frankenstein, 608, monster
Franklin, Ben, 159
Fraser, James, 525, handwriting expert
Fratiano, Jimmie 'The Weasel,' 348, 354, 404-5
Freedman, L., 396, woman lawyer
Frenchy's Cove, 602
Fresno, Ca., 340
Friars Club, 335
Friday, Ofc., 333-4
Friedan, Betty, 406, Womens activist, 407-8, pro-choice, 'right to my own body,' 427
Friedman, Arnie, 411, reporter
Friedman, Judge Leonard, 511-2 case law, 538, 556, 558, 563
Friends Of The River, 469
Funk & Wagnall dictionary, 54, bigoted, 549, huckster

Gage, Dennis, 240-1, fireman, 246
Galatea, 370
Gallagher, Hugh, 132, 601, 603
G.A.P. Development Co., 325-6
Garcia, Arthur A., 319-20
Garfield, Rita, 90-1, 95, 100, 104-5
Garziano, Carol, 478-9, 481-4, 486-9
Gates, Darryl, 382, LAPD Chief, intell. files, 382
Geary, Patrick, 18, 56
Geffensky, Ralph, 495, aka Geffen, Magistrate, 496
George, 143
Georgia Street Receiving Hosp., 333-5

Genovese, Family, 546, Mafia
Ghitterman, Hourigan, Grossman, Finestone & Perren, 431, law firm
Gianini, A.P., 472-3, Bank Of Italy
Gilbert, Judge, 470
Gill, Ron, 228, lawyer in Berenson & Nordman law firm
Gillespie, John, 614, Ventura Undersheriff
Gilliam, Jr., 8-9, baseball player
Ginsberg, 397-8, pawnshop owner
Gius, Judas, 198, 237-8, Letters To The Editor, 239, the old Judas kiss, 240, 249-50, 253, 255, 257, 327, 384, 408, 415-7, 420-1, 426, 430, 434, 459-61, 477, 492, 514, 521, Letters To The Editor, 523-4, 604
Glass House, 371, LAPD Hdqrs.
Glasser, Ira, 389, ACLU
Glitman, Maynard, 559-60
Godzilla, 314, 509
Goldblatz, Rabbi Izzy, 426
Goldenring, Ira, 420, lawyer
Godfather, 545, (see list)
Goldman, J., 545, LA Times
Goldstein, Barceloux & Goldstein, 290-1, law firm
Golgotha, 624, Crucifixion
Grand Jury, 118-20, 122, 124, 126-7, 138, 141-4, 146-8, 154, 156, 163-4, 167, 174-9, 181-2, 185, 198, 211, 230, 249-50, 255, 268, 380, 409, 419, 442, 474-5, 519, 524-5, 541, 606-7, 611, 613-4, 622-3
Grand Oligarch, 172, 174
Grant, Armand, 557
Great Britain, 501
Green Patrol, 392, 537-8
Greenson, Dr., 617
Grodinsky, Justice Joseph R., 431, aka Joe Grodin, 450, 493, 509, 561
Grossman, Israel G., 614
Groucho, 498
Gruber, Jack, 589, gangster, 591
Guerin, Thomas, 134-5, lawyer, 137, 139-40, 179
Guns, 502, for Israel
Gurion, Ben, 393, Israeli prime minister
Gustafson, Roy, 374-5, Ventura D.A.
Gutierrez, Judge A., 446, extension cord case, petition for removal, 447-8
Gutstein, Robert A., 614

INDEX 637

Hadden, Judge Joseph, 469, 532, 'you ain't never going to get in court, do you hear me? Never.'
Haerle, Paul, 428, lawyer
Hair, William, 189, 191, 233-6, 290, 300-1, 304-5, 309, 315, 464-5
Haley, Judge, 86
Haley, Katherine, 233-4, aka Katherine Hoffman, 464, 467, 469, 544
Hallbrecht, Seigfried, 387
Hambleton, Richard, 526, harbor commissioner
Hamilton, Capt., 346-9
Hamilton, Paul, 301-3, 309-10, 315-6
Hamm, Robert, 130, county clerk, 131, 137, 161-3, 185-7, 252, 257-8, 267-8, 384, 460
Hanawalt, Richard, (Dick) 53-5, 57-8, 60-1, 70, 596
Harbor, College, 550
Harbor Division, 336
Harbortown Marina Hotel, 521
Harding, Mrs., 90
Hardy, James, 525, (see Larry Stone)
Harrington, Ron, 514, lawyer, 521-3, whitewash
Harris, John J., 525, handwriting expert
Harrison, Rubbish Co., 496
Harry's Place, 569-70
Hart, Gary, 503-4
Harter, Merle, 1, 30
Harth, Leonora F., 422, plaintiff in Argo case
Harvard University, 628, (see New England Regional Primate Research Center)
Hastings, Judge J. H., 194
Hauser, Joseph, 381-2, Judge Pregerson's footpad, 381-2, 384, 424-5
Hawkes, Norman R., 542, County auditor
Hayes, Capt. Floyd, 117, 342
Haymaker, Kenneth, 141-2, 179, 248
Haynes, Sgt., 111
Hazelwood, Richard J., 428
Heaton, Judge Richard, 135-40, 179, 212, 250, 288-9, 293, 599, 600-3
Helen, 245
Henderson, James, 382-3, U.S. Prosecutor
Henricksen, Barbara, 177
Herro, William, 123-4

Hertz Rent-A-Car, 338
Hetrick, Wm. Morgan, 598-600
Higgins, Ray, 604
High Priest, 414, human sacrifice
Hill, Sgt. Gerald, 588
Hill, Irving, Federal Judge, 320-2
Hilltop Bar, 205, 451
Hilton, James, 465, Lost Horizon
Hinkle, Wm., 420, Ventura Dep. D.A., 421, 447
Hintzlestein, Steven, 431, aka Judge Hintz, 497-501, 506, 531, 543-4
Hirschman, R., 430, lawyer
Hitler, Adolph, 538
Hoffa, Jimmie, 620-1
Hoffman Family Ranch, 231
Hoffman, Walter, 233
Hollings, Sen. Ernest, 388
Hollywood Division, 334, 342, 347
Hollywood Legion Stadium, 343
Hollywood Palladium, 343
Hollywood Race Track, 568
Hollywood Receiving Hospital, 334
Hollywood & Vine, 342
Holocaust, The, 393-4
Holt, Bob, 604-5
Holy War, 504, 563, 593, 615, 630
Home Savings Bank of Ventura, 472
Honey Bees, 420-2, 434
Hooks, Bob, 141
Hopman, Lt. Jonas, 17, 26-30, 108
Horowitz, Judge David, 554-5
Horral, C.B., 330, LA Police Chief
Howard Estate, 287
Hronesh, James, 6, 10, 11, 17-8, 25-33, 51, 53-8, 60, 70-2, 75, 82, 93-5, 99, 100, 106-8, 123, 131, 133, 138, 141, 156, 163, 176
Hubka, Sgt. Floyd, 345
HUD, 528, loans
Huddle, Elaine, 405
Hudson, Mrs. Marjorie, 419-20, Grand Juror
Hugginson, Mr., 20
Hugginson, Mrs., 18, 21, 23
Hughes, Lloyd, 203
Hunt, E. Howard, 581, Super Patriot, 582-90, 593
Hunt, Capt. Reid, 611-2
Hunter, Judge John, 447, Municipal Court Presiding Judge, 448-52, all firemen are police officers, 454, 456-8, conditions of release
Huntington, Stanley, 260-5, 269-70

638   INDEX

Husbands, Victor, 255, 260-2,
   Resource Management Agcy.,
   288-9, 468
Hymie Town, 504
Hymie's Book, 347, 352, bookmaker,
   354, 356

Iggy, 76-8
Imperial Family of Russia, 576-8
Imperial Seal, 578
Inglewood Police Dept., 568
Ipatiev House, 576, 578
Iran, 326, 622, arms fiasco, 623
IRS, 590, 597
Ivan The Terrible, 551

Jack, 124, 130
Jackson, B., 47
Jackson, Jesse, 503-5
Jackson, Sgt. LAPD, 376
Jacobs, Arthur, 617
Jacobs, Henry (Hank), 572-6, 591
Jacobson, Geraine, 285, 384-5, 423,
   562
Jaeman, Allen, 36-7, 44-6
Jalaty, Al, 57-8, Port Hueneme Police
   Chief, 61, 63, 93, 205, Ventura
   Sheriff, 207, 229, 480-4, 486-7, 606,
   611-2, Sheriff Emeritus, 614
James, Jessie, 629, special U.S.
   Counsel
Japanese Jakuza, 546, crime family
Jarvis, Howard, 256, Prop. 13, 419
Javits, Jacob, U.S. Sen., 391
Jefferson, Thomas, 298
Jerusalem, 503
Jesus Christ The Savior, 413-5, 593,
   2nd crucifixion
Jew Lobby, 387, 389
Jew World Conspiracy, 379, 558
Jewett, Franklin R., 175-7, 250
Jewish Defense League, (JDL) 395-6,
   427, 459, 501-2, 505, 538, 541, 557,
   559, 563, 608
Jewish High Command, 388
Jewish Judges, 380, 426
Jewish TV Network, 407, 412-3, corp.
   for Public Broadcasting
Jewish Vendetta, 380
John, 581-2, fake assassination plot,
   584-5, 612
Johnson, Harold Wm., 512, con-man,
   514-8
Johnson, Jay, 514, lawyer, 521
Johnson, Pres. Lyndon B., 199, 443,
   585, 592-3, 626-7, 630
Johnson, Judge Melinda Ann, 431-2,
   514
Johnson, R.W., 276-8, Dep. Clerk for
   Pregerson, 282, 295-6
Johnston, Catherine E., 526, Treas.,
   Tax Collector, Public Adm. Ventura
   county
Johnston, James A., 526, witness to
   will
Jones, Bill, 141
Jones, Sgt. Bob, 131-2
Jones, Joan, 147
Judicial Council, 119-20, 124, 144, 422,
   464
Judicial Elections, 180, voters rights to
   elect representative of their choice,
   197, never on ballot, 419-27
Judicial Immunity, 383
Judicial System, 510, 536, 539, 545,
   563, 605
Judicial Tower of Babel, 511
Justice Department, 311, 553, 621-2,
   Organized Crime Task Force
Justice Lady, 231

Kahane, Rabbi Meir, 501, 504-5, 538
Kaufman, Judge Irving, 546-7
Kampelman, Max, 559-60, lawyer
Kampfer, Myron, 562
Kantor, Seth, 590, 592
Kaus, Judge Otto, 194, as State
   Appeal Court Judge, 213, 215, 223,
   322-3, 'Not To Be Published,' 381,
   383, 416, 450, 493, 509, 561, 563
Kay, Saul, 522, con-man, 523, 'it's a
   good deal'
Keegan, Judge, 86
Kennedy, Edward, (Teddy), 618-9, 622
Kennedy, Jackie, 579
Kennedy, Joe, 618
Kennedy, John F., 372
Kennedy, Pres. John F., 199, 376, 443,
   565-6, financing Israel, 567, 572,
   579-87, 589-94, 612, 616-21, 626-7
Kennedy, Robert, (Bobby), 199, 307,
   311, 594, 616-8, 620-1
Kennedys, 311, 575, 619, 621
Kerensky, Republic, 548, 577
KGB, 460, Grey Shirts

INDEX 639

Kimball, Eve, 319-23, 508-9, 517, 539-40
Kimche, David, 623, Mishpucka Israeli spy
King David Hotel, 509
King & I Lounge, 565
King, Mal, 58, Chief Investigator DA Bureau of Investigation-Ventura County, 61-4, 67-8, 73-5, 89-91, 93-4, 119-20, 141, 167, 179, 289, 480, 482-4, 486-7, 603-6, 611
King, Capt. Robert, 351
Kinkle, George, 291, lawyer
Kissing Judge, 218-20
Kissinger, Henry, 610
KKK, 541
Klein, Judge Joan Dempsey, 396-8, 416
Kleinman, 396, woman lawyer
Koehn, J., 396, woman lawyer
Koen, Elizabeth, 271, Spec. Dep. Atty. Gen., California
Kohn, Aron, 586
Kornblit, Majir, 394
Kornblit, Manya, 394
Kornblum, Ronald, 325, Ventura County Coroner
Kossoris, Peter, 595-6, 605, Ventura County Dep. DA
Korth, W.H., 262, Mgr. Weights & Measures
Kozinsky, Judge Alex, 628-9
Kramer, Levin, Nessen, Kamin & Frankel, 614, law firm
Kremlin, 594
Kritzman, Edward M., 223, Dist. Court Clerk
Kruschev, 594
Kuhn, Glen, 7-8, 11, 17-8, 24-33, 37, 43, 50-5, 57-62, 65, 68-74, 81-84, 87, 93, 95-8, 100, 106-8, 123, 133, 141, 163, 176

La Conchita, 467
L.A. Daily Journal, 444, Local Rules
Lagomarsino, Emilio, (Red), 247-50, 281, American Commercial Bank, 327, 467, 470-4, 482, 520-1, 526, 541
Lagomarsino, Robert, 247-8, U.S. Congressman, 432, 467, 470-1, 520, 526
Lake Casitas, 231, 234, water hole, moot, 237, 374, 437-8, 464, 469, 544

Land, Ann, 445-6, Sen. Thurmond's Secretary
Lansky, Meyer, 586, Mishpucka criminal financial genius
Laskey, Willard, 477, 480-9, 492-3
Las Vegas, 485, 490
Lawford, Peter, 567, Malibu house, 584, 616, 618, 621
Lawyers Row, 196
Leader, The, 608-10, 614-5
Lefleur, 554-6, Madam
Lenin, Nikolai, 416, aka Vladimir Illick Ulianov, 548-9, Communist leader, 550, Jewish World conspiracy, 576-8
Lennie, 36
Leonard, Herbert, 367, TV Producer
Leonard, Roger, 357, hoodlum, 366-8, 376, 565
Levine, Leonard, 554, lawyer
Levy, Helen, 147
Lewellen, Royce, 319-20
Lewis, Clair, 326
Lewis, Louie, 612-3, financier
Lewis, Judge Marvin, 38-41, 43-6, 48-52, 88, 94, 325-6, 426, 479, 489-94, warning to lawyers, 601
Liberace, 460
Libertatia, 552, Romanian newspaper
Likud Party, 392, 537
Lin, 397-8
Lincoln Heights City Jail, 296, 336, 338
Linquini, Don Sonny, 426
Local Rules, 273-4, 294-5, 300-2, 304, 310, 314, 441-2, 444, Petition for removal
Locigno, Sammy, 356-68, Big man in Hollywood, 565, live TV interview, 589, 617, 622
Lockwood, Roy, 528, corruption fighter
Loebl, James D., 233-6, Ojai mayor, 464-9
Lola, 17, 26, 29, 30, 32, 107
Long, James, 490, Portland Oregonian reporter
Longfellow, Henry Wadsworth, 399
Lopez, Jesus, 5, 6
Los Angeles Daily News, 411-2
Los Angeles District Atty. Bureau of Investigation, Criminal Intell. Section, 351, 362, 400, 464, 566, 585, 604

640 INDEX

Los Angeles Police Dept. (LAPD) 7, 8, 16, 111, 286, Intell. Div., 330, 338, 340, 348, Metro Div., 351, 369, 371-2, 394, 564, 579
Los Angeles Sheriff Dept., 347
Los Angeles Times, 408-10
Los Padres Natl Forest, 464, 466-7, 470, 476
Louisa, 373-4, Madam
Lowen, Cliff, 150, ABC Investigator, 152, 265
Lubin, Eli, 346-7
Lucifer, 391, Satan's chosen people
Luther, 549, death to usurers
Lynch, Mrs., 84-5

Mac Donald, J. Ken, 207-8, 252, 255, 289, 465, 481, 484
Machamer, Caton, 112, 342
Madden, Judge, 86
Mafia, 226, 285, 299, 305-6, 346-9, 353-5, The Family, 359, 361-2, Dogma, Omerta, 367-8, 381-2, 389-90, 394, 396, 398, 404-5, 424-6, 471-7, 480, 490, 493-4, 496, 520-21, 524, 527, 545-6, 555-6, 563, 571, 576, 584, Carlos Marcello, 586-7 no motive, 590 Mafia & Mishpucka clash, 605, Menachem Begin, 618, subserviant to the Mishpucka, 622
Magic Bullet, 586, 590
Magurski, Mike, 401, wrestler
Mahon, 256, County auditor
Major Blakeny Corp. v. Jenkins, 536, case law
Maldonado, Augustine, 374-5, 403, 604
Manetho, 549, Egyptian Priest
Manson, Charlie, 408-10, 555
Marcello, Carlos, 381, 424-5, 586, 591, 629
Marciano, Rocky, 353
Marcie, 373, hooker
Mark of Cain, 413
Marlinsky, Fred, aka Marlow, 612-3
Maronowsky, Dorothy, aka Maron, 469, 527-31
Marshall, Consuello B., 291-5, U.S. Dist. Court Judge, 300, 304-5, 309-12, memorandum, 313-7, 319
Martin, Arthur, 423-4, lawyer
Martin, Judge Bonnie Lee, 423-4, 510
Martin, Deke, 16
Martin, Lane, 18, 56-7, 75, 94, 114,

156, 169, 246-7, 328, 474, 477
Martinez, Ben, 27-8, 93, 141-2, 167, 176-7, 183
Marx, Karl, 548-9, 558
Mary, 47
Mason, Clark, 238, Star Free Press Reporter
Masonic Lodge, 392
Master Plan, 466
Matillija Ranch, 464-5
Maverick, Internatl. Airlines, Inc., 326, 597-9
Max, 570-1, bar owner
Maxie's Bar, 488
Maxwell, Blynn, 47, lawyer
Maynard, Harry L., 97, Civil Service Commissioner 109-10, 117, 122, Banker 125, 167-8, Conspirator, 176-7, 281
Mc Bride, James L., 186-7, Ventura County Counsel, 189-91, threatening phone call, 193-4, 213, 215-8, conspiracy with Pregerson, 221, 233, 236, 241-2, stalling Appeal, 270-1, 274-7, 280-1, Civil Service Rules, 283, 285
Mc Claren, Fire Capt., 241
Mc Closkey, Paul N., 387, U.S. Rep.
Mc Cormick, John, 39-41, 43, 88, 100-5, 108-9, 167
Mc Daniel, Judge, 86
Mc Dill, S.R., 596, counselor-therapist
Mc Gee, Kevin, 450-3, 456, Dep. DA
Mc Gee, Michael, 256, County Exectutive for Budget Finance & Federal Revenue Sharing
Mc Grath, Judge Charles, 174, 429
Mc Kesson, Wm., (Big Bill), 75, 584, LA Dist. Atty.
Mc Kinney, Robt. M., 235, Gen. Mgr. & Chief Engineer, (CMWD)
Mc Mahon, Robt. E., 491, retired cop
Mc Meeking, Corey, 295, Sup. of Federal Clerks, "Judge Pregerson's Local Rules supercede the Federal Rules"
Mc Quillan, Larry, 410, reporter
Meade, Sgt. Bill, 206-7
Mediterranean Fleet, 560
Meece, Edwin, 389, Pres. Counselor, 442, 554-5, Atty. Gen., 622
Meiners Oaks Sanitary Dist., 465
Melody Room, 349, 354, 356
Meltzer, Happy, 346-7, gangster

INDEX 641

Members of The Natl Reporters Committee, 412, (list of names)
Mendez-France, Pierre, 393
Mercadante, Mary, 369-77, 565-7, 617, 619
Mercouris, 335
Metropolitan Development Co., 287-92, 300-03, 305, 308, one hundred thousand dollar document, 309-11, proxy statement, 313, 417
Metropolitan Div., 336, 340, 342, 569
Metzenbaum, Howard, 388, Ohio Sen.
Middle East, 598
Mike Lyman's Restaurant, 348
Mikel, Don, 595-7, Minister
Milano, Peter John, 622, aka Jimmy Caci, 629
Miller, Royal M., 85
Milligan, Bud, 174, Pres. Bank Of A. Levy, 177, 197
Mills School, 467
Minelli, Liza, 172-3, money, money, money
Mishna, 414, Jew law, 415-6, 493, 501, 508-10, total chaos, 512, 529, 531, 535-6, 538-40, 545, 558-9, 627
Mishpucka, 384, Judges, 385-6, extortion & protection racket, 389, sub-groups, 390, 394, revenue bond scam, 359-6, 398, 405-8, 411-3, Judas goat, 417-8, 424-6, 428-30, 440, 444, 454-5, 459-60, 463-6, 468-71, 473-4, 476, 478-80, 489-90, 492-5, 499-502, 505-13, Black Robe leader, 516, 519-22, 524, 527-9, 531, 536, 538, 540-8, 550, 552-4, 556, 558-61, 563, 571, 576-8, modus operandi, 578, 586-7, 589-95, 600-1, 604-6, 612-8, eating America alive, 622-3, 626-9
Mitchum, Robt., 343
Mizrahi, Dina, 396
Mobley, Robt. L., 174-5, VP Bank of A. Levy, 177, 181
Moceri, 'Leo The Lip,' 404
Mondale, Walter, 503-5
Monroe, Marilyn, 372, 376, 431, 564-7, 572, 576, 616-22
Montalvo Hill, 173-4, 178, 181, 228, 522
Moral Majority, The, 407-8
Morley Construction Co., 227-8
Morgan, Vickie, 553-6
Mormans, 9, 10, 32, 40, 43, 84

Morris, Roscoe, 477, 487
Morrissey, v. Morrissey, 498, case law
Mosk, Stanley, 373-4, State Supreme Court Justice, drug smuggler
Mount Calvary, 413
Moute, Lawrence, 525, handwriting expert
Moya, Luis, 374-5, murderer, 403, 604
Murphy, Audie, 134, WW11 hero, 400, 579-81, movie actor, 583-5, 591, American patriot, 612
Murray, Eunice, 617
Musso-Franks Restaurant, 348
Myra, 573, Madam
Mythology, 195-6, Clotho, Lachesis, Atropos

Nagelsztajn, Harry, 394
National Abortion Rights Action League, 406, B'nai B'rith, 408
National Football League, 282, 382
National Guard Armory, 442, burglary, 502-3, 608
National Security, 585, at stake, 593
National Security Advisor, 442, 502
National Transportation Safety Board, (NTSB) 524
Nazi, 393, 541, 548, 550-1, 557
Nazi Beast, 380, 386
Nazi Brown Shirt, 392, 537-8
Nelson, Lars, 410, reporter
Neue Rheinische Zietung, 549, Marx's newspaper
New England Regional Primate Research Center, 628, AIDS
New Government Center, 174-5, real estate scam, 177-9, Sup. Robinson frameup, 181-3, nullified Due Process of Law, 185, 190-1, Mc Bride's threats, 194, 197-8, Judge Berenson & Ben Nordman bond scam, 207, 213, 227-30, construction co. scam, 233, 239-40, 246-7, Fire Dept. threats, 250, 256, 260, 266, 268, 302, 423, 449, 474, 522-3, 527
New Oil Ordinance, 470
Nichols, Sgt. Lee, 336, 338-40
Nicholson, George, 431-2, Asst. Dep. Atty. Gen.
Nimmea, David, 556, Asst. U.S. Atty.
Nixon, Pres. Richard M., 298, 444
Noble Jurists, 194

642 INDEX

Nofziger, Lynn, 543-4, Pres. Reagan's campaign financier
Noguchi, Thomas, 417, LA coroner
Non-Judicial Foreclosure law, 495-6, Mishpucka racket
Nordman, Ben, 147-8, 173-7, 181, 185, 187, 189, 191-4, 197, 201, 213, 228-30, 232-7, 241, 249-51, 255-6, 258, 264, 276-8, 281, 285, 287, environmental impact report, 288-93, 296-7, 300-1, 303-5, 309-11, 315-6, Fed. Commissioner, 350-1, 381, 383, 409-11, 417-9, 422-3, 426, 430, 462, 464, 468-9, 471, 474, 478-9, 481, 489-91, 502, 520, 522, 525, 543, 606
'Not To Be Published,' 509, Mishna treason,

Oak Dale Park, 287, 291
Oak View Journal, 232, 237, 239
Oak View Sanitation Dist., (OVSD) 465
Oakland Raiders, 282, Al Davis, 382, 449, 613
O'Hara, Jack, 352-3, 356-60, 362-4, 567, 589, 617
Ojai Meeting-Mishpucka Dons, 406, (list of names)
Ojai Oil Co., 466
Old Chinatown, 336-40, 569
Old Courthouse, 2, 175-7, 182, 185, 206-7, 514
Oligarch, 251
Olympic Stadium, 335, 341-3, 568
Orange Julius, 348
Ordin, Andrea, 201, U.S. Atty. Gen. LA, 311
Ordin, Robt., 201, U.S. Magistrate, 311
Orrock, Dennis, 512-5, Ventura mayor, 517-8, 522-25
Ortega, James, 295, Dallas lawyer
Oswald, Lee Harvey, 579-90, 592, 613
Otash, Freddie, 219-20, former LA Vice Ofc., 225, Tinseltown private eye, 617-9, 77 Sunset Strip, 620-2
Overcoat Charlies, 353, New York hoods
Oxnard Police Dept., 5, 94, 350

Pacht-Ross, 300, law firm, 301, 306,

(cont'd) 308-10, 313, 315, 318, shysters, 410, 417
Padelford, Sumner, 97-8, Civil Service Commissioner 100, 102-3, 105, 108
Page, Vincent C., 85
Paik, Harkjoon, 31-3, Dep. Public Defender 39-44, 46, 48-50, 53, 74, 88, 101, 103-5
Palestine Liberation Org., 393
Palmer, Al, 74-5, 81-2, 89-92, 95-8, 100, 104, 110, 125-7, 158-60, 229, 513
Palmer, Jerry, 462-5, lawyer, 475-94, warning to lawyers
Palo Verde, Ariz., 395, nuclear plant
Pan Card Club, 480
Pancoast, Marvin, 553-4, 556
Parkland Hospital, 589
Pass Club, 477, card room, 478-90, 493
Pass Club Property Inc., 479
Patterson, W. E., 421, lawyer
Patton, Sgt. Ed., 40-1, 50-3, 94, 350, 377-8, 604
Paxton, Sgt. Doug, 39-40, 88, 101, 350, 374, 603-4
Peace, 591-2, 594
Peace Corps, 566, 575, 591
Pearl, 21
Pearl Harbor, 393, 582
Peck, William, 465, lawyer, partner of Mayor Loebl, 467, school board member, 468-70, Superior Court Judge, 529-33, 536
Pedroff, P., 523, County Budget Adm.,
Peled, Yoav, 392, 537-9, 556, 558, 563
Penfield, Dr. Douglas, 63, Grand Jury foreman, 68, 73, 90-1, 93-5, 97, 118-20, corrupt Grand Jury foreman, 144, 167, 176-7, 211
Pentagon, 563
Pentateuch, 414, first five books of bible
Perkins, Robt., 235, CMWD
Perle, Richard, 560, read The Armegeddon Network by Michael Saba
Perrenowsky, Steven Z., 341, aka Judge Perren
Petrochem, 465-7, refinery, 470
Pfotenhauer, Judge Jay, 429
Phillips, Abe, 227, bail bondman, 335, 338, 350-1, 358-9, 370-2, Mercadante rapist, 375-7, 502, 565, 607-10, 619
Phillips, Hymie, 227, bail bonds, 502

INDEX   643

Phillips, 'Yummie,' 485-6, Vegas gambler, 492
Philpot, Marty, 401-3, IRS Intell., 520
Phoenix Oil Co., 466
Pianezzi, Pete, 404-5, Italian scapegoat for Jews
Pic'l, Dean, 81-3, lawyer, 86-9, 91, 95-103, 108-10, 118, 121-4, 127, 136, 178, 197, 212, 513-4
Pig & Whistle Restaurant, 342
Pink Pagoda Restaurant, 337
Piscitelli, Georgie, 356-8, gangster, 368, 372, 376, 565-7, 572, 617, 619-20, 622
Plaza De Las Palmas, 527-8, redevelopment
Plotkin, Jerry, 394, 411
Plymouth House, 352, Hollywood night club, 356
Poe, Ofc., J.M., 588
Point Mugu Naval Air Station, 471
Political Action Com., 407-8, (PAC)
Pollack, Judge Richard, 133
Porter, Bill, 238-9
Powell, Terrell, 191-4, 207, 209-10, 213, 215-8, 221, 230, 240, 267-8, lawyer, 271-2, 274-8, 283, 285, 289, 291-5, 299, 304, 520
Powers, Charles T., 387, Times staff writer
Pregerson, Dean, 227
Pregerson, Fed. Judge, Harry, 215-8, 221-5, City Terrace, 227, acquired real estate, 229-30, 240, 243, 250, 267, 270, 272-9, 281-4, 294-7, 300, 304, 310-12, 314, 319, 335, 338, treasonous judge, 377, 381-4, 403, Gaugin painting, 416, 424-6, 430, 439, 441, 445, 450, 471, 475, 502, 509, 607-10, 612-3
President of the U.S., 298-9, 578, assassination
Presiding Judge of the Superior Court, 120, 127, 139, 144, 178, 197, 214, 237, 293, 306, 420-2, 429, 477
Pretoria, 627-8
Prohibition, 472-3, Eighteenth Amendment, 474, Repeal of
Protection Bureau, 458-9, Grey Shirts
Public Defender, (refer to Ventura County Pub. Def.)
Public Employees Assoc. of Ventura City, 380, 513-4
Public Employees Assoc. of Ventura

(cont'd) County, 74-5, 81-2, 110, 125, 157-9, 179, 208, 229
Pygmalian, 390, Cyprian sculptor

Queen Bee Club, 582, Japan

Rabbi Juda, 414, The Holy, 501
Rabbis, 414-5, 558, 567
Radin, Judge Sara K., 411-2
Rafeedie, Judge Edw., 495-6
Raft, George, 359
Raider Construction Co., 430, (see Ventura Enterprises, page 413)
Rains, Omer, 418, State Sen., 428, bagman
Rancho Mi Solar, 223, 232, 236
Ray, 374, Fed. Drug Agent
Reagan, Ronald, 127, as Gov., 133, 155, 174, 296, as Pres., 381, 410, 432, 442-3, 446, 470-1, Air Force One, 476, re-election, 503, 505-6, 519-20, 543, 546, 553-4, 626-9
Real Estate Invest. Trust Corp., 178
Real, Judge Manuel, 270-2, 520
Red Devil Bar, 570
Redevelopment Agy., 469, 474, 527
Regnier, Richard A., 420-1, lawyer
Reid, Judge, 86
Reiman, Charlie, 18, Ventura City Mgr., 56-7, 75, 91-2, 94, 119, 141, 156, 163, 169, 176, 230, 246, 248, 250, 474
Reinhardt, Stephen R., 381-2, Federal Appeal Court, 383-4, LA Police Commissioner, 424-5, 450, 613
Remember The Maine, 583
Responsa Project, 558-60, Operation Responsa, 627, Jew secret communications
Revenue Bonds, 187, 191-2, 194, 228, 256, 395
Revenue Sharing Funds, 256-7
Revere, Paul, 399
Rhoades, Janice, 533-5, Court clerk
Rice, Baxter, 268
Richardson, Hazel M., 543, Reagan for re-election, 1984
Richie, 245-6
Riewer, Mrs. Pat, 419, Grand Juror
Rishe, Melvyn, 623, lawyer
River Ridge Raddison Hotel, 613
Rivkin, 'Buzzie,' 485-6, Vegas gambler

644 INDEX

Rizzuto, Phillip, 381
Roberti, David, 389, State Sen.
Robinson, Judge Aubrey, Jr., 623
Robinson, Edw. G., 568
Robinson, 'Robby,' 27, 56-7, 75, 92-4, 119, 141-2, 156, 163-4, 169, 176-7, 179-80, 230, 246-50, threats-"last nail in coffin," 469, 474, 477, 595, 600, 605
Rogers, Sally, 444-6, Sen. Thurmond's Secretary
Rohatyn, Felix, 613, Jewish bond salesman
Romanov Families, 577-9
Rondeli's Italian Restaurant, 352, 357-8, 360-1, 567, 616
Rooney, Mickey, 401
Roosevelt, Loren, 335, Highway Patrolman
Roost Cafe, 404
Roselli, John, 354
Rosenberg, Ethel & Julius, 546-8, spies, 554
Rosenfeld, Charlie, 394
Rosenthal, A.M., 613
Rosenthal, Harold, 391, aide on Jewish affairs
Ross, N. Joseph, 309-11, 316, 318
Rothert, Judge, 86
Rothman, 'Hooky,' 568, gangster
Roussey, R.H., 173-4
Ruben, Lawrence, aka Eddie Pollack, 614
Rubenstein, Dimitri, 578
Rubenstein, Jacob, 614, scam artist
Rubin, Irving, 395-6, 427, 459, 538, 546-7, 550, 557, 559, 563, 608
Rubin, Sherry, 559, 563
Rubinstein, Elyakim, 623, Israeli Cabinet Secy.
Ruby, Jack, (Jacob Rubenstein) 567, 569-71, Mishpucka, 586-93, "act of overthrowing the government," 609, 630
Rudin, Milton, 617, lawyer
Rudolph, Arthur L., 551-2, scientist
Ruidoso, N. Mex., 580, 612
Rummel, Sammy, 346, Hollywood lawyer
Runyon, Damon, 486
Russell, John, 5, 7, 12, 16-7, 102
Russia Immigrating Jew Criminals, 382
Ruven, Ele & Esther, 398, Mishpucka drug dealers, murder and mayhem

Safeway Market, 468
Salomon, Elaine & Sol, 398
Salvador, 153-4
Sam, 36-7
Sam's Pawn Shop, 341
San Buena Ventura, 1
Sandanistas, 541
Santa Monica Pier, 349
Santa Paula Daily Chronicle, 384-5
Sanzo, Jack, 360-5, bookie, 367-8
Satan, 413-5, wealth & political power, 502-58
Savitch, Jessica, 412-3, TV commentator
Savitch, Judge Leon, 395, 413
Scantlan, Kenny, 52
Scapegoats, 502-3, KKK, Blacks, Neo-Nazis, Southern Baptists, Moral Majority, Eastern States Catholics, 577, 595, 622, 630
Schade, Edw. C., 294-5, Asst. clerk, U.S. Supreme Court
Schaefer, Rudy, 287-8, 305
Schechter, Dorothy, 186, 191, 213-4, 242, 270, 280-3, 322, 380, 383, 466, 468, New oil ordinance, 475, 541
Schechter, Thomas L., 168
Scheinbaum, Stanley, 389, ACLU
Schierenbeck, Insp. Walter, 433-5, 438, 453, 459
Schmidt, J. Scott, 412, Pres. of Daily News
Science of Civil Government, 431-2, politics
Sciortino, Sam, 381-2
Scripts, John P., 239, newspapers, 249, 408
SEC, 308, 310, 417, 614
Seiderman, Bert, 492
Seigle, 'Bugsy,' 346, gangster
Seigle, David, 614
Seymour, Phillip, 469, lawyer
Shah of Iran, 597
Shangri-la, 465
Shatila & Sabra, 563, Arab refugee camps
Shakespeare, Marguerite, 320-3, Federal Decision, case no. 65-637, Judge Irving Hill, vindictive diatribe
Shaw, Ernie, 108-10, Ventura Police Capt., 125, 167-8
Shaw, Judge Robt., 132, 141-2, 163-4, 188-9, 191-4, 213, 216, 233, 602-5
Shell Oil Co., 465, refinery

INDEX 645

Sherbinsky, Neal, aka Sher, 551-2, Justice Dept., 556
Sheriff, 319
Short, Elizabeth, 340, Black Dahlia
Shultz, George, 563, Secy. of State
Sica Brothers, 354
Simon, Paul, 629, Illinois Senator
Sinatra, Frank, 408
Singapore Charlie's Joint, 339
Sible, Randy, 12, 13, 15, 17, 524-5
Sixty Minutes, TV program, 402
Sloan, Aubrey Edw., 326, aka 'Bud' or 'Haystack'
Smalley, Beatrice, 266, lawyer for ABC, 268-9
Smith, Lt. A.J., 111, 331, 333, 335
Smith, Charlene, 324-6, 477, 488-9, 595, 601
Smith, Judge, 86
Smith, Keely, 622, singer
Smith, Lee, 12-7, 33-5
Smith, Lyman, 324-7, 488-9, 595-601
Smith, Martin 'Bud,' 374-5, 377-8, 426
Smith, William French, 410-11, U.S. Atty. Gen.
Smokehouse Restaurant, 401-2
Sneed, 270, 272, 275, Fed. Appeal Judge
Soares, Judge Robt., 436, 438-9
Soderquist, Ofc., 331-3
Solkovitz, Craig, 257-8, Camarillo Daily News reporter, 267, 384-5, 407
Solkovitz, Judy, 407, Pres. United Teachers Union
Solomon, Steve, 261, County Environmental Health Agt., 263, 384-5
Sosna, Marvin, 93, Grand Juror, 249-50, Editor Thousand Oaks Chronicle, 384
South Africa, 627
Southern California Gas Co., 467, pipeline
Southern California Public Powers Authority, 395, 413
South Gate Arena, 337, 339
South Gate City, 338
South Western Law School, 90
Spindel, Bernard, 620, wiretapper
Sportmans Lodge, 237, 357-8
Spykerman, Fire Capt., 435, 452-3, 456-7, 459
Star Free Press, 90, 104-5, 157, 194,

(cont'd) 198, 237-40, 249, 255, 415-7, 420, 426, 430, 459-60, 476-7, 492, 503, 513-4, Letters To The Editor, 521, 523-5, 597, 604
Stare Decisis, 511
Stebelskyi, Ivan, 551, alleged Nazi
Stein, Ofc. Gene, 115-7
Stein, Jerry, 394
Stein, Tamar, 300-1, 305-6, 308-9, 312-3, 318
Stein, Theodore Jr., 430, lawyer
Steinberg, Robt., 553-6, lawyer
Stephen, Judge Clark, 194
Stevas, Alexander L., clerk of U.S. Supreme Court, 294-5
Stevenson, Adlai, 389, Illinois Sen.
Stewart, Mrs., Vilate, 419, Grand Juror
Stompanato, Johnny, 355, 565-7, 572, 617, 620-2
Stone, Herbert, 614
Stone, Larry, 525
Stone, Judge Steven, 429-31, (see Blitzberg), 450, 469-70, 493, 509, 517, 529, 536, 540, 544-5, 560, 563, 598-9, 601
Storch, Judge Larry, 429, Mishpucka bloodline, 477-9, 481, 511, 525-6, 546, 598
Strickland, Bill, 247, former Ventura Police Chief
Summers, Anthony, 564-7, author, 569, 572-2, 574, 576-7, 585-6, 590-1, 616-9, 621-2
Symbionese Army, 379

Taft, John E., 496-9, electric contractor
Tail Of The Cock Restaurant, 403, Los Feliz Dr.
Tang, 270, 272, 275, Fed. Judge
Tang's Chinese Restaurant & Bar, 338
Tannenbaum, Harry, 571, 586
Tate, La Bianco, 408, Manson family murders
Taylor, Joan, 324
Teamsters Union, 620-1
Tel Aviv, 503
Temple Rabbis, 426
Temples of Holy Judah, 511
Terrible Turk, The, 611-2
Texas School Book Depository, 590
TGY Stores, 468

646 INDEX

Thomas, Chuck, 239
Thousand Oaks Chronicle, 93
Thurman, Betty, 26, 29, 30, 65, 75, 106-8, 123
Thurman, David, 107
Thurmond, Strom, U.S. Sen., 307, Chm. Senate Judiciary Committee, 439-40, 443, Cannizzaro files, 444-6, 470, 546, 629
Tia Juana, 226
Tice, William, 449, Jury foreman, extension cord case, 454
Tieri, Frank, 545, Mafia
Tierney, Lawrence, 343
Tinkler, Donald, 84-5
Tinseltown, 342-3, 619
Tippit, Ofc., J.D., 587-9, 591
Tivnan, Ed, 618-9, writer, 621
Tod, 290, old friend, 297-9, 383
Todd, Wm., 86-8, lawyer, 123
Tolmach, Jane, 101
Tossopulos, Vanetta, 304-5, 309-11, 314, 316-9
Tranelone, John, 546, Mafia
TransAmerica Corp., 472-3
Traynor, Judge Roger, 86
Tregoff, Carol, 352
Tribune Company, 411
Trifa, Valeria, 552, Arch Bishop
Trojan Horse, 407
Trom, Clara, 562
Trom, Stanley, 562, lawyer
Trombino, Tony, 347
Trotsky, Leon, 548, (see Bronstein), 576-8
Trottsky, Stephen, 551, aka Trott, 556, song writer, 560, appointed Federal Atty. Gen., & Federal Judge
Troxell, Wayne, 525
Truman, Harry, 127
Trust Deed, 495
Trust Deed Services Co., 495-6
Tsar, Nicholas, 11, 576-8
Tsarina, Alexandria, 576
Turkebtahn, Nathan, 227, 338, 607, 609-10, 612, 614
Turner Construction Co., 228-9
Turner, Lana, 355, 372, 565, 567, 572, 617, 620, 622
Turner, Richard K., 127, Governor Reagan's Asst. Legal Affairs Secretary
Twenty Twenty TV program, 402
Two Tonys, 347-9, Italian hoods

Union Bank, 228-9
Union Depot, 339, railroad station
United Nations Hdqtrs., 593
United Teachers of LA, 407, political organization
Universal Studios, 580
University Div., LAPD, 331, 340-1, 568, 570
Unlawful Detainer, 498-9
Unruh, Jesse, 418, 'Big Daddy,'
Untouchables, 307-8, a class of American citizens, 506, 521
U.S. Attorney General, 311
U.S. Congress, 442
U.S.S. America, 627, aircraft carrier
U.S.S. Liberty, 388-9, Intell. ship, 560, SOS, 627
U.S. Supreme Court, 274, exercise their power of supervision over lower courts, 275, Certiorari, 290-1, Village of Bell Terri v. Borass, N.Y., case law, 294, letter from U.S. court clerk, 295-9

Valenti, Jack, 626, Hollywood agent & Pres. Johnson's aide
Van de Kamp, John, 431-2, LA Dist. Atty., 629, Atty. Gen.
Vaughn, Lane, 295, Texas lawyer
Ventura County Board of Supervisors, 310, stipulation agreement
Ventura County Branch of The American Association of University Women, 155-7
Ventura County Bldg. Dep., 151, 153, 262, 287-8, 456
Ventura County Criminal Justice Planning Committee, 174, 177, 179-80, 289
Ventura County Election Dept., 252-3, 255, 257-8, 395, 561-2
Ventura County Fire Dept., 240, 242
Ventura Planning Dept., 150-3, 236, 465, 467
Ventura County Public Defender, 1, 3-7, 15, 29, 31, 37, 41, 46, 48, 53, 65-6, 69, 73-4, 86, 90, 96, 106, 158, 171, 408, 585
Ventura County Public Facilities Corp., 177, a non-profit corp. owned by Judge Jerome Berenson & Ben Nordman, 185, 187, 194, 196, 213, 215, 227, 233, 236, 256, 289, 410,

INDEX 647

(cont'd) 423, 430, 522, 542-3, (see list of bank deposits), 606
Ventura County Recorder, 495, escrow
Ventura County Resource Management Agency, 262
Ventura County Sheriff's Dept., 350, 477, bribery
Ventura Enterprises Co., 413, (see Raider Constr. Co.)
Ventura Group Seven, 522, financial scam artists
Ventura Police Dept., 2, 4, 30-2, 92, 108, 169, 247, 325, 350, 600
Ventura Realty Co., 248, 'Red' Lagomarsino, 250, 474
Ventura River, 231
Ventura County Water Dist., 464
Vera, 30-1, 33, 41
Veterans of Foreign Wars, 541
Vidal, Yvonne, 535, Secy.
Viet Nam's Holocaust, 592, 594
Villa, 378, informant
Vogelbaum, Ron, 261, Planning Dept. Agt., 263, 384-5
Volz, Fred, 255, Editor Ojai Valley News, 257
Von Braun, Werner, 551, rocket scientist

Wachs, Joel, 394, 628
Walker, Gen. Edw., 582
Walker, Machine Gun, 335
Walker, Marion, 236, CMWD Dir., also Dir. of Ventura County Public Facilities Corp.
Wall, Richard, 428
Wallace, Michael H., 543-4 Reagan's campaign financier & gambling racketeer
Walsh, Bill, 516, coach
Walsh, Lawrence E., 623, U.S. Prosecutor
War & Peace, 591
Warburton, Judge, 86
Ward, Carl E., Jr., 173, 478-84, 487, 489-91, 543, crooked lawyer & gambler
Ward, Carl E., Sr., 173, 478
Warren, Chief Justice Earl, 592-3
Warren Commission, 579, Kennedy Assassination, 585-6, 590
Wasserman, Lew, 406, 626, high level Mishpucka

Watergate, 298, 480, Republican fiasco
Watt, James, 388, Secy. of Interior
Watts, 628, Black Ghetto
Webster, Wm. H., 425, Dir. of FBI, 439, 545-6
Webster's Dictionary, 304
Weeks, Constance, 492, Juror
Weinberger, Casper, 555, Secy. of Defense, 575, 591-2, 610
Weiner, George, 363, Mickey Cohen's sister's husband
Weiner, Howard B., 85
Weingart, Ben, 417, developer, 431, 511
Weinstein, Sammy, 394
Weisberg, Stanley, 554, lawyer
Weiss, Harry, 369-73, lawyer, 565
Wells Fargo Bank, 97, 177
West, Judge Phillip, 61-3, 90, 132-3, 602-3, 605, killed during judicial election
Whalen, Jack, (O'Hara), 352, 'The Enforcer'
White Bib Cafe, 132, 237, 248-9, secret meeting, 327
White, Marie, 530-1, Citizens Advocates
White, Dr. Walter, 391, Western Front Christian Organization
Wiesel, Elie, 552, racial & religious agitator
Wiesenthal, Simon, 538, great Nazi hunter, 551, 557
Wilcox, Wm., 600
Willard, Judge Robt., 186, 188
Williams, County inspector, 203
Williams, Willie, 539-40
Wilson, Sen. Pete, 626, Century City
Wilson, Wm., 389, Vatican Envoy
Wise, Miriam, 559
Wittenberg, Richard, 229-30, Ventura County Chief Administrator, 380, 383, 419, 466, 468, New Oil Ordinance, 523
Witter, Dean, 441, Stocks & Bonds
Women Lawyers of Ventua, 396
Wong, Benny, 340, drug dealer, 377-8
Wood, Timothy M., 543, Oregon Atty. Gen.
Woodard, Lt. Bill, 375, 604
Woods, Sue, 428
World Peace, 591-2, 594
Wright, Donald, 150, 153

648 INDEX

Wright, Frank, 588, witness to Ofc. Tippit murder

Yaroslavsky, Zev, 394, LA City Councilman
Yegansky, Judge Kenneth, aka Yegan, 431, 494
Yeman, 563
Yiddish, 578

Zakaria, Joseph, 398, Israeli drug smuggler & killer
Zohn, Martin S., 313-4, Pacht-Ross lawyer, conspirator with Magistrate Tossopulos
Zundel, Ernst, 550, printer, victim of Mishpucka persecution

SYNOPSIS

DISASTERS, CRISIS AND CHAOS, starkly striking at the heart of America - directly caused, created by the Senators infamous, traitorous cover-up since 1987.

Fervently I had hoped my suspicions of the Senators treason was wrong - but my hopes were in vain, their reaction, their swift, evil acts to cover-up dashed all such expectations.

After my contact with the Senators in 1987 hundreds of people have been murdered - killed for no other reason than they had 'gotten in the way.'

1963, in Ruidoso, New Mexico we had talked to Sheriff Bill Decker's friend - not for twenty four years after this meeting did I mention John's name. In this book, printed in 1987 I used only his first name John and changed his physical description to protect his identity. John was Senator John Tower, it can be revealed now because John is dead - another victim.

Tower had coveted the office of Secretary of Defense because his vast experience well qualified him. But Caspar Weinberger needed the office in order to keep the lid on his treasonous sabotage of the military and spying for the Mishpucka.

Weinberger had far more political influence and finances to spread around than did John, he became the Secretary of Defense. Tower was very bitter at the foul tactics and lies Weinberger and the Mishpucka media used against him. John made it known he was going to write a book. Shortly after that John Tower was dead, killed in a mysterious airplane crash identical to Audie Murphy's fatal, and unexplained plane crash.

Tower was involved in the 'phony' assassination that was turned into the 'real' assassination. Others even more culpable were George Bush's father and Arlen Specter. Hunt had failed to look to his flank (a monumental blunder). A man close to Specter at that time will remain unnamed for now - Specter and this man were the secret Mishpucka agents monitoring Hunt's operation and manipulated the 'phony' assassination into the 'real' assassination, both are presently U.S. Senators.

'Everything is connected,' all the catastrophes currently assaulting our country - I knew that loyal Americans had to understand this, give it deep thought. A very knowledgable man, Thomas Pynchon, said, "Paranoia is the leading edge of the awareness that everything is connected." Absolutely, yes, everything <u>is</u> connected.

So, Americans are <u>not</u> paranoid over the horrendous disasters that seem to be over-whelming our country - they are merely "on the leading edge of <u>awareness</u> that everything is connected."

On June 2, 1976 an investigative reporter for the Phoenix Arizona

Republic newspaper, Don Boles, was blown up in his car and killed in Phoenix. Two days later they tried to kill me in my driveway. Boles was about to expose the Mishpucka's Palo Verde nuclear plant scheme - massive corruption - four billion dollars involving their Southern California Public Powers Authority bond-sellers, and several U.S. Senators - and I was jamming up the Mishpucka bond-sellers on their two hundred and fifty million dollar bond sale for their Ventura County Public Facilities Corporation. The Mishpucka's bond-records were being kept in the First Interstate Bank in L.A. Billions and billions of dollars of their secret bond transactions and who really owned them. I was putting on pressure - they secretly removed the records and a man took them to a new, secure location in Phoenix. To conceal this theft of records a fire was set and the floor on which the records were kept at the bank was incinerated. In the process a man was murdered. The Los Angeles District Attorney Ira Reiner covered-up the crime.

Then a terrible disaster befell the evil Mishpucka - a major calamity, one that could totally annihilate the Mishpucka's spy and sabotage machine not only in America but world-wide. Two intrepid San Francisco Police Department detectives had been investigating the Anti-Defamation League of the B'nai B'rith. The ADL is the heart and brain of the Mishpucka's espionage and assassination operations along with the (JDL) Jewish Defense League and the thousands of other crazy Jew Organizations they have set up to eat the heart out of America. The Senators aid and abet them by allowing them to function tax-exempt.

The two detectives raided the ADL offices in Los Angeles and San Francisco and seized more than two tons of secret files. The files revealed that for over seventy years the ADL had been spying on and keeping clandestinely obtained information on American politicians, businessmen, religious leaders etc., etc., for the purpose of blackmail and forcing them to do their bidding. The records disclosed that ADL agents had infiltrated and were sabotaging the police and sheriffs departments across the nation and had turned high ranking, key FBI and CIA agents into nothing more than paid-informants and saboteuers for the Mishpucka. The records revealed that the Mishpucka had secret bank accounts, huge amounts of money that Jew lawyers and Hollywood leaders used to pay these treasonous Americans for doing their dirty work.

But, as always the Mishpucka's insidious political influence and unlimited money interfered with and smashed America's judicial system and due process of law. They got to the San Francisco District Attorney - a cowardly, greedy politician Arlo Smith dismissed the criminal charges - he sold out America's future and hope - how much money does the Mishpucka have to give these scum who call themselves Americans to sell their soul?

Like the Italian 'lover-boys' Sammy Lo Cigno, Georgie Piscitelli, Johnny Stompanato and Joe Di Carlo worked for and were paid by the Mishpucka's, Mickey Cohen and Menachem Begin to degrade and pick the brains of wealthy, important women and politicians, so did Ronald Goldman (a lover-boy) and Fay Resnick (a drug dealer) work for the Mishpucka's, Stanley Scheinbaum and Ira Glasser the powerful heads of the Los Angeles Police Commission in their scam to frame O.J. Simpson.

Shortly after the gruesome murders lawyer Johnnie Cochran and O.J. Simpson announced a reward of half a million dollars for information leading to the persons who actually committed the crimes.

I gave Cochran information revealing that persons connected to the L.A.P.D. were responsible for the murders and for planting evidence to frame Simpson and claimed the reward.

However, these persons were not police officers, they were police commissioners. Cochran set up his defense strategy based on this information. But, instead of naming and exposing the Police Commission, Cochran twisted the facts to make the police officers the scapegoats.

Lawyer Robert Shapiro and broadcaster Larry King both fanatical Mishpuckas are livid at Cochran and F. Lee Bailey for daring in their summation to the jury to equate the plight of Black people in the same breath with the persecution of Jews thus minimizing and jeopardizing their holocaust business.

To this date Cochran has reneged on his word and refuses to pay the reward. But, Simpson still faces the next trial in Santa Monica.

On top of this, Irving Rubin the demented leader of the JDL (Jewish Defense League) screams from the roof-tops his vicious threats at Marlin Brando for exposing the fact that the Jews own and control Hollywood and use their power to pour out Anti-American propaganda, "Brando, I am going to make your life a living hell forever for what you have said."

Scheinbaum, Glasser and Norman Dorsen are powerful leaders of the ACLU and are the lawyer architects of the New World Order Constitution that they intend to jam down the throat of America.

The murders of Ronald Goldman and Nicole Simpson are complications of the Mishpucka's vicious spying operation - they had received very disturbing reports from their spies that O.J. Simpson was connecting with Louis Farrakhan and that the Black people in Hollywood were getting wise to how the Jew lawyers and talent agents controlled the actors and the TV and movie industry. If this situation was allowed to exist and continue the Mishpucka could lose their power in Hollywood and the Democrats grip over the huge national Black vote. This black vote problem led to William Clinton's selection through Mayor Tom Bradley of the Warren Christopher

Commission to Hollywoodize the Rodney King affair. This was designed to bring the black people together again to vote as a solid-block for Clinton.

It was no coincidence that a seedy ambulance chaser, Mickey Kantor and the wife of a Federal Judge, Andrea Ordin were picked for the Warren Christopher Commission and for their part in the Christopher farce they would be appointed important positions in Clinton's cabinet. Through my efforts Andrea Ordin who was slated for Attorney General was blocked as was Zoe Baird and Kimba Wood, but Clinton finally pressured Janet Reno in as Attorney General.

Everything is 'connected' - Waco, what they wanted there was to recover guns that could be tracked to National Guard burglaries and then could be traced further to Menachem Begin and then to the government of Israel - the knowledge of Jew agents conducting their sabotage and assassination operations within the United States could have stopped cold all the billions of dollars the Washington, D.C. politicians send to the Jews in Israel.

In Oklahoma City, what the Mishpucka wanted there was records and documents stored in government offices - records of trillions of dollars of their treachery in bond dealings, Savings and Loan and Wall Street depredations of giant corporations would have been exposed - as in the First Interstate Bank fire all these documents were stolen and taken to a secret location before the Oklahoma City bombing which was then set-up to conceal the fact that the files had been removed.

The Mishpucka (the Jew Crime Family) could care less how many innocent people they kill - Menachem Begin and the King David Hotel explosion - the murder of American sailors on the U.S.S. Liberty - John Kennedy, Robert Kennedy, it goes on and on.

On this day as I sit here and write the Mishpucka has just won the election in Israel - President Clinton and Secretary of State Warren Christopher were supposedly backing Shimon Peres and promoting peace between the Arabs and Jews - now Netanyahu, a fanatical Mishpucka, a dedicated Halacha assassin responsible for the murder of Prime Minister Rabin is no sooner elected than Clinton invites him to the White House.

An article in the New York Times, a Mishpucka newspaper, written by Serge Schmemann, a Mishpucka reporter starts off the Mishpucka propaganda by conning America - Prime Minister Netanyahu is really an American with America's interest at heart - Schmemann says, "Netanyahu's image was massaged by an American, Arthur Finkelstein." If Arthur Finkelstein is an American I am Fu Manchu....

Prime Minister Yahoo's father, Benzion Netanyahu was a fanatical follower of a right wing school of Zionism (Halacha) that held clear back in 1925 that the Jew claim to the entire land of Israel was unquestionable and nonnegatiable.

In 1987 I had warned the U.S. Senators of the Bar-Ilan University in Israel where they teach the Jew-law of Halacha - this is the law wherein the Rabbis can order the murder of anyone they believe is interfering with their beliefs - it is inevitable that a new and terrible escalation of war between the Jews and Arabs is at hand - America and its innocent people will be inexorably drawn into this conflict by Prime Minister Yahoo and new and terrible catastrophes will strike at the heart of America because of insane Jew conspiracies...

President Clinton and other politicians who follow will continue to give Prime Minister Yahoo billions and billions of American dollars supposedly because the Jews are our friends.

In the future it is intended that the author will periodically make intellegence reports called 'A Notice to The People' exposing the Mishpucka's secret conspiracies to use America's power for their purposes, thus they will ultimately destroy America's sovereignty.

The book was ready to hit the press but the first intelligence report, 'Notice to the People' will hurriedly be inserted as new evidence and documentation are exploding on the National scene. Although addressed to Lawyers and Politicians it includes all Americans, we are all victims of the Dossier and Secret File terror.

LAWYERS AND POLITICIANS

Each and everyone of you have Dossiers...Secret Files that can be used against you by your enemies.

It's like the 'Great White Shark,' if he wants you, he is going to get you - -

Eighty million Dossiers the Federal Bureau of Investigation has made - that's a Dossier for one out of every three persons in America. Oregon's U.S. Congressman, Wes Cooley is under direct, merciless attack by his enemies use of his Dossier. Lies, innuendo, intimate details of a persons life, infidelities, drinking and drug habits, plain vicious gossip, anything bad you've been overheard saying about a judge, - whether any of it's true or not it's all there.

The news media claims they are getting their information on Cooley from their own day to day investigations - this is false, Cooley's Dossier was secretly released by the FBI to his enemies way back when he first voted in Congress for measures his enemies didn't want.

This conspiratorial plot by these vicious people was generated and in place long before the media was ever tuned in.

How could just a few FBI Agents possibly come up with eighty million Dossiers?

Here is how it works...it breaks down to county's, each and every county in the fifty states of the U.S. - FBI Agents assigned to each county have informants in every courthouse, a court clerk, election clerk, court deputy, file clerk, Dist. Attorney, Public Defender, Judge etc., etc.. They have an informant among law offices, political staffs, process servers, bail bondsmen, escrow officers, bankers, jail-house inmates, drug dealers etc., etc..

These informants feed the FBI Agents every bit of so-called inside information on local people, gossip, confidential police reports, client-lawyer relationships, political movements, etc., etc.. FBI Agents funnel all of this information and gossip to FBI Headquarters in Washington, D.C. where it becomes part of the individual's Dossier. Dossiers are revealed in this book.

In Jackson County, Oregon, a lawyer, James Dietz was handling a civil case for this author who held a First Trust Deed on property in California. The people who bought the property obtained lawyers and filed bankruptcy. When the bankruptcy was over the author wanted to file foreclosure but lawyer Dietz in collusion with California lawyers George Benz, Charles J. Conway, Jr. and Randolph Joyce, stalled the author for months to give the California lawyers who held a Second Trust Deed time to file foreclosure ahead of the author and get the property in their name. Lawyer Dietz then combined with the California lawyers to defraud the author of $250,000.00. Dietz was secretly paid $10,000.00 by the other lawyers to defraud his client.

Now, lawyer James W. Dietz has combined with April Sevcik, President of General Credit Service, Inc. 2724 Jacksonville Hwy, Medford, Oregon to collect $8338.32 plus $2358.26 interest, a total of $10,696.58 that Dietz claims is owed him for lawyer fees.

Lawyer Dietz has been sued for misconduct by other lawyers in Medford in the past.

The California lawyers, George Benz, Charles J. Conway, Jr. and Randolph Joyce are associates of another lawyer Carl E. Ward who was involved in the assassination of John F. Kennedy and Carl's brother Robert Ward who was arrested in a plot to assassinate President Bush and all four past Presidents, Ronald Reagan, Jimmie Carter, Richard Nixon, Gerald Ford and their wives at the dedication of Reagan's Library in Simi Valley, just a few miles from the setting of the Rodney King v. L.A.P.D. trial. This conspiracy of assassination was covered up by the Secret Service and Robert Ward was released.

Carl E. Ward and Michael H. Wallace who were Ronald Reagan's Presidential Campaign Chief Financial Officers were arrested in Portland, Oregon for gambling operations run through a phony church set-up, the Church of the Conceptual Truth. They were laundering money through the Bank of A. Levy in Oxnard, California which was owned by U.S. Commissioner Ben Nordman and his partner, Judge Jerome Berenson. The lawyers were members of Nordman and Berenson's law firm. Lawyer Dietz was involved with the California lawyers in county and cross-state furnishing of information to the FBI on other members of the Oregon Bar to be placed in Dossiers. Another politician who is now running for election against Cooley for the purpose of syphoning votes from him was also involved as a member of Reagan's Presidential Finance Committee.

Presently the U.S. Senate Judiciary Committee is holding hearings into the FBI's release of Dossiers to President William Clinton - strangely, Senators Joseph Biden, Arlen Specter and others were made well aware of this situation many years ago, yet, today they sit there and pretend that they know nothing about it.

Senator Dianne Feinstein's also presently on the Senate Judicial Committee. A few years back she pressured the Director of the FBI, former Federal Judge William Webster to secretly give Dossiers to the Anti-Defamation League to be used against politicians and bring them around to vote the way the ADL wanted. Under Feinstein's pressure William Webster wrote a directive to the commanding agents of all the FBI's major Field Offices in the U.S. to give the ADL records and Dossiers on anyone they want.

The three California lawyers filed a phony civil lawsuit against the author and persecuted and harassed him for five solid years with mis-use and abuse of process, interrogatories, depositions, needless court hearings forcing the author to travel thousands of miles back and forth from Oregon to California.

Their alleged client was a lying drug-addict who claimed to have been injured in the authors place of business.

The California lawyers tried to force the author into arbitration hearings for settlement which the author adamantly refused and demanded a jury trial.

Lawyer George Benz who persecuted the author in a two day jury trial used every trick and lie that shysters can devise - but, the author won the trial one hundred percent with an innocent verdict.

The judge polled the jury, and ordered that the author be paid damages and costs by the lawyers and their client. The foreman of the twelve person jury was a Black man, the others of various races. The jurors deliberated about four hours and came down with a decision in the author's favor. The jury system of America worked in absolute fairness without any 'professional juror-selectors.'

After the trial George Benz accosted the jury foreman outside the courthouse and threatened him but there were numerous witnesses and Benz was forced to back off.

The author's lawyer, George Dyer refused to file documents with the court to claim the damages and costs and the judge also refused to order Dyer to file the documents. The author lost thousands of dollars and five years of horrific persecution and harassment and even though the court awarded costs and damages the author received not a penny. This is the way the court system is being run and Senators Biden, Dianne Feinstein, and Arlen Specter and the others on the Senate Judiciary Committee will cover-up the Dossier and secret file terror the same as their phony Senate hearings covered-up the Ruby Ridge and Waco and Oklahoma City murders of innocent American Citizens.

The power of the Dossier, secret file. Democrat Dianne Feinstein was running for the U.S. Senate. She was losing to Republican Michael Huffington, a rich oil man who had spent $28 million of his own money.

A Hollywood premium Madam, Heidi Fleiss was arrested, she had kept a little Black-Book listing her customers. Fleiss had so many names of prominent politicians and judges in her Black-Book that according to her she could have changed the NAFTA vote if she wanted. The FBI got the little Black-Book and made secret files, a Dossier on all of Fleiss' Johns.

Dianne Feinstein and the ADL who had made secret connections with the head of the FBI to get any of their classified, secret records they wanted has obtained the Dossiers on all the John's in Fleiss' Black-Book. What do you know - right there in the R's, the Dossier on staunch Republican Richard Riordan, the powerful Mayor of Los Angeles - suddenly a big switch, just a few weeks before the election here comes staunch Republican Riordan on the TV, waltzing, hugging and fawning over staunch Democrat Dianne Feinstein - with Mayor Riordan's powerful political influence, endorsement and votes Feinstein became a U.S. Senator.

Now Feinstein sits on the powerful Senate Judiciary Committee where she along with other treacherous, treasonous Senators can cover-up their so called 'Dossier, Secret File Investigation.'

The Judiciary Committee is making Craig Livingstone a scapegoat to cover-up the fact that it was really the President's Counsels, Nussbaum and Cutler who ordered the files from the FBI - this was the same MO as when Dianne Feinstein wanted to become a U.S. Senator - now she wants to become the President.

The expose of who really ordered the secret Dossiers will lead to other extraordinary truths - the facts of how a foreign country is interfering into and sabotaging America's government process and sovereignty.